INTERNATIONAL DEVELOPMENT IN FOCUS

The Role of Intergovernmental Fiscal Transfers in Improving Education Outcomes

SAMER AL-SAMARRAI AND BLANE LEWIS, EDITORS

WORLD BANK GROUP

1818 H Street NW, Washington, DC 20433
Telephone: 202-473-1000; Internet: www.worldbank.org

1 2 3 4 24 23 22 21

ISBN: 978-1-4648-1693-2
DOI: 10.1596/978-1-4648-1693-2

Cover design: Debra Naylor / Naylor Design Inc.

Contents

Boxes

Figures

Maps

Tables

Acknowledgments

This study was prepared by a team led by Samer Al-Samarrai (World Bank) and Blane Lewis (Australian National University), who conceptualized the overall report, co-authored several chapters, and provided guidance and direction for the country case studies. The study benefited from a series of workshops and discussions with authors of the country case studies and other colleagues that included Leandro Costa, Louisee Cruz, André Loureio, and Ursula Mello (Brazil); Assenka Hristova and Lars Sondergaard (Bulgaria); Xiaoxia Wang and Binzhen Wu (China); Juanita Bodmer and Pedro Cerdán-Infantes (Colombia); Kebede Feda and Tanya Savrimootoo (Sudan); and Alasdair Fraser, Marlaine Lockheed, and Elizabeth Ninan (Uganda). The team is grateful to Hieu Nguyen and Marianne Vital for providing research assistance for the overall study. Dina Abu-Ghaida, Ana Belver, Kai Kaiser, and Yevgeniya Savchenko (of the World Bank) and Paul Smoke (New York University) provided very useful comments at the initial concept stage of the study. The team is also grateful for comments and advice received on the draft chapters and final study from Pablo Acosta, Cristian Aedo, Rythia Afkar, Juan Diego Alonso, Jurgen Blum, Fabiano Calbano, Peter Darvas, Rafael De Hoyos, Paolo Dudine, Sebastian Eckardt, Ning Fu, Kjetil Hansen, Kai Kaiser, Dessilava Kuznetsova, Jessica Lee, Rafael Moreno, Desislava Nikolova, Elizabeth Ninan, Diana Sekaggya-Bagarukayo, Kirill Vasiliev, Tim Williamson, and Noah Yarrow. We are also grateful for the support of Jaime Saavedra (Global Director, Education Practice, World Bank) and Omar Arias (Practice Manager, Global Knowledge and Innovation, Education Practice, World Bank) at every stage of the study. Amy Fine and Fiona Mackintosh edited the report. Cindy Fisher and Janice Tuten of the World Bank Publishing Program managed the publication process. Financial support for this work was provided by the Results in Education for All Children (REACH) trust fund.

About the Contributors

Samer Al-Samarrai is a senior economist in the World Bank's Education Global Practice. Since joining the Bank in 2011, Samer has worked in Africa and East Asia and as the thematic lead for the World Bank's Education Finance and Reform Group. He was a co-author of *World Development Report 2018: Learning to Realize Education's Promise* and co-authored reports including *Assessing Basic Education Service Delivery in the Philippines* and *Teacher Reform in Indonesia: The Role of Politics and Evidence in Policy Making*. Before joining the World Bank, he was a senior policy analyst on the Global Monitoring Report team at UNESCO, where he was responsible for developing key themes and coordinating research on the challenges countries faced in achieving the Education for All goals. Between 2001 and 2008, Samer was a research fellow in the Institute of Development Studies at the University of Sussex. He holds a PhD in economics from the University of Sussex and a BSc and MSc from the London School of Economics.

Juanita Bodmer is a consultant at the World Bank, based in Colombia. Previously, she worked with the Colombian National Ministry of Education and at the Colombian Ministry of Finance and Public Credit. She holds a BA in economics from the University of the Andes and a master's degree in public administration in international development from the Kennedy School of Government at Harvard University.

Pedro Cerdán-Infantes is a senior economist in the World Bank's Education Global Practice, based in Colombia. Since joining the Bank in 2009, Pedro has spent six years in East Asia. He has managed projects in early childhood development, basic education, and tertiary education and has authored and co-authored a number of reports and papers, including "Mobilizing Resources for Education and Improving Spending Effectiveness: Establishing Realistic Benchmarks Based on Past Trends" and "Spending More or Spending Better: Improving Education Financing in Indonesia." Before joining the Bank, Pedro was a research fellow at the Inter-American Development Bank and a junior professional associate at the World Bank. He holds a master's degree in public administration in international development from the Kennedy School of Government at Harvard University.

Louisee Cruz is a consultant in the World Bank's Education Global Practice. She has conducted a series of analytical studies on pre-university education on topics such as education reforms, literacy policies, results-based financing, vocational education and training, and ed-tech programs. She has also contributed to the preparation and supervision of World Bank education projects in Brazil. Previously, Louisee worked as a research manager at J-PAL Latin America and as a policy analyst at the Lemann Foundation. She holds a double MSc in public policy and human development from Maastricht University and the United Nations University and a BA in international relations from the University of São Paulo.

Kebede Feda, a senior economist in the World Bank's Education Global Practice, works on education operations and analytical work in the Africa region. He holds a PhD and master's degree in economics from American University.

Alasdair Fraser is an independent consultant. He has worked on public expenditure and education in several countries, mostly for a UK-based nongovernmental organization, the Overseas Development Institute. He holds an MSc in economics from the University of Edinburgh and an MA in economics from the University of Glasgow.

Assenka Hristova is founder and executive director of the Institute for Research in Education and managing partner of Industry Watch Group Bulgaria. Her main areas of experience include economics of education, public finance, and labor market economics. Much of her research work is focused on efficiency and effectiveness of education, monitoring and assessment of public policies and programs in education, and development of evaluation methodologies and tools for quality assessment in school education. Her research interests include the adaptability of technical and vocational education and training to labor market demands, graduate tracking, and skills anticipation. Her consultancy support has focused on improving the employability and quality of the labor force. She participates in various World Bank projects contributing to better evidence-based education policy in Bulgaria. She is a board member of the Bulgarian Macroeconomic Association and senior member of the European Expert Network on Economics of Education. She holds a master's degree in economics and finance from the University of National and World Economy, Bulgaria.

Blane Lewis joined the Arndt-Corden Department of Economics, Crawford School of Public Policy at Australia National University (ANU) as a senior fellow in 2014. He is the director of ANU's Indonesia Project and the lead editor of the *Bulletin of Indonesian Economic Studies.* His research focuses on issues related to local public finance and political economy in Indonesia. He teaches courses on quasi-experimental methods in economics. Before joining ANU, Blane worked for many years as a policy adviser in Indonesia, mostly on intergovernmental fiscal relations and decentralization, with Harvard Institute for International Development, Research Triangle Institute, and the World Bank, among others. He has worked in other developing and transition countries, including Bangladesh, Belize, the Democratic Republic of Congo, Arab Republic of Egypt, Haiti, India, Kenya, Madagascar, Niger, the Philippines, Poland, Togo, and

Vietnam. He holds a BA in mathematics from Lawrence University, and an MA and PhD in urban economics from Cornell University.

Marlaine Lockheed has four decades of experience advising governments, donor agencies, and private organizations on evidence-based reforms for education quality, gender equity, and school effectiveness. In her 19 years at the World Bank, she held several research and senior management positions, including those with responsibilities for global education policy and practice, as well as for education policy and lending for the 14 countries of the Bank's Middle East and North Africa region. Before joining the Bank, she was principal research scientist at Educational Testing Service. She has taught at Harvard, Princeton, and Stanford, and has served on the boards of numerous professional associations and scientific journals. She is an author of more than 100 journal articles and book chapters and of 13 books, including the influential *Improving Primary Education in Developing Countries*, and has worked in more than 40 developing countries across all regions. She holds a bachelor's degree from Reed College and a doctorate from Stanford University.

André Loureiro, a Brazilian national, is a senior economist in the World Bank's Education Global Practice in the Latin America and the Caribbean region. Since joining the Bank in 2013, André has been leading the preparation and supervision of projects with the objective of improving quality and access to education, as well as analytical work on education policies and human development. His projects and studies include effective use of learning assessment, curriculum reform, accelerated learning programs, full-time schooling, technical education, education financing, and strengthening the management capacity of schools and education secretariats. André holds a PhD in economics from the University of Edinburgh and a master's degree in economics from the Federal University of Ceará in Brazil.

Ursula Mello is a consultant for the World Bank, currently involved in the analysis of World Bank education projects in Brazil. She is a postdoctoral researcher at the Institute for Economic Analysis, Consejo Superior de Investigaciones Científicas and an affiliated professor at Barcelona Graduate School of Economics. In her research, she uses applied microeconometrics methods to investigate key issues for educational and labor market policies. In education, her recent work concentrates on the impact of large reforms on the higher education admissions process and the composition of the student body as well as individual incentives and choices. On the topic of labor, her work focuses on intergenerational mobility and labor market adjustments to economic shocks. Ursula holds a PhD and a master's degree in economics from Universidad Carlos III de Madrid.

Tanya Savrimootoo is an economist in the World Bank's Education Global Practice, based in Washington, DC. She has contributed to Public Expenditure Reviews in the education sector for the Democratic Republic of Congo, Côte d'Ivoire, and Nigeria, and has led analytical work on education financing in Sudan. Tanya holds a BA in economics with a secondary concentration in mathematics from Bates College and an MA in economics from American University.

Lars Sondergaard is a program leader in the World Bank's Human Development Global Practice, focusing on health, education, and social protection and jobs in EU member countries. Lars has more than 16 years of experience working with governments and development partners on a range of topics related to education, health, and social protection, with a focus on how to improve the efficiency of spending. He has written and co-written many publications at the World Bank, including "Skills, Not Just Diplomas: The Path for Education Reforms in ECA." Before joining the World Bank in 2005, he was a senior economist at the European Central Bank. He has a PhD and an MA in economics from Georgetown University.

Xiaoxia Wang is an assistant professor at Capital University of Economics and Business. She holds a PhD degree in economics from Tsinghua University.

Binzhen Wu is an associate professor and vice chair of the department of economics and deputy director of the National Institute for Fiscal Studies at Tsinghua University. Her research interests include public economics, development economics, and education economics. She has presided over research projects on education, household consumption and income, and taxation funded by the National Natural Science Foundation. She has published papers in journals including *Games and Economics Behavior*, *Journal of Development Economics*, *Journal of Economic Perspectives*, *Journal of Comparative Economics*, and *Economic Development and Cultural Change*. She holds a PhD in economics from the University of Wisconsin–Madison and a master's degree in economics from Peking University.

Executive Summary

Access to schooling in developing countries has increased rapidly over the last 20 years with many more children, and particularly poor children, starting earlier and staying in school for longer than ever before (World Bank 2018). These improvements have been due in part to greater investment in education. Global public spending on education has more than doubled in real terms since the early 2000s. The largest increases have been registered in low-income countries where public education spending increased from 3.5 percent of gross domestic product (GDP) in 1998–2001 to 4.1 percent in 2014–17 (Al-Samarrai, Cerdan-Infantes, and Lehe 2019).

Despite increases in investment and improvements in access, many countries continue to face a learning crisis. Across the world, 53 percent of all ten-year-old children are unable to read a short age-appropriate text with comprehension. The proportion of children in learning poverty increases to 90 percent in low-income countries (World Bank 2019). Changing this picture will require further increases in funding for education. Estimates show that low-income countries would have to increase public education spending to approximately 6 percent of GDP to provide good quality learning opportunities for all (Education Commission 2016). But spending more will not be enough. Research in many countries points to large spending inequalities and inefficiencies that limit the effectiveness of education funding. Addressing the twin financing challenges of inadequate and ineffective spending can support efforts to tackle the learning crisis and contribute to the achievement of national and international education goals (see figure ES.1). The COVID-19 pandemic makes addressing these challenges even more critical to prevent the pandemic's short-term economic shock from lowering long-term development prospects.

The vast majority of the world's children live in countries where subnational governments are responsible for providing basic education services. Over the last 30 years, many countries have introduced reforms to decentralize basic public services. These reforms are expected to improve service delivery outcomes because subnational governments are better placed than central governments to understand what types of services are needed and how best to provide them. Because citizens are closer to their subnational governments, they are also better able to hold them accountable for the services available. Education, and basic

FIGURE ES.1

The link between financing and education sector objectives

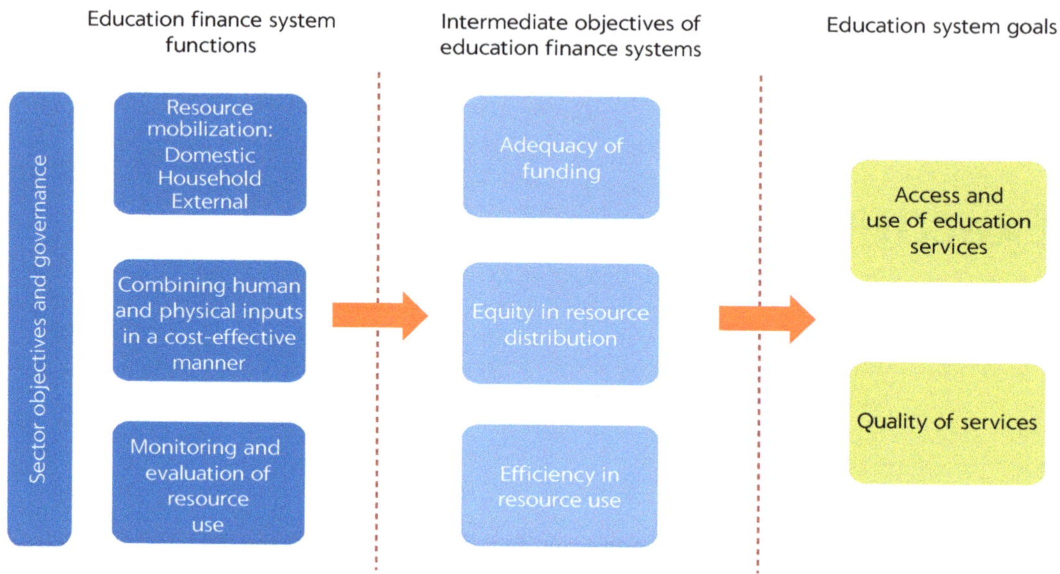

Source: World Bank; see chapter 1.

education (preprimary, primary and lower secondary schooling) in particular, have been at the forefront of decentralization reforms.[1] Recent estimates indicate that 84 percent of the world's children live in countries where government primary and secondary schools are run by subnational governments.[2]

Given the central role subnational governments play, the success of efforts to improve education outcomes will depend critically on how they use public funding to tackle the twin financing challenges of adequacy and effectiveness. In countries where education has been decentralized, a large share of public funding is managed and spent by subnational governments. Figure ES.2 shows the share of total education spending in a selection of countries that have decentralized basic education services. It shows that in most countries, subnational governments account for over 50 percent of total public education spending. If the focus is narrowed to basic education only, this share would be significantly higher. For example, subnational governments account for over 80 percent of government spending on primary and secondary education in Uganda.[3] How effectively subnational governments are able to translate these funds into good-quality education services will determine to a large degree the proportion of children in primary and secondary school that leave with the skills they require to continue to learn and lead productive lives.

Although subnational governments manage and make decisions on the use of public education funding, they often rely on transfers from the central government. In decentralized countries, intergovernmental fiscal transfers account for a large share of subnational government revenues. This dependence on transfers extends to subnational education funding. In Sudan, for example, central government fiscal transfers provide states with approximately three-quarters of all public education funding. In Indonesia, two-thirds of all public education funding in 2013 was allocated through fiscal transfers between the central government and provincial and district governments. Beyond core funding, transfer systems can also provide an effective system for channeling funds to protect

FIGURE ES.2

Subnational public education spending as a percentage of total public education spending, 2010–18

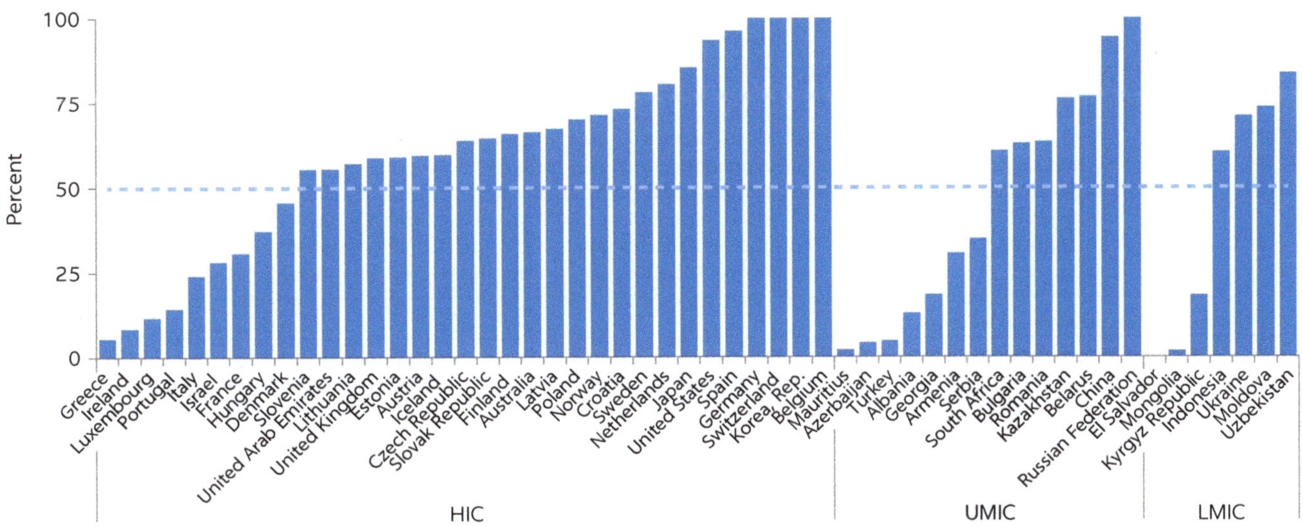

Source: World Bank calculations using Fiscal Decentralization Dataset, International Monetary Fund, Washington, DC (accessed May 8, 2020), https://data.imf.org/?sk=1C28EBFB-62B3-4B0C-AED3-048EEEBB684F.
Note: Average share calculated from all available data between 2010 and 2018. HIC = high-income country; LMIC = lower-middle-income country; UMIC = upper-middle-income country.

education systems during times of crisis. For example, in the United States, federal stimulus packages have used existing transfer mechanisms to provide additional financial support to local education systems during the financial and COVID-19 crises.

ASSESSING THE USE OF FISCAL TRANSFERS TO ADDRESS EDUCATION FINANCE CHALLENGES

Because transfers account for a large share of subnational spending, the way they are designed and implemented can help address key financing challenges. Most countries use a combination of general- and specific-purpose transfers to support subnational governments' delivery of education services (see table ES.1). General-purpose transfers are unconditional fiscal transfers that subnational governments may allocate across their responsibilities, including education, according to their own preferences and needs. Central governments often complement these general transfers with conditional or specific-purpose transfers. These transfers to subnational governments are targeted for use in particular sectors and relate to providing certain inputs or are tied to improvements in sector-specific outputs or outcomes.[4]

This study consists of seven country case studies that explore how fiscal transfers affect education sector financing and ultimately sector outcomes. Country case studies were conducted in Sudan, Uganda, Indonesia, Colombia,

TABLE ES.1 **How fiscal transfers address critical education finance challenges**

FINANCE CHALLENGE OR TRANSFER OBJECTIVE	RELATED FISCAL TRANSFER OBJECTIVE	TRANSFER APPROACHES TO SUPPORT EDUCATION CHALLENGE IN CASE STUDY COUNTRIES
Resource mobilization		
Adequacy	To address vertical imbalances and ensure subnational governments have sufficient funds to deliver on their responsibilities	Most countries use a combination of general and specific transfers to increase subnational resources for education, although the mix varies considerably among Sudan, Colombia, Indonesia, Brazil, and China. Others, such as Uganda, rely almost exclusively on specific-purpose transfers, and in Bulgaria these transfers are designed to provide subnational governments with minimum levels of funding for education based on estimates of per student costs.
Effective use of education funding		
Equity	Equalizing revenues across subnational governments at a particular level	All case study countries use general-purpose transfers to address inequalities in revenue between subnational governments. However, their design can sometimes be an important driver of subnational spending inequalities, as in Sudan and Indonesia. Most case study countries, including Brazil, Colombia, Bulgaria, and China, also use specific-purpose transfers to address equity issues, and these transfers provide more education funding to poorer subnational governments and narrow spending inequalities. In Uganda, specific transfers allocated on the basis of the student, rather than the school-age population, drive education spending inequalities.
Efficiency	Ensuring that spatial spillovers and other externalities are accounted for and promoting the efficient use of inputs to deliver outputs demanded by citizens	Inefficiency in the education sector is tackled mostly through specific-purpose transfers. Transfers based on per capita or per student allocation mechanisms are common, as in Uganda, Colombia, Brazil, Bulgaria, and China, and ensure there is a link between spending and outputs such as enrollment. In Indonesia, the main transfer associated with efficiency supports capital spending and includes a requirement that subnational governments contribute to the overall transfer allocation. Other transfers, with different objectives, can sometimes include perverse incentives that make education spending inefficient, such as in Indonesia and Colombia.
Performance	Improve results or outcomes by linking transfers to results	Performance-based specific-purpose transfers for education are used in Uganda, Indonesia, and Colombia. The state of Ceará in Brazil uses a general-purpose transfer that is allocated on the basis of performance in the education sector.

Source: World Bank.
Note: Chapter 2 provides further details on transfer types and how they link to different types of objectives.

Brazil, Bulgaria, and China. The selection of case studies was driven primarily by the need to cover a broad set of country experiences and to capture countries at different stages of economic development and decentralization. As a result, the case studies provide a broad set of examples of how fiscal transfers have been used to address education sector challenges at different stages of development.[5]

Challenge 1: Providing adequate resources for education

Transfers can play a critical role in helping subnational governments adequately fund the services for which they are responsible, including the provision of basic education. Although all transfers provide subnational governments with additional resources, they do not automatically result in higher spending on education. General transfers increase the overall amount of revenue available, but subnational governments can, and often do, choose to use these funds on other priority sectors. Even conditional or specific-purpose transfers may not increase overall spending on education because fiscal resources are fungible.

The evidence from the case studies generally shows that intergovernmental fiscal transfers are successful at increasing subnational spending on education. The analysis in the case studies show that the receipt of general- and specific-purpose transfers resulted in subnational governments spending more on education, although specific-purpose transfers often had a larger effect. For example, in Brazil and China, the estimated marginal effect for education-specific conditional transfers was higher than that for unconditional transfers. However, differences in the effect of general- and specific-purpose transfers on subnational education spending is likely to be dependent, to an extent, on their relative size. For example, specific-purpose transfers had a greater effect on subnational spending in Brazil, where these transfers made up approximately 62 percent of municipal spending, than in Indonesia, where they accounted for only 11 percent.

Although transfers generally increase public education spending, only a few countries use the transfer system to ensure that all subnational governments have adequate funds for education. Some countries have designed specific-purpose transfers that are based on the actual costs associated with providing education to each student. These schemes are distinctive because they provide guaranteed and predictable funding for education that is insulated, to a large degree, from government budget fluctuations. For example, in Bulgaria, the central government uses a unified per student cost standard to allocate specific-purpose funds for municipally owned schools.

In contrast to transfers based on cost standards, some countries have designed transfers so as to guarantee an annual minimum level of per student funding. For example, in Brazil, federal funds for education are allocated in a way that ensures a minimum level of per student funding in all states based on a set of specific annual revenues. Transfer schemes of this kind are not associated with the actual costs of service provision, but they aim to narrow spending inequalities by establishing a funding floor and ensuring through the transfer system that all subnational governments have adequate funds to reach this floor. However, because these types of transfers are funded through taxes, revenue can change from year to year, making overall funding levels volatile, leading to unpredictable and constantly changing minimum spending levels for education. This can make planning and budgeting difficult for subnational governments and affect how effectively public education spending is used.

Challenge 2: Encouraging more effective use of public funding for education

Improving equity

Education spending inequalities between subnational governments can be large (see figure ES.3). In Sudan, the state with the highest funding per student spends approximately 21 times the amount spent in the state with the lowest funding levels. These subnational spending inequalities frequently reinforce patterns of poverty between subnational governments. World Bank public expenditure reviews and other studies have shown that, in approximately one-half of developing countries with available data, there was a negative and statistically significant relationship between subnational poverty rates and education spending (Manuel et al. 2019). A similar pattern was found in some of the case studies,

FIGURE ES.3

Subnational education spending and poverty rates, Sudan and Uganda

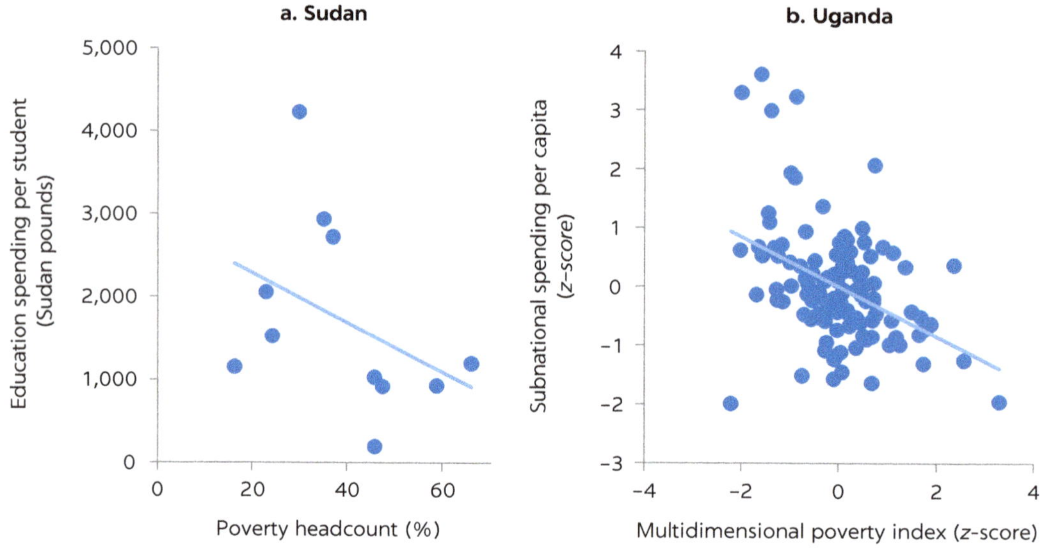

Source: World Bank; see case studies in chapters 4 and 5.

including Sudan and Uganda (see figure ES.3). There are relatively few countries that show an opposite and statistically significant relationship.

Because transfers can fund a large share of subnational education spending, the way in which they are distributed is critical to improving spending equity between subnational governments. Addressing horizontal imbalances in revenue between subnational governments is a major objective of most fiscal transfer systems. Most of the case study countries have general-purpose transfers that are designed to reduce inequalities of this kind across the whole set of subnational responsibilities (see table ES.1). For example, in China, equalization general-purpose transfers make up approximately two-thirds of all transfers to provinces and counties. These transfers are allocated according to formulas that include estimates of subnational fiscal gaps, which measure the gaps between subnational revenues and expenditure obligations, as well as population size and levels of economic development.

Most of the case study countries also have specific-purpose transfers that aim to narrow inequalities in subnational spending on education. In Brazil, the Fund for the Development of Basic Education (FUNDEB) addresses equity issues by guaranteeing minimum levels of education spending among municipalities. Prior to the introduction of the Fund for the Development of Primary and Lower Secondary Education (FUNDEF), FUNDEB's predecessor, in 1996, there were large differences in education spending between municipalities, which were driven by the limited revenues of poorer municipalities. Before the program started, the wealthier South, Southeast, and Central West regions in Brazil were spending almost twice as much per student as the poorer regions in the North and Northeast (Gordon and Vegas 2005). These spending disparities led to significant differences in education outcomes and exacerbated more general socioeconomic inequalities between regions. FUNDEB and its predecessor FUNDEF aimed to narrow spending inequalities by redistributing a portion of federal, state, and municipal tax revenues among all municipalities to guarantee a minimum level of spending per student across all municipalities. The funds have

FIGURE ES.4
The distribution of municipal education spending in Brazil with and without FUNDEB

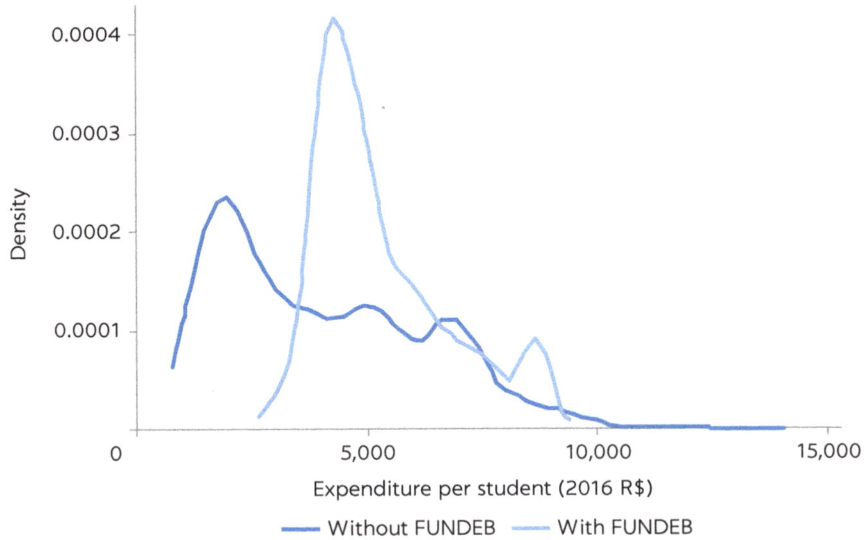

Source: World Bank using Summary Report on Budget Execution (RREO) from the Information System on Education Budgets (SIOPE). See case study in chapter 8.
Note: FUNDEB = Fund for the Development of Basic Education; R = Brazilian real.

been successful at narrowing spending inequalities between municipalities and particularly in increasing the funding of education in the poorest states (Cruz and Silva 2020; Gordon and Vegas 2005). A World Bank simulation of per student funding also shows that inequality in per student spending has been significantly smaller since the introduction of FUNDEB (see figure ES.4).

Improving efficiency

This section focuses on the extent to which transfers affect the spending efficiency of education funding. In the broader literature on intergovernmental transfers described in chapter 2, a key objective of an effective transfer system is to compensate subnational governments for benefit spillovers to neighboring jurisdictions. Clearly if education investment decisions are made without accounting for the benefits that come from these investments outside the jurisdiction, subnational governments will underinvest.

Transfers can be used to help subnational governments internalize externalities and invest in education in ways that are optimal for the nation as a whole. They can also improve the technical efficiency of education spending and improve overall spending efficiency. Figure ES.5 shows scatter plots of learning outcomes compared with spending levels per student in Bulgaria and Colombia. In both countries, some municipalities appear to use their resources more effectively than others to deliver education services. Within each panel, municipalities in quadrant A spend less than the average municipality on education but have better than average outcomes. For example, Bello municipality in Colombia spends about 2.5 million pesos per student and has an average learning score of 40 percent, which is 8 percentage points higher than the average for all municipalities. In contrast, municipalities in quadrant C are relatively inefficient. They spend more than the average municipality but have outcomes below the national average for all municipalities. Clearly, other factors, such as cost

FIGURE ES.5

Subnational learning outcomes and spending per student, Bulgaria and Colombia

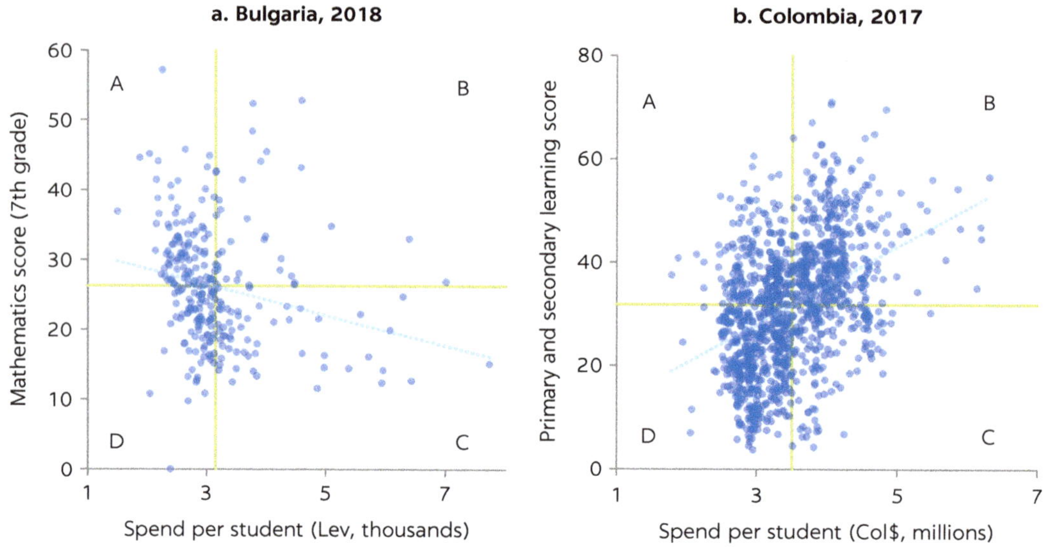

Source: World Bank; see case studies in chapters 7 and 9.

differences across subnational governments, also explain some of the variation, but more detailed econometric work in the case studies, as well as other more rigorous approaches to measuring inefficiency, all demonstrate significant spending inefficiencies at the subnational level (De Witte and López-Torres 2017; Sutherland, Price, and Gonand 2010).

The design and implementation of fiscal transfers can sometimes drive inefficiencies in public education spending. For example, in Indonesia, the formula for the largest general transfers includes incentives for district governments to spend more on hiring civil servants than on nonsalary spending. In education, this has resulted in a tendency to hire more teachers than is required to comply with minimum service standards and maximum class sizes and is an important driver of inefficiency (Lewis and Smoke 2017; World Bank 2012).

However, carefully designed transfers can increase spending efficiency in education. In the early 1990s, the education systems in many countries in Europe and Central Asia were becoming more inefficient as a result of declines and changes in the school-age population. These demographic shifts often resulted in the existence of many small schools, small class sizes, and low student-teacher ratios. Moreover, the existing input-based funding mechanisms were giving municipalities and schools no incentives to adjust to the new reality. Per capita financing mechanisms were introduced that linked transfer allocations to student numbers. Municipalities could no longer afford to fund their existing school networks, which gave them an incentive to find ways to increase spending efficiency (Alonso and Sanchez 2011). In Bulgaria, the introduction of per capita financing has led to the merging or closing of some schools, which has significantly increased efficiency. Overall, the allocation of education funding on a per student basis has increased class sizes and student-teacher ratios and has put the education sector in Bulgaria on a more sustainable financial footing. Although some inefficiency in spending remains, per capita funding formulas also act as automatic stabilizers that adjust financing mechanisms immediately in response to demographic shifts and other factors that may drive spending inefficiency.

Strengthening the link between spending and sector results

Fiscal transfers can create incentives for subnational governments to expand access to education services and improve learning. As the country case studies and other research have shown, intergovernmental fiscal transfers increase subnational education spending, and this additional funding has the potential not only to increase access to education but also to improve learning outcomes (de Carvalho Filho and Litschig 2020; Olsson and Valsecchi 2015). Econometric analysis in the case studies in Brazil, Colombia, Indonesia, and Uganda shows that both transfers and subnational education spending have a positive and significant impact on student achievement. For example, in the Indonesia case study, a 10 percent increase in subnational per capita education spending increased students' test scores by 0.6 percent. Although the relationship is significant, it is not very strong, and there is considerable variation in the effectiveness of subnational entities in translating funding into outcomes. In an effort to strengthen the link between funding and outcomes, fiscal transfers in some countries, particularly specific-purpose transfers, have been designed to include stronger incentives for subnational governments to focus on improving the performance of schools and students.

Transfers can be designed to provide direct incentives to encourage subnational governments to expand education access. In particular, transfers that include a per student allocation can act as a strong incentive for subnational governments to enroll more students. When education transfers include a per student element, subnational governments know that if they expand access, they will receive funding from the central government to help cover the costs of providing more school places. This has had the effect of reducing the cost burden on subnational governments and, in turn, on households, while also narrowing inequalities in access to basic education. Many countries use these types of transfers to encourage and sustain widespread access to basic education (OECD 2017).

China's New Mechanism to Guarantee Rural Compulsory Education Financing, introduced in 2006, strengthened the incentives for provincial governments to increase access to basic education. The New Mechanism introduced a specific-purpose transfer that was allocated to provinces on a per student basis and was designed to cover elements of nonsalary funding and to compensate subnational governments for the revenue they lost as a result of the abolition of tuition fees, which was implemented at the same time. The share of per student funding covered by the transfer varied depending on the socioeconomic characteristics of each province. For example, the central government transfers covered 80 percent of the administrative expenses and lost fee income of the least developed provinces in the west and 60 percent of those of the central provinces. Initially, the wealthier eastern provinces did not receive any funds through the compulsory specific-purpose education transfer, but this changed in 2015 when they received transfers amounting to 50 percent of their total expenses.

The New Mechanism reforms have been credited with contributing to the increases in enrollment and completion rates in basic education since the early 2000s. Moreover, spending inequalities between provinces have narrowed since the introduction of the reforms, but the evidence is mixed on whether this was the direct result of the reforms. Nevertheless, the reforms appear to have increased levels of enrollment in primary and secondary education and narrowed enrollment outcomes between provinces and counties.[7] There is also evidence that the reforms had positive effects on attainment and learning outcomes and that these effects were larger for students from disadvantaged backgrounds (Ha and Yan 2018; Xiao, Li, and Zhao 2017).

The FUNDEB and FUNDEF transfers in Brazil also improved education outcomes particularly in poorer municipalities. Research studies have also shown that these funds have increased enrollment in basic education particularly in poorer municipalities, improved education quality, and narrowed achievement gaps (Cruz 2018; Cruz and Rocha 2018; Gordon and Vegas 2005). A recent study exploring the impact of FUNDEB on student achievement in upper secondary schools found that it had increased average achievement in both Portuguese and mathematics and that the gains were greater for poorer students (Silveira et al. 2017).

In some countries, the transfer system has also aimed to incentivize improvements in education quality and student learning outcomes. Compared with transfers that support increasing access to schooling, there is less evidence available on the effectiveness of performance-based transfers that focus on learning outcomes, particularly in developing countries. However, recent evidence from the use of performance-based transfers in the state of Ceará in Brazil show that they can be an effective tool to improve performance, but their effectiveness depends on solid and comprehensive information systems, good implementation capabilities of subnational governments, and careful design to avoid any negative consequences such as the risk of transfers of this kind widening existing inequalities (see box ES.1)

BOX ES.1

Using performance-based incentives to improve education outcomes in Brazil

In 2008, an innovative reform of the fiscal transfer system in the state of Ceará in Brazil linked an important general transfer to learning outcomes. States are obligated to transfer 25 percent of consumption tax revenues to their municipalities as a general-purpose transfer. A funding formula dictates how most of these funds are transferred but states have discretion over how they transfer a quarter of the total transfer. Since 2008, the state of Ceará has allocated 72 percent of these discretionary funds based on municipalities' performance in the education sector. These transfers are a very significant revenue source for municipalities and represent as much as one-third of all revenue for poorer municipalities in Ceará (Loureiro and Cruz 2020).

The discretionary transfer amount is determined by a primary "education quality index" that is designed both to improve performance and to increase equity between students within municipalities. A comprehensive census-based learning assessment is used to calculate the index. The assessment consists of indicators on early grade literacy, learning measured at the end of primary school, and the proportion of children transitioning to the next grade. Municipalities are allocated transfer resources based on their scores on these indicators as well as on the magnitude of their educational improvements over the preceding year.

Rigorous evaluations have shown that the performance-based reform to the fiscal transfer program has improved learning outcomes in most municipalities in Ceará. Even though the transfer was not a specific-purpose transfer, evidence shows that it led municipalities to increase their spending on basic education and narrowed per capita differences in transfers between municipalities (Franca 2014). Moreover, it appears that the transfers also narrowed learning gaps between poor and wealthy municipalities (Brandão 2014). Because these outcomes were based on the use of existing revenue sources, the reforms have also increased the overall efficiency of spending in the state of Ceará and its municipalities (Loureiro and Cruz 2020; Wetzel and Viñuela 2020).

Based on the successful experience in Ceará, a recent amendment of the Brazilian constitution has changed the allocation mechanism for FUNDEB (the main education fund transfer) to introduce a mandatory results-based component to the formula. In particular, the amendment includes an allocation of federal top-up funds to states based on improvements in results.

GUIDING PRINCIPLES FOR EFFECTIVE TRANSFER MECHANISMS[8]

Strengthening fiscal transfer mechanisms to tackle financing challenges and improve education outcomes is difficult. In the absence of conflicting objectives between central and subnational governments, differences in subnational government capacity, and externalities and information asymmetries, a single general transfer may provide the optimal system. However, these conditions are rarely met, and a country's overall political and economic context plays an important role in both how the intergovernmental transfer is set up and the opportunities that exist for reform.

The case studies show that countries typically use a mix of different transfers to address different objectives in the education sector. There is no one-to-one correspondence between specific finance challenges and particular transfers. For example, faced with inadequate subnational government funding for education, central governments may use a combination of general and specific transfers to increase general levels of funding and to ensure that specific inputs are funded. Tackling education spending inequalities across subnational governments may in some cases require changes to allocation rules for general transfers and in other cases require the design of a specific education transfer that aims to compensate subnational governments that are unable to fund education adequately. The choices that countries make will depend on both the technical and political feasibility of different options.

The study draws its findings from the case studies and the broader literature to identify a set of guiding principles to help strengthen education finance in decentralized systems (see figure ES.6). The reform of fiscal transfer systems frequently involves changes that do not align with the interests of all stakeholders. Existing weaknesses in transfer systems often are not the result of poor design and execution but rather reflect a suboptimal equilibrium based on past and current economic and political factors. Given the different starting points of countries and their potential for reform, it will not always be possible to apply all the principles, particularly in the short term. However, they provide a roadmap for the direction toward which reforms should move as well as a set of principles against which an existing system or any proposed reforms can be assessed.[9]

Drawing on the findings of the study, the following are the main guiding principles for the effective design of intergovernmental fiscal transfers for education:

- *Align transfers with national objectives and subnational responsibility.* It is critical to align the incentives inherent in fiscal transfer systems with national education goals, which requires a good understanding of how fiscal transfer systems work and how they affect the decisions subnational governments make in delivering education services.
- *Avoid perverse incentives.* In designing and implementing transfers, it is important to eliminate or reduce any perverse incentives that can limit funding effectiveness (Lewis and Smoke 2012). For example, transfers can sometimes encourage subnational governments to devote a large share of spending on particular inputs, resulting in large spending inefficiencies.
- *Define clear, focused, and nonconflicting transfer objectives.* Transfers that have unclear aims or try to achieve multiple objectives often fail to improve outcomes effectively.

FIGURE ES.6

Guiding principles for effective design of intergovernmental fiscal transfers for education

Source: World Bank; see chapter 3.

- *Make funding predictable and limit fragmentation.* Transfers that rely on government revenues can be unpredictable, but there are often other factors that make education funding volatile. Reducing the volatility of transfers can ensure that public funding for education is used effectively. The study shows that in many countries education systems are funded by multiple transfers, often with similar objectives, which can make it difficult for subnational governments to budget, plan, and execute the use of these funds. For many countries, reducing the number of intergovernmental transfers for education, by, for example, consolidating transfers with the same objectives, has the potential to improve both the adequacy and effectiveness of education spending.
- *Use easy-to-understand and transparent transfer formulas.* The ability of subnational governments to understand allocation rules and how their own actions can affect the level of funding they receive is critical to good transfer design. Transparency in the design of transfers is also important to ensure

that stakeholders can hold different levels of government accountable. Both require good quality information on the characteristics of subnational populations and education systems.

- *Account for differences in the costs of education provision.* Ensuring that transfers account for differences in subnational characteristics that affect the costs of providing education can help narrow inequalities and improve national education outcomes.
- *Take account of subnational government capacity.* Subnational governments differ in their capacity to use funding effectively to improve education outcomes. Funding alone is not enough to support lagging regions in their efforts to improve outcomes and catch up with other parts of the country. Strengthening the capacity of subnational governments to improve education outcomes often goes hand-in-hand with reform of the transfer system.
- *Focus on equity and on education outputs and outcomes.* The study shows the potential that well-designed fiscal transfers have for improving equity between subnational governments. Many of the other guiding principles relate to equity by, for example, accommodating cost differences and strengthening the capacity of weaker subnational governments. However, it is important to keep a focus on equity and ensure that the overall system supports national goals to provide learning for all. Allocating transfers on the basis of outputs or outcomes is also important, providing subnational governments with more flexibility in how they deliver education services and helping ensure that education funding is used more effectively.

The reform of fiscal transfer systems is constrained by a variety of political economy factors. There are numerous stakeholders involved in the reform process, cutting across all levels of government and involving many nongovernment actors. Desirable changes frequently do not align with the interests of all concerned parties. Therefore, it may not always be politically feasible to implement technically viable and useful changes to fiscal transfers. Second-best solutions are often all that can be accomplished. However, the principles outlined here can provide a roadmap for the direction that reforms should take over the longer term and serve as a way of assessing the benefit of any proposed changes to existing fiscal transfer systems.

NOTES

1. See Dyer and Rose (2005) and Channa and Faguet (2016) for discussions of the potential benefits and actual effects of decentralization in the education sector.
2. The estimates are based on the Fiscal Decentralization Dataset, International Monetary Fund, Washington, DC (accessed May 8, 2020), https://data.imf.org/?sk=1C28EBFB-62B3-4B0C-AED3-048EEEBB684F, and OECD/UCLG (2019).
3. See chapter 5.
4. Chapter 2 outlines the main transfer types and how they link to broad policy objectives.
5. Chapter 3 provides further details on the characteristics of the different case study countries.
6. The per student intergovernmental fiscal transfers analyzed in this section are similar in effect to per student transfers to schools. Evaluations have shown that providing transfers directly to schools has been successful in increasing access to education and attainment (McEwan 2015; Snilstveit et al. 2015).
7. See, for example, Shi (2016). Studies have shown that the impact of the reforms was different in different regions as well as for different levels of education. Ding et al. (2020) concluded that the new transfers did not lead to any significant increases in spending on

education because they substituted for other "off-budget" spending, including tuition fees. This may also help to explain their positive impact on outcomes since the burden of funding shifted from households to governments, which removed the cost constraints on households associated with school attendance.

8. The guiding principles focus on the education sector but are drawn from the broader literature on fiscal transfers (see, for example, Bahl (2000); Boadway and Shah (2007); and Smoke and Kim (2003)) as well as findings from the case studies and associated author workshops.
9. The summary provides a short description of the principles. See chapter 3 for further details and examples.

REFERENCES

Al-Samarrai, Samer, Pedro Cerdan-Infantes, and Jonathan David Lehe. 2019. "Mobilizing Resources for Education and Improving Spending Effectiveness: Establishing Realistic Benchmarks Based on Past Trends." Policy Research Working Paper 8773, World Bank, Washington, DC.

Alonso, J.D., and A. Sanchez, eds. 2011. *Reforming Education Finance in Transition Countries: Six Case Studies in Per Capita Financing Systems*. Washington, DC: World Bank.

Bahl, Roy. 2000. "Intergovernmental Transfers in Developing and Transition Countries: Principles and Practice." World Bank, Washington, DC.

Boadway, R., and A. Shah, eds. 2007. *Intergovernmental Fiscal Transfers: Principles and Practice*. Washington, DC: World Bank.

Brandão, Júlia Barbosa. 2014. "O rateio de ICMS por desempenho de municípios no Ceará e seu impacto em indicadores do sistema de avaliação da educação." Fundação Getulio Vargas, School of Public and Business Administration, Rio de Janeiro.

Channa, Anila, and Jean-Paul Faguet. 2016. "Decentralization of Health and Education in Developing Countries: A Quality-Adjusted Review of the Empirical Literature." *World Bank Research Observer* 31 (2): 199–241.

Cruz, Gabriela, and Rudi Rocha. 2018. "Efeitos do FUNDEF/B sobre frequência escolar, fluxo escolar e trabalho infantil: uma análise com base nos Censos de 2000 e 2010." *Estudos Econômicos (São Paulo)* 48 (1): 39–75.

Cruz, Tassia. 2018. "Teacher Hiring Decisions: How Do Governments React to an Exogenous Redistribution of Education Funds?" *Economics of Education Review* 67 (C):58–81.

Cruz, Tassia, and Talita Silva. 2020. "Minimum Spending in Education and the Flypaper Effect." *Economics of Education Review* 77 (C): 102012.

de Carvalho Filho, Irineu, and Stephan Litschig. 2020. "Long-Run Impacts of Intergovernmental Transfers." *Journal of Human Resources*. doi: 10.3368/jhr.57.3:0917-9064R2.

De Witte, Kristof, and Laura López-Torres. 2017. "Efficiency in Education: A Review of Literature and a Way Forward." *Journal of the Operational Research Society* 68 (4): 339–63.

Ding, Yanqing, Fengming Lu, and Xiaoyang Ye. 2020. "Intergovernmental Transfer under Heterogeneous Accountabilities: The Effects of the 2006 Chinese Education Finance Reform." *Economics of Education Review* 77 (C): 101985.

Dyer, C., and P. Rose. 2005. "Decentralisation for Educational Development? An Editorial Introduction." *Compare* 35 (2): 105–13.

Education Commission. 2016. *The Learning Generation: Investing in Education for a Changing World*. New York: International Commission on Financing Global Education Opportunity.

Franca, E.M. 2014. "Repasse da cota-parte do ICMS aos municípios cearenses: Avaliação das mudanças ocorridas no período de 2009 a 2011." Universidade Federal do Ceará.

Gordon, Nora, and Emiliana Vegas. 2005. "Educational Finance Equalization, Spending, Teacher Quality, and Student Outcomes: The Case of Brazil's FUNDEF." In *Incentives to Improve Teaching: Lessons from Latin America*, edited by E. Vegas, 151–82. Washington, DC: World Bank.

Ha, Wei, and Fang Yan. 2018. "Does Money Matter? The Effects of Block Grants on Education Attainment in Rural China: Evidence from Intercensal Population Survey 2015." *International Journal of Educational Development* 62 (September): 174–83.

Lewis, Blane D., and Paul Smoke. 2012. "Incentives for Better Local Service Delivery." In *Fiscal Decentralization in Indonesia a Decade after Big Bang*. Jakarta: Ministry of Finance.

———. 2017. "Intergovernmental Fiscal Transfers and Local Incentives and Responses: The Case of Indonesia." *Fiscal Studies* 38 (1): 111–39.

Loureiro, Andre, and Louisee Cruz. 2020. *Achieving World-Class Education in Adverse Socioeconomic Conditions: The Case of Sobral in Brazil*. Washington, DC: World Bank.

Manuel, Marcus, Dan Coppard, Amy Dodd, Harsh Desai, Richard Watts, Zach Christensen, and Stephanie Manea. 2019. "Subnational Investment in Human Capital." Development Initiatives, Bristol, UK.

McEwan, P. 2015. "Improving Learning in Primary Schools of Developing Countries: A Meta-Analysis of Randomized Experiments." *Review of Educational Research* 85 (3): 353–94.

OECD. 2017. *The Funding of School Education*. Paris: OECD.

OECD/UCLG. 2019. *2019 Report of the World Observatory on Subnational Government Finance and Investment—Key Findings and Country Profiles*. Paris: OECD.

Olsson, Ola, and Michele Valsecchi. 2015. "Resource Windfalls and Local Government Behavior: Evidence from a Policy Reform in Indonesia." doi.org/10.2139/ssrn.2685721.

Shi, Xinzheng. 2016. "The Impact of Educational Fee Reduction Reform on School Enrollment in Rural China." *Journal of Development Studies* 52 (12): 1791–1809.

Silveira, Iara Maira da, João Eustáquio de Lima, Evandro Camargos Teixeira, and Rubicleis Gomes da Silva. 2017. "Avaliação do efeito do FUNDEB sobre o desempenho dos alunos do ensino médio no Brasil." Institute for Applied Economic Research, Brasilia.

Smoke, Paul, and Yun-Hwan Kim. 2003. *Intergovernmental Fiscal Transfers in Asia: Current Practice and Challenges for the Future*. Mandaluyong, Philippines: Asian Development Bank.

Snilstveit, B., J. Stevenson, D. Phillips, M. Vojtkova, E. Gallagher, T. Schmidt, H. Jobse, M. Geelen, and M. Pastorello. 2015. *Interventions for Improving Learning Outcomes and Access to Education in Low- and Middle-Income Countries*. New Delhi: International Initiative for Impact Evaluation.

Sutherland, Douglas, Robert Price, and Eric Gonand. 2010. "Improving Public Spending Efficiency in Primary and Secondary Education." *OECD Journal: Economic Studies* 2009 (1): 1–30.

Wetzel, Deborah L., and Lorena Viñuela. 2020. "Intergovernmental Fiscal Transfers and Performance Grants in Brazil." In *Intergovernmental Transfers in Federations*, edited by Serdar Yilmaz and Farah Zahir, 204–23. Cheltenham, UK: Edward Elgar Publishing.

World Bank. 2012. *Making Better Use of Teachers: Strengthening Teacher Management to Improve the Efficiency and Equity of Public Spending*. Jakarta: World Bank.

———. 2018. *World Development Report 2018: Learning to Realize Education's Promise*. Washington, DC: World Bank.

———. 2019. *Ending Learning Poverty: What Will It Take?* Washington, DC: World Bank.

Xiao, Yun, Li Li, and Liqiu Zhao. 2017. "Education on the Cheap: The Long-Run Effects of a Free Compulsory Education Reform in Rural China." *Journal of Comparative Economics* 45 (3): 544–62.

Abbreviations

BOS	School Operational Assistance Program (Indonesia)
CPA	Comprehensive Peace Agreement (Sudan)
CTE	Certified Territorial Entities (Colombia)
DAK	specific purpose grant (Indonesia)
DAU	general purpose grant (Indonesia)
DBH	tax and nontax revenue sharing (Indonesia)
DPD	dynamic panel data
ECE	early childhood education
EMIS	education management information system
EU	European Union
FFAMC	Fiscal and Financial Allocation and Monitoring Commission (Sudan)
FMoE	Federal Ministry of General Education (Sudan)
FMoF	Federal Ministry of Finance (Sudan)
FMoHE	Federal Ministry of Higher Education (Sudan)
FNDE	National Fund for Education Development (Brazil)
FUNDEB	Fund for the Development of Basic Education (Brazil)
FUNDEF	Fund for the Development of Primary and Lower Secondary Education (Brazil)
GDP	gross domestic product
GER	gross enrollment ratio
GPS	General Participation System (Colombia)
ICMS	Tax on the Circulation of Goods and Services (Imposto Sobre Circulação de Mercadorias e Serviços) (Brazil)
IDEB	National Index of Education Quality (Brazil)
IGFT	Inter-Governmental Fiscal Transfer Program (Uganda)
LG	local government (Uganda)
MoES	Ministry of Education and Science (Bulgaria)
MoES	Ministry of Education and Sports (Uganda)
MoFPED	Ministry of Finance, Planning and Economic Development (Uganda)
NAPE	National Assessment of Progress in Education (Uganda)

OECD	Organisation for Economic Co-operation and Development
OLS	ordinary least squares
P	primary school
PAIC	Literacy at the Right Age Program (Brazil)
PISA	Programme for International Student Assessment
PLE	Primary Leaving Examination (Uganda)
PPP	purchasing power parity
PSEA	Preschool and School Education Act (Bulgaria)
RBF	results-based financing
S	secondary school
SACMEQ	Southern Africa Consortium for Monitoring Educational Quality (Uganda)
SAEB	Basic Education Evaluation System (Brazil)
SAR	special administrative region
SIEQ	Synthetic Index of Education Quality (Colombia)
SMC	school management committee (Uganda)
SMoE	State Ministries of Education (Sudan)
SMoF	State Ministries of Finance (Sudan)
TVET	technical and vocational education and training
UCS	unified cost standard (Bulgaria)
UNEB	Uganda National Examinations Board
UPE	universal primary education
USE	universal secondary education

CURRENCY

Col$	Colombian peso
€	euro
lev	Bulgarian lev
R$	Brazilian real
RF	Rwanda franc
Rp	Indonesian rupiah
SD	Sudanese pound
U Sh	Uganda shilling
US$	US dollar
¥	Chinese yuan

INTRODUCTION, PRINCIPLES, AND SYNTHESIS OF FINDINGS

1 Introduction

SAMER AL-SAMARRAI AND BLANE LEWIS

Access to schooling in developing countries has increased rapidly over the last 20 years with many more children, and particularly poor children, starting earlier and staying in school for longer than ever before (World Bank 2018). These improvements have been due in part to greater investment in education. Global public spending on education has more than doubled in real terms since the early 2000s. The largest increases have been registered in low-income countries where public education spending increased from 3.5 percent of gross domestic product (GDP) in 1998–2001 to 4.1 percent in 2014–17 (Al-Samarrai, Cerdan-Infantes, and Lehe 2019).

Despite increases in investment and improvements in access, many countries continue to face a learning crisis. Across the world, 53 percent of all ten-year-old children are unable to read a short age-appropriate text with comprehension. The proportion of children in learning poverty increases to 90 percent in low-income countries (World Bank 2019). Changing this picture will require further increases in funding for education. Estimates show that low-income countries would have to increase public education spending to approximately 6 percent of GDP to provide good quality learning opportunities for all (Education Commission 2016). But spending more will not be enough. Research in many countries points to large spending inequalities across regions and different socioeconomic groups. Spending inefficiencies are also common. School inputs do not reach schools, teachers are not deployed where they are most needed, or funding is used to support activities that have little impact on learning. Addressing the twin financing challenges of inadequate and ineffective funding can support efforts to tackle the learning crisis and contribute to the achievement of national and international education goals (see figure 1.1). The COVID-19 pandemic places even greater focus on addressing these financing challenges to protect education investments and prevent the pandemic's short-term economic shock from lowering long-term development prospects.

The vast majority of the world's children live in countries where subnational governments are responsible for providing basic education services. Over the last 30 years, many countries have introduced reforms to decentralize basic public services. Education, and basic education (preprimary, primary and lower secondary schooling) in particular, have been at the forefront of these reforms in

FIGURE 1.1

The link between financing and education sector objectives

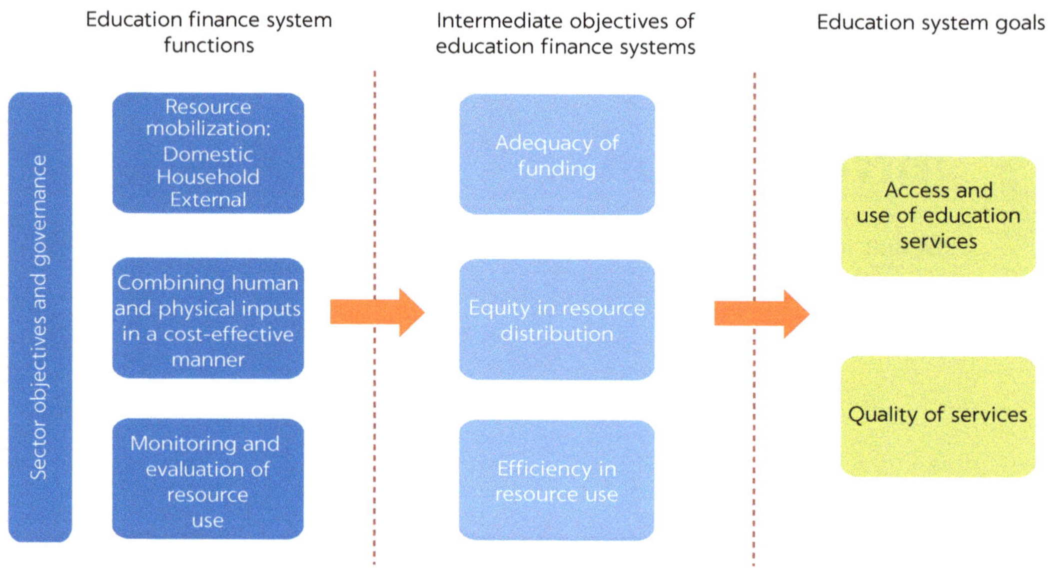

Source: World Bank.

many countries.[1] Recent estimates indicate that 84 percent of the world's children live in countries where government primary and secondary schools are run by local governments.[2]

Given the central role local governments play, the success of efforts to improve education outcomes will depend critically on how they use public education funding. In countries where education has been decentralized, a large share of public funding is managed and spent by subnational governments. Figure 1.2 shows the share of total education spending in a selection of countries that have decentralized basic education services. It shows that in most countries, subnational governments account for over 50 percent of total public education spending. If it were possible to focus only on basic education this share would be significantly higher. How effectively subnational governments are able to translate these funds into good quality education services will determine to a large degree the proportion of children in primary and secondary school that leave with the skills they require to continue to learn and lead productive lives.

Although subnational governments manage and make decisions on the use of public education funding, they often rely on transfers from the central government. In decentralized countries, intergovernmental fiscal transfers account for a large share of subnational government revenues. This dependence on transfers extends to subnational education funding. In Sudan, for example, central government fiscal transfers provide states with approximately three-quarters of all public education funding. In Indonesia, two-thirds of all public education funding in 2013 was allocated through fiscal transfers between the central government and provincial and district governments. Beyond core funding, transfer systems can also provide an effective system for channeling funds to protect education systems during times of crisis. In the United States, for example, federal stimulus packages have used existing transfer mechanisms to provide additional financial support to local education systems during the financial and COVID-19 crises.

FIGURE 1.2

Subnational public education spending as a percentage of total public education spending, 2010–18

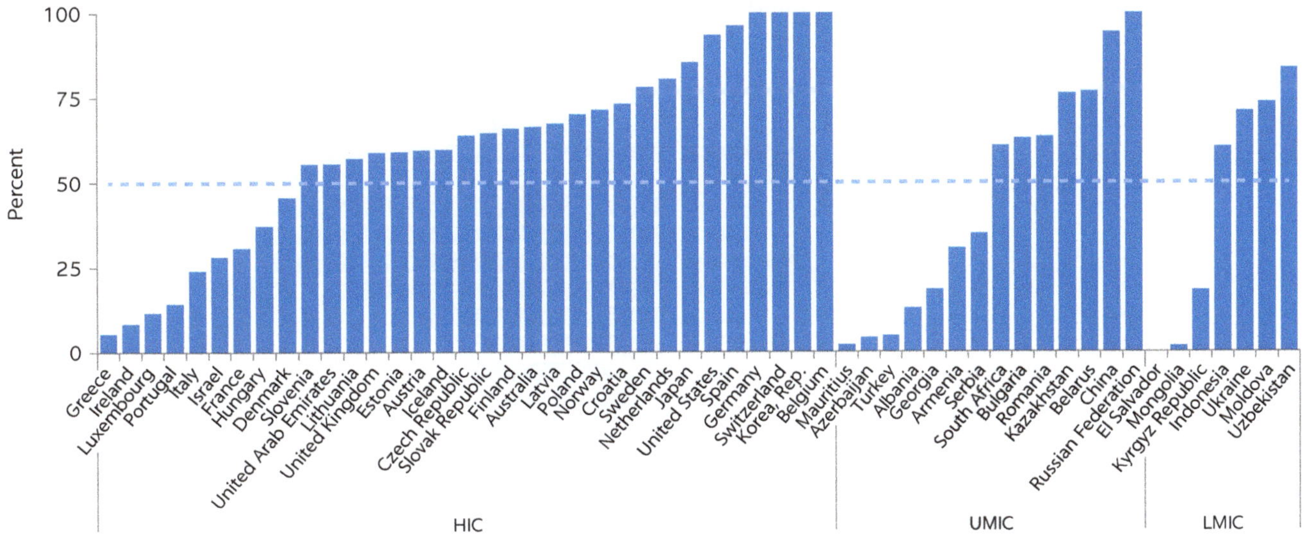

Source: World Bank calculations using Fiscal Decentralization Dataset, International Monetary Fund, Washington, DC (accessed May 8, 2020), https://data.imf.org/?sk=1C28EBFB-62B3-4B0C-AED3-048EEEBB684F.

Note: Average share calculated from all available data between 2010 and 2018. HIC = high-income country; LMIC = lower-middle-income country; UMIC = upper-middle-income country.

Because transfers account for a large share of subnational education spending, the way they are designed and implemented has important implications for how much subnational governments spend on education. Without transfers, the revenues of many subnational governments would be insufficient to provide education services to all children. How transfers are designed, for example, whether they are general transfers or specific to the education sector, influences their overall effect on subnational education spending. Some transfers elicit large increases in subnational education spending while others have only a limited effect. Some countries, through careful costing exercises, have also used transfers to ensure that all children, regardless of where they live, have access to a minimum standard of education.

Intergovernmental fiscal transfers also affect how equitably public funds for education are distributed. In many countries, large spending inequalities exist across regions. An analysis of recent public expenditure reviews shows that in many countries these differences are large. In Nigeria, for example, education spending per capita in the highest-spending region was nearly six times higher than that in the lowest-spending region (see figure 1.3). Subnational spending differences also tend to reinforce existing patterns of poverty and disadvantage. For example, in Tanzania, the relationship between district per capita spending on education and levels of poverty is negative and statistically significant (see figure 1.3). Transfer systems can help narrow spending inequalities by providing poorer subnational governments with additional funding to make up for their more limited revenues. This in turn can help narrow differences in school quality and ultimately differences in learning achievement between children living in different parts of a country.

FIGURE 1.3

Indicators of subnational public education spending per capita inequalities

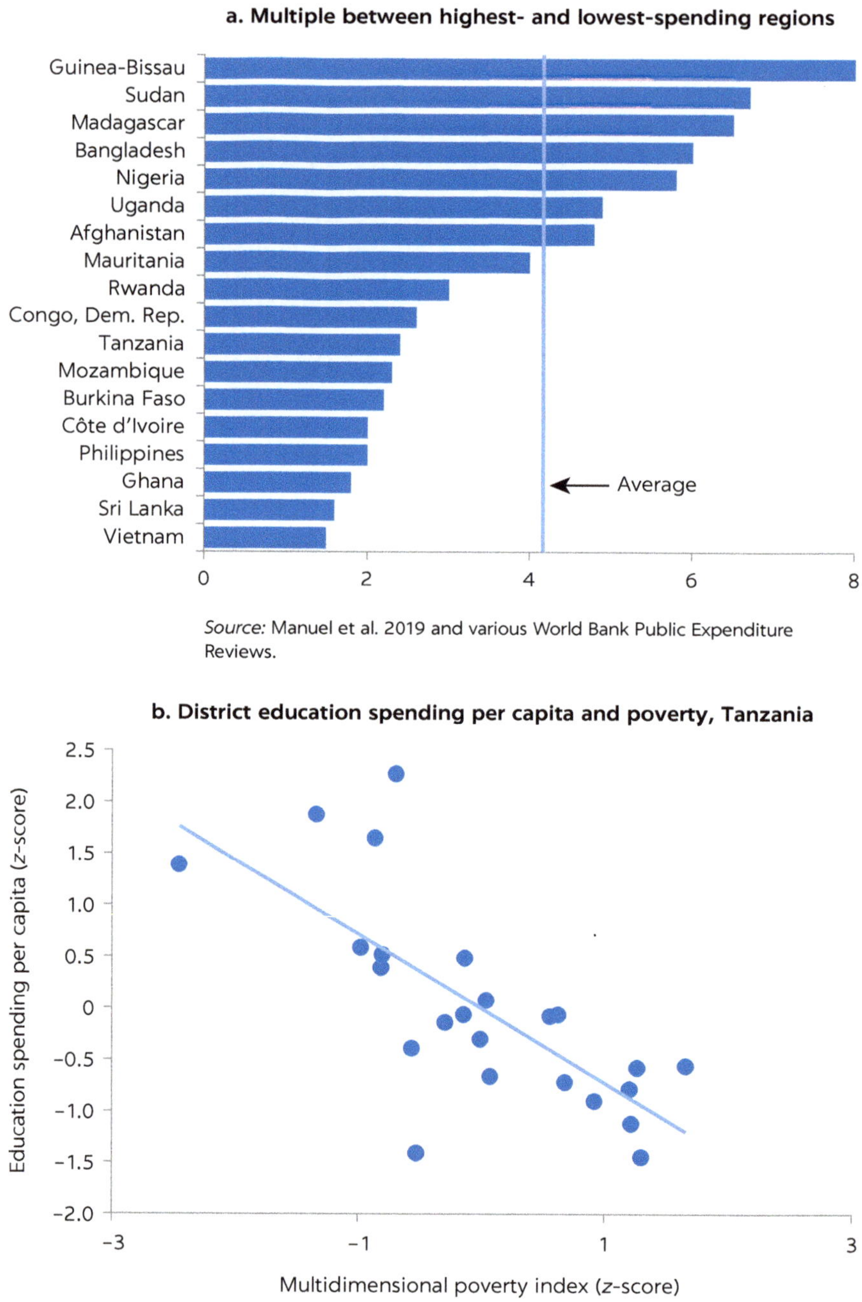

Source: Manuel et al. 2019.
Note: Data for Tanzania are from 2017–18.

Transfers can also create incentives for subnational governments to concentrate on specific results or to improve efficiency. Differences in how subnational governments translate funding into student learning outcomes are typically large. In Brazil, for example, some municipalities achieve average learning assessment scores three or four times higher than other municipalities even though they spend similar amounts per student. Some of these differences are likely explained by differences in the cost of provision and the socioeconomic conditions of municipal populations. However, differences also arise because some municipalities are more efficient in how they use their resources by, for example, ensuring that schools have the right balance between inputs and that governance and accountability systems work to ensure that resources are not wasted or used for other purposes. Intergovernmental transfers can create incentives for subnational governments to deliver education services more efficiently. For example, transfers can be designed to reward local governments for improved performance thus improving how resources are used.

Although intergovernmental fiscal transfers have the potential to drive improvements in subnational education systems, they sometimes fail to deliver. For example, many of the countries outlined in figure 1.3 rely on intergovernmental fiscal transfers to fund their education systems and yet large spending disparities remain between different regions. In other cases, the design of transfers can introduce implicit incentives that drive inefficiencies in education spending. For example, the formula for determining the size of transfers can introduce incentives to spend more on some educational inputs and neglect others, which can lead to suboptimal outcomes and drive inefficiency. Transfer formulas can also add to spending inequality by providing similar levels of funding to all subnational governments, ignoring differences in population and socioeconomic characteristics that can drive large differences in education outcomes.

The main purpose of this study is to assess how fiscal transfers affect public funding for education and how they ultimately affect student schooling and learning outcomes. Whereas research and analysis on education finance does not always look at the impact of fiscal decentralization reforms, research on fiscal transfers often does not explore in detail the impact on education outcomes. This study aims to fill this gap and provide a useful resource for both education and public sector reform practitioners and policy makers. Through a careful analysis of how fiscal transfers have affected education systems in different contexts, the study develops a set of principles to support improvements in the design and implementation of transfer systems with a specific focus on education service provision.

The study is centered around seven country case studies designed to answer a set of common research questions using a similar approach. Country case studies were conducted in Sudan, Uganda, Indonesia, Colombia, Brazil, Bulgaria, and China. The selection of case studies was driven primarily by the need to cover a broad set of country experiences and to capture countries at different stages of economic development and decentralization. As a result, the case studies provide a broad set of examples of how fiscal transfers have been used to address education sector challenges at different stages of development. While these factors were of primary importance, some of the case studies were also selected to exploit an existing evidence base on these issues or to explore countries where reforms in this area were taking place and the authors were engaged in related work.

The country case studies follow a common approach that first explores the complexities of public education funding in a decentralized system. They then analyze how intergovernmental transfers affect levels of subnational spending and how they influence the link between spending and education outcomes. They explore how different types of transfers have been used to address educational inequalities and improve spending efficiency. For example, the study assesses the use of performance-based transfers to improve learning outcomes and the use of equity transfers to narrow inequalities in access and completion.

The study also draws together the main findings from the case studies and assesses how fiscal transfer systems can improve the adequacy, equity, and efficiency of public education spending. The synthesis (chapter 3) uses the case studies and evidence from other countries to propose a set of principles to guide improvements in the design and implementation of intergovernmental fiscal transfer mechanisms that can drive improvements in education outcomes.

Chapter 2 outlines the key principles of fiscal decentralization including a framework for analyzing intergovernmental fiscal transfers. It also provides a brief review of the academic literature on the impact of transfers on education spending and the impact of spending on education outcomes. Chapter 3 provides a synthesis of the findings from the seven country case studies and draws out a set of guiding principles for improving the design and implementation of fiscal transfers aimed at supporting education service delivery. The remaining chapters provide the detailed case studies and dig deeper into the issues outlined in chapter 3.

NOTES

1. See Dyer and Rose (2005) and Channa and Faguet (2016) for discussion of the potential benefits and actual impact of decentralization in the education sector.
2. The estimates are based on the Fiscal Decentralization Dataset, International Monetary Fund, Washington, DC (accessed May 8, 2020), https://data.imf.org/?sk=1C28EBFB-62B3-4B0C-AED3-048EEEBB684F and OECD/UCLG (2019).

REFERENCES

Al-Samarrai, Samer, Pedro Cerdan-Infantes, and Jonathan David Lehe. 2019. "Mobilizing Resources for Education and Improving Spending Effectiveness: Establishing Realistic Benchmarks Based on Past Trends." Policy Research Working Paper 8773, World Bank, Washington, DC.

Channa, Anila, and Jean-Paul Faguet. 2016. "Decentralization of Health and Education in Developing Countries: A Quality-Adjusted Review of the Empirical Literature." *World Bank Research Observer* 31 (2): 199–241.

Dyer, C., and P. Rose. 2005. "Decentralisation for Educational Development? An Editorial Introduction." *Compare* 35 (2): 105–13.

Education Commission. 2016. *The Learning Generation: Investing in Education for a Changing World.* New York: International Commission on Financing Global Education Opportunity.

Manuel, Marcus, Dan Coppard, Amy Dodd, Harsh Desai, Richard Watts, Zach Christensen, and Stephanie Manea. 2019. "Subnational Investment in Human Capital." Development Initiatives, Bristol, UK.

OECD/UCLG. 2019. *2019 Report of the World Observatory on Subnational Government Finance and Investment—Key Findings and Country Profiles.* Paris: OECD.

World Bank. 2018. *World Development Report 2018: Learning to Realize Education's Promise.* Washington, DC: World Bank.

World Bank. 2019. *Ending Learning Poverty: What Will It Take?* Washington, DC: World Bank.

2 Key Principles of Fiscal Decentralization

BLANE LEWIS

Chapter 2 outlines key principles of fiscal decentralization, as drawn from the academic literature, including: (1) the rationale for devolving service provision and financing responsibilities to subnational governments; (2) guidelines for assigning particular expenditures and revenues across levels of government; and (3) a framework for designing and allocating intergovernmental transfers. Implications for education sector decentralization are discussed. Finally, the literature on the impact of transfers on education spending and the impact of spending on education outcomes is briefly reviewed and some outstanding issues and policy questions are highlighted.

RATIONALE FOR FISCAL DECENTRALIZATION

The decentralization of responsibility for the provision and financing of services from central governments to subnational governments is a pervasive phenomenon in developing and transition countries (Martinez-Vazquez and Vaillancourt 2011; Smoke and Loffler 2013). In theory, decentralization results in a better match between subnational public service delivery and diverse citizen preferences. The expected benefits are a function of the relative physical proximity of subnationals to their respective constituents. Greater proximity allows subnationals to determine citizen demand for services more accurately than the central government and to tax and spend more effectively based on that understanding (Oates 1972). Proximity also supports the strengthening of horizontal accountability. Because citizens are physically closer to their subnational governments, they are better able to insist that their demands for more and better services be met. They may also be more encouraged to hold subnationals accountable when they are obliged to pay taxes and charges for services. In any case the increased demand-side accountability reinforces independent improvements to subnational service supply. In theory, the overall outcome is more efficient subnational public service delivery (Lewis 2017a; Lewis and Smoke 2017; Martinez-Vazquez and Vaillancourt 2011; Oates 1972; Smoke and Loffler 2013; Tiebout 1956).

Worldwide experience of developing and transition countries that are decentralizing their public sectors suggests, however, that the theoretical benefits of decentralization may not be so easily attained. For one thing, decentralization programs are in many, perhaps most, cases undertaken for purely political reasons and are not necessarily explicitly intended to achieve public service efficiency or horizontal accountability objectives (Eaton, Kaiser, and Smoke 2011). Even where such potential gains are recognized and sought out, practice shows that the increased physical proximity between subnational government decision-makers and their citizens, in and of itself, may be inadequate to generate expected improvements in subnational service delivery and related outcomes. A significant amount of quantitative and qualitative research on the impact of decentralization on services is particularly mixed, ranging from strongly positive to deeply negative and everything in between (Bardhan and Mookherjee 2006; Boadway and Shah 2007; Channa and Faguet 2016; Connerley, Eaton, and Smoke 2010; Faguet 2014; Martinez-Vazquez and Vaillancourt 2011; Lewis 2017a; Lewis and Smoke 2017; Smoke 2001, 2014).

The academic literature highlights a number of political economy factors that may cause decentralization's uneven service delivery. Perhaps the most well-known finding in this context is that subnationals in developing and transition countries often suffer from elite capture or clientelism (Bardhan and Mookherjee 2000, 2012; Smoke 2014). Under elite capture, fiscal resources are diverted away from the delivery of basic services demanded by most citizens and toward proscribed uses or beneficiaries, especially the rich and powerful. Under clientelism, some benefits may be susceptible to redirection to key political constituencies in the run-up to elections. Elite capture and clientelism may exist at both the central and subnational levels, of course, but they may be especially problematic subnationally because of the relatively greater cohesiveness of special interest groups and reduced voter awareness (Bardhan and Mookherjee 2000).[1] Other basic political economy and governance features, such as the establishment of subnational jurisdiction boundaries (and the creation of new subnational units), central government interference in subnational decision-making, subnational government form (directly versus indirectly elected subnational executives), the size and functioning of subnational legislatures, and formation and structure of executive-legislative coalitions, among many others, may also constrain successful decentralized service delivery (Lewis 2018, 2019; Lewis and Hendrawan 2019).

EXPENDITURE ASSIGNMENT

The guiding principle for assigning public service responsibilities across levels of government is Wallace Oates's decentralization theorem (Oates 1972). A closely related standard is subsidiarity, which is the recognized basis for assigning services in the European Union, among other places (McLure and Martinez-Vazquez 2000). Both imply that expenditures should be assigned to the lowest level of government compatible with the size and scope of the benefit area of delivered services (Bahl 2008). These principles argue for decentralizing most public service delivery to the lowest level of government—unless there are particularly good reasons for not doing so. Some of those "particularly good reasons" relate to macroeconomic stabilization, risk-pooling, economies of scale, and spatial externalities (Boadway and Eyraud 2018). These latter standards may be thought of as mitigating criteria that imply at least some involvement of higher levels of government in service provision.

Government stabilization functions are designed to address common macroeconomic shocks, and these are most appropriately carried out at the central level. Services that require risk-pooling, such as those related to social insurance programs, are usually claimed to be more efficiently carried out centrally. Some services with especially strong economies of scale—major transportation systems, for example—can be more efficiently provided centrally. Finally, public services for which benefits (costs) spill over to a large extent across jurisdictional boundaries may warrant higher-level government provision, because lower levels may tend to under- (over-) supply them. Overall, these principles suggest that the central government should assume responsibility for national public goods and social insurance programs, while subnational governments should provide local public goods (Boadway and Eyraud 2018).

Expenditure assignments among subnationals at the same level need not be uniform; some asymmetry may be desirable given the different characteristics of subnationals (for example, urban versus rural) and uneven capacities. Finally, even in the case of subnational provision, central government should likely maintain at least some policy authority (Martinez-Vazquez and Vaillancourt 2011; Boadway and Eyraud 2018).

Although these principles provide broad guidance in expenditure assignment, in practice many different assignments may be consistent with the standards. Perhaps the most important point in this context is that any service assignment that is undertaken should be clear to all parties involved and rigorously enforced.

TAX ASSIGNMENT

It is usually argued that the assignment of authority over taxes should come after decisions have been made regarding the decentralization of expenditures across the various levels of government in a country. That is, in principle, finance should follow function. This suggests, among other things, that any revenues that are directly associated with the provision of services should be placed under the authority of the government providing those services. Beyond that, taxes may be assigned across levels of government based on two additional principles: efficiency in tax administration and fiscal needs (Bahl 2008; Bird 2011; Shah 1999). Mobile tax bases are more efficiently managed from the center, for example, in order to minimize tax competition. The fiscal needs criterion highlights again the importance of a prior assignment of service responsibilities, because the financial needs of a government cannot be accurately derived until expenditure assignments have been determined (Bird 2011). A final principle of tax assignment is that governments at all levels require sufficient tax base and rate authority "at the margin," so that any rise in service demand can be financed out of marginal increases in own-tax revenues. Insufficient own-source revenues—vertical fiscal imbalances—reduce subnational government fiscal discipline and weaken horizontal accountability (Eyraud and Lusinyan 2013; Gadenne 2017).

In practice, the application of these principles implies that the central government should probably be assigned corporate and personal income taxes, multistage sales taxes (value-added taxes—VAT), taxes on unequally distributed natural resources, and international trade taxes, among others. Second-tier governments might hold authority over single-stage sales taxes; taxes on alcohol, motor fuels, lotteries, and vehicles; provincial road congestion charges; and excises. Finally, property taxes should be assigned to lower government tiers, as should local road tolls, market taxes, and user charges of various kinds (Bahl 2008; Boadway and Eyraud 2018; Shah 1999).

Tax assignments across countries of the world vary significantly, even among those nations that have attempted to apply the broad principles outlined above. Those differences notwithstanding, a common result is that subnationals, especially those at the lowest tiers of government, will in all likelihood have an insufficient amount of revenue to finance the services they have been charged with delivering. That is, it is typical for countries to decentralize significant expenditures to subnationals while maintaining a relatively more substantial role for the central government in raising tax revenues. This internationally ubiquitous outcome highlights the unavoidable and essential role played by intergovernmental transfers in filling resource gaps (Bahl and Linn 1992).

INTERGOVERNMENTAL TRANSFERS

Transfer objectives

The four most commonly stated objectives for intergovernmental transfers are adequacy, equity, efficiency, and performance. These objectives are relevant for transfer systems in general and for transfers specific to education. For transfer systems in general, adequacy refers to addressing vertical imbalances between levels of government (assuring that each subnational level has sufficient funds to deliver on its responsibilities); equity refers to accommodating horizontal imbalances (equalizing net fiscal capacity across subnational governments at a particular level); efficiency is linked to the idea of preserving an "internal common market" (for example, guaranteeing that all subnational governments at a certain level have enough money to deliver a minimum standard of services, thereby encouraging the efficient flow of labor, capital, and goods across borders), addressing spatial spillovers and other externalities, and promoting the efficient use of inputs and the delivery of outputs demanded by citizens; and performance refers to transfers that encourage any of the many "results" that the central government would like to promote. Objectives are often mutually compatible. Meeting minimum service standards, for instance, discussed here as a means of achieving efficiency goals, may also promote adequacy, equity, and even performance objectives. On the other hand, transfer objectives may sometimes be in tension with one another. Intergovernmental transfers that focus purely on equalizing net fiscal capacity across subnational units, for example, may not do much to promote the efficient use of service delivery inputs or encourage subnational government service performance (Bahl and Linn 1992; Boadway and Shah 2007; Shah 1994).

For education, adequacy means that transfers are sufficient for schools to educate all students to desired levels; equity refers to equalizing the net fiscal capacity of schools or the provision of transfers for poor students to support their enrollment and learning; efficiency means that funding focuses on delivering a minimum level of education to all students, addresses benefit spillovers to neighboring jurisdictions, or is allocated to school activities that promote the technical or cost-efficient use of inputs and resources by schools, or, at the margin, are most likely to lead to education outputs desired by the community; and performance means promoting education outputs or outcomes of various types through the transfer system.

Transfer types

There are many different ways to classify transfer types. A common one follows, based on Boadway and Shah (2007):

- General nonmatching
- Conditional input-based nonmatching
- Conditional input-based matching
  - Open-ended
  - Closed-ended
- Conditional output-based nonmatching

General grants are lump sum transfers to subnational governments that can be spent on any functions that the subnational government chooses. Conditional nonmatching transfers, sometimes referred to as "sectoral block grants," are transfers to subnational governments that are targeted for use in particular sectors. Conditional matching grants are also meant to be spent on indicated functions and require some counterpart contribution by the recipient government. Such grants can be either open-ended, with no firm limit on the size of the grant or closed-ended, where grant magnitude is restricted. Conditional output-based nonmatching grants target, as the name implies, improvements in sector-specific outputs or outcomes.

The general idea is that individual types of grants, as classified above, should be matched with objectives. General nonmatching transfers are usually preferred for addressing adequacy concerns, for example. General nonmatching transfers are also typically viewed as the most appropriate mechanisms to tackle problems related to equity and horizontal imbalances. Conditional input-based nonmatching or conditional input-based matching grants are often used to encourage spending on particular types of activities or functions to enhance efficiency; the former are usually thought to be most appropriate to address minimum service standards and the latter to deal with spillovers and externalities. And conditional output-based grants are preferred for dealing with performance objectives. Again, these matches work for both the transfer system, in general, and as it relates to education, specifically. The links between grant objectives and grant types are summarized in table 2.1.

TABLE 2.1 **Transfer type by objective**

	TRANSFER OBJECTIVE			
TRANSFER TYPE	ADEQUACY	EQUITY	EFFICIENCY	PERFORMANCE
General	√	√	n.a.	n.a.
Conditional input-based nonmatching	n.a.	n.a.	√	n.a.
Conditional input-based matching	n.a.	n.a.	√	n.a.
Conditional output-based	n.a.	n.a.	n.a.	√

Source: World Bank.
Note: √ = applicable; n.a. = not applicable.

TABLE 2.2 **Allocation of transfers**

	DETERMINING THE POOL OF FUNDS		
ALLOCATING THE POOL OF FUNDS	SPECIFIED SHARE OF NATIONAL REVENUE	AD HOC	REIMBURSEMENT OF EXPENDITURE
Origin of collection	General nonmatching	n.a.	n.a.
Formula	General nonmatching or conditional input-based nonmatching (sectoral block grants)	General nonmatching or conditional input-based matching or nonmatching	n.a.
Cost reimbursement	Conditional input-based matching or nonmatching	General nonmatching or conditional input-based matching or nonmatching	General nonmatching or conditional input-based matching or nonmatching or conditional output-based nonmatching
Performance-based	n.a.	Conditional output-based matching or nonmatching	n.a.
Ad hoc	General nonmatching, conditional input-based matching or nonmatching	General nonmatching or conditional input-based matching or nonmatching	n.a.

Source: Adapted from Bahl and Linn 1992.
Note: n.a. = not applicable.

Transfer allocation mechanisms

The allocation of transfers has two components: determining the total pool of funds available for transfers and distributing that pool across individual units (such as governments and schools). There are three basic ways to determine the pool of funds: as a specified share of national government tax or nontax revenue; as a function of annual ad hoc decision-making; or based on the reimbursement of approved expenditures. The five principal means of allocating the pool of funds are: origin of tax or nontax revenue; formula; reimbursement of costs; performance-based; and ad hoc. A sixth means of allocating funds is based on subnational government proposals to the central government. This is not a typical method of distributing grant funds, although some countries, such as Indonesia, employ it to a limited extent.

Allocation mechanisms can also be matched to transfer types. One way of matching fiscal transfer types with distribution arrangements is shown in table 2.2.

EDUCATION SECTOR DECENTRALIZATION

The provision of education is among the most decentralized of all government functions. Benefit areas for education tend to be reasonably local for primary, secondary, and vocational schools. There may be some education benefit spillover across neighboring jurisdictions (or even nationally), but where there is evidence that subnational governments underprovide schooling because of positive externalities they can be encouraged to increase supply through conditional input-based matching grants. Because macroeconomic stabilization and risk-sharing are not particularly noteworthy in the sector, there is no obvious need to centralize education responsibilities based on these standards.

Education functions of special note include teacher recruitment, promotion, and payment; school maintenance, rehabilitation, and construction; standard setting; curriculum design and teaching methods; textbook production and distribution; and student evaluation. Of these, teacher payment and school maintenance, rehabilitation, and construction are mostly assigned locally, while all other subfunctions tend to be shared among subnational governments and the central government, with the latter maintaining significant control over policy.

With respect to education finance, subnational governments typically employ various community funding schemes, such as school fees, contingencies, and ad hoc contributions. In addition, the central government often assigns a particular revenue source to be used by subnational governments to finance education; the property tax is especially important in this context. These two sources of finance are rarely sufficient to cover the costs associated with providing education, however. This deficiency suggests a strong role for intergovernmental transfers in financing education at the subnational level (Rondinelli 1999).

There is significant disagreement, however, about the types of intergovernmental transfers that should be employed to support the funding of local education. Public finance experts tend to view the use of general grants as optimal, on adequacy and equity grounds. Most seem to prefer a minimalist approach to the use of conditional grants in the sector, viewing their employment as necessary only to address specific efficiency concerns such as ensuring minimum standards in education or accommodating education benefit spillovers. Education sector specialists, on the other hand, appear to favor a much more pronounced role for conditional grants, in order to ensure sufficient levels and growth of funding in the sector, perhaps, or to address a broader range of efficiencies, such as the optimal use of teaching inputs. Interest in performance grants is apparent across both camps, but experience in the use of such mechanisms in the education sector is so far quite limited and approaches for advancing their employment in a more significant way are contentious. In sum, consensus on the use of intergovernmental transfers in the education sector remains elusive.

IMPACT OF FISCAL TRANSFERS IN EDUCATION: A LITERATURE REVIEW

Impact of transfers on education spending

The impact of intergovernmental fiscal transfers on subnational education spending depends, in theory, on the type of transfer. It is typically claimed, for example, that conditional transfers have a larger effect on education spending than general transfers because conditional transfers must be spent in the education sector; general transfers can be spent by subnationals on any function—education or others—according to their preferences (Gamkhar and Shah 2007; Gruber 2010; Shah 1994). Therefore, targeted conditional grants are more likely to induce increases in education spending.

Among conditional transfers, both open- and closed-ended, matching grants are thought to stimulate education spending the most. Such grants both provide additional funds to subnational governments—the income effect—and lower the cost of spending in education—the price or substitution effect. The two effects work together to increase spending by a potentially considerable amount, sometimes by more than the amount of the grant itself. (In the case of closed-ended matching grants, the subsidy applies only until the maximum size of the grant is reached.) Conditional nonmatching grants may also be useful in increasing education spending, but their impact may not be as large as that of matching grants. The latter have only an income effect, which reduces the overall spending impact, typically to an amount that is less than the size of the transfer. Note that for conditional nonmatching transfers, if the amount of the grant is less than what subnational governments would have otherwise spent on education, the expected impact is indistinguishable from that of a general grant (Gamkhar and Shah 2007).

The available empirical evidence is quite mixed with regard to the theoretical propositions described in the previous paragraphs. Some research does, in fact, suggest that conditional grants are more stimulative of local education spending than general grants. Lewis (2013) shows, for example, that an extra rupiah of closed-ended matching capital grant in Indonesia leads to an increase in local government capital spending on education and health of 0.50 rupiah, whereas an additional rupiah of general purpose grant leads to a rise in education and health capital spending of only 0.01 rupiah. At the same time, a substantial amount of research implies that general grants may have a larger impact on spending, in general, than theory would predict. That is, the effect of a general transfer to subnational governments on spending should, in theory, be equivalent to the effect of a transfer directly to local community private income. Gamkhar and Shah (2007) review a large number of studies and find that an extra US$1.00 of general grants leads to a nearly US$0.60 increase in subnational spending. However, an additional US$1.00 of private income results in an increase of only US$0.10 in spending at most. The differential impact is often referred to as the flypaper effect—money sticks where it lands (Gramlich 1969; Henderson 1968; Inman 2008). Some evidence suggests that the impact of conditional closed-ended matching grants on subnational education spending may be significantly lower than anticipated. In a rare study on the topic, McGuire (1973) found that an extra US$1.00 of federal matching education grants to local governments in the United States led to between a US$0.82 and US$0.98 increase in total local spending, but that 64–69 percent of that spending was allocated to noneducation sectors. On the other hand, substantial empirical evidence shows that nonmatching conditional grants in the education sector have broadly the expected impact. A wide-ranging survey by Fisher and Papke (2000) found that a US$1.00 increase in nonmatching conditional grants to state governments in the United States resulted in a US$0.30 to US$0.70 increase in education spending.

Impact of spending on education outcomes

How does public spending, in turn, affect education outcomes? This key policy question has generated a significant amount of academic work over the years. As before, the empirical evidence is quite mixed. Some research indicates that spending has an insubstantial impact, if any, on education outcomes. Hanushek (1995) reviews the experience of many developing countries across major regions of the world and finds an unsystematic relationship between public spending and education outcomes of various kinds. Mingat and Tan (1992, 1998) also find little association between public expenditures and education outcomes across a large sample of developed and developing countries.

Other research on the impact of spending on education outcomes offers more ambiguous results. Incentive payments for teachers in Chile had positive effects on math and language test scores but had no significant impact on enrollment (Contreras and Rau 2012). The No Child Left Behind program in the United States had a positive effect on children's math test scores but had no impact on reading scores (Dee and Jacob 2011). In Jakarta, Indonesia, Al-Samarrai et al. (2018) show that the city's performance grant program led to improvements in test scores among students in junior secondary school but not among those in primary school. The analysis also suggests that any positive results may have been more a function of competition among schools to secure performance funding rather than an increase in the availability of resources per se.

Finally, other empirical work suggests more positive and robust effects related to the influence of public spending on education service delivery. Gupta, Verhoeven, and Tiongson (2002) find a strong correlation between public spending and education and health outcomes for a cross-section sample of 50 transition and developing countries. Jackson, Johnson, and Persico (2014) demonstrate the existence of a very significant relationship between public education spending and a variety of school outcomes in the United States for a nationally representative panel of children born between 1955 and 1985. Baldacci, Guin-Siu, and de Mello (2003) show for 94 transition and developing countries that public spending can be effective in improving education and health outcomes, as long as underlying problems related to income and gender inequality are resolved. Rajkumar and Swaroop (2008) examine a panel of 90 developed and developing countries and conclude that the effect of spending on education and health outcomes is significantly improved as the quality of governance rises. Litschig and Morrison (2013) demonstrate that a 20 percent increase in local government spending over a period of four years in Brazil led to a rise in enrollment of about 7 percent and an increase in literacy rates of approximately four percentage points. de Carvalho Filho and Litschig (2017) find that these positive effects endured, albeit at diminished levels, for up to 15 years after the initial increase in education spending. Lewis (2017b) shows that Indonesian local government spending positively affects education and other outcomes, especially when local governance conditions are accommodating.

Outstanding issues and policy questions

The technical issues related to the investigation of the impact of transfers on education spending and the effect of spending on education outcomes are summarized in the preceding sections. Among the most important, perhaps, is the potential endogeneity of explanatory variables. That is, it has been argued by many researchers that transfers should in many cases be treated as endogenous in the determination of spending and that spending should be taken as endogenous in the determination of outcomes (see, for example, Gamkhar and Shah 2007; Lewis 2013, 2016). Other technical problems with the estimation of transfer and spending effects include, among others, possible omitted explanatory factors, neglecting grant conditions when examining the impact of transfers on spending, and the disregard of plausible dynamic effects (Gamkhar and Shah 2007). If these technical issues are not handled well in model specification and estimation, the empirical results will be biased. These difficulties may help explain both why the results diverge to such a large extent from what theory predicts and why the empirical results differ so much across individual studies.

For policy purposes, the definition of "spending" is critical to the examination of transfer impact on spending and spending impact on outcomes. In many, perhaps most, analyses researchers have focused on the effects of transfers on education spending and of education spending on education outcomes. However, this ignores the fact that spending on other functions may also have an impact on education outcomes. For example, expenditure on health and social protection (health insurance and subsidies to the poor), the environment (protecting clean water from pollutants), infrastructure and low-income housing (clean water and sanitation access), security and law and order (provision of a safe environment for the delivery of subnational public services), and even administration (which includes supply of back office functions for subnational government and its service delivery units) may well positively influence education outcomes. If so, a narrow focus on education spending may miss an important part of the story (Lewis 2017b).

NOTE

1. On the other hand, capture and clientelism may be comparatively stronger at the central level when electoral competition for higher office is negligible or national electoral outcomes are highly uncertain (Bardhan and Mookherjee 2000).

REFERENCES

Al-Samarrai, S., U. Shrestha, A. Hasan, N. Nakajima, S. Santoso, and W.H.A. Wijoyo. 2018. "Introducing a Performance-Based Component into Jakarta's School Grants: What Do We Know about its Impact after Three Years?" *Economics of Education Review* 67 (December): 110–36.

Bahl, R.W. 2008. "The Pillars of Fiscal Decentralization." CAF Working Paper 2008/07, CAF, Caracas.

Bahl, R.W., and J.F. Linn. 1992. *Urban Public Finance in Developing Countries*. Washington, DC: World Bank.

Baldacci, E., M.T. Guin-Siu, and de Mello, L. 2003. "More on the Effectiveness of Public Spending on Health Care and Education: A Covariance Structure Model." *Journal of International Development* 15 (6): 709–25.

Bardhan, P.K., and D. Mookherjee. 2000. "Capture and Governance at Local and National Levels." *American Economic Review* 90 (2): 135–39.

——. 2006. "Decentralisation and Accountability in Infrastructure Delivery in Developing Countries." *Economic Journal* 116 (508): 101–27.

——. 2012. "Political Clientelism and Capture: Theory and Evidence from West Bengal, India." Working Paper, 2012/97, Helsinki, World Institute for Development Economics Research.

Bird, R.M. 2011. "Subnational Taxation in Developing Countries: A Review of the Literature." *Journal of International Commerce, Economics and Policy* 2 (1): 139–61.

Boadway, R., and L. Eyraud. 2018. "Designing Sound Fiscal Relations Across Government Levels in Decentralized Countries." Working Paper 18/271, International Monetary Fund, Washington, DC.

Boadway, R.W., and A. Shah, eds. 2007. *Intergovernmental Fiscal Transfers: Principles and Practices*. Washington, DC: World Bank.

Channa, A., and J.P. Faguet. 2016. "Decentralization of Health and Education in Developing Countries: A Quality-Adjusted Review of the Empirical Literature." *World Bank Research Observer* 31 (2): 199–241.

Connerley, E., K. Eaton, and P.J. Smoke, eds. 2010. *Making Decentralization Work: Democracy, Development, and Security*. Boulder, CO: Lynne Rienner Publishers.

Contreras, D., and T. Rau. 2012. "Tournament Incentives for Teachers: Evidence from a Scaled-Up Intervention in Chile." *Economic Development and Cultural Change* 61 (1): 219–46.

de Carvalho Filho, I., and S. Litschig. 2016. "Long-Run Impacts of Intergovernmental Transfers." *Journal of Human Resources*. doi: 10.3368/jhr.57.3:0917-9064R2.

Dee, T.S., and B. Jacob. 2011. "The Impact of No Child Left Behind on Student Achievement." *Journal of Policy Analysis and Management* 30 (3): 418–46.

Eaton, K., K.A. Kaiser, and P.J. Smoke. 2011. *The Political Economy of Decentralization Reforms: Implications for Aid Effectiveness*. World Bank: Washington, DC.

Eyraud, L., and L. Lusinyan. 2013. "Vertical Fiscal Imbalances and Fiscal Performance in Advanced Economies." *Journal of Monetary Economics* 60 (5): 571–87.

Faguet, J.P. 2014. Decentralization and Governance. *World Development* 53 (C): 2–13.

Fisher, R.C., and L.E. Papke. 2000. "Local Government Responses to Education Grants." *National Tax Journal* 53 (1): 153–68.

Gadenne, Lucie. 2017. "Tax Me, But Spend Wisely? Sources of Public Finance and Government Accountability." *American Economic Journal: Applied Economics* 9 (1): 274–314.

Gamkhar, S., and A. Shah. 2007. "The Impact of Intergovernmental Fiscal Transfers: A Synthesis of the Conceptual and Empirical Literature." In *Intergovernmental Fiscal Transfers: Principles and Practice*, edited by R. Boadway and A. Shah, 225–58. Washington, DC: World Bank.

Gupta, S., M. Verhoeven, and E.R. Tiongson. 2002. "The Effectiveness of Government Spending on Education and Health Care in Developing and Transition Economies." *European Journal of Political Economy* 18 (4): 717–37.

Gruber, J. 2010. *Public Finance and Public Policy*. New York: Macmillan.

Gramlich, E.M. 1969. "A Clarification and Correction: Alternative Federal Policies for Stimulating State and Local Expenditures." *National Tax Journal* 22 (2): 286–90.

Hanushek, E.A. 1995. "Interpreting Recent Research on Schooling in Developing Countries." *World Bank Research Observer* 10 (2): 227–46.

Henderson, J.M. 1968. "Local Government Expenditures: A Social Welfare Analysis." *Review of Economics and Statistics* 50 (2): 156–63.

Inman, R.P. 2008. "The Flypaper Effect." National Bureau of Economic Research Working Paper w14579, NBER, Cambridge, MA.

Jackson, C.K., R. Johnson, and C. Persico. 2014. "The Effect of School Finance Reforms on the Distribution of Spending, Academic Achievement, and Adult Outcomes." National Bureau of Economic Research Working Paper w20118, NBER, Cambridge, MA.

Lewis, B.D. 2013. "Local Government Capital Spending in Indonesia: Impact of Intergovernmental Fiscal Transfers." *Public Budgeting & Finance* 33 (1): 76–94.

———. 2017a. "Does Local Government Proliferation Improve Public Service Delivery? Evidence from Indonesia." *Journal of Urban Affairs* 39 (8): 1047–65.

———. 2017b. "Local Government Spending and Service Delivery in Indonesia: The Perverse Effects of Substantial Fiscal Resources." *Regional Studies* 51 (11): 1695–1707.

———. 2018. "Local Government Form in Indonesia: Tax, Expenditure, and Efficiency Effects." *Studies in Comparative International Development* 53 (1): 25–46.

———. 2019. "Legislature Size, Local Government Expenditure and Taxation, and Public Service Access in Indonesia." *Studies in Comparative International Development* 54 (2): 274–98.

Lewis, B.D., and A. Hendrawan. 2019. "The Impact of Majority Coalitions on Local Government Spending, Service Delivery, and Corruption in Indonesia." *European Journal of Political Economy* 58 (June): 178–91.

Lewis, B.D., and P. Smoke. 2017. "Intergovernmental Fiscal Transfers and Local Incentives and Responses: The Case of Indonesia." *Fiscal Studies* 38 (1): 111–39.

Litschig, S., and K.M. Morrison. 2013. "The Impact of Intergovernmental Transfers on Education Outcomes and Poverty Reduction." *American Economic Journal: Applied Economics* 5 (4): 206–40.

Martinez-Vazquez, J., and F. Vaillancourt, eds. 2011. *Decentralization in Developing Countries.* Cheltenham, UK: Edward Elgar Publishing.

McGuire, M. 1973. "Notes on Grants-in-Aid and Economic Interactions Among Governments." *Canadian Journal of Economics* 6 (2): 207–21.

McLure, C., and J. Martinez-Vazquez. 2000. "The Assignment of Revenues and Expenditures in Intergovernmental Fiscal Relations." World Bank Institute, Washington, DC.

Mingat, A., and J.P. Tan. 1992. *Education in Asia: A Comparative Study of Cost and Financing.* Washington, DC: World Bank.

——. 1998. "The Mechanics of Progress in Education. Evidence from Cross-Country Data." Policy Research Working Paper 2015, World Bank, Washington, DC.

Oates, W.E. 1972. *Fiscal Federalism.* Cheltenham, UK: Edward Elgar Publishing.

Rajkumar, A.S., and V. Swaroop. 2008. "Public Spending and Outcomes: Does Governance Matter?" *Journal of Development Economics* 86 (1): 96–111.

Rondinelli, D. 1999. "What Is Decentralization?" In *Decentralization Briefing Notes*, edited by Jennie Litvak and Jessica Seddon, 2–5. Washington, DC: World Bank.

Shah, A. 1994. *The Reform of Intergovernmental Fiscal Relations in Developing and Emerging Market Economies.* Washington, DC: World Bank.

——. 1999. *Fiscal Federalism and Macroeconomic Governance: For Better or for Worse?* Washington, DC: World Bank.

Smoke, P. 2001. *Fiscal Decentralization in Developing Countries: A Review of Current Concepts and Practice.* Geneva: United Nations Research Institute for Social Development.

——. 2014. "Why Theory and Practice Are Different: The Gap Between Principles and Reality in Subnational Revenue Systems." In *Taxation and Development: The Weakest Link?*, edited by R.M. Bird and J. Martinez-Vazquez, 287–325. Cheltenham, UK: Edward Elgar Publishing.

Smoke, P., and G. Loffler. 2013. *The Role of Decentralisation/Devolution in Improving Development Outcomes at the Local Level.* Brooklyn, NY: Local Development International LLC.

Tiebout, C.M. 1956. "A Pure Theory of Local Expenditures." *Journal of Political Economy* 64 (5): 416–24.

3 Assessing the Effects of Intergovernmental Fiscal Transfers on Education Financing and Outcomes

AN OVERVIEW OF SEVEN CASE STUDIES

SAMER AL-SAMARRAI AND BLANE LEWIS

INTRODUCTION

Chapter 3 presents evidence from seven country case studies on how intergovernmental fiscal transfers have been used to strengthen education systems and improve education outcomes. The chapter explores how the case study countries have used transfers to provide adequate funding for basic education, narrow education inequalities, increase efficiency, and incentivize better performance from various actors in the education sector. Although it draws mostly on the evidence presented in the case studies, it also includes examples from other countries, mostly high-income countries, to supplement this evidence where necessary. Because the transfer systems in the case study countries have very different characteristics and are at different stages of development, no attempt at a systematic comparison across case studies is made. The chapter concludes with some principles for the design and implementation of effective transfers for education.

The case study countries differ in their stages of economic development and the number and size of their subnational jurisdictions. Gross national income (GNI) per capita varies from US$590 in Sudan to over US$10,410 in China (see table 3.1). Although all of the case study countries have decentralized, there is considerable variability in the size of the basic education systems that their subnational governments manage. For example, in the Latin American case studies, the average municipality has a total population of approximately 10,000 children of school age (between 5 and 19 years old) compared to the subnational governments in the African case studies, which manage systems comprising approximately 90,000 students (see table 3.1).

The type and scale of the education challenges faced by the countries also differ. Increasing access to education is a significant challenge for countries with low per capita income levels but less of a challenge for wealthier countries. For example, the secondary education system in Sudan is able to enroll only 47 percent of the secondary-school-aged population, whereas in Brazil, Bulgaria, and Colombia, secondary schooling is available to almost all children (see table 3.1). Large differences related to levels of income are also evident in basic education

TABLE 3.1 **Economic and education characteristics of case study countries**

	SUDAN	UGANDA	INDONESIA	COLOMBIA	BRAZIL	BULGARIA	CHINA
GNI per capita (US$)	590	780	4,050	6,510	9,130	9,410	10,410
Poverty headcount (%)	—	69.9	24.2	10.9	9.2	3.1	5.4
States/provinces/regions	18	—	34	33	27	—	31
Districts/municipalities	189	175	508	1,101	5,570	265	2,861
Average district population age 5–19	82,739	102,654	138,480	10,854	8,303	3,835	86,528
Responsibility for basic education	S	D	D	D	D & S	D	D
Public primary education spending per child (US$ PPP)	106	92	1,465	2,549	3,163	3,779	2,910
Primary GER (%)	77	103	106	115	115	89	99
Secondary GER (%)	47	31	87	96	101	98	104
Learning-adjusted years of schooling	4.4	4.5	7.9	8.5	7.6	10.3	9.7
Learning poverty (%)	—	83	—	48	48	12	18
Income group	LIC	LIC	UMIC	UMIC	UMIC	UMIC	UMIC
Geographic region	AFR	AFR	EAP	LAC	LAC	ECA	EAP

Sources: World Bank 2020; UNESCO Institute of Statistics Database, UNESCO, Paris (accessed May 8, 2020), http://data.uis.unesco.org/#; and Al-Samarrai, Cerdan-Infantes, and Lehe 2019.

Note: Poverty headcount data are from the latest year available between 2015 and 2018 and are based on the US$3.20-a-day poverty line (2011 PPP). Learning poverty data range between 2011 and 2016. GNI per capita is for 2019. All other data are for 2017. AFR = Africa; D = district; EAP = East Asia and the Pacific; ECA = Europe and Central Asia; GER = gross enrollment rate; GNI = gross national income; LAC = Latin America and the Caribbean; LIC = low-income country; PPP = purchasing power parity; S = state; UMIC = upper-middle-income country; US$ = US dollar; — = not available.

learning outcomes. A child born today in Uganda is expected to receive 4.5 learning-adjusted years of schooling compared to 10 years in Bulgaria and China (see table 3.1). In all of the case study countries, these averages also mask large disparities between regions, socioeconomic groups, and other markers of disadvantage. In Brazil, for example, an average of 48 percent of 10-year-olds are unable to read a simple text. However, learning poverty is much higher in the north where more than two-thirds of 10-year-olds in many municipalities are unable to read.

Although subnational governments are responsible for delivering basic education services, they rely heavily on central governments for funding. Subnational governments have the main responsibility in all of the case study countries for the delivery of pretertiary education services.[1] They are also responsible for at least half of all public education spending, and in Colombia and China, they supply over three-quarters of total public education spending (see figure 3.1). In most cases, they are responsible for an even greater share of basic education spending. For example, subnational governments in Brazil are responsible for 97 percent of public spending on early childhood, primary, and secondary education. Despite spending the bulk of public funding for education, subnational governments tend to have relatively limited revenues of their own and thus have to rely on transfers from higher levels of government (see figure 3.1). The lower levels of government can often be even more heavily reliant on higher levels of government. For example, counties in China depend on transfers from higher levels of government for over 80 percent of their revenues compared to an average for all subnational governments of only 58 per cent. Because lower levels of government are mostly responsible for providing basic education services, transfers are likely to be a very important source of funding for the subsector.

FIGURE 3.1

Fiscal transfers and subnational spending on education, 2016–18

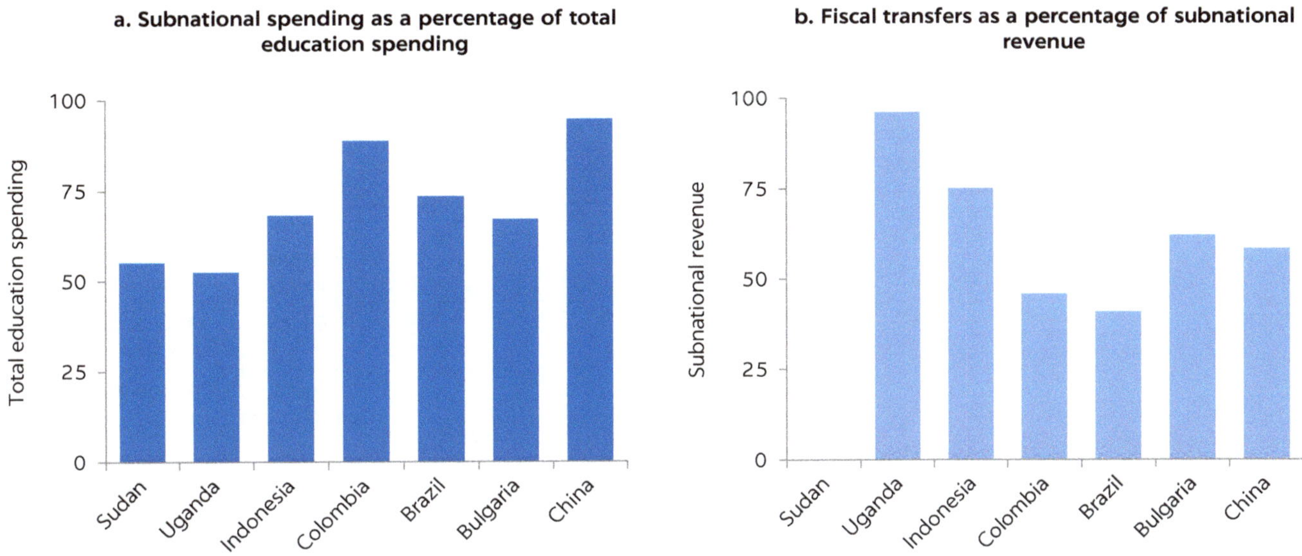

Source: Case studies in chapters 4–10.
Note: Subnational spending refers to state or regional and district or municipality levels of government where applicable. Information for Sudan in panel b is not available.

The way in which transfers from central governments are used to finance subnational education services varies. Chapter 2 outlined the characteristics and objectives of the intergovernmental transfers that are commonly provided to subnational governments. The case study countries use a variety of transfers to enable subnational governments to deliver the education services for which they are responsible (see table 3.2). General transfers are used in most of the countries, but the extent of their importance varies. In Sudan, over three-quarters of education funding in recent times came in the form of general transfers, while in Bulgaria, the bulk of education funding currently consists of conditional or specific-purpose transfers (Alamir et al. 2014). Conditional transfers account for over 80 percent of the transfers used for education in Colombia and Uganda but only 38 percent in China.

In the case study countries, the aim of transfers is to increase the funding for and improve the outcomes of subnational education services. Although the number of transfers differs significantly among the countries, most of them use transfers to address inadequacies and inequalities in the resources available to subnational governments. In some cases, this is done through general transfers that aim to reduce vertical or horizontal fiscal imbalances more generally, while in other cases, conditional or specific-purpose transfers are used to guarantee a minimum level of education funding for each child. For example, in Brazil and China, conditional transfers from the central government provide sufficient funding to ensure a minimum level of spending per student by all subnational governments.[2] Efficiency is also an objective of the conditional transfers used in many of the case study countries. In some cases, these transfers aim to reduce inefficiencies by addressing spatial spillovers and other externalities or to promote the efficient use of inputs and the delivery of outputs demanded by citizens (see chapter 2). In others, they aim to address spending inefficiencies in the education sector specifically. Providing per student transfers is a common approach to increasing efficiency, particularly in

TABLE 3.2 **Characteristics of intergovernmental fiscal transfers supporting education**

	NUMBER OF TRANSFERS		OBJECTIVES	
	GENERAL	SPECIFIC-PURPOSE OR CONDITIONAL	GENERAL	SPECIFIC-PURPOSE OR CONDITIONAL
Sudan	1	2	Adequacy, equity	Adequacy
Uganda	3	9	Equity	Adequacy, equity, performance
Indonesia	2	3	Adequacy, equity	Equity, efficiency, performance
Colombia	1	4	Equity	Adequacy, equity, performance
Brazil	4	3	Equity, performance	Adequacy, equity, efficiency
Bulgaria	0	4	Equity	Adequacy, equity, efficiency
China	3	10	Equity	Adequacy, equity, efficiency

Source: Case studies in chapters 4–10.

countries where demographic changes have resulted in a mismatch between service provision and demand, as has happened in many European countries over the past 30 years.[3] Some of the case study countries also use transfers that aim to provide incentives to various actors in the education sector to improve their performance. For the most part, this is done through the use of conditional transfers that allocate funds based on some measure of performance. For example, in Uganda, a measure of the quality of education management performance is included in the formula used to allocate a share of transfers to fund school infrastructure. The state of Ceará in Brazil stands out as the only case included in the report that has a general transfer that is allocated in part on the basis of education outcomes, including learning.

HOW EFFECTIVE HAVE COUNTRIES BEEN IN USING FISCAL TRANSFERS TO ENSURE ADEQUATE FUNDING FOR EDUCATION?

A key objective of many intergovernmental fiscal transfers is to address imbalances between the revenue raising abilities and public spending responsibilities of subnational governments. Transfers can play a critical role in helping subnational governments adequately fund the services for which they are responsible, including the provision of basic education. Although all transfers provide subnational governments with additional resources, they do not automatically result in higher spending on education. General transfers increase the overall amount of revenue available, but subnational governments can, and often do, choose to use these funds in other priority sectors. Even conditional transfers may not increase overall spending on education because fiscal resources are fungible. For example, subnational governments may lower their spending on education from other sources so that the net effect on spending maybe less than the original amount of the conditional transfer. This suggests that it is important to explore whether these displacement effects reduce the effect of intergovernmental transfers on levels of subnational spending on education.

On the whole, intergovernmental fiscal transfers in the case study countries are successful in increasing subnational spending on education. Most of the case studies used the same approach to explore the causal effects of transfers on subnational education spending (World Bank 2021). Their analyses showed that the receipt of general transfers resulted in subnational governments spending more on education, although specific-purpose transfers often had a larger effect. Table 3.3 summarizes the marginal effects of fiscal transfers on subnational education spending in the case study countries. It shows that a US$1.00 increase in general transfers leads to an increase of up to US$0.38 in subnational education spending. Other studies in the case study countries and elsewhere have produced similar findings on the effect of general transfers on subnational education spending (Arvate, Mattos, and Rocha 2015; Boadway and Shah 2007).

The effects of general transfers and specific-purpose transfers on subnational education spending can differ (Das et al. 2013; Ding, Lu; and Ye 2020).[4] Wherever it was possible for the case studies to distinguish between different types of transfers, the findings showed that unconditional transfers always tended to increase subnational education spending. For example, in Bulgaria and Indonesia, the marginal effect for unconditional transfers was 0.66 and 0.11, respectively. In China, a recent study also found that general transfers raised counties' education spending more than increases in a county's own revenues (Ding, Lu, and Ye 2020). The effects of conditional transfers on subnational education spending in the case study countries were more mixed. In Brazil and China, the estimated marginal effects for education-specific conditional transfers were higher than those for unconditional transfers. In Indonesia, a specific-purpose transfer aimed at reducing inefficiencies had no statistically significant impact on total subnational education spending, even though a US$1.00 increase in general transfers raised total education spending by US$0.11. The overall impact of different transfers is likely to be dependent, to an extent, on their relative size. It is possible that smaller conditional transfers are likely to have less impact. In Brazil, conditional transfers make up approximately 62 percent of municipality education spending compared to less than 14 percent for districts in Indonesia, which may account for the difference in their estimated effect on subnational spending in the two countries. In contrast, own revenues and general transfers are negligible in Uganda, which implies that levels of subnational education spending are largely determined by specific-purpose transfers.

TABLE 3.3 Marginal effects of fiscal transfers on subnational education spending

	INDONESIA	BRAZIL	BULGARIA	CHINA (PROVINCE)	CHINA (COUNTY)
Total transfers	0.11**	n.a.	0.66***	0.25**	n.a.
General purpose	0.18***	0.38***	n.a.	n.a.	0.1***
Specific purpose	−0.08	0.62***	n.a.	n.a.	1.6***
Dependent variable	per capita	per capita	per student	per capita	per capita

Source: Case studies in chapters 6, 8, 9, and 10.
Note: n.a. = not applicable. Significance levels: * = 10 percent, ** = 5 percent, and *** = 1 percent.

The specific purpose of conditional transfers can also affect their impact on overall public spending levels or on particular elements of subnational spending. In some cases, specific-purpose transfers have relatively little effect on overall spending. Although the unconditional equalization transfer and the conditional transfer in Bulgaria both had a statistically significant impact on subnational education spending, the impact of per student transfers for capital spending was not statistically significant. In Indonesia, the specific-purpose transfer had no effect on total spending, but more detailed analysis has shown that it increased subnational capital spending (Lewis 2013).

Although transfers generally increase public education spending, only a few countries use the transfer system to ensure that all subnational governments have adequate funds for education. Some countries have designed specific-purpose transfers that are based on the actual costs associated with providing education to each student. These schemes are distinctive because they provide guaranteed and predictable funding for education provision that is insulated, to a large degree, from government budget fluctuations. For example, China rolled out a new mechanism to guarantee financing for rural compulsory education in 2007. The new mechanism includes a specific-purpose transfer that provides provinces with a minimum guaranteed level of central government funding to cover their education administrative costs.[5] The funding levels are based on per student cost standards for groups of provinces. Currently, the transfer is equivalent to approximately US$92 and US$121 for each primary and junior secondary school student, respectively, and accounts for 30 percent of total basic education funding. In Bulgaria, the central government uses a unified per student cost standard to allocate specific-purpose funds to municipally owned schools. These standards were developed to cover all of the major costs of running schools, including staffing. In 2019, the average per student transfer in Bulgaria was US$942 with some variation in cost standards between different regions and different education levels.

In contrast to transfers based on cost standards, some countries have designed transfers to guarantee an annual minimum level of per student funding. In Brazil, federal funds for education are allocated in a way that ensures a minimum level of per student funding in all states. The Fund for the Development of Basic Education (FUNDEB) is a specific-purpose transfer that supports state and municipal funding of pretertiary education (see box 3.1). It derives its funds from specific revenues mandated for use in the education sector. States are required to share these revenues equally among all state and municipal schools according to their enrollment rates. Federal funds are added to this overall funding pool to set an annual minimum level of per student spending across all of Brazil. In practice, federal funds are used to increase per student spending levels in the poorest states. Although the fund has been credited with considerably increasing education funding, the endogeneity of the pool of funds used for the transfer, which is based on annual revenue receipts, has led to considerable volatility and unpredictability in minimum spending levels. For example, as a result of the financial crisis and the negative effect it had on overall government revenues, the minimum expenditure per student fell by 26 percent between 2008 and 2009 from US$419 to US$308. Transfer schemes of this kind are not associated with the actual costs of service provision because they aim to narrow spending inequalities by establishing a funding floor and ensuring through the transfer system that all subnational governments have adequate funds to reach it.

HOW EFFECTIVE ARE FISCAL TRANSFERS IN INCREASING THE EQUITY OF PUBLIC EDUCATION SPENDING?

Education spending inequalities between subnational governments can be large. Figure 3.2 shows the range of differences in per capita public education spending between subnational governments in the case study countries. To make the distributions comparable, subnational spending per capita is expressed in multiples of spending per capita in the median district. It is clear that differences in subnational spending per capita are quite large in most countries. In 2007, for example, the interquartile range for education spending across counties in China was equivalent to 0.6 times the median. This implies that a county at the 25th percentile of the per capita spending distribution spent less than two-thirds (¥275) of that of a county at the 75th percentile (¥491). Inequalities in state-level spending are even greater in Sudan. West Kordofan, at the 25th percentile, spends about one-third as much (SD933) as Northern State (SD2,724), at the 75th percentile, on the average primary and secondary school student. Looking beyond the interquartile range also highlights the sizeable proportion of subnational governments that have either very low or very high levels of relative spending.

These subnational spending inequalities frequently reinforce patterns of poverty between subnational governments. World Bank public expenditure reviews and a recent study have shown that, in approximately one-half of developing countries with available data, there was a negative and statistically significant relationship between subnational poverty rates and education spending (Manuel et al. 2019). A similar pattern was found in some of the case studies including Sudan and Uganda (see figure 3.3). There are relatively few countries that show the opposite relationship to a statistically significant extent.

FIGURE 3.2

Distribution of subnational education spending in case study countries

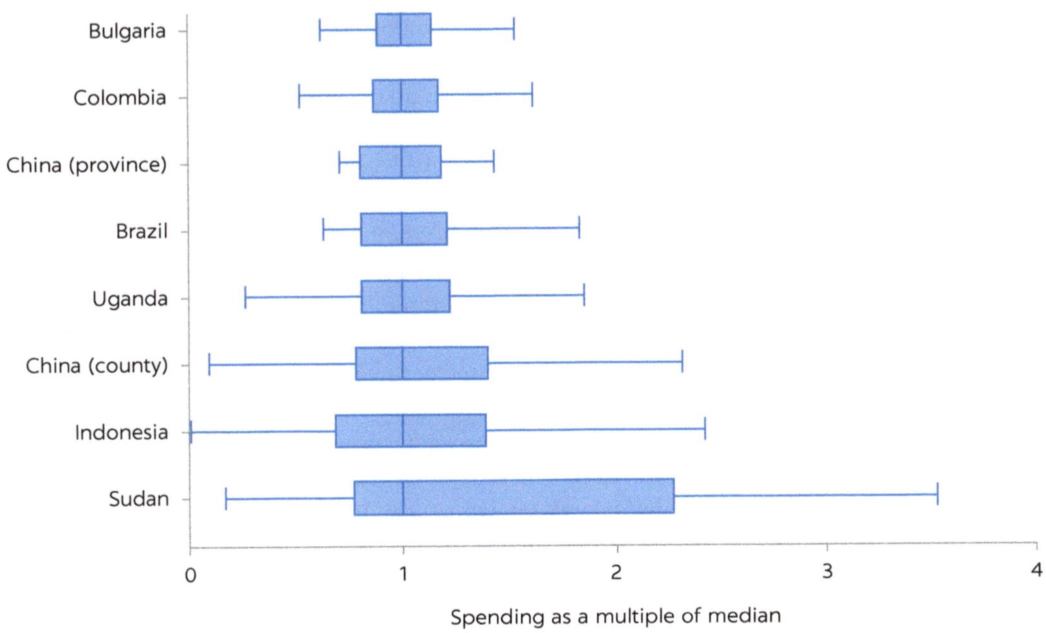

Source: Case studies in chapters 4–10.

Note: The figure shows a box-plot of spending per student or per capita as multiples of its median value.

FIGURE 3.3

Subnational education spending and poverty rates in Sudan and Uganda

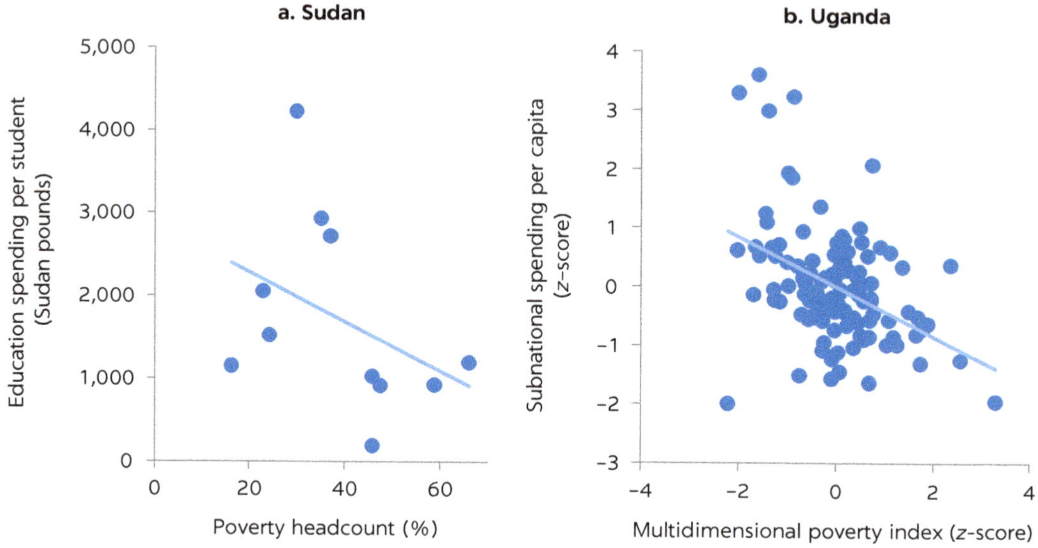

Source: Case studies in chapters 7 and 9.

Two underlying factors generally explain lower education spending by poorer subnational governments. First, poorer subnational governments cannot provide adequate funding for education because their overall budgets are too small. Second, preferences for education investment differ between subnational governments, resulting in different decisions on how much to spend on education. For example, the Pohuwato and Tangerang Selatan districts in Indonesia both devote about 20 percent of their budgets to education, but this results in large differences in education spending per capita, with Pohuwato spending US$316 and Tangerang Selatan US$105 per capita. Also, despite having similar budgets per capita, the Sibloga district in Sumatra and the Yahukimo district in Papua devote 25 percent and 8 percent of their budgets, respectively, to education.

Because transfers can fund a large share of subnational education spending, the way in which they are distributed is critical to improving spending equity between subnational governments. Addressing horizontal imbalances in revenues between subnational governments is a major objective of most fiscal transfer systems. Most of the case study countries use general-purpose transfers that are designed to reduce inequalities of this kind across the whole set of subnational responsibilities. For example, in China, equalization general-purpose transfers make up about two-thirds of all transfers to provinces and counties. These transfers are allocated according to formulas that include estimates of subnational fiscal gaps, which measure the difference between subnational revenues and expenditure obligations, as well as population size and levels of economic development. Many countries also establish specific-purpose transfers that aim to address education spending inequalities more directly. In Colombia, the allocation formula for per student specific-purpose transfers to municipalities tends to provider higher levels of funding for poorer municipalities.

The ways in which general-purpose transfers are designed can have unintended consequences for funding levels for education. In Indonesia, the rules for distributing general transfers among subnational governments result in large differences in per capita transfer amounts, which are the key driver of inequality in subnational education spending. The aim of the general-purpose grant (DAU) in Indonesia is to equalize levels of public funding across districts, and, in 2018, the DAU accounted for 45 percent of total district revenues. The allocation formula for these transfers is designed to equalize funding among subnational units but not among individuals. This results in districts with large populations receiving lower per capita transfers than districts with smaller populations (see figure 3.4). Because population size is a critical driver of education costs, these types of allocation rules lead to significant inequalities in education funding.

Most of the case study countries also have specific-purpose transfers that aim to narrow inequalities in subnational spending on education. In China, for example, the new education funding mechanism, introduced in 2006, includes specific-purpose transfers that vary in value depending on the ability of provinces and counties to fund their education systems from their own revenues or from their general-purpose transfers. For example, the central government transfers 80 percent of nonsalary costs in the poorer Western Provinces, 60 percent in the Central provinces, and nothing in the wealthier Eastern Provinces. In Colombia, the main specific-purpose transfer in education, accounting for over 50 percent of total central government transfers, is allocated based on a formula that takes into account a set of fiscal, socioeconomic, and education-specific characteristics. This differs from the approach taken in Bulgaria, where the bulk of education spending is made up of per student transfers and where municipalities have relatively little autonomy or revenues to change these allocations significantly (see figure 3.2 and the section titled *How effective have countries been in using fiscal transfers to ensure adequate funding for education?*). The way these resources are allocated, however, tends to be pro-poor and provides more funding to the poorer subnational governments with the weakest education systems.

FIGURE 3.4

Allocation of general-purpose transfers among districts in Indonesia, 2016

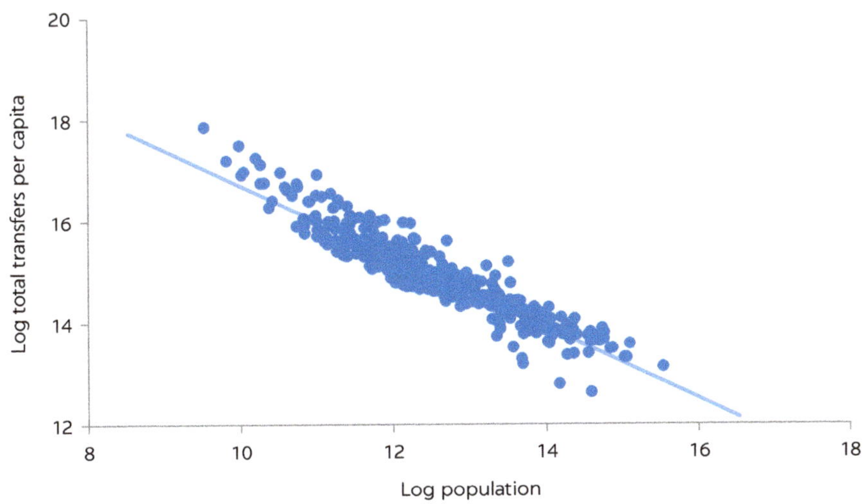

Source: Case study in chapter 6.

In Brazil, FUNDEB addresses equity issues by guaranteeing minimum levels of education spending among municipalities (see box 3.1).

Prior to the introduction of FUNDEB's predecessor in 1996, there were large differences in education spending between municipalities, which were driven by the limited revenues of poorer municipalities. Before the program started, the wealthier South, Southeast, and Central West regions in Brazil were spending almost twice as much per student as the poorer regions in the North and Northeast (Gordon and Vegas 2005). These spending disparities led to significant differences in education outcomes and exacerbated more general socioeconomic inequalities between regions. FUNDEB and its predecessor FUNDEF aimed to narrow spending inequalities by redistributing a portion of federal, state, and municipal tax revenues among all municipalities to guarantee a minimum level of spending per student across all municipalities. The funds have successfully narrowed

BOX 3.1

The nuts and bolts of Brazil's Fund for the Development of Basic Education (FUNDEB)

FUNDEB was established in 2006 as the successor to the Fund for the Development of Primary and Lower Secondary Education (FUNDEF), established in 1996. The main objective of these funds has been to narrow spending inequalities between municipalities in Brazil. Following on from the success of FUNDEF, FUNDEB was established with a larger revenue base and its coverage extended from primary and lower secondary education to cover all cycles of pretertiary education as well as adult education.

FUNDEB is financed by a share of various mandated state and municipal taxes, including motor vehicle and land taxes, as well as by federal funds equivalent to 10 percent of the state and municipal governments' contributions. FUNDEB allocates funds in two stages. First, the funds generated within a state are allocated on the basis of a formula that ensures that municipalities receive the same per student allocation for students in the same cycle of education and with the same characteristics. Second, the federal contribution is distributed to the states with the lowest levels of per student funding in a way that sets a minimum level of spending per student. In 2018, US$3.7 billion was allocated through FUNDEB. States and municipalities are obligated to use 60 percent of the funds they receive from FUNDEB on teachers' remuneration.

FUNDEB's allocation formula effectively guarantees a minimum amount of spending for each student in all states and municipalities. In 2018, the fund guaranteed average spending per student of US$1,235. The sizes of the transfers to municipalities are dependent on the number of children enrolled in pretertiary education, which has given a strong incentive to municipalities, particularly poor municipalities, to increase access. However, because tax revenues are the main source of funds for FUNDEB, the minimum spending level changes each year with fluctuations in the tax base. This can result in significant unpredictability in education funding, particularly for the poorest municipalities that are most dependent on the fund.

In 2020, an amendment to Brazil's constitution introduced several reforms to FUNDEB to improve spending equity and to introduce a results-based component to the transfer. The federal top-up to FUNDEB is set to increase to 23 percent of state and municipal contributions by 2026. Under these changes, a greater proportion of these funds will be allocated to those municipalities and states with the lowest levels of per student spending, which is expected to narrow spending inequalities further.[a]

a. The amendment has also introduced a results-based element to transfers that requires states to spend a minimum of 10 percent of the funds received from their Imposto Sobre Circulação de Mercadorias e Serviços (ICMS) excise tax revenues on improving education performance.

spending inequalities between municipalities and in particular have increased the funding of education in the poorest states (Cruz and Rocha 2018; Cruz and Silva 2020; Gordon and Vegas 2005). A World Bank simulation of per student funding also shows that inequality in per student spending has been significantly smaller since the introduction of FUNDEB (see figure 3.5).

Although transfers can help narrow spending inequalities and raise spending in poorer regions, they are not designed or intended to completely eliminate spending inequality in a decentralized system. Some of the differences in subnational education spending are deliberate attempts to compensate for differences in the costs of providing education in different parts of a country or to different population groups (see box 3.2). The costs of providing schooling in remote and sparsely populated areas are often higher than the costs of providing it in urban areas, and additional costs are usually incurred to provide marginalized children with opportunities similar to those available to other children. For example, the formula for the main education transfer in Bulgaria provides additional funding for students from vulnerable groups. Education spending also differs because of the overall fiscal position of subnational governments. Differences in the ability of subnational governments to raise revenue and inequalities in the share of national revenues that they receive through transfers can also result in spending differences. In Colombia, for example, subnational education spending is lower in poorer municipalities that have more limited own-source revenue even though they receive higher per student transfers from the central government. Finally, some subnational populations will have stronger preferences for education and be willing to allocate a greater share of their revenues to education than to other priorities.

FIGURE 3.5

Distribution of municipal education spending, with and without FUNDEB, in Brazil

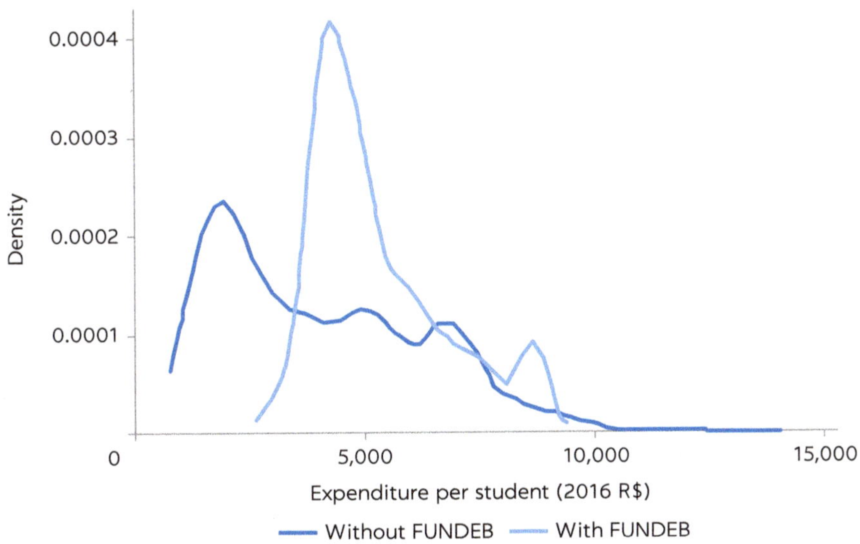

Source: World Bank using Summary Report on Budget Execution (RREO) from the Information System on Education Budgets (SIOPE).
Note: FUNDEB = Fund for the Development of Basic Education; R$ = Brazilian real.

BOX 3.2

Reducing school funding inequality in the United States

Many states in the United States have introduced school funding reforms to reduce spending inequalities between school districts. Reforms in 28 states have included the following:

- Formulas that guarantee a minimum level of spending per student, with states filling the gap between the contribution that districts can feasibly make from their own resources and the guaranteed minimum
- Per student spending limits to reduce expenditure differences across districts
- Equalization schemes that use taxes from all districts to redistribute funding to lower-income districts
- States providing matching funds to districts

An analysis of these reforms found that they had been effective in narrowing spending inequalities and increasing the educational attainment of children from low-income families.

Source: Jackson, Johnson, and Persico 2016; OECD 2017.

HOW EFFECTIVE ARE FISCAL TRANSFERS IN INCREASING THE EFFICIENCY OF PUBLIC EDUCATION SPENDING?

This section focuses on the extent to which transfers affect the efficiency of education spending. In the broader literature on intergovernmental transfers described in chapter 2, a key objective of an effective transfer system is to compensate subnational governments for benefit spillovers to neighboring jurisdictions. Clearly if education investment decisions are made without accounting for the benefits that come from education outside the jurisdiction in which the investments are made, subnational governments will have an incentive to underinvest. Transfers can be used to help subnational governments internalize these externalities and invest in education in ways that are optimal for the nation as a whole instead of just for the specific subnational government. Although this is an important objective of the transfer system, this section focuses on how the transfer system can affect the technical efficiency of spending in education.

Subnational spending inefficiencies in education are often substantial. The extent of these inefficiencies can be seen by looking at levels of spending and education outcomes. Figure 3.6 shows scatter plots of learning outcomes compared with spending levels per student in Bulgaria and Colombia. In both countries, some municipalities appear to use their resources more effectively than others to deliver education services. Within each panel, municipalities in quadrant A spend less than the average municipality on education but have better than average outcomes. For example, Bello municipality in Colombia spends about 2.5 million pesos per student and has an average learning score of 40 percent, which is 8 percentage points higher than the average for all municipalities. In contrast, municipalities in quadrant C are relatively inefficient. They spend more than the average municipality but have outcomes below the national average for all municipalities. Clearly, other factors are also involved in the link between spending and education outcomes and may explain the inefficiencies outlined in figure 3.6. For example, municipalities in quadrant C may incur higher costs of provision than other municipalities because they are more sparsely populated or may serve more

FIGURE 3.6

Subnational learning outcomes and spending per student in Bulgaria and Colombia

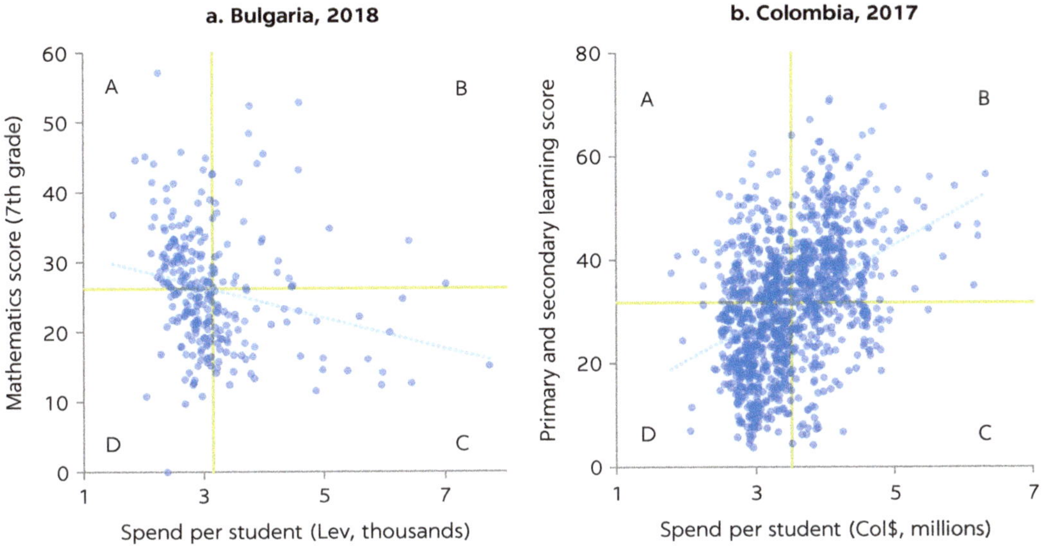

Source: Case studies in chapters 7 and 9.

disadvantaged students, both of which may increase the costs of provision or lower outcomes compared with other municipalities. However, more detailed econometric work in the case study countries as well as other more rigorous approaches to measuring inefficiency all demonstrate significant spending inefficiencies in most countries at the subnational level (De Witte and López-Torres 2017; Sutherland, Price, and Gonand 2010).

The design and implementation of fiscal transfers can affect the efficiency of public education spending. In Indonesia, the formula for the largest general transfers includes incentives for district governments to spend more on hiring civil service teachers than on nonsalary spending. In education, this has resulted in a tendency to hire more teachers than is required to comply with minimum service standards and maximum class sizes (Lewis and Smoke 2017; World Bank 2012). Because salary spending accounts for approximately three-quarters of subnational education spending, the perverse incentives included in the transfer's allocation formula is a major driver of this inefficiency. The transfer system can also affect efficiency in other ways. In Colombia, for example, the main specific-purpose transfer for education allocates funds according to a per student formula, which can increase efficiency. However, a top-up transfer is provided to those municipalities that cannot cover their payroll costs from the main transfer, which reduces their incentive to use funds efficiently. In Brazil, the fixed pool of education funding mandates that a specific share of overall revenues be spent on education. This can result in inefficient spending, particularly in states where levels of funding for education are already high. A recent study showed that, if all subnational governments in Brazil were able to spend as efficiently as top-performing municipalities and states, student achievement in primary and lower secondary education might be 40 percent higher (World Bank 2017).

Carefully designed education transfers can increase spending efficiency in the sector. In the early 1990s, the education systems in many countries in Europe and Central Asia were becoming more inefficient as a result of declines and changes in the school-age population. These demographic shifts often resulted in many small schools, small class sizes, and low student-teacher ratios. Moreover, the existing input-based funding mechanisms were giving municipalities and schools no incentives to adjust to the new reality. Per capita financing mechanisms were introduced that linked transfer allocations to student numbers. Municipalities could no longer afford to fund their existing school networks, which gave them an incentive to find ways to increase spending efficiency (Alonso and Sanchez 2011). In Bulgaria, the introduction of per capita financing has led to the merging or closing of some schools, which has significantly increased efficiency. Overall, the allocation of education funding on a per student basis has increased class sizes and student-teacher ratios and has put the education sector in Bulgaria on a more sustainable financial footing. Although some inefficiency in spending remains, per capita funding formulas also act as automatic stabilizers that adjust funding immediately in response to demographic shifts and other factors that may drive spending inefficiency.

CAN FISCAL TRANSFER MECHANISMS FOSTER BETTER EDUCATION OUTCOMES?

Fiscal transfers can create incentives for subnational governments to expand access to education services and improve learning. As the country case studies and other research have shown, intergovernmental fiscal transfers increase subnational education spending, and this additional funding has the potential not only to increase access to education but also to improve learning outcomes (de Carvalho Filho and Litschig 2020; Olsson and Valsecchi 2015). Econometric analysis in the case studies in Brazil, Colombia, Indonesia, and Uganda shows that both transfers and subnational education spending have a positive and significant impact on student achievement. For example, in the Indonesia case study, the author found that a 10 percent increase in subnational per capita education spending increased students' test scores by 0.6 percent. Although the relationship is significant, it is not very strong, and there is considerable variation in subnational entities' effectiveness in translating funding into outcomes (see figure 3.6). To strengthen the link between funding and outcomes, fiscal transfers in some countries, particularly specific-purpose transfers, have been designed to include stronger incentives for subnational governments to focus on improving the performance of schools and students.

Transfers can be designed to provide direct incentives to encourage subnational governments to expand education access. In particular, transfers that include a per student allocation can act as a strong incentive for subnational governments to enroll more students; subnational governments know that if they expand access, they will receive funding from the central government to help cover the costs of providing more school places. This has had the effect of reducing the cost burden on subnational governments and, in turn, on households, while also narrowing inequalities in access to basic education.[6] Many countries use these types of transfers to encourage and sustain widespread access to basic education (OECD 2017).

China's New Mechanism to Guarantee Rural Compulsory Education Financing (the New Mechanism), introduced in 2006, strengthened the incentives for provincial governments to increase access to basic education. The New Mechanism introduced a compulsory specific-purpose education transfer.

This specific-purpose transfer was allocated to provinces on a per student basis and was designed to cover elements of nonsalary funding and to compensate subnational governments for the revenue they lost as a result of the abolition of tuition fees, which was implemented at the same time. The share of per student funding covered by the transfer varied depending on the socioeconomic characteristics of each province. For example, the central government transfers covered 80 percent of the administrative expenses and lost fee income of the least developed provinces in the west and 60 percent of those of the central provinces. Initially, the wealthier eastern provinces did not receive any funds through the compulsory specific-purpose education transfer, but this changed in 2015 when they received transfers amounting to 50 percent of their total expenses.

The New Mechanism reforms have been credited with contributing to the increases in enrollment and completion rates in basic education since the early 2000s. Spending inequalities between provinces have narrowed since the introduction of the reforms, but the evidence is mixed on whether this was the direct result of the reforms. Nevertheless, the reforms appear to have increased levels of enrollment in primary and secondary education and narrowed enrollment outcomes between provinces and counties.[7] There is also evidence that the reforms had positive effects on attainment and learning outcomes and that these effects were larger for students from disadvantaged backgrounds (Ha and Yan 2018; Xiao, Li, and Zhao 2017).

The FUNDEB and FUNDEF transfers in Brazil raised education spending and improved education outcomes particularly in poorer municipalities. Research studies have also shown that these funds have increased enrollment in basic education particularly in poorer municipalities, improved education quality, and narrowed achievement gaps (Cruz and Rocha 2018; Cruz 2018; Gordon and Vegas 2005). A recent study exploring the impact of FUNDEB on student achievement in upper secondary schools also found that it had increased average achievement in both Portuguese and mathematics and that the gains were greater for poorer students (Silveira et al. 2017).

In some countries, the transfer system has also aimed to incentivize improvements in education quality and student learning outcomes. Compared with transfers that support increasing access to schooling, there is less evidence available on the effectiveness of performance-based transfers that focus on learning outcomes, particularly in developing countries. These transfers have aimed to make funding directly conditional on improvements in some measure of school or student performance. The limited amount of available evidence echoes findings from studies that have examined performance-based transfers in developed countries and other sectors (see box 3.3). The findings show that these transfers can strengthen performance incentives, but their effectiveness depends on strong information systems, good implementation capabilities of subnational governments, and careful design to avoid negative consequences, such as the risk of widening existing inequalities.

In 2008, an innovative reform of the fiscal transfer system in the state of Ceará in Brazil linked an important general transfer to learning outcomes. Value-added consumption taxes are a key source of revenue for state governments in Brazil. States are obligated to transfer 25 percent of these revenues to their municipalities as a general-purpose transfer. Most of the funds are transferred on the basis of fiscal capacity indicators that measure the contribution of each municipality to overall state revenues, but the state has discretion over how it

BOX 3.3

The No Child Left Behind Act in the United States

Federal funding accounts for only about 2 percent of total public education funding in the United States. The 2001 No Child Left Behind Act made a substantial proportion of these funds conditional on the states' measuring learning outcomes and using these indicators to set annual school improvement targets. States were required to test students in reading and mathematics and report the results achieved by specific disadvantaged groups. States also committed to achieving state-defined student learning proficiency levels over a 10-year period. Within this timeframe, schools were given annual achievement targets, and the state would introduce remedial measures and sanctions if a school failed to meet them. For example, states could shut schools down, convert schools into charter schools, or use other improvement strategies if schools continued to miss their annual targets. Each state had to prepare and implement plans that included these elements in order to qualify for federal funding.

The overall weight of evidence suggests that the No Child Left Behind policy improved learning outcomes and reduced inequality. Studies have used different approaches to identify its impact. A comprehensive study of the effects of the Act shows that it led to increases in per student district education spending, specifically increases in teachers' pay, and in the proportion of teachers with graduate qualifications. It also appears to have increased the amount of instructional time spent on mathematics and reading (the two subjects included in the Act's assessment requirements). There is also evidence that it led to improvements in mathematics achievement, particularly in the early grades, and that these improvements were larger at the bottom of the achievement distribution. However, it does not appear to have had as significant an impact on reading achievement. Overall, the improvements identified in the evidence fell short of the targets that the state plans originally set.

Despite these generally positive findings, the No Child Left Behind Act faced significant resistance, and the 2015 Every Child Succeeds Act changed many elements of the original Act. Although the original Act resulted in increased instructional time spent on mathematics and reading, it diverted time and resources away from other subjects that were not included in testing. Moreover, even in the tested subjects, instruction was focused on the tested items rather than on the subject as a whole. The Act was also criticized for giving schools an incentive to inflate their overall achievement scores, and, in extreme cases, the pressure to meet targets encouraged cheating. As a result, the subsequent Every Child Succeeds Act expanded indicators of performance beyond test scores and limited the ability of the federal government to tie state funding to specific requirements, including using test scores to evaluate teachers.

Source: Dee and Jacob 2010; Klein 2015, 2016; Koretz 2017;National Research Council 2011.

transfers a quarter of the total transfer to municipalities. Since 2008, the State of Ceará has allocated 72 percent of these discretionary funds based on municipalities' performance in the education sector, with the remaining funds being allocated based on their performance on health and the environment. These transfers are a very significant revenue source for municipalities and represent as much as one-third of all revenue for poorer municipalities in Ceará (Loureiro and Cruz 2020).

The amounts transferred are determined by a primary "education quality index" that is designed both to measure performance and to increase equity between students within municipalities. The index consists of indicators on early grade literacy, learning measured at the end of primary school, and the proportion of children transitioning to the next grade. Municipalities are allocated transfer resources based on their scores on these indicators as well as on the magnitude of their educational improvements over the preceding year.

This ensures that those municipalities with relatively low levels of learning can still receive sizeable allocations if they make progress in a given year. The index also takes into account the distribution of each indicator and the proportion of students taking the assessments used to calculate its indicators. This prevents the incentives from widening inequalities within municipalities.

A comprehensive census-based learning assessment is used to calculate the index, and the results are disseminated to the public. The state's monitoring and evaluation systems were overhauled and strengthened as an essential element of the implementation of the performance-based transfer. In addition, the Permanent Basic Education Assessment System was expanded to cover additional grades and assessments in mathematics and Portuguese. It now tests all students in selected grades every year. The state funds the expanded evaluation system to avoid any municipal interference in the assessment process. The institution that administers the performance-based transfer makes publicly available all data, the index calculations, and the final transfer amounts.

Rigorous evaluations have shown that the performance-based reform to the fiscal transfer program has improved learning outcomes in most municipalities in Ceará. Even though the transfer was not a specific-purpose transfer, evidence shows that it led municipalities to increase their spending on basic education and narrowed per capita differences in transfers between municipalities (Franca 2014). The performance-based transfer was introduced when many other reforms were enacted aimed at improving the quality of education (Costa and Carnoy 2015). However, evaluations that aimed to isolate the causal impact of the transfers themselves have found that they have had positive, significant, and relatively large positive effects on student enrollment and learning outcomes (Lautharte, Oliveira, and Loureiro 2021; Petterini and Irffi 2013). Moreover, it appears that the transfers also narrowed learning gaps between poor and wealthy municipalities (Brandão 2014). Because these outcomes were based on the use of existing revenue sources, the reforms have also increased the overall efficiency of spending in the state of Ceará and its municipalities (Loureiro and Cruz 2020; Wetzel and Viñuela 2020).

The evidence from Brazil highlights the potential of performance-based transfers to improve education outcomes, but the evidence base is still limited. Although some countries, mostly in the developed world, have introduced performance-based fiscal transfers in the education sector, they are still relatively rare, and evaluations of their impact are rarer still. Performance-based transfers for education have been introduced in Colombia and Indonesia, and, although no formal evaluations have been completed, there is some evidence that weaknesses in their design and implementation have limited their impact on education outcomes. Evidence on the use of performance-based transfers in other sectors is also sparse but suggests that they have the potential to improve outcomes, although the size of their impact has been mixed (Gertler, Giovagnoli, and Martinez 2014; Glassman and Sakuma 2014; Lewis 2014). Transfers of this kind can also face resistance from politicians, bureaucrats, and stakeholders that may receive less funding than before, because they increase accountability and focus on poor performance and inefficiency (Shah 2010). Although there is relatively limited evidence on performance-based fiscal transfers, the evidence on the use of results-based financing in education more generally suggests that two factors are critical for maximizing the impact of transfers of this kind—careful design and the provision of complementary interventions (see box 3.4).

BOX 3.4

What do we know about the use of results-based financing in education?

Results-based financing can increase the effectiveness and efficiency of education spending. It aims to strengthen the incentives for different actors, including teachers, students, and government bureaucracies, to improve education outcomes.

A recent review of the evidence on results-based financing identified cases where it had been successful. It found that teacher incentives tend to reduce absenteeism and improve learning outcomes in developing countries and that conditional cash transfers increase educational attainment and, in some cases, student achievement. However, the review also highlighted cases in which it had been unsuccessful in improving outcomes and, in some cases, had even widened inequalities in education outcomes. It also highlighted other related factors that were important determinants of the success of results-based financing interventions. These included:

- *Political commitment.* A survey of results-based financing practitioners highlighted political commitment as the most important factor in the success of results-based financing initiatives.
- *Complementary interventions.* Evidence suggested that results-based financing is more effective when combined with other supporting interventions. For example, performance-based grants to schools worked better when they were combined with capacity-building or technical assistance. Technical capacity was also cited by practitioners as an important precondition for the success of results-based financing.
- *Robust information and financial management systems.* The collection of regular and reliable information on key education results (such as learning achievement) was a prerequisite for the success of results-based financing. Similarly, effective public financial management systems are required to manage results-based transfers.
- *Avoiding common drawbacks in design.* Any potential for actors in the education system to game or cheat results-based financing mechanisms can reduce their effectiveness. Careful design and early evaluation efforts can often minimize these risks.

Source: Lee and Medina 2019.

GUIDING PRINCIPLES FOR EFFECTIVE TRANSFER MECHANISMS[8]

Strengthening fiscal transfer mechanisms to tackle financing challenges and improve education outcomes is difficult. In the absence of conflicting objectives between central and subnational governments, differences in subnational government capacity, and externalities and information asymmetries, a single general transfer may provide the optimal system. However, these conditions are rarely met, and a country's overall political and economic context plays an important role in both how the intergovernmental transfer is set up and the opportunities that exist for reform.

The case studies show that countries typically use a mix of different transfers to address different objectives in the education sector. There is no one-to-one correspondence between specific finance challenges and particular transfers. For example, faced with inadequate subnational government funding for education, central governments may use a combination of general and specific transfers to increase general levels of funding and to ensure that specific inputs are funded. Tackling education spending inequalities across subnational governments may in some cases require changes to allocation rules for general transfers and in other cases require the design of a specific education transfer that aims to compensate subnational governments that are unable to fund education adequately. The choices that countries make will depend on the technical and political feasibility of different options.

The findings from the case studies and the broader literature can be used to identify some guiding principles to help strengthen education finance in decentralized systems (see figure 3.7). The reform of fiscal transfer systems frequently involves changes that do not align with the interests of all stakeholders. Existing weaknesses in transfer systems often are not the result of poor design and execution but rather reflect a suboptimal equilibrium based on past and current economic and political factors. Given the different starting points of countries and their potential for reform, it will not always be possible

FIGURE 3.7

Guiding principles for effective design of intergovernmental fiscal transfers for education

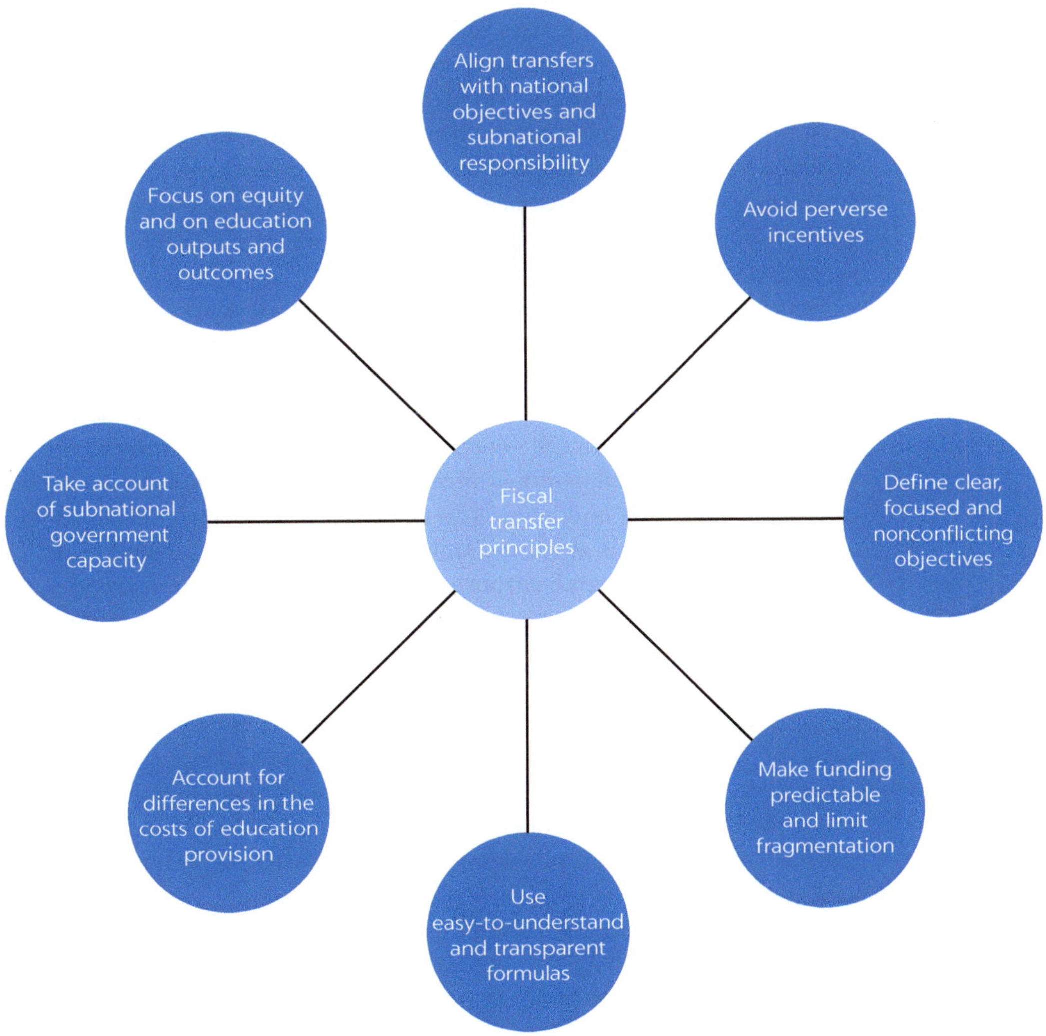

Source: World Bank.

to apply all the principles, particularly in the short term. However, they provide a roadmap for the direction toward which reforms should move as well as a set of principles against which an existing system or any proposed reforms can be assessed.

Drawing on the findings of the study, the following are the main guiding principles for the effective design of intergovernmental fiscal transfers for education:

Align transfers with national objectives and subnational responsibility

Decentralized financing systems need to support the achievement of national education goals (Boadway and Shah 2007; Shah 2006). It is critical to align the incentives inherent in fiscal transfer systems with national education goals, which requires a good understanding of how fiscal transfer systems work and how they affect the decisions subnational governments make in delivering education services. The case studies have demonstrated many ways in which transfers affect the incentives that subnational governments face in delivering education services. For example, the use of per student formulas in fiscal transfer mechanisms provided incentives for subnational governments to expand access to basic education and were aligned with national objectives to provide education for all.[9] In the state of Ceará, Brazil, performance-based transfers provided strong incentives for municipalities to improve learning outcomes and narrow inequalities between schools. Although it may not be feasible or desirable to introduce direct links between transfers and learning outcomes, carefully designed transfers can support national objectives for increased adequacy, equity, and efficiency in public education spending.

Decentralized financing can help subnational governments identify and respond to the needs and demands of their citizens. Putting important education financing decisions in the hands of subnational officials can also help citizens to hold those officials accountable for meeting their demands and needs. Finding an appropriate balance between central government priorities and the needs of subnational citizens can be challenging, but it is vital for improving education outcomes. The design of fiscal transfer systems will often require decisions about the appropriate mix of general- and specific-purpose transfers. General-purpose transfers provide greater autonomy to subnational governments to support their own priorities and use funds to deliver services in ways that are sensitive to subnational characteristics. On the other hand, specific-purpose transfers leave less room for subnational decision-making but ensure that allocated funds are used for specific services and in many cases specific inputs. Country political and economic factors will determine the appropriate mix of transfers, including the extent to which national and subnational priorities align and whether accountability mechanisms are adequate to ensure that funds are used appropriately at the subnational level.

Whatever the appropriate mix of fiscal transfers, it is important to direct public funding to the level of government that is responsible for delivering education services (Bahl 2000; Bird and Smart 2002). Mismatches between funding and responsibilities negatively affect the ability of subnational governments to manage their education systems effectively and can lead to duplication of activities and spending inefficiencies (Pritchett 2015). In some cases, misalignments occur because the overall decentralization framework is unclear. In other cases, central governments fund schools directly rather than using the transfer system to allocate funds to subnational governments to fulfill their roles. In Sudan, for example, the central government directly funds the purchase and distribution of textbooks in all schools rather than providing funds to subnational governments. In Indonesia, until 2013, the central government provided grants directly to schools, bypassing subnational governments that often already had their own school grants programs (Al-Samarrai et al. 2015). In some other cases, major school input decisions (such as hiring teachers and opening or closing schools) are made by a level of government that bears no responsibility for financing these decisions.[10] Aligning funding with a clear framework of roles and responsibilities for each level of government can prevent these weaknesses and improve the allocation and use of public education resources.

Avoid perverse incentives

In designing and implementing transfers, it is important to eliminate or reduce any perverse incentives that can limit funding effectiveness (Lewis and Smoke 2017). The case studies have shown that school finance in decentralized systems is complex because schools receive funding through many different channels. There is little analysis of how financing systems affect incentives within the sector, but they can drive inefficiency and inequality in education spending. The Indonesia case study shows that the country's large general transfer incorporates an implicit incentive to hire excessive numbers of civil service teachers, which in turn drives spending inefficiencies in the education sector. Perverse effects are often largely unintended, but they can be significant and can affect a wide range of subnational fiscal outcomes, accountability relationships, and service delivery performance (Lewis and Smoke 2017). Eliminating unintended perverse incentives should be a first step in any reform of intergovernmental transfers in education.

Define clear, focused, and nonconflicting transfer objectives

The objectives of transfers should be clear, focused, and consistent. At the outset it is important to identify the overall objectives for education financing and assess the extent to which existing fiscal transfers address these objectives. Transfers that have unclear aims or try to achieve multiple objectives often fail to improve outcomes effectively. In Colombia, for example, the formula for education transfers mixes different indicators of enrollment and learning achievement. In Uganda, development transfers are based partly on subnational government performance, and partly on an equity basis, with districts registering relatively poor education outcomes receiving more. Conflicting elements in transfer formulas are difficult for subnational officials and schools to understand and act upon. It is also more difficult to evaluate the impact of transfers on spending and outcomes in the education sector. Transfers tend to work better in general when they have a limited number of objectives that are clear and consistent (Shah 2006).

Make funding predictable and limit fragmentation

As with financing more generally, transfers should provide a stable and predictable source of education funding (Shah 2006). However, the funding pool for transfers can often be unpredictable, resulting in large annual fluctuations in the availability of public education funds. For example, in Brazil, the FUNDEB transfer is procyclical because it is funded from tax revenues that ebb and flow throughout the economic cycle. This often starves education systems of funding during economic crises when needs are greatest. But central officials are often reluctant to guarantee intergovernmental transfer funding when their own revenues are in doubt, as doing so would strain their own fiscal positions. It can be tricky to stabilize transfers that are dependent on tax revenues, but the case studies have highlighted other causes of unpredictability that may be easier to avoid. For example, in Sudan, fluctuations in funding arise from differences between planned and actual transfers, a possible result of weaknesses in central government planning and budgeting. In Colombia, the transfer formulas are adjusted on an annual basis, which makes it difficult for municipalities to use funds effectively and leaves little time for them to act on the incentives that some of the transfers are designed to strengthen. To ensure that education funding is used optimally, transfers should be designed in ways that reduce these fluctuations and help subnational governments plan their spending most effectively.

General- and specific-purpose grants both have roles to play in funding education, but care must be taken to avoid fragmentation in the transfer system. General-purpose transfers tend to be used more frequently to increase adequacy and equity, whereas specific-purpose grants tend to be better at promoting efficiency and performance (Bird and Smart 2002; Shah 2006). However, the proliferation of transfers, especially specific-purpose transfers, makes it difficult for recipients to effectively budget, plan, and execute those funds (Lewis 2013). Many of the case study countries use a multitude of transfers and financing mechanisms to channel funding to schools. In most instances, these channels have different fund use and reporting requirements, which not only makes planning and budgeting more difficult but significantly increases the time that schools, and school principals, spend on fund management rather than on maximizing learning. For many countries, reducing the number of intergovernmental transfers for education, by, for example, consolidating transfers with the same objectives, has the potential to improve both the adequacy and effectiveness of education spending. Limiting the number of financing mechanisms can also free up subnational governments to focus on improving education performance within their jurisdictions.

Use easy-to-understand and transparent formulas

The ability of subnational government actors to understand allocation rules and how their own actions can affect the level of funding they receive is critical to good transfer design. It is more difficult for subnational governments to act on the incentives in fiscal transfers when funding formulas are complicated or the indicators used are difficult to understand. In Colombia, for example, funding formulas have ten different indicators for education performance alone. This makes it difficult for municipal governments to identify the key improvements and actions needed to secure greater funding and ultimately reduces the incentive effects of the transfer. However, the keys to good transfer design are not always reducing the indicators or making the formula simple. In the state of Ceará in Brazil, a successful performance-based transfer has a relatively complicated mathematical formula, but municipalities know that in order to secure greater funding they need to improve retention and learning, particularly in their poorer performing schools. Good communication of how funding formulas work and the actions required to improve transfer amounts are important to ensure that subnational governments are able to act on the incentives inherent in many transfers.

Transparency in the design of transfers is also important to ensure that transfer systems are accountable (Shah 2006). Accountability for the use of funds depends crucially on publicly available information on how they are allocated and how they flow through the financing system. A public expenditure tracking survey in Uganda in 1995 found that districts delivered only 76 percent of intended funding to schools. In an effort to address the leakage of funds, the government made public the transfer of funds to district offices and schools. This greater transparency in transfers was one element in a set of reforms that resulted in districts passing on a far greater proportion of funding to schools than before (Hubbard 2007; Reinikka and Svensson 2011). Ensuring that stakeholders have the required information on how transfers work also helps to guarantee that funds are used for their intended purposes and that the incentives that they create are effective. In the state of Ceará in Brazil, disseminating the details of the performance-based transfer was a key element of its success in improving education outcomes (Loureiro and Cruz 2020).

The most effective transfer systems have access to good quality information on subnational populations and education systems (Boex and Martinez-Vazquez 2007). Without good information, it is challenging for intergovernmental fiscal transfers to support improvements in education effectively. Using transfers to achieve key education objectives requires indicators that are easy to understand, that can be accurately measured on a regular basis, and that measure important aspects of education systems (Lewis, McCulloch, and Sacks 2016). Some of the information systems in the case study countries contain comprehensive data on education systems that are used in the transfer system. For example, the performance-based transfers in the state of Ceará in Brazil are possible only because the state has a credible annual census-based learning assessment, which provides the data needed to measure performance. On the other hand, weak information systems can hamper the effectiveness of transfer systems. For example, Sudan has very limited information on education indicators for states and localities, making it difficult to allocate funding accurately or effectively.

Account for differences in the costs of education provision

Ensuring that transfers account for differences in subnational characteristics that affect the costs of providing education can help narrow inequalities and improve national education outcomes. Almost all of the case study countries use subnational demographic and socioeconomic characteristics in funding formulas to improve equity in spending and education outcomes. However, in Indonesia the funding formula for the main fiscal transfer excluded district population size, which resulted in large differences in the per capita distribution of funds between subnational governments. Although many of the case study countries transferred funds on the basis of differences in population size and characteristics, very few included adjustments in their allocation formulas to address differences in the costs of education provision. Costs diverge among regions because the prices of key inputs vary (for example, the cost of delivering textbooks to remote mountainous regions is higher than that for urban schools) and because different population groups may need more support to complete education than others. Poorer municipalities often incur high costs in providing education services and are disadvantaged further if transfer mechanisms fail to take this into account. Accommodating these differences in the design of transfers will help all localities afford a minimum level of education provision (Kim and Smoke 2003). Bulgaria and Colombia demonstrate how transfers can account for differences of this kind, as can many countries in the Organisation for Economic Co-operation and Development (OECD 2017). However, accounting for service delivery cost differentials across subnational governments is not easy to do well technically, and once mistakes are made, they are difficult to correct. The aforementioned case of Indonesia is instructive. Rectifying the now well-understood problems of cost adjustments in transfer distributions would necessitate allocating more funds to large urban areas, especially on Java, a nearly impossible task politically.

Take account of subnational government capacity

Subnational government capacity constraints also need to be accounted for if transfers are to support equitable and effective use of education funding. Subnational governments differ in their capacity to use funding effectively to improve education outcomes. Funding alone is not enough to support lagging regions in their efforts to improve outcomes and catch up with other parts of the country. Strengthening the capacity of subnational units to improve education outcomes often goes hand-in-hand with reform of the transfer system (Smoke 2017). Capacity building programs should avoid central "supply-driven" approaches that are mechanical, standardized, and technical and that ignore unique subnational needs and governance environments (Smoke 2017). In Brazil, providing technical assistance to states and municipalities was a key feature in the introduction of the performance-based grant and helped increase the impact of the transfer (Lautharte, Oliveira, and Loureiro 2021). In Uganda, subnational governments that perform badly are required to develop and implement performance improvement plans, with the support of the central government, to address weaknesses in the management of education services.

Focus on equity and on education outputs and outcomes

The study shows the potential that well-designed fiscal transfers have for improving equity between subnational governments. Many of the other guiding principles relate to equity by, for example, accommodating cost differences and strengthening the capacity of weaker subnational governments. However, it is important to keep a focus on equity and ensure that the overall system supports national goals to provide learning for all.

Allocating transfers on the basis of outputs or outcomes is also important and provides subnational governments with more flexibility in how they deliver education services. The transfers described in the case study countries range from transfers designed to finance the provision of specific education inputs (such as teachers and textbooks) to transfers that are based on outputs (such as enrollment) or performance (such as student learning outcomes) of subnational education systems. Input-based transfers are restrictive and do not give subnational governments any autonomy over how to provide education services, which is often identified as an important benefit of decentralization. In contrast, transfers based on outputs or performance can achieve national objectives without undermining subnational choices on how best to deliver education services.

Transfers based on outputs and outcomes can also help ensure that education funding is used effectively. The case studies show that output-based and performance-based transfers can work in the education sector. In China, for example, the transfer system increased incentives for provincial governments to expand education access in basic education and contributed to large increases in enrollment and completion rates. Rigorous evaluations of the performance-based transfer in the state of Ceará in Brazil also demonstrated that transfers of this kind can improve student retention and learning outcomes. These types of transfers require good-quality information systems, strong government implementation capabilities, and careful design. Currently, only a relatively small number of developing countries are likely to meet these criteria for implementing transfers of this kind. In these countries it is important that reforms to fiscal transfer systems aim to strengthen information systems and build capabilities so that, in the medium to long term, transfers are designed in ways that promote a stronger link between funding and education outcomes.

POLITICAL ECONOMY CONSTRAINTS

The reform of fiscal transfer systems is constrained by a variety of political economy factors. There are numerous stakeholders involved in the reform process, cutting across all levels of government and involving many nongovernment actors as well. Desirable changes frequently do not align with the interests of all concerned parties. Therefore, it may not always be politically feasible to implement technically viable and useful changes to fiscal transfers. Second-best solutions are often all that can be accomplished.

Education transfer formulation and implementation is a multi-institutional affair. Central government departments of finance and education, among other line agencies, subnational governments, national and subnational parliaments, and nongovernmental and private sector entities of various kinds are all likely to be involved. The sheer number of involved parties creates challenges for grant design and execution. For example, the clarity and consistency of transfer goals may easily be sacrificed as the number of stakeholders involved in grant design rises, objectives multiply, and the inevitable political compromises are made (Smoke 2017). Some education sector grant authorities may expressly avoid transparency in setting objectives so that the parties involved are free to read their own interpretations into the stated ambitions. In other cases, some institutions may be benefiting from the status quo, making reforms especially challenging.

Some parties may be unhappy with increased clarity and simplicity in grant design, if, for example, such attributes endanger their efforts to corrupt associated budgets (Lewis and Hendrawan 2020). The development of stronger information and monitoring systems for allocation and use of transfers might well disadvantage interest groups who profit from opaqueness, who will likely resist needed reforms (Lewis and Hendrawan 2020). And the existence of perverse incentives embedded in education transfers, their unintentional nature notwithstanding, likely benefits certain groups, thus making their elimination politically challenging (Lewis and Smoke 2017).

Striking the appropriate balance between the achievement of national objectives and facilitating subnational responsiveness to citizen demands is perhaps the hardest of all principles to carry out. During the past decade enthusiasm for decentralized service delivery has waned to a certain extent, especially among central governments, but also among academics and other observers (Malesky, Nguyen, and Tran 2014). In response to their own dissatisfaction with subnational service outcomes, whether warranted or not, some central governments have adopted policy approaches that have made matters worse. Ministries of finance, for example, have expressed their discontent by focusing more attention on the development of specific-purpose grants, which give them more control over how funds are spent. Specific-purpose grants in the education sector have proliferated in many countries in recent times, leading to significant fragmentation in funding and challenges for subnational governments and school planning and budgeting (Lewis 2013). Specific-purpose grants are also particularly attractive targets of rent-seeking and corruption (Williams 2017).

The dissatisfaction with decentralized education has also led national departments of education to directly intervene in tasks that have been officially devolved to subnational governments and schools. School building programs are a particular case in point. Some central governments continue to engage in school construction even though that task has been decentralized. These interventions create confusion among citizens with respect to the division of labor between central and subnational governments in education decision-making and service delivery and weaken downward accountability (Lewis 2016). In any event, such actions have made it more difficult for subnational governments to deliver education outcomes effectively. In many cases, therefore, it seems that central governments' perception of generally poor subnational performance has led them to take actions that constrain subnational governments' ability to improve that performance.

Improving how education is financed for the majority of the world's children will require designing and implementing better intergovernmental transfer systems. This chapter has highlighted approaches to the effective design and distribution of transfers aimed at improving education outcomes and at the same time indicated various political challenges associated with making the needed technical reforms. The case studies that follow provide greater context and more details of the examples highlighted here and emphasize the complexity of education finance systems and the myriad challenges involved in ensuring that they contribute to better student learning outcomes.

NOTES

1. In all of the case study countries, subnational governments are responsible for early childhood, primary, and secondary education. The responsibility for technical and vocational secondary education is not always held at the subnational level. In Bulgaria, for example, it is a shared responsibility between the central and municipal governments.
2. How each country sets the minimum level of spending per student differs. In China, the minimum level of funding is set independently of the pool of funding available. However, this funding only ensures a minimum level of operational spending, which usually accounts for approximately 40 percent of total spending. In Brazil, the minimum varies and is based on the revenues that are raised each year.
3. See, for example, the Bulgaria case study (chapter 9) and Alonso and Sanchez (2011).

4. The effects described here relate to how transfers affect reported public education spending and do not take account of whether they displace private spending or other forms of public spending. In some cases, these displacement effects can be substantial.
5. Administrative costs include administration and management of schools and systems, teacher training, recreational activities, electricity, heating, transportation, library management, and the maintenance of facilities.
6. The per student intergovernmental fiscal transfers analyzed in this section are similar in their effects to per student transfers to schools. Evaluations have shown that providing transfers directly to schools has been successful in increasing access to education and attainment (McEwan 2015; Snilstveit et al. 2015).
7. See, for example, Shi (2016). Studies have shown that the impact of the reforms was different in different regions as well as for different levels of education. Ding, Lu, and Ye (2020) concluded that the new transfers did not lead to any significant increases in spending on education because they substituted for other "off-budget" spending, including tuition fees. This may also help to explain their positive impact on outcomes; the burden of funding shifted from households to governments, which removed the cost constraints on households associated with school attendance.
8. The guiding principles focus on the education sector but are drawn from the broader literature on fiscal transfers (see, for example, Bahl (2000); Boadway and Shah (2007); and Smoke and Kim (2003)) as well as findings from the case studies and associated author workshops.
9. See, for example, the Brazil (chapter 8) and China (chapter 10) case studies.
10. In Ukraine, for example, the responsibility for funding schools' recurrent costs was held by a level of government different from the one that held decision-making authority to open or close schools. As a result, when demographic changes meant that fewer school places were needed, the number of schools was not adjusted downward. Although this disconnect has since been addressed, it led to an increase in the number of schools with low levels of enrollment, which, from a financing viewpoint, was inefficient (Herczynski 2017).

REFERENCES

Al-Samarrai, Samer, Pedro Cerdan-Infantes, and Jonathan David Lehe. 2019. "Mobilizing Resources for Education and Improving Spending Effectiveness: Establishing Realistic Benchmarks Based on Past Trends." Policy Research Working Paper 8773, World Bank, Washington, DC.

Al-Samarrai, Samer, Tazeen Fasih, Amer Hasan, and Daim Syukriyah. 2015. "Assessing the Role of the School Operational Grant Program (BOS) in Improving Education Outcomes in Indonesia." Report AUS4133, World Bank, Washington, DC. https://openknowledge.worldbank.org/handle/10986/22102.

Alamir, M.A., M.T. Geiger, R. Bladon, N.M. Yehia, H. El-Tayeb Alyn, A.M. Ali, M. Yanez Pagans, J. Claussen, O.H. Fjeldstad, and S.A.I. Mustafa. 2014. *Sudan State-Level Public Expenditure Review: Meeting the Challenges of Poverty Reduction and Basic Service Delivery*. Background papers, vol. 2. World Bank, Washington, DC.

Alonso, J.D., and A. Sanchez, eds. 2011. *Reforming Education Finance in Transition Countries: Six Case Studies in Per Capita Financing Systems*: Washington, DC: World Bank.

Arvate, Paulo Roberto, Enlinson Mattos, and Fabiana Rocha. 2015. Intergovernmental Transfers and Public Spending in Brazilian Municipalities. FGV EESP: Escola de Economia de São Paulo, Fundação Getulio Vargas (Brazil).

Bahl, Roy. 2000. "Intergovernmental Transfers in Developing and Transition Countries: Principles and Practice." World Bank, Washington, DC.

Bird, Richard M., and Michael Smart. 2002. "Intergovernmental Fiscal Transfers: International Lessons for Developing Countries." *World Development* 30 (6): 899–912.

Boadway, R., and A. Shah, eds. 2007. *Intergovernmental Fiscal Transfers: Principles and Practice*. Washington, DC: World Bank.

Boex, Jameson, and Jorge Martinez-Vazquez. 2007. "Designing Intergovernmental Equalization Transfers with Imperfect Data: Concepts, Practices, and Lessons." In *Fiscal Equalization*, edited by Jorge Martinez-Vazquez and Bob Searle, 291–343. New York: Springer.

Brandão, Júlia Barbosa. 2014. "O rateio de ICMS por desempenho de municípios no Ceará e seu impacto em indicadores do sistema de avaliação da educação." Fundação Getulio Vargas, School of Public and Business Administration, Rio de Janeiro.

Costa, Leandro Oliveira, and Martin Carnoy. 2015. "The Effectiveness of an Early-Grade Literacy Intervention on the Cognitive Achievement of Brazilian Students." *Educational Evaluation and Policy Analysis* 37 (4): 567–90.

Cruz, Gabriela, and Rudi Rocha. 2018. "Efeitos do FUNDEF/B sobre frequência escolar, fluxo escolar e trabalho infantil: uma análise com base nos Censos de 2000 e 2010." *Estudos Econômicos (São Paulo)* 48 (1): 39–75.

Cruz, Tassia. 2018. "Teacher Hiring Decisions: How Do Governments React to an Exogenous Redistribution of Education Funds?" *Economics of Education Review* 67 (C): 58–81.

Cruz, Tassia, and Talita Silva. 2020. "Minimum Spending in Education and the Flypaper Effect." *Economics of Education Review* 77 (C): 102012.

Das, J., S. Dercon, J. Habyarimana, P. Krishnan, K. Muralidharan, and V. Sundararaman. 2013. "School Inputs, Household Substitution and Test Scores." *Applied Economics* 5 (2): 29–57.

de Carvalho Filho, Irineu, and Stephan Litschig. 2020. "Long-Run Impacts of Intergovernmental Transfers." *Journal of Human Resources*. doi: 10.3368/jhr.57.3:0917-9064R2.

De Witte, Kristof, and Laura López-Torres. 2017. "Efficiency in Education: A Review of Literature and a Way Forward." *Journal of the Operational Research Society* 68 (4): 339–63.

Dee, Thomas S., and Brian A. Jacob. 2010. "The Impact of No Child Left Behind on Students, Teachers, and Schools." *Brookings Papers on Economic Activity* (Fall 2010): 149–207.

Ding, Yanqing, Fengming Lu, and Xiaoyang Ye. 2020. "Intergovernmental Transfer under Heterogeneous Accountabilities: The Effects of the 2006 Chinese Education Finance Reform." *Economics of Education Review* 77 (C): 101985.

Franca, E.M. 2014. "Repasse da cota-parte do ICMS aos municípios cearenses: Avaliação das mudanças ocorridas no período de 2009 a 2011." Universidade Federal do Ceará.

Gertler, Paul, Paula Giovagnoli, and Sebastian Martinez. 2014. *Rewarding Provider Performance to Enable a Healthy Start to Life: Evidence from Argentina's Plan Nacer*. Washington, DC: World Bank.

Glassman, Amanda, and Yuna Sakuma. 2014. "Intergovernmental Fiscal Transfers for Health: Overview Framework and Lessons Learned." Center for Global Development, Washington, DC.

Gordon, N., and E. Vegas. 2005. "Educational Finance Equalization, Spending, Teacher Quality, and Student Outcomes: The Case of Brazil's FUNDEF." In *Incentives to Improve Teaching: Lessons from Latin America*, edited by E. Vegas, 151–82. Washington, DC: World Bank.

Ha, Wei, and Fang Yan. 2018. "Does Money Matter? The Effects of Block Grants on Education Attainment in Rural China: Evidence from Intercensal Population Survey 2015." *International Journal of Educational Development* 62 (September): 174–83.

Herczynski, J. 2017. *Education Finance in Ukraine: Selected Strategic Issues*. Stockholm: SKL International.

Hout, Michael, and Stuart W. Elliott, eds. 2011. *Incentives and Test-Based Accountability in Education*. Washington, DC: National Academies Press.

Hubbard, P. 2007. "Putting the Power of Transparency in Context: Information's Role in Reducing Corruption in Uganda's Education Sector." Working Paper Series 135, Center for Global Development, Washington, DC.

Jackson, C. Kirabo, Rucker C. Johnson, and Claudia Persico. 2016. "The Effects of School Spending on Educational and Economic Outcomes: Evidence from School Finance Reforms." *Quarterly Journal of Economics* 131 (1): 157–218.

Kim, Yun-Hwan, and Paul Smoke. 2003. "The Role and Challenges of Intergovernmental Fiscal Transfers in Asia." In *Intergovernmental Fiscal Transfers in Asia: Current Practice and Challenges for the Future*, edited by Paul Smoke and Yun-Hwan Kim, 1–19. Mandaluyong, Philippines: Asian Development Bank.

Klein, A. 2015. "No Child Left Behind: An Overview." *Education Week*, April 10. https://www.edweek.org/policy-politics/no-child-left-behind-an-overview/2015/04.

——. 2016. "The Every Student Succeeds Act: An ESSA Overview." *Education Week*, March 31. https://www.edweek.org/policy-politics/the-every-student-succeeds-act-an-essa-overview/2016/03.

Koretz, Daniel. 2017. *The Testing Charade: Pretending to Make Schools Better*. Chicago: University of Chicago Press.

Lautharte, I., J. Oliveira, and A. Loureiro. 2021. "Incentives for Mayors to Improve Learning: Evidence from State Reforms in Ceará, Brazil." Policy Research Working Paper 9509, World Bank, Washington, DC.

Lee, Jessica D., and Octavio Medina. 2019. "Results-Based Financing in Education: Learning from What Works." World Bank, Washington, DC. https://openknowledge.worldbank.org/handle/10986/31250.

Lewis, Blane D. 2013. "Local Government Capital Spending in Indonesia: Impact of Intergovernmental Fiscal Transfers." *Public Budgeting & Finance* 33 (1): 76–94.

——. 2014. "Indonesian Intergovernmental Performance Grants: An Empirical Assessment of Impact." *Bulletin of Indonesian Economic Studies* 50 (3): 415–33. doi: 10.1080/00074918.2014.980378.

——. 2016. "Is Central Government Intervention Bad for Local Outcomes? Mixed Messages from Indonesia." *Journal of Development Studies* 52 (2): 300–13.

Lewis, Blane D., and Adrianus Hendrawan. 2020. "The Impact of Public Sector Accounting Reform on Corruption: Causal Evidence from Subnational Indonesia." *Public Administration and Development* 40 (5): 245–54.

Lewis, Blane D., Neil McCulloch, and Audrey Sacks. 2016. "Measuring Local Government Service Delivery Performance: Challenges and (PARTIAL) Solutions in Indonesia." *Journal of International Development* 28 (5): 808–17. doi: doi:10.1002/jid.3106.

Lewis, Blane D, and Paul Smoke. 2017. "Intergovernmental Fiscal Transfers and Local Incentives and Responses: The Case of Indonesia." *Fiscal Studies* 38 (1): 111–39.

Loureiro, Andre, and Louisee Cruz. 2020. *Achieving World-Class Education in Adverse Socioeconomic Conditions: The Case of Sobral in Brazil*. Washington, DC: World Bank.

Malesky, Edmund J., Cuong Viet Nguyen, and Anh Tran. 2014. "The Impact of Recentralization on Public Services: A Difference-in-Differences Analysis of the Abolition of Elected Councils in Vietnam." *American Political Science Review* 108 (1): 144–68.

Manuel, Marcus, Dan Coppard, Amy Dodd, Harsh Desai, Richard Watts, Zach Christensen, and Stephanie Manea. 2019. "Subnational Investment in Human Capital." Development Initiatives, Bristol, UK.

McEwan, P. 2015. "Improving Learning in Primary Schools of Developing Countries: A Meta-Analysis of Randomized Experiments." *Review of Educational Research* 85 (3): 353–94.

OECD. 2017. *The Funding of School Education*. Paris: OECD.

Olsson, Ola, and Michele Valsecchi. 2015. "Resource Windfalls and Local Government Behavior: Evidence from a Policy Reform in Indonesia." doi.org/10.2139/ssrn.2685721.

Petterini, Francis Carlo, and Guilherme Diniz Irffi. 2013. "Evaluating the Impact of a Change in the ICMS Tax Law in the State of Ceará in Municipal Education and Health Indicators." *EconomiA* 14 (September–December): 171–84.

Pritchett, Lant. 2015. "Creating Education Systems Coherent for Learning Outcomes: Making the Transition from Schooling to Learning." Working Paper 15/005, Research on Improving Systems of Education (RISE), Oxford, UK.

Reinikka, Ritva, and Jakob Svensson. 2011. "The Power of Information in Public Services: Evidence from Education in Uganda." *Journal of Public Economics* 95 (7): 956–66.

Shah, Anwar. 2006. "A Practitioner's Guide to Intergovernmental Fiscal Transfers." Policy Research Working Paper 4039, World Bank, Washington, DC.

——. 2010. "Sponsoring a Race to the Top: The Case for Results-Based Intergovernmental Finance for Merit Goods." Policy Research Working Paper 5172, World Bank, Washington, DC.

Shi, Xinzheng. 2016. "The Impact of Educational Fee Reduction Reform on School Enrollment in Rural China." *Journal of Development Studies* 52 (12): 1791–1809.

Silveira, Iara Maira da, João Eustáquio de Lima, Evandro Camargos Teixeira, and Rubicleis Gomes da Silva. 2017. "Avaliação do efeito do Fundeb sobre o desempenho dos alunos do ensino médio no Brasil." Institute for Applied Economic Research, Brasilia.

Smoke, Paul. 2017. "Looking Beyond Conventional Intergovernmental Fiscal Frameworks: Principles, Realities, and Neglected Issues." In *Central and Local Government Relations in Asia*, edited by Naoyuki Yoshino and Peter J. Morgan, 64–99. Cheltenham, UK: Edward Elgar Publishing.

Smoke, Paul, and Yun-Hwan Kim. 2003. *Intergovernmental Fiscal Transfers in Asia: Current Practice and Challenges for the Future*. Mandaluyong, Philippines: Asian Development Bank.

Snilstveit, B., J. Stevenson, D. Phillips, M. Vojtkova, E. Gallagher, T. Schmidt, H. Jobse, M. Geelen, and M. Pastorello. 2015. *Interventions for Improving Learning Outcomes and Access to Education in Low- and Middle-Income Countries*. New Delhi: International Initiative for Impact Evaluation.

Sutherland, Douglas, Robert Price, and Eric Gonand. 2010. "Improving Public Spending Efficiency in Primary and Secondary Education." *OECD Journal: Economic Studies* 2009 (1): 1–30.

Wetzel, Deborah L., and Lorena Viñuela. 2020. "Intergovernmental Fiscal Transfers and Performance Grants in Brazil." In *Intergovernmental Transfers in Federations*, edited by Serdar Yilmaz and Farah Zahir, 204–23. Cheltenham, UK: Edward Elgar Publishing.

Williams, Martin J. 2017. "The Political Economy of Unfinished Development Projects: Corruption, Clientelism, or Collective Choice?" *American Political Science Review* 111 (4): 705–23.

World Bank. 2012. *Making Better Use of Teachers: Strengthening Teacher Management to Improve the Efficiency and Equity of Public Spending*. Jakarta: World Bank.

——. 2017. *Overview*. Vol. 1 of *A Fair Adjustment: Efficiency and Equity of Public Spending in Brazil*. Washington, DC: World Bank.

——. 2020. World Development Indicators. Washington, DC: World Bank. https://datatopics.worldbank.org/world-development-indicators/.

——. 2021. *The Role of Intergovernmental Fiscal Transfers in Improving Education Outcomes. Annex*. Washington, DC: World Bank.

Xiao, Yun, Li Li, and Liqiu Zhao. 2017. "Education on the Cheap: The Long-Run Effects of a Free Compulsory Education Reform in Rural China." *Journal of Comparative Economics* 45 (3): 544–62.

II COUNTRY CASE STUDIES

4 Sudan Case Study

TANYA SAVRIMOOTOO AND KEBEDE FEDA

INTRODUCTION

Context of the study

This chapter takes a close look at the decentralized nature of the education finance system in Sudan and explores potential ways to increase the equity and efficiency of public spending. The challenges to ensuring equity and efficiency in education spending in Sudan, which are identified in this chapter, are not new, as many of the same observations have been made in a number of reports on this topic since 2010. However, the Sudanese Revolution of 2019 has created a unique opportunity to usher in deep transformative reforms that can have a significant impact on the goal of ensuring that all Sudanese children have access to quality education.

The chapter is structured as follows. First is an overview of the education sector, including its structure, management, and performance. The next section describes education finance in the context of decentralization, including the financing framework, public expenditures, and links to learning outcomes. The final section suggests some key policies to strengthen Sudan's education finance system.

Country context

Sudan has a population of about 43 million people and, as of 2019, was administratively divided into 18 states and 189 localities. In 2011, after many years of conflict, South Sudan seceded from Sudan to form its own country. The secession triggered economic hardship for the population of Sudan and precipitated the fall of the 30-year regime of Omar al-Bashir. Sudan's oil revenues declined substantially, from 54 percent of total revenues in 2003 to just under 24 percent by 2013. The decline in revenue has contributed to budgetary shortfalls and undermined fiscal stability. Since 2018, Sudan has undergone a sociopolitical revolution that has fundamentally changed the path of the country. The Sudanese Revolution, which started in December 2018, culminated in the swearing in of the Interim Government in September 2019. This officially marked the end of the al-Bashir regime and will have significant repercussions for the country's governance structure.

Sudan's revolution was fueled by its youth. It is estimated that about 47 percent of the total population is currently under the age of 17. Figure 4.1 shows the population pyramid by age and sex since 2000, including projections for 2030. The projections show that demand for education services can be expected to continue to grow, putting an even higher premium on ensuring that education finance mechanisms maximize the equity, efficiency, and effectiveness of public spending, especially as the fiscal outlook remains challenging in the short term.

An estimated 36.1 percent of the population of Sudan live below the national poverty line, although there are significant geographic disparities; some regions experience higher rates of poverty, including the Darfur states at over 60 percent of the population in South and Central Darfur. Map 4.1 shows the map of poverty rates by state in Sudan (panel a) and the share of youths aged 15- to 24-years-old who are not in school or working (panel b). In some states, a large share of young people is neither in school nor working. Those engaged in economic activities also tend to come from areas with high poverty rates, which may be indicative of the prevalence of either underemployment or low productivity opportunities. For Sudan to effectively harness the productive potential of these young people, it will be necessary to increase access to quality education for all.

FIGURE 4.1
Population pyramid of Sudan, 2000–30

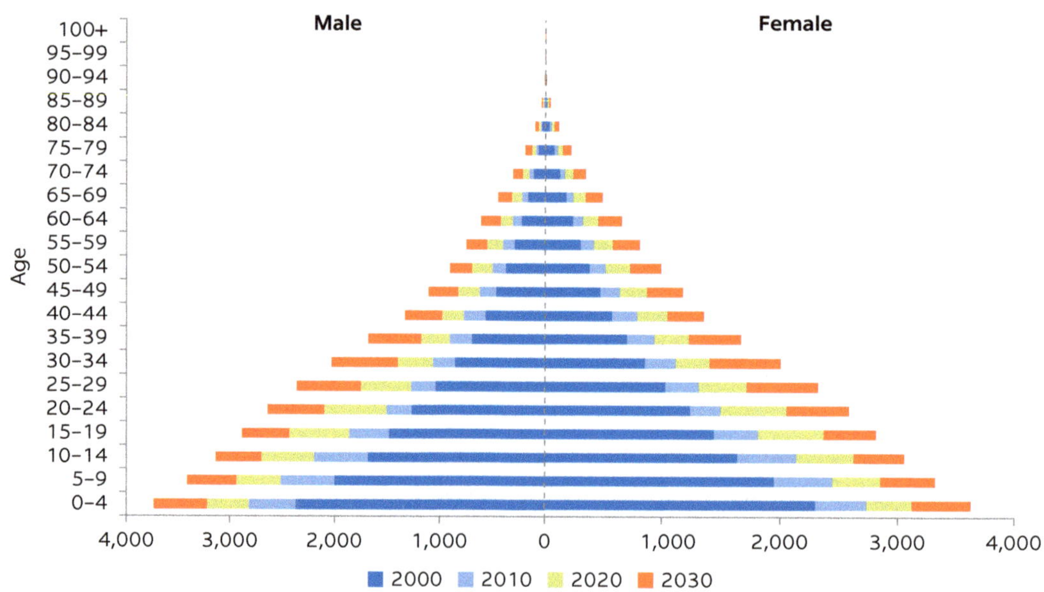

Source: UN Population Division Standard Projections Database, United Nations, New York (accessed May 2020), https://population.un.org/wpp/.

MAP 4.1
Poverty and youth activity in Sudan

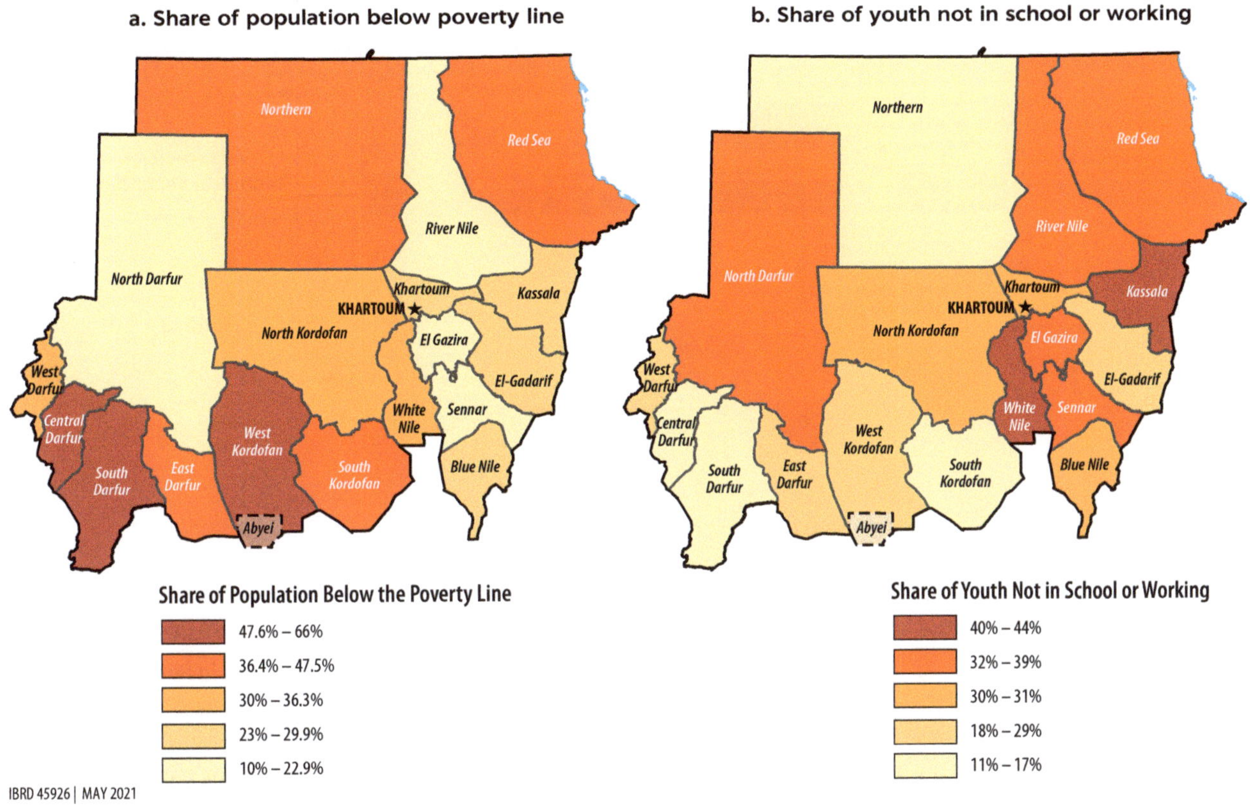

Source: World Bank calculations based on data from National Household Budget and Poverty Survey 2014–15.

EDUCATION SECTOR CONTEXT

Education structure

The education sector in Sudan is divided into two years of noncompulsory preschool starting at age 4, followed by eight years of basic education starting at age 6, after which students take the basic education examination. Based on their performance on the examination, students may enroll either in two years of vocational school or in three years of upper secondary education (either academic or technical). Those who have earned their secondary school certificates may then go on to study at a university or other higher education institution (see figure 4.2). It should be noted that the newly appointed government of Sudan has announced its intention to revert to a system of six years of basic education, followed by three years of junior secondary education and three years of upper secondary education, but this is still under discussion.

As of 2019, there were 18,634 preschools, 20,432 basic education schools (of which 16,438 were run by the government), and 4,493 secondary schools (of which 2,940 were run by the government). At the higher education level, there were 36 public universities, 71 private universities and colleges, 18 technical colleges, and 9 research centers. There were about 942,000 children enrolled in preschool, 6.2 million children enrolled in basic education, and a little over 1.1 million children enrolled in secondary school.

FIGURE 4.2
General education ladder in Sudan

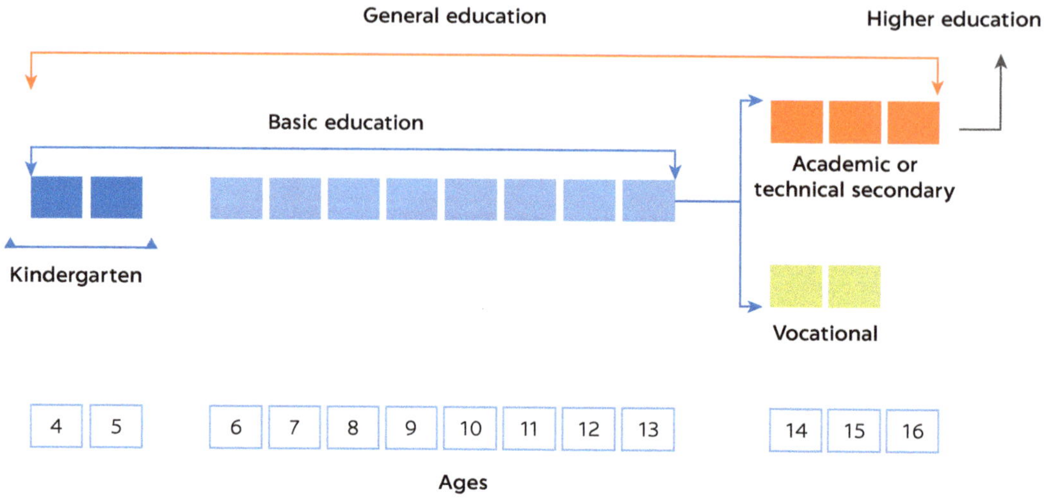

Source: Adapted from Federal Ministry of Education 2018a.

Education management

The allocation of responsibilities for education management in Sudan has evolved over time, with a trend toward devolving administrative and fiscal responsibilities to subnational levels of government. The origins of the decentralization process in Sudan date as far back as postindependence days,[1] although the path to the current system has been unstable, with frequent changes to the structure of subnational governments, their responsibilities, and their degree of autonomy. In more recent times, however, there have been two watershed events that have shaped the current education system: the adoption of a federal structure for the country in 1994, leading to the division of existing regions into new states and to the establishment of lower tiers of government; and the 2005 Comprehensive Peace Agreement (CPA) and Sudan's 2005 Interim National Constitution (INC). The latter, in particular, was fundamental to the creation of a decentralized system for delivering education. Under this system, education responsibilities are shared by three levels of government: (1) the federal level through the Federal Ministry of General Education (FMoE) and the Federal Ministry of Higher Education (FMoHE); (2) the state level through the State Ministries of Education (SMoE); and (3) localities through local governments (mahalliyas).

The federal level is responsible for planning, setting policy, and the general oversight, coordination, and monitoring of the sector. This includes the development and maintenance of standards and the development of policy in three key areas: (1) secondary school certification; (2) the qualification framework for teachers; and (3) development of curricula for basic and secondary education through the National Center for Curriculum and Education Research (NCCER). The states are responsible for the delivery of secondary education, human resource management, coordination among local Directorates of Education, and certification of students in basic education. Localities are responsible for delivering basic education. Table 4.1 summarizes the roles and responsibilities of the three tiers of government.

Under this decentralized system, many key functions and responsibilities, both administrative and fiscal, fall under the mandate of the states. Teacher management is one example. The recruitment and transfer of teachers in secondary

TABLE 4.1 **Education roles and responsibilities of national and subnational governments**

FUNCTION	FEDERAL GOVERNMENT	STATE GOVERNMENT	LOCALITIES
Policy	Sets standards, norms, and policies such as curriculum standards, teacher qualification framework, and secondary school certification	Implements policies and regulations	Implements policies and regulations
Financing	Responsible through the Federal Ministry of Finance for making federal transfers to states, the most important source of funding for education service delivery Responsible through the FMoF for making direct transfers of grants to higher education institutions Manages the budgets of the FMoE and the FMoHE	Responsible for funding secondary education	Responsible for funding basic education
Curriculum	Supervises the NCCER, the semiautonomous agency responsible for developing and supporting the national curriculum framework for basic and secondary education	Responsible for setting the preschool curriculum through SMoE Implement secondary education curriculum	Implement preschool and basic education curriculums
Facilities and infrastructure	Sets policies and establishes frameworks, such as the National School Construction Strategy, which includes norms, standards, technical specifications, bills of quantities, and local competitive bidding documents	Responsible for the construction of secondary schools In practice, about 80 percent of schools are constructed by local communities	Responsible for the construction of preschool and basic education schools In practice, however, approximately 80 percent of all schools are constructed by local communities
Teachers and education staff	Responsible through the National Center for Teacher Training for the one-year accreditation process for basic education teachers	Responsible through SMoE and SMoF for the recruitment and transfer of teachers for secondary education Although localities are responsible for the recruitment and transfer of teachers at the basic education level, most states actually carry out this role, especially when localities have limited capacity	Responsible for the recruitment and transfer of teachers for basic education level This can be done either by the state or the local government depending on the capacity of the local government as well the state's willingness to devolve responsibility to the locality (see State government in this table 4.1) Volunteer teachers are hired directly by the schools and constitute 10 percent of total teachers in basic education and 6 percent in secondary education
Quality assurance	Responsible through the Directorate of Quality Assurance–General Education for setting inspection framework and policies	State inspectors supervise secondary school teachers In practice, basic and secondary school teachers are supervised by state and local inspectors or head teachers, or a combination of all three depending on capacity (see Localities in this table 4.1)	Local inspectors supervise basic education teachers In practice, state inspectors may also carry out inspections in basic education schools Head teachers also carry out supervision of teachers

Sources: 2018 Rapid Survey Database, Ministry of Education, Khartoum, Sudan, and interviews for this chapter.
Note: FMoE = Federal Ministry of General Education; FMoF = Federal Ministry of Finance; FMoHE = Federal Ministry of Higher Education; NCCER = National Center for Curriculum and Education Research; SMoE = State Ministries of Education; SMoF = State Ministries of Finance.

education is the responsibility of state government. At the basic education level, this is technically the responsibility of the localities, although the state government may step in depending on the capacity of the local government and the degree of autonomy granted to localities in each state. The situation varies from state to state. The recruitment of volunteer teachers is the responsibility of school education councils, which are school-based management committees consisting of parents, teachers, and members of the community. The costs of volunteer teachers are covered by contributions from parent-teacher associations (PTAs).

Figure 4.3 shows the distribution of staff and volunteer teachers in the general education system.

Volunteer teachers are financed by PTA contributions collected at the school level. Their salaries represent about 18 percent of all PTA contributions nationwide (see figure 4.4). The percentage varies significantly across states, ranging from 2 percent in Blue Nile to between 30 and 39 percent in Central Darfur, West Darfur, West Kordofan, East Darfur, and North Kordofan. The heavy dependence on PTA contributions to finance volunteer teachers on the western front of Sudan may be indicative of the particular challenges these states face in financing key education inputs from state budgets.

Teacher deployment is the mandated responsibility of the state at the secondary level and of localities at the basic education level. However, some states also assume this role for basic education, especially where localities have limited capacity. As a result, the capacity for ensuring effective deployment is significantly constrained. Teachers can decide to move to another state, but they cannot be required to do so, and there are currently no incentives to motivate teachers to take positions in remote locations or in areas where they are most needed across Sudan. Figure 4.5 shows the correlation between the number of students and the number of teachers at the basic and secondary levels. The R-squared indicator represents the percentage of the variation in the number of teachers allocated to government primary schools attributable to the number of students; the remainder is related to other unexplained factors

FIGURE 4.3

Number of teachers in the general education system

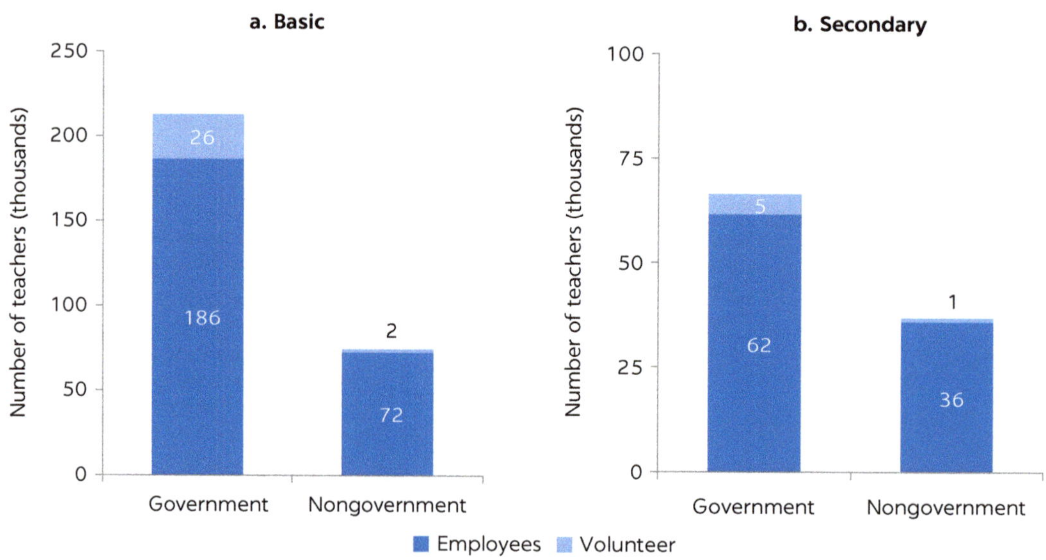

Source: 2018 Rapid Survey Database, Ministry of Education, Khartoum, Sudan.

FIGURE 4.4

Share of PTA contributions that finance volunteer teachers' salaries, by state

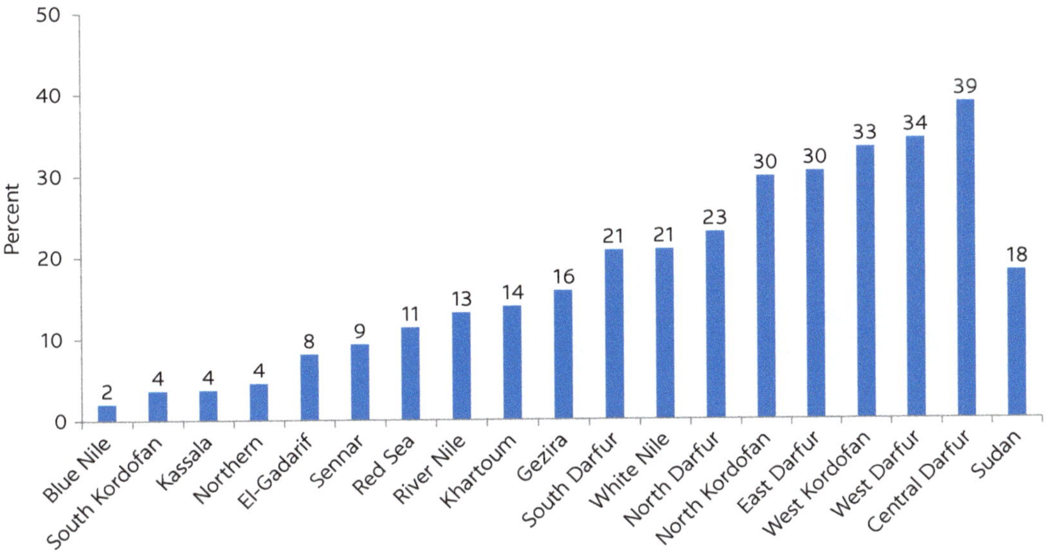

Source: 2018 Rapid Survey Database, Ministry of Education, Khartoum, Sudan.
Note: PTA = parent-teacher association.

FIGURE 4.5

Correlation between the number of students and teachers at the basic and secondary levels

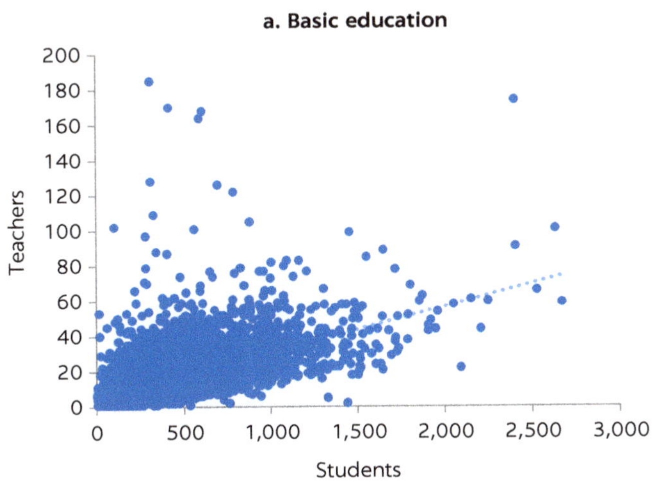

Source: 2018 Rapid Survey Database, Ministry of Education, Khartoum, Sudan.
Note: R^2 = 0.3842. Each dot represents one school.

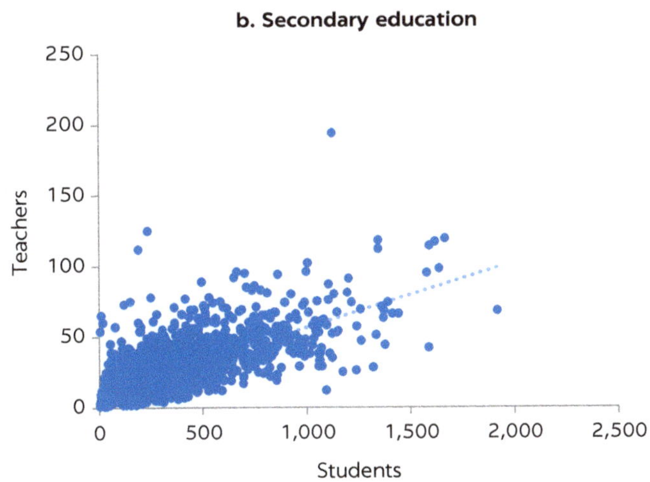

Source: 2018 Rapid Survey Database, Ministry of Education, Khartoum, Sudan.
Note: R^2 = 0.4909. Each dot represents one school.

(referred to as the degree of randomness). The degree of randomness can be as low as 8 percent in Zimbabwe or 13 percent in The Gambia, for example, which reflects intercountry differences in the mechanisms used to recruit and deploy teachers.

Figure 4.6 shows the student-teacher ratio at the basic education level across states. Although the ratio for Sudan is about 26 students per teacher, there are important variations across states, ranging from a low of 13 in Northern state to a high of 36 in North Kordofan. To assess how much the ratio varies among localities, we divided the ratio at the 80th percentile of schools by the ratio at the 20th

FIGURE 4.6

Student-teacher ratio in basic education, by state

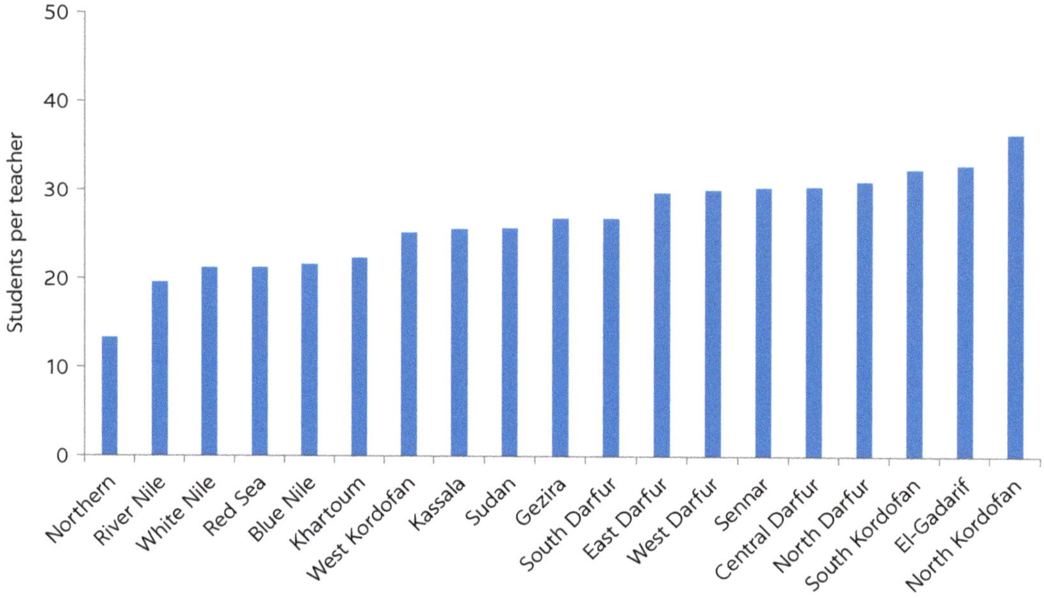

Source: 2018 Rapid Survey Database, Ministry of Education, Khartoum, Sudan.
Note: Includes volunteer teachers.

percentile by locality and found a gap of 3.02. A value greater than 2 is usually thought to be symptomatic of either political economy and patronage problems, or a lack of data or mechanisms to distribute resources efficiently among localities or a combination of those factors. Although the student-teacher ratio itself is not very high by recommended standards, there may be efficiencies to be gained by allowing greater coordination between states and perhaps by reducing dependence on volunteer teachers in some areas.

Education sector performance

Sudan faces two main challenges: (1) an unfinished agenda of providing access to education to all; and (2) generally low learning achievement levels, with very slow improvements over time and large disparities among states. The government's latest Education Sector Strategic Plan for 2018–19 to 2022–23 acknowledges these challenges and formulates a strategy aimed at increasing access to and equity in both basic education and secondary education and at improving the quality of education by increasing access to quality preschool and by strengthening students' foundational skills.

Although access has increased over time, gross enrollment ratios (GER) remain low. Even at the basic education level, the GER is only 94 percent. Figure 4.7 shows the GER by level of education and disaggregated by gender, area of residence, and wealth quintile. It should be noted that the net enrollment ratio at the basic education level is about 74 percent and at the secondary level (not shown) only 28 percent, indicating a significant issue of students not enrolling on time. The GERs are also lower for girls, for children from rural areas, and for students from the poorest households (the bottom 40 percent of wealth quintiles) in all levels of education.

FIGURE 4.7
Gross enrollment ratio by gender, residence, and wealth

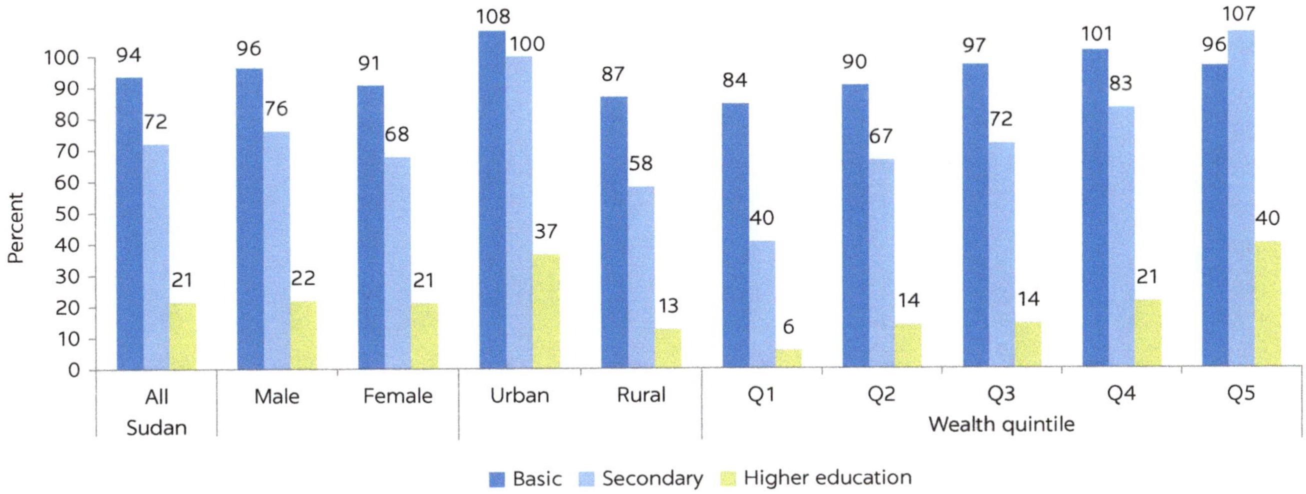

Source: World Bank calculations based on data from National Household Budget and Poverty Survey 2014–15.

FIGURE 4.8
Gross enrollment ratio, by state

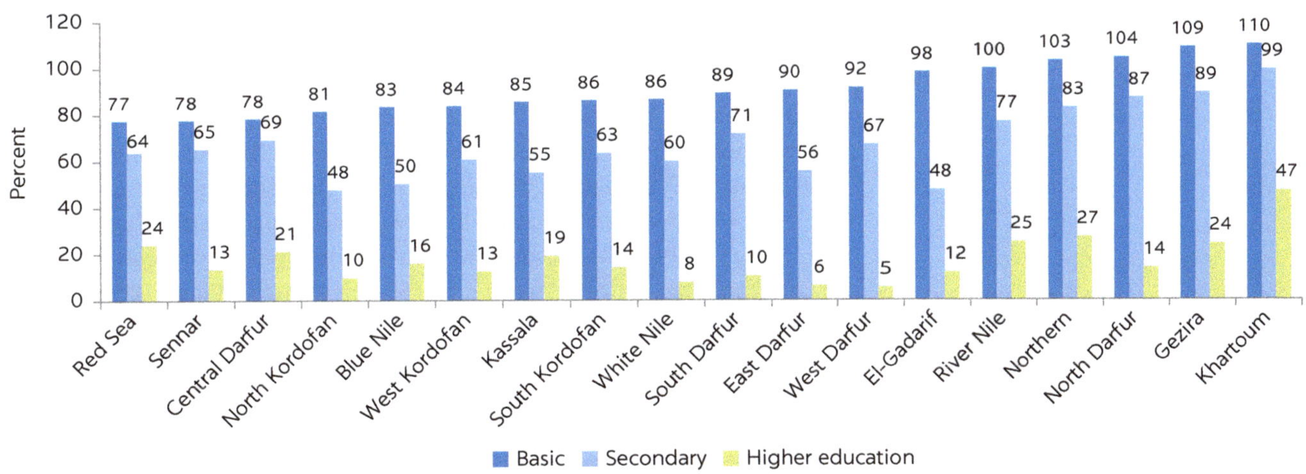

Source: World Bank calculations based on data from National Household Budget and Poverty Survey 2014–15.

Figure 4.8 shows the GER disaggregated by state and level of education. Although the GER at the national level is 94 percent, access varies significantly from state to state. For example, in 2014–15, the GER ranged from about 77 percent in Red Sea to 110 percent in Khartoum at the basic education level. Similarly, although the national GER averaged 72 percent at the secondary level, it ranged from a low of 48 percent in El-Gadarif to a high of 99 percent in Khartoum.

Figure 4.9 shows the gender parity index (GPI) disaggregated at the state level. Parity has not yet been achieved in most states, even in basic education. The gap tends to widen at the secondary level. There are some notable variations across states, with the GPI ranging from a low of between 84 and 87 percent in Kassala and the Darfur states at the basic education level and the even lower 57 percent at the secondary level, for example, in West Kordofan. According to

FIGURE 4.9

Gender parity index, by state

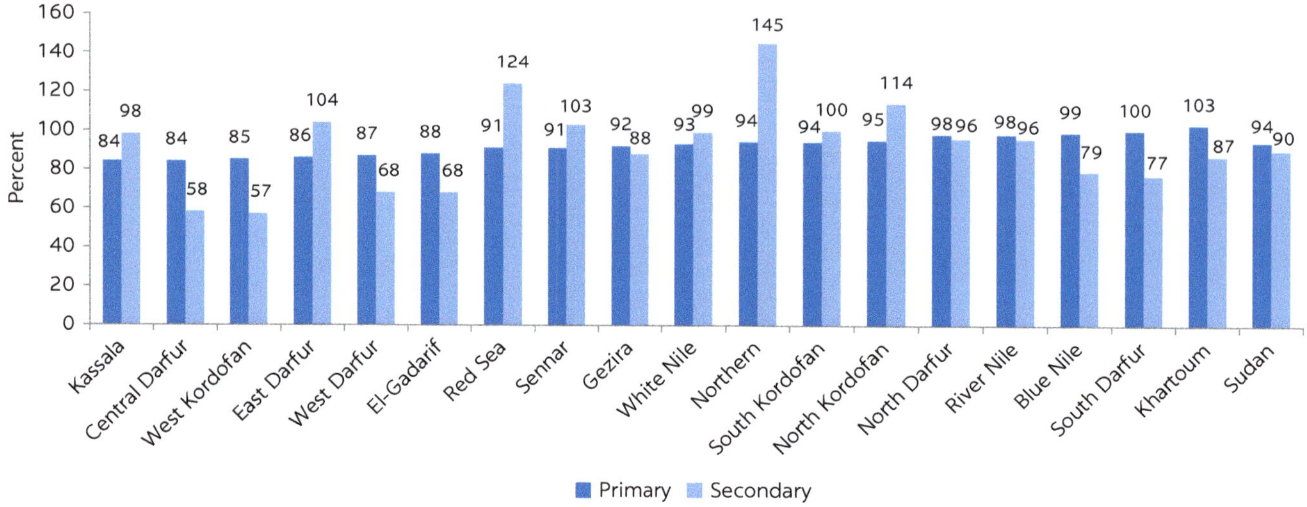

Source: World Bank calculations based on data from National Household Budget and Poverty Survey 2014–15.

feedback from state officials we consulted, this may be a result of region-specific cultural norms, especially among the nomadic tribes.

The survival rate from grades 1 to 8 stands at approximately 80 percent for Sudan, meaning that a child who enrolls in grade 1 has an 80 percent chance of reaching grade 8.[2] Figure 4.10 shows the disparities between urban and rural areas in panel a and the disparities among states in panel b. Even though survival rates are relatively high across Sudan, there are clear state-specific disparities, with West and Central Darfur and Blue Nile having particularly low survival rates. There are also strong disparities between urban and rural areas. There are no significant disparities between girls (80.8 percent) and boys (80 percent); these data are not shown.

About 22 percent of children between ages 6 and 13 are out of school (OOS) in Sudan. Figure 4.11 shows the OOS rate across basic and secondary school age cohorts disaggregated by gender, area of residence, and wealth and categorized by those who have never been to school and those who have dropped out. Among children between ages 6 and 13, the OOS rate is largely made up of children who have never enrolled in school (19.5 percent) and is higher among girls (24.1 percent), children from rural areas (28.8 percent), and those from the poorest households (25.6 percent for children from the bottom two wealth quintiles). At the secondary school level (children ages 14 to 16), the OOS rate is 24.5 percent at the national level and is characterized by a large share of students who have dropped out of the education system (14 percent). Again, the rate is higher among girls (25.7 percent), children from rural households (30.9 percent), and those from the poorest households (28.5 percent for the bottom two wealth quintiles).

The disaggregation of the OOS rate among states reveals strong disparities within Sudan. Figure 4.12 shows the OOS rate for the age 6 to 13 cohort across all 18 states and disaggregated by those who have never attended school and those who have dropped out. The OOS rate ranges from a low of 4.8 percent in Khartoum state to a high of 41.8 percent in Central Darfur.

Learning outcomes in Sudan are generally poor, and improvements over time have been gradual and uneven across states. There have been two recent rounds

FIGURE 4.10
Survival rates, grades 1 to 8

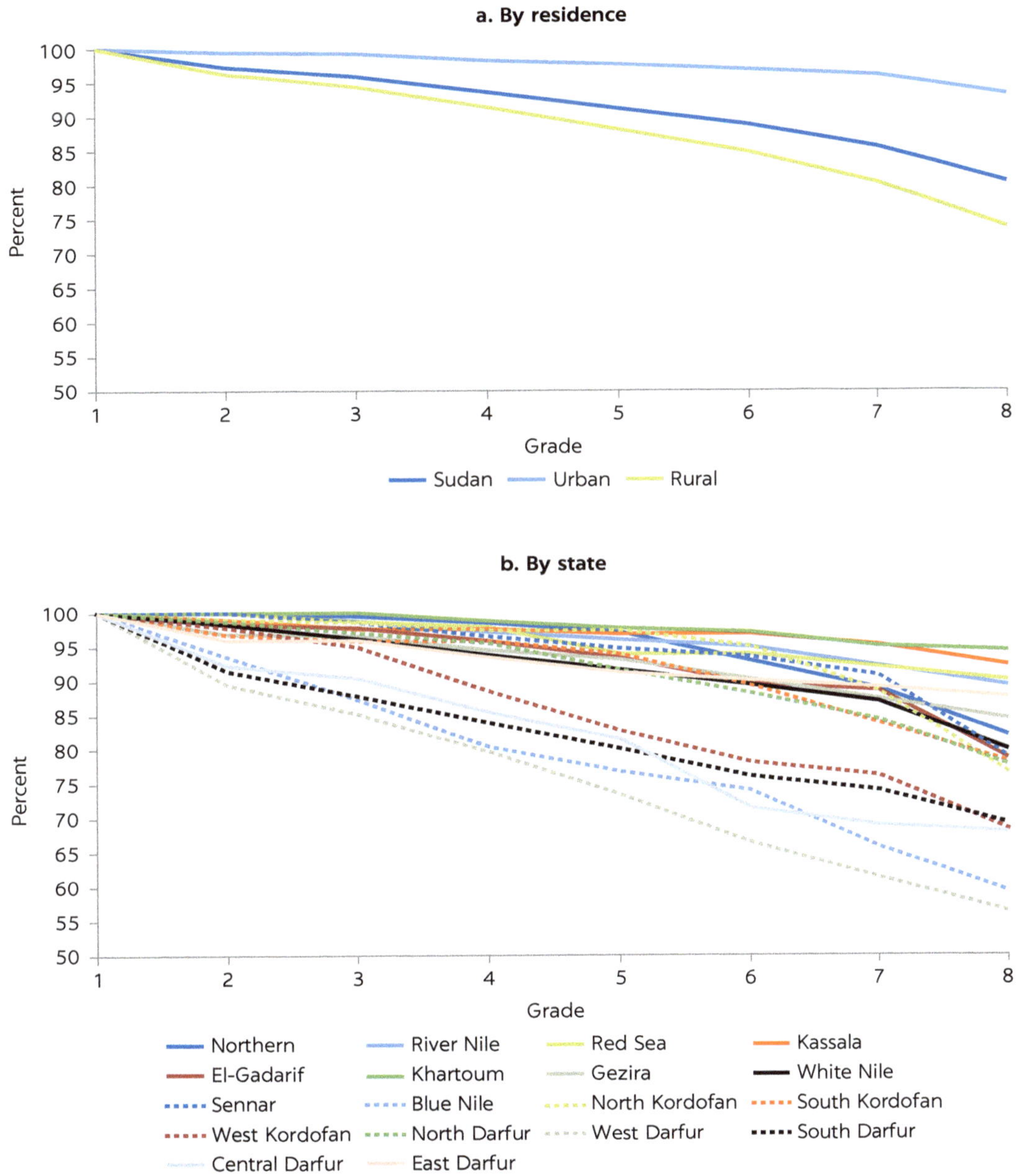

Source: Multiple Indicator Cluster Survey Database, UNICEF, New York, New York (accessed June 2019), https://microdata.worldbank.org/index.php/catalog/2656.

of learning assessments: (1) the Early Grade Reading Assessment (EGRA) and the Early Grade Mathematics Assessment (EGMA) for students in grade 3 in 2014–15, and (2) the same assessments for students in grades 3 and 6 in 2017–18. Figure 4.13 shows the share of nonreaders in grade 3 in 2014–15 and in 2017–18 by state. As indicated, even though the share of nonreaders decreased overall from 40.2 percent to 38.7 percent, the experience has been uneven across states. Although some states have successfully reduced the share of nonreaders (River Nile dropped from 37.3 percent to 18.6 percent, and Central Darfur dropped from 71 percent to 56.2 percent), other states experienced an increase (El-Gadarif rose from 45 to 61 percent).

FIGURE 4.11
Out-of-school rates, by education level

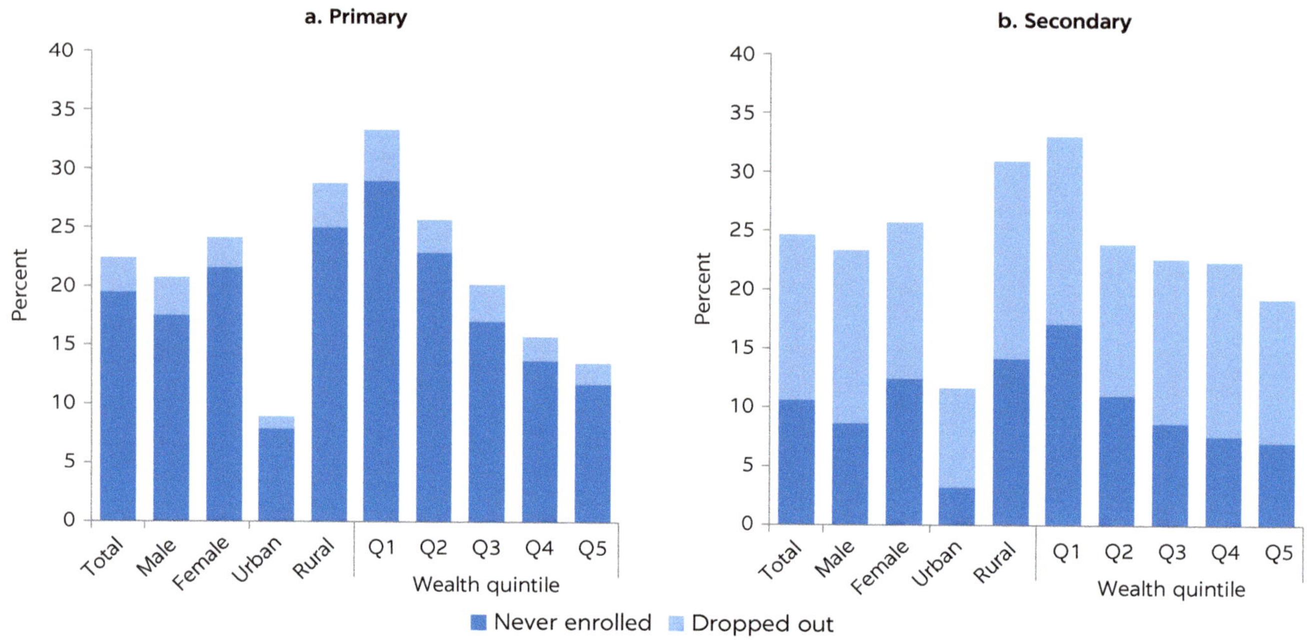

Source: World Bank calculations based on data from National Household Budget and Poverty Survey 2014–15.

FIGURE 4.12
Out-of-school rates for children ages 6 to 13, by state

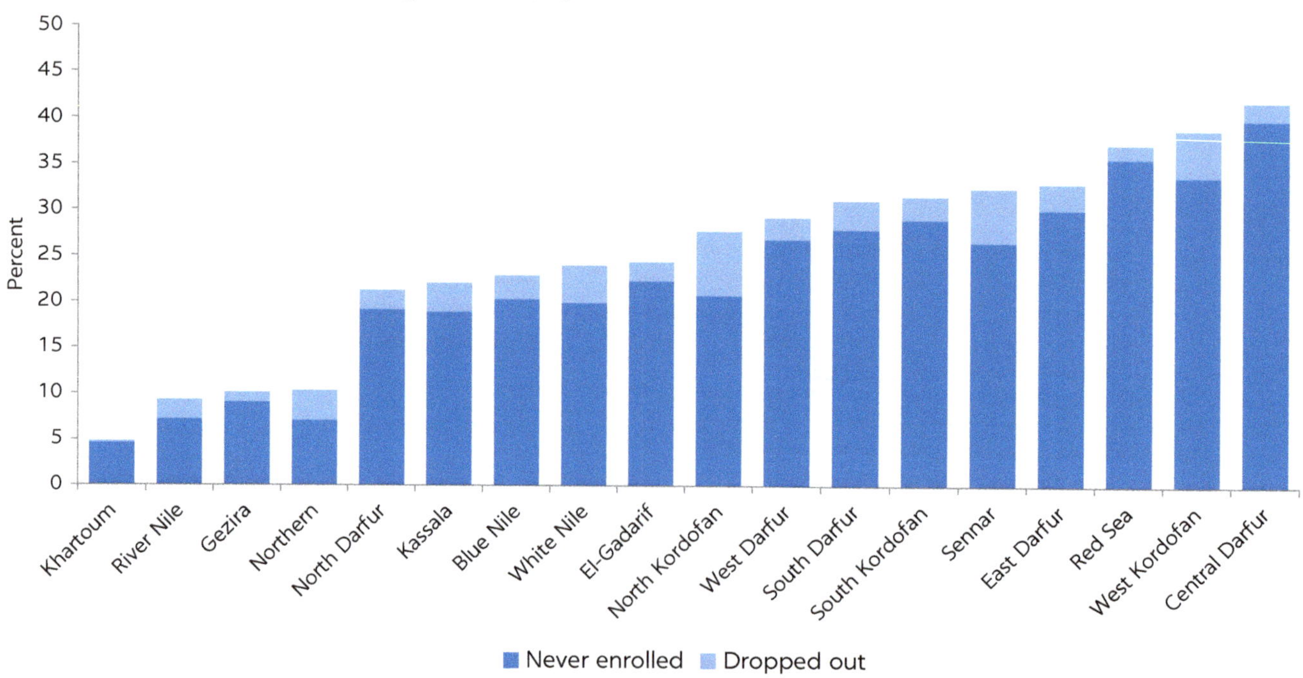

Source: World Bank calculations based on data from National Household Budget and Poverty Survey 2014–15.

FIGURE 4.13
Share of nonreaders in grade 3, by state, 2014/15 and 2017/18

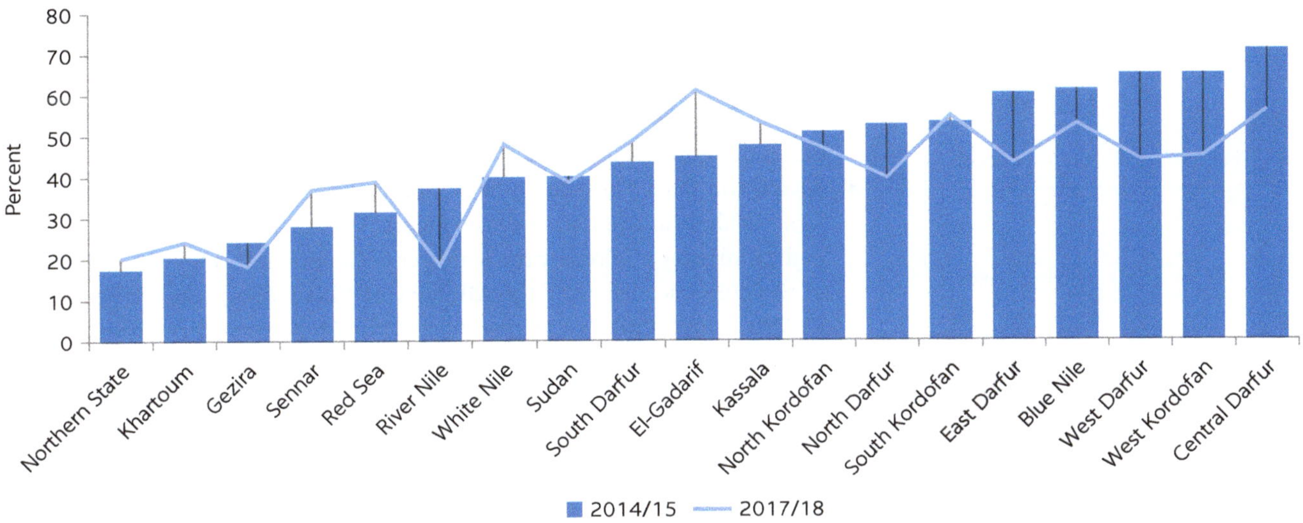

Source: Federal Ministry of Education 2018b.

EDUCATION SECTOR FINANCING

Education sector financing framework

Just as for education management, decentralization has been applied to the education finance structure in Sudan. As mandated by the Interim National Constitution (INC), the provision and financing of secondary education is the responsibility of the state, while the responsibility for basic education lies with the locality. In practice, however, decentralization has been a challenge. The allocation of roles and responsibilities for education finance differs from state to state, in part due to the varying capacity of states and localities to raise revenue and implement policies.

Public spending on education at the subnational level is financed by federal transfers and revenues raised at the state and local levels. At the federal level, there are four different transfer mechanisms used to channel funds to the states:

- *Current transfers.* These are nonearmarked, unrestricted transfers that are allocated from the federal government to states based on a vertical allocation formula determined by the Fiscal and Financial Allocation and Monitoring Commission (FFAMC). The formula takes into account population size, agriculture requirements, security, education needs, health, financial performance, distance to the center and port, and off-budget support. These are the largest of all federal transfers, and it is usually assumed that they are used to pay the salaries of civil servants, including teachers and other staff in the education sector.
- *State development transfer.* This transfer is driven by ongoing or completed state development projects and state development projects that are planned for the forthcoming budget year in all sectors (infrastructure, commodity projects, and service projects, including for education and health). The transfer is allocated by the federal government on an ad hoc or discretionary basis.

Between 2016 and 2018, education projects received between 4 and 5 percent of all federal development transfers (about SD 277.5 million in 2018).

- *Specified transfer.* These are direct transfers from the federal government to state bodies (such as higher education institutions, police, and prison systems). Transfers to higher education institutions are categorized as grants and are off-budget because they are distributed directly from the central government to the institutions.
- *Special transfers.* These amount to 2 percentage points of the current transfers, withheld at the source by the federal level. This fund is supervised by a high committee chaired by the Minister of General Education and composed of the Undersecretary of the Ministry of Finance, representatives of the FFAMC, the Council of Ministers, and the Undersecretary of Ministry of General Education. This transfer funds key inputs at the state level based on priorities identified by the high committee through consultation with ministry of education officials at the state level. They are used to finance seating, textbooks, laboratory equipment, teacher training, and rehabilitation of schools. In 2019, a special transfer was used by the federal government to purchase and distribute grade 5 textbooks.

Table 4.2 summarizes the main transfer mechanisms between the federal government and the states that support the provision of education financing at the subnational levels. The transfer mechanisms are not aimed at narrowing the equity gaps in the education sector, and there are no built-in performance-based incentives to encourage states to focus on improving education outcomes. The transfers are mostly aimed at ensuring the adequacy of education financing, although there is no mechanism for assessing whether the available financing is meeting the basic requirements of the sector. The states' opinions of the effectiveness of the special transfers are somewhat mixed. During the consultation workshop held for this study some state representatives indicated that the withholding of 2 percentage points of funds from the current transfers further constrained their ability to finance priorities in their own states. Others expressed their appreciation for the efficiency gains that have arisen from the special transfer.

Federal transfers fluctuate depending on the level of federal revenues. Prior to South Sudan's secession in 2011, federal revenues were largely driven by nontax revenues, especially revenues accrued from the production and exportation of oil. However, nontax revenues have decreased since the secession because most oil producing fields are located in South Sudan. Sudan and South Sudan have also failed to reach an agreement on acceptable terms for refining and transporting oil, which has deepened Sudan's reliance on tax revenues since 2011. Tax revenues as a share of total federal revenues increased from 41 percent in 2009 to 83 percent in 2017 (Central Bank of Sudan 2019; El-Hassan El-Battahani and Gadkarim 2017).

The principles underlying the transfer of resources between different levels of government in Sudan is rooted in the Wealth Sharing Protocol, adopted under the CPA to correct the imbalances in revenue generation across states while ensuring that states are capable of exercising their constitutionally mandated responsibilities. The FFAMC was formed following the adoption of the CPA and given the responsibility both for determining the vertical share of revenue from the federal government to the states and for equalizing horizontal transfers between the states (World Bank 2014). The FFAMC reported directly to the

TABLE 4.2 **Transfer mechanisms between the federal government and the states for education**

TRANSFERS	CURRENT TRANSFER	STATE DEVELOPMENT TRANSFER	SPECIFIED TRANSFER	SPECIAL TRANSFER
Type	General transfer, nonearmarked	Project-based transfer, including but not limited to education projects	Targeted transfers for specific purposes, including higher education	Education-specific transfer
Objectives	General support for state budgets including education expenditures (adequacy)	Ad hoc support for selected ongoing development projects (adequacy)	Provision of off- budget grant directly to public higher education institutions (adequacy)	Economies of scale in acquisition of education inputs (efficiency)
Use of resources	Support for overall state budgets, including salaries and, in some cases, nonsalary recurrent spending	Support for ongoing development projects, including education projects	Support for higher education institutions as a grant, not earmarked for specific spending categories	Used to finance specific inputs such as textbooks and managed centrally; priorities are determined by the FMoE and the high committee every year
Determination of pool of funds	Based on projected revenues for the year, using past levels of revenues and expenditures as proxies; usually represents between 25 and 33 percent of total federal revenues	Ad hoc allocation	Off-budget support in form of grants	2 percentage points of the current transfer is earmarked
Allocation of pool	Horizontal allocation formula determined by the FFAMC based on a set of eight criteria	Varies based on states' planned, ongoing, or completed development projects	Varies depending on the institution receiving direct support (for example, higher education institutions or prisons); grant amount is based on previous year's allocation	Varies depending on the program being supported; for example, the distribution of textbooks among states depends on enrollment numbers
Issues and policy challenges	Little evidence that allocation decisions are aligned with the criteria; moreover, there are strong concerns about budget credibility	No clear rationale underpinning the allocations for state development transfers; conflict about who should be funding these projects; some states indicate that they receive little support from the federal level whereas the federal government wants states to rely less on federal funds	Higher education institutions do not systematically report on their use of the grants	Unclear how well-aligned these funds are with the states' needs; some states have indicated that they prefer to manage these resources directly

Source: World Bank.
Note: FFAMC = Fiscal and Financial Allocation and Monitoring Commission; FMoE = Federal Ministry of General Education.

president's office until its operations were suspended after the investiture of the new government in September 2019. However, although the principle underlying the equalization of transfers was well-understood, it lacked clarity and specificity on, for example, whether the equalization should be achieved by providing equal access to services such as health and education, by increasing access to funding, or by some other approach. There was also a complete lack of transparency on what factors were used to determine the vertical share of transfers from the federal government. Federal transfers to states between 2012 and 2018 have ranged between 25 and 33 percent of total federal revenues.

The horizontal allocation formula that is currently used by the FFAMC at times contradicts the objective of redressing funding imbalances across states. Table 4.3 outlines the eight criteria used to determine the horizontal allocations and the relative weights placed on each. The formula-based allocation system was introduced in Sudan in 1998 to equalize funding across states, taking into account the expenditure responsibilities and own-revenue capacity of each state, and to reimburse them for specific costs. The formula has been changed several times over the years. The criteria consist of both formula-based and discretionary factors. Each of the eight factors has its own set of elements, which together constitute the score for each factor. The final score for the state is then computed from the scores across all eight factors. For example, a state with a high teacher-student ratio receives a score of 3, while a state that has more students overall receives a score of 5. States with security issues receive higher scores than states without security issues.

The education criteria themselves (student-population ratio, teacher-student ratio, and number of students) do not capture critical equity aspects such as the share of out-of-school (OOS) children or disparities in access across gender and between urban and rural areas. Moreover, states that are able to generate more own-revenue and those that are able to carry a budget surplus are favored in the allocation formula, which defeats the underlying objective of achieving greater equity across states. For example, states that carry a budget surplus are allocated more points (three) than those with a budget deficit (one) in the overall scoring. It should be noted that the exact application of the formula is not made explicit by the FFAMC, neither is it communicated to the subnational levels, so any nuances in the interpretation of the formula may not be fully captured.

There is little to no evidence that this formula is being applied. The complexity of the formula has made it difficult for the federal government to clearly communicate the basis on which it decides the amount of federal resources to be transferred to the states, which creates a lack of transparency and prevents the achievement of the intended equalization objective.

Figure 4.14 shows the distribution of federal transfers in 2018 compared with the population size and poverty rates in each state. Although it is clear from panel a that population size is correlated to some extent with transfer size, panel b confirms that there is a very weak correlation with the share of population living under the national poverty line. This further reinforces the possibility that the allocation formula fails to adequately account for socioeconomic disparities between states.

The fiscal autonomy of states is also limited by a lack of capacity to generate their own revenues. Most states, despite decentralization, depend to a large extent on federal transfers to finance their constitutionally mandated basic services, including teacher salaries, which is the largest item in the state education budgets.

Figure 4.15 shows the percentage of federal transfers as a share of total state revenue in 2017 and 2018. The level of dependence on federal grants varies significantly across states from as low as 26 percent in Khartoum state to as high as 89 percent in Central Darfur. The share of federal transfers represents at least 50 percent of the revenues of all states in Sudan except for Khartoum state.

The actual levels of state revenue also vary widely. Figure 4.16 shows total state revenues by source. "National government transfers" are unallocated,

TABLE 4.3 **Horizontal allocation formula factors and weights**

FACTOR	ELEMENTS	WEIGHT
Population size		
	Population	12
	Population density	5
	Urban population	8
		25
Agricultural requirements		
	Livestock	7
	Agricultural area	8
		15
Security		
	Police	4
	Prisons	5
	Security situations	4
	When state created	2
		15
Education		
	Student-population ratio	5
	Teacher-student ratio	3
	Number of students	5
		13
Health		
	Hospital beds per capita	4
	Doctors per capita	4
	Midwives per capita	1
	Number of health facilities	3
		12
Fiscal performance		
	Total revenue and recurrent expenses	2
	Budget surplus	3
	Budget deficit	1
	Improvement on revenue	2
	Inflation	2
		10
Distance to center and port		
	Less than 500 km	1
	500–1,000 km	3
	More than 1,000 km	4
		8
Off-budget support		**2**

Source: FFAMC 2017.

FIGURE 4.14

Size of transfers in relation to states' population size and poverty rates

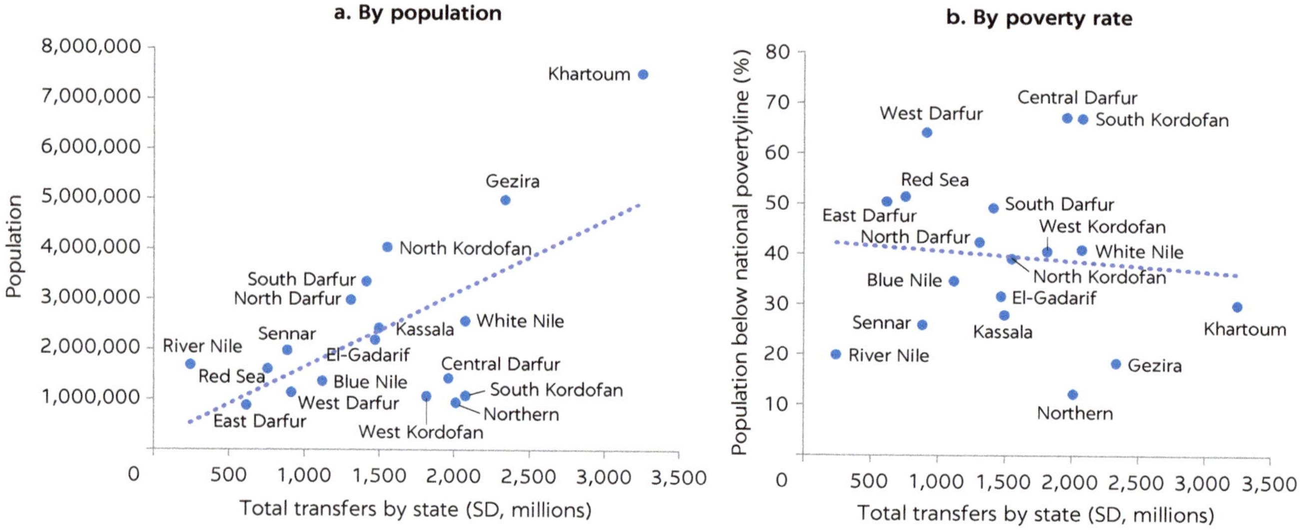

Source: Data from case study and World Bank calculations based on data from National Household Budget and Poverty Survey 2014–15.
Note: SD = Sudanese pound.

FIGURE 4.15

Federal transfers as a percentage of total state revenues, 2017 and 2018

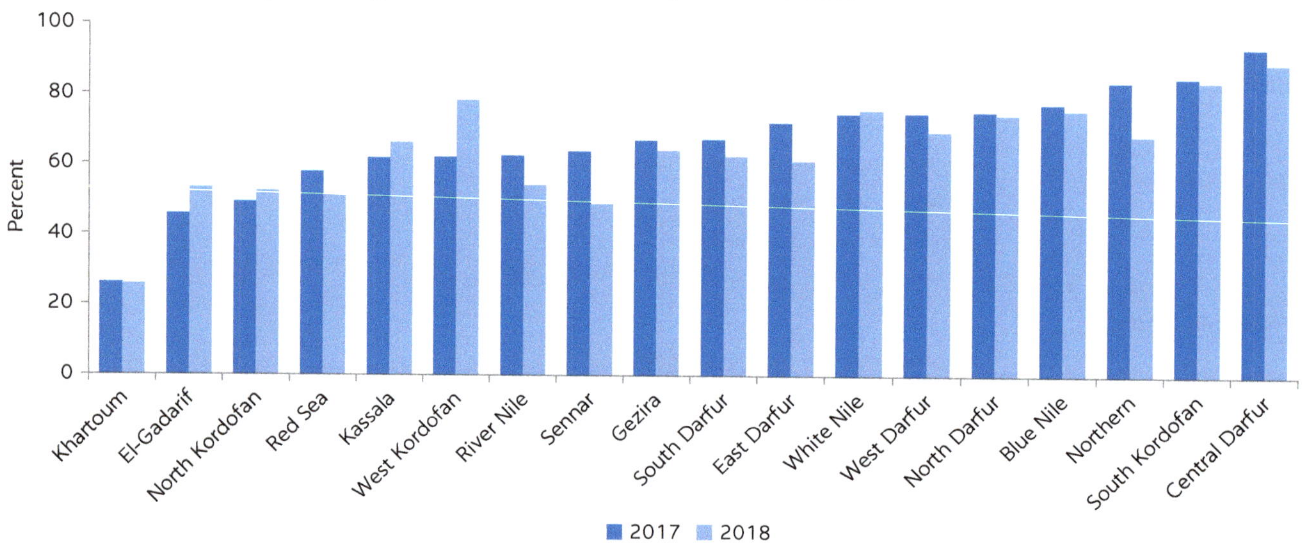

Source: Administrative data from the Ministry of the Federal Government.

unearmarked transfers from the federal government to the states; "government transfers" are earmarked transfers for both education and other sectors combined. The disparities between states are wide. Khartoum, the state with by far the highest revenues, has about 3.5 times more revenue than Gezira, the state with next highest revenues. Khartoum receives about 13 percent of all federal transfers provided to the states, while its self-generated revenues represent about 74 percent of the state's total revenues. In comparison, Central Darfur receives about 7.1 percent of all federal transfers to all states, while its self-generated revenues represent about 11 percent of the state's total revenues.

FIGURE 4.16

State revenue mobilization, by source

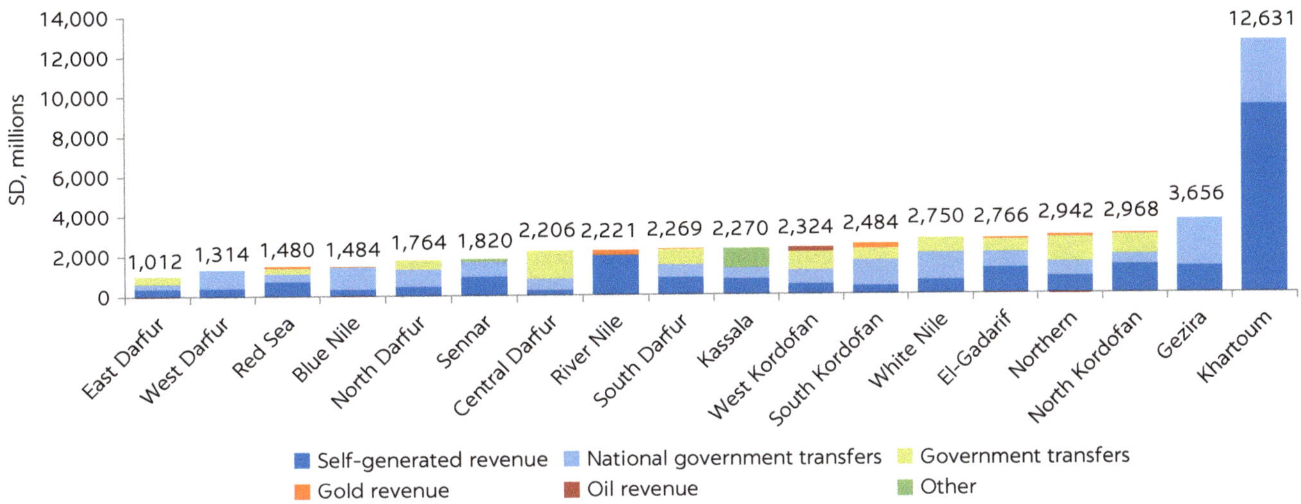

Source: Administrative data derived from the Ministry of the Federal Government.
Note: SD = Sudanese pound.

FIGURE 4.17

Self-generated revenues and federal transfers, by state

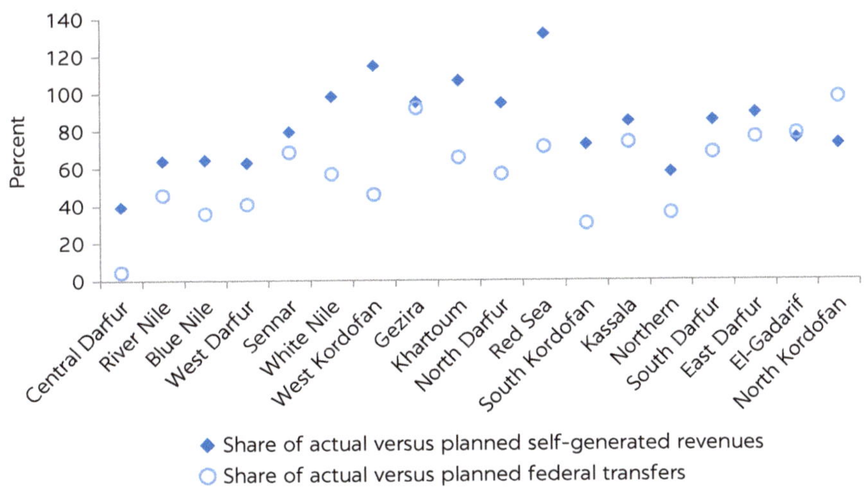

Source: Administrative data derived from the Ministry of the Federal Government.

The weaknesses of the education finance mechanisms in Sudan tend to reflect the overall challenges faced by the country in fully implementing the decentralization process in accordance with the law. First, there is limited clarity and understanding of the roles and responsibilities of the various tiers of government. Second, the states' limited capacity to generate revenue and collect taxes has reinforced their dependence on federal transfers to finance the delivery of basic services, thus undermining their ability to fully finance the education sector. Third, the lack of transparency in the allocation formulas, the lack of adherence to those formulas, and a tendency to rely on the discretionary allocation of funds are all constraining the ability of all levels of government to adequately, efficiently, and effectively fund the education sector.

The unpredictability of actual federal transfers to states compared to planned transfers also hinders proper planning at the subnational level. Figure 4.17 shows the share of actual versus planned federal transfers and self-generated revenues. Self-generated revenues tend to be more predictable than federal transfers; 12 of the 18 states were able to generate 70 percent or more of their planned own revenue. In contrast, the reliability of federal transfers varies significantly among the states, ranging from lows of 4.3 percent in Central Darfur and 29.9 percent in South Kordofan to highs of 91.9 percent in Gezira and 97.4 percent in North Kordofan. During our joint consultations with officials from the State Ministries of Finance (SMoFs) of all 18 states, many were surprised by this variation, which contributed to a lack of trust in the federal government or in the allocation formulas being used or both.

Education budgets and expenditures

With the exception of direct financing for the FMoE and the FMoHE and for higher education institutions, education budgets are in large part determined at the state level. The SMoE have, since 2019, adopted a medium-term expenditure framework (MTEF) approach to preparing their budgets. The MTEF helps the ministries clearly identify their priorities in both the short and medium terms and budget for them accordingly over the upcoming three years. However, as is often the case, actual allocations, which are determined by the State Ministries of Finance, depend on and are constrained by other factors, including limited revenue mobilization by the states. States are usually constrained by a limited budget, which tends to be increased only incrementally from year to year. Even so, using the MTEF approach in the planning phase of the budget has strong merits because it reflects the state's actual needs. During our consultation workshops with representatives from the SMoF and SMoE, it became clear that, although states are expected to submit their plans based on the MTEF approach, some of them still develop their budgets based on the previous year's allocation rather than using the latest available data on needs in the education sector. State officials pointed out that a lack of readily available data hinders their planning.

To finance their education expenditures, states depend on federal transfers, state-level self- generated revenues, and locality-level generated revenues. Current transfers, which are not earmarked, represent the largest share of federal transfers, which are used mostly to finance public sector salaries, including those of teachers. However, once states have received current transfers, there is no way of distinguishing among the various sources of funds and how they will be used across sectors. Figure 4.18 depicts the funds flow in the education sector, including sources of revenue and end beneficiaries. The figure shows that states receive their share of federal transfers as determined by the horizontal allocation formula. Once the states have received these transfers, they are added to any self-generated revenues by states and localities to finance education spending at the basic and secondary levels. Secondary education is financed by the states. Although localities are mandated to finance basic education, states often take on this responsibility because localities lack the revenues necessary to carry it out. Funding for higher education is channeled from the Federal Ministry of Finance (FMoF) directly to the higher education institutions in

FIGURE 4.18
Fund flows in education

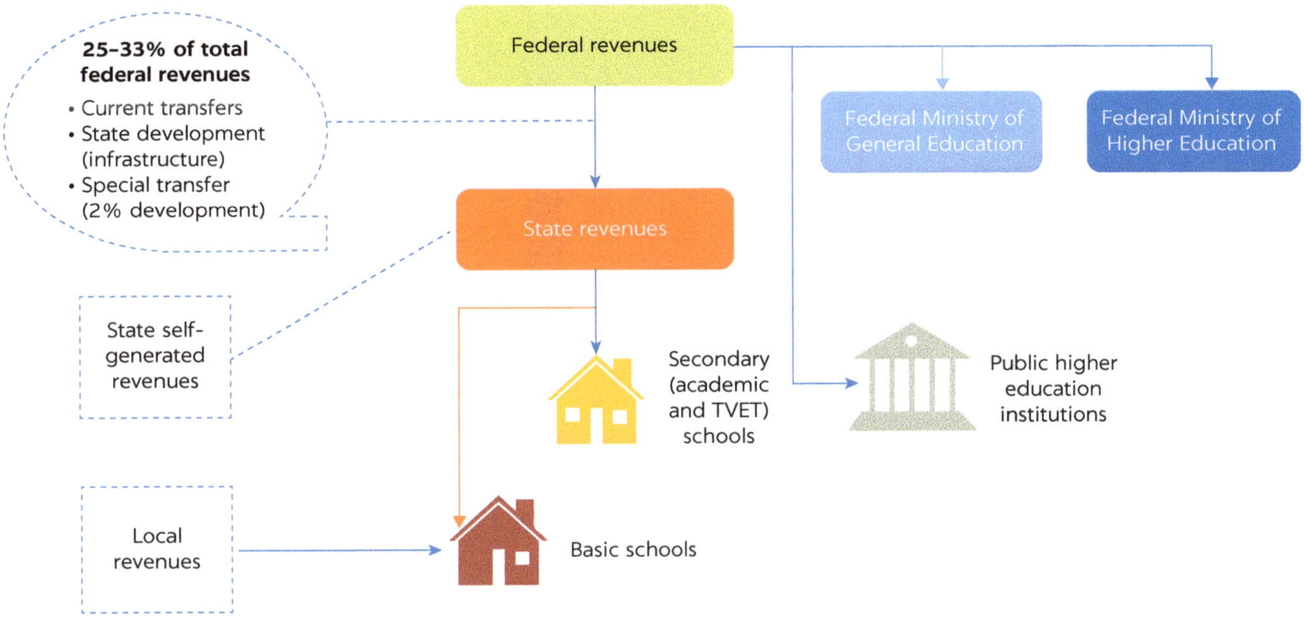

Source: World Bank.
Note: TVET = technical and vocational education and training.

the form of grants. Federal revenues also finance the FMoE and the FMoHE and their Khartoum-based offices.

Although localities are responsible in theory for both the financing and delivery of basic education, financing arrangements vary from state to state. In many cases, the state finances all employee salaries, including those in basic education. The state then "charges" localities for the costs of those basic education salaries, but in name only. Localities then use their own revenues to finance nonsalary inputs to basic education. The amount of revenue available varies depending on the revenue-generating capacity of each locality, and the state funds even the nonsalary education costs in some localities. No clear formula allocates state transfers to localities. It should be noted that private schools do not receive any support from the government.

Spending on education in Sudan is low, especially by international benchmarks. Sudan spends about 9 percent of its total public spending on education, which is equivalent to 1.3 percent of its gross domestic product (GDP). This is far below the levels of 4 to 6 percent of GDP and 20 percent of total public spending recommended by the Incheon Declaration at the 2015 World Education Forum. In comparison, education spending by Sub-Saharan African countries averages about 16.6 percent of total public spending and 4.4 percent of GDP. Figure 4.19 contrasts Sudan's education spending levels with those of other Sub-Saharan African countries and with international benchmarks.

The trend in public education spending in Sudan has consistently been below expected levels, even prior to the 2011 secession by South Sudan. Over the last two decades, it has fluctuated between 1.3 and 2.7 percent of GDP, while public education spending as a share of total public spending has fluctuated between 7.3 and 12 percent. These persistently low spending levels, even during the periods of strong economic growth prior to the secession

FIGURE 4.19
Comparison of education spending levels

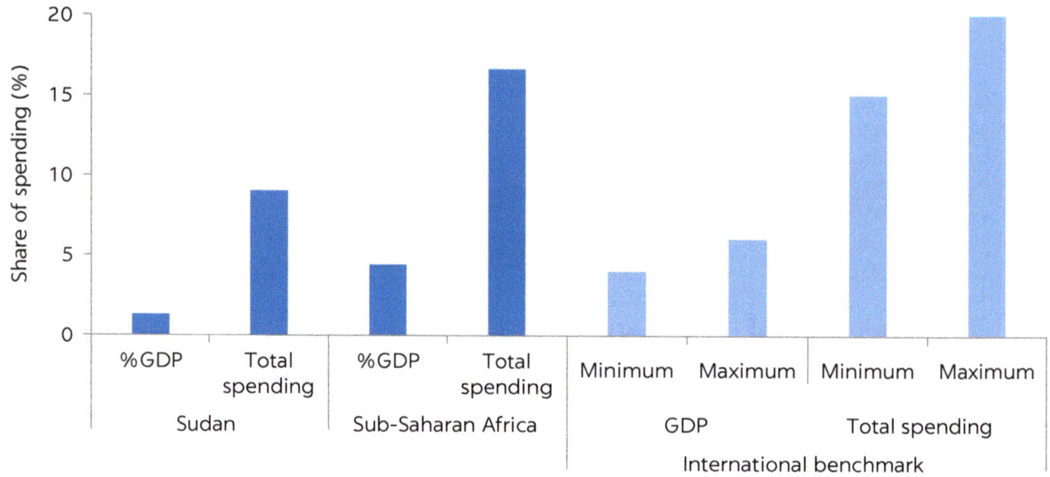

Source: Administrative data collected from Ministry of Finance.
Note: GDP = gross domestic product.

FIGURE 4.20
Spending on education as a share of total public spending and GDP

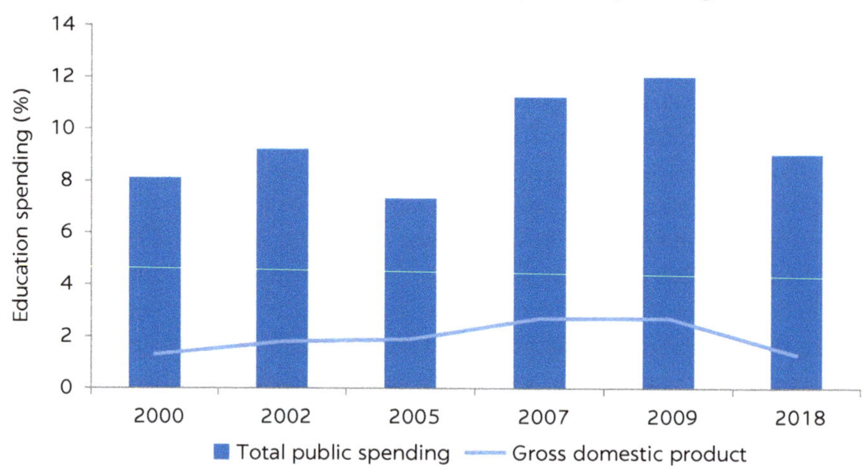

Source: Administrative data collected from Ministry of Finance and World Bank 2012.

(8.4 percent GDP growth in 2000 during the Oil Decade) reflect the challenges of ensuring a nationwide prioritization of education under a decentralized system when there are large disparities in revenue generation between subnational governments and no clear agreed or enforced minimum education spending levels. Figure 4.20 shows trends in education spending in Sudan between 2000 and 2018.

Education has not been prioritized in the government's budget. The consolidated budgets (federal and state) for 2018 indicate that Sudan's budget allocation to education amounted to about SD 15.28 billion (US$2 billion) out of a total budget of SD 179.2 billion. Figure 4.21 shows the breakdown of the consolidated budget by spending areas. Social protection expenditures receive the largest budget share with 27 percent. With only a total of about 16 percent combined,

FIGURE 4.21
Breakdown of consolidated budgets, by sector and for education

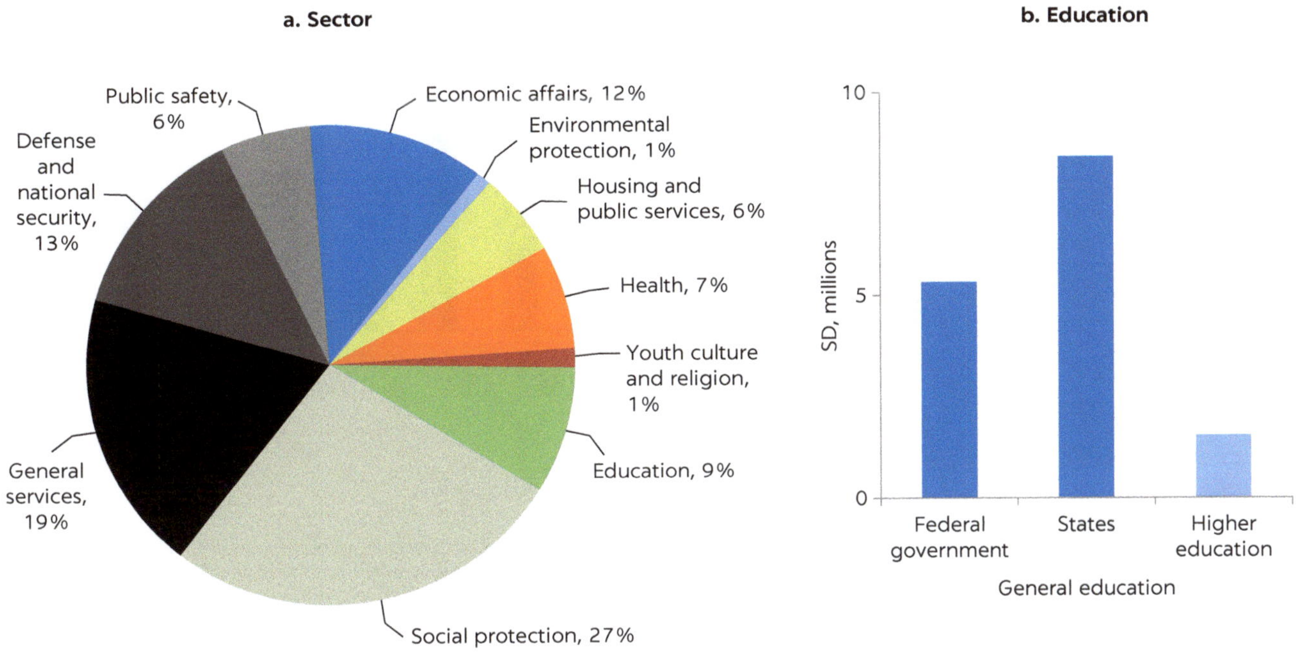

Source: Administrative data collected from Ministry of Finance.
Note: SD = Sudanese pound.

health and education have clearly not been a high priority. Higher education received about SD 1.5 billion in 2018, or about 10 percent of total spending on education. The figure also shows that, out of the SD 15.28 billion spent on education in 2018, over 55 percent was executed at the state level.

The collection of data on public expenditures is a complicated endeavor in Sudan. The data that are currently available at the federal level are not sufficient to enable the development of a detailed analysis of spending trends and do not allow for disaggregation by levels of education. There are currently no systematic reporting mechanisms between the FMoE and SMoE regarding education expenditures. Education expenditures at the state level are reported to the federal level on paper reports. Also, the FMoF tends to extract information from states only as necessary, usually for budget preparation purposes. The remaining data are not systemically collected or recorded and, because they are on paper, are prone to being discarded or misplaced.

To better understand spending on education at the state level, we prepared a questionnaire for state-level officials regarding their education expenditures. Figure 4.22 presents our findings from those states that provided us with complete data. Spending on education ranged from a low of 29 percent of the state budget in South Kordofan to a high of 95 percent in Northern State in 2017. Education represents a significant share of the total state budget in some states. This is not entirely surprising; the education sector employs the largest share of civil servants in every state—salary expenditures alone are likely to account for a large share of state spending. In states where security is an ongoing issue, spending on security is likely to reduce the share of spending on education.

FIGURE 4.22

Share of education spending in state budgets, 2015 and 2017

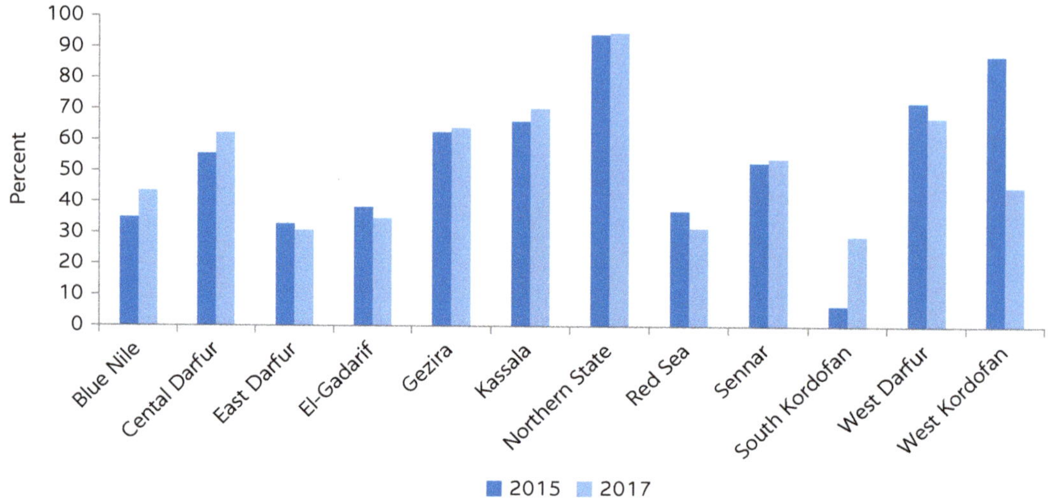

Source: Administrative data collected from state officials by questionnaire between April 2019 and January 2020.
Note: We omitted from the analysis any states for which the data were inconsistent, unreliable, or missing.

FIGURE 4.23

Salaries as a share of total state education spending, 2016–18

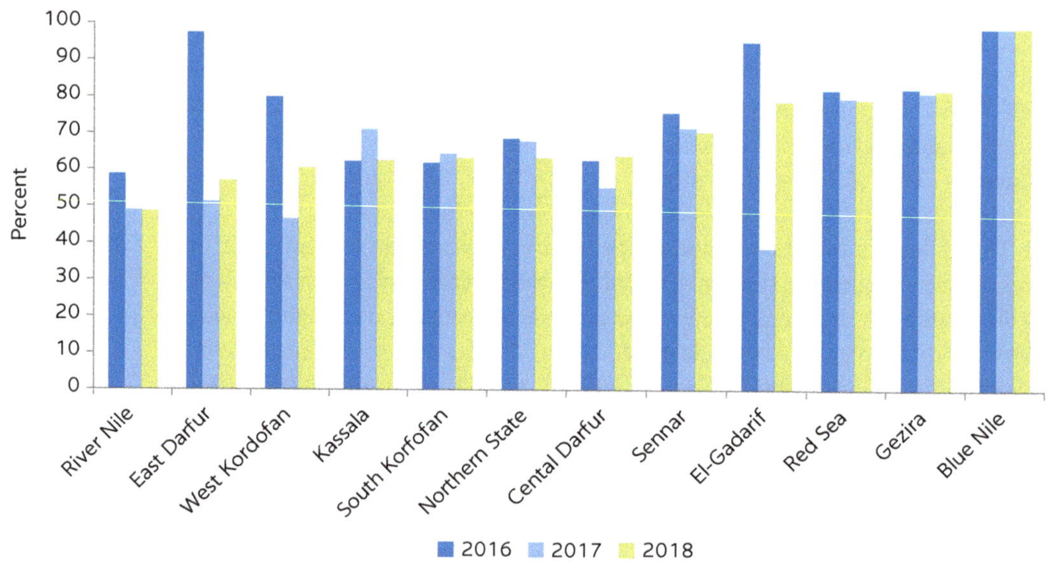

Source: Administrative data collected from state officials by questionnaire between April 2019 and January 2020.

According to the data submitted by the state officials, salaries represent the largest share of total education spending, ranging from 49 percent in River Nile to 99 percent in Blue Nile (see figure 4.23). These shares are influenced by the levels of capital investment in the education sector in each state. In River Nile for example, spending on capital expenditures, such as construction, contributes to the lower-than-average share of the state budget spent on salaries.

FIGURE 4.24
Actual budget allocation in states, by level of education, 2017

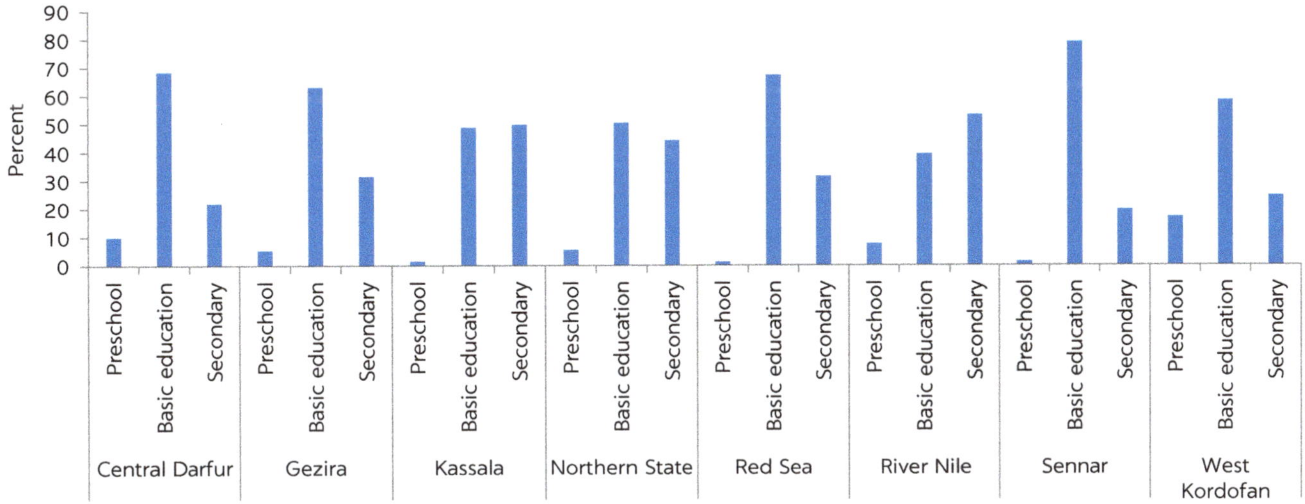

Source: Administrative data collected from state officials by questionnaire between April 2019 and January 2020.

FIGURE 4.25
Predictability of state education budgets, 2016–18

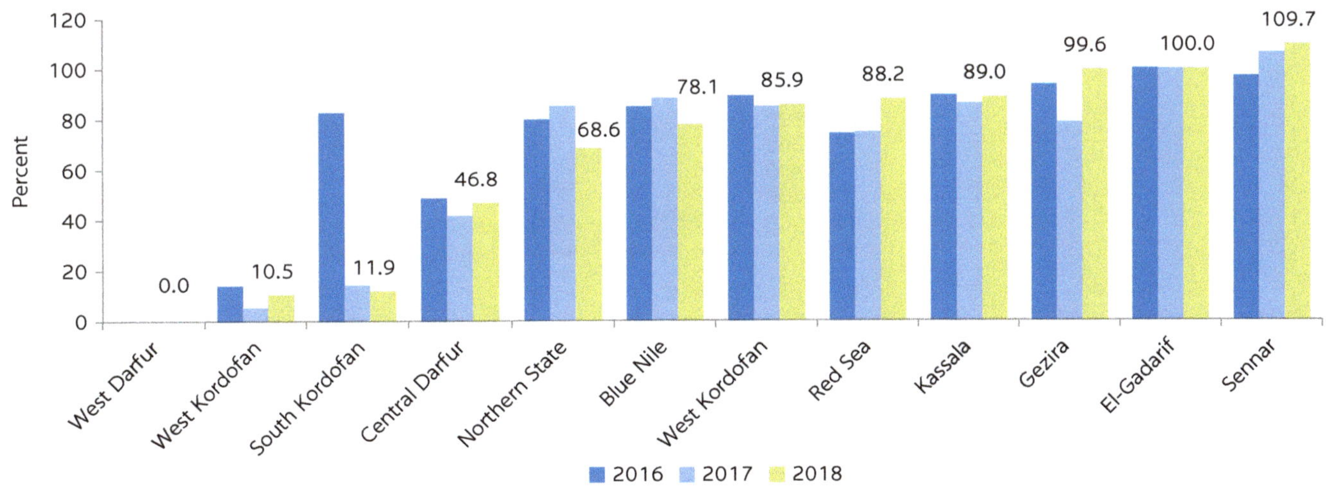

Source: Administrative data collected from state officials by questionnaire between April 2019 and January 2020.

Actual public spending across levels of education indicates that basic education tends to account for the largest share of total spending (see figure 4.24). Some of the states that provided us with data, however, such as Northern State and River Nile, spend as much if not more on secondary education. This may be driven by the higher costs of running secondary schools, including higher salaries and other operating costs, and higher relative demand; River Nile accounts for 4.6 percent of all national enrollment at the secondary level.

Figure 4.25 depicts the predictability of state education budgets (actual spending as a share of planned spending) over time. Predictability levels vary across states from 46.8 percent in Central Darfur to 89 percent in Kassala in

FIGURE 4.26

Public unit costs, by level of education, 2018

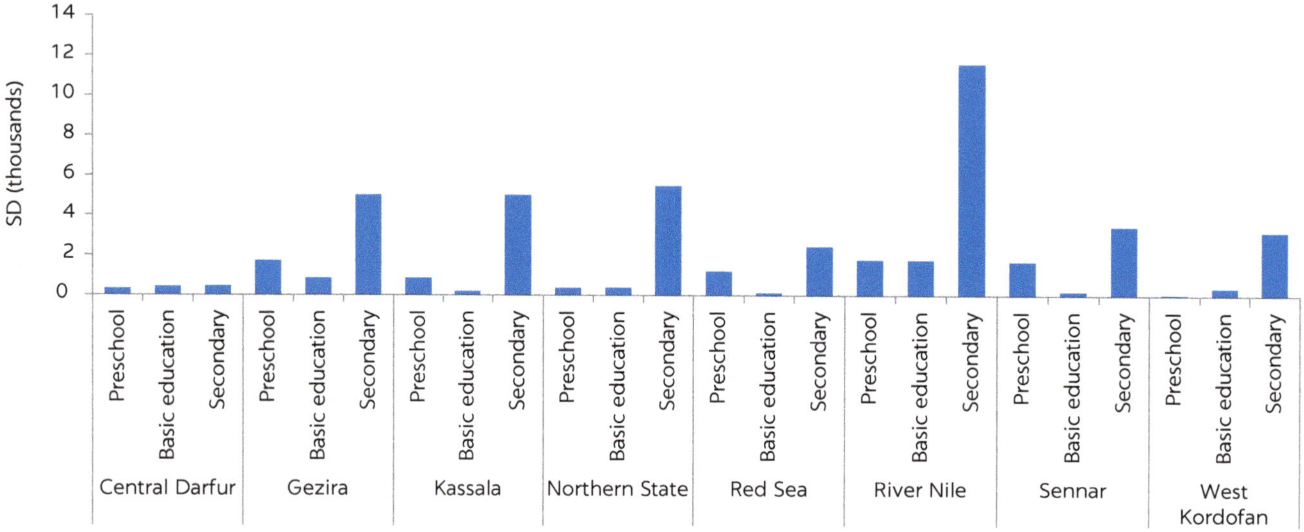

Source: Administrative data collected from state officials by questionnaire between April 2019 and January 2020.
Note: SD = Sudanese pound.

FIGURE 4.27

Comparison of government funding per student

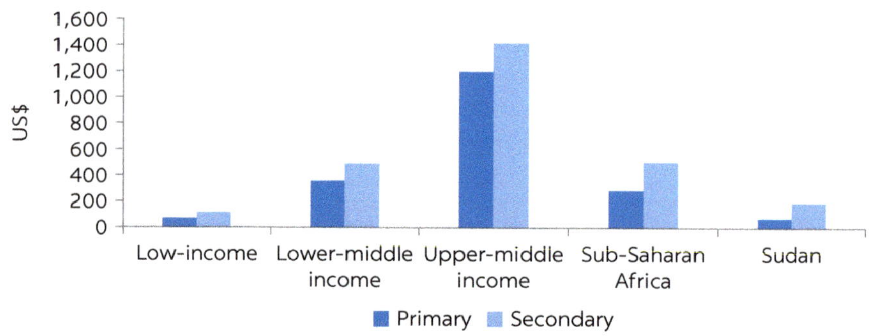

Source: Administrative data collected from state officials by questionnaire between April 2019 and January 2020 and Education Statistics Database, UNESCO Institute of Statistics, Paris, France, http://data.uis.unesco.org/.

2018. In states where federal transfer predictability is relatively high, such as Kassala and Red Sea, actual education budget expenditures tend to be closer to the planned expenditures.

Figure 4.26 indicates that public unit costs in basic education range from a low of SD 169.6 per student in Sennar to a high of SD 1,745 per student in River Nile. At the secondary level, the range is from SD 437.1 in Central Darfur up to SD 11,583 in River Nile. The data indicate the potential for efficiency gains in many states. However, a more detailed analysis would be necessary to explore the underlying reasons for these disparities.

Public spending levels as reported by the states indicate that per capita spending at the basic education and secondary levels in Sudan is comparable to the averages reported for low-income countries. Figure 4.27 compares per capita public spending on basic and secondary education in Sudan, Sub-Saharan Africa, and low-income, lower-middle-income, and upper-middle-income countries. Based on the averages of states for which we have full data, we estimate that spending per student in Sudan is equivalent to US$68.9 for basic education and US$188.2 for secondary education. These are far below the averages for other lower-middle-income countries.

Household spending on education also varies significantly across states (see figure 4.28).[3] Nationwide, households spend an average of about SD 391 per capita for basic education, but at the state level, the amount ranges from SD 171 in Blue Nile to SD 826 in Khartoum. Household spending per capita on secondary education averages SD 1,067 at the national level but ranges from SD 583 in Blue Nile to SD 1,933 in Khartoum.

Education finance and education outcomes

Sudan ranks 139th out of 157 countries on the World Bank's Human Capital Index (HCI) with a score of 0.38 (see figure 4.29). This indicates that a child born in Sudan today will be only 38 percent as productive at age 18 as she could be if

FIGURE 4.28

Household unit expenditure, by level of education, by state

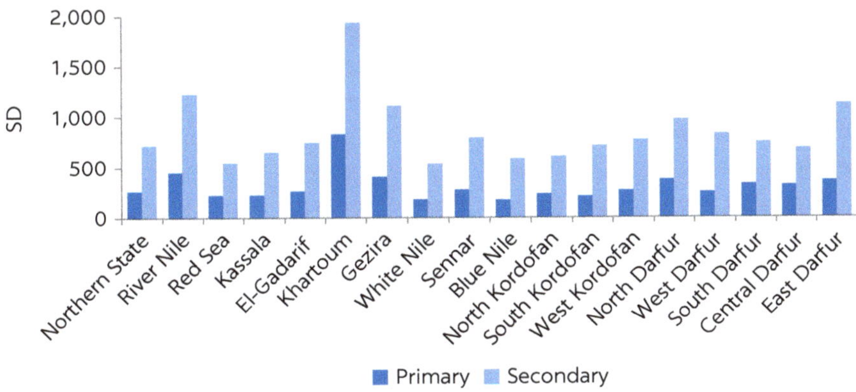

Source: World Bank calculations based on data from National Household Budget and Poverty Survey 2014–15.
Note: SD = Sudanese pound.

FIGURE 4.29

Comparison of countries in the Human Capital Index, 2019

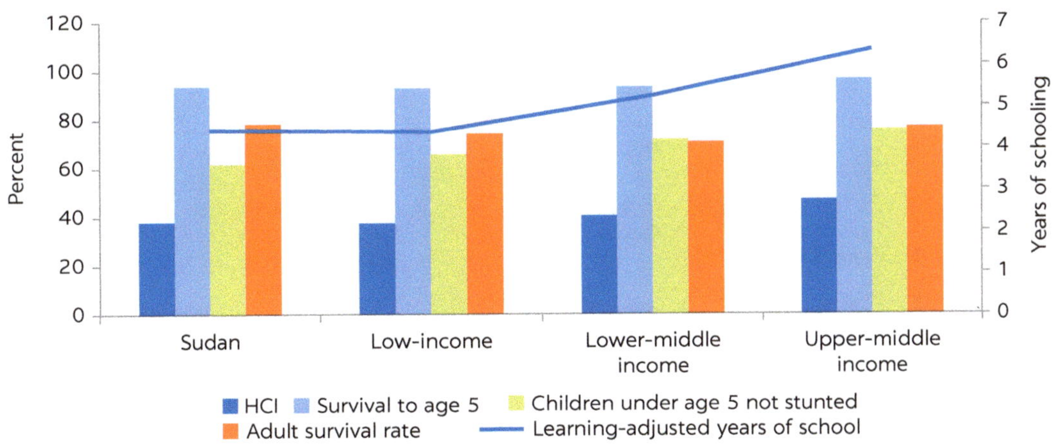

Source: Human Capital Index Database, World Bank, Washington, DC (accessed December 2019), https://www.worldbank.org/en/publication/human-capital.

she enjoyed a complete education and full health. A significant reason for this low score is the country's poor education indicators, including learning outcomes.

Figure 4.30 compares the average share of children in grade 3 who cannot read a single word according to the 2018 National Learning Assessment (NLA) with the share of population living under the national poverty line. The figure shows a clear correlation between poverty and illiteracy and suggests that a person born to a poor household is likely to remain poor. The highest shares of students who cannot read a single word by grade 3 tend to come from states with very high poverty levels. Ensuring equitable access to quality education in Sudan will be critical to closing the poverty gap and achieving greater economic prosperity for all. This further reinforces the need for federal transfer mechanisms that redress the imbalances in available resources across states.

The level of education spending matters, but how the funds are spent matters more for improving learning outcomes in Sudan. Figure 4.31 shows a very weak relationship between states' public spending per student and average scores in reading and mathematics on the 2017 NLA in grade 6. South Kordofan and West Kordofan, for example, have higher scores on both reading and mathematics than Blue Nile despite spending only one-fourth as much on education. The discrepancy reflects differences in how public education funding is used at the state level and whether, for example, it has been spent on activities that will improve learning outcomes, such as teacher training, and learning materials, such as textbooks.

Similarly, spending per student does not seem to be correlated with GERs. Figure 4.32 compares states' public education spending per capita with their GERs. Although spending levels vary significantly across states, GERs do not

FIGURE 4.30

Poverty and reading levels, by state

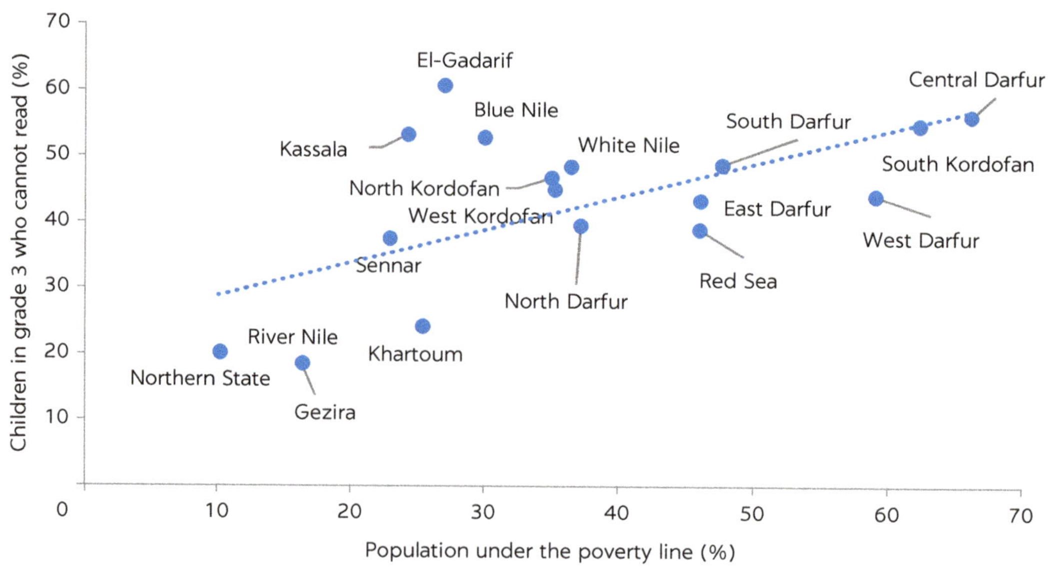

Source: World Bank calculations based on data from National Household Budget and Poverty Survey 2014–15 and Federal Ministry of Education 2018b.

FIGURE 4.31

State education spending per student and National Learning Assessment outcomes in grade 6

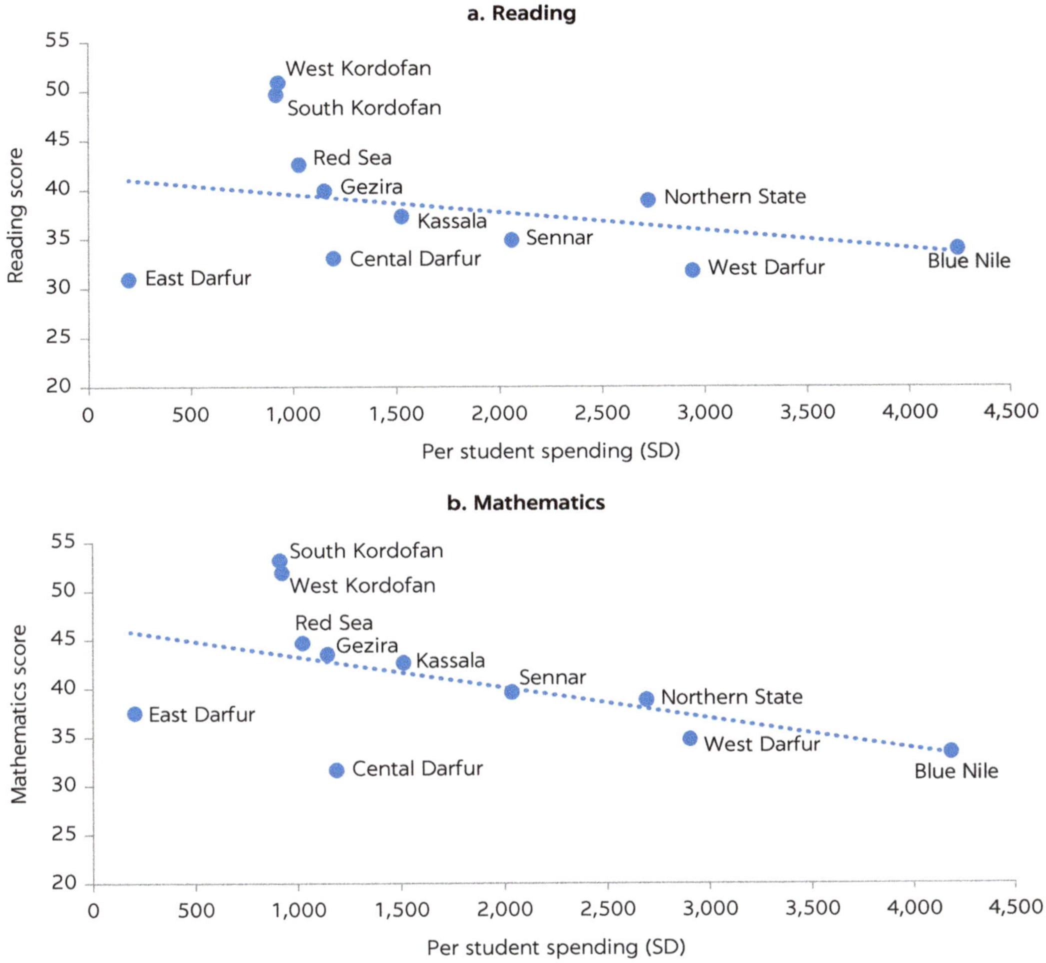

Source: Administrative data collected from state officials by questionnaire between April 2019 and January 2020 and Federal Ministry of Education 2018b.
Note: SD = Sudanese pound.

FIGURE 4.32

State education spending per student and GERs

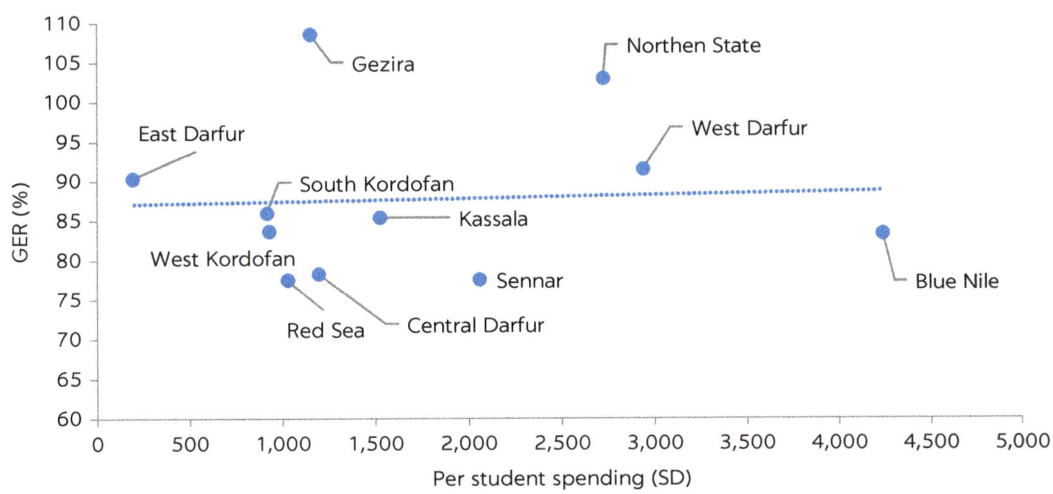

Source: Administrative data collected from state officials by questionnaire between April 2019 and January 2020 and World Bank calculations based on data from National Household Budget and Poverty Survey 2014–15.
Note: GER = gross enrollment ratio; SD = Sudanese pound.

vary to the same extent. This may reflect inefficiencies that cause some states (such as Blue Nile) to outspend others (such as Kassala) and yet achieve a similar GER.

LIMITATIONS OF THE STUDY

One of the key challenges that has been repeatedly highlighted in several publications on education spending in Sudan has been the lack of readily available data. There are several reasons for this. First, there is considerable fragmentation of reporting and accountability in the sector. Under the current federal system, there is no uniform requirement for SMoF or SMoE to report to the FMoF on spending at the subnational levels. The Federal Ministry of General Education cannot plan effectively without sufficient information to understand how best to support education outcomes across states. Second, much of the existing reporting is still done on paper, which complicates the process of tracking and tracing data, particularly for establishing trends. Paper records are often misplaced, and there is no database or systematic process for recording state-level public education expenditures at the central level. Instead, the central level simply extracts the specific information that it needs to prepare the consolidated budget from the paper reports prepared by states. Because there is currently no nationwide database of actual education expenditures by level of education, every request for information from the federal government triggers a new cycle of data collection from the states, which often both takes time and is incomplete. Third, reporting on education spending is not uniform across all states and localities. This makes it impossible to compare data across states. During the preparation of this chapter, it became very clear that this weakness in the sector would significantly limit our ability to deepen the analysis. This needs to be addressed rapidly to lay the foundation to conduct evidence-based policy making and, particularly, to effectively analyze the equity and efficiency of total public spending.

TABLE 4.4 Education policy proposals for Sudan

CHALLENGES	POLICY RECOMMENDATIONS	RESPONSIBLE STAKEHOLDER AND COLLABORATING ACTORS	TIMEFRAME
Equitable quality education			
Current spending levels and funding mechanisms in education hinder the ability of states and localities to address some of the key challenges and reduce disparities between states in resources and learning outcomes	• Increase spending on education at all levels of government to ensure basic minimum standards for learning are met in all states	FMoF, FMoE, SMoF, SMoE, and localities	Short term

continued

TABLE 4.4, *continued*

CHALLENGES	POLICY RECOMMENDATIONS	RESPONSIBLE STAKEHOLDER AND COLLABORATING ACTORS	TIMEFRAME
	• Improve the functional allocation of the budget to drive better learning outcomes		Short term
	• Set clear, measurable criteria in the formula to address the vertical and horizontal allocation imbalances and to ensure that budget allocations are pro-poor		Short term
	• Prioritize spending on education at the national level; determine a minimum spending amount per student to easily measure the adequacy of spending and allow for the reprioritization of budgets over time • Prioritize use of funds to achieve the Sustainable Development Goals in education		Short term
	• Use special transfers (2% fund) to support targeted interventions to eliminate or reduce disparities between states, including for gender disparities, nomadic tribes, and conflict areas, and to increase internal efficiency to increase school survival rates, especially in rural areas • Explore the use of matching grants to incentivize states to increase spending on inputs to strengthen students' foundational skills		Short term
Accountability and transparency			
Weak coordination among all three tiers of government leads to inconsistencies in financial resource management and creates the risk of misuse of resources	• Improve coordination among the three tiers of government by clarifying the roles and responsibilities of each tier and enforcing consistent approaches across all states, while ensuring all levels are well equipped to fulfill their responsibilities	FMoF, FMoE, SMoF, SMoE, and localities	Short to medium term
A lack of predictability of transfers and budgets hinders state and local planning	• Increase the predictability of transfers and budgets, which is particularly poor in states such as Central Darfur, and contributes to a lack of transparency between tiers of government—particularly important given the high dependence on transfers to fund basic service delivery	FMoF, SMoF	Short to medium term
Capacity, efficiency, and data reporting mechanisms			
The lack of systematic and comprehensive reporting mechanisms and data collection prevent the use of evidence-based planning	• Strengthen data collection and reporting and use data systematically in decision-making; rely on data and evidence for strategic decisions; standardize budget data reporting • Ensure clear, transparent, and systematic reporting across all three tiers of government for proper planning and decision-making	FMoF, FMoE, SMoF, SMoE, and localities	Short term
A lack of capacity hinders the effectiveness of the MTEF budgeting approach	• Provide states with clear guidelines on how to report, plan, and execute budgets; build adequate capacity in states to prepare budgets	FMoF, FMoE, SMoF, SMoE, and localities	Short term
Inefficient use of resources, particularly teachers, contributes to inefficiency of the education system	• Facilitate strategic deployment of teachers across state lines to increase efficiency in resource use and reduce disparities	FMoF, SMoF	Short term

Source: World Bank.
Note: FMoE = Federal Ministry of Education; FMoF = Federal Ministry of Finance; MTEF = medium-term expenditure framework; SMoE = State Ministries of Education; SMoF = State Ministries of Finance.

CONCLUSION AND POLICY DIRECTIONS

This study provides an overview of education finance in Sudan and outlines some of the key challenges it faces in ensuring that federal transfers increase equity among states not only of resources but also of students' learning outcomes. Table 4.4 summarizes the main conclusions of the study and proposes key recommendations.

NOTES

1. For example, the introduction of the Provincial Administrative Act of 1960 represented a step toward strengthening the administrative ability of the states to represent the central government within each state's borders (El-Hassan El- Battahani and Gadkarim 2017).
2. It should also be noted that repetition rates are relatively low in Sudan (3 to 4 percent in basic education) relative to averages in Sub-Saharan Africa and that the transition rate to secondary education is high at 90.7 percent (97.9 percent after accounting for repeaters).
3. Spending data from the National Household Budget and Poverty Survey 2014–15 are not disaggregated by category.

REFERENCES

Alamir, M.A., M.T. Geiger, R. Bladon, N.M. Yehia, H. El-Tayeb Alyn, A.M. Ali, M. Yanez Pagans, J. Claussen, O.H. Fjeldstad, and S.A.I. Mustafa. 2014. *Sudan State-Level Public Expenditure Review: Meeting the Challenges of Poverty Reduction and Basic Service Delivery*. Background papers, vol. 2. Washington, DC: World Bank.

Central Bank of Sudan. 2019. 59th Annual Report. http://www.cbos.gov.sd.

El-Hassan El-Battahani, A., and Hassan Ali Gadkarim. 2017. *Governance and Fiscal Federalism in Sudan 1989–2015: Exploring Political and Intergovernmental Fiscal Relations in an Unstable Polity*. Bergen, Norway: Michelsen Institute.

Federal Ministry of Education. 2018a. *Draft Education Sector Analysis*. Khartoum: Federal Ministry of Education.

——. 2018b. *National Learning Assessment Report*. Khartoum: Federal Ministry of Education.

FFAMC (Fiscal and Financial Allocation and Monitoring Commission). 2017. *2017 Guidelines*. Khartoum: FFAMC.

World Bank. 2012. *The Status of the Education Sector in Sudan*. Washington, DC: World Bank.

5 Uganda Case Study

ALASDAIR FRASER[1] AND MARLAINE LOCKHEED

INTRODUCTION

Uganda was an early leader in expanding primary school enrollment, supported by "unusually authentic and powerful" fiscal decentralization reforms in the 1990s (World Bank 2013). However, improvements in learning and retention[2] have not followed. In part, this is due to Uganda's high poverty rates, low revenue generation, and the low share of government financing devoted to education.[3] However, the government's de-emphasis of local government support since 2006 and the increasing number of local governments are also responsible. Despite recent funding increases, local governments lack the resources and capacity to carry out their responsibilities, which include monitoring and inspecting primary schools, and there are many opportunities for political patronage.

As in many countries, the education decentralization process has not proceeded uniformly. Prior to Uganda's independence in 1962, a local government structure was introduced, but this structure was abolished under the second president. Since the adoption of the 1995 Constitution, Uganda has implemented extensive political and fiscal decentralization, with many responsibilities for the delivery of primary, secondary, and some postsecondary education devolved to local governments (LGs). This chapter focuses on primary and secondary education, which are delivered through LGs and account for the vast majority of students. LG education provision is accompanied by firm fiscal oversight from the central government's Ministry of Finance, Planning and Economic Development (MoFPED) and by budget limits on personnel costs set by the Ministry of Education and Sports (MoES) and the Ministry of Public Service (MoPS). Since 2002, the central government has increasingly intervened in, while reducing its real-terms fiscal contribution to, primary and secondary education. This has resulted in such anomalies as teaching personnel policies not being funded in the budget. Also, over the past two decades, the central government has curtailed the ability of LGs to generate their own revenue.

The vast majority of the central government's financial support to local governments has been earmarked for specific purposes, including universal primary education (UPE) and universal secondary education (USE). Conditional grants, which included formula-based allocations and, later, performance-based allocations, were introduced in 1997. These systems and practices have been eroded since the mid-2000s. Efforts to reestablish a rules-based transfer system started in 2016–17. Decades of experience with decentralization in education and a relatively strong public financial management system position Uganda as a good case study to examine the relationship between funding mechanisms and education outcomes.

The education sector has in recent years struggled to improve the quality of teaching and learning. The 2016–21 manifesto of the ruling party[4] emphasizes improving quality, raising teacher salaries, and strengthening infrastructure. The government's National Development Plan 2015–16 to 2020–21 also emphasizes improving quality along with supporting early childhood development (ECD) and strengthening school inspections. However, the reforms that have been implemented have generally not been focused on quality improvements. In contrast, donors have supported interventions aimed at improving quality, particularly in early grade reading, but the coverage and durability of the gains made under these projects remain to be seen.[5] Overall, Uganda's learning assessments indicate that quality has deteriorated since 2011, in marked contrast to what has happened in Kenya and Tanzania.[6]

The current education finance system is based on the intergovernmental transfers architecture introduced after 1995. Funding from the central government to LGs takes the form of multisectoral unconditional grants, and sectoral conditional grants. Outside the transfer system, there are subventions from the central government (Williamson 2010). Grants to LGs for education are ring-fenced through the annual budget process, whereas subventions, which consist mostly of donor project resources, are sent to LGs at the discretion of the central government.

Transfers have been provided to LGs for the purpose of providing UPE since 1996 and USE since 2007.[7] Since 2012, the Inter-Governmental Fiscal Transfer (IGFT) Reform Program[8] has aimed to (1) increase the adequacy of LG budgets; (2) ensure greater equity between LGs by reimposing and revising objective allocation formulas; and (3) increase the efficiency of local service delivery through an annual performance assessment and targeted assistance and reforms based on its results. The MoFPED has been a lead actor in implementing these reforms since 2015–16, and thus Uganda provides an interesting recent example of both the opportunities and limits of finance-led improvements to primary and secondary education.

Currently, Uganda faces four major education challenges. First and most important is to improve the quality of learning, particularly at the primary education level.[9] This involves ensuring that all primary schools meet at least the minimum conditions for teaching and learning.[10] Second is to increase the efficiency of the system so that teachers attend school and teach more often, more students progress through grades on time,[11] and a higher share of students transitions from primary to secondary school. Third is to increase access to secondary education, while maintaining quality. In 2019–20, the gross enrollment rate for secondary education was only 21 percent (MoES 2019a). The fourth challenge is to increase children's readiness for primary school by expanding preprimary education, particularly in underserved areas. In 2016–17, fewer than 15 percent of children in Uganda were enrolled in preprimary education.[12] Meeting these four education challenges has implications for a fifth challenge: meeting the recurrent and development costs for improved access, equity, efficiency, and learning.

EDUCATION DECENTRALIZATION: THE CHARACTERISTICS OF THE SYSTEM

Uganda has a long history of political, administrative, and fiscal decentralization related to education as enshrined in the Constitution and subsequent acts, decrees, and policies over three-quarters of a century (see table 5.1). However, the depth of decentralization since 1995 has been limited relative to many other countries. The central government has retained control over the number of teachers hired, the management of secondary teachers and of secondary education inspections, the curriculum, and language and examination policies (Steffensen et al. 2004). Notably in 2005, the appointment of the LG Chief Administrative Officer was shifted to the central government.

TABLE 5.1 **History of decentralization in Uganda**

YEAR	LEGAL OR REGULATORY BASIS	ACTION AND EFFECT	DIRECTION
1949	Local Government Ordinance	Introduction of local governments	Decentralization
1962	Constitution	Independence; devolved powers to kingdoms and local governments	Decentralization
1967	Constitution	Directed abolition of devolved systems and recentralization to the MoLG	Centralization
1970	Education Act	Laid out central Ministry of Education responsibilities for education	Centralization
1971	Local Governments Act	Directly legislated abolition of devolved systems and recentralization to the MoLG	Centralization
1993	Local Governments Statute	New administrative and fiscal decentralization policies	Decentralization
1995–97	Constitution of 1995; Local Governments Act 1997	New decentralization policies including establishment of the Local Government Finance Commission	Decentralization
2002	Fiscal Decentralization Strategy (FDS)	Strategy to streamline the system of transfers and increase local governments' discretion in response to recentralization	Decentralization
2002	Education Service Act	Formalized the Education Service Commission's responsibility for educational personnel and allowed for the delegation of responsibility to the DSC; implementation and power has been limited in practice	Decentralization
2005	Constitution including constitutional amendment	Increased number of districts; required senior LG technical officials to be appointed by the central government; disbanded the LG tender board; created more LGs with fewer powers	Centralization
2008	Education (Pre-Primary, Primary and Post-Primary) Act	Repealed the Education Act of 1970 and gave "full effect" to the government's decentralization of education, UPE, universal preprimary education, and training policies; proscribed the collection of almost all fees by government primary schools; clear delegation and communication, and other support to LGs to help them implement the Act, has been mixed	Decentralization
2010	Constitution and LGs Act Amendment	Cities' legislation elaborated; not enacted outside Kampala	No effect
2012	Education Service Commission Regulations	Elaborated education service employment regulations; little acknowledgment of LGs' roles and confirmed central powers	Centralization
2014–16	LGs Act, guidelines for decentralized payroll	Decentralized payroll implementation; initial results suggest slightly more errors but more government responsiveness to local needs	Decentralization
2018	Cabinet decision	Shift of oversight of discretionary grants from the OPM to the MoLG	Not yet clear

Source: Gazettes (database), Uganda Legal Information Institute, Kampala (accessed August 2020), ulii.org; Whitworth and Williamson 2010; Williamson 2010; Lewis 2014; MoLG 2014; World Bank 2013, 2017; Lwanga, Munyambonera, and Guloba 2018; Ernst & Young 2019.
Note: DSC = District Service Commission; LG = local government; MoLG = Ministry of Local Government; OPM = Office of the Prime Minister.

The most extensive decentralization policies were enacted in the mid-1990s, while subsequent education-related acts and regulations spelled out the responsibilities of central ministries and LGs. The pattern of decentralization following the 1995 Constitution was aligned with the Poverty Eradication Action Plan, in which UPE was a central policy. As a result, the central government constrained LGs' discretion over education funding to ensure that ringfenced financing would be spent on UPE (a major campaign point in the 1996 election) and subsequently on USE in 2006. A reduction in budget support from several donors from 2012 and 2013 coincided with a shift in government priorities toward infrastructure following 2010–11.[13] As in many countries, Uganda has experienced waves of both decentralization and recentralization policies (Lewis 2014; Eaton, Kaiser, and Smoke 2010; Ministry of Local Government 2014).

Uganda's education and governance systems

The education system

Pretertiary education consists of seven years of compulsory primary school (P1 to P7), four years of lower secondary school (S1 to S4) and two years of upper secondary school (S5 to S6). Early childhood education (ECE), which consists of two years, received negligible government support up until the present day; it is a major but not yet implemented component of the newest education sector plan for 2020–25 (MoES 2019). Postsecondary government-supported education is provided through 65 technical and vocational education and training (TVET) centers and 124 teacher training colleges, both of which are funded through LGs, and 10 national universities, which are funded by the central government.

Most primary students are educated in schools provided by LGs and funded by the central government through transfers. More than half of all Ugandan secondary schools are private, and approximately 1,000 of these were government-subsidized (about one-third of total private schools) until 2016–17 (MoES 2016).[14] School enrollments in 2018–19 were estimated to be 9.3 million students in primary, 1.1 million students in lower secondary, and 139,000 students in upper secondary (MoES 2019). The public education system comprises 12,400 government primary schools employing about 135,000 teachers and 1,883 government secondary schools and formerly government-aided private secondary schools employing about 35,000 government teachers. The estimated gross enrollment ratio (GER) in 2019–20 for primary education was 115 percent,[15] for lower secondary, about 28 percent, and for upper secondary, about 7 percent. The net enrollment rate (NER) is about 93 percent at the primary level and 23 percent at the lower secondary level according to the Education Sector Strategic Plan for 2020–2025 (ESSP) (MoES 2019). Access to lower secondary and upper secondary schools is determined by examinations.

National and subnational governance

Uganda is a unitary state, with several layers of local government (see figure 5.1). Although the country is divided into four regions and fifteen subregions, there are no regional or subregional governments. Districts and municipal councils (referred to as LGs throughout) have the main legislative responsibility for delivering primary, secondary, teacher training, and technical education, while the MoES is responsible for setting standards and policy, evaluating all levels of education, and inspecting postprimary schools.

FIGURE 5.1
LGs in Uganda, 1980–2020

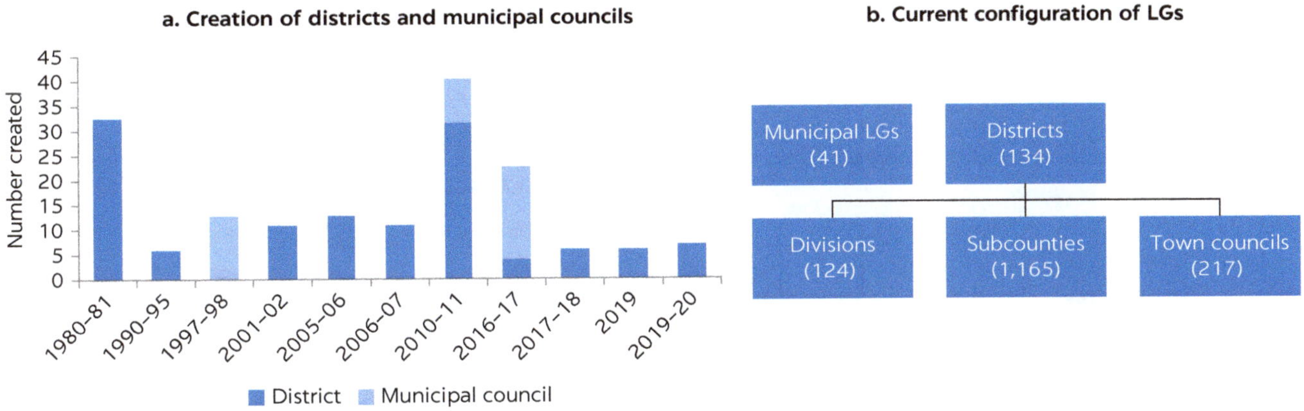

Sources: Panel a. World Bank calculations based on government budget estimates and World Bank 2013. Panel b. Budget 2019–20, Online Transfer Information Management System (database), Republic of Uganda (accessed August 2020), otims.go.ug.
Note: LG = local government.

The Local Governments Act of 1997 established the details of decentralization and specified that "the system of local government shall be based on the district as a unit" and gave the districts the right to subdivide.[16] In the education sector, municipal councils, which cover urban areas, are treated as districts.[17] The number of districts and municipalities has steeply increased over time.[18] There were 39 districts listed in the 1995 Constitution, and, as of 2020, there were 134 districts and 41 municipalities [19] (see figure 5.1, panel a), with LG creation, which is a parliamentary power, often corresponding to the election cycle. The next level of local government, known collectively as the lower local governments (LLGs), consists of 1,165 subcounties and 124 town councils below districts and 228 municipal divisions below municipalities.[20] Below this, there are approximately 10,000 parishes. The total number of various lowest-level units (cells, villages, and zones) was about 69,000 in 2014. The Kampala City Council Authority is administered as a central government agency. Local governments elect their representatives in a multiparty system.

The proliferation of LGs strains the management capacity of smaller LGs and LLGs, which have the formal responsibility for providing primary education. Only three LGs have fewer than 25,000 inhabitants (see figure 5.2, panel a), but more than half of all LLGs do (figure 5.2, panel b). Therefore, although district councils may devolve the provision of nursery, primary, and adult education to LLGs, most primary education responsibilities have been retained by districts and municipalities.

Responsibilities for education service delivery

The responsibilities related to delivering basic education services are largely decentralized, but the responsibilities for education finance are not. The Local Governments Act of 1997 specified that the government is responsible for education policy[21] and devolves to district and municipal councils the responsibility for providing "education services, which cover nursery, primary, secondary, trade, special education, and technical education"[22] (with the exception that municipal councils are not responsible for providing nursery schools). District councils are also responsible for "aiding and supporting the establishment and maintenance

FIGURE 5.2
LGs and LLGs, by population

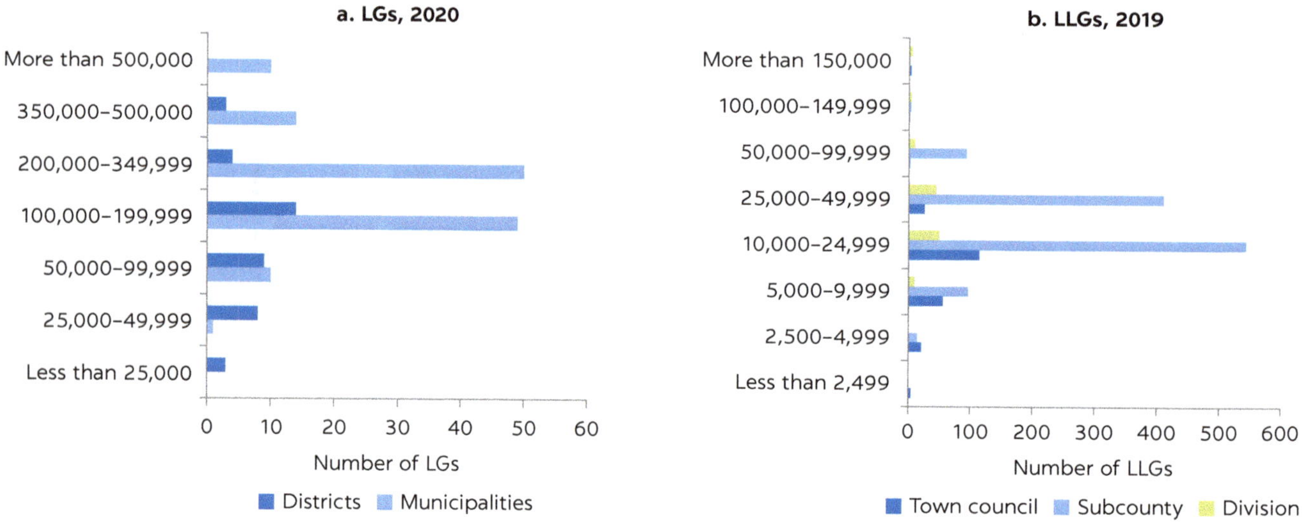

Source: MoFPED 2020.
Note: LG = local government districts and municipalities; LLG = lower local government divisions, subcounties, and town councils.

of schools . . . providing bursaries to assist in the education of children of persons residing in the district."[23]

The Education (Pre-Primary, Primary, and Post-Primary) Act, 2008 (the Education Act) further elaborated the responsibilities of various stakeholders in education and training, including the government, parents, and "foundation bodies." The Act states that the government of Uganda has responsibility for education in six broad categories shown in table 5.2. In practice, some policy areas are contested, and the central government tends to have the upper hand. The Education Act did not fully address the subject of responsibility for financing other than to proscribe the collection of fees by schools.

Some of the key central government responsibilities noted in table 5.2 are carried out for the MoES by formally autonomous bodies. The National Curriculum Development Commission (NCDC) is responsible for curriculum design, and the Uganda National Examinations Board (UNEB) designs and administers national examinations and government learning assessments. Within the ministry, the Directorate of Education Standards (DES) is responsible for inspecting secondary schools and oversees the development of inspection tools for primary schools.

The division of responsibility between the central and local governments for teacher management is evolving. Under the Education Act, the Education Service Commission (ESC), a central body, is responsible for all government education personnel. In recent years, however, the District Service Commissions (DSCs) at the LG level have played a larger role in meeting requests from schools to hire primary teachers, leaving the central ESC responsible for appointing secondary teachers and nonteaching personnel and for developing and improving the quality of those personnel and the services that they provide.

Local governments are given most direct management responsibilities for primary education and have spending authority over grant transfers and their own revenues (see section titled *Alignment of funding with responsibilities*). For personnel management, the DSC of each district can hire registered

TABLE 5.2 **Government responsibilities under the Education Act**

FUNCTION	CENTRAL GOVERNMENT	LOCAL GOVERNMENT
Policy	• Setting policy on all matters concerning education and training • Setting and maintaining the national goals and broad aims of education • Encouraging the development of a national language	n.a.
Teachers	• Registering and licensing of teachers (primary, secondary, postprimary) • Recruiting, deployment, and promotion of teaching and nonteaching staff (postprimary)	• Recruiting, deployment, and promotion of teaching and nonteaching staff (primary) • Management, monitoring, supervising, and disciplining of staff and students (primary) • Ensuring teachers' welfare
Curriculum and instruction	• Providing learning and instructional materials • Developing and controlling the national curriculum • Determining the language of instruction	n.a.
Evaluation and supervision	• Evaluating academic standards through continuous assessment and national examinations • Developing management policies for all government and government-aided schools and private schools	• Ensuring the supervision of student performance in both public and private schools
Institutions	• Ensuring the equitable geographic distribution of education institutions • Regulating, establishing, and registering educational institutions • Providing buildings (de facto)	• Ensuring the equitable geographic distribution of education institutions • Providing and maintaining buildings (de jure and de facto)
Financing	• Restricting collection of fees by government schools and government-aided schools	• Passing on capitation grants to schools

Source: World Bank based on the Education Act, 2008.
Note: n.a. = not applicable.

primary teachers and primary school inspectors within approved personnel budget limits, with the input of the District Education Officer (DEO).[24] Two recent surveys have found serious shortcomings in some districts with teacher job vacancies and redeployment, noting that key stakeholders such as headmasters and DEOs are not fully involved in the process (Ernst & Young 2019; Lwanga, Munyambonera, and Guloba 2018). In addition, LGs are authorized to procure and supervise improvements in school infrastructure and to procure and supervise the construction of new schools.

Schools themselves have only limited responsibilities, which include hiring contract teachers and nonteaching school staff, procuring instructional materials in addition to those provided by MoES (typically, the textbook budget is minimal and donor-dependent), and procuring small school improvements and administrative necessities (Najjumba, Habyarimana, and Bunjo 2013). Head teachers and school management committees (SMCs), which usually meet only once or twice a year, appear to have, relative to many countries, few mandated responsibilities with respect to teachers, curriculum, or finance (Najjumba, Habyarimana, and Bunjo 2013; Twaweza 2018a, 2018b). Headmasters perceive the DEO as the major decision-maker for teacher transfers or suspensions, as well as the person to whom they submit requests related to school improvements. Teachers are often paid allowances from the capitation grant resources, although this is officially discouraged (National Planning Authority 2018c).

Alignment of funding with responsibilities

Virtually all funding for education originates from the central government. Local governments' own revenues for supporting education are minimal,[25] and LGs have only limited discretion over the funds they receive from the central government because these resources are largely in the form of sector-specific wage and nonwage conditional grants. (See discussion in section titled *The IGFT in education*.)

Central government budgetary support for education, which totaled US$915 million in 2019–20, has declined by 50 percent as a share of GDP since 1997–98. Despite large increases in the school-age population and notwithstanding recent increases particularly in secondary and higher education financing, the government shifted its emphasis to other sectors, and budget support to education was reduced following the end of a large primary school and classroom building program in 2007–08.

Approximately half of the national budget for education is retained at the central level to support the central government's education responsibilities, including the operating costs of the MoES, selected TVET institutions, higher education, examinations and curriculum design, and a small budget line for textbooks for primary and secondary education. Some donor projects are also budgeted as part of the central ministry. During the 2010s, the central government budget for its central responsibilities increased, particularly for higher education (see figure 5.3).

The remaining half of the national budget for education is transferred every year to LGs and schools to fund their delivery of education services.[26] These transfers from the central government constitute over 98 percent of the LGs' budgeted education expenditures for primary and secondary education, primary teaching colleges, and other postsecondary technical and vocational colleges.

The central government has paid capitation grants to schools since 1997 to enable them to carry out their teaching and learning responsibilities. However, these grants are small (for example, only US$3.86 per primary student in 2019–20) and are not adequate to enable schools to procure textbooks and other instructional materials for all their students. School headmasters and SMCs have few other official resources to draw from to carry out their responsibilities. Other resources at the school level can sometimes include unofficial fees in the form of voluntary contributions from parents,[27] which one study found

FIGURE 5.3

Centrally funded education expenditures per capita, 1997/98–2019/20

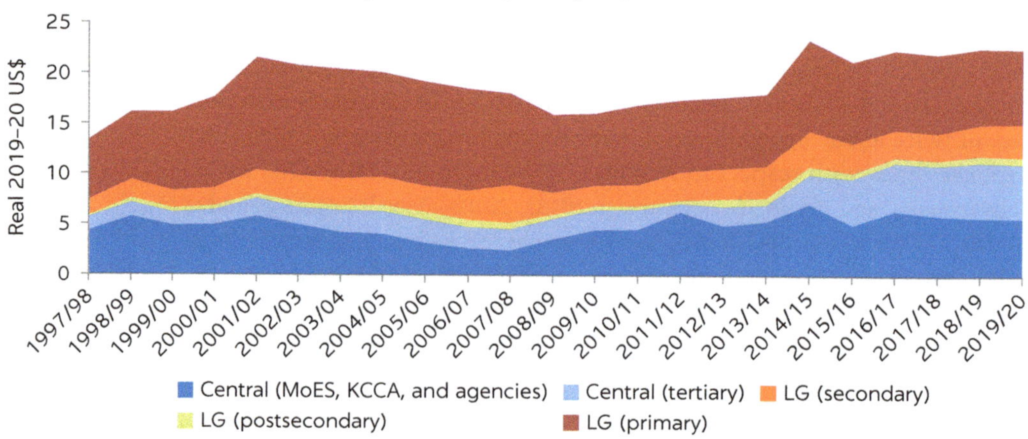

Source: Hedger et al. 2010; World Bank calculations using data from MoFPED Budget Books.

Note: KCCA = Kampala City Council Authority; LG = local government; MoES = Ministry of Education and Sports; MoFPED = Ministry of Finance, Planning and Economic Development; US$ = US dollar.

outstripped the amount of the capitation grant per school by a factor of more than five in 2015 and provided a median US$11.50 per student per year to government primary schools (Uganda Bureau of Statistics 2016b).[28] Teachers' salaries are paid directly by the MoFPED, based on payrolls prepared by LGs.

Current education challenges

Access

Ensuring access to schooling involves not only providing an adequate number of schools but also an adequate amount of actual instruction. In most districts in Uganda, there is widespread access to government primary schools, and these schools provide primary education to most school-age children. Recent surveys have shown that only 10 to 15 percent of children between ages 6 and 14 were out of school, although a high share were repeating a grade and some were attending nongovernment schools (Twaweza 2019a).[29] Actual instruction is compromised by the limited availability of instructional materials, teacher absenteeism, and insufficient infrastructure. For example, recent visits by researchers from Twaweza to a random sample of P2 classrooms in over 900 schools showed that only 37.5 percent of the classes had textbooks for at least half of the students, and teachers were absent from a fifth of the classrooms visited, while other in-school distractions accounted for another fifth of teachers' time, reducing actual instructional presence by over 40 percent (Twaweza 2019a). In addition, these classroom visits recorded severe infrastructure shortcomings.

Access to preschool and secondary education is limited. Government support does not cover preprimary classes, and as of 2019, three-quarters of preschool-age children (ages 4 and 5) remained out of school. Fewer than 35 percent of 3- to 5-year-olds had experienced any type of preschool.[30]

Access to secondary education is constrained by a lack of schools at that level, despite the government's announced commitment to achieving USE. As of 2016–17, only 56 percent of primary school graduates had continued to lower secondary school (MoES 2019a; Uganda Bureau of Statistics 2017). Examinations restrict access to both lower secondary and upper secondary schooling, while informal fees and strategic exclusion of weaker students from examinations are likely to be additional barriers.[31]

Equity

Significant differences in access to primary schooling remain, with lower enrollment rates in poorer rural areas than in more affluent urban areas. Well over half of all children between ages 6 and 14 in Karamoja subregion were out of school in 2015 (Twaweza 2016a). The private sector share of primary enrollment is highest in the most affluent subregions. However, private schools are also relied on in poorer regions with few government schools (see figure 5.4). Financing to cover teachers' wages is not distributed according to need, and there are large disparities among districts as will be discussed in the section titled *Decentralization and equity.*

Gender parity in access has been achieved in primary education but not in secondary education, and more girls than boys passed the Primary Leaving Examination (PLE) in 2019.[32] At the secondary level, gender differences in access remain pronounced, with transition rates from primary to lower secondary and from lower secondary to upper secondary favoring males (see figure 5.5). In 2014,

FIGURE 5.4

Children aged 6 to 14, by education type and subregion, 2015

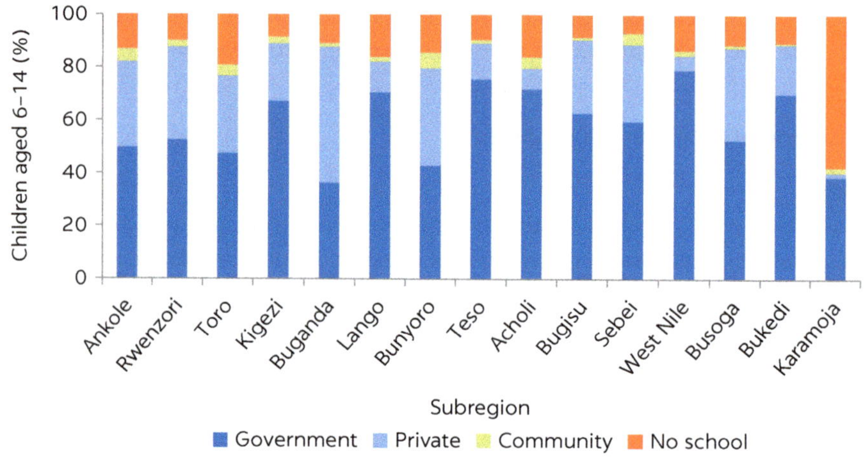

Source: Twaweza 2015.
Note: Subregions are sorted left to right from richest to poorest by 2015–16 poverty headcount in Uganda Bureau of Statistics 2016a.

FIGURE 5.5

Secondary school enrollment, by grade and gender, 2016/17

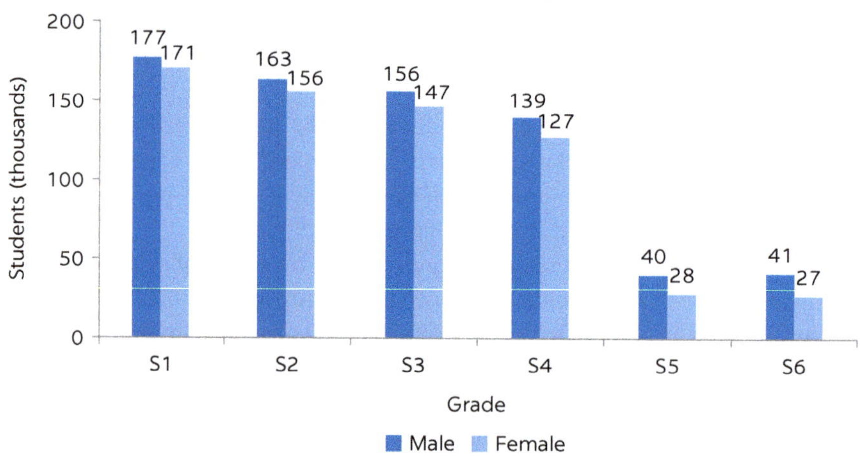

Source: Uganda Bureau of Statistics 2017.
Note: S = secondary school.

the net secondary enrollment rate for males (42.8 percent) was higher than that for females (38.7 percent), and the gender parity index was 0.89. The GER for the first year of lower secondary (S1)[33] was 63.3 percent for males and 58.9 percent for females (Uganda Bureau of Statistics 2017). In 2017, fewer girls than boys enrolled in lower secondary (S1 to S4), and a significantly lower share of girls enrolled in upper secondary (S5 to S6): 34 percent of boys and 24 percent of girls. Repetition rates are similar for both genders.

With respect to learning outcomes, girls outperform boys in early grade assessments, but fall behind in the upper primary and secondary grades. Girls outperformed boys on National Assessment of Progress in Education (NAPE) tests of P3 numeracy and English literacy but underperformed relative to boys on P6 numeracy (UNEB 2014a). Boys outperformed girls on the P6 Southern Africa Consortium for Monitoring Educational Quality (SACMEQ) IV test in both reading and mathematics (MoES 2013). At the lower secondary level, girls and boys performed comparably on NAPE tests of English literacy, but S2 girls fell behind S2 boys in both mathematics and biology (UNEB 2014b).[34]

Efficiency

The education system is inefficient in three main respects: (1) high early grade repetition rates; (2) low primary completion rates; and (3) inequitable teacher distribution. Exceptionally high enrollments in P1 and high primary GERs overall are partly accounted for by very high repetition rates (estimated at 21 percent in the primary system and up to 41 percent in P1) and disguised early childhood enrollment in P1 (Brunette et al. 2017). In 2017, enrollments in P1 were almost 40 percent higher than those in P2 and close to three times as high as those in P7 (see figure 5.6).[35] Uganda's rate of early grade progression is the third lowest among 103 low- and middle-income countries for which data are available (Bashir et al. 2018). The primary completion rate in Uganda has been estimated at 53 percent.

Teacher distribution is highly inefficient, with only a weak relationship between the number of students and teachers in a school. Disparities between schools with the same number of students are large, with schools enrolling 1,000 students having anywhere from no government teachers to more than 30 government teachers (see figure 5.7).

Quality

There are serious shortcomings in the quality of education provided to most students in Uganda, both in learning outcomes and in the conditions for learning. Recently, three large-scale learning assessments—the long-running NAPE, Uwezo, and SACMEQ—all pointed to persistent low levels of learning by primary and lower secondary students. Several Early Grade Reading Assessments (EGRAs)[36] as well as a refugee-focused Uwezo survey in 2019 (Twaweza 2019) have also found poor learning levels in early grades, although some donor-financed programs produced some significant learning gains when they were implemented (Brunette et al. 2019).

FIGURE 5.6

Enrollment, by grade and PLE candidates and PLE passed, 2017

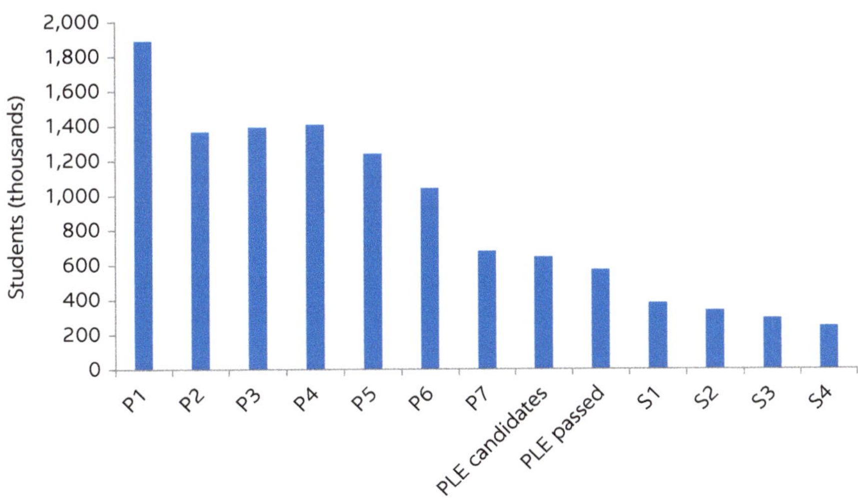

Source: Uganda Bureau of Statistics 2017.
Note: Includes public and private schools. P = primary school; PLE = Primary Leaving Examination; S = secondary school.

FIGURE 5.7

Enrolled students and government teachers per primary school, 2015

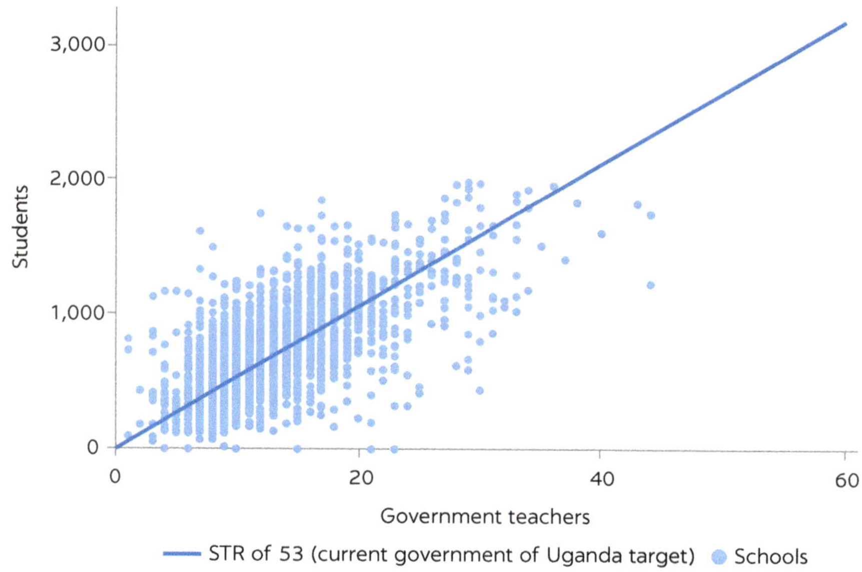

Source: Twaweza 2015.
Note: Dark blue line = student-teacher ratio (STR) of 53 (Uganda target). Data points represent 3,347 schools in 112 districts. Schools with no government teachers are not shown.

UNEB administers NAPE, which is a sample-based large-scale assessment of student performance in primary and lower secondary school. NAPE has assessed literacy and numeracy in P3 and P6 since 1996, and both subjects plus biology in S2 since 2008 (Kanjee and Acana 2013). On the most recent primary-level NAPE, in 2018, which tested 62,319 students in 1,558 schools across 122 LGs, only about half the students at either P3 or P6 could be considered "proficient" in either reading English or numeracy. On the lower secondary level NAPE, in 2014,[37] the percentage of students performing "adequately or better" was 49 percent for English, 41 percent for mathematics, and 20 percent for biology (UNEB 2014b).

Uwezo, a citizen-led household and school survey, includes a learning assessment of fundamental literacy and numeracy skills that is pegged to what would be expected of children in P2. The most recent assessment, in 2018, surveyed 45,670 children in 954 schools in 32 districts and characterized a very small share of children in P3 as having "full competence" at either reading or numeracy, while the results for students in P6 were broadly similar to those on the 2018 NAPE (see figure 5.8). Several recent donor-supported projects are funding education quality improvements. Their outcomes may have come too late to be reflected in the Uwezo and NAPE findings;[38] their short-term effects have been large and significant in most cases, but with variations in early learning outcomes for different regional languages (Brunette et al. 2019).

Since 2000, Uganda has also participated in SACMEQ, an assessment of reading and mathematics for P6 students across Southern and Eastern Africa. The most recent SACMEQ assessment, in 2014, tested 6,125 students in 245 schools sampled from 13 of the 15 regions and found that Uganda's students performed close to the average of the 14 countries that participated in both mathematics and reading, and that more than two-thirds of the country's P6 students read at an "acceptable" level.[39]

FIGURE 5.8
Primary students reaching performance standard on NAPE and Uwezo

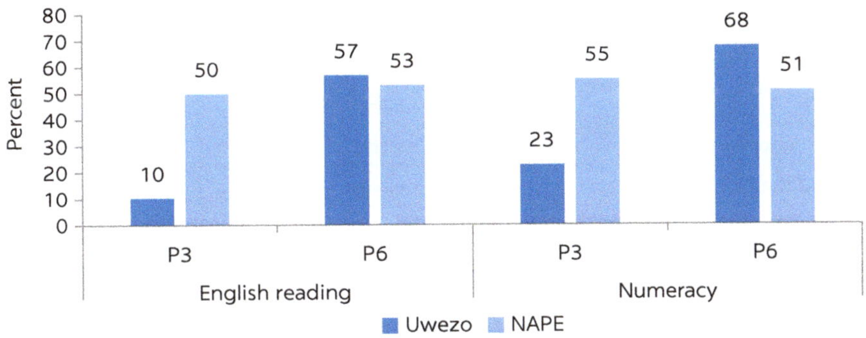

Sources: Data for NAPE are from Universalia 2020; data for Uwezo are from Twaweza 2019a.
Note: Performance standards are "proficient" for NAPE and "fully competent" at P2 level for Uwezo. NAPE = National Assessment of Progress in Education; P = primary school.

Scores on the PLE also provide some evidence of student learning. However, these examinations are also used to filter students progressing from primary to lower secondary education. Given the limited number of places available in secondary schools, it is unwise to rely on these exams as a measure of learning. Also, analysis in 2016 suggested that the PLE assesses a relatively narrow band of ability at the lower end of the skills spectrum (Allen et al. 2016). Another recent analysis concluded that the PLE exam was "very poorly aligned" with the upper end of the primary curriculum (Atuhurra and Kaffenburger 2019).[40]

Financing

The additional cost of meeting the need for universal, effective primary and lower secondary education is likely to be significantly more than central government allocates to LGs, although some reforms could lead to efficiency gains or savings. Particularly given Uganda's low unit costs and the resulting opportunity to focus additional spending on improving quality, more and better education is likely to lead to better economic outcomes in the long run. Measures taken at the preprimary and primary levels are likely to cost less than measures taken at the secondary level both because so few students continue to secondary education and because current per student primary education financing is so low. The necessary measures would raise Uganda's spending per student to a level similar to that in other low-income countries but would require difficult political choices among other spending priorities.

Indicative estimates, covering a six-year period, are shown in table 5.3. Primary education costs would be lower for all measures if concurrent reforms were adopted to ensure that fewer children repeated grades and learned more in each grade they attended. The resulting increased demand for secondary education would, however, increase costs. The costs of providing early childhood education (ECE) for all would be offset by the reduction in the number of underage children in P1, many of whom (estimates range from 40 to 60 percent of P1 enrollees) are disguised ECE attendees (Brunette et al. 2017; Weatherholt et al. 2019). ECE attendees are less likely to repeat later on, which would yield further savings in later grades (UNICEF and Ministry of Education Rwanda 2019; Weatherholt et al. 2019).

TABLE 5.3 **Estimated costs of adequate inputs for universal education, 2019–25**

	ADDITIONAL COST (US$)	
POLICY MEASURE OR PROGRAM	SIX-YEAR TOTAL	AVERAGE PER YEAR
Preprimary and primary levels		
Expand early childhood GER to 50 percent by 2025	111 million	18.5 million
Implement automatic promotion and improve instructional quality	72 million	12 million
Improve transition to lower secondary by abolishing the PLE	23 million	3.8 million
Lower secondary level		
Open new schools	1.2 billion	200 million
Add capitation grant for new students	99 million	16.5 million
Add salaries for new teachers	308 million	51.3 million
Introduce new lower secondary curriculum	158 million	26.3 million
Introduce new school safety measures	30 million	5 million
Total	**2 billion**	**333 million**

Source: World Bank 2019b, table 6.
Note: Totals are rounded. Six-year total = U Sh (Uganda shilling) 7.294 trillion; average per year = U Sh 1.215 trillion; GER = gross enrollment ratio; PLE = Primary Leaving Examination; US$ = US dollar.

Some interventions have been cost-effective in improving education outcomes, including a package of teacher training, ongoing teacher support, resources for teachers, and classroom learning materials (Bashir et al. 2018); and giving information to students about earnings returns to education (Evans and Yuan 2017; Nguyen 2008). Multipronged interventions targeted at the furthest-behind schools have also been shown to be highly effective (Eble et al. 2020; Eble et al. 2021). Designing a realistic curriculum that is coherent with examinations has been effective in similar contexts (Allen et al. 2016; Bashir et al. 2018). Fairer distribution of existing teachers at the national level and within LGs might motivate teachers by delivering a "fairer deal." However, some interventions are difficult to deliver through the government without greater accountability throughout the sector (Bold et al. 2018), and little progress is possible without sustained attention to early learning quality from government policy makers. Communities and teachers need clear communication and support from the central and local governments regarding what is expected of teachers professionally and to support the adoption of teaching techniques that actually enable children to learn, as have recently been implemented in Kenya (Piper et al. 2018).

Capacity

Insufficient resources translate into inadequate capacity. The ability of the central government and LGs to address the issues discussed in this section is highly compromised by a lack of capacity at all levels. For instance, each primary school inspector covers more than 50 government primary schools as well as many schools in the private sector and has a wider mandate than that in many other countries (National Planning Authority 2018a). As many as 46 percent of teaching positions in teacher training colleges are unfilled, making these colleges unable to provide necessary in-service and preservice training (National Planning Authority 2018a). As of 2015, because of the lack of in-service teacher trainers, only 55 percent of the government primary teaching workforce received any training over a two-year period (Twaweza 2015).[41] Poor quality and insufficient intensity of in-service teacher training to update teaching techniques has been shown to render the current teacher in-service training system ineffective (Kerwin and Thornton 2020). And inadequate capacity ultimately has a negative effect on the quality of education that is provided in government schools.

FISCAL TRANSFER MECHANISMS

Characteristics of transfers to education

This section first briefly describes the financing of LGs in general and then LG financing for education. Details of the Inter-Governmental Fiscal Transfer (IGFT) program are described in box 5.1.

BOX 5.1

The Inter-Governmental Fiscal Transfer program: An ongoing reform

Intergovernmental grants from the central government to LGs began with the 1997 Local Governments Act, but the current IGFT program has its origins in the 2002 Fiscal Decentralization Strategy (FDS). This strategy was devised in response to several issues related to transfers, including fragmentation (many different earmarked grants, including those to address postconflict and donor priorities), a lack of LG autonomy, and a lack of incentives to encourage LGs to raise their own revenue. Some of the FDS was implemented with mixed results. Few LGs took up the opportunity for autonomy to reallocate resources among subsectors and sectors; the low level of the nonwage transfers from the central government, which fell in real terms between 2003–04 and 2011–12, may have limited the extent to which LGs had any real discretion. In education, transfers effectively failed to cover any management costs, including the costs of the LG inspectorate functions, until the 2010s.

Following concerns over the fragmentation, inequity and inadequacy of funding in the mid 2010s, the IGFT Reform Program was developed to (1) reduce the number of grants to give LGs more discretion to respond to local needs while still reflecting national policies as set out in annual sector guidelines; (2) increase equity by shifting from ad hoc allocations among LGs to formula-based allocations, which gave bigger allocations to those LGs that received the lowest per capita amounts; (3) increase the adequacy of grants to improve service delivery; and (4) increase the efficiency of expenditures by beginning a shift away from input-based controls to performance-based and output-based management.

Implementation of the IGFT Reform Program began in 2016 with a reduction in the number of subgrants and a reintroduction of formula-based allocations.

Further implementation of actions proposed in the FDS, including a redesign and revival of the LG grant-linked performance assessment system for LGs, paved the way for US$200 million in World Bank financing support in 2017 to provide fiscal space to improve the adequacy and equity of funding in the health and education sectors and support improved LG management of resources.

As of 2020, the World Bank board approved US$300 million in additional support to the IGFT Reform Program, which extended the support to water and micro-scale irrigation. It also deepened the engagement in education and health, including supporting the recruitment of teachers and health workers in LGs with the greatest shortages, and focusing on school and health facility performance.

Successes have included large increases to nonwage health and education grants and the revival of the local government performance assessment system. Improvements in equity have been marked in health, nonwage recurrent grants, discretionary grants, and water and environment. Improvements in equity were less apparent in education, in part because per pupil grant equity already had priority over school-age population-based equity efforts.

The IGFT system

Most of the resources available to LGs are transferred from the central government in two classes of grants, conditional and unconditional, as well as subventions provided by the MoES and donors for specific purposes. Little information is publicly available on the budget or actual expenditures for LG subventions. Therefore, our analysis has necessarily focused on the grant system. Overall, LG grant financing amounted to 20 percent of government domestic revenues in 2019–20, a decline from 30 percent in 2008–09 (MoFPED 2020b). LG education grants amounted to 3 percent of GDP in 2019–20, considerably down from their peak of 5.7 percent in 2002–03.

Since the introduction of the current IGFT system in 1997–98, the majority of LG transfers from the central government have been conditional grants of three types: (1) wage grants; (2) nonwage recurrent grants; and (3) development grants.[42] Nonwage and development grants are currently allocated according to formulas.[43] Since 2007, the value of nonwage conditional grants has varied according to policy revisions, nominal erosion, and reforms (Hedger et al. 2010), but since 2017–18, there has been a significant increase in nonwage grants to LGs (see figure 5.9).

In 2019–20, unconditional grants represented 35 percent of the grants given to LGs, second only to the 36 percent share in 1998–99. However, the provision of unconditional development grants remains concentrated only in certain areas of the country.

As of 2019–20, LGs' own revenues account for no more than an average of 4 percent of total reported LG financing, although larger municipalities tend to raise more. In 1965, local-government-raised revenue accounted for 15 percent of total revenue, but by 2002, the share had fallen to 4 percent (Simson 2017a; Simson 2017b). Since 2018–19, rules regarding the budgeting and release of LGs' own revenue have become stricter, which may have reduced LGs' incentive to raise or report their own revenues.

FIGURE 5.9

All-sector LG financing, by class and type of grant, 1997/98–2019/20

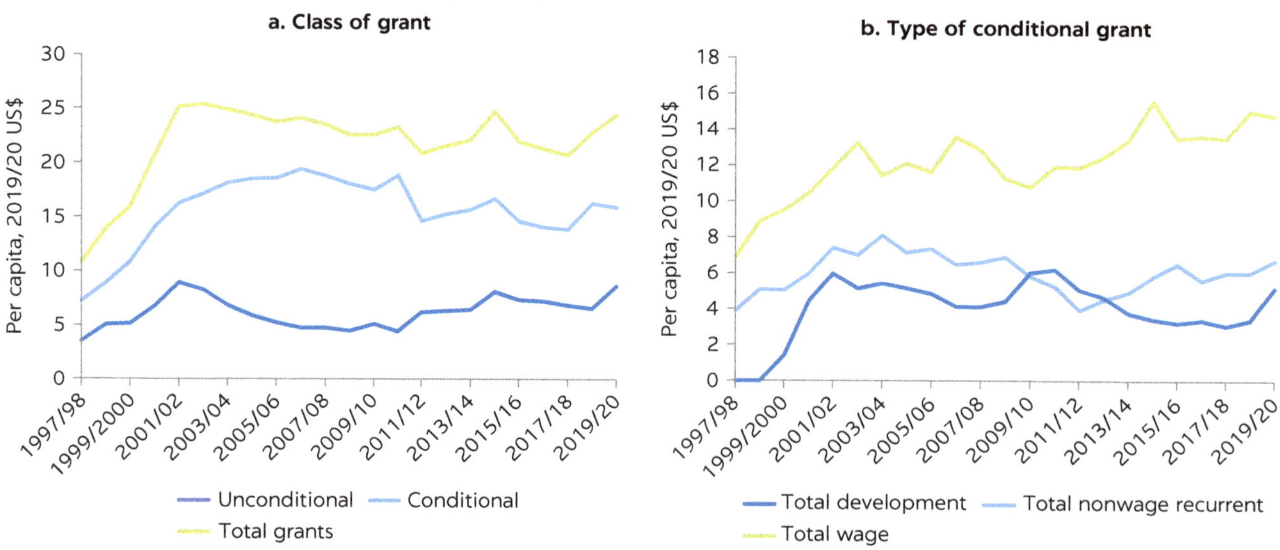

Source: Long 2020.

Note: Panel a. Conditional grants predominate in post-2001/02 allocations, and both kinds of grants are approaching their real historical peak under current reforms. Panel b. Wages have been buoyant, but other categories have been recovering since 2017/18. LG = local government; US$ = US dollar.

The IGFT in education

LG education financing comes from four sources: (1) conditional grants, which the central government provides to LGs to fund their education activities; (2) unconditional grants, which the central government provides to LGs to be allocated to whichever sector they choose (although little of this funding goes to education); (3) LGs' own-source revenues, which are officially negligible; and (4) subventions—mainly donor funds—that the central government provides to LGs but manages from the center. Conditional education grants and subventions account for over 98 percent of total LG financing for education, while neither LG own-source revenues nor unconditional grants play any significant role in education financing.

Eighty-six percent of total LG funds for education are transferred in the form of conditional wage, nonwage, and development grants, which are designated for the education sector (see table 5.4). Three-quarters of these grants are designated for wages, while 91 percent of the nonwage recurrent grants consist of

TABLE 5.4 Financing architecture for LG education

	IGFT GRANT SYSTEM							
GRANT CLASS	CONDITIONAL OR SECTORAL; LGs CANNOT REALLOCATE THESE GRANTS ACROSS SECTORS OR TO OTHER PURPOSES			UNCONDITIONAL OR MULTISECTORAL; LGs TO ALLOCATE SOME OF THESE RESOURCES TO EDUCATION[a]			ADDITIONAL CENTRAL GOVERNMENT SUBVENTIONS	OWN-SOURCE REVENUES
Grant type	Wage	Nonwage recurrent	Development	Wage	Nonwage recurrent	DDEG	Donor funding (US$60m, of which US$13 million is for primary education); additional government capital expenditure (US$8 million); nonwage (US$0.8 million)	Can be allocated to nonwage recurrent or development budget lines
Subgrants	Primary; secondary; skills development	Primary and LG administration;[b] secondary; skills development	Conditional development; new secondary school construction; ad hoc	District; urban	District; urban	District; urban; USMID[c] Refugee; PRDP; LRDP		
Value (capitation to education institutions)	US$358 million	US$80 million (US$73 million)	US$41 million	US$2.9 million	US$0.3 million	US$2.1 million	US$69 million	US$0.9 million
Share of grants (capitation to education institutions) (%)	74	17 (15)	9	1	0	0	n.a.	n.a.
Share of financing (capitation to education institutions) (%)	64	14 (13)	7	1	0	0	12	0

Source: Government of Uganda, LG Education Guidelines, Kampala (accessed March 2020), budget.go.ug.

Note: Values are 2019–20 US$. DDEG = Discretionary Development Equalization Grant; IGFT = Inter-Governmental Fiscal Transfer; LG = local government; LRDP = Luwero-Rwenzori Development Program; n.a. = not applicable; PRDP = Peace, Recovery and Development Plan; US$ = US dollar; USMID = Uganda Support to Municipal Infrastructure Development.

a. In reality, much of the unconditional nonwage recurrent funds cover administration and prior years' policy commitments. DDEG is more flexible (MoES 2019b).

b. Includes inspection and administration, as well as the primary schools' capitation grant. It is anticipated that a small Special Needs Education subgrant will be incorporated into the primary subgrant from 2020–21.

c. USMID (Uganda Support to Municipal Infrastructure Development) is a World Bank project that funds municipalities and refugee-hosting districts using formula- and performance-based grants.

capitation grants, which are passed through to schools and to LG tertiary institutions. LG own-source resources account for less than 1 percent of finance for education, and LGs allocate less than 3 percent of their unconditional development grants to education.[44] LGs have discretion over very few resources for education, but they also tend not to allocate the resources over which they have discretion to the education sector.

The number of conditional grants for education was reduced from 15 in 2014–15 to 9 in 2019–20. The MoES also stipulates the purpose and eligible spending for each subgrant in the education grant guidelines (MoES 2019b). The vast majority of recurrent allocations are earmarked for salaries and capitation payments to individual schools. LGs usually use the small residual allocations in recurrent grants to cover their costs of administration and inspection. In recent years, the guidelines specified individual secondary school construction projects for most of the value of the increases in education development grants, limiting discretion. Locally raised and development revenues are genuinely discretionary, but LGs seem to prefer not to spend these resources on education, which receives just 2 percent of LGs' discretionary capital grant expenditures and 2 percent of their own-source revenue (see figure 5.10).

Figure 5.11 shows the flow of funds to government primary, secondary, and LG postsecondary education and teachers.

Objectives of transfers

Each transfer attempts to balance the government's general objectives for LG grants, which were clarified in the recent IGFT reform, with sectoral priorities and historical patterns of grant allocations and the distribution of teachers and schools. Because transfers constitute the vast majority of LG spending, the government's transfer objectives strongly influence LGs' objectives.

FIGURE 5.10

Share of own-source revenue budgeted by LGs, by sector

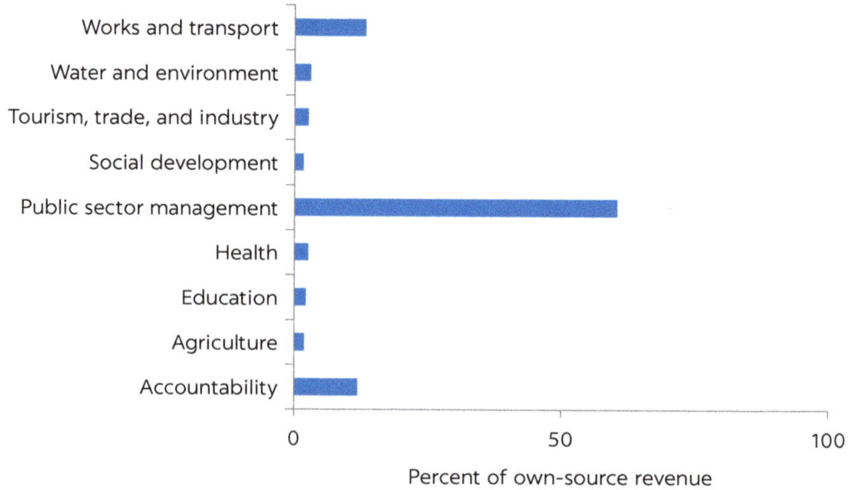

Source: World Bank calculations based on data from LG budget estimates.
Note: LG = local government.

FIGURE 5.11

Flow of funds for basic and LG postsecondary education

US$, millions

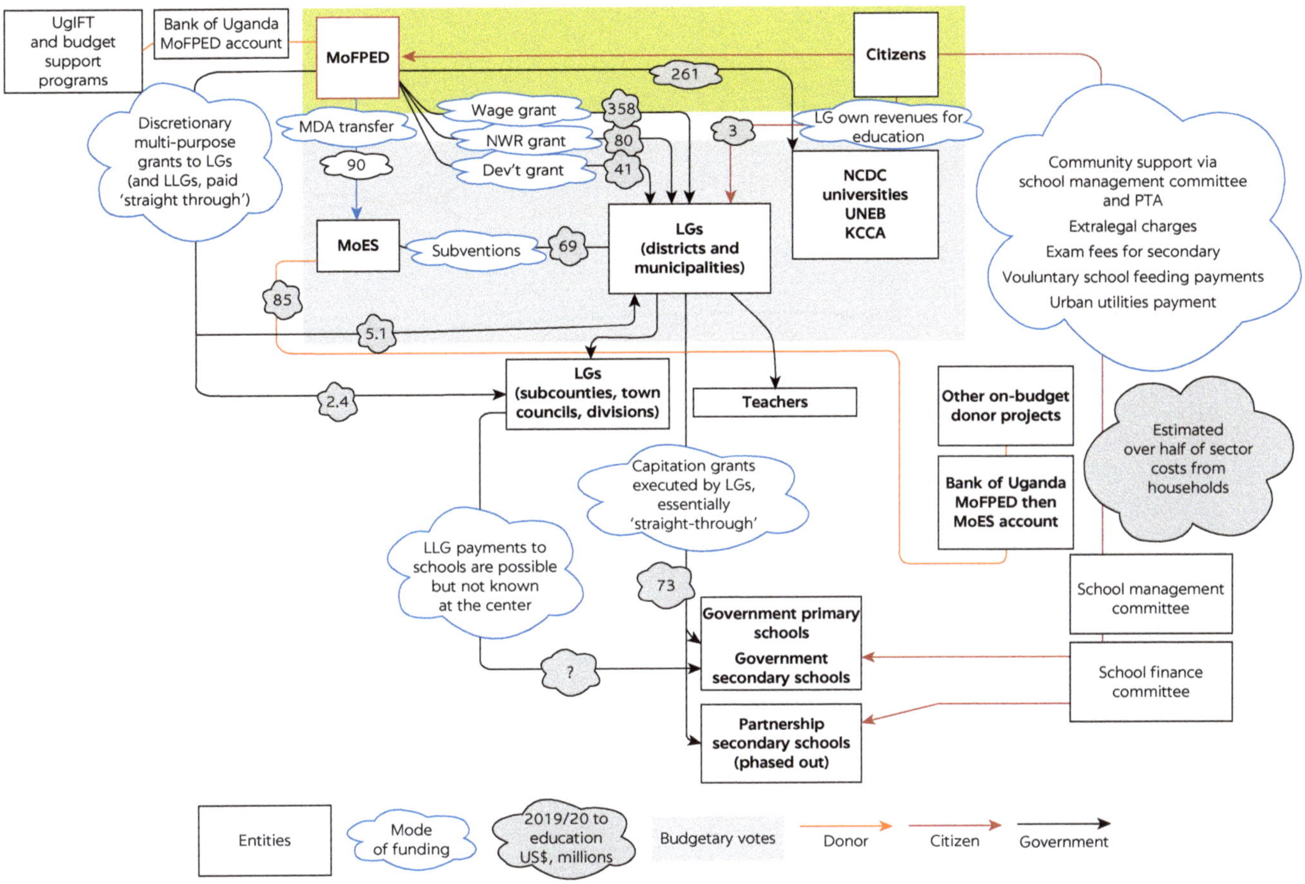

Source: World Bank.

Note: Some entities not shown for simplicity. Subventions amount is an upper estimate (ACODE-U 2020). KCCA = Kampala City Council Authority; LG = local government; LLG = lower local government; MDA = Ministries, Departments, and Agencies; MoFPED = Ministry of Finance, Planning and Economic Development; NCDC = National Curriculum Development Commission; NWR = nonwage recurrent; PTA = parent-teacher association; UgIFT = Uganda Intergovernmental Fiscal Transfers; UNEB = Uganda National Examinations Board; US$ = US dollar.

The rest of this section focuses on the progress toward achieving the current IGFT reform objectives since 2015–16.[45] Reforms build on good levels of grant transparency, execution, and timeliness.[46] Until 2019–20, the reforms focused on the nonwage grants (20 percent of the grant total) rather than on the wage grants because of the high cost of reforms associated with achieving staff deployment equity, and the sensitivities around wage reforms in general.

Adequacy

The financing provided to LGs through the intergovernmental transfer system is not enough to enable them to fulfill their mandated responsibilities to provide education services. Since 2017–18, the government and external donors[47] have increased the amount transferred to LGs, but their resources remain low by international standards (see figure 5.12). The financing challenge is exacerbated by Uganda's rapidly growing population.

FIGURE 5.12

Government education expenditures, by purpose, 1997/98–2019/20

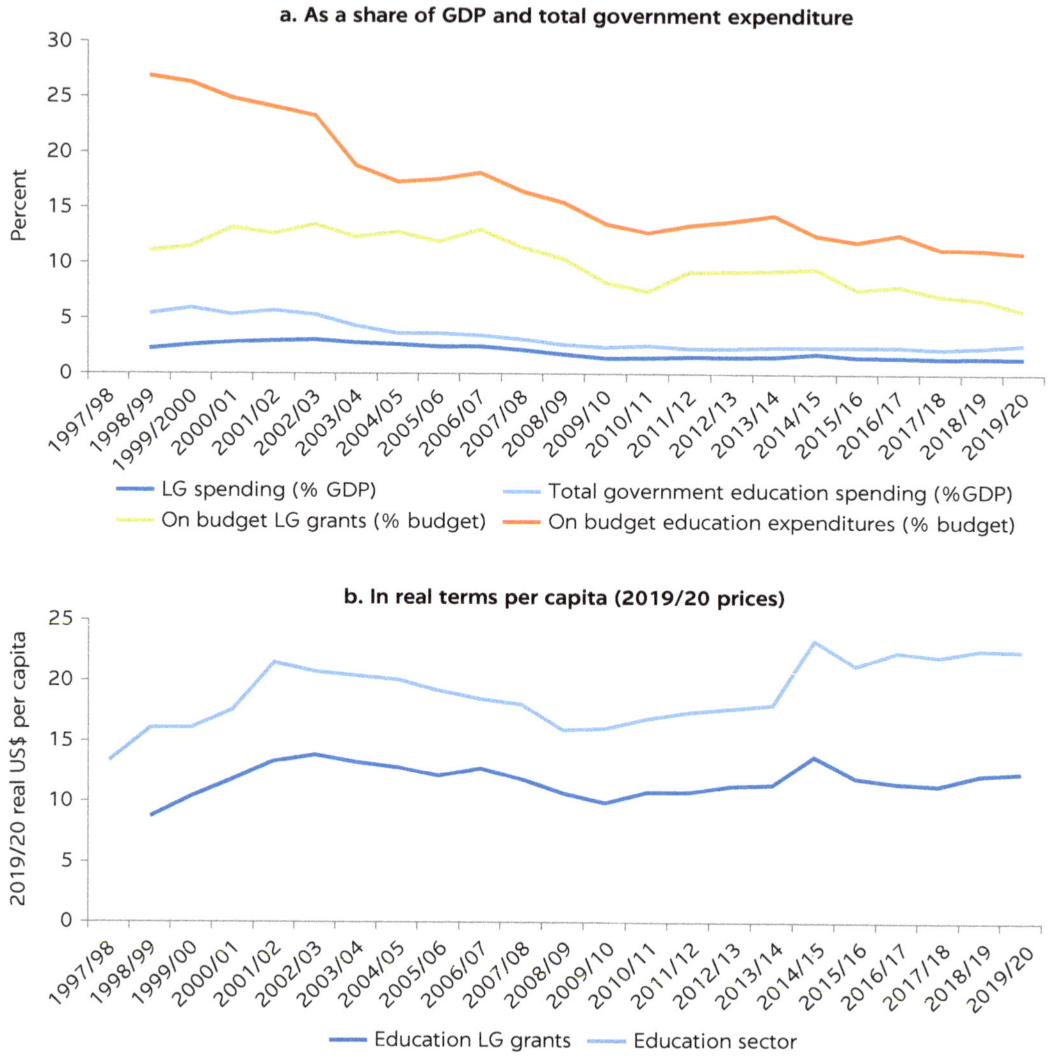

Sources: World Bank calculations based on government estimates and Long 2020.
Note: GDP = gross domestic product; LG = local government; US$ = US dollar.

In 2019–20, US$288 million plus a share of the US$7.5 million budgeted centrally for basic education (P1 to P7 and S1 to S4) was spent on LG-provided primary education in Uganda.[48] With an estimated 7.4 million children in LG primary schools, this amounts to US$39 per year per primary school student. Despite significant recent increases, this is close to the lowest level of government funding per primary student in the world.[49] Eighty-seven percent of the value of the primary education grant is earmarked for wages, leaving only about US$5 per student per year for all other types of expenditures. Teachers' wages in Uganda are low by international standards, although a primary teacher is paid approximately 2.5 times GDP per capita, which is similar to that in other countries of Sub-Saharan Africa. Reforms since 2015–16 and a wage agreement implemented beginning in 2019–20 have ensured that wage grant levels increased, but it is only in 2020 as part of the additional financing discussions with the World

Bank that policy makers are addressing concerns that additional teachers be posted to LGs with the highest student-teacher ratios.

After the LGs have passed the capitation grants on to schools, only approximately US$1 per student remains to cover the LGs' oversight and inspection costs and any other nonconstruction education initiatives. With respect to evaluation and supervision, LGs are responsible for inspecting the more than 12,000 government primary schools and all private schools, but collectively employ fewer than 350 staff for this purpose (National Planning Authority 2018b); this issue may be addressed under ongoing reforms. The central government plays a significant role in setting standards and providing oversight, including conducting secondary school inspections, but it is also significantly understaffed.

The fixed component of the capitation grant per primary school in 2019–20 is worth 64 percent of its real value in 2007–08 (as quoted in Kayabwe et al. 2014).[50] The per student amount, which has been increased by 50 percent since 2018–19 to US$3.86 per year, is about 45 percent of its 1997–98 real value. Analysis by the National Planning Authority in 2018 recommended quadrupling current capitation grant levels, to fully fund a limited range of school-level interventions (National Planning Authority 2018c).

A total of US$167 million is budgeted for the provision of secondary education at the local government level, which amounts to US$229 per year per student. Approximately 55 percent of the grant total for secondary education consists of wages, leaving about US$100 per enrolled student for other expenditures. There is a capitation grant provision for USE (S1 to S4) of US$50 per student per year and for universal upper secondary education and training (S5 to S6) of US$65 per student per year. Despite the vast disparity in capitation per student (see figure 5.13, panel b), the low number of students attending government secondary schools means that the aggregate levels of nonwage government financing for primary and secondary education are very similar (see figure 5.13, panel a).

FIGURE 5.13

Grants for students at primary, secondary, and tertiary levels, 1997/98–2019/20

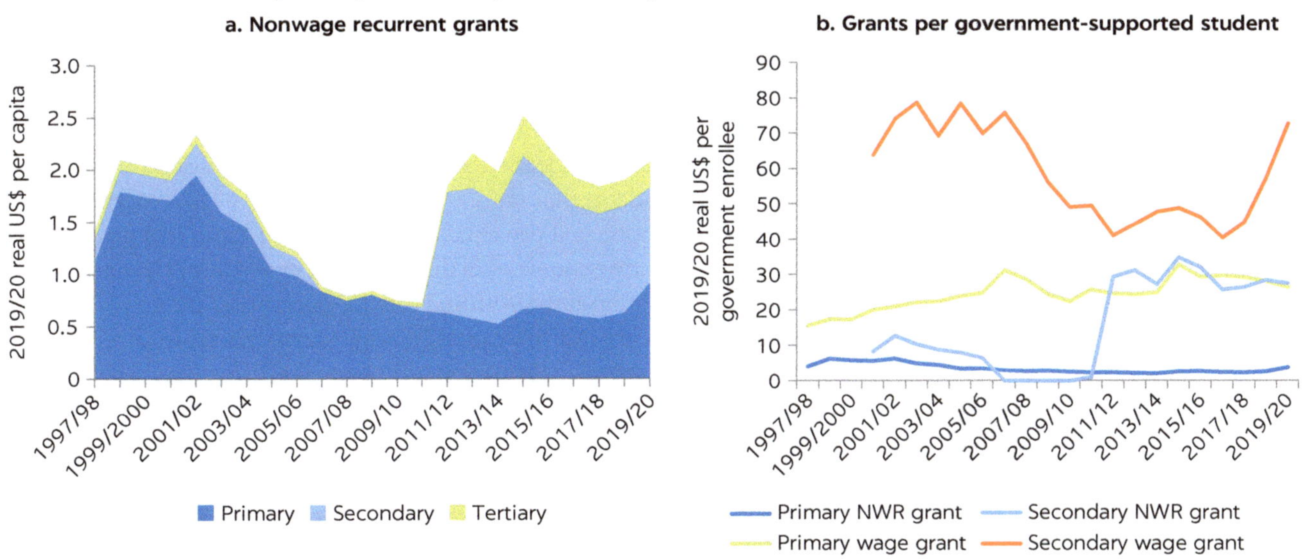

Source: Long 2020.
Note: Panel b does not include capital expenditure financing. NWR = nonwage recurrent; US$ = US dollar.

The government's 2016–2021 manifesto and previous policy pronouncements promised to ensure at least one secondary school in every subcounty; extensive construction ensued at a cost of US$29 million annually. LG oversight costs make up the balance. School fees, even in government schools, constitute the majority of schools' noncapital resources (MoES 2016). Total financing for secondary schools from the central government has increased markedly over the past four years, despite the gradual removal of capitation grants for students enrolled in private secondary "partnership" schools starting in 2015–16. The government had been subsidizing these schools to increase access without having to construct schools or pay teachers directly, but decided to withdraw its support. Secondary nonwage recurrent grants shifted into the central government budget between 2007–08 and 2011–12, subsequently returning to LGs' transfers.

LGs receive regular increments from the central government to fund their tertiary education responsibilities, but funding for critical elements of the sector remains low, and recent donor support has not yielded more or better in-service and teacher training services (National Planning Authority 2018c). The entire LG-funded postsecondary subsector, which includes 124 teacher training colleges, receives approximately U Sh 99 billion in total, including salaries. This is less than 60 percent of the government's subsidy to just one national tertiary institution, Makerere University.

Funding for in-service teacher training, which was not initially covered by the IGFT reforms, has had ad hoc increases but continues to be low.

Equity

Vertical equity in per student funding among different education levels is still a far-off goal. The large and widening gap between primary and secondary education capitation spending is indicative of central government priorities having shifted from UPE to secondary and postsecondary levels. The share of the education sector budget for UPE fell from 65 percent prior to the adoption of the USE policy in 2006–07 to just 33 percent in 2019–20 (Hedger et al. 2010). The vertical differences between primary, secondary, and postsecondary per student funding are not unique to Uganda but are among the widest in the region.

The reforms to the IGFT since 2015 have focused on per capita equity among LGs. In 2015, grants were biased toward western Uganda at the expense of the north and east (MoFPED and ODI 2016; Manuel et al. 2019). Since 2016–17, the formula-based grants have been allocated according to a "hold-harmless principle" to ensure that no LG allocation was reduced in nominal terms from the year before. Figure 5.14 shows that more populous LGs receive less central government funding per capita and per child, but this funding gap is less pronounced than in some of the other countries in this study (for example, in Uganda, the per capita ratio for education at the 90th and 10th LG percentiles is 2.5 and figure 3.2 in chapter 3 shows greater interquartile ranges among LGs in several other countries). Often, there are good reasons for per capita differences. The extreme outliers in figure 5.14 reflect private school attendance in populous periurban areas and the provision of extra money for remote islands; school attendance by refugees also can affect differences (Long 2020; World Bank 2021).

Wage financing continues to increase incrementally rather than on the basis of need or student numbers, thus contributing to these inequalities, which is fully discussed in the section titled *Elements of formulas used to allocate funds*.

FIGURE 5.14
Grants to LGs

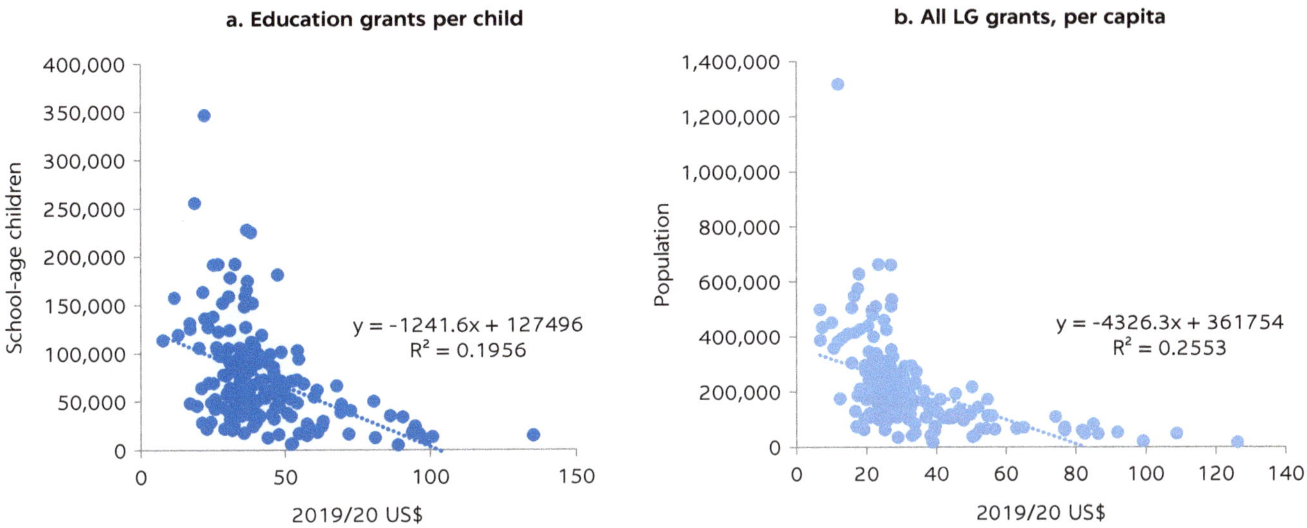

Source: World Bank calculations based on government of Uganda budget estimates 2019/20.
Note: Refugees excluded. LG = local government; US$ = US dollar.

Formula-based LG allocations for the education sector differ from those for other sectors. In the education nonwage recurrent formula, the emphasis is on service use, in the form of government school enrollment, rather than on population or poverty headcounts. Therefore, nonwage recurrent funding tends to be driven by the existing numbers of schools and teachers, which is shown in figure 5.14 (Long 2019, 2020).

The allocation for the "one secondary school per subcounty" policy, which was introduced in 2019–20, reflects equity concerns to some extent.[51] This policy accounted for U Sh 106 billion of the U Sh 153 billion development grant in 2019–20. Development funding for secondary schools appears to be awarded on a rotating basis, with at least one school under construction in most districts in 2018–19. However, the policy requires larger sums to be allocated to fewer LGs each year, unlike a formula-based allocation, and it has a more rural bias than the formula-based grants.

Progress toward increasing equity in education grant funding has been mixed since 2015–16 (see figure 5.15), with some recent slippages, notably in the conditional development grant, stemming from a redesign to favor secondary school construction in 2019–20. Secondary nonwage recurrent and wage grants have recently become more equitable as weights for nonwage recurrent grants have shifted to reflect the school-age population and as more government secondary teachers have been recruited. No similar changes have been made to the procedure for allocating primary school teachers. Nonwage recurrent grants are somewhat closely related to population levels but are heavily determined by enrollment (see figure 5.16). The number of LGs increased from 133 to 175 since 2015–16, which accounts for some of the divergence.

Elements of formulas used to allocate grant funds

All of the nonwage recurrent subgrants to education and 30 percent of the development grant value are allocated according to objective criteria. Table 5.5 shows

FIGURE 5.15

Ratio of highest to lowest LG grants per capita, 2015/16–2019/20

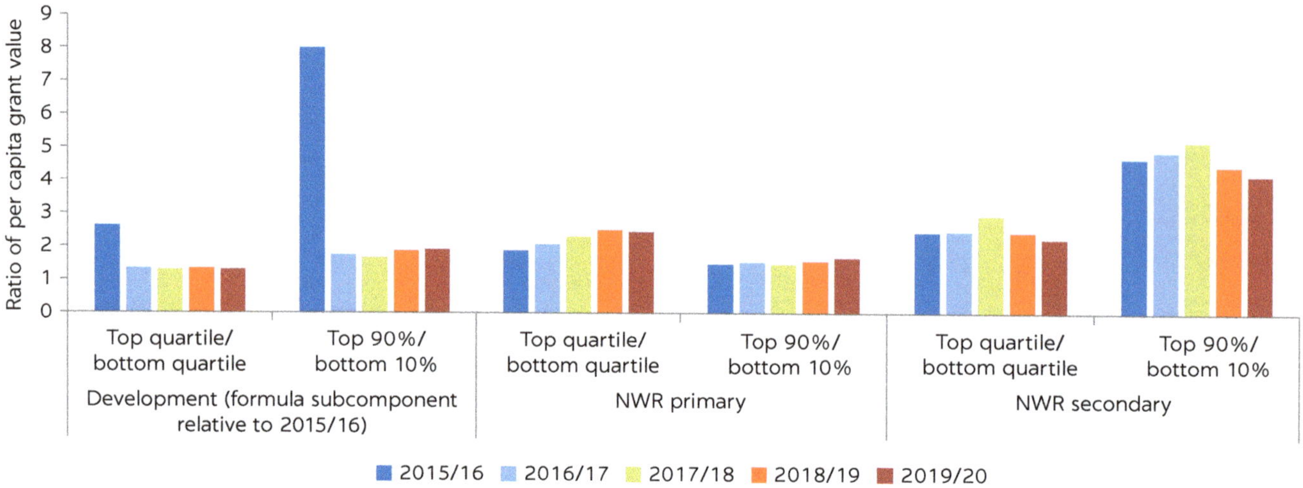

Source: Long 2020.
Note: LG = local government; NWR = nonwage recurrent.

FIGURE 5.16

Nonwage recurrent grants for primary education and GERs in government schools

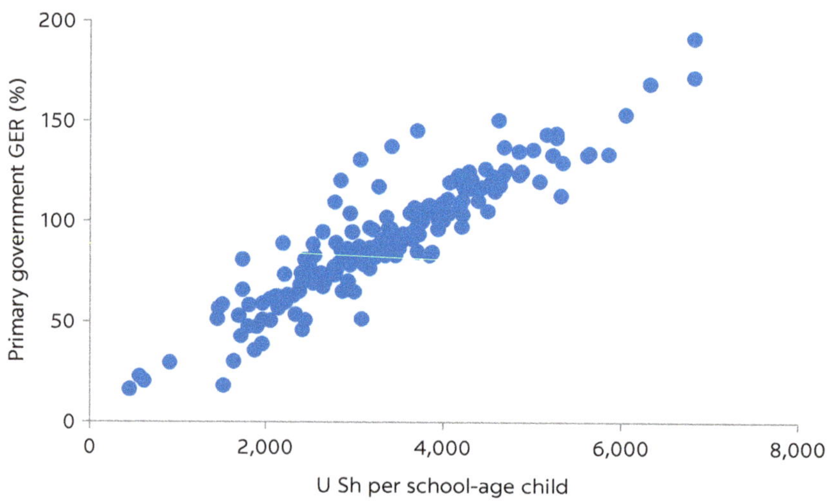

Source: Budget 2019–20, Online Transfer Information Management System (database), Republic of Uganda (accessed August 2020), otims.go.ug.
Note: Differences in primary GERs in government schools account for most of the variation per school-aged child. GER = gross enrollment rate; U Sh = Uganda shilling.

the allocation of 98 percent of the LG conditional grant value for education, although the allocation system is currently being reformed.[52] Higher formula shares for enrollment reduce the space for formula variables that respond to out-of-school need and adversely affect low-enrollment LGs. As part of the reform program, since 2018–19, 15 percent of the current education development grant (a share that is expected to rise)[53] has been allocated according to how well LGs perform on a variety of measures. The annual LG Performance Assessment is conducted by the Office of the Prime Minister (MoFPED 2020a).[54] The grant allocations to LGs for the year following the assessment are determined in

TABLE 5.5 **Allocation of the largest education LG subgrants, 2019–20**

percent

	WAGES (PRIMARY, SECONDARY, SKILLS)	PRIMARY NONWAGE RECURRENT	SECONDARY NONWAGE RECURRENT	CONDITIONAL DEVELOPMENT GRANT
Objective criteria				
Enrollment	0	93.1	97.4	0
Exam performance (LGs with lower scores receive more resources)	0	0.9	0.2	4.9
Out-of-school population	0	0	0	3.4
Total school-age population	0	0	0	4.2
Fixed per LG allocation	0	0.5	0	2.1
Number of facilities	0	4.7	0.7	0
Hold-harmless policy (no LG loses resources from formula-based grants relative to pre-2015–16 ad hoc allocations)	0	0.3	1.6	0
Hard-to-reach population	0	0.3	0.1	0.3
Land area (larger LGs get more funding)	0	0.3	0.1	0
Island population	0	0	0	0.1
Annual LG performance assessment				
LG performance	0	0	0	15.0
Incremental and input based budgeting				
Secondary school construction	0	0	0	70.0
Incrementally budgeted	100	0	0	0

Source: Online Transfer Information Management System (database), Republic of Uganda (accessed August 2020), otims.go.ug; MoFPED 2020d.
Note: Nonwage recurrent grants include capitation grants. LG = local government.

accordance with their scores. Only the development grant is allocated based on the score; development activities are less recurrent than the LGs' obligations that are funded by the nonwage and wage grants, therefore any variation in the amount awarded will not disrupt recurring activities. The objectives of these performance-linked grants, which operate in four different sectors, are to reward LGs for carrying out their responsibilities well but also to identify any underperforming LGs. The Ministry of Local Government (MoLG) is responsible for identifying any underperforming LGs and for providing them with modest levels of targeted technical assistance.[55]

Efficiency and discretion

There is some evidence suggesting that LGs with more discretion are more efficient (Rasul and Rogger 2018; Rasul, Rogger, and Williams 2018; Williams 2017). However, in Uganda, LGs appear to have little appetite for more expenditure discretion without more resource autonomy, and the central government has shown little appetite for granting either.

A public expenditure tracking survey in Uganda in 1995 found that only 20 percent of the centrally allocated capitation funds intended for schools actually reached the schools (Reinikka and Svensson 2004). Following the combined introduction of UPE in 1997, elimination of primary school fees, introduction of conditional grants, direct transfer of capitation grants from the newly created LGs to schools, and publishing grant disbursement figures, the share of funds reaching the schools increased to 90 percent in 1999. In absolute terms, however, leakage was not reduced significantly, and transparency and publicity requirements, although important elements of the reforms, did not produce the efficiency savings (Hubbard 2007).

Ninety-three percent of the primary education nonwage subgrant, 96 percent of the secondary education nonwage recurrent subgrant, and all of the tertiary nonwage recurrent subgrants are capitation grants, which go directly to schools. Within the amount of the nonwage recurrent grant retained by LGs, a minimum per school amount is budgeted for inspections (see figure 5.17). After inspections, LGs are left with less than US$0.30 per school-age child per year to fund their oversight responsibilities and to pursue their own policy priorities to support education. Moreover, the central government has issued additional directives in an attempt to require LGs to spend these small amounts on additional inspection and sports activities, leaving LGs little scope to respond to locally identified needs, to top up capitation grants, or to conduct any other policy initiatives.

Figure 5.18 shows the increase in resources controlled by the LGs' district offices for school inspections and district administration, which have increased from almost nothing prior to 2016–17.

The value of development grants to LGs has increased in recent years, and LGs' autonomy over their use has increased but remains limited. Figure 5.19 tracks the shift from full central government earmarking to increased LG autonomy followed by a more recent slippage back to greater "joint" control. The government's policy commitment to building schools in all subcounties resulted in this partial roll-back of LG autonomy. As a result, there was far more development spending in the secondary education subsector in 2019–20.

FIGURE 5.17

Total value of nonwage recurrent grants, by purpose and recipient, 2019/20

US$, millions

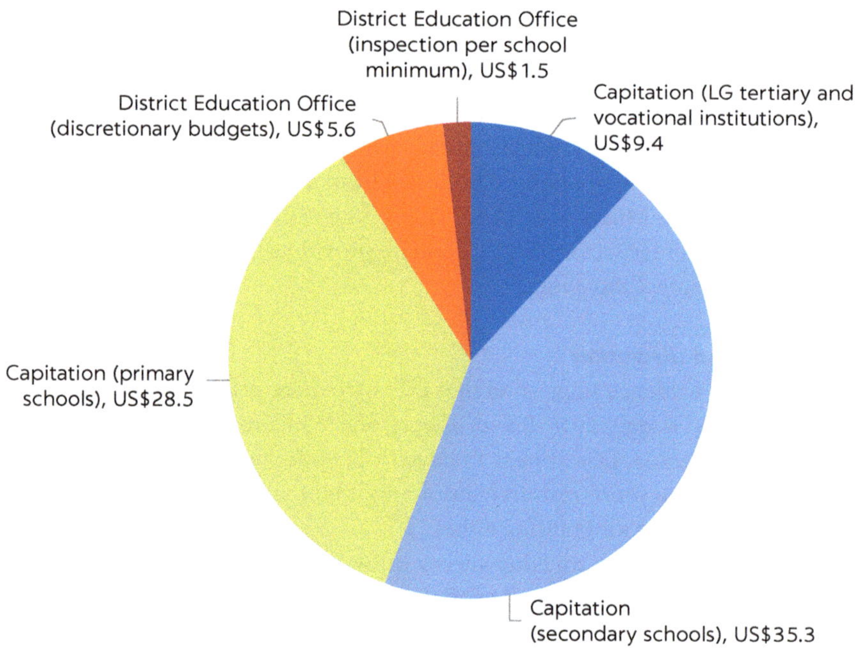

Source: Budget 2019–20, Online Transfer Information Management System (database), Republic of Uganda (accessed August 2020), otims.go.ug.

FIGURE 5.18

Nonwage recurrent grant financing for education, by function, 2014/15–2019/20

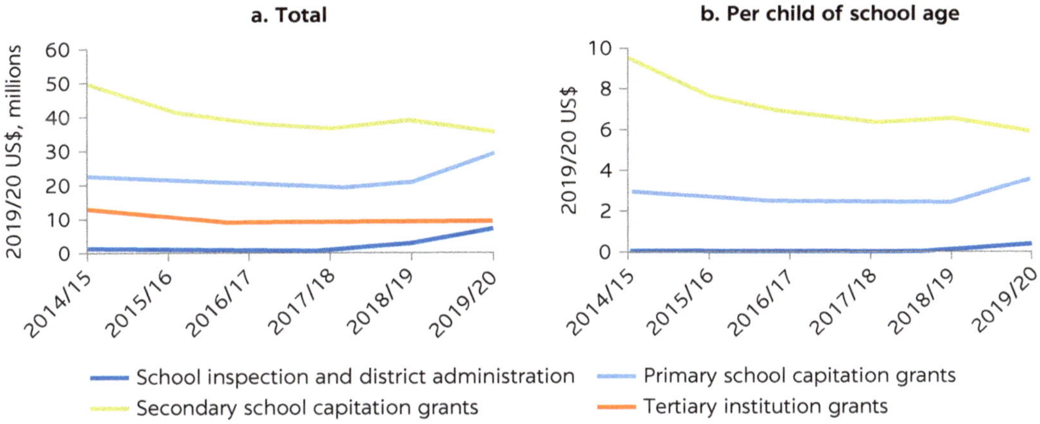

Source: Budget 2019–20, Online Transfer Information Management System (database), Republic of Uganda (accessed August 2020), otims.go.ug.
Note: The downward slope of the secondary school capitation grant line reflects the removal of subsidies to partnership schools, which were government-aided private sector secondary schools. The value of the capitation grant per remaining student (in government secondary schools) has been sharply increased.

FIGURE 5.19

Adequacy and extent of LG autonomy over development grants, 2012/13–2019/20

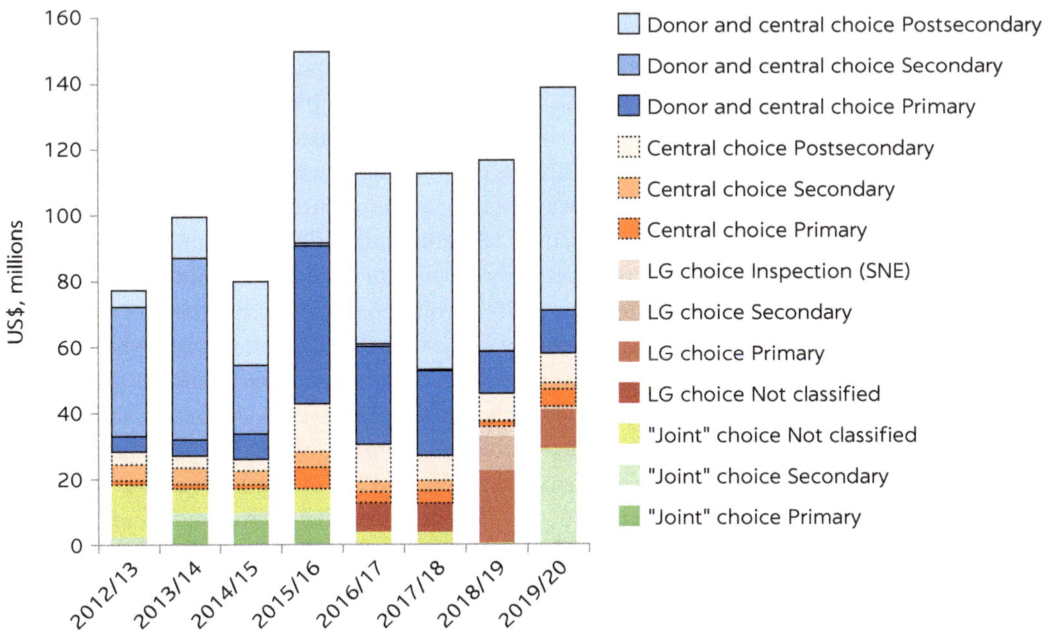

Source: World Bank calculations based on data from MoES 2019b.
Note: Bars with outlines are centrally determined, while those without outlines (especially bars in red) provide more autonomy to LGs. The figure includes donor and central government resources for primary, secondary, and postsecondary TVET provision delivered by LGs. LG = local government; SNE = special needs education; TVET = technical and vocational education and training; US$ = US dollar.

LGs enjoy even less autonomy over subventions for education (estimated at U Sh 257.2 billion in 2019–20) than over grants (ACODE-U 2020). LG policy makers receive little prior information from the central government about their extent or how they are to be used, which hinders their planning and reduces transparency (Williamson 2010). Donor-provided education sector support through the central government also encourages centralization.

Who is incentivized and how?

The central government sets budget limits for teachers' wages and determines them overwhelmingly on the basis of the previous years' allocation. There is a relatively close association between the number of schools and the number of teacher posts but a weaker link between the number of students and the number of teacher posts. The allocation of additional teachers and other staff to LGs is not based on a public set of rules, although the government has expressed a national target student-teacher ratio of 53. LGs are incentivized to lobby the central government for additional teachers, but their bargaining power varies, and it is difficult to analyze this dynamic because there is less transparency about workforce deployment than financing.

In the case of nonwage recurrent grants, the main incentive in the grants system is for schools to enroll students, with LG assistance. This contrasts with the intended design of the ongoing reforms, which emphasized the number of school-age children in the allocation formula. Grants based on the number of children, rather than number of students, would therefore provide resources to enable LGs to identify and enroll out-of-school children. LGs are limited in their ability to respond to this incentive, however, because of a lack of human capital, limited budgets, and limited autonomy. There is no effective system in place to verify school enrollment, which creates a risk that schools might exaggerate their numbers of students. LGs may find it complex and expensive to (1) recruit and retain students in more remote areas; (2) construct enough primary school classrooms[56]; and (3) certify and license schools in a streamlined and transparent manner. The publication in the newspapers of capitation grant levels may provide some incentives for LGs and school leadership to be honest in their reporting of expenditures. But this incentive is likely not decisive—the direct capitation grant might be. LGs almost always pass capitation grants on to the schools in full, but often parents are not aware of their value or purpose (Twaweza 2018a).

In most LGs in Uganda, over 85 percent of children are already enrolled in school, but they are not necessarily learning or even progressing through grades. It would be relatively easy to verify enrollment numbers, but the central government rarely does so. In contrast with the way the capitation grant was designed before 2008, when more was paid for students enrolled in higher grades, the current design gives LGs and schools no incentives to encourage students to progress to later grades. Given schools' extensive reliance on parents' contributions, the lack of any effective oversight, and the endemic repetition of grades, many perverse incentives reward increasing enrollment without increasing progression rates.

Schools have few direct incentives to improve learning for the majority of students, and incentives based on examinations and tests have been shown elsewhere to have perverse effects (Lockheed 2008). The lack of a clear accountability system compounds the problem (see Cilliers, Mbiti, and Zeitlin 2018a in a similar context). The longstanding transparency about schools' exam performance through newspapers and noticeboards incentivizes schools to present only "perfect candidates" for the exams, enabling them to appear higher up the league tables.[57] To counteract this, a portion of the nonwage recurrent grant is targeted to LGs who let weaker students sit the PLE.[58] Places at schools with higher pass rates are prized, and the informal fees charged by schools may reflect that. Children are tested throughout primary school, although there are some concerns about the quality of the commercial tests that teachers buy (Allen et al. 2016). Schools must buy copies of the syllabus for primary education, while the secondary syllabus is available online.[59] The budgets for secondary exams held by UNEB are far higher than those for primary school tests.[60]

Recent donor interventions are working to make inspections more effective in supporting teachers, and the central government may have new teacher development planning legislation in the pipeline. The DFID is also supporting school-based and LG-based management interventions, which support better school resource prioritization and a focus on teacher and student behaviors to support learning, in 26 LGs. Sustaining and scaling up these reforms in the absence of further donor support is likely to be challenging. Uganda has conducted trials of direct incentives and enhanced the monitoring of teachers (Cilliers et al. 2018b), and government schools often provide their teachers with additional allowances funded from the capitation grant (National Planning Authority 2018c). However, official initiatives have been confined to nongovernmental organization pilot programs and research projects.

The performance assessment process has the potential to address some of the issues related to both access and learning. The LG performance assessment, the results of which are linked to the allocation of the development grant, gives LGs an incentive to meet to discuss education delivery issues, fill any vacant but funded teaching and inspection positions, and conduct school inspections, all of which help to improve learning. As shown in table 5.5, the objective proportion of the education development grant in 2019–20 was awarded 50 percent on the basis of each LG's score on the assessment (weighted by underlying formula variables) and 50 percent on the basis of the formula variables alone. Formulas are structured to balance competing aims—providing rewards for good performance without penalizing citizens for the failure of their LGs.

In the three successive performance assessments, education management scores have improved (see figure 5.20).

Although LGs were incentivized through linking a portion of the value of their development grants to performance assessments in 2018–19, 2019–20 and 2020–21, there is still only limited understanding among LGs of the reasons for basing grant allocations on their performance. It is likely that the assessment

FIGURE 5.20

Average LG performance assessment scores, 2017/18–2019/20

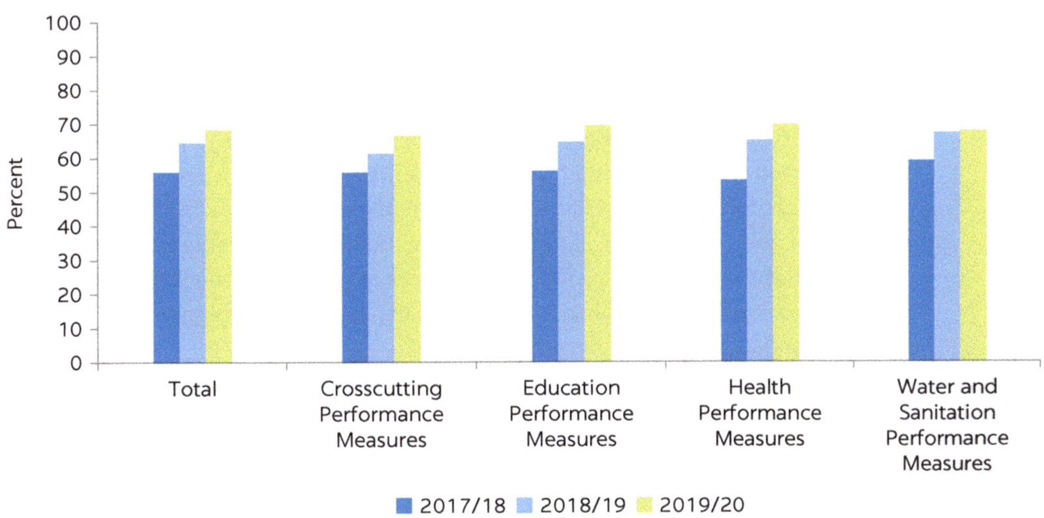

Source: Office of the Prime Minister 2019, 2020.

process and the publicity around it contributed strong incentives to improve management performance.

More fundamentally, there is need to strengthen the links between measured LG management performance and the obstacles to student learning examined earlier in this chapter. This has been acknowledged by the government, and a refocus of the performance indicators, combined with the introduction of a school-level performance improvement framework, was underway in late 2020.

Notwithstanding the need to improve the measures in the performance assessment and the importance of maintaining a credible assessment, the Uganda case points to the potential for a combination of nonfinancial and financial incentives delivered through performance grants to play a positive role in improving results.

Central government systems to support local service delivery

The MoFPED is a key actor in the current round of IGFT reforms. These reforms include shifting financing toward critical service delivery areas, including primary education, which has been deemphasized in recent years. An important question is the extent to which increasing formula-based financing and providing performance incentives can improve learning. It is likely that significant learning gains will require the full attention of the MoES, particularly regarding teacher management and training.

A principle underlying the current round of reforms is that the formulas are based on objective and independent data that cannot be directly influenced by LGs, including survey data from the Uganda Bureau of Statistics. Although the Bureau is the source of the majority of data for LG grant formula allocations in other sectors, in the education sector, the most valuable information on enrollment counts, which determine the lion's share of formula-allocated spending, is collected by the LGs with MoES oversight.

Uganda's current education management information system (EMIS) is not regularly updated. Primary school enrollment data is collected by MoES for calculating grant allocations, but not by the EMIS section.

EFFECTS OF THE DECENTRALIZED FINANCE SYSTEM ON SUBNATIONAL SPENDING AND EDUCATION OUTCOMES

How has Uganda's lengthy experience with education decentralization affected the sector? Has it changed spending, increased access, reduced inequity, or improved quality over time? Clearly, the central government's provision of fiscal transfers to LGs to support their provision of basic education has contributed to high if not universal enrollment. However, Uganda's population is growing rapidly, and this will require more classrooms and more teachers, particularly in urban areas (World Bank 2020). Such an expansion in enrollment has yet to be achieved in lower secondary education.

Evidence regarding improved learning outcomes or conditions for learning is less clear. What is clear is that, throughout Uganda, students start and exit primary school late, and many do not complete it. In this section, we review the available evidence and report the findings of our analysis of decentralized financing on education spending and outcomes. We focus on primary education for reasons of space and availability of data and because control over primary education is more decentralized than that over secondary.

Effect of transfers on subnational and household spending

Because local governments raise so little of their own revenue, LGs could not fund public education without central government support. It is, therefore, tautological to inquire whether transfers affect subnational spending.

Household expenditure shares for education rose from 5.0 percent in 2012–13 to 7.8 percent in 2016–17, which coincided with a fall in real levels of government spending. Combining various survey data from 2014 to 2019 suggests that, overall, households outspend the government on P1 to S4 education.[61]

Effect of transfers on education outcomes

In principle, fiscal decentralization has the potential to result in a number of positive education outcomes, including increasing access, equity, and efficiency, all of which should improve learning. Evidence of the effects of Uganda's recent reforms is scarce and geographically incomplete, and the data may have quality limitations; but it is clear from multiple sources that the potential educational benefits of fiscal decentralization have not yet been realized.

The Service Delivery Indicator survey conducted in 2013 showed a clear link between the availability of resources and improved learning at the school level (Wane and Martin 2016). However, we have used more recent LG-level data in our analysis and have found a less definite link. The panel and dynamic panel data analyses that we used show that increased financing has a positive association with increased access—a 1.0 percent increase in primary education grant financing is associated with increases in the primary GER of roughly 0.5 percent at the LG level (World Bank 2021). However, we were unable to demonstrate any association between government financing and improved performance on primary level exams. Further analysis at the school level might shed more light. In this section, we look at changes in access (enrollment and service delivery), equity (variations among districts in enrollment and service delivery), efficiency (early grade repetition, primary school completion, and teacher deployment) and learning (exam and test results).

Decentralization and access to education

Access to schooling involves both the availability of schools and the availability of actual instruction.

The adoption of the UPE policy resulted in a large increase in primary enrollment after 1996, with steadily increasing total enrollment numbers since then. The USE policy, which is controlled to a greater extent by the central government, was introduced at a time when there was less enthusiasm for decentralization. It resulted in slightly increased secondary enrollment but enrollment has stagnated since 2009 (see figure 5.21, panel a).

GERs, however, tell a different story. Primary GERs have been sustained at over 115 percent, while secondary GERs have declined in recent years (see figure 5.21, panel b).

The high primary GERs reflect the presence of a large number of underage and over-age children, particularly in P1. Regression analyses undertaken for

FIGURE 5.21

Growing primary enrollment and low and stagnating secondary enrollment, and high primary GER and falling secondary GER, 1996/97–2019/20

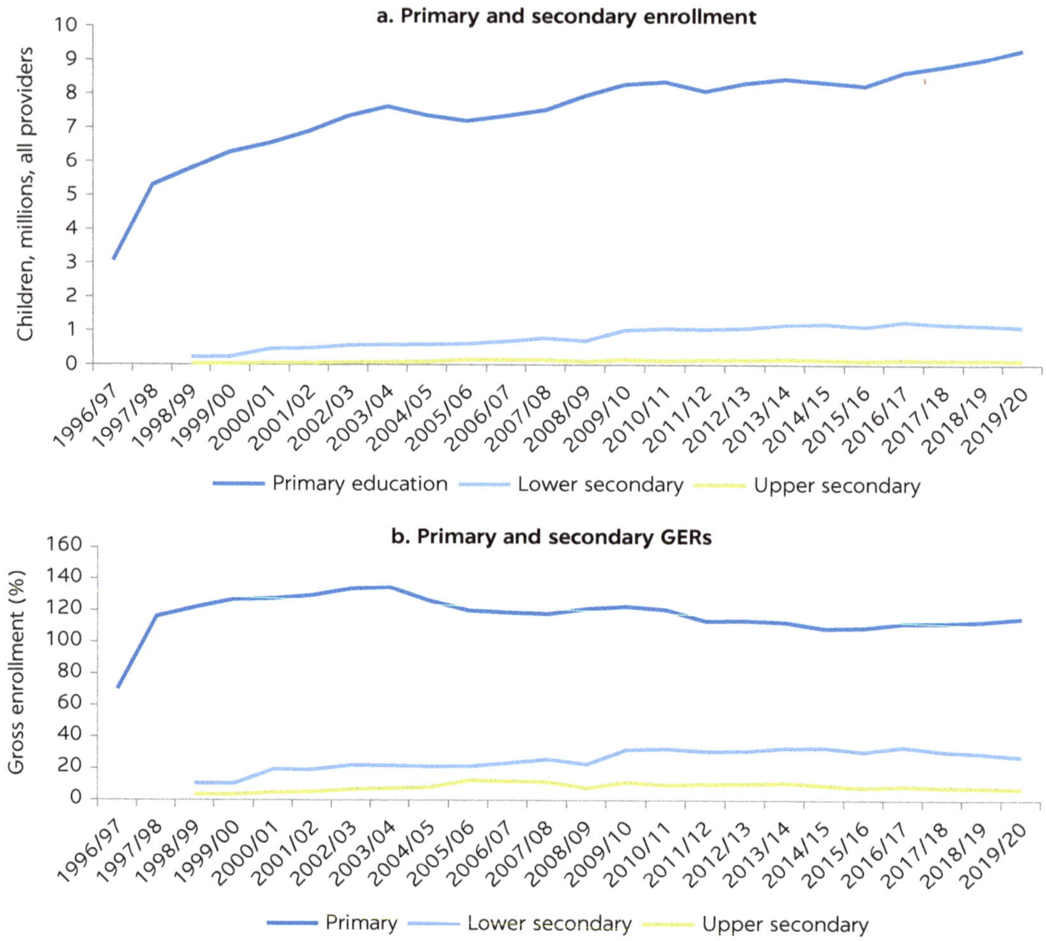

Source: World Bank 2020.
Note: Data after 2017 are projected, based on the Education Sector Strategic Plan 2020–2025 and MoFPED 2020d. Prior data are from the Education Statistical Abstracts and EMIS reports, https://www.ubos.org/publications/statistical/, and from Simson 2017b. Population denominators are from Global Burden of Disease Collaborative Network 2018. GER = gross enrollment rate.

this case study indicate that LG-level increases in both education nonwage per capita grants and education wage per capita grants are associated with increases in primary GERs.

The declining secondary GERs reflect both the elimination of capitation grants to support students in previously government-aided private secondary partnership schools[62] and the limited availability of secondary school places for a fast-growing population. The recent net decline in secondary enrollees in Uganda from the removal of support for previously government-subsidized private secondary school places, has been estimated at about 10 percent (O'Donoghue et al. 2019). Notwithstanding the new school construction and nationalization of private schools, it may take at least five years to reverse this reduction.

Learning conditions for students are poor on average and remain uneven, with high levels of school crowding, particularly in the early grades. Student-classroom ratios remained roughly constant between 2011 and 2017 and tend to be higher in government schools than in private schools (see figure 5.22).

FIGURE 5.22

Student-classroom ratio, 2009/10–2016/17

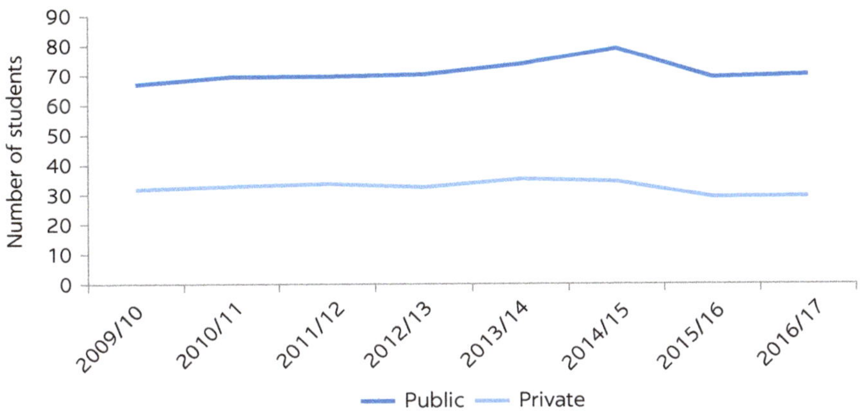

Source: EMIS 2011–17 (unpublished database), MoES, Kampala, Uganda, and World Bank, Washington, DC (accessed July 2020).

FIGURE 5.23

Average class sizes for primary grades P1–P7

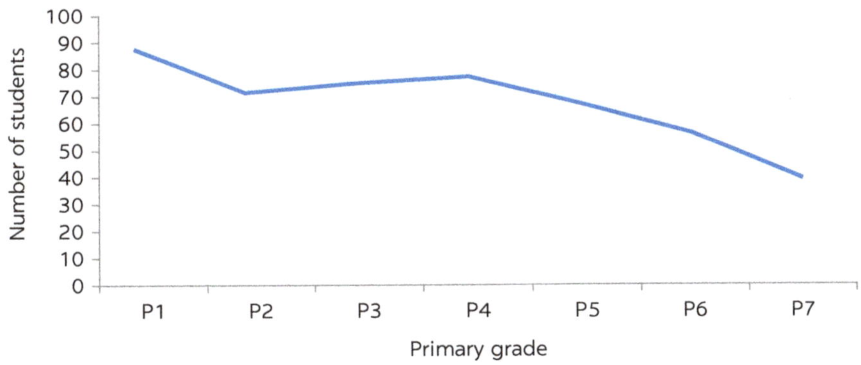

Source: Twaweza 2018b.

Class sizes are extremely large in P1 and P2 (see figure 5.23). Student-teacher ratios in government primary schools have risen to 56 to 1 in 2019–20 from 43 to 1 in 2015 (MoES 2019a). There is wide variation in student-teacher ratios between and within LGs, and both student-classroom and student-teacher ratios are high in rural LGs and in the north and east of the country.

The share of Primary 4 classes in which at least half the children had access to textbooks appears to have increased, from 5.6 percent in 2013 to 51 percent in 2018 for classes in government schools as a result of recent interventions funded by the Global Partnership for Education (GPE) (Wane and Martin 2016; Twaweza 2019b).[63] Government schools did slightly better on this measure than private schools.

The increase in the number of districts may have some role to play in school creation. We can't say why, but it may be for political or technical reasons, such as increased oversight. Table 5.6 shows that, based on 2019–20 data on school creation over the previous four years, the 76 LGs that have recently experienced splits (either as a "child" of a "parent" district or the "parent" district itself) were unable to create new schools in aggregate, despite having more students.

TABLE 5.6 **Primary enrollment and school creation**

percent

	SPLIT (EITHER A "PARENT" OR A "CHILD" LG) IN THE PAST 4 YEARS (LGs = 76)	"CHILD" (ANNUALIZED RATE SINCE SPLIT) (LGs = 34)	"CHILD" LGs 4- TO 10-YEARS-OLD, NO SUBSEQUENT SPLITTING (LGs = 52)	NOT SPLIT IN THE PAST 4 YEARS AND OVER 10-YEARS-OLD (LGs = 47)	NOT SPLIT IN PAST 4 YEARS (LGs = 99)
Increase in number of schools in 2019/20 relative to 2016/17	0.2	5.9	4.4	0.5	2.0
Urban schools	n.a.	n.a.	-0.6	0.3	-0.1
Increase in number of students in 2019/20 relative to 2016/17 or split	5.8	10.5	6.8	2.3	4.1
Urban schools	n.a.	n.a.	3.8	3.0	3.4

Source: Database of Releases to Schools, Ministry of Education and Sports and Ministry of Finance, Planning and Economic Development (accessed October 2020) https://budget.go.ug/sites/default/files/19_20_Q4_from_16_17_Facilities_IPFs_and_Release_advice%20v1_0.xlsx 2020.
Note: Our analysis excluded schools that switch between local governments (LGs), except for switches caused by an LG split, to enable us to identify new schools. The number of LGs dates from 2016/17. Average of percentages is at the LG level. n.a. = not applicable.

In contrast, the 34 new "child" districts created more schools and absorbed more students in the years after splitting.[64] LGs that were between four- and ten-years-old added schools at a faster percentage rate than older or younger LGs. The number of government-supported primary schools has fallen in municipalities since 2016–17, which should raise some concerns given Uganda's rapid pace of urbanization.[65]

Decentralization and equity

Substantial variation in both enrollment and service delivery exist among and within districts. Decentralization is expected to narrow these variations and to increase equity, but the limited amount of available data do not show any increase in equity as of 2019–20.

Government primary GERs differ widely across districts, ranging from about 20 percent to nearly 200 percent (see figure 5.24). The variations depend on several factors, including private sector choices, especially in richer areas, the size of the refugee population, and the amount of population movement since the 2014 census. The government primary GER in Karamoja (where out-of-school problems are persistent) is exceptionally low, while that in Madi-Okolo (a refugee hosting area) is exceptionally high. Grade repetition varies substantially across districts and is strongly correlated with the GER, meaning that the higher the GER, the higher the level of grade repetition (Weatherholt et al. 2019).

As previously discussed in the section entitled *Elements of formulas used to allocate funds*, the centrally allocated teaching budget does not follow enrollments very closely. The student-classroom ratio varies considerably among LGs, from an average of 19 pupils per classroom to over 150 (see figure 5.25, panel a). Similarly, the primary school wage subgrant[66] per primary student—a proxy for the student-teacher ratio—varies by a factor of almost ten between US$15 to US$145 (see figure 5.25, panel b). The student-teacher ratio worsened between 2015 and 2018 by an average of three students per teacher, having improved (been reduced) by five students per teacher between 2011 and 2015. The average student-teacher ratio in 20 of the 31 LGs sampled in the 2018 Uwezo survey

FIGURE 5.24

GERs in government primary schools, by LG, 2019/20

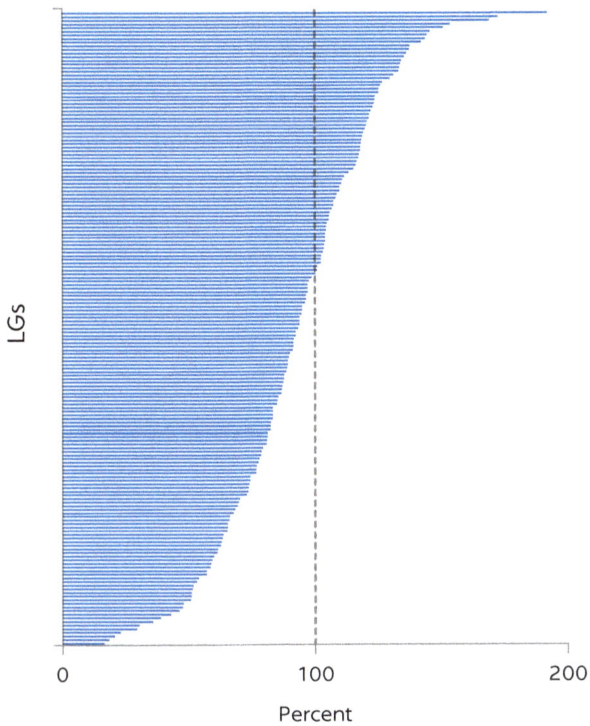

Source: MoFPED 2020c.
Note: Each bar shows the GER for an individual LG. GER = gross enrollment ratio; LG = local government.

(Twaweza 2018b) was considerably higher than the central government's estimate of the student-teacher ratio for 2019.

Through the full decentralization of the primary payroll to LGs in 2015–16, LGs were granted full autonomy to deploy teachers. Incentives to improve teacher deployment were introduced in the performance assessment of 2017. Our analysis did not find any improvement in the equity of teacher allocations within most of the 31 LGs surveyed in the 2018 Uwezo survey (Twaweza 2018b). We measured equity in teacher allocation using the standard deviation of the student-teacher ratio within an LG for government-funded staff in government schools, with a higher standard deviation indicating less equitable teacher allocation. In fact, equity within districts appears to have worsened (see figure 5.26). The standard deviation within 21 of the 31 districts increased between 2015 and 2018, remained relatively unchanged in five districts, and declined in five districts. The ratio of students to government primary teachers between 2011 and 2018 at the 90th percentile of LGs, was half that at the 10th percentile of LGs, and this was a persistent pattern over the seven years from Uwezo 2011 to 2018.

Although the analysis in the previous paragraph is only an indication, it is impossible to claim that teacher deployment has become more equitable; this is unfortunate given the greater responsiveness from LGs to issues raised, as well as other improvements reported by Ernst & Young (2019). LGs may have legitimate reasons for the current diverse allocation of teachers, but our analysis suggests that the central government needs to give more attention to this issue, following a final school survey from the MoES expected in 2020; a draft survey

FIGURE 5.25

Overall student-classroom ratio and government wage grant per government student

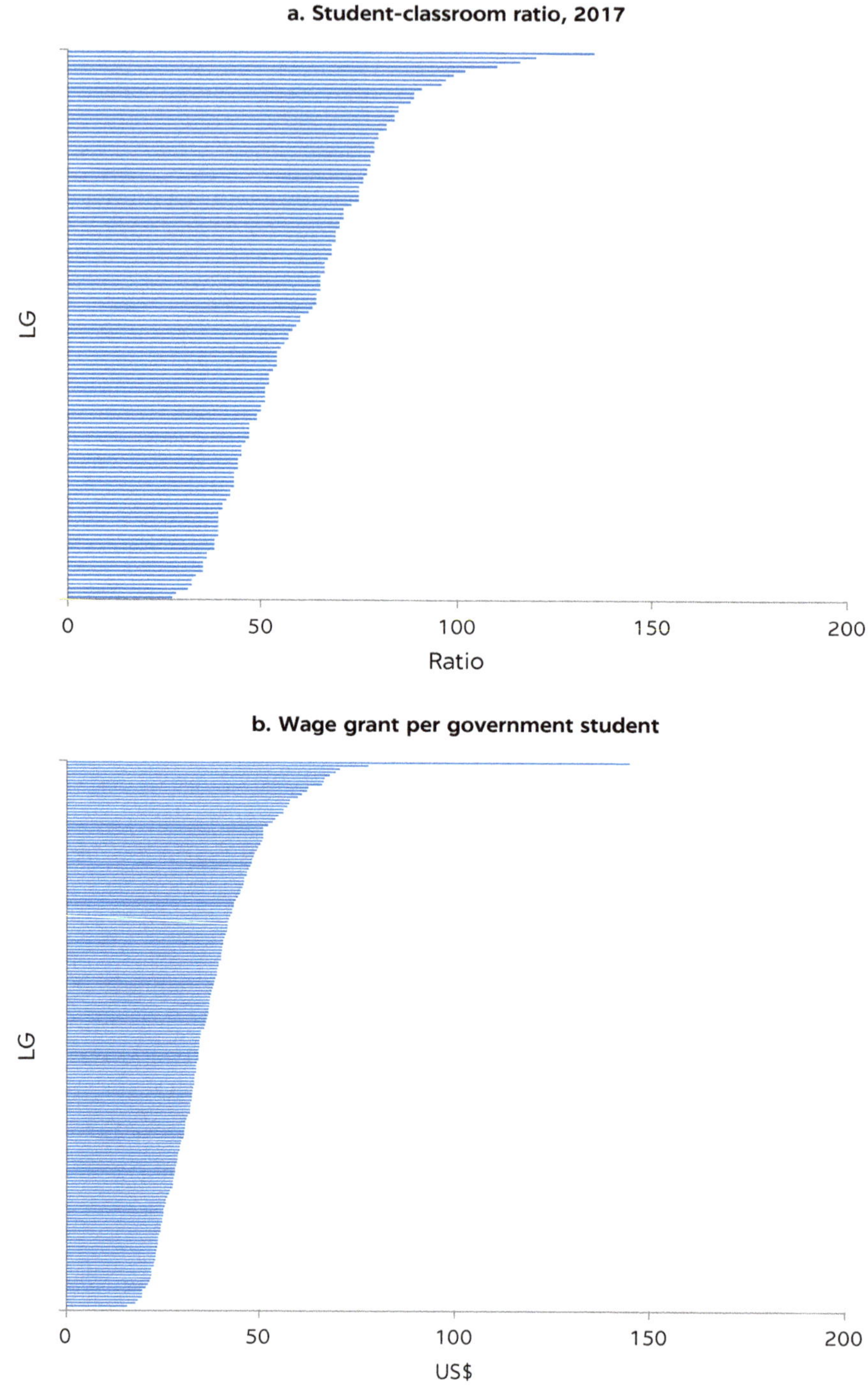

Sources: EMIS 2011–17 (unpublished database), MoFPED 2020c, Online Transfer Information Management System (database), Republic of Uganda (accessed August 2020), otims.go.ug.
Note: Each bar shows the value for an individual local government (LG). US$ = US dollar.

FIGURE 5.26

Standard deviation and change in student-teacher ratio, within LG

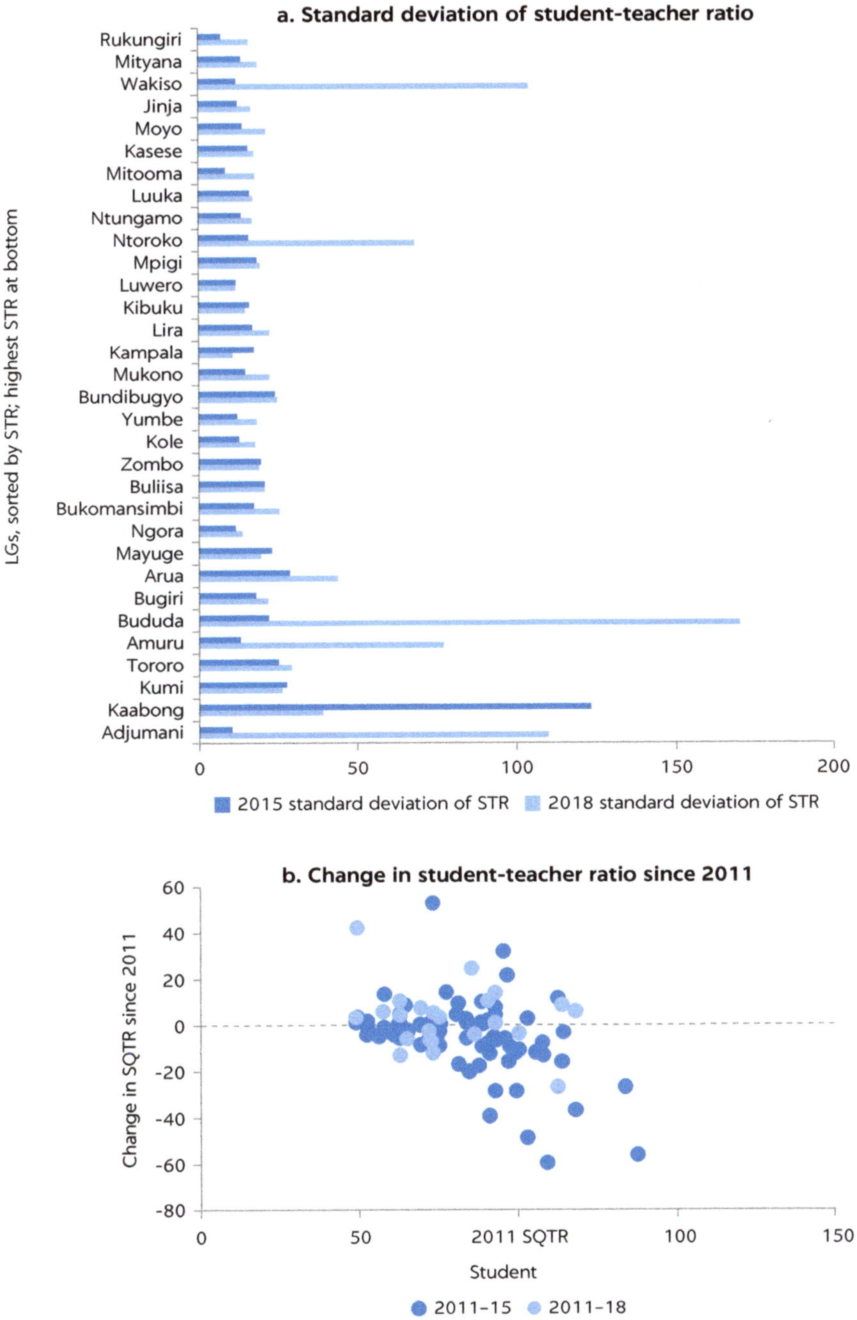

Sources: Panel a: Twaweza 2015, 2018b; panel b: Twaweza 2011, 2015, 2018b.
Note: There were 788 government schools in the 2018 Uwezo survey and 775 in the subsample of the 2015 Uwezo survey. LG = local government; SQTR = student-qualified teacher ratio. STR = student-teacher ratio.

was completed in mid-2019 but not released. It may be, as with curriculum redesign in 2007, that teacher deployment is not a failure on the part of LGs, but an indication that what is needed is more support and clear communication to LGs from the central government (Altinyelkin 2010).

The current teacher deployment does not appear to be sufficient for higher-enrollment schools, although undersupply to some low-enrollment

FIGURE 5.27
Government teachers versus students, per school

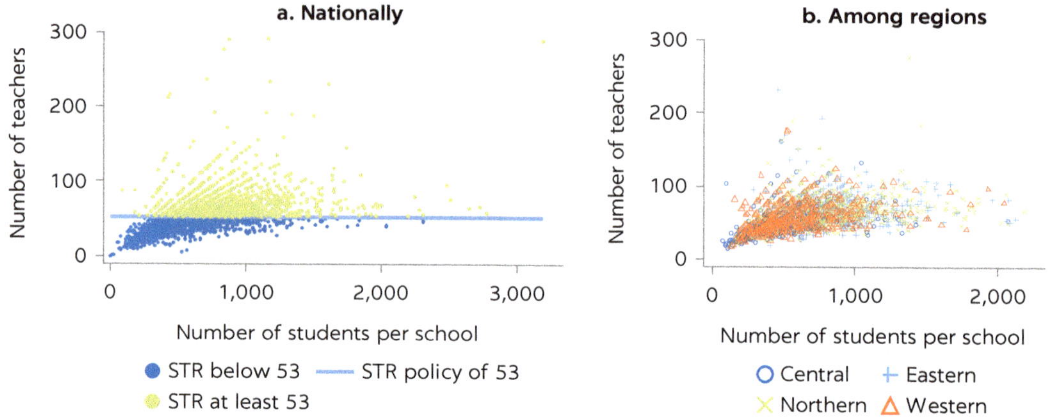

Source: Twaweza 2015.
Note: Government schools only. STR = student-teacher ratio.

schools is also a problem. Figure 5.27, using data from 3,347 schools, shows the comparison to the government's target student-teacher ratio of 53. The student-teacher ratio is on average significantly higher in the north and east regions than elsewhere.

Decentralization and efficiency

Proxy indicators of low efficiency in education include high rates of early grade repetition, low primary completion rates, and inequitable teacher deployment. Recent data show few, if any, improvements in these indicators.

Early grade repetition is particularly pronounced in Uganda (Bashir et al 2018), with rates as high as 30 to 40 percent in P1 and P2 (Weatherholt et al. 2019). Several recent surveys report high levels of repetition throughout primary grades (Hares, Minardi, and Rossiter 2020; Twaweza 2019a). One study found that head teachers consistently underreport repetition rates (Weatherholt et al. 2019). The Uganda Demographic and Health Survey (Uganda Bureau of Statistics and ICF 2018), the definitive national government source, estimates that about one-quarter of primary school students are repeating. Children who had attended preprimary school were less likely to repeat primary 1.

Although the absolute number of students completing primary school has risen, primary completion rates have fallen and remain well below averages for Sub-Saharan Africa (see figure 5.28, panel a). As a result, lower shares of children are completing primary school than did before the introduction of the USE policy when the central government's focus on and investment in the primary school system was higher. At 53 percent, the 2018 primary completion rate was about a quarter lower than the average for Sub-Saharan Africa at 69 percent. Participation in P7 as a share of the age group has actually fallen since 2002, while USE resulted in a small "level effect," and not a sustained trend toward universal coverage. The transition rate from primary to secondary remains very low (see figure 5.28, panel b).

FIGURE 5.28

School completion and progression rates

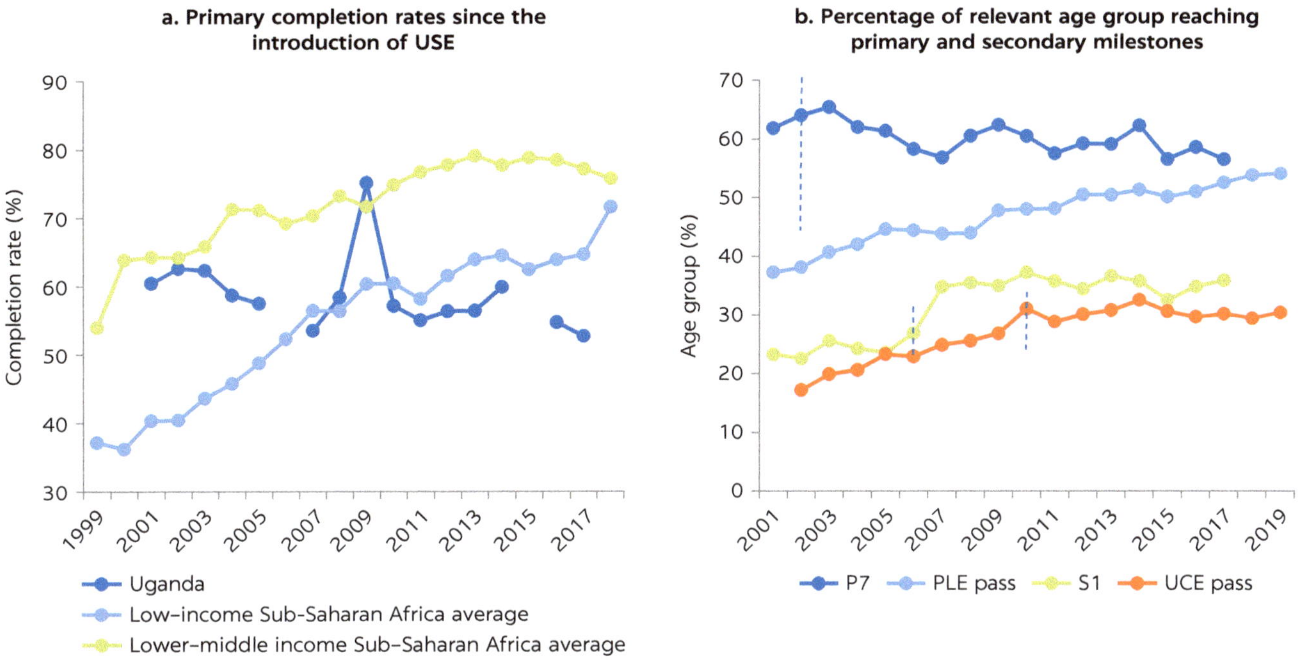

Sources: Panel a: EMIS 2011–17 (unpublished database), MoES, Kampala, Uganda, and World Bank, Washington, DC (accessed July 2020). Panel b: Education Statistical Abstracts and UNEB website. Dotted vertical lines in panel b mark the first P1 cohort to complete UPE (P7) in 2002, the introduction of USE in 2006, and the first S1 cohort to complete USE in 2010.
Note: P = primary school; PLE = Primary Leaving Examination; S = secondary school; UCE = Uganda Certificate of Education; UNEB = Uganda National Examinations Board; UPE = universal primary education; USE = universal secondary education.

More recently, when we divided the number of children who sat the PLE in 2019 (that is, those who reached P7) by the number of children enrolled in P2 in 2013 (that is, the same cohort of pupils, allowing for a year of repeating), we found a similar low primary completion rate. Only 52 percent of all children enrolled in P2 in 2013 were enrolled in P7 in 2019.[67] This figure varied substantially among districts, with lower poverty rates consistently correlated with higher completion rates; the association is significant in a series of LG-level regressions (see figure 5.29).

LG completion rates also correlate strongly with scores on learning tests taken about the time a child could be expected to be in an examination year. This was true of the 2015 Uwezo survey for P3 and P7 students' competence in both language and math and, although less significantly, for the 2015 NAPE for students in P3 and the 2018 NAPE for students in P6. Scores on NAPE's early year tests have a greater association with completion than scores on later year tests. Neither the indicator for LGs that had split, nor the linear variable of the age of the LG, was associated with completion rates.

We found considerable variation in the student-teacher ratios among districts, and this indicator has not improved over time, suggesting that decentralization has had little positive impact. Inefficiency in teacher deployment was shown in figure 5.26, with the number of teachers assigned to a school only weakly related to the number of students enrolled. In addition, the poor correlation between the student-teacher ratio and the student-classroom ratio at the LG

FIGURE 5.29

Primary completion rates and poverty rates

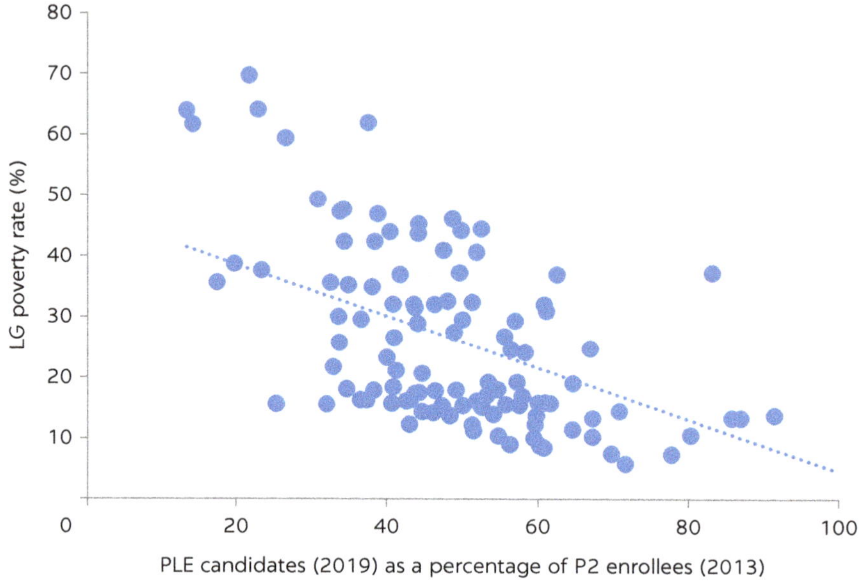

Source: UBoS 2016a, UBoS 2013.
Note: LG = local government; P = primary school; PLE = Primary Leaving Examination.

level suggests inefficiency in both, but the current set of reforms will aim to improve teacher deployment equity by targeting the furthest-behind LGs. Growth in student numbers between 2013 and 2019–20 was not correlated with the 2017 student-teacher ratio. One reason for the inelasticity is that in practice LGs usually cannot afford to construct many new primary schools. In 2019–20, only 27 out of 175 LGs received enough money from the nonearmarked development subgrant to construct a single primary school during two years of receiving funds (MoES 2019b).

Decentralization and learning

If decentralization was supposed to improve the conditions for learning, then learning should have improved as well. However, the available data do not indicate any steady improvements in learning over time since decentralization was first implemented. Moreover, the service delivery indicators that should be related to improved learning show little correlation with learning outcomes.

The percentage of P3 students who were rated as proficient in English on the NAPE test increased from 45.5 percent in 2007 to 57.6 percent in 2010, dropped in 2011, and increased to 64.2 percent in 2014 before falling to 49.9 percent in 2018. By comparison, the percentage of P6 students rated as proficient declined from 49.6 percent in 2007 to 38.3 percent in 2014, before improving to 53.1 percent in 2018. In the case of the numeracy test, P3 student performance improved markedly between 2007 and 2008 and remained stable until 2015, after which it deteriorated. The performance of P6 students on the numeracy test also improved from 2007 to 2008 and remained stable until 2010, after which it steadily deteriorated until 2014 before improving in 2015 and 2018 (Universalia 2020). "Older" districts had a higher share of students whose scores were classified as proficient, but the NAPE 2018 data do not include students in districts that were created after 2015–16 (see figure 5.30).

The Uwezo assessments also showed little improvement in student scores associated with greater decentralization between 2011 and 2018 (Twaweza 2011, 2018b). The assessments between 2011 and 2015 covered about 80 LGs, but in 2018 the assessment was carried out in only 30 LGs. Table 5.7 shows a large variation in the scores of the different LGs, but most scores fell or stagnated. Even when comparing the scores of the same LGs in 2015 and 2018, significant improvements were not evident.

The Uwezo surveys indicate that, by the end of primary education, 80 percent or more of those students who were still enrolled had reached full P2 competence (see figure 5.31).

In 2014, SACMEQ tested a stratified random sample of 5,261 students in 245 schools in Uganda and students in 13 other countries.[68] Its results show that P6 student performance in reading and mathematics had improved in all countries between 2007 and 2013 and that Uganda's students had achieved larger improvements than average. However, the performance of Uganda's students in absolute

FIGURE 5.30

LG scores on NAPE English and numeracy assessments, by age of LG, 2018

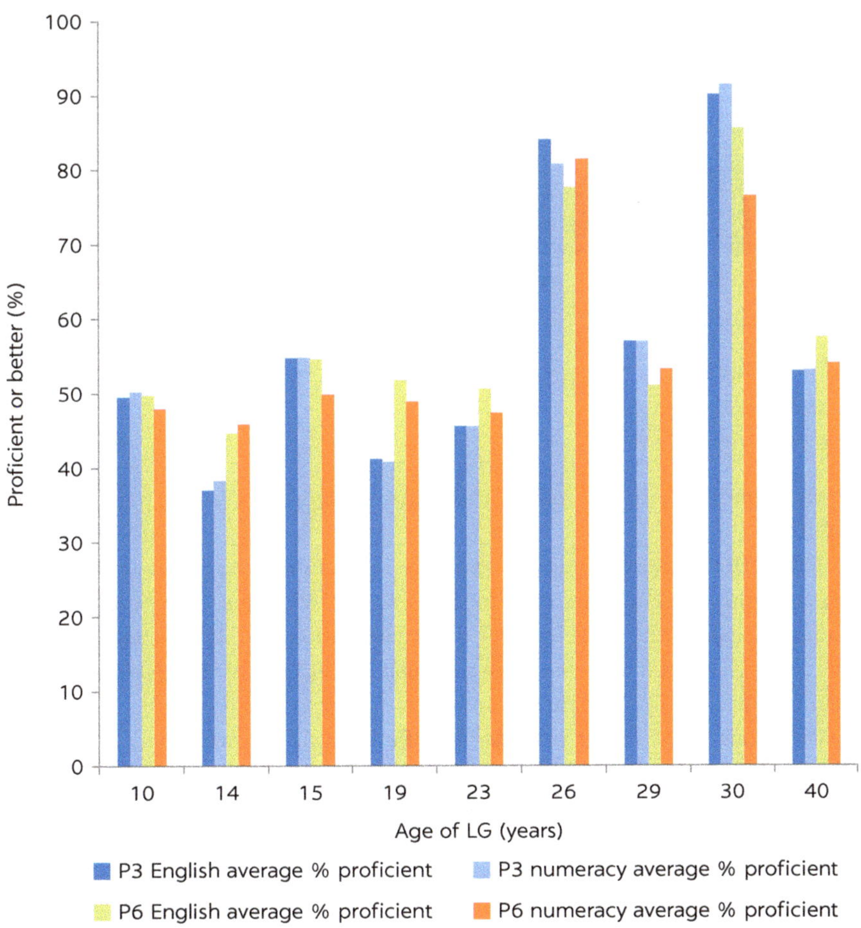

Source: NAPE 2018.
Note: LG = local government; NAPE = National Assessment of Progress in Education.

TABLE 5.7 **Percentage of P4–P7 students with full P2 competency on Uwezo assessments**

	ENGLISH					LOCAL LANGUAGE	NUMERACY				
	2011	2012	2013	2015	2018	2018	2011	2012	2013	2015	2018
LGs average (%)	52	57	56	55	52	35	63	55	59	64	58
Top decile of LGs (%)	67	70	73	73	65	56	75	68	72	74	66
Bottom decile of LGs (%)	39	44	42	41	37	11	52	43	48	55	49
Standard deviation (%)	11	10	13	12	11	19	9	9	10	8	8
Number of LGs	79	80	80	79	30	14	79	80	80	79	30

Sources: Twaweza 2011, 2012, 2015, and 2018b.
Note: P4–P7 cohorts were equally weighted at the LG (local government) level. P = primary school.

FIGURE 5.31
Percentage of students with full P2 competence in numeracy and English, by primary grade

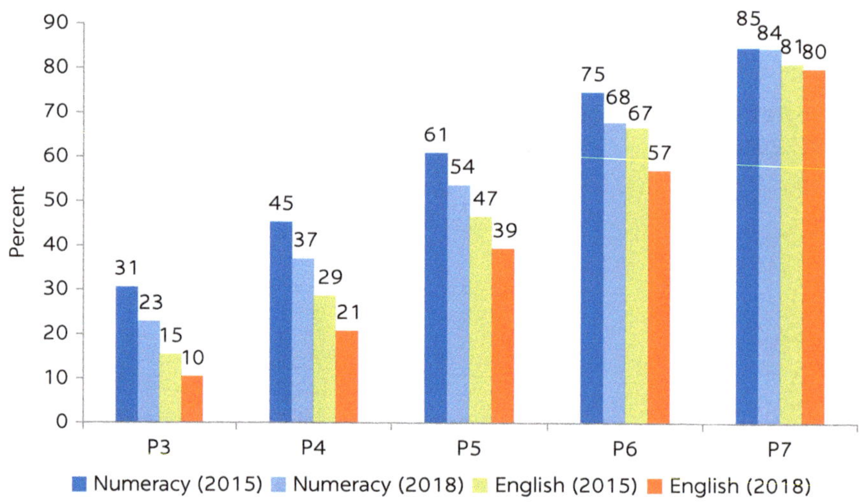

Sources: Twaweza 2011, 2015, 2018b.

terms remained slightly below the regional average for the participating countries.

The performance of Uganda's students on examinations taken at the end of primary and lower secondary school has varied over time. The percentage of students passing the PLE increased between 2002 and 2006, then dropped sharply until 2008. The percentage rose again until 2012, at which time the rate stabilized at about 87 percent.

Variations in the inputs provided in different LGs are associated with variations in levels of early learning. Correlations between the average government primary school size (enrollment divided by the number of schools) in an LG and the share of private sector enrollment in the Uwezo data suggest strongly that students in those LGs where a large percentage of children attend government schools rather than private sector schools attend larger schools. Further correlations suggest that larger average school size is associated with lower levels of learning. These correlations may indicate ways in which variations in the adequacy of financing can affect learning.

Regressions carried out for this study (World Bank 2021) suggest that lower poverty rates, lower repetition rates, and lower student-classroom ratios are correlated with higher NAPE, Uwezo, and PLE scores at the LG level. The positive correlation between the share of students who are out of school and higher scores suggests selection effects. Analysis using student scores on the most recent Uwezo assessment in government schools also suggests that household wealth quintile and textbook availability have a small effect and that grade progression has a very large effect.[69]

KEY POLICY DIRECTIONS TO STRENGTHEN THE DECENTRALIZED EDUCATION FINANCE SYSTEM

Although LGs have overseen an expansion in basic education, the analysis in this chapter has shown that the fiscal decentralization framework and systems for primary and secondary education currently in place are not delivering the results that were expected. Specifically:

- Despite extensive political and nominal fiscal decentralization, education trends reveal a sustained learning crisis, inequitable access to secondary education by both gender and socioeconomic status, inefficient distribution of both primary school teachers and classrooms, and inadequate levels of funding for nonwage expenditures.
- Fiscal decentralization is largely nominal; conditional grants from the central government to LGs provide virtually all funds for basic education service delivery and their use is centrally conditioned. LGs have few discretionary fiscal resources and little ability to raise them.
- After more than 20 years of fiscal decentralization, access to services across and within LGs is inequitable. Grants to cover wages are allocated on the basis of a bargaining process with little transparency between the central government and LGs. As a result, student-teacher ratios diverge sharply among LGs. The distribution of schools and classrooms is inequitable, and enrollment is linked to the limited availability of classrooms and teachers.
- Conditional grants for education are based on the number of students enrolled rather than on the number of school-age children. This is not unusual. Because enrollment is not independently verified, however, this incentivizes primary repetition and overenrollment and does nothing to improve learning, increase primary school completion, or improve the transition from primary to lower secondary.
- Although recent increases have started to reverse the impact of a decade of decline, the level of financing for education services is inadequate. In particular, the central government's allocation to capitation grants to primary schools remains very small and is inadequate for procuring enough of the instructional materials and other school operational inputs needed to improve learning.
- The capacity to implement education decentralization policies is weak because of inadequate funding for routine LG management and oversight of service delivery; insufficient capacity development and technical support to LGs for in-service or preservice teacher training and inspection officers or LG officers responsible for education service delivery; an absence of clarity about delegated responsibilities; and a lack of effective data and accountability mechanisms.

- Expanding access to secondary education without fixing systemic issues in primary education will compound inefficiencies in the sector. Policies aimed at achieving universal lower-secondary education are necessary but will sharply increase the education budget. However, expansion of funding for preprimary education is required to reduce early grade repetition, which may deliver subsequent efficiency gains.

There are some promising signs that progress is being made toward creating a finance system that enables LGs to deliver education effectively. The current use of formula-based allocations for the majority of nonwage allocations and safeguards to ensure that grants get to schools in a timely fashion puts Uganda ahead of many other countries.

The existing fiscal decentralization system needs to be better financed to enable adequacy and equity of service delivery and further strengthened with clear goals and incentives for key actors to improve teaching and learning (Pritchett 2015). Enrollment-based nonwage recurrent grants could incentivize access to education if the central government put in place an effective system for checking enrollment figures and incentives were established for the transition from primary to lower-secondary school and grade-to-grade progression. The formula could be revised to give greater weight to nonenrollment factors, which could enhance support for more disadvantaged areas and increase the nonwage resources provided to schools. In parallel, budgetary increases could be focused on teacher recruitment in underserved areas using objective criteria.

Efforts are needed on multiple fronts to improve the quality of early year education and to increase access to preschool education. Education is the engine of broad-based economic growth. The learning deficit evident in the current system cannot be addressed by focusing adequate spending only on those students who can transition to secondary education and on the lucky few who continue on to tertiary education. The education funding formula and teacher rosters should also include allocations for preschool enrollments. Failing to ensure learning quality and accountability costs money. Low attendance rates by primary school teachers and limited time on task together cost perhaps two-fifths of the entire primary school budget but yield little benefit. Providing insufficient resources for ECE and failing to effectively implement the curriculum together result in about half of all students repeating P1. Repetition throughout the system results in GERs far above 100 percent and in many children never reaching P7.

Funding for nonwage grants, funding per primary student, and funding for primary teaching colleges must be increased. Many aspects of the system remain virtually unfunded, including in-service teacher training and management and oversight of the system. Staffing is lower than is needed for effectiveness, including in primary schools, primary teaching colleges, and school inspectorates. As for the schools themselves, despite large increases since 2017–18, the government's overall funding levels per primary student remain among the lowest in the region and the world.

The central government must recognize that the greatest returns from resources come from sustained support for what happens in classrooms, rather than from building classrooms, recruiting teachers, and paying for supervisory visits to LGs. For example, the Ministry of Public Service must give more attention and support to decentralizing the payroll and to ensuring that teachers are distributed effectively and fairly among LGs. In turn, LG leaders should recognize that, even though the education budget is large compared to those of other sectors, it is not adequate to meet the country's education needs and should be a priority among LGs' own-financed expenditures. Despite recent funding increases and promising policy pronouncements, the central government does not yet provide LGs with the financing or capacity-building support needed to build a high-quality education system and has not yet granted enough financial and operational autonomy to either LGs or schools.

Access to lower-secondary schooling needs to be expanded in a cost-effective way. Discontinuing the subsidies paid for supporting students in private secondary schools could lead to a higher demand for places in government secondary schools; expanding government-implemented secondary education for all will require employing more teachers and building more schools than would be necessary if other delivery models remained available.

NOTES

1. Alasdair Fraser was a consultant on the Overseas Development Institute (ODI) technical assistance program. Views expressed in this chapter do not necessarily represent the views of the DFID or the UK Foreign Commonwealth and Development Office (FCDO), the government of Uganda, the ODI, or the World Bank.
2. Kan and Klasen (2018) document fewer years of schooling completed after the introduction of universal primary education (UPE).
3. Per capita income in Uganda was US$643 in 2019, and government revenue amounted to approximately 14 percent of gross domestic product (GDP). Government expenditures on education amount to 2.7 percent of GDP. Population growth is among the highest in the world, averaging over 3 percent annually between 2000 and 2017 (World Bank 2020).
4. The National Resistance Movement (NRM) Manifesto 2016–2021: Steady Progress: Taking Uganda to Modernity Through Jobs-Creation and Inclusive Development was promulgated in 2016.
5. Twaweza (2019a) found that more than one-fifth of students progressing to primary 7 (P7) are unable to read or do math at a primary 2 (P2) level.
6. Both Uwezo surveys and National Assessment of Progress in Education (NAPE) assessments reflect this pattern (UNEB 2014a).
7. The current system of LG grant support from the central government began in 1995 (Williamson 2010).
8. The IGFT Reform Program originated with the 2002 Fiscal Decentralization Strategy (FDS).
9. The average Ugandan child born in 2019 will complete seven years of schooling, the equivalent of only 4.5 years of quality schooling (World Bank 2019b). Moreover, learning outcomes may have worsened since the 2014 estimate on which this assessment is based.
10. In 2007, only 11 percent of primary schools in Uganda had more than 4 out of 6 essential conditions for effective teaching (Bashir et al. 2018).
11. As many as 30 to 40 percent of students in primary 1 (P1) are age 8 or older, and 41 to 52 percent (according to reports from teachers and parents) of P1 students repeat the grade (Weatherholt et al. 2019).
12. The gross enrollment rate for preprimary education was 14 percent. UNESCO Institute for Statistics (database), UNESCO, Paris (accessed August 2020), http://uis.unesco.org/en/country/ug.
13. The expenditure framework in the 2010–11 National Development Plan explicitly increased the share of the budget allocated to the energy and mineral development sector from 7 to 25 percent over four years, thus reducing the share to LG-delivered sectors including education. The full reduction was not implemented.
14. Government-aided private schools received "partnership" capitation grants for enrolled students until 2016–17, after which the grants started to be phased out, a process that is due to be completed in 2020–21.

15. The GER has been consistently high since shortly after UPE was introduced, which is a sign of inefficiency. This will be discussed further in the section titled *Education Challenges*.
16. Cities were given similar rights in 2015, but no cities had been created within the LG fiscal system as of June 2020. In practice, subdivision is to some extent controlled by central government.
17. Municipal LGs are treated as equivalent to district LGs in budgeting for education but not in LG legislation.
18. Districts that subdivide create two districts, the original "parent" district and a new "child" district.
19. According to the 2019–20 Budget (MoFPED 2019). As of 2020, 23.4 percent of LGs were municipal councils, and as of 2018, 23.8 percent of Ugandans lived in an urban area, including those governed by town councils and municipal councils.
20. Counts from the 2019–20 Budget (MoFPED 2019). Lower levels (parishes, cells, villages and zones) are not shown in figure 5.1.
21. Local Governments Act of 1997, part 1 (21).
22. Local Governments Act of 1997, part 2 (1).
23. Local Governments Act of 1997, part 2 (1).
24. Payroll management was decentralized to LGs starting in 2013–14, and pension and gratuities payments were decentralized starting in 2015–16.
25. Subnational revenue collection authority rests at the subcounty level, and these revenues may not be fully reflected in municipal and district budgets. See Green (2015).
26. Unspent balances held by the LGs must be returned to the central government at the end of the fiscal year, although LGs can ask the central government for extensions, particularly to complete capital projects.
27. Only in urban areas are these parental contributions formalized; parents are supposed to contribute U Sh 10,400 per term per student toward the cost of hiring additional workers, including contract teachers, under the UPE policy.
28. Karlan and Linden (2016) report a lower average of US$7 per pupil in 2012–13.
29. Only 2 percent of children age 14 had completed primary school; 90 percent were still in primary school.
30. Twaweza (2019a) reported that 21.2 percent of 4-year-olds and 33.8 percent of 5-year-olds were in school (many in P1), whereas Weatherholt et al. (2019) found that 34 percent of sampled P1 students had attended any form of preprimary schooling and just 13 percent had attended a registered early childhood education (ECE) program.
31. Cilliers et al. (2018a) find this to be true in Tanzania.
32. Population estimates for 2020 show that there is gender parity in the school-age population. Males ages 5 to 14 account for 14.6 percent of the national population, while females ages 5 to 14 account for 14.3 percent. The estimated primary school population (ages 6 to 12) is 3.73 million males and 3.63 million females, while for secondary education (ages 13 to 18), the numbers are 2.59 million and 2.66 million, respectively.
33. Defined as the number of students enrolled in S1 divided by the number of 13-year-olds in the population.
34. In mathematics, 48.7 percent of boys and 33.7 percent of girls performed "adequately" or better, while in biology, 26.9 percent of boys and 13.4 percent of girls performed "adequately" or better.
35. Coverage of the private sector in Uganda's education management information system (EMIS) is patchy, and the private sector predominates at the secondary level.
36. EGRAs orally assess basic foundation skills for literacy acquisition in early grade students, including prereading skills such as listening comprehension.
37. As of late 2020, the results from the 2018 NAPE for lower secondary students had not been published.
38. In addition, UNEB revised the NAPE methodology in 2018 so the scores are not comparable over time.
39. "Acceptable" in the report on Uganda is equivalent to level 5 of the SACMEQ scale. More than one-third of students have dropped out of school by P6 (see figure 5.6), which produces selection effects.
40. See Atuhurra and Alina (2018) for a description of curriculum and examination mismatch in Uganda.
41. The National Planning Authority (2018a) has claimed that, based on a small survey, 30 percent of teachers had never had any in-service professional development.

42. These are discussed in greater detail in the section titled *The IGFT in education*. All sectoral grants are conditional grants because LGs must spend them within the designated sector.
43. Although a participatory process was used in 2015 to develop allocation formulas for nonwage and development grants under the IGFT reform program, changes have been made annually, and decision-making power is retained by the central government.
44. A recent overhaul of the grant guidelines for the Discretionary Development Equalization Grant (DDEG), the multisectoral capital grant to LGs, may increase this share.
45. The current reform agenda builds on the Fiscal Decentralization Strategy (FDS) of 2002 and the Local Government Finance Commission (LGFC) review of 2012 and tackles issues outlined in a Public Expenditure Review conducted by the MoFPED and other agencies in 2013 (World Bank 2013). A definitive statement, the IGFT Reform Program document, is expected to be published as part of the Uganda Intergovernmental Fiscal Transfers (UgIFT) program.
46. The execution of budgeted transfers to LGs is excellent compared with most other developing countries. Transparency about releases of transfers to LGs is also high, as is budget transparency generally in Uganda (International Budget Partnership 2017).
47. The World Bank currently supports the IGFT with US$500 million. The Department for International Development (DFID) provided technical assistance support through the Overseas Development Institute (ODI) for the fiscal decentralization reform program to the MoFPED and other agencies to operationalize the IGFT.
48. The Uganda Teacher and School Effectiveness Program (UTSEP), a project funded by the Global Partnership for Education and the World Bank, added a further U Sh 56 billion in 2019–20.
49. UNESCO's Institute for Statistics places Uganda 130th among 134 reporting countries for primary education spending per enrollee from 2013 to 2019. UNESCO Institute for Statistics (database), UNESCO, Paris (accessed September 2020), http://uis.unesco.org/en/country/ug.
50. The fixed component was U Sh 900,000 per year in 2007–08 and in 2019–20 was set at U Sh 1.35 million.
51. The number of lower local governments (LLGs) increased from 968 as of 2010 (Uganda Bureau of Statistics 2012) to 1,506 as of 2019–20 (Budget 2019–20, Online Transfer Information Management System (database), Republic of Uganda (accessed September 2020), otims.go.ug.
52. A full description of the formulas is available in World Bank (2021).
53. The performance assessment score is also used to allocate 15 percent to 50 percent of other sectors' development grants.
54. Education sector performance measure is based on: (1) human resource planning and management; (2) monitoring and inspection; (3) governance and oversight transparency and accountability; (4) procurement and contract management; (5) financial management and reporting; and (6) social and environmental safeguards (Office of the Prime Minister 2019, 2020).
55. See MoFPED, Local Government Performance Improvement Plans, budget.go.ug/PIPs. Reimbursements to the government from Uganda Intergovernmental Fiscal Transfers (UgIFT) program, a large multisector World Bank project, are conditional on the successful implementation of performance assessments. Other requirements are the transparent allocation and execution of agreed formulas (aimed at improving equity) and annual real-term, nonwage budget increases until 2023–24 (aimed at improving adequacy), of which three years have already been completed.
56. See World Bank (2020) for a projection of classroom needs.
57. Cilliers, Mbiti, and Zeitlin (2018a) found that, in Tanzania, after examination results were widely published, the performance of schools in the bottom quintile of achievement in each district improved partly because less-able pupils were strategically excluded from taking the examination.
58. Donor work funded by the DFID (Crawfurd and Elks 2018) has attempted to shift the government's secondary school focus toward rewarding the most-improved secondary schools with additional capitation grants, based on the difference between the PLE and later exam attainment, but this has not been integrated into the grant's design.
59. Publications, National Curriculum Development Center, Kampala (accessed July 2020), https://www.ncdc.go.ug/publications.

60. Budget 2019–20, Online Transfer Information Management System (database), Republic of Uganda (accessed August 2020), otims.go.ug.
61. Household consumption figures for 2019 are from World Bank (2019a). Household spending shares on different levels of education are from the National Education Accounts of 2014 (Government of Uganda et al. 2016). Shares of household education spending for 2012–13 and 2016–17 are from the national household surveys of those years (Uganda Bureau of Statistics 2016a, 2016b).
62. The number of government-supported secondary students in both partnership and government schools has declined by an estimated 30 percent over the past four years according to capitation grant records.
63. Also as reported in the 2018 Uwezo survey as an average of 933 classes (Twaweza 2018b). However, the survey methods differed as the Service Delivery Indicators study recorded "in-use books" and made classroom visits unannounced (Wane and Martin 2016).
64. For a discussion of the likely resource capacity of a district in the first few years after it has been created, see Green (2015).
65. Urban areas are expected to more than triple in total population before 2050, and rural areas are expected to increase their total population by 46 percent (United Nations 2018).
66. Wage grant values per teacher are similar across LGs, making this a good proxy for the student-teacher ratio.
67. P1 was not used because of the disguised preprimary enrollment and chronic repetition issues described in Weatherholt et al. (2019) and Brunette et al. (2017). LGs are not disaggregated in the enrollment data in the 2013 and 2014 Statistical Abstracts or in the PLE 2019 outcomes. We used 2013, rather than 2014, data for enrollment, because of recording issues in the Statistical Abstract.
68. Similar sample-based SACMEQ assessments were carried out in 2000 and 2007.
69. See Twaweza (2019a) for a full explanation.

REFERENCES

ACODE-U. 2020. "An Analysis of the Proposed National Budget FY 2019/20 and Proposals for Reallocation." Advocates Coalition for Development and Environment, Kampala, Uganda.

Allen, R., P. Elks, R. Outhred, and P. Varley. 2016. "Uganda's Assessment System: A Road Map for Enhancing Assessment in Education." Health & Education Advice & Resource Team, Oxford, UK.

Altinyelkin, H.K. 2010. "A Converging Pedagogy in the Developing World? Insights from Uganda and Turkey." In *Global Education Policy and International Development: New Agendas, Issues and Policies*, edited by A. Verger, M. Novelli, and H.K. Altinyelken, 201–22. London: Bloomsbury.

Atuhurra, J., and V. Alina. 2018. "Basic Education Curriculum Effectiveness in East Africa: A Descriptive Analysis of Primary Mathematics in Uganda Using the 'Surveys of Enacted Curriculum'." Working Paper 87583, University Library of Munich, Munich, Germany.

Atuhurra, J., and M. Kaffenburger. 2019. "System (In)Coherence Seen Through a Curriculum Lens: Ugandan Teachers Face Conflicting Demands from Curriculum and Examination Bodies." Research on Improving Systems of Education (RISE) (blog), May 23, https://riseprogramme.org/blog/system_incoherence_curriculum.

Bashir, S., M. Lockheed, E. Ninan, and J.P. Tan. 2018. *Facing Forward: Schooling for Learning in Sub-Saharan Africa*. Washington, DC: World Bank.

Bold, T., M. Kimenyi, G. Mwabu, A. Ng'ang'a, and J. Sandefur. 2018. "Experimental Evidence on Scaling Up Education Reforms in Kenya." *Journal of Political Economy* 168 (December): 1–20.

Brunette, T., L. Crouch, C. Cummiskey, A. Dick, C. Henny, R. Jordan, K. Merseth, R. Nabacwa, J. Pressley, and T. Weatherholt. 2017. "Repetition of Primary 1 and Pre-primary Education in Uganda." Working Paper, 2017-02, RTI International, Research Triangle Park, NC.

Brunette, T., B. Piper, R. Jordan, S. King, and R. Nabacwa. 2019. "The Impact of Mother Tongue Reading Instruction in Twelve Ugandan Languages and the Role of Language Complexity,

Socioeconomic Factors, and Program Implementation." *Comparative Education Review* 63 (4): 591–612.

Cilliers, J., I. Mbiti, and A. Zeitlin. 2018a. "Can Public Rankings Improve School Performance? Evidence from a Nationwide Reform in Tanzania." Working Paper 19/027, Research on Improving Systems of Education (RISE), Oxford, UK.

Cilliers, J., I. Kasirye, C. Leaver, P.M. Serneels, and A. Zeitlin. 2018b. "Pay for Locally Monitored Performance? A Welfare Analysis for Teacher Attendance in Ugandan Primary Schools." *Journal of Public Economics* 167 (November): 69–90.

Crawfurd, L., and P. Elks. 2018. "Testing the Feasibility of a Value-Added Model of School Quality in a Low-Income Country." *Development Policy Review* 37 (4): 470–85.

Eaton, K., K. Kaiser, and P. Smoke. 2010. *The Political Economy of Decentralization Reforms: Implications for Aid Effectiveness*. Washington, DC: World Bank.

Eble, A., I. Fazzio. R. Lumsdaine, P. Boone, B. Bouy, J. Hsieh, C. Jayanty, S. Johnson, and A.F. Silva. 2020. "Large Learning Gains in Pockets of Extreme Poverty: Experimental Evidence from Guinea Bissau." Working Paper 27799, National Bureau of Economic Research, Cambridge, MA.

Eble, A, C. Frost, A. Camara, B. Bouy, M. Bah, M. Sivaraman, J. Hsieh, C. Jayanty, T. Brady, P. Gawron, P. Boone, and D. Elbourne. 2021. "How Much Can We Remedy Very Low Learning Levels in Rural Parts of Low-Income Countries? Impact and Generalizability of a Multi-Pronged Para-Teacher Intervention from a Cluster-Randomized Trial in The Gambia." *Journal of Development Economics* 148 (January): 102539.

Ernst and Young. 2019. *Situational Analysis of the Teachers' Payroll Management and Capacity Building Needs Assessment for Payroll Managers Under UTSEP*. London: Ernst & Young.

Evans, D., and F. Yuan. 2017. "The Economic Returns to Interventions that Increase Learning." 2018 World Development Report Background Paper, World Bank, Washington, DC.

Government of Uganda, International Institute for Educational Planning and IIEP-Pôle de Dakar. 2016. *National Education Accounts Report*. Kampala: Government of Uganda.

Green, E. 2015. "Decentralization and Development in Contemporary Uganda." *Regional and Federal Studies* 5 (5): 491–508.

Hares, S., A.L. Minardi, and J. Rossiter. 2020. "Grade Repetition in Developing Countries: Repeat to Fail or Second Time's a Charm?" Center for Global Development, Washington, DC.

Hedger, E., T. Williamson, T. Muzoora, and J. Stroh. 2010. "Sector Budget Support in Practice: Education Sector in Uganda." Overseas Development Institute, London.

Hubbard, P. 2007. "Putting the Power of Transparency in Context: Information's Role in Reducing Corruption in Uganda's Education Sector." Working Paper 136, Center for Global Development, Washington, DC.

IHME (Institute for Health Metrics and Evaluation). 2018. *Global Burden of Disease Study 2017 Population Estimates 1950–2017*. Seattle, WA: IHME.

International Budget Partnership. 2017. *Open Budget Survey 2017*. Washington, DC: International Budget Partnership.

Kan, S., and S. Klasen. 2018. "Evaluating UPE in Uganda: School Fee Abolition and Educational Outcomes." Discussion Paper 245, Courant Research Centre, Göttingen, Germany.

Kanjee, A., and S. Acana. 2013. "Developing the Enabling Context for Student Assessment in Uganda." SABER-Student Assessment Working Paper 8, World Bank, Washington, DC.

Karlan, D., and L. Linden, 2016 "Loose Knots: Strong versus Weak Commitments to Save for Education in Uganda." NBER Working Paper 19863, National Bureau of Economic Research, Cambridge, MA.

Kayabwe, S., and R. Nabacwa with J. Eilor and R.W. Mugeni. 2014. *The Use and Usefulness of School Grants: Lessons from Uganda*." Paris: International Institute for Educational Planning.

Kerwin, J., and R. Thornton. 2020. "Making the Grade: The Sensitivity of Education Program Effectiveness to Input Choices and Outcome Measures." Working Paper. http://dx.doi .org/10.2139/ssrn.3002723.

Lewis, J. 2014. "When Decentralization Leads to Recentralization: Subnational State Transformation in Uganda." *Regional and Federal Studies* 24 (5): 571–88.

Lockheed, M. 2008. "Measuring Progress with Tests of Learning: Pros and Cons for 'Cash on Delivery Aid' in Education." Working Paper 147, Center for Global Development, Washington, DC.

Long, C. 2019. "Note on Education Sector" (unpublished manuscript July 2020, Overseas Development Institute, London.

——. 2020. "Intergovernmental Fiscal Transfers Equity (unpublished manuscript July 2020), Overseas Development Institute, London.

Lwanga, M., E. Munyambonera, and M. Guloba. 2018. "Effectiveness of the Public Payroll Decentralisation Reforms in Uganda." Research Series 141, Economic Policy Research Center, Kampala.

Manuel, M., D. Coppard, A. Dodd, H. Desai, R. Watts, Z. Christensen, and S. Manea. 2019. "Subnational Investment in Human Capital." Overseas Development Institute, London, and Development Initiatives, Bristol, UK.

MoES (Ministry of Education and Sports). 2013. *Addressing the Challenges of Providing Quality Education for All in Uganda (SACMEQ Project IV Report)*. Kampala: MoES.

——. 2016. *Uganda Secondary School Survey Data*. (unpublished), Kampala: MoES.

——. 2019a. *Education Sector Strategic Plan 2020–25*. Draft. Kampala: MoES.

——. 2019b. Budgeting and Implementation Guidelines for Primary and Secondary Schools, Kampala: MoES.

MoFPED (Ministry of Finance, Planning and Economic Development). 2020a. "Local Government Performance Assessments." budget.go.ug/lgpas.

——. 2020b. "Government of Uganda Intergovernmental Fiscal Transfer Reform Program: Update for PFM Working Group." Presentation by Ministry of Finance Planning, and Economic Development, Kampala, Uganda, June 15.

——. 2020c. "2019/20 Indicative Planning Figures." Kampala: MoFPED. https://budget.go.ug/sites/default/files/19_20_Approved_IPFs_LG_Grants.xlsx.

——. 2020d. *Approved Estimates of Revenue and Expenditure (Recurrent and Development. Vol. II: Local Government Votes*. Kampala: MoFPED. https://budget.go.ug/sites/default/files/National%20Budget%20docs/LG%20%20APPRO VED%20ESTIMATES%20BOOK%20%20FY%202019-20%20FINAL%20COPY.pdf.

MoFPED and ODI (Overseas Development Institute). 2016. "Reform to Transfers to Local Governments in Uganda: Allocation Formulae and Simulations Medium Term Roll-out Plan, November 2016." (unpublished note), MoFPED and ODI, Kampala, Uganda and London, UK.

MoLG (Ministry of Local Government). 2014. *Decentralization and Local Development in Uganda*. Kampala: MoLG.

Najjumba, I.M., J. Habyarimana, and C.L. Bunjo. 2013. *Improving Learning in Uganda, Volume 3: School-Based Management, Policy, and Functionality*. Washington, DC: World Bank.

National Planning Authority. 2018a. *Comprehensive Evaluation of the Universal Primary Education (UPE) Policy. Thematic Report 3: Primary Teacher Training for Producing Competent Teachers to Deliver UPE*. Kampala: National Planning Authority.

——. 2018b. *Comprehensive Evaluation of the Universal Primary Education (UPE) Policy. Thematic Report 4: Efficacy of School Inspection in Supporting the Delivery of UPE*. Kampala: National Planning Authority.

——. 2018c. *Comprehensive Evaluation of the Universal Primary Education (UPE) Policy. Thematic Report 5: Financing and Costing of UPE*. Kampala: National Planning Authority.

Nguyen, T. 2008. "Information, Role Models and Perceived Returns to Education: Experimental Evidence from Madagascar." Job Market Paper, Massachusetts Institute of Technology, Cambridge, MA.

O'Donoghue, J., L. Crawfurd, J. Makaaru, P. Otieno, and R. Perakis. 2019. *A Review of Uganda's Universal Secondary Education Public Private Partnership Programme*. London: Education Partnerships Group.

Office of the Prime Minister. 2019. *Local Government Performance Assessment Report—FY 2018/2019 National Synthesis Report*." Kampala: Office of the Prime Minister.

——. 2020. *Local Government Performance Assessment Report—FY 2019/2020 National Synthesis Report*. Kampala: Office of the Prime Minister.

Piper, B., J. Destefano, E. Kinyanjui, and S. Ong'ele. 2018. "Scaling Up Successfully: Lessons from Kenya's Tusome National Literacy Program." *Journal of Educational Change* 19 (August): 293–321.

Pritchett, L. 2015. "Creating Education Systems Coherent for Learning Outcomes: Making the Transition from Schooling to Learning." Working Paper 15/005, Research on Improving Systems of Education (RISE), Oxford, UK.

Rasul, I., and D. Rogger. 2018. "Management of Bureaucrats and Public Service Delivery: Evidence from the Nigerian Civil Service." *Economic Journal* 128 (608): 413–46.

Rasul, I., D. Rogger, and M. Williams. 2018. "Management and Bureaucratic Effectiveness: Evidence from the Ghanaian Civil Service." Policy Research Working Paper 8595, World Bank, Washington, DC.

Reinikka, R., and J. Svensson. 2004. "Local Capture: Evidence from a Central Government Transfer Program in Uganda." *Quarterly Journal of Economics* 119 (2): 679–706.

Simson, R. 2017a. "(Under)privileged Bureaucrats? The Changing Fortunes of Public Servants in Kenya, Tanzania and Uganda, 1960–2010." PhD diss., London School of Economics and Political Science. http://etheses.lse.ac.uk/3618/.

Simson, R. 2017b. "Supplementary Material, (Under)privileged Bureaucrats? The Changing Fortunes of Public Servants in Kenya, Tanzania and Uganda, 1960–2010." PhD diss., London School of Economics and Political Science. http://etheses.lse.ac.uk/3618/.

Steffensen, J., P. Tidemand, H. Naitore, E. Ssewankambo, and E. Mwaipopo. 2004. *Final Synthesis Report—A Comparative Analysis of Decentralization in Kenya, Tanzania, and Uganda*. Washington, DC: World Bank.

Twaweza. 2011. "Uwezo Uganda Learning Assessment Dataset." Dar es Salaam, Tanzania. https://www.uwezo.net/publications/datasets/.

——. 2012. "Uwezo Uganda Learning Assessment Dataset." Dar es Salaam, Tanzania. https://www.uwezo.net/publications/datasets/.

——. 2015. "Uwezo Uganda Learning Assessment Dataset." Dar es Salaam, Tanzania. https://www.uwezo.net/publications/datasets/.

——. 2016a. *Are Our Children Learning? Five Stories on the State of Education in Uganda in 2015 and Beyond: The Fifth Uwezo Annual Learning Assessment Report*. Dar es Salaam, Tanzania.

——. 2016b. *Are Our Children Learning? Uwezo Uganda Sixth Learning Assessment Report*. Dar es Salaam, Tanzania.

——. 2018a. "Preparing the Next Generation: Ugandans' Experiences and Opinions on Education." Research Brief 8, Dar es Salaam, Tanzania.

——. 2018b. "Uwezo Uganda Eighth Learning Assessment Dataset." Dar es Salaam, Tanzania. https://www.uwezo.net/publications/datasets/.

——. 2019a. *Are our Children Learning? Uwezo Uganda Eighth Learning Assessment Report*. Dar es Salaam, Tanzania.

——. 2019b. *Uwezo Learning Assessment in Refugee Contexts in Uganda*. Dar es Salaam, Tanzania.

Uganda Bureau of Statistics. 2012. "Sub-County Boundaries, Uganda, 2010." http://purl.stanford.edu/yg674hb9000.

——. 2013. *Uganda National Household Survey Report*. Kampala: Uganda Bureau of Statistics. https://ubos.org/wp-content/uploads/publications/04_20182012_13_UNHS_Final_Report.pdf.

——. 2016a. *Uganda National Household Survey Report*. Figure 3.4. Kampala: Uganda Bureau of Statistics. https://www.ubos.org/wp-content/uploads/publications/03_20182016_UNHS_FINAL_REPORT.pdf.

——. 2016b. Uganda National Household Survey Dataset. World Bank Microdata Catalog. https://microdata.worldbank.org/index.php/catalog/3460/.

——. 2017. *Education: A Means for Population Transformation*. Kampala: Uganda Bureau of Statistics.

Uganda Bureau of Statistics and ICF. 2018. *Uganda Demographic and Health Survey 2016*. Kampala, Uganda, and Rockville, MD: Uganda Bureau of Statistics and ICF.

UNEB (Uganda National Examinations Board). 2014a. *Achievement of Primary School Pupils in Uganda in Numeracy and Literacy in English*. Kampala: UNEB.

——. 2014b. *Achievement of S2 Students in Uganda in English Language, Mathematics and Biology*. Kampala: UNEB.

——. 2018. *Achievement of Primary School Pupils in Uganda in Numeracy and Literacy in English*. Kampala: UNEB.

United Nations. 2018. *World Population Prospects*. New York: United Nations.

UNICEF and Ministry of Education Rwanda. 2019. *Understanding Dropout and Repetition in Rwanda*. New York: UNICEF.

Universalia. 2020. *Summative Evaluation of GPE's Country-Level Support to Education: Uganda*. Quebec, Canada: Universalia.

Wane, W., and G. Martin. 2016. "Education Service Delivery in Uganda." Service Delivery Indicators Report AUS5359, World Bank, Washington, DC.

Weatherholt, T., R. Jordan, L. Crouch, E. Barnett, and J. Pressley. 2019. "Challenge and Drivers of Over-Enrollment in the Early Years of Primary School in Uganda." *International Journal of Early Childhood* 51 (April): 23–40.

Whitworth, A., and T. Williamson. 2010. "Overview of Ugandan Economic Reform since 1986." In *Uganda's Economic Reforms: Insider Accounts*, edited by F. Kuteesa, Emmanuel Tumusiime-Mutebile, Alan Whitworth, and Tim Williamson, 1–34. Oxford: Oxford University Press.

Williams, M. 2017. "The Political Economy of Unfinished Development Projects: Corruption, Clientelism, or Collective Choice?" *American Political Science Review* 111 (4): 705–23.

Williamson, T. 2010. "Fiscal Decentralization." In *Uganda's Economic Reforms: Insider Accounts*, edited by F. Kuteesa, Emmanuel Tumusiime-Mutebile, Alan Whitworth, and Tim Williamson, 310–36. Oxford: Oxford University Press.

World Bank. 2013. *Service Delivery with More Districts in Uganda: Fiscal Challenges and Opportunities for Reforms*. Washington, DC: World Bank.

World Bank. 2014. *Uganda Teacher and School Effectiveness Project Appraisal Document*. Washington, DC: World Bank.

——. 2017. *Uganda Intergovernmental Fiscal Transfers Program Project Appraisal Document*. Washington, DC: World Bank.

——. 2019a. "Households and NPISHs Final Consumption Expenditure (% of GDP)—Uganda." https://data.worldbank.org/indicator/NE.CON.PRVT.ZS?locations=UG.

——. 2019b. *Uganda Economic Update, 13th Edition, May 2019: Economic Development and Human Capital in Uganda—A Case for Investing More in Education*. Washington, DC: World Bank.

——. 2020. *Uganda Demographic Study*. Washington, DC: World Bank.

——. 2021. *The Role of Intergovernmental Fiscal Transfers in Improving Education Outcomes. Annex*. Washington, DC: World Bank.

6 Indonesia Case Study

BLANE LEWIS

District-level spending in Indonesia positively affects both access to and the quality of education. How much is spent in each district is largely determined by the magnitude of fiscal transfers that each district receives from the central government. These intergovernmental fiscal transfers are allocated very inequitably across districts, which vary in their ability to achieve the education objectives desired by their citizens. This ultimately results in an inequitable distribution of education outcomes. A number of perverse incentives embedded in the current system of fiscal transfers encourage overspending on teachers at the expense of expenditure on other inputs, including teaching materials and capital. The resulting inefficiency of spending suggests that many districts could supply more and better education, even without any additional resources. As a technical matter, both the inequitable allocations and the perverse incentives could easily be overcome, but politically, they are significantly more challenging to solve. The use of performance-based grants might be one way to improve education outcomes, but these are likely to be difficult both to design and to execute. Furthermore, performance-based funding has been used in other sectors in Indonesia with little success. Not only are technical reforms to the intergovernmental fiscal system needed, but longstanding governance challenges at the local level will also need to be overcome.

INTRODUCTION

In countries where the public sector is decentralized, local government spending can positively influence service outcomes, including those in education, at least under certain conditions (Lewis 2017b). In most decentralized developing countries, local government spending is to a large extent financed by intergovernmental fiscal transfers of various kinds from the central government. Thus, it is important to know exactly how these transfers affect local spending, which in turn influences education outcomes. If transfers that result in local government spending help determine education outcomes, it is crucial that those transfers be allocated equitably across local governments to assure that they have a fair chance of achieving education objectives desired by their citizens. It is also important to analyze the incentives and disincentives that transfers offer to local governments to ensure that the money is spent efficiently to maximize the supply of education services demanded by citizens.

Indonesia is an interesting case in this context. Indonesia is a unitary country and for many years was one of the most centralized countries in the world (Lewis 2014a). The government launched an extremely ambitious program of public sector decentralization in 2001. Since then, the 34 provinces and, especially, the 508 districts (excluding the capital city of Jakarta) have assumed substantial responsibility for delivering public services in education and other sectors. Provincial and district spending has increased from 26 percent of total public spending in 2001 to about 42 percent in 2018 and as of 2020 accounts for about 50 percent of total public sector expenditures, net of subsidies and interest charges. District spending makes up approximately 75 percent of the subnational total. Tables 6.1, 6.2, and 6.3 show the profile of subnational expenditure in rupiah, as a percent of total public spending, and as a percent of gross domestic product (GDP) between 2001 and 2018.

TABLE 6.1 **Spending, by level of government, 2001–18**

Rp tn, constant 2010

	2001	2003	2005	2007	2009	2011	2013	2015	2017	2018
Central	612.2	539.3	627.5	694.2	679.4	822.3	971.6	922.2	923.1	1,022.6
Province	48.5	68.6	61.2	82.9	87.4	95.1	137.4	145.4	179.4	188.2
District	167.7	229.3	229.2	317.3	327.5	359.6	465.7	519.6	548.4	538.0
Total	828.4	837.7	917.9	1,094.5	1,094.3	1,277.1	1,574.7	1,587.2	1,650.8	1,748.7

Source: World Bank calculations based on Ministry of Finance data.
Note: Central and province spending, exclude transfers to lower level government. Rp = Indonesian rupiah; tn = trillions.

TABLE 6.2 **Spending, by level of government as a share of total government spending, 2001–18**

percent

	2001	2003	2005	2007	2009	2011	2013	2015	2017	2018
Central	74	64	68	63	62	64	62	58	56	58
Province	6	8	7	8	8	7	9	9	11	11
District	20	27	25	29	30	28	30	33	33	31
Total	100	100	100	100	100	100	100	100	100	100

Source: World Bank calculations based on Ministry of Finance data.
Note: Figures may not total due to rounding.

TABLE 6.3 **Spending, by level of government as a share of GDP, 2001–18**

percent

	2001	2003	2005	2007	2009	2011	2013	2015	2017	2018
Central	15	12	12	12	11	11	12	10	9	10
Province	1	2	1	1	1	1	2	2	2	2
District	4	5	4	5	5	5	6	6	6	5
Total	20	18	13	19	17	18	19	18	17	17

Source: World Bank calculations based on Ministry of Finance data.
Note: GDP = gross domestic product.

However, there has been significantly less decentralization of authority over tax revenues. About 53 percent of provincial spending and about 85 percent of combined provincial and district spending is financed by intergovernmental transfers. Transfers to provincial and district governments account for about one-third of the central government's spending budget. Tables 6.4, 6.5, and 6.6 show the share of transfers in the central, provincial, and district budgets between 2001 and 2018.

Intergovernmental fiscal transfers in Indonesia are distributed very inequitably across districts (Lewis 2014a). The district with the highest per capita transfers, for example, has 40 times more transfer revenue than the district with the lowest per capita transfers, after adjusting for the differential costs of service delivery between districts. In addition, incentives and disincentives are embedded in the intergovernmental transfer system. Perverse incentives in the general purpose grant, for example, encourage district governments to overspend on

TABLE 6.4 **Total fiscal transfers, 2001–18**

Rp tn, constant 2010

	2001	2003	2005	2007	2009	2011	2013	2015	2017	2018
Fiscal transfers, province	36.1	45.2	49.3	49.1	57.9	61.7	89.4	89.8	127.6	124.3
Fiscal transfers, district	170.8	202.9	196.1	301.2	304.1	345.7	397.1	446.4	459.3	462.2
Total fiscal transfers, subnational	206.9	248.1	245.5	350.4	361.9	407.4	486.5	536.2	586.9	586.5
Revenue, province	59.4	82.0	97.5	83.5	106.9	130.0	176.2	189.2	236.5	235.9
Revenue, district	183.1	220.2	214.0	325.2	328.9	378.7	445.4	514.8	550.3	542.4
Total revenue, subnational	242.5	302.2	311.5	408.7	435.8	508.7	621.6	704.0	786.8	778.2

Source: World Bank calculations based on Ministry of Finance data.
Note: Fiscal transfers include all types of transfers received by district or province budget (total revenue minus own-source revenue). Fiscal transfers at district level include some transfers from the province-level government; therefore, the total fiscal transfers in table 6.4 will be different from the total transfer to regions recorded in the central government budget. Figures may not total due to rounding. Rp = Indonesian rupiah; tn = trillions.

TABLE 6.5 **Total fiscal transfers as a share of subnational government revenue, 2001–18**

percent

	2001	2003	2005	2007	2009	2011	2013	2015	2017	2018
Fiscal transfers, province government	61	55	51	59	54	47	51	47	54	53
Fiscal transfers, district government	93	92	92	93	92	91	89	87	83	85
Total fiscal transfers, subnational government	85	82	79	86	83	80	78	76	75	75

Source: World Bank calculations based on Ministry of Finance data.
Note: Fiscal transfers include all types of transfers received by district or province budget (total revenue minus own-source revenue). Fiscal transfers at district level include some transfers from the province-level government; therefore, the total fiscal transfers in table 6.4 will be different from the total transfer to regions recorded in the central government budget. Figures may not total due to rounding.

TABLE 6.6 **Total fiscal transfers as a share of central government expenditure, 2001–18**

	2001	2003	2005	2007	2009	2011	2013	2015	2017	2018
Transfers to regions (Rp tn 2010 constant)	190.5	253.3	261.4	348.4	333.4	382.7	438.5	485.6	541.3	532.5
Total central government expenditure (Rp tn 2010 constant)	802.7	792.5	888.9	1,042.6	1,012.8	1,205.1	1,410.2	1,407.8	1,464.3	1,555.0
Fiscal transfers as a share of central government expenditure (%)	24	32	29	33	33	32	31	34	37	34

Source: World Bank calculations based on Ministry of Finance data.
Note: Transfers to regions are as recorded in the central government budget. Total central government expenditure includes transfer, subsidy, and interest payments. Rp = Indonesian rupiah; tn = trillions.

personnel, such as teachers, at the expense of spending on other important inputs, including capital. This reduces the efficiency of district expenditures. Both features of intergovernmental fiscal transfers will be discussed in more detail.

Provinces and districts spend a large share of their intergovernmental transfers and other revenues on education. As of 2018, in provinces, this share was about 37 percent of the total, while in districts the share was about 28 percent of their available funds. Note that provincial budget shares increased significantly in 2017 with the transfer of responsibility for senior secondary school from districts to provinces that year, and district education budget shares declined considerably as a result of this reassignment. Overall, about 30 percent of all subnational spending was allocated to the education sector as of 2018. Tables 6.7 and 6.8 show the importance of education spending in provincial and district budgets between 2001 and 2018.

Access to education has increased steadily, on average, in recent years. Between 2005 and 2017, net enrollment rates for primary, junior secondary, and senior secondary school increased from 90 to 96 percent, 62 to 76 percent, and 41 to 61 percent, respectively. However, improvements in the quality of locally provided education have been much more modest. Between 2003 and 2015, Indonesia's performance on the Organisation for Economic Co-operation and Development's (OECD) Program for International Student Assessment (PISA) increased by 15 points in reading and mathematics and by about 8 points in science, but its average PISA score (395 points) still lags considerably behind the OECD average (490 points). Indonesia is near the bottom of the list of all countries that participate in PISA.

The two challenges facing Indonesia are: (1) the need to allocate intergovernmental transfers more equitably and to expunge any perverse incentives embedded in the system; and (2) to continue to expand education access, especially at the secondary school level, while at the same time enhancing at a substantially more rapid rate the quality of education at all levels. These challenges are inextricably linked.

TABLE 6.7 Subnational education spending, 2001–18

Rp tn, constant 2010

	2001	2003	2005	2007	2009	2011	2013	2015	2017	2018
Province	3.5	7.8	6.7	11.8	10.7	15.2	16.6	22.2	65.6	70.6
District	59.8	74.1	70.4	88.9	103.9	136.6	158.4	169.8	150.1	148.1
Subnational (province and district)	63.3	81.9	77.2	100.6	114.6	151.7	192.0	192.0	215.7	218.7

Source: World Bank calculations based on Ministry of Finance data.
Note: Figures may not total due to rounding. Rp = Indonesian rupiah; tn = trillions.

TABLE 6.8 Subnational education spending as a share of subnational budgets, 2001–18

percent

	2001	2003	2005	2007	2003	2011	2013	2015	2017	2018
Province	7.2	113	11.0	14.2	12.2	15.9	12.1	15.3	36.6	37.5
District	35.7	32.3	30.7	28.0	31.7	38.0	34.0	32.7	27.4	27.5
Subnational (province and district)	29.3	27.4	26.6	25.1	27.6	33.4	29.0	28.9	29.6	30.1

Source: World Bank calculations based on Ministry of Finance data.

EDUCATION DECENTRALIZATION

The education system in Indonesia is the world's fourth largest, after those of China, India, and the United States. At the pretertiary level, which consists of early childhood education and primary and secondary school, it encompasses about 250,000 schools, 50 million students, and 2.8 million teachers. Early childhood education in Indonesia comprises two years of schooling, and primary comprises six years, followed by three years each for junior and senior secondary school. Primary and secondary school are compulsory (World Bank 2013).

Public and private secular schools dominate the primary and secondary education system with about 85 percent of the total. Islamic schools make up the remaining 15 percent. Secular schools are under the general authority of the Ministry of Education and Culture (MoEC); the Ministry of Religion (MoRA) oversees Islamic schools (OECD 2015). The average public school has over 500 students, twice as many as the average private school. Islamic schools are about half the size of private secular schools. Student teacher ratios (STR) in Indonesia are among the lowest in the world. The STRs for public and private secular primary and secondary schools are 20:1 and 12:1, respectively; the STR for Islamic schools is 7:1 (OECD 2015). However, these averages mask significant variations across Indonesia's regions.

Responsibilities for education service delivery

Prior to 2001, schools were directly managed by the central government education ministry and its geographically deconcentrated field offices. After 2001, when authority over most public services was decentralized to subnational governments, districts assumed the bulk of responsibility for managing early childhood, primary, junior secondary, and senior secondary public schools, including those functions related to curriculum development and teachers. In 2017, authority for managing public senior secondary schools was reassigned to the provinces.

Nevertheless, the central government retains considerable authority over education decisions. The Ministry of Administrative and Bureaucratic Reform (MenPAN) and the National Civil Service Board (BKN) determine national civil servant teacher quotas and play key roles in hiring teachers. The MoEC sets national quotas for teacher certification and takes the lead on implementing the government's teacher certification program and coordinating its activities with the districts. The MoEC also sets regulations and technical guidelines for teacher deployment. Responsibility for the redistribution of teachers across schools is held by districts (within districts), provinces (between districts), and the central government (between provinces) (World Bank 2013). The MoEC outlines general principles for the curriculum, which can be adapted locally.

The MoEC retains the responsibility for developing national education policies and setting national education standards for all non-Islamic pretertiary schools. It also has a full mandate over all functions related to tertiary education. The MoRA manages all aspects of Islamic schooling. Table 6.9 summarizes the responsibilities for nontertiary and non-Islamic education across government levels, including financing.

TABLE 6.9 **Education responsibilities across levels of government**

FUNCTION	CENTRAL	PROVINCE	DISTRICT
Policy	√	n.a.	n.a.
Financing	√	√	√
Curriculum	√	√	√
Facilities and infrastructure	n.a.	√	√
Teachers and education staff	√	√	√
Quality assurance	√	n.a.	n.a.

Source: World Bank.
Note: √ = responsibility of the government level specified; n.a. = not applicable.

Financing education spending

Districts and provinces have significant authority over how they manage their budgets across all functions, including education. Both districts and provinces are constitutionally mandated to spend at least 20 percent of their budgets on education but are otherwise free to spend their budgets according to their wishes and the demands of their citizens.[1] The majority of districts spend significantly more than the mandated 20 percent of their budgets on education. Provinces were less likely to adhere to the 20 percent rule, but since they took over responsibility for senior secondary schools, the majority of provincial governments have adhered to this mandate. At present, there are no sanctions for not meeting the spending mandate.

The funding that districts and provinces use to finance the delivery of education services comes from both own-source revenues and intergovernmental transfers. Own-source revenues make up just under half of provincial budgets but only about 15 percent of district budgets. The most important transfers from the central government to the subnational level are tax and nontax revenue sharing (DBH), a general purpose grant (DAU), and specific purpose grants (DAK), which now include teacher certification grants and the School Operational Assistance Program (BOS).[2] These transfers will be discussed in more detail in the next section. The MoEC also spends some of its own budget directly in the regions through the Dekonsentrasi (Dekon) and Tugas Pembantuan (TP) mechanisms or on its own account. These funds can be thought of as in-kind transfers. Dekon is organized through the provinces and is supposed to be used only for routine activities. TP is coadministered by provinces, districts and schools (or a combination) and is meant to be used only for capital works. Dekon and TP do not form part of either provincial or district budgets; the funds are administered through the central government's project accounts. Both mechanisms are meant to finance the central government's education responsibilities in the provinces and districts, although this rule is widely breached in practice (Lewis 2016). Direct spending by the central government in the provinces and districts, to build schools for example, also contravenes the law but is nevertheless widely practiced. Finally, the MoRA directly finances Islamic schooling through its decentralized offices at the provincial level. Figure 6.1 maps the flow of funds from the major sources of revenue that finance education spending at the subnational level. Overall, the figure illustrates the fractured nature of funding faced by districts. Such fragmentation creates major challenges for local government planning, budget formulation and execution, and education service delivery (Lewis 2013).

FIGURE 6.1
Public transfers and funds flows

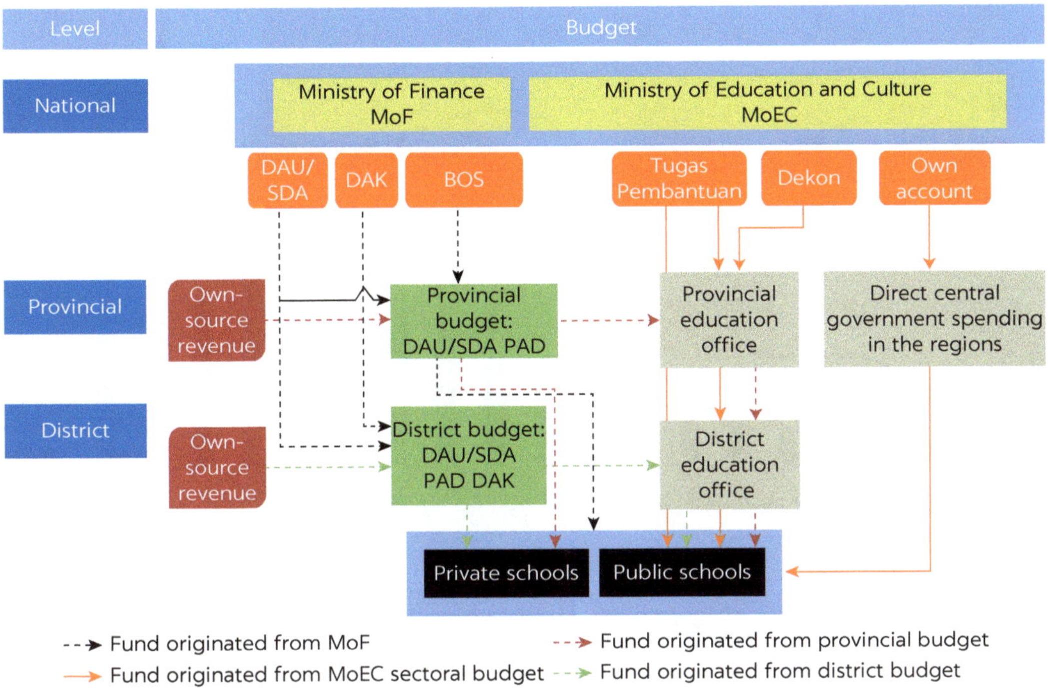

Source: Adapted from World Bank 2013.
Note: Teacher certification grants are allocated directly to districts in the same manner as DAK. Fund flows to Islamic schools, which receive funds directly from the Ministry of Religion (MoRA), are not shown. BOS = School Operational Assistance Program; DAK = specific purpose grant; DAU = general purpose grant; MoEC = Ministry of Education and Culture; MoF = Ministry of Finance; SDA = natural resource revenues; PAD = pendapatan asli daerah (own-source revenue).

Figure 6.2 illustrates trends in total public spending on education since 2001. Total education spending has increased significantly over the past nearly two decades. Consolidated education expenditures (national and subnational spending combined) have risen from 11 percent to 18 percent of total public sector spending. Education spending as a percentage of GDP increased from 2.2 percent in 2001, peaked at 3.4 percent in 2015, and declined to 3.1 percent in 2018. As previously noted, the bulk of education spending is carried out at the subnational level, mostly by districts.

It is difficult to determine the extent to which education spending in Indonesia is "adequate." It is clear, however, that Indonesia spends considerably less on education than other countries in the region as a percentage of GDP, including Thailand, China, Malaysia, Vietnam, Mongolia, Lao People's Democratic Republic, Papua New Guinea, and Timor-Leste (World Bank 2019a). The education spending shortfall results at least in part from the relatively small size of the public sector in Indonesia. This, in turn, is a function of Indonesia's comparatively low tax-to-GDP ratio. Total public spending relative to GDP was only about 15 percent as of 2020, considerably lower than other countries in the region.

Figure 6.3 shows how total public sector spending across a number of important government functions was distributed between the central, provincial, and district governments in 2016. Subnational governments dominate spending in the education sector. Education expenditures by districts and provinces make up about 56 percent and 6 percent of the total, respectively.

FIGURE 6.2

Education spending in Indonesia, 2001–18

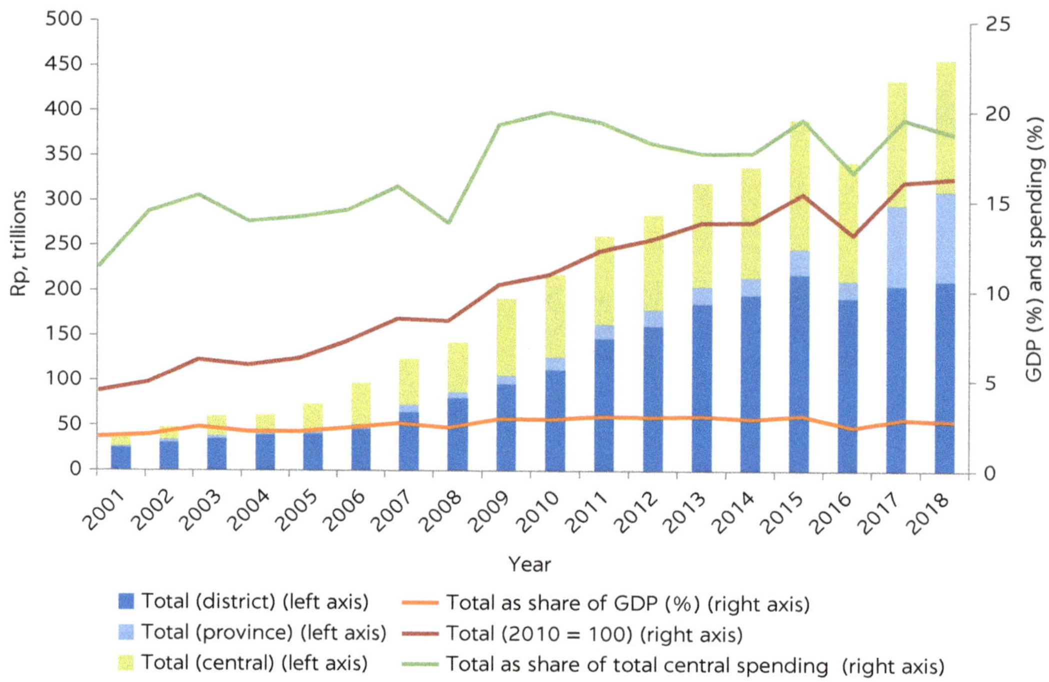

Source: World Bank based on Ministry of Finance data.
Note: Central government data represent audited realized spending. Subnational data (province and district) represent realized data, except for the province level in 2015, which is the budgeted amount. Realized spending data may not capture subnational education spending that was coded under "general administration" such as, for example, BOS and education administrator salaries. BOS = School Operational Assistance Program; GDP = gross domestic product; Rp = Indonesian rupiah.

FIGURE 6.3

Share of general government expenditure, by level of government, 2016

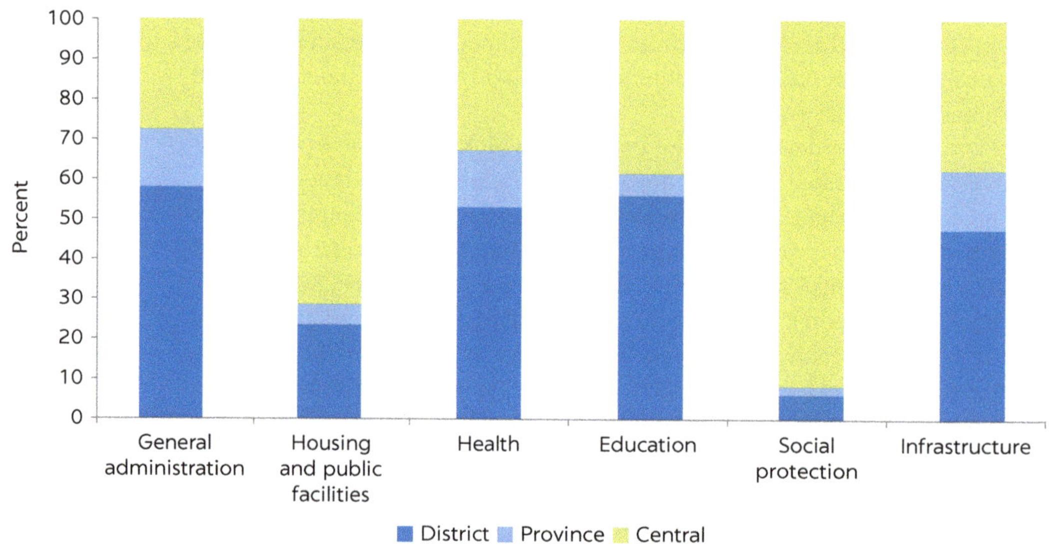

Source: World Bank Consolidated Fiscal Database using Ministry of Finance data.
Note: General administration at the central level excludes subsidies and interest payments. School Operational Assistance Program (BOS) spending may be classified as general administration spending for some subnational governments.

Provinces took over responsibility for senior secondary education in 2017, and, as a result, their share of the education budget increased and the districts' share declined. Overall, the subnational share of education spending has remained reasonably constant since decentralization started in 2001 at between 60 and 68 percent. See tables 6.10, 6.11, 6.12, and 6.13.

TABLE 6.10 **Subnational education spending, 2001–18**

Rp tn, constant 2010

	2001	2003	2005	2007	2009	2011	2013	2015	2017	2018
Province	3.48	7.76	6.72	11.76	10.71	15.17	16.56	22.23	65.59	70.60
District	59.31	74.13	70.43	88.89	103.59	136.56	158.40	169 82	150.10	148.11
Subnational (province and district)	63.29	81.88	77.16	100.65	114.59	151.73	174.96	192.05	215.70	218.71

Source: World Bank Consolidated Fiscal Database using Ministry of Finance data.
Note: Figures may not total due to rounding. Rp = Indonesian rupiah; tn = trillions.

TABLE 6.11 **Subnational education spending as a share of total subnational spending, 2001–18**

percent

	2001	2003	2005	2007	2009	2011	2013	2015	2017	2018
Province	1.6	2.6	2.3	2.9	2.6	3.3	2.7	3.3	9.0	9.7
District	27.7	24.8	24.3	22.2	25.0	30.0	26.3	25.5	20.6	20.4
Province and district	29.3	27.4	26.6	25.1	27.6	33.4	29.0	28.9	29.6	30.1

Source: World Bank Consolidated Fiscal Database using Ministry of Finance data.
Note: Figures may not total due to rounding.

TABLE 6.12 **Education spending, by level of government, 2001–18**

Rp tn, constant 2010

	2001	2003	2005	2007	2009	2011	2013	2015	2017	2018
Central	30.01	44.63	50.92	69.94	91.75	91.06	98.23	111.94	101.04	102.54
Province	3.48	7.76	6.72	11.76	10.71	15.17	16.56	22.23	65.59	70.60
District	59.81	74.13	70.43	88.89	103.8.9	136.56	158.40	169 32	150.10	148.11
Total	93.30	126.51	128.08	170.59	206.35	242.78	273.20	303.99	316.74	321.26

Source: World Bank Consolidated Fiscal Database using Ministry of Finance data.
Note: Figures may not total due to rounding. Rp = Indonesian rupiah; tn = trillions.

TABLE 6.13 **Spending by level of government as a share of total education spending, 2001–18**

percent

	2001	2003	2005	2007	2009	2011	2013	2015	2017	2018
Central	32	35	40	41	44	38	36	37	32	32
Province	4	6	5	7	5	6	6	7	21	22
District	64	59	55	52	50	56	58	56	47	46
Total	100	100	100	100	100	100	100	100	100	100

Source: World Bank Consolidated Fiscal Database using Ministry of Finance data.
Note: Figures may not total due to rounding.

Education outcomes and challenges

Access to all levels of schooling have increased significantly over recent years. Figure 6.4 illustrates the trends in net enrollment rates for primary, junior secondary, and senior secondary school from 2005 to 2016. The net enrollment rate for primary school was already high by 2005 (91 percent) and had increased further by 2016 (96 percent). Net enrollment rates for junior and senior secondary school rose from 62 percent and 41 percent to 76 percent and 61 percent, respectively, over the period.

Improvements to the quality of education have been less evident. Figure 6.5 shows Indonesia's scores on the PISA math, reading, and science modules from 2003 to 2015. Although some progress is apparent, the improvements have been quite modest. Among the 70 countries that take the PISA, Indonesia remains near the bottom of the list, ranking 64th, 62nd, and 63rd in math, reading, and science, respectively. At current rates of improvement, it will take about 50, 69, and 134 years, respectively, for Indonesian students to reach the averages in those three areas of testing (World Bank 2019a).

FIGURE 6.4

Net enrollment rates, 2005–16

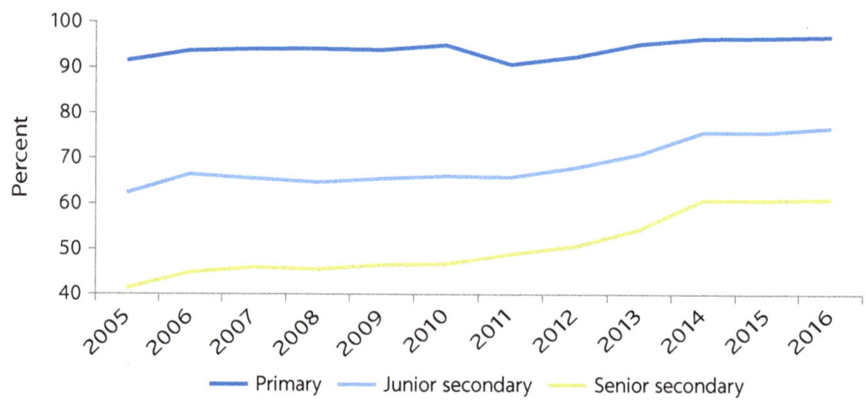

Source: World Bank calculations based on Central Bureau Statistics data.

FIGURE 6.5

Indonesia's PISA scores, 2003–15

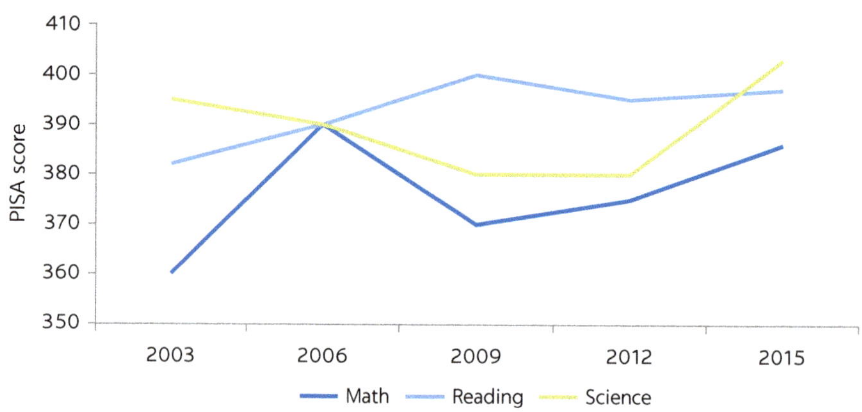

Source: World Bank 2019a.
Note: PISA = Programme for International Student Assessment.

The challenge for Indonesia moving forward is to continue to expand access to education, especially at the secondary school level, while substantially improving the quality of education at all levels. Achieving both objectives will depend at least in part on how education services are financed, especially through the intergovernmental fiscal system, discussed in the next section.

FISCAL TRANSFER MECHANISMS

The Indonesia system of intergovernmental fiscal transfers comprises DBH, DAU, DAK, and other kinds of grants. DBH, through which the central government distributes a portion of national tax revenues to local governments, involves both tax and nontax mechanisms. The tax mechanisms (*pajak*) consist of revenue from property taxes, the personal income tax, and the tobacco excise tax;[3] the nontax mechanisms consist of natural resource revenues (SDA) from forestry, fisheries, mining (geothermal and other), and gas and oil. The DAU is a fiscal equalization instrument. There are two types of DAK: capital (DAK *fisik*) and noncapital (DAK non-*fisik*). Officially, districts that receive a capital grant are meant to provide counterpart funds in the amount of 5 percent of the grant, but in recent years the matching component seems to have been relaxed. The noncapital DAK consist of teacher certification grants and BOS. Other grants include special autonomy funds (Dana Otsus) for Ache, Papua, and West Papua; a special transfer to Yogyakarta (Dana Keistemewaan); and a small regional incentive grant (DID). Provinces also make transfers to districts from their own-source revenue (raised from motor vehicle taxes, a fuel tax, a surface water tax, and a cigarette tax).[4] All transfers except the DID are judged according to inputs rather than results. The DID is the government's only ongoing incentive-based (performance) grant, although other transfers—especially the DAU—include implicit (and perverse) incentives. The focus in the present subsection is on DBH, the DAU, and DAK (*fisik*) grants.

Transfer objectives

Each of the major transfers has its own specific objectives. Officially, DBH is intended to reduce fiscal imbalances between the central government and the subnational governments by raising the revenue of districts and provinces. However, the real aim of the DBH is political. Its introduction fulfilled the political objective of persuading resource-rich provinces not to secede from the nation at the beginning of decentralization, and this is a continuing objective. The clear aim of the DAU is to increase equity in fiscal resources among provinces and among districts according to their fiscal needs and capacities, and particularly to counteract the very concentrated distribution of DBH allocations in certain provinces and districts. The stated objectives of the DAK are: (1) to reduce inefficiencies that are a function of spatial (benefit) spillovers, especially in education, health, and infrastructure; (2) promote the application of minimum service standards across all functions; and (3) foster economic stabilization by stimulating increased capital spending. In practice, DAK allocations are very strongly associated with DAU distributions; therefore, implicitly at least, the DAK also reduces inequity (see figure 6.6). Overall, the system of intergovernmental transfers in Indonesia is mostly concerned with correcting horizontal fiscal imbalances.

FIGURE 6.6
DAK and DAU transfers

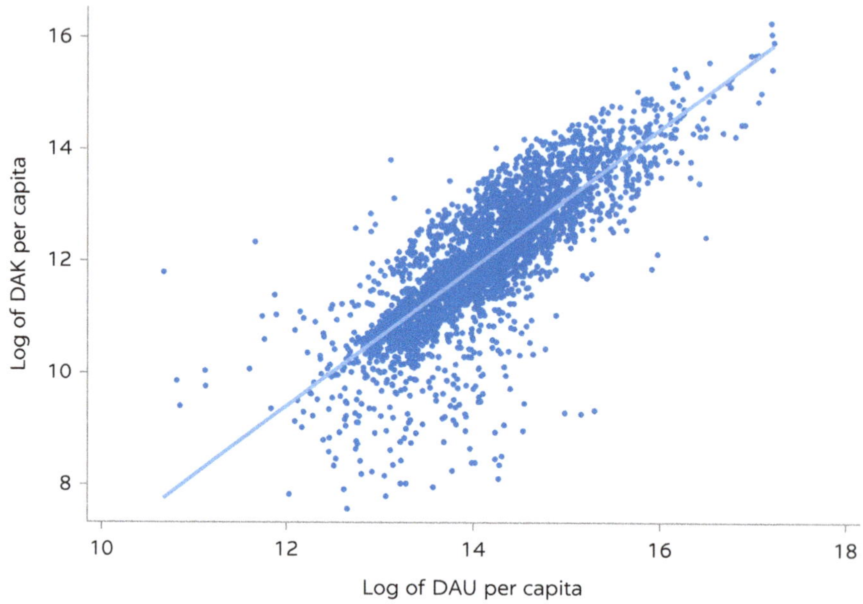

Source: World Bank calculations based on data from the Ministry of Finance.
Note: DAK = specific purpose grant; DAU = general purpose grant.

Pools of finance for transfers

DBH pools of finance are set as fixed percentages of total actual tax and natural resource revenues. Provincial pools are applicable only for their originating provinces, that is, those provinces in which the revenues are produced. For many shared revenues, district pools also apply only to their originating districts, while for other revenues, district pools vary across originating and non-originating districts within their originating provinces. Finally, for some revenues, pools apply to all districts, whether originating or not. Table 6.14 provides the details.

The pool of finance for the DAU is fixed in law as a minimum of 26 percent of total planned domestic revenues, net of amounts otherwise shared with subnational governments (for example, through the various revenue sharing schemes). Recently, the DAU pool has been set at about 27 percent of revenues. Districts receive 90 percent of the total pool and provinces get 10 percent.[5]

The pool of finance for the DAK varies from year to year based on negotiations between the Ministry of Finance and the National Parliament. The Parliament takes a keen interest in DAK transfers and has argued strongly for an increase in their funding levels in the national budget. This may be due at least in part to the significant rent-seeking opportunities for national and local politicians associated with the transfer (Lewis 2014b).

Transfer allocation mechanisms

DBH revenues are, for the most part, are allocated to the places where the revenues were generated. Thus, all revenues raised within a given province are returned to the province of origin except for revenues associated with fisheries. The same is true for districts in most cases, although some revenues are

TABLE 6.14 **Revenue sharing pools of finance as a share of total revenues**

percent

REVENUE SOURCE	ORIGINATING PROVINCES	ORIGINATING DISTRICTS	ALL DISTRICTS IN ORIGINATING PROVINCES	ALL DISTRICTS (EQUAL SHARES)
Property tax	16.2	64.8	n.a.	10.0
Property transfer tax	16.0	64.0	n.a.	20.0
Personal income tax	8.0	12.0	n.a.	n.a.
Tobacco excise tax	0.4	0.8	0.8	n.a.
Forestry license	16.0	64.0	n.a.	n.a.
Forestry royalty	16.0	32.0	32.0	n.a.
Fisheries	n.a.	n.a.	n.a.	80.0
Mining royalty	16.0	64.0	n.a.	n.a.
Mining land rent	16.0	32.0	32.0	n.a.
Geothermal mining	16.0	32.0	32.0	n.a.
Oil	3.1	6.2	6.2	n.a.
Gas	6.1	12.2	12.2	n.a.

Source: Republic of Indonesia, Law 33/2004 on Fiscal Balance.
Note: n.a. = not applicable.

distributed to nonoriginating districts within the originating provinces. Revenue from fisheries is allocated in equal proportions across all districts in the country as is some portion of the revenues raised from the property tax and the property transfer tax. Note that the allocations make no allowances for differences in population size between provinces and districts.

DBH transfers are distributed quarterly. The first two tranches are based on some (usually equal) percentage of provisionally estimated amounts, while the third and fourth tranches are derived from the difference between definitive totals to be allocated (actual revenues) and the previous tranches. Occasionally, further adjustments must be made to align distributions with actual revenues; these are made in the first quarter of the following year.

Allocations of the DAU to the districts comprise a basic allocation and a fiscal gap allocation.[6] (Allocations of the DAU to provinces follow similar procedures.) The relative sizes of the two separate allocations in total DAU distributions are determined administratively every year. In recent years, the basic allocation has amounted to about 45 percent of the total.

The basic allocation is determined as a simple function of a district's spending on personnel as a share of total spending by all districts on personnel. The fiscal gap allocation is derived from the difference between a district's fiscal needs and its fiscal capacity. Its fiscal needs are estimated based on a number of proxies including population size, geographic area, poverty, a service delivery cost index, the human development index, and per capita gross regional domestic product (GRDP). Fiscal capacity is the sum of a district's other revenues, consisting of own-source revenues and tax and nontax revenue sharing. DAK and other transfer revenues are not included in the estimation of district fiscal capacity. DAU allocations are distributed monthly in equal installments, usually in the first week of the month.

There are two special points to note regarding DAU allocations. First, allocations are based on place-based norms not per capita norms, similar to DBH allocations. This results in very unequal per capita distribution of transfers.

Second, at least two possible perverse incentives are embedded in the DAU allocation formula. The first involves spending on personnel. The current allocation formula implies that the more a district spends on personnel relative to other districts, the larger its basic DAU allocation (and thus its total DAU allocation) will be. This gives districts a strong incentive to increase their spending on staff such as teachers, even if their student-teacher ratios are already low, which may have negative consequences for other aspects of education quality. The second potential disincentive involves the generation of own-source revenues. The fiscal gap allocation formula reduces the DAU allocation as a district's own-source revenues increase. This would seem to give the districts a strong disincentive to increase their own-source revenues.

Lewis and Smoke (2017) provide some empirical evidence to show that, in practice, the DAU allocation formula leads districts to increase their personnel spending but not to reduce their generation of own-source revenues. Districts or provinces may want to increase their own-source revenue for other reasons; for example, this income is typically used to fund variable staff allowances. These motivations may prevail over any disincentives embodied in the allocation formula (Lewis and Smoke 2017).

Until recently allocations of the DAK *fisik* were determined by three sets of criteria: general, special, and technical. The general criteria focused on the fiscal capacity of regions. The special criteria involved conditions in districts or provinces, including whether they were from lagging, border, or coastal regions. The technical criteria concentrated on general local infrastructure conditions as assessed by the line ministries.

Since 2017, however, DAK *fisik* allocations have been based on proposals for capital projects from districts. (Provinces no longer receive DAK *fisik* transfers.) The proposals are vetted by technical ministries and Bappenas, the national planning ministry, and the final decisions are made by the Ministry of Finance. The grants are distributed in three tranches over the course of the year: 30 percent of total planned allocations in February if the districts have approved their budgets and reported on their previous year's grant spending; 45 percent after the districts demonstrate that 90 percent of the first tranche has been spent; and 25 percent after the districts demonstrate that 90 percent of the second tranche has been spent.

DAK non-*fisik* allocations follow a different distribution system. Teacher certification grants are uniform lump sum transfers allocated to districts based on the number of teachers being certified. The allocations are made on a quarterly basis. BOS is a capitation (per student) grant allocated directly to schools (through provinces) on a monthly basis.

Table 6.15 summarizes transfer objectives, types, pool determination, pool distribution, and use of transferred funds for DBH, the DAU, and DAK *fisik* specific purpose grants.

Transfer allocation trends

Figure 6.7 shows the magnitude of transfers over time. Transfers have increased significantly in the aggregate. The DAU is the largest individual transfer, although its comparative significance has declined somewhat over the years. The DAK has become relatively more important in recent years, while DBH has become comparatively less significant. Own-source revenue has grown the fastest of all revenue sources, and its importance in budgets has grown.

TABLE 6.15 **Objectives, types, pool determination and distribution, and use of transfers**

	DBH	DAU	DAK
Objectives	Adequacy and political	Equity	Efficiency and equity
Types	General	General	Specific (input-based) matching, closed ended
Pool determination	Fixed percentages of national revenues	Minimum 26% of domestic revenues	Ad hoc
Pool distribution	Point of origin	Formula	By rules; since 2017, by proposal
Use	No restriction (except 0.5% of oil and gas revenue sharing should be allocated to education)	No restriction	Capital

Source: World Bank.
Note: DAK = specific purpose grant; DAU = general purpose grant; DBH = tax and nontax revenue sharing.

FIGURE 6.7
Composition of district revenue, 2001–18

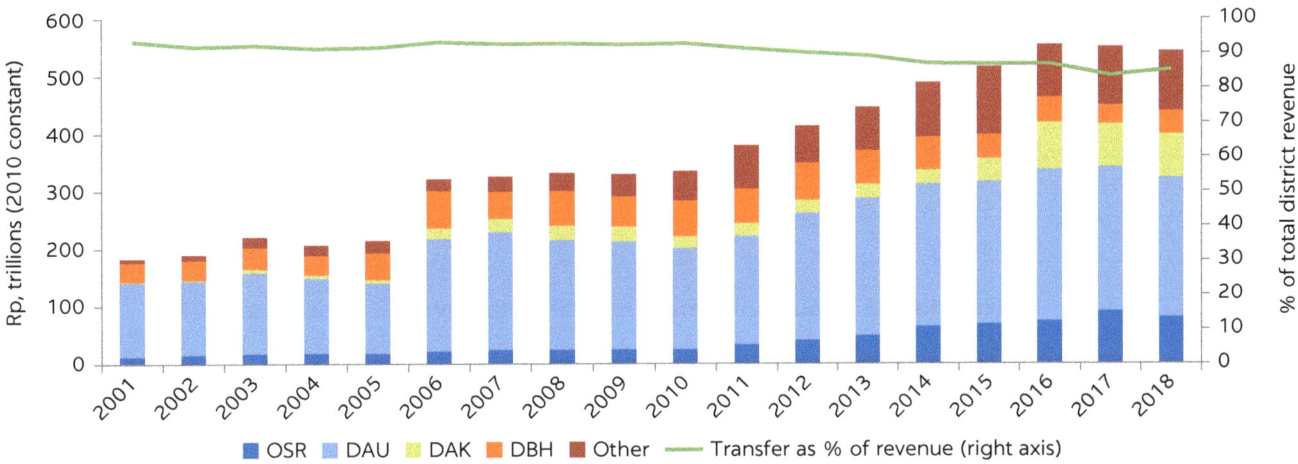

Source: World Bank calculations based data from the Ministry of Finance.
Note: DAK = specific purpose grant; DAU = general purpose grant; DBH = tax and nontax revenue sharing; OSR = own-source revenue; Rp = Indonesian rupiah.

Nevertheless, transfers still make up the vast bulk of district revenues, amounting to about 85 percent.

Transfer distribution among districts

The allocation formula for the DAU is not per capita based. In other words, allocations are made with the objective of equalizing the net fiscal capacities of districts rather than of individuals within districts. The formulas for DBH and DAK also are not per capita based. The consequence is that the amount of transfer per capita declines significantly for districts with higher populations. Figure 6.8 illustrates the striking relationship between districts' transfers and their population sizes.

This antipopulation bias has significant implications for the distributional equity of transfers. Figure 6.9 shows a strong negative relationship between transfers and population, with the negative relationship holding for all revenue sources, but particularly for the DAU.

FIGURE 6.8
Transfers and population size

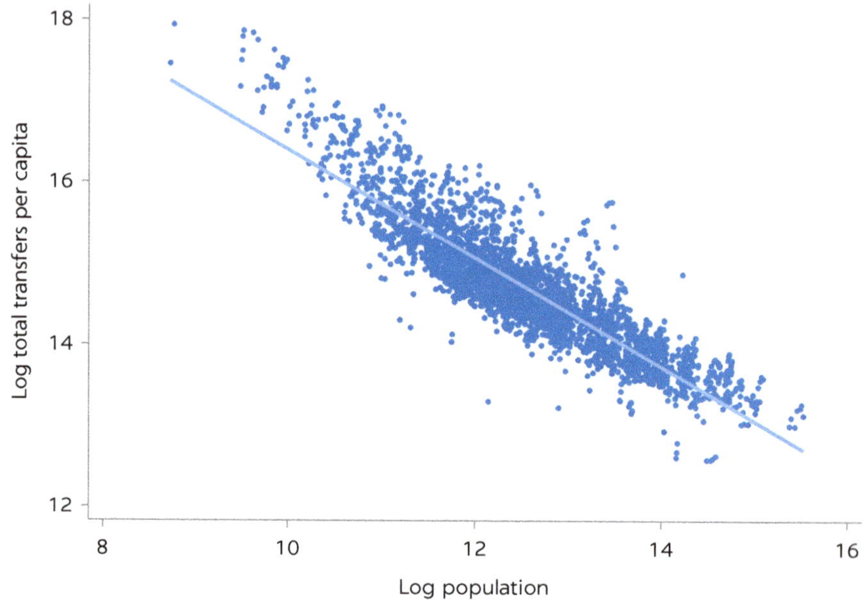

Source: World Bank calculations based data from the Ministry of Finance.

FIGURE 6.9
Median district population versus median total revenue per capita, 2017

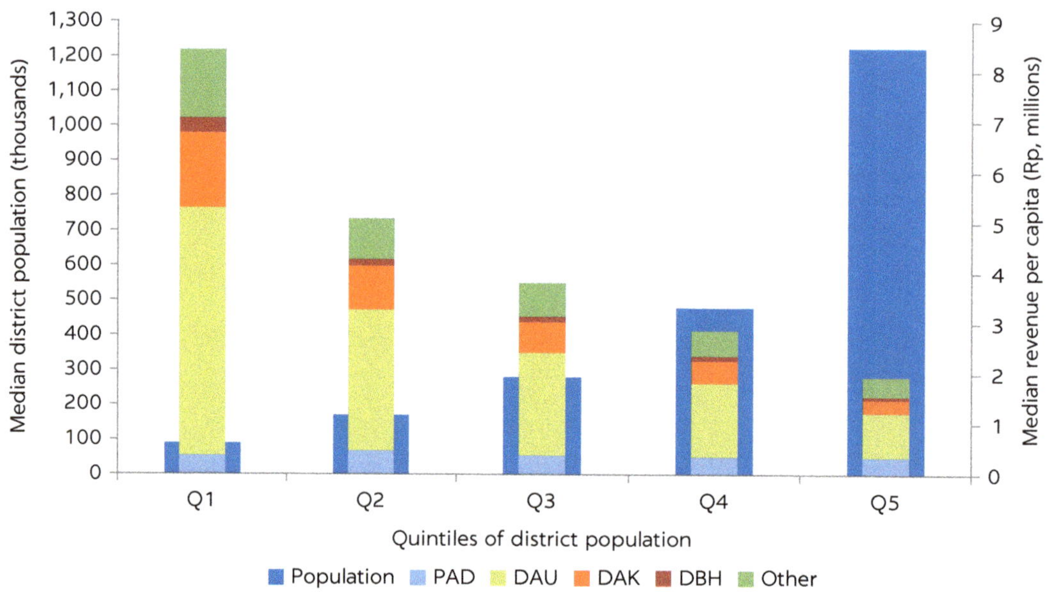

Source: World Bank 2019b.
Note: DAK = specific purpose grant; DAU = general purpose grant; DBH = tax and nontax revenue sharing; PAD = pendapatan asli daerah (own-source revenues); Rp = Indonesian rupiah.

FIGURE 6.10

District transfers per capita adjusted for service delivery costs, 2016

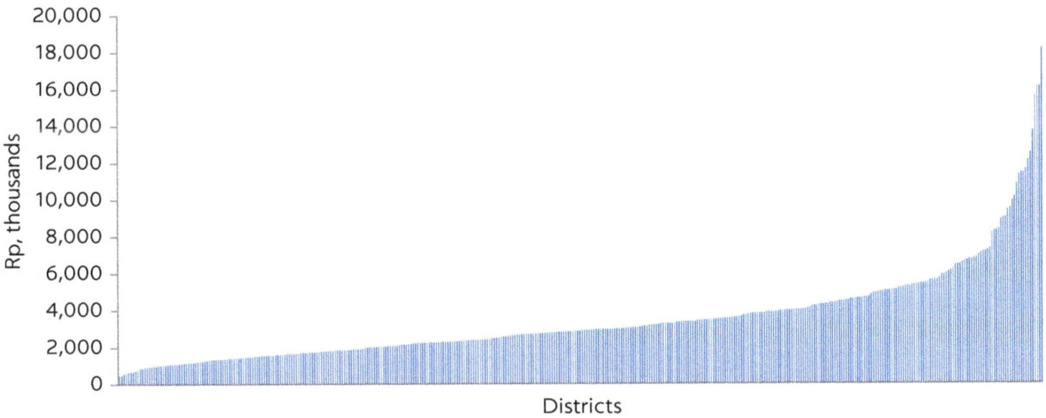

Source: World Bank calculations based on data from Ministry of Finance.
Note: Rp = Indonesian rupiah.

Specifically, the district with the highest transfers per capita has 68 times the amount of transfers as the district with the lowest transfers per capita. Of course, per capita transfers should not necessarily be equivalent in all districts because the cost of delivering services varies from place to place. However, even after adjusting for differences in service delivery costs, using the Ministry of Finance's service cost index, which is used in the DAU allocation formula, transfers are still very inequitably distributed across districts. After adjusting for service delivery costs, the ratio of the highest per capita transfers to the lowest is 40.

Figure 6.10 shows average district per capita transfers after adjusting for service costs ranked from lowest to highest; the unequal distribution of per capita transfers can clearly be seen.

EFFECTS OF TRANSFERS AND SPENDING ON SERVICE OUTCOMES

Given the inequitable distribution of intergovernmental fiscal transfers across districts and given the assumption that transfers strongly influence education expenditure, it might be expected that district education spending per capita would also be inequitable. Figure 6.11 shows district education spending per capita in 2016 after adjusting for service delivery costs. The figure demonstrates that the distribution of education spending is indeed quite unequal, although not as unequal as the per capita allocation of transfers. The maximum-minimum ratio for district per capita spending on education is 21.

The ranking of districts by how much they spend on education has some similarities to the ranking of districts by how much they receive in intergovernmental transfers. The simple correlation coefficient between the two distributions is 0.88. This provides some initial, albeit rather crude, evidence to suggest that intergovernmental transfers may determine education spending to some extent.

Figure 6.12 shows the relationship between per capita transfers to districts (in total and by specific instrument) and total per capita district spending.

FIGURE 6.11

District education spending per capita adjusted for service delivery costs, 2016

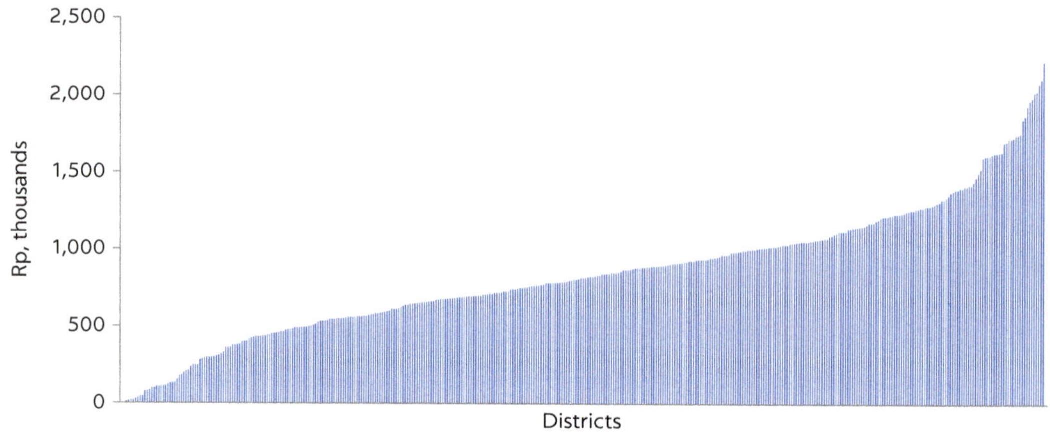

Source: World Bank calculations based on data from Ministry of Finance.
Note: Rp = Indonesian rupiah.

FIGURE 6.12

Transfers and total spending

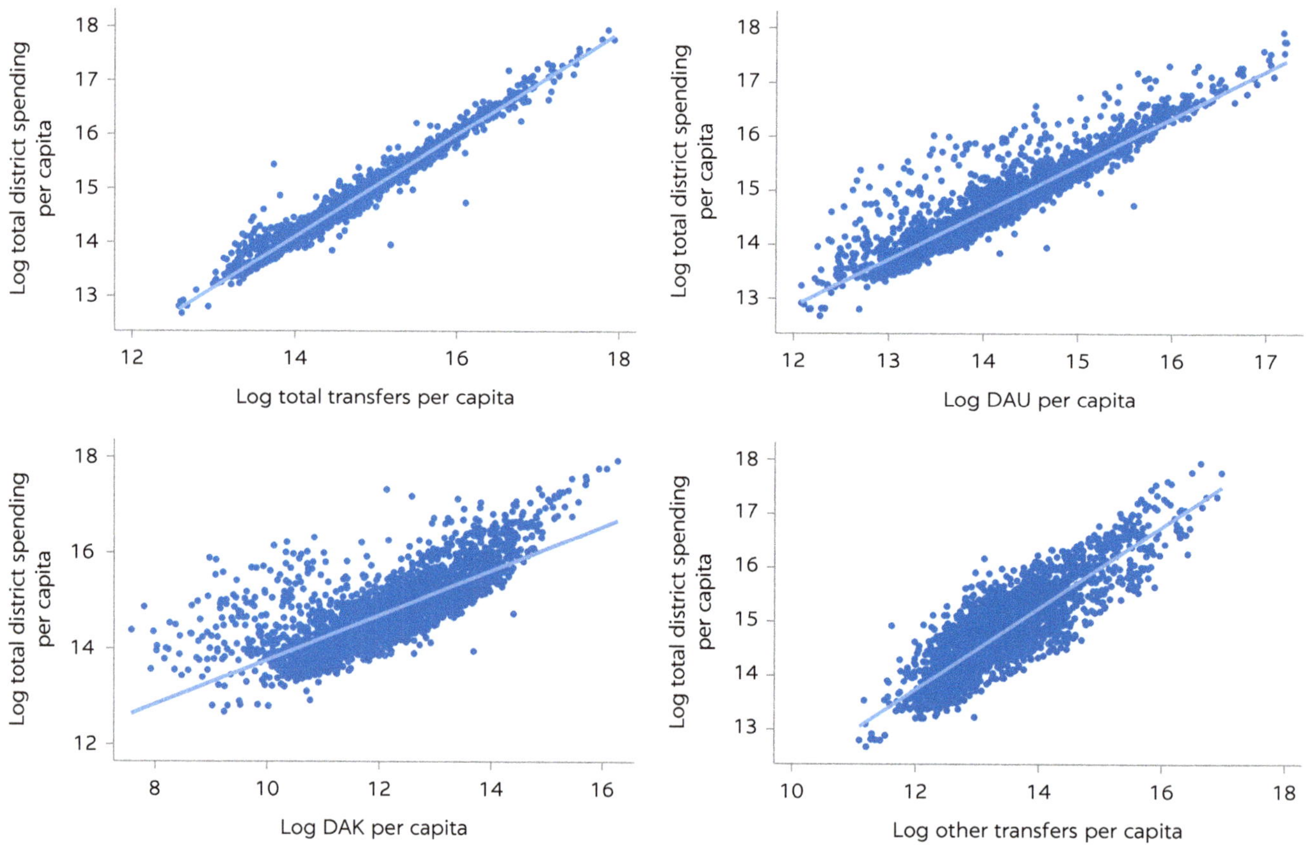

Source: World Bank calculations based on data from Ministry of Finance.
Note: DAK = specific purpose grant; DAU = general purpose grant.

The association between transfers and spending is clearly strong. Regression estimates (World Bank 2021), which control for other possible influences on total spending as well as the possible endogeneity of some transfers, suggest that the elasticity of total per capita spending with respect to total transfers per capita is around 0.85, which is relatively large. Furthermore, the regression results indicate that the DAU has the greatest influence among all transfers on total spending. The estimated elasticity of total per capita spending with respect to per capita DAU transfers is about 0.45.

Figure 6.13 illustrates the relationship between districts' per capita transfers and per capita education sector spending. Again, the relationships are strong, although perhaps not as robust as those for intergovernmental transfers and total district spending. Econometric analysis indicates that the elasticity of district per capita education spending with respect to total transfers per capita is about 0.45. As before, the DAU has the most significant influence on education spending. The elasticity of per capita education spending with respect to per capita DAU is approximately 0.50. See World Bank (2021) for the detailed regression results.

One curious finding from the regression results (World Bank 2021) is that the DAK have no statistically significant impact on district spending, either in total or for education. DAK is meant to stimulate capital spending, not spending in

FIGURE 6.13

Transfers and education spending

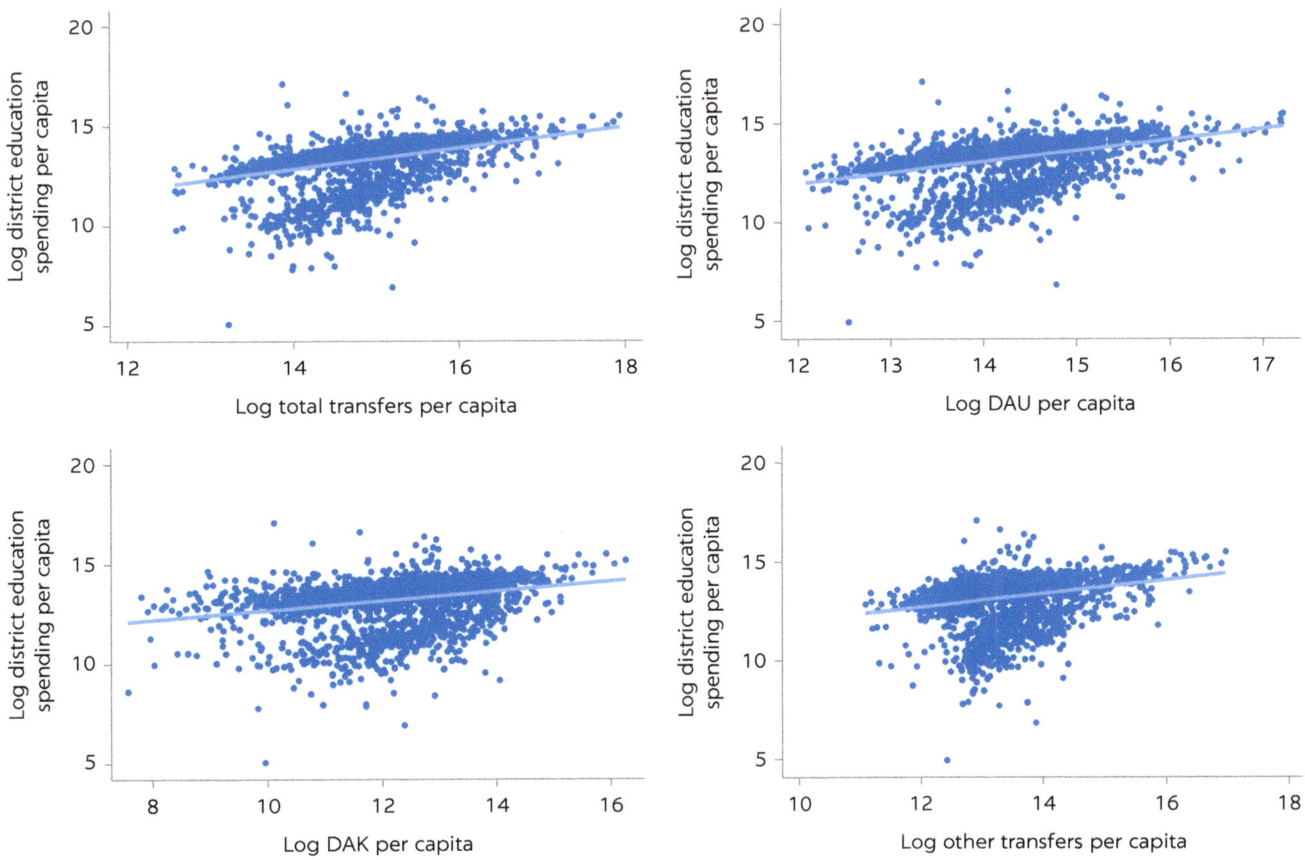

Source: World Bank calculations based on data from Ministry of Finance.
Note: DAK = specific purpose grant; DAU = general purpose grant.

general, and Lewis (2013) has shown that DAK does indeed have a strong positive effect on capital spending in the education sector. It is also plausible that DAK negatively affects routine spending as districts shift any additional fiscal resources to support DAK-financed capital projects. If this is true, then DAK's positive impact on capital spending might be cancelled out by its negative effect on routine spending, thus voiding its net effect on aggregate spending. Lewis (2014b) provided some evidence to suggest that the DAK may crowd-in additional capital spending at least under certain circumstances, which supports this argument. A final issue of concern regarding DAK transfers is that the magnitude of annual allocations is quite volatile across districts, creating challenges in planning and completing capital projects in education and other sectors. This may also help explain the weak effects of DAK on spending.

The relationship between district spending and education outcomes is examined next. Figure 6.14 illustrates the association between district total and education spending and education access, as measured by net enrollment rates, and education quality, as proxied by national test scores. The figure shows no clear relationship between district spending and education outcomes.

But simple scatterplots do not account for several important aspects of the relationship between spending and education outcomes. First, they do not accommodate the likelihood that education outcomes in one period depend on outcomes in the previous period. Second, they do not account for the possible

FIGURE 6.14

District spending and education outcomes

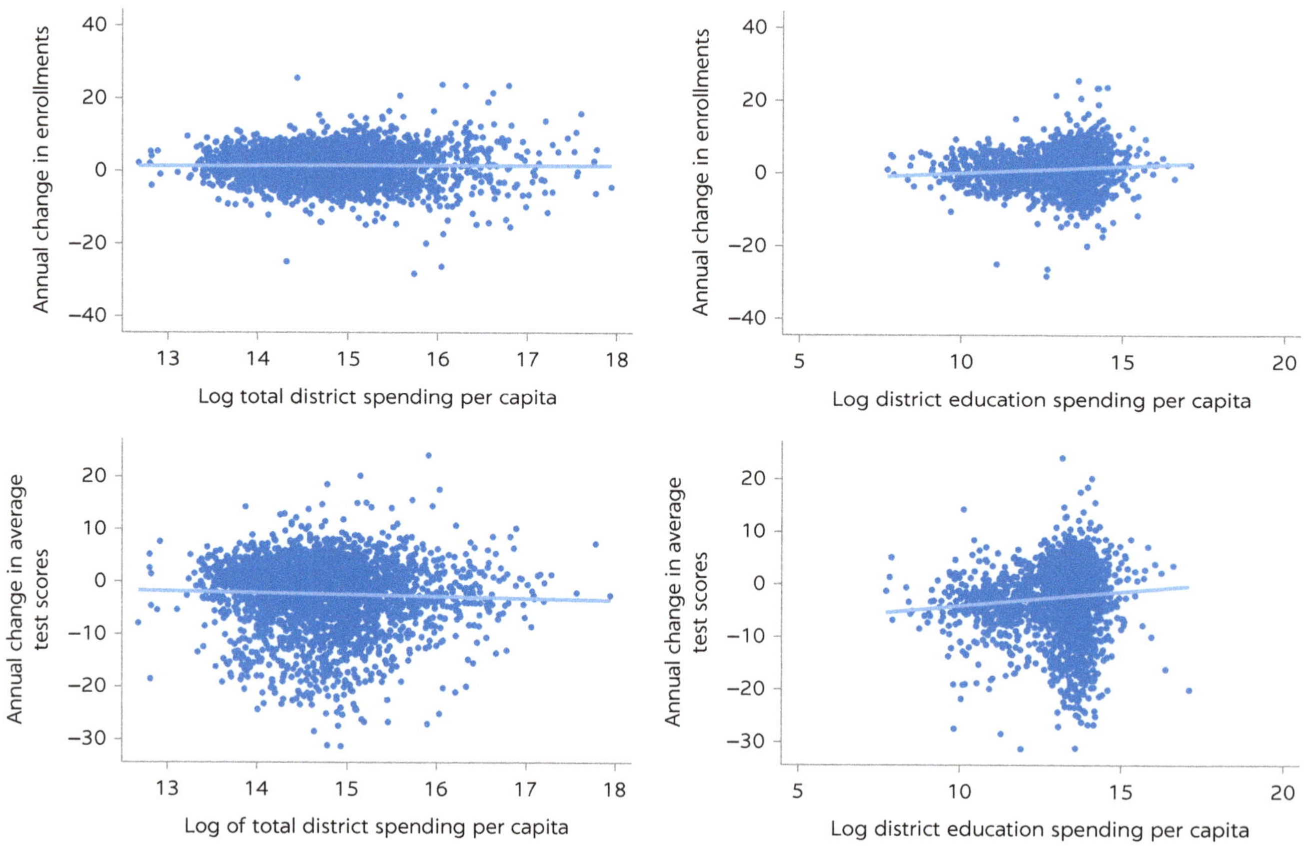

Source: World Bank calculations based on data from Ministry of Finance.

endogeneity of district spending in determining outcomes. Finally, they do not control for other possible influences on education outcomes.

The regressions represent an attempt to overcome all these problems (World Bank 2021, tables 2.3, 2.4, 2.5, and 2.6). The results suggest that a 1 percent increase in total spending leads to a 0.029 increase in enrollment rates and a 0.062 increase in average test scores. These are modest effects. In addition, the regression results imply that a 1 percentage point increase in the education budget share leads to a 0.10 increase in enrollment rates and a 0.04 increase in average test scores, although these results are not statistically significant at conventional levels.

The lack of impact that education spending has on test scores is perhaps odd. There is some indication, however, that at least some districts do not classify BOS as education spending but rather as administrative expenditure. If so, then the fact that BOS is not included in the calculation of education spending in many districts might dilute the estimated effectiveness of education expenditures on test scores. On the other hand, it may simply be that increased education spending does not have any impact on the quality of education as measured by test scores. Kurniawati et al. (2018), for example, argue that education sector investments have not led to any substantive improvements in education quality in Indonesia.

One way to illustrate the impact of district expenditures on education outcomes after accounting for the influence of outcomes in the previous period, spending endogeneity, and covariate effects is to create scatter plots that show the relationship between district expenditures and predicted education outcomes from the estimated regression equation. As figure 6.15 shows, the relationship between spending and predicted outcomes is now positive.

In sum, intergovernmental transfers determine district spending to a large extent, and district spending positively influences local education outcomes on average, at least to a limited extent. These relationships suggest that the inequitable distribution of transfers and spending in Indonesia may lead to inequitable educational opportunities and outcomes. As a result, some districts receive considerably more funds than others and therefore spend significantly more as well and vice versa. The districts that receive lower transfers are relatively disadvantaged because they have fewer opportunities to improve their performance, which is reflected in their outcomes.

The inequity in education outcomes is illustrated in figure 6.16, which shows the frequency distribution of district enrollment and test scores in 2016. In that year, enrollment rates varied from about 10 percent to 85 percent, and district test scores ranged from about 40 to 80 (out of 100). District education outcomes in Indonesia are indeed unequal, and this chapter argues that these unequal outcomes are to some extent a function of the unequal distribution of transfers.

Overall, the analysis raises at least two additional questions. First, why does local government spending have such a muted impact on various education outcomes? Second, what other policies or factors might positively or negatively influence such outcomes?

Research indicates a number of elements that mitigate the positive effects of local spending on school enrollment and test scores in Indonesia. Suryadarma et al. (2006) demonstrate that teacher absenteeism has a strong negative effect on student achievement in test scores. Suryadarma (2012) shows that district corruption constrains the positive impact of spending on school enrollment. Lewis (2017b) finds that the spending of local governments that manage their

FIGURE 6.15

Predicted education outcomes and district spending

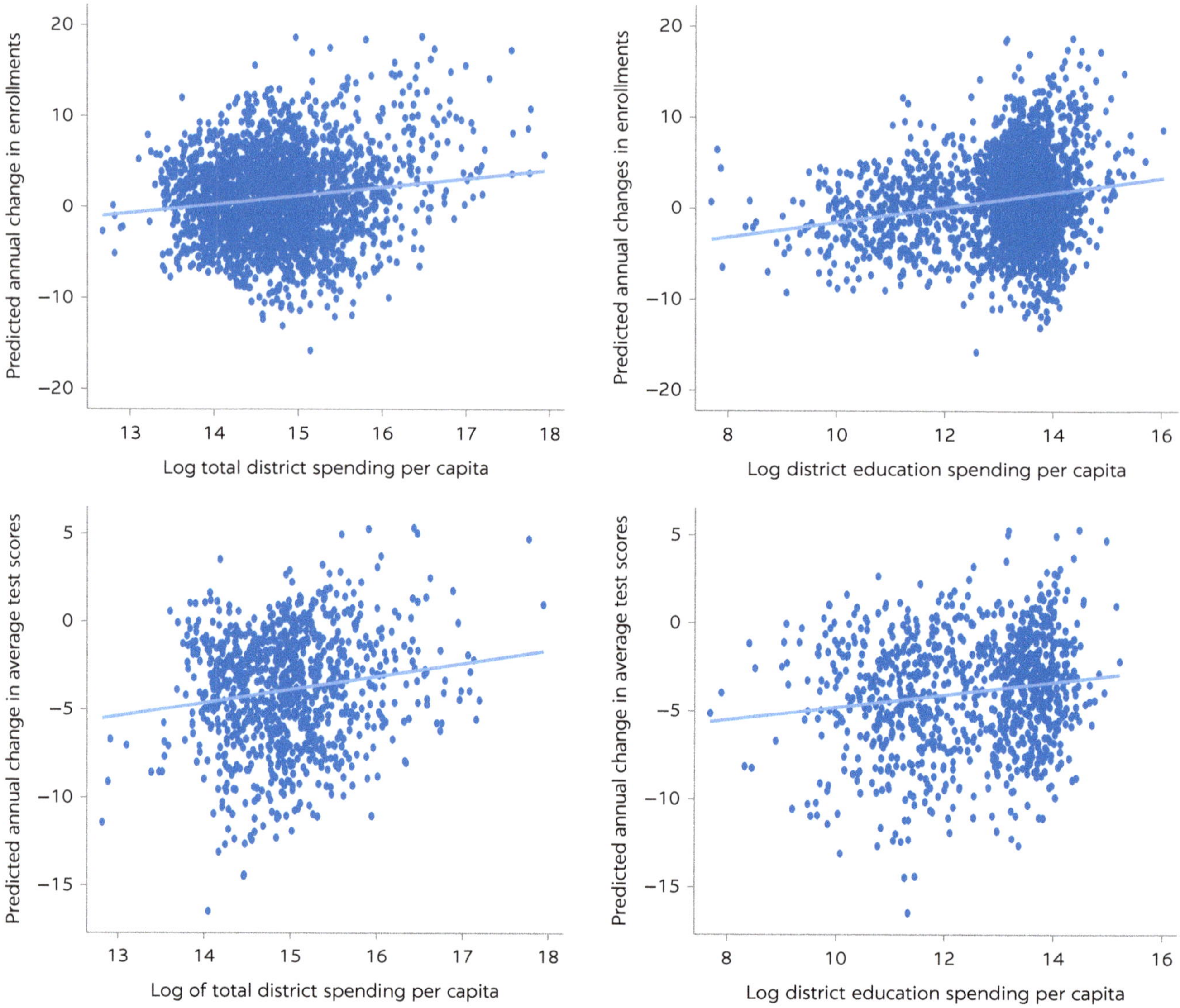

Source: World Bank calculations based on data from Ministry of Finance.

budgets more effectively (and by implication are arguably less corrupt) has a stronger positive impact on school enrollment; at the same time, the author shows that increasing district dependence on intergovernmental fiscal transfers moderates the positive spending effects of those generally better performing local governments. Agustina, Hanjani, and Lewis (2021) demonstrate that the spending of poorly governed districts is more likely to lead to weak service delivery outcomes across all major sectors, including education.

Recent research shows that some education policy initiatives do not, in any event, have the intended effects on outcomes in the sector. Lewis and Nguyen (2020) find no evidence that Indonesia's compulsory schooling program has increased educational attainment, largely due to weak implementation efforts. In addition, Lewis (2020) shows that the government's vaunted 20 percent rule (which insists that all levels of government spend at least 20 percent of their

FIGURE 6.16
Distribution of district enrollment rates and test scores, 2016

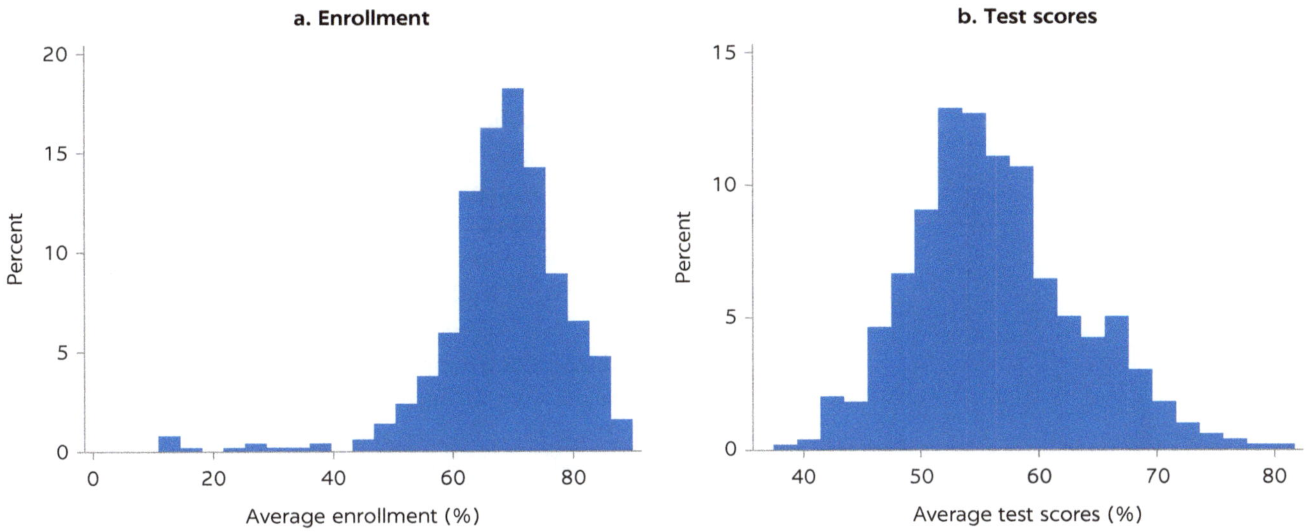

Source: World Bank calculations based on Ministry of Education and Culture data.

budgets on education functions) has no discernable impact on enrollment at any level of schooling.

Political economy factors related to local service delivery present mixed effects. Lewis (2017a) shows that district splitting, which is largely politically motivated, has no impact on school enrollment. Lewis (2016) demonstrates that direct central government spending in the regions (through so-called deconcentration mechanisms) negatively affects local service delivery, including that in the education sector. Lewis (2019) finds that expanding local legislature size, and the attendant increasing fragmentation in decision-making, leads to weaker education and other sector outcomes. Finally, Lewis, Nguyen, and Hendrawan (2020) establish that local electoral accountability—as proxied by the performance of reelected incumbent mayors—has no significant effect on education or other local service outcomes.

The analysis suggests that improving the distributional equity of intergovernmental transfers, while clearly needed, may not in and of itself lead to the desired enhanced education outcomes. In this context, ameliorating governance conditions will be especially important and, given the deeply embedded nature of the problems, may prove particularly challenging.

POLICY DIRECTIONS

Any reform of intergovernmental transfers in Indonesia should focus on making the allocation of per capita transfers more equitable across districts and on removing perverse spending incentives in the system. A more equitable distribution of transfers would provide all districts with a more uniform chance of both increasing access to education and improving its quality. Removing perverse incentives would encourage districts to spend their resources more efficiently and would also increase the supply and improve the quality of education services.

In this context, revising the allocations of the DAU should be the first priority. This reform should involve at least two important changes: estimating per capita fiscal needs and removing the basic allocation. Estimating fiscal needs in the fiscal gap formulation per capita instead of per district would make DAU distributions more equitable. Expunging the basic allocation would reduce incentives for districts to overspend on teachers and would encourage them to spend more efficiently. An additional possible reform, although less urgent, would be to replace own-source revenues with potential own-source revenues in the estimation of fiscal capacity in the allocation formula, thereby eliminating any disincentives to generate more own-source revenue. A simple way to address these three issues is provided in World Bank (2019b).

The allocation of DBH and DAK could also be made more equitable. Instead of distributing DBH to districts on a lump-sum basis, the funds could be adjusted for the size of the population within each district. In addition, although DAK allocations are now awarded based on proposals from the districts, those allocations could also be adjusted to reflect district population size. These reforms would reinforce the recommended reforms for the DAU in enhancing the equity of all transfers in the system.

As a technical matter, these reforms should be quite easy to implement, but politically they are likely to be more challenging. As in the adoption of any reform there would be winners and losers. Simulations suggest that if the recommended reforms were adopted, then large, mostly urban districts on Java would receive more funds and smaller, more rural areas off Java would receive less. Because of the longstanding antiurban and anti-Java biases, many Indonesians might find these distributional outcomes unpalatable. Although decision-makers in the Ministry of Finance might be persuaded, past experience suggests that legislators in Parliament would likely be significantly more recalcitrant. Reform is not impossible, of course, but it may prove more than a little difficult.

Apart from these technical reforms to the intergovernmental fiscal system, it will also be necessary to address longstanding governance issues at the local level, with reducing corruption the most urgent priority. A significant amount of research suggests that the impact of spending on education outcomes is strongly conditional on the governance environment, in general, and on the existence of rent-seeking and other forms of corruption, in particular. As governance improves, local spending is likely to have a more positive effect on education outcomes. This is not the place to discuss possible specific reforms to reduce corruption but only to highlight the importance of such reforms in achieving education objectives.

Another possible reform relates to performance grants. There is currently a great deal of interest in the use of intergovernmental performance grants to stimulate improvements in local education spending and service outcomes. The notion is theoretically compelling, but it is incredibly challenging in practice to design and implement effective performance grants. The design choices are numerous, which gives policy makers and planners ample opportunity to make crucial mistakes. Also, local governments are very adept at gaming performance grant systems to capture the benefits internally, no matter how well they are designed (Lewis and Smoke 2009, 2012). Pilot projects in Indonesia suggest that intergovernmental performance grants in sectors other than education (such as infrastructure) have had only a modest impact in improving local spending and service outcomes (Lewis 2014a). Monitoring and accountability arrangements, such as audits, embedded in performance grant design appear to have been more effective than financial incentives in improving outcomes.

Unfortunately, the small positive local spending and service delivery effects seem to have disappeared after performance grant programs were rolled out nationally. All this is not to argue categorically against the use of performance grants in education but only to stress that the endeavor is difficult and that the experience in Indonesia at least has not been particularly auspicious.

Although these policy directions pertain specifically to Indonesia, they are also very likely to be relevant for other countries as well. Making intergovernmental fiscal transfers more equitable, removing perverse incentives embedded in transfer systems, and improving local governance conditions are objectives shared by many countries, including those studied in this volume. The introduction to this book provides an indication of the importance of these various difficulties and suggests some ways forward to overcome the challenges.

NOTES

1. Districts are also required to spend 10 percent of their budgets on health and 25 percent of general intergovernmental transfers (shared revenues and the general purpose grant) on infrastructure. These spending mandates are aspirational, and there are currently no consequences for not meeting them.
2. Prior to 2017, DAK was a specific purpose capital grant. In 2017, teacher certification grants and BOS were rolled into DAK. As of that year, the capital grant became known as DAK *fisik* and the teacher certification grants and BOS became known as DAK non-*fisik*.
3. Urban and rural property tax sharing between the central and subnational governments was discontinued in 2014 when these taxes were decentralized to districts. Property taxes in the estates, forestry, and mining sectors continue to be shared.
4. The central government also transfers funds to villages in the Dana Desa program. These grants are not discussed here.
5. Interestingly, the pools of finance did not change when the responsibility for senior secondary school education was reassigned from the districts to the provinces. The government's argument for not reallocating this funding pool was that provinces already had sufficient funding to carry out the new function.
6. The DAU allocation formula is detailed in World Bank (2021).

REFERENCES

Agustina, C.D., Hanjani, C., and Lewis, B.D. 2021. "Quality of Subnational Spending and Services: Which Factors Explain Differences in the Quality of Subnational Spending in Indonesia?" World Bank, Jakarta.

Kurniawati, S., D. Suryadarma, L. Bima, and A. Yusrina. 2018. "Education in Indonesia: A White Elephant?" *Journal of Southeast Asian Economies* 35 (2): 185–99.

Lewis, B. 2012. "Incentives for Local Service Delivery: International Experience and Options for Indonesia." In *Fiscal Decentralization in Indonesia a Decade after Big Bang*, edited by Directorate General of Fiscal Balance, Ministry of Finance, 255–88. Jakarta: Ministry of Finance.

Lewis, B. 2013. "Local Government Capital Spending in Indonesia: Impact of Intergovernmental Fiscal Transfers." *Public Budgeting & Finance* 33 (1): 76–94.

———. 2014a. "Indonesian Intergovernmental Performance Grants: An Empirical Assessment of Impact." *Bulletin of Indonesian Economic Studies* 50 (3): 415–33.

———. 2014b. "Twelve Years of Fiscal Decentralization: A Balance Sheet." In *Regional Dynamics in a Decentralized Indonesia*, edited by Hal Hill, 135–55. Singapore: Institute of Southeast Asian Studies.

——. 2016. "Is Central Government Intervention Bad for Local Outcomes? Mixed Messages from Indonesia." *Journal of Development Studies* 52 (2): 300–13.

——. 2017a. "Does Local Government Proliferation Improve Public Service Delivery? Evidence from Indonesia." *Journal of Urban Affairs* 39 (8): 1047–65.

——. 2017b. "Local Government Spending and Service Delivery in Indonesia: The Perverse Effects of Substantial Fiscal Resources." *Regional Studies* 51 (11): 1695–1707.

——. 2019. "Legislature Size, Local Government Expenditure and Taxation, and Public Service Access in Indonesia." *Studies in Comparative International Development* 54 (2): 274–98.

——. 2020. "Local Mandated Education Spending: Indonesia's Misguided 20 Percent Rule." Arndt-Corden Department of Economics Working Paper, Australian National University, Canberra.

Lewis, B.D., and H.T. Nguyen. 2020. "Assessing the Causal Impact of Compulsory Schooling Policy in Indonesia." *International Journal of Educational Research* 104 (101693).

Lewis, B.D., H.T. Nguyen, and A. Hendrawan. 2020. "Political Accountability and Public Service Delivery in Decentralized Indonesia: Incumbency Advantage and the Performance of Second Term Mayors." *European Journal of Political Economy* 63 (June): 101910.

Lewis, B.D., and P. Smoke. 2009. "Incorporating Subnational Performance Incentives in the Indonesian Intergovernmental Fiscal Framework." In *Proceedings: 101st Annual Conference on Taxation*, National Tax Association Annual Conference, Miami, Florida, November 20–22.

——. 2017. "Intergovernmental Fiscal Transfers and Local Incentives and Responses: The Case of Indonesia." *Fiscal Studies* 38 (1): 111–39.

OECD (Organisation for Economic Co-operation and Development). 2015. *Education in Indonesia: Rising to the Challenge*. Paris: OECD.

Suryadarma, D. 2012. "How Corruption Diminishes the Effectiveness of Public Spending on Education in Indonesia." *Bulletin of Indonesian Economic Studies* 48 (1): 85–100.

Suryadarma, D., A. Suryahadi, S. Sumarto, and F.H. Rogers. 2006. "Improving Student Performance in Public Primary Schools in Developing Countries: Evidence from Indonesia." *Education Economics* 14 (4): 401–29.

World Bank. 2013. *Spending More or Spending Better: Improving Education Finance in Indonesia*. Washington, DC: World Bank.

——. 2019a. *Public Expenditure Review, Draft Chapter on Education*. Jakarta: World Bank.

——. 2019b. *Public Expenditure Review, Draft Chapter on Intergovernmental Fiscal Transfers*. Jakarta: World Bank.

——. 2021. *The Role of Intergovernmental Fiscal Transfers in Improving Education Outcomes. Annex*. Washington, DC: World Bank.

7 Colombia Case Study

JUANITA BODMER AND PEDRO CERDÁN-INFANTES

CONTEXT

Colombia decentralized the provision of education services almost 30 years ago.[1] The National Political Constitution of 1991 transferred decision-making power and resources to local governments at two levels (municipalities and states[2]) with the aim of increasing the efficiency of spending and improving social results and equity by closing regional gaps in resources. These objectives have only been partially met. Although access to education has increased significantly and regional gaps in basic education have narrowed to some extent, learning outcomes have not improved at a similar pace and regional inequities in resources and outcomes persist in both access to postsecondary education and learning outcomes. This case study shows that the ways in which decentralization and intergovernmental fiscal transfers have been designed and implemented are partly responsible for these results.

Since 1991, access to education has increased significantly, although it has stagnated in recent years, particularly since 2005. Between 1996 and 2017, both gross enrollment rates and net enrollment rates have increased at all levels (see figure 7.1). Total net enrollment rate for all levels increased from 76 percent in 1996 to 85 percent in 2017, while the total gross enrollment rate increased from 86 percent to 96 percent in 1996 to 2017, respectively. The total number of students enrolled in the system went down, however, between 2010 and 2017,[3] and enrollment rates are stubbornly low in postsecondary and early childhood education.

Quality has not improved at the same pace and learning outcomes remain low. Results for public school students on the Programme for International Student Assessment (PISA) test show that between 2009 and 2018 the gap in average math and reading scores between countries of the Organisation for Economic Co-operation and Development (OECD) and Colombia fell from 105 points to 98 points, which is not a significant improvement (see figure 7.2). More worrisome is the fact that 50 and 65 percent of students in Colombia score at or below level 1 in reading and math, respectively, as compared with 23 and 24 percent of students in OECD countries. The share of high performers (levels 5 and 6) accounts

FIGURE 7.1

Net enrollment rates, by education level, 1996–2017

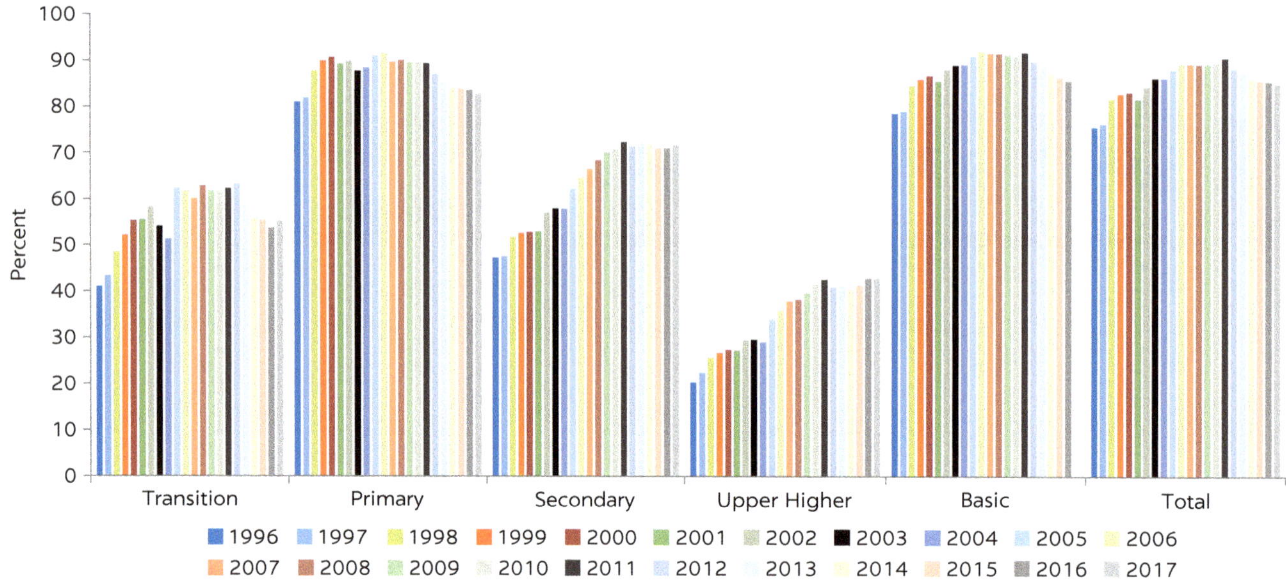

Source: World Bank calculations based on data from the National Ministry of Education.

FIGURE 7.2

PISA test results

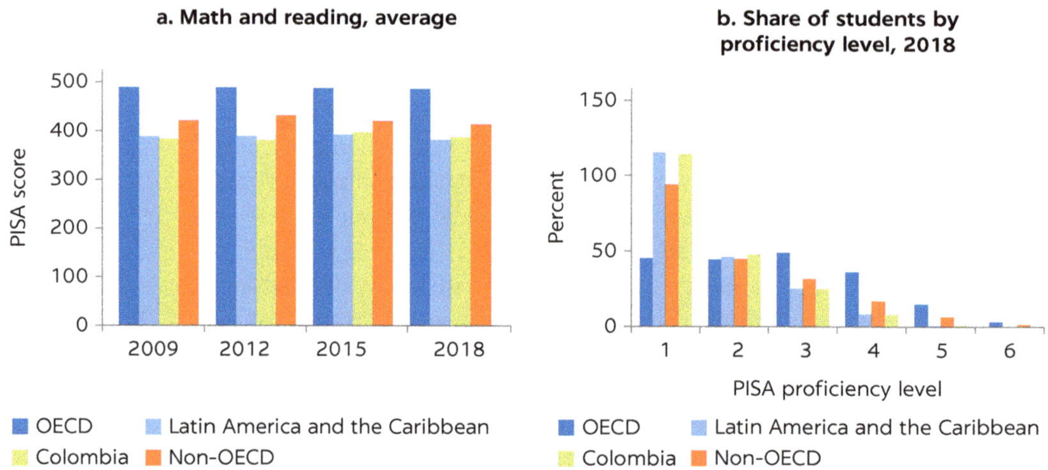

Source: PISA 2018 Results (Volume I) (database) OECD, Paris (accessed June 2020), https://www.oecd-ilibrary.org/education/pisa-2018-results-volume-i_79c489df-en;jsessionid=kK-ijxJDHcn9ojAJBN61MztF.ip-10-240-5-109.

Note: OECD = Organisation for Economic Development; PISA = Programme for International Student Assessment.

for less than 1 percent of students in Colombia for both tests but above 8 percent of students in OECD countries. The trends are similar if we include private schools. Improving learning outcomes is the biggest challenge in the education sector.

Colombia falls below the OECD country with the lowest score—Chile—but this difference narrowed from 26 to 18.5 points between 2009 and 2018. Compared to Mexico, the top performer in Latin America and the Caribbean, Colombia improved from 32.5 points behind in 2009 to 23 points behind in 2018. Finally, compared to non-OECD countries, Colombia improved from 185.5 points below the top performer in 2009 to 183 points below in 2018 (see table 7.1). Again, the data show that even though there is some improvement, progress is slow.

High inequalities in access and quality across income levels and differences between urban and rural areas and among population groups are behind these disappointing trends in learning outcomes and the stagnation of enrollment growth. For example, net enrollment rates in upper secondary education are 57 percent for the richest quintile of the population and 21 percent for the poorest quintile and 47 percent and 31 percent in urban and rural areas, respectively. Learning outcomes mirror these inequalities. In 2018, the lowest quintile trails the richest quintile by the equivalent of three years of schooling, while rural areas trail urban areas by one year of schooling. On Prueba Saber 9—the national standardized test—the gap between the richest and the poorest students in the lowest performance level is 23 percentage points in reading (1 percent versus 24 percent) and 30 percentage points in math (4 percent versus 34 percent).[4]

Regional inequality is one of the main drivers of these results, and the gap in outcomes among regions is closing too slowly. Poorer regions have worse outcomes. Figure 7.3 shows negative correlations between poverty rates and upper secondary gross enrollment rates and poverty rates and learning outcomes (using the Synthetic Index of Education Quality—SIEQ).[5] The rate of convergence is too slow for the large gaps observed. By using a conditional convergence model (mimicking the neoclassical growth model and conditional on fiscal performance, homicide rates, poverty, rurality, and the electoral representativeness of the elected mayor), a study conducted by the Comptroller General of the Republic (La Contraloría General de La República) in 2017 showed that if current trends were to continue, it would take up to 23, 15, and 17 years to close the gap between the municipalities with the lowest social outcomes and other municipalities in net enrollment rates in primary, secondary, and upper secondary education, respectively. For learning outcomes, at the current trends in convergence among regions, closing the gap would take 24 years (Comptroller General of the Republic 2017).

The relatively slow progress in achieving better education outcomes and closing regional gaps is a sign that the decentralization system as it is designed in Colombia might not be enough to achieve these objectives. As this chapter shows, this is partly because of the way the roles and responsibilities in the

TABLE 7.1 **Highest and lowest PISA exam results for public schools, 2009 and 2018**

	2009				2018			
	OECD	LATIN AMERICA AND THE CARIBBEAN	NON-OECD	COLOMBIA	OECD	LATIN AMERICA AND THE CARIBBEAN	NON-OECD	COLOMBIA
Lowest	Chile (410.5)	Peru (348)	Qatar (337.5)	384.5	Chile (406.5)	Dominican Republic (324.5)	Dominican Republic (324.5)	388
Highest	Finland (538.5)	Mexico (417)	Hong Kong SAR, China (570)		Estonia (522.5)	Mexico and Uruguay (411)	China[a] (571)	

Source: PISA 2018 Results (Volume I) (database) OECD, Paris (accessed June 2020), https://www.oecd-ilibrary.org/education/pisa-2018-results-volume-i_79c489df-en;jsessionid=kK-ijxJDHcn9ojAJBN61MztF.ip-10-240-5-109.
Note: OECD = Organisation for Economic Co-operation and Development.
a. Beijing, Shanghai, Jiangsu, and Zhejiang.

FIGURE 7.3

Correlation between poverty and education outcomes

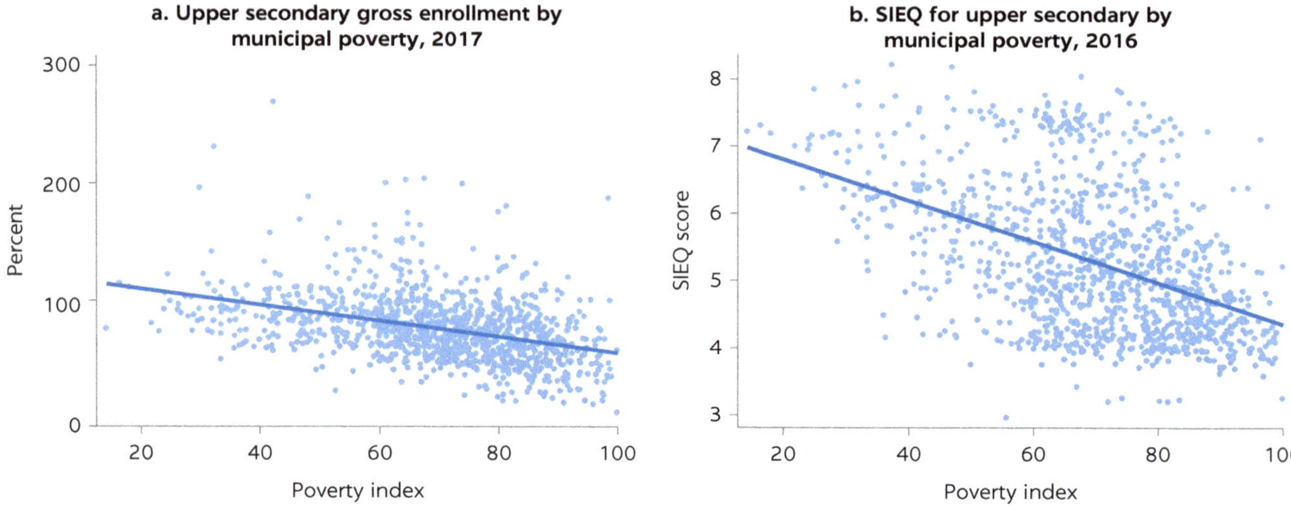

Sources: Poverty index data are from Terridata (database), National Planning Department, Bogotá (accessed October 2019), https://terridata.dnp.gov.co/index-app.html#/descargas.
Panel a: Municipal gross enrollment rates are from the Municipal Statistics for Preschool, Basic, and Upper Higher Education Database, National Ministry of Education, Bogotá (accessed in October 2019), https://www.datos.gov.co/Educaci-n/MEN_ESTADISTICAS_EN_EDUCACION_EN_PREESCOLAR-B-SICA/nudc-7mev.
Panel b: SIEQ calculated by the Colombian Institute for Education Evaluation 2015–16.
Note: SIEQ = Synthetic Index of Education Quality.

education system are organized and how fiscal transfers have operated, with unclear objectives and incentives and complex and unpredictable formulas. These factors coupled with low local government capacity have limited the effectiveness of decentralization.

The chapter first describes how decentralized education services operate in Colombia and how responsibilities for service delivery are divided among different levels of government. Next, it describes how fiscal transfers work and their evolution since 1991, highlighting potential issues with the design and implementation of the transfers. Next, it evaluates the impact of these fiscal transfers on local resources, efficiency, equity, and outcomes. Based on the analysis, the chapter provides policy directions to improve the efficiency and effectiveness of fiscal transfers in education in Colombia.

HOW IS THE DECENTRALIZATION OF THE EDUCATION SYSTEM ORGANIZED?

Colombia decentralized the provision of four social services—education, health, water and sanitation, and sports and culture—in 1991. Decentralization of these four services was accompanied by a fiscal decentralization that included the local collection of taxes. The main sources of tax revenue for local governments are limited and generate high inequalities in local government revenue. States rely mainly on taxes on alcoholic beverages and tobacco, whereas municipalities rely on taxes on property, industry and commerce, and gasoline. Most local government spending comes from fiscal transfers from the central government (about 45 percent for municipalities and 43 percent for states in 2018[6]). Education transfers account for more than half of total transfers.

There are four levels of government involved in the management of the education system: the central government, states, municipalities, and schools. Their roles have changed, falling into two distinct periods. In 1991, the country decentralized responsibilities to three different administrative levels: 32 states, 1,101 municipalities, and schools. Although municipalities are subregions of states, the two levels are politically and administratively independent, and the first wave of decentralization (1993–2001) distributed responsibilities and resources to both levels for different purposes. States were responsible for service provision, and municipalities were responsible for quality investments. Since 1994, schools have been responsible for curriculum design.

This structure was modified in 2001 with the establishment of Certified Territorial Entities (CTEs) (Entidades Territoriales Certificadas), which initially included all of the states and all municipalities with more than 100,000 inhabitants (including Bogotá, which is a special district). This effectively gave large municipalities a higher level of autonomy by transferring the responsibility for service provision to them directly (instead of to their state governments). Small municipalities continued under the same structure, responsible only for quality investments and dependent on the state governments for service provision. Since 2004, municipalities with fewer than 100,000 habitants that meet capacity requirements can also ask their state for a certification to administer both the provision of services and quality investments.[7]

Schools were not given any functions under the 1991 decentralization scheme. The General Education Law of 1994 assigned curriculum design to schools but did not provide any resources for undertaking this function. Only in 2013, as a result of a constitutional mandate, did it become mandatory for the central government to transfer resources to schools, even though these resources were not meant to cover the pedagogical function that had been assigned to them.

A total of 96 CTEs in 32 states and Bogotá and 63[8] large municipalities are responsible for service provision with certified and uncertified municipalities continuing to receive some transfers for quality improvements. Figure 7.4 shows the institutional structure under which education is provided.

This structure establishes parallel systems of management for certified and uncertified municipalities. Certified municipalities are responsible for both service provision and quality improvements in their own schools. Uncertified municipalities depend on their states for service provision, while they retain some responsibility for quality investments that are executed, in theory, in coordination with their states. In practice, uncertified municipalities do not generally have the capacity to manage the resources for quality improvements effectively and strategically, spending 38 percent of these resources on school feeding, transportation, and infrastructure.[9]

Uncertified municipalities tend to be more rural, have a larger number of smaller schools, higher poverty rates, and worse education outcomes (see table 7.2). Although certified municipalities represent less than 6 percent of total municipalities, they contain over 60 percent of total population and are on average more urban and denser than other municipalities. Certified municipalities have more private schools, fewer but larger public schools, and higher student-teacher ratios than other municipalities. Elacqua et al. (2019) found

FIGURE 7.4

Institutions responsible for education service provision in Colombia

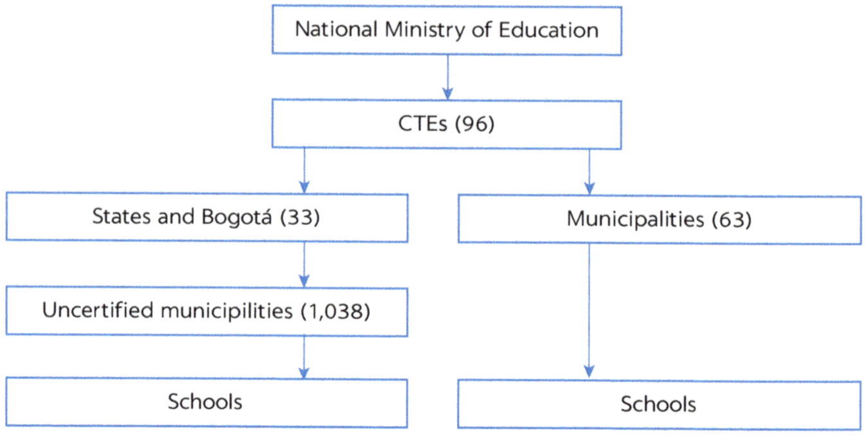

Source: World Bank.
Note: CTE = Certified Territorial Entity.

TABLE 7.2 **Local providers of education, 2017**

	CERTIFIED MUNICIPALITIES (62 AND BOGOTÁ)	UNCERTIFIED MUNICIPALITIES (1,038)
Total population	29,893,089	19,267,664
Average population	474,493	18,562
Multidimensional poverty (0 = richest; 100 = poorest)	45	71
Mortality of children under 1 year (per 1,000 newborns)	10	11
Homicides (per 100,000 habitants)	26	24
Prenatal controls (appointments attended during pregnancy)	7	6
Density (number of people per square km)	15,251	76
Rurality (1 = Cities and 4 = Dispersed Rural)[a]	1	3
Total enrollment	5,778,884	4,310,498
Total net enrollment rate (%)	91	83
Public enrollment	4,178,568	3,987,186
Public share of total enrollment (%)	72	93
Schools	2,580	6,856
Average public school size	1,563 students	571 students
Total number of public teachers	148,594	173,667
Average student-teacher ratio	28:1	21:1
Average per student transfer (US$)	722	889
Average per student expenditure (US$)	846	1,049

Sources: Terridata (database), National Planning Department, Bogotá (accessed October 2019), https://terridata.dnp.gov.co/index-app.html#/descargas; Municipal Statistics for Preschool, Basic, and Upper Higher Education Database, National Ministry of Education, Bogotá (accessed in October 2019), https://www.datos.gov.co/Educaci-n/MEN_ESTADISTICAS_EN_EDUCACION_EN_PREESCOLAR-B-SICA/nudc-7mev; Public Teachers in Preschool, Basic, and Upper Higher Education Database, National Ministry of Education, Bogotá (accessed in October 2019), https://www.datos.gov.co/Educaci-n/MEN_DOCENTES-OFICIALES_EPBM/fjw5-pzau.
Note: km = kilometer; US$ = US dollar.
a. "Rurality" is an index calculated by the National Planning Department in which *1* stands for cities, *2* for intermediate cities, *3* for rural, and *4* for dispersed rural.

that, compared to uncertified municipalities, certified municipalities have a lower percentage of low-performing students and better-quality teachers.

It is also important to note the large inequalities within these groups of municipalities. The poverty rate within certified municipalities ranges between 14 percent and 98 percent. In uncertified municipalities the variation is smaller, but still significant. In uncertified municipalities, the student-teacher ratio is about 18:1 for the bottom 25th percentile and 24:1 for the 75th percentile. In the case of certified municipalities, the teacher-student ratio is of 25:1 for the 25th percentile and 30:1 for the 75th percentile.

Who is in charge of what?

The logic behind the allocation of functions in the sector since decentralization is, generally, that the national government is responsible for designing policies and standards (which are not necessarily binding) and setting overall goals and targets for the system, while CTEs are responsible for implementing these policies and designing and implementing their own programs. CTEs are also responsible for the financing of these programs, with their own resources and with support from central government transfers, and for the management of teachers and other human resource issues (such as teacher deployment and salary payments), although teacher hiring is done centrally through a competitive process. Infrastructure is also maintained by certified and uncertified municipalities. Importantly, because Colombia does not have a binding national curriculum, schools have the fundamental role of designing and implementing their curriculums. Table 7.3 presents a summary of the distribution of functions as established in Law 715 of 2001 (Fiscal Transfer Law) and Law 115 of 1994 (General Education Law).

Although Colombia has made significant efforts to define roles in more detail through multiple decrees and regulations, two fundamental problems remain with the allocation of functions. First, some key functions are not allocated formally to any actor. Second, some functions are allocated to several actors, fragmenting decision-making and implementation responsibilities, and creating coordination problems. The financing system contributes to these problems through misalignments between functions allocated and funding provided.

The crucial functions that are not allocated under the current system are textbook production and distribution and teacher training. Because they have not been allocated to a specific entity, these functions either are not being carried out at all or are being carried out by different actors, thus creating a coordination problem. This situation leads the central government to invest in unassigned functions, such as its purchase in 2016 of over 10 million textbooks. However, when curricular autonomy is at the school level, textbooks are a central component in the promotion of pedagogical content; thus textbook policies should be at the forefront of the management of the system and a function clearly allocated in the system.

Some functions, however, like school infrastructure development and maintenance are allocated to every entity, which can create coordination problems that translate into poor and inefficient delivery. Similarly, the decentralized system currently allocates the function of financing programs to improve quality to municipalities (both certified and uncertified), states, and the central

TABLE 7.3 **Allocation of functions across entities**

FUNCTION	NATIONAL GOVERNMENT	CTEs	UNCERTIFIED MUNICIPALITIES	SCHOOL PRINCIPALS
Teacher recruitment	Design and implement teacher selection	n.a.	n.a.	n.a.
Teacher promotion	Design and carry out evaluations for promotion; regulate promotions	Administer promotions	n.a.	n.a.
Teacher payment	Establish salary scales	Administer payments	n.a.	n.a
Teacher training	Regulate teacher training	n.a.	n.a.	n.a.
Teacher supervision	Regulate teacher and principal evaluations	Evaluate school principals	n.a.	Evaluate teacher performance
Teacher transfers	Regulate transfers	Administer teaching staff	n.a.	n.a.
School maintenance and construction	n.a.	Finance infrastructure, school maintenance, and endowment	Finance infrastructure, school maintenance, and endowment	n.a.
Standard setting	Set technical parameters, standards, and ratios for personnel assignments; define per capita amounts for fiscal transfers to cover costs of education inputs	n.a.	n.a.	n.a.
Curriculum design and teaching methods	Establish technical curricular and pedagogical norms without interfering with school autonomy	n.a.	n.a.	Design the school curriculum
Textbook production and distribution	n.a.	n.a.	n.a.	n.a.
Programs to improve quality and increase access	Promote, finance, and evaluate education programs to improve access and quality; provide incentives for quality improvements	Promote, finance, and evaluate education programs to improve access and quality	Promote, finance, and evaluate education programs to improve access and quality	Design improvement plans
Support for implementation of policies and programs	Provide technical assistance to CTEs; evaluate the performance of local governments	Provide technical, financial, and administrative assistance to municipalities (states only); certify municipalities (states only); provide technical, financial, and administrative assistance to schools	n.a.	n.a.
Information systems	Design and maintain information systems	Administer information systems and provide high-quality information	Provide high-quality information	Provide high-quality information
Financial	Distribute fiscal transfers	Administer fiscal transfers; use own-source revenue to finance education services	Administer fiscal transfers	Administer fiscal transfers

Source: World Bank based on Law 115 of 1994 and Law 715 of 2001.
Note: CTE = Certified Territorial Entity; n.a. = not applicable.

government. This function is very broad, allowing most investment projects to be included in this rubric. In practice, for reasons that go beyond the distribution of roles (such as lack of reliable information and poor-quality school improvement plans), many initiatives are not coordinated or aligned with the needs of schools (Cerdán-Infantes and Zavala 2017).

Finally, responsibility for curriculum design and teaching methods, a crucial function for education quality and learning, is allocated jointly to the national government, which is responsible for designing and setting standards, and school principals, who are in charge of designing and implementing their own curriculum within their schools. CTEs are given no functions related to curriculum design or teaching methods; therefore, they can choose whether to invest in these important activities. Schools, however, are not given any funding for this important task.

Evidence of the existence of coordination problems can be found in the various guidelines that have been produced by the national government to illustrate to local entities the ways in which they can use the resources they receive through the transfer system (see table 7.4).

Table 7.4 shows clearly that many functions overlap among entities, including the responsibility for financing utilities, the internet, pedagogical needs, transportation, the food program, endowments, and school maintenance and construction.

The problems that arise from the assignment of roles and responsibilities to different levels of government are compounded by the misalignment between these roles and the financing system. The next section explores how the system is financed and how these misalignments create significant difficulties in improving access and quality.

HOW IS THE SYSTEM FINANCED?

Trends in overall education spending

Total public spending for basic education and upper secondary education has not changed significantly as a percentage of gross domestic product (GDP) since 2010, moving from 3.2 percent in 2010 to 2.8 percent in 2018. A decrease in the number of students enrolled in the system in recent years, however, from 9.4 million in 2010 to 8.2 million in 2018, resulted in an increase in real per student spending from US$743 in 2010 to US$990 in 2018, a 33 percent increase in 8 years (see figure 7.5).

Per student expenditures for primary and secondary education in Colombia are similar to those of Mexico. When compared to Chile, however, data show that Colombia is behind in per student expenditures, although the gap fell from US$1,717 in 2013 to US$1,289 in 2015. Per student expenditures for primary education and postsecondary (nontertiary) education in OECD countries are three times those of Colombia and, the differences are not significant, moving from US$6,174 in 2013 to US$6,134 in 2015. Compared to other countries in Latin America and the Caribbean, as a percentage of GDP, the level of public education

TABLE 7.4 **Guidance to CTEs on permitted use of transfers**

	PERMITTED USE OF RESOURCES RECEIVED BY CTEs FROM THE CENTRAL GOVERNMENT FOR SERVICE PROVISION	PERMITTED USE OF TRANSFERS RECEIVED BY MUNICIPALITIES (CERTIFIED AND UNCERTIFIED) FROM THE CENTRAL GOVERNMENT FOR INVESTMENT PURPOSES	PERMITTED USE OF TRANSFERS RECEIVED BY SCHOOLS FROM THE CENTRAL GOVERNMENT TO GUARANTEE GRATUITY FOR STUDENTS[a]
Teaching and administrative staff	X	n.a.	n.a.
Teacher training	n.a.	X	n.a.
Construction and maintenance of infrastructure and utilities	X	X	X
Purchasing goods and services for the proper functioning of schools	X	X	X
Provision of education inputs	X	n.a.	n.a.
Educational and pedagogical endowments	n.a.	X	X
Promotion of education quality	X	X	X
Fee to private schools to provide services to students belonging to the public system	X	n.a.	n.a.
Internet	X	n.a.	X
Transportation	X	X	X
Food program	X	X	n.a.
Administrative expenses	X	n.a.	n.a.
Single-shift school day	X	n.a.	n.a.
Special education needs	X	n.a.	n.a.
Boarding schools	X	n.a.	n.a.
Provision of services to imprisoned teenagers	X	n.a.	n.a.
Costs of providing degrees, certifications, reports, and manuals	n.a.	n.a.	n.a.
Insurance of school property	n.a.	n.a.	n.a.
Services from third parties that are required for the school's proper functioning	n.a.	n.a.	n.a.

Source: National Ministry of Education 2016.
Note: CTE = Certified Territorial Entity; n.a. = not applicable; X = permissible use.
a. Schools mandated to educate children without cost to their families.

expenditure in Colombia is above that of Peru and Mexico and below the levels in Argentina and Chile. (See figure 7.6.)

Ninety-four percent of the public expenditures in basic and upper secondary education are spent at the subnational level, and only 6 percent are spent by the central government on projects and programs aimed at increasing enrollment and learning. The trend observed in figure 7.7 reflects the importance of decentralization for the provision of education in the country.[10]

FIGURE 7.5
Education expenditures per student and as a percentage of GDP, 2010–18

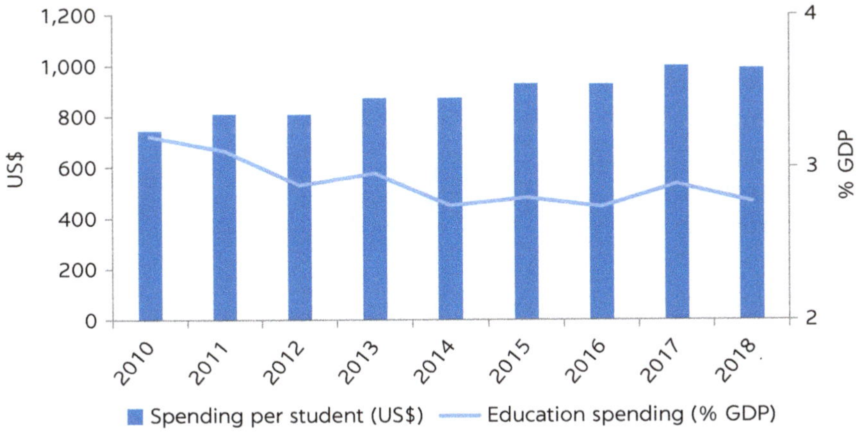

Sources: GDP database from NADS, available at https://www.dane.gov.co/index.php/estadisticas-por-tema/cuentas-nacionales/cuentas-nacionales-trimestrales/historicos-producto-interno-bruto-pib accessed in October 2019; enrollment calculated by the National Ministry of Education, available at https://www.mineducacion.gov.co/1759/w3-propertyname-3377.html?_noredirect=1 accessed in June 2020; education expenditure calculated based on public budget laws from 2010–18 and "Investment Expenditures" database from the Unique Territorial Form, UTF database available at https://sisfut.dnp.gov.co/app/login accessed in October 2019.
Note: US$1 = Col$ 3.39. GDP = gross domestic product.

FIGURE 7.6
International and Colombian education expenditures

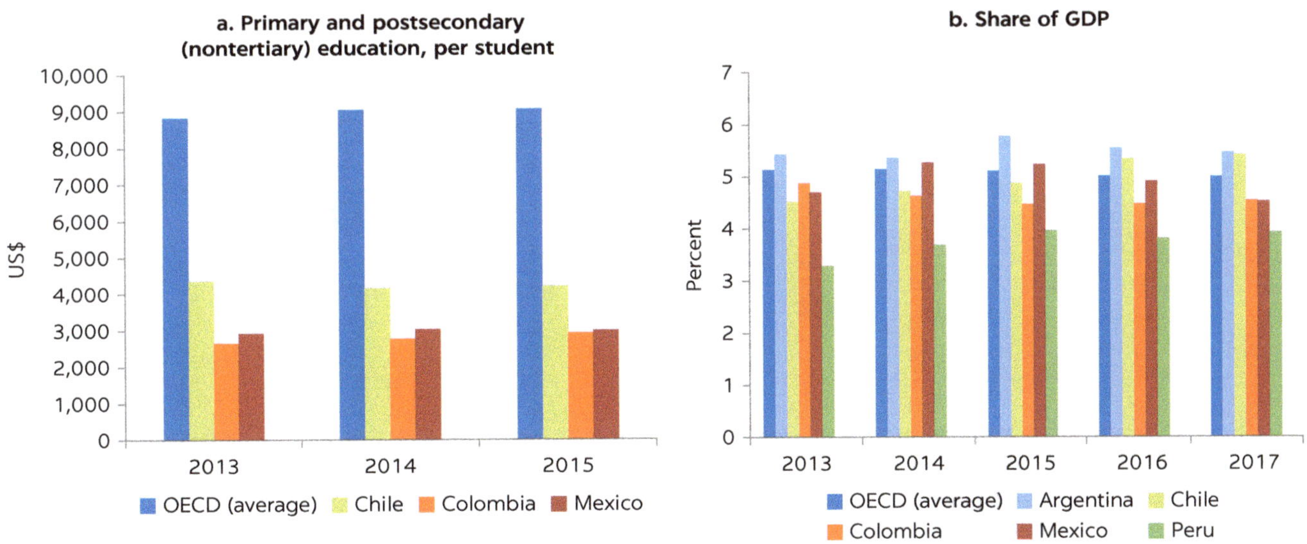

Sources: Panel a: Education Spending Database, OECD, Paris (accessed April 2021), https://data.oecd.org/eduresource/education-spending.htm#indicator-chart; panel b: World Development Indicators Database, World Bank, Washington, DC (accessed April 2021), https://databank.worldbank.org/reports.aspx?source=2&series=SE.XPD.TOTL.GD.ZS&country=#.
Note: Panel b includes tertiary education. GDP = gross domestic product; OECD = Organisation for Economic Development; US$ = US dollar.

Although most education expenditures are executed at the subnational level, there is great variation across municipalities, especially between certified and uncertified municipalities. Unlike certified municipalities, uncertified municipalities do not receive resources to cover costs; those resources are sent to their respective states. Figure 7.8 shows that when resources to cover costs are included, uncertified municipalities have higher per student

FIGURE 7.7

Subnational and central government spending, 2005–18

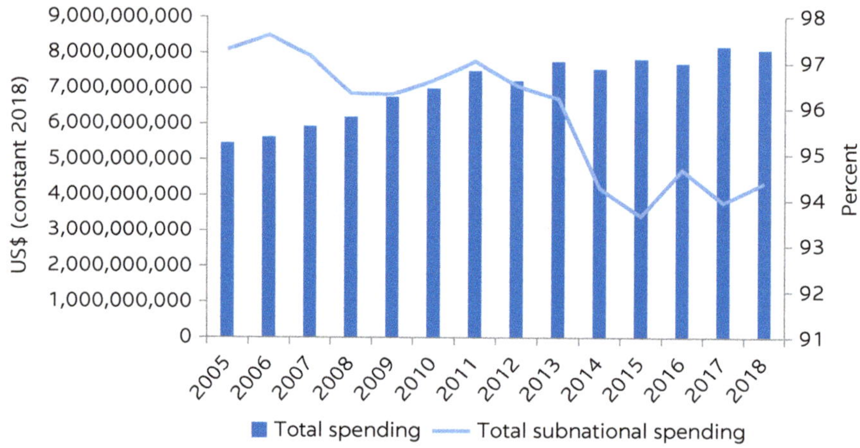

Sources: Education expenditures calculated based on public budget laws from 2010–18 and Investment Expenditures Database, Unique Territorial Form (accessed October 2019), https://sisfut.dnp.gov.co/app/login.
Note: US$1 = Col$ 3.39.

FIGURE 7.8

Municipal education spending, 2017

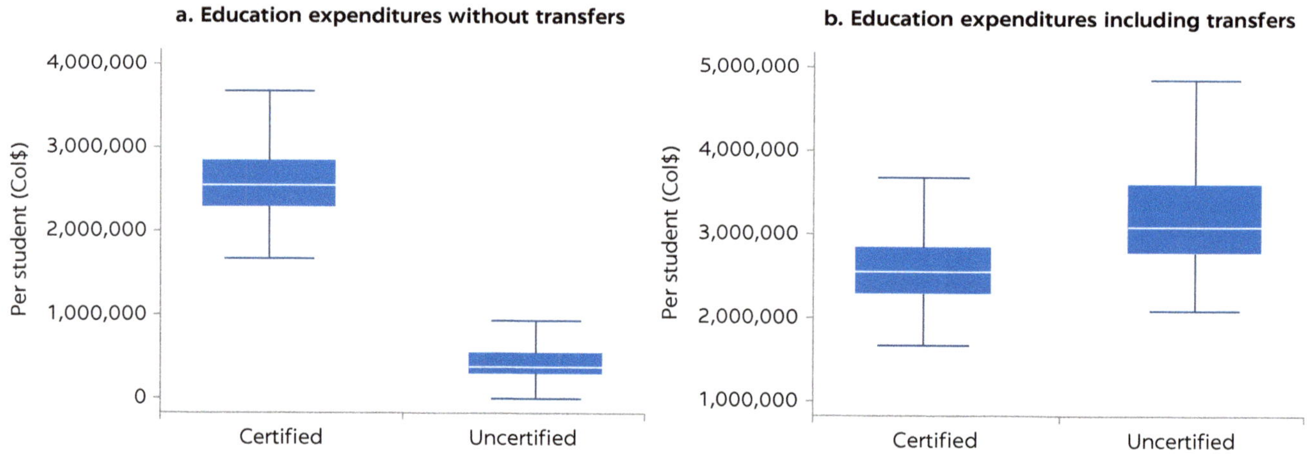

Sources: Municipal education expenditures calculated using data from the Investment Expenditures Database, Unique Territorial Form (accessed October 2019), https://sisfut.dnp.gov.co/app/login, and data from the Information and Consultation System for Distribution of Territorial Resources Database, National Planning Department, Bogotá (accessed October 2019), https://sicodis.dnp.gov.co/ReportesSGP/SGP_Historicos.aspx. Enrollment data are from the Municipal Statistics for Preschool, Basic, and Upper Higher Education Database, National Ministry of Education, Bogotá (accessed October 2019), https://www.datos.gov.co/Educaci-n/MEN_ESTADISTICAS_EN_EDUCACION_EN_PREESCOLAR-B-SICA/nudc-7mev.
Note: 95% confidence intervals.

expenditures than certified municipalities (their own municipal revenues plus their states' own-source revenue as an additional financing source compared to certified municipalities, which have only their own revenue). However, when resources to cover costs are excluded from the calculation, certified municipalities have much higher per student spending than their uncertified counterparts. Finally, certified municipalities have a much higher variation in per student spending, although this might be a result of the difference in sample size between certified municipalities (62 plus Bogotá) and uncertified municipalities (1,038).

Subnational spending in education and the role of intergovernmental transfers

Subnational spending has four main sources of funding. Figure 7.9 shows that in 2018, approximately 84 percent of spending in the education sector was financed through earmarked education transfers from the national budget through the decentralization fiscal transfer mechanism (the General Participation System or GPS). An additional 7 percent was financed through local authorities' own-source revenue, while other transfers made through the GPS for the school food program and early childhood education and general purpose represent 0.73 percent. Royalties (transfers from the central government that are not part of the GPS) represent 3 percent. Therefore, approximately 88 percent of public education spending comes from transfers made by the national government in the form of royalties and GPS transfers.

These data show that fiscal transfers made through the GPS, the main financing source of public education in Colombia, are highly fragmented (earmarked education transfers, food program transfers, early childhood transfers, and general-purpose transfers spent at the discretion of municipal governments on education) and managed separately, creating administrative burdens that can be avoided with better alignment.

FIGURE 7.9
Subnational education spending by financing source, 2018

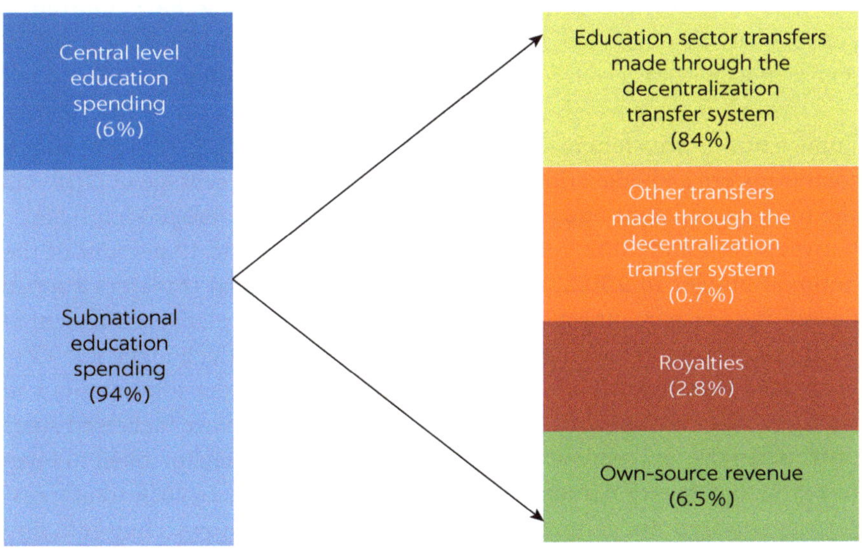

Source: World Bank calculations based on education expenditure data from public budget laws from 2010–18 and Investment Expenditures Database, Unique Territorial Form (accessed October 2019), https://sisfut.dnp.gov.co/app/login.

How do fiscal transfers work?

Decentralization and the history of Colombia's transfer system can be divided into two periods—1993 to 2001 and 2001 to 2021. Each period was focused on different policy objectives and had different ways of calculating the total amount of resources to be transferred and different mechanisms for allocating the transfers among different levels of government. Between 1993 and 2001, under Law 60 of 1993, the main objectives were to increase equity and access to services between regions of Colombia, the total amount of transfers was a fixed percentage of the central government's revenue, and the transfers were distributed across states and municipalities and sectors in fixed percentages.

A fundamental problem with this system was that the size of the budget allocated to fiscal transfers was set as a percentage of national current revenue, thus making it highly volatile and vulnerable to economic downturns. In 1999, Colombia went through an economic crisis that resulted in a decrease of 8.4 percent in national current revenue, which had two negative effects (National Planning Department 2002). First, it decreased the amount of transfers distributed to local governments, which put pressure on the provision of social services. Second, local governments incurred debt to maintain their previous expenditure levels, which created a dangerous fiscal and macroeconomic imbalance.[11]

The government reformed the system in 2001. Efficiency was introduced as an objective, in addition to the existing objectives of equity and access to social services, and learning as an objective was introduced through decrees in 2011. These objectives were promoted through funding and performance-based formulas. Under the new system the total amount of transfers would grow annually in real terms (until 2016 when the formula reverted to depending on the average of the growth of revenue of the previous four years), and these would first be distributed across sectors in fixed percentages and then across levels of government. Finally, in 2013, and as a result of a mandate from the Constitutional Court, gratuity—the obligation of the state to exonerate families from the costs of sending their children to school—was also included as one of the priorities for the education sector, and schools have received funds for this mandate since then.

These changes have also been accompanied by changes in the relative importance of transfers in GDP and the national budget. Figure 7.10 shows total transfers and education-specific transfers as a percentage of GDP and the total government budget. Total fiscal transfers increased significantly between 1994 and 2002, reaching 5 percent of GDP and 19 percent of the national budget in 2002. After the 2001 reform, fiscal transfers started decreasing as a percentage of GDP, and then remained relatively constant at about 3.8 percent between 2011 and 2019. As a share of the budget, transfers decreased significantly after the 2001 reform, when the total amount of transfers was uncoupled from increases in revenue, but have increased since 2016, when the total pool of resources for transfers was again linked to revenue growth. Education transfers follow the same pattern. In 2019, total transfers accounted for almost 18 percent of the national budget, and education-specific transfers for 10 percent.

The GPS is described in figure 7.11. First, the pool of resources to be transferred for all sectors was determined based on inflation until 2016, and on trends in revenue over the previous four years since 2016. Until 2016, if the economy grew at more than 4 percent per year, additional resources were provided, earmarked for

FIGURE 7.10
Education and total fiscal transfers, 1994–2019

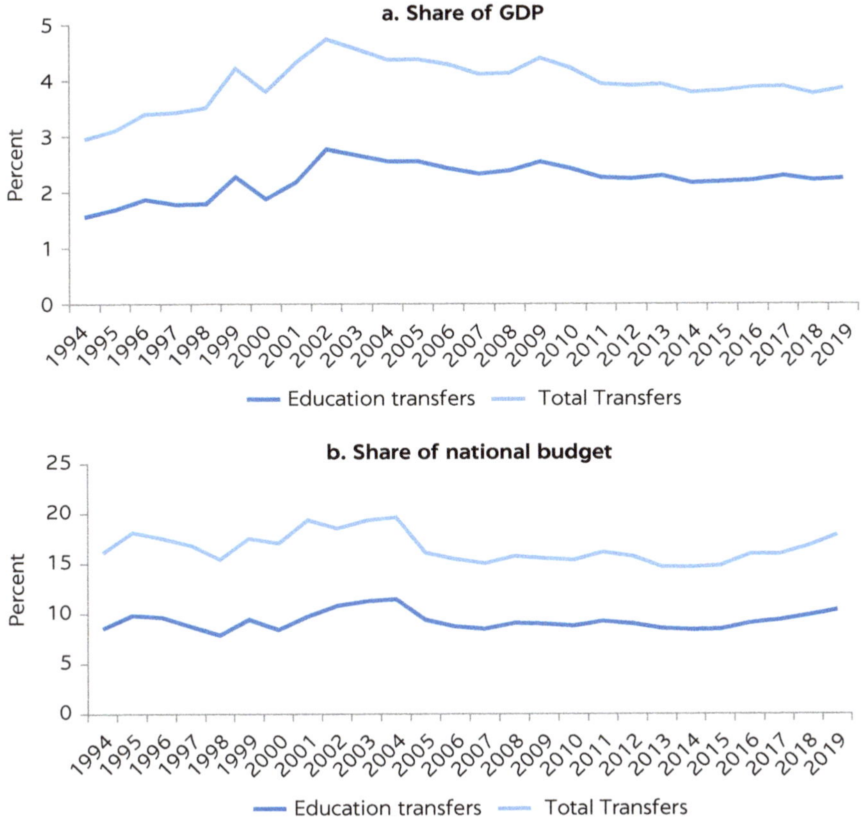

Sources: GDP data are from GDP Database, National Administrative Department of Statistics, Bogotá (accessed October 2019), https://www.dane.gov.co/index.php/estadisticas-por-tema/cuentas-nacionales/cuentas-nacionales-trimestrales/historicos-producto-interno-bruto-pib; national budget data were collected from public budgets laws 1994–2018; education and total fiscal transfers data are from the Information and Consultation System for Distribution of Territorial Resources Database, National Planning Department, Bogotá (accessed October 2019), https://sicodis.dnp.gov.co/ReportesSGP/SGP_Historicos.aspx.

early childhood education. Second, total GPS resources are divided across sectors according to fixed percentages—education receives the largest share of resources, with 56.16 percent of the transfers. Only 11 percent of total transfers are unconditional. Third, these resources are then distributed among local governments by the National Ministry of Education and the National Planning Department under three different headings: (1) provision of service, under which resources are distributed to all CTEs to cover the costs of providing services (to increase access and equity); (2) quality, under which resources are distributed to all municipalities, both certified and uncertified, for investment purposes (to improve quality and equity); and (3) gratuity, under which resources are distributed to schools to cover costs related to attending school that would otherwise have to be covered by the student's family. Formulas are used to calculate the per student amount to be distributed to different entities for each type of transfer.

In addition to these three allocations, a fourth allocation known as the complement is provided to CTEs that do not receive enough resources in the initial distribution to cover their costs. The need for the complement together with its effects on efficiency will be analyzed later in this chapter.

FIGURE 7.11

The GPS fiscal transfer system, 2001

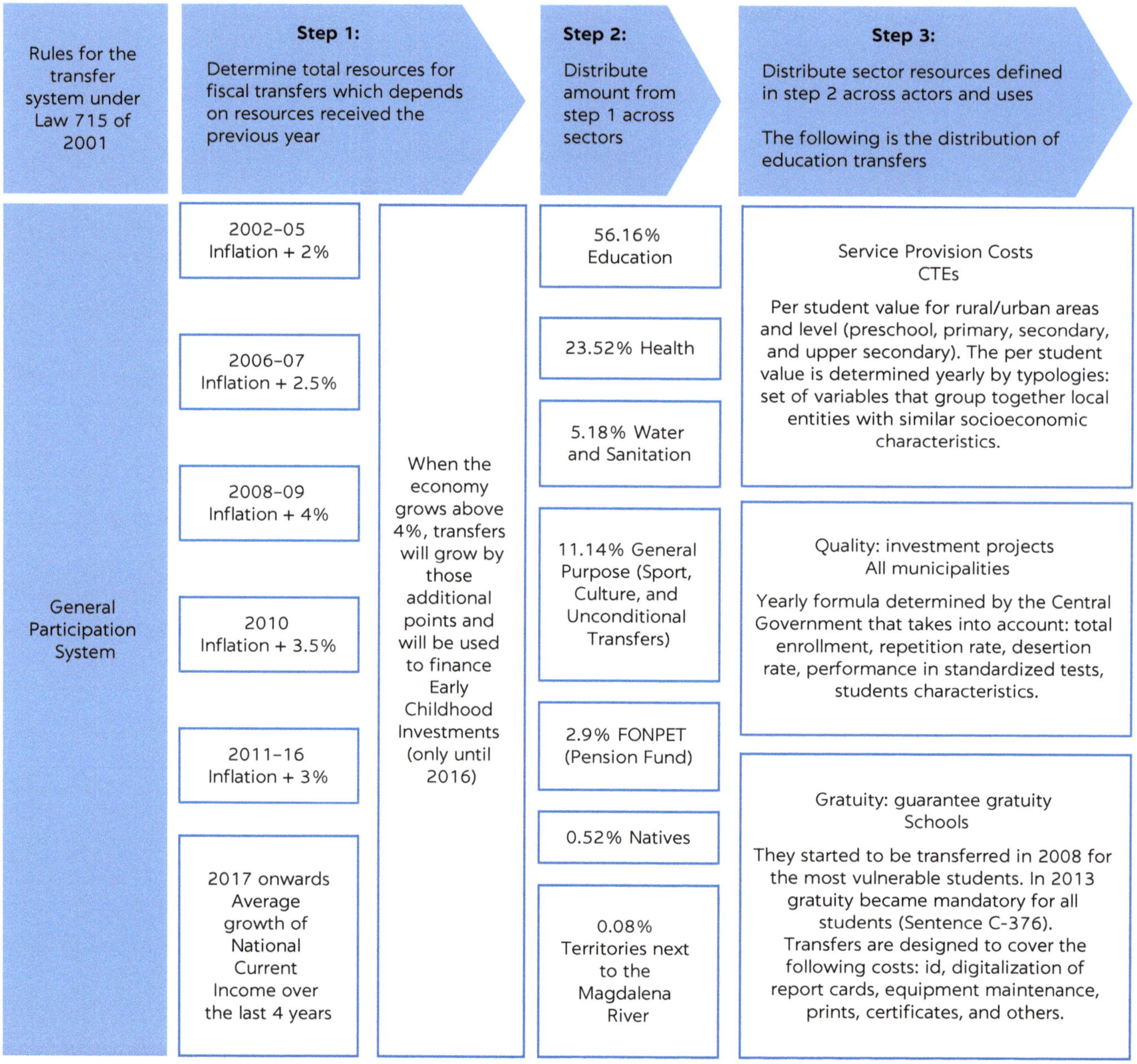

Source: World Bank based on Law 715 of 2001.
Note: CTE = Certified Territorial Entity; GPS = General Participation System.

In addition to the GPS and the complement, additional earmarked transfers for the school feeding program and for early childhood education, where it is offered, are distributed using different mechanisms and formulas. Together they account for less than 0.1 percent of total transfers. Local governments can spend their general purpose transfers (which account only for 11 percent of total transfers) on education, although, in practice, only 5 percent of these resources are spent on education.[12] Virtually all transfers for education are earmarked and the GPS accounts for most of them.

FIGURE 7.12
Allocation of education transfers, 2005–19

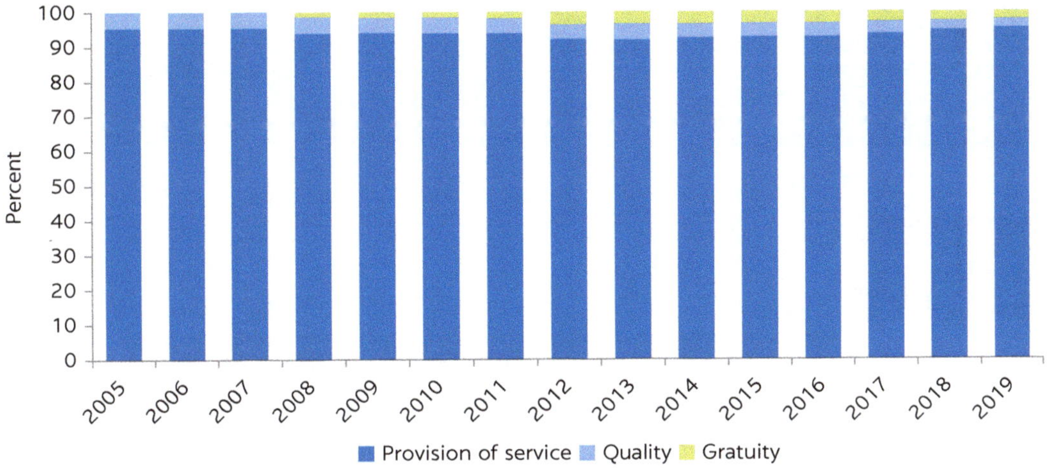

Source: Data from the Information and Consultation System for Distribution of Territorial Resources Database, National Planning Department, Bogotá (accessed October 2019), https://sicodis.dnp.gov.co/ReportesSGP/SGP_Historicos.aspx.
Note: The distribution patterns shown include resources from surpluses of the FONPET (pension fund) that have been transferred to the education sector since 2016 to supplement insufficient funds from regular transfers.

Earmarked education transfers

The transfers for service provision and the complement have accounted for most of the transfers since the reform of the transfer system in 2001, increasing from 92 percent at their lowest point in 2013 to 95 percent in 2019. Resources for municipalities under the quality heading have decreased from 4.7 percent of earmarked education transfers in 2013 to 2.5 percent in 2019. Gratuity resources, which were introduced in 2008 and are transferred directly to schools, have also decreased from 3.5 percent of total fiscal transfers in 2013 to 2.3 percent in 2019 (see figure 7.12).

Each of these allocations is distributed according to formulas that are set at the discretion of the national government and that try to capture the different objectives established for each of them: increasing access, reducing regional inequity, increasing efficiency, and improving learning outcomes. Provision of service resources are allocated across CTEs through a funding formula that determines a per student value for rural and urban areas and levels of education and that is calculated according to typologies—a set of variables that groups together local CTEs according to their regional and socioeconomic characteristics. Gratuity and quality transfers are distributed among municipalities (certified and uncertified) and schools, respectively, based on performance-based formulas that incorporate access, learning, and socioeconomic characteristics (such as rurality and poverty). Each of these formulas and their evolution in time can be found in World Bank (2021).

Figure 7.13 summarizes the resources flows in the education system in Colombia that have been explained and described so far in this chapter.

Supporting systems

The transfer system in Colombia uses information extensively and has a wide range of supporting systems that facilitate the allocation and distribution of transfers as well as the monitoring of education outcomes. The main supporting information systems are:

FIGURE 7.13

Financial flows between entities in the education sector

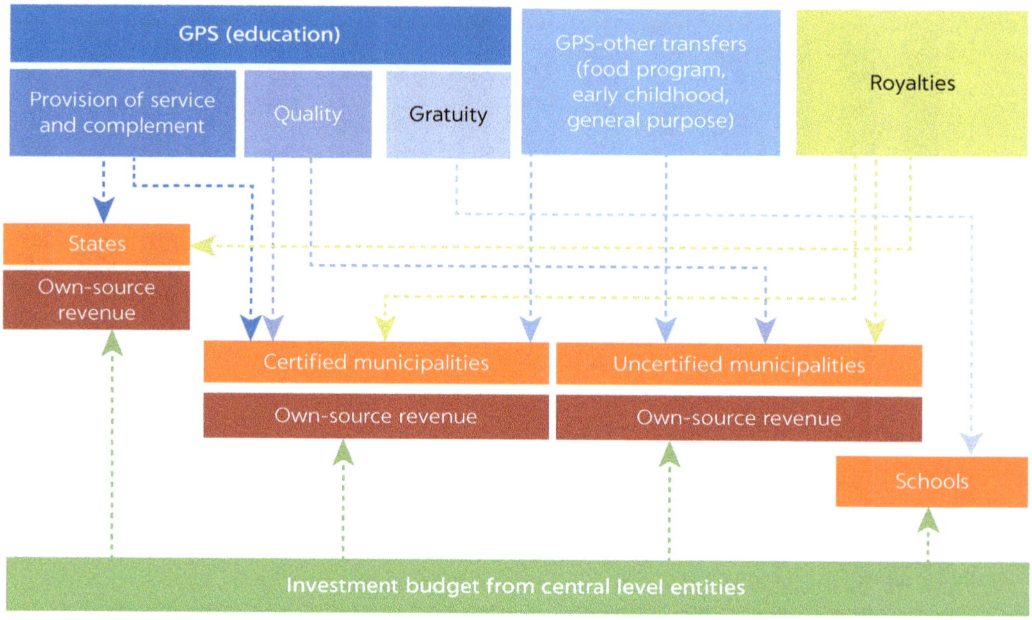

Source: World Bank.
Note: GPS = General Participation System.

- *SIMAT (Integrated Enrollment System).* This system enables administrators to organize, manage, and control enrollment in public education and is the main tool used to calculate enrollment rates. All students who are or have ever been enrolled in the public system are registered in SIMAT, which makes it possible to track students through time.
- *Saber tests and the SIEQ.* The national government requires standardized Saber tests to be administered annually to students in grades 3, 5, 9, and 11 in all schools in Colombia, both public and private. Tests in math and reading for grades 3, 5, and 9 are administered to a random sample of children in each school, with science and citizenship sometimes included, but not yearly. The test for grade 11 is taken by all students; it includes additional subjects, such as natural sciences, in addition to math and reading. These test results, together with information on enrollment and school environment, are used yearly by the Ministry of Education to calculate the SIEQ.[13] This index ranges between 0 and 10 and its simplicity makes it easy for local entities to ascertain their relative position in education outcomes and their progress. The index is calculated for all schools, all CTEs, and the country as a whole.
- *3A Annex.* This database contains information on all public teachers in the country, including personal information, the school to which they are assigned, their pay scale, and their higher education qualifications. It is used to track and manage the sector's teaching staff.
- *School Monitor.* This online platform supports schools and quality management. The school provides information about its needs in areas such as infrastructure, pedagogy and teaching, school environment, community involvement, and administration.

The national government actively uses SIMAT, the Saber tests, and the 3A Annex to allocate and distribute fiscal transfers and other resources to states and municipalities. It is not currently using School Monitor, however, the system that contains information on school needs and areas of improvement, to target resources, programs, or projects aimed at improving education outcomes, which may cause misalignments between targeting and needs.

Although the transfer system in Colombia appears to feature characteristics of a high-performing system (such as per capita amounts, formula-based transfers, and incorporating equity and performance in its formulas), its implementation limits the effectiveness of these features. We discuss these limitations next.

Main design and implementation issues for fiscal transfers for education

Transfers are a zero-sum game: resources for the provision of service, quality, and gratuity transfers compete with each other. The allocation of education-specific transfers (provision of service, quality, and gratuity) is a zero-sum game[14] because the amount of resources available for all transfers is predetermined exogenously at 56.16 percent of GPS (see box 7.1). Any increase in budget for one of the three allocations must be subtracted in whole or in part from one or both of the other two. Although this design feature has the advantage of creating fiscal stability, its main disadvantage is that the budget for investments by municipalities and schools competes with the budget for provision of service transfers, a budget that has been increasing due to increasing salary expenditures. These increases are likely to continue to put pressure on the transfer system, absorbing resources for service provision and reducing resources for both quality investments and gratuity transfers to schools.[15]

With 88 percent of service provision transfers spent on salaries in 2018,[16] increases in salary expenditures put significant pressure on the transfers. We used available data to calculate a rough approximation of the cost of the two main agreements—the 12 percent salary increase for all teachers and the new evaluation for promotion. (See World Bank (2021) for a detailed explanation of

BOX 7.1

Distribution of education transfers as a zero-sum game

Zero-sum games are interactions in which what one actor wins, another loses (Mas-Colell, Whinston, and Green 1995). The distribution of transfers among provision of service, quality, and gratuity can be considered a zero-sum game because each of them is allocated mostly to one group in the education sector: teachers (the main beneficiaries of the provision of service allocation), local mayors (quality transfers), and education communities from each school (the main beneficiaries of the gratuity transfers). The final distribution of total transfers (which is a fixed amount) is the result of the interaction among these three actors and the political power they hold when dealing with the central government. Consequently, each of these groups faces different collective action problems (Olson 1965) (that is, even though it is desirable for the group as a whole to push for more favorable policies, it might not be in the interest of some individual group members to do so). Collective action problems can be overcome when the group is small or well-organized (Krugman and Obstfeld 2006). Each of the groups that interacts in the distribution of fiscal transfers for education in Colombia represents constituencies of different sizes (teachers or mayors or education communities from each school) and has different capabilities and resources to organize as a group. Therefore, each group has a different level of political power to negotiate and push for policies that benefit its interests before the national government, which ultimately affects the final distribution of education transfers.

the methodology.) Together, these two agreements total almost US$487 million, which represents 8 percent of the total education-specific transfers made through the GPS in 2017. Because our calculations are for only one year and do not take into account any promotions that may have taken place since 2016, this number is likely a lower bound.

The competition between the different transfer budgets can be expected to get worse in the upcoming years because the formula to determine total transfers was changed in 2016, and it no longer guarantees a yearly real increase. Under this scenario, if the new formula—average growth in national current income over the previous four years—results in lower transfers, the provision of service budget will take up an increasing share of the available resources, thus severely limiting the amount available to municipalities and schools to invest in quality and pedagogical investments.

The existence of the complement limits the incentives for efficiency improvements embedded in the per capita formulas. The effectiveness of formula funding is undermined by the complement, the additional transfer local governments receive if the amount allocated for service provision does not cover salary costs. Between 2013 and 2014, the complement represented 7 percent of total education transfers, but that amount declined after the introduction of a cost-based formula (see figure 7.14). In 2018 and 2019, when additional resources beyond the education budget were transferred to cover CTEs' payroll expenses, the complement increased. In 2019, reflecting in part negotiated salary increases, the complement amounted to 13 percent of total education transfers, and 89 percent of CTEs received a complement. The importance of the complement is likely to increase in upcoming years.

The existence of the complement negates the purpose of having a formula-based funding system. After the complement, resources received by CTEs do not depend on the formula but on their actual costs. Thus, the formula is meaningless for the 89 percent of CTEs that received the complement in 2019. Additionally, the complement eliminates the incentive for efficiency embedded in per capita formulas. Because the formula incorporates the "efficient" number of teachers that each CTE should have, local authorities should have an incentive to manage their teaching staffs efficiently to release resources for other expenses. The existence of the complement, however, eliminates this incentive. Since CTEs do not suffer the financial consequences of not managing their teaching staff efficiently, they have no incentive to do so.

Human resources management is highly inflexible in other ways. Even if CTEs had the incentive to manage human resources more efficiently, they would still need to have the ability to do so. Unfortunately, there are other impediments to flexibility in managing their teaching staff. Teacher transfers are not transparent and are difficult to implement. Legally, CTEs have the authority to transfer teachers according to their needs. There is evidence, however, that they are unable to exercise this authority. Estimates from the national government show that, in 2017, over 10,000 teachers (3 percent of the total) could have been reallocated (5,451 within their jurisdiction and 4,705 between jurisdictions), which would have yielded yearly savings up to Col$ 0.461 billion (about US$136 million) or 2.26 percent of total education transfers. Administrative and political economy barriers might be preventing CTEs from reassigning teachers (Ministry of Finance and Public Credit 2018). Teacher hiring is done transparently and

FIGURE 7.14

Education resources transferred through the complement, 2013–19

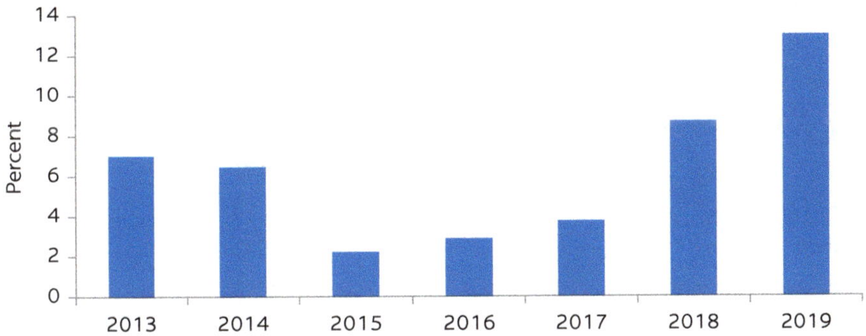

Source: Data are from the Information and Consultation System for Distribution of Territorial Resources Database, National Planning Department, Bogotá (accessed October 2019), https://sicodis.dnp.gov.co/ReportesSGP/SGP_Historicos.aspx.

competitively but teacher transfers are vulnerable to political capture by local governments. Also, CTEs fear that forcing teachers to transfer to another location (especially when the transfer involves changing municipalities) will create legal disputes that they want to avoid. Dismissing teachers is also very difficult. The only mechanism for dismissing teachers is failure on the mandatory performance evaluation carried out by the principal. With almost all teachers systematically passing that evaluation with high scores, the mechanism has never been used.[17]

Pedagogical functions are not aligned with budget allocation. As shown in table 7.3, General Education Law 115 of 1994 made all schools responsible for the development of their own curriculum, with the curricular standards designed by the Ministry of Education serving only as suggestions. Originally, however, schools were given no budget to fulfill this crucial pedagogical function. The gratuity transfers implemented in 2013 were meant to cover the costs of educating students rather than pedagogical expenses. Table 7.5 shows how gratuity transfers were initially calculated in 2013.

As shown in figures 7.12 and 7.15, since their formal introduction in 2013, the resources available for gratuity transfers have decreased in real terms (absolute and per student), that is, schools are receiving less money than before. If the resources received by schools in 2013 were just enough to cover the costs shown in table 7.5, then clearly schools are not receiving the financial support from the national government that they need to carry out the crucial pedagogical functions that have been assigned to them, including designing the curriculum.

The absence of a national binding curriculum is not the rule internationally and its impact on learning is unclear. However, transferring a critical function like curricular design to schools without the resources to fulfill it might easily hinder school principals and teachers from improving their pedagogical practices and, therefore, learning outcomes. Although having national standards such as "Basic Learning Rights—Derechos Básicos de Aprendizaje" and curricular meshes[18] might help, having the resources to implement them locally is still a fundamental part of improving pedagogical practices at the school level.

TABLE 7.5 **Assignment of per student gratuity transfers, 2013**

PURPOSE OF TRANSFER	PER STUDENT VALUE, URBAN PRIMARY AND SECONDARY (US$)
Identification system	1.23
Report cards	2.06
Equipment maintenance	4.13
Prints	2.21
Certificates	2.65
Others	5.40
Total (urban primary and secondary)	*17.68*
Urban preschool	20.05
Urban upper secondary	26.55
Rural preschool	24.78
Rural primary and secondary	21.82
Rural upper secondary	33.03

Sources: National Planning Department 2013.

FIGURE 7.15

Trend in per student gratuity transfers, 2013–18

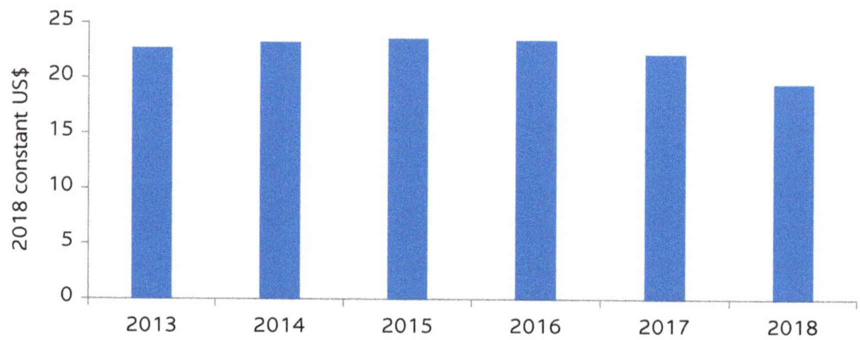

Source: Data are from the Information and Consultation System for Distribution of Territorial Resources Database, National Planning Department, Bogotá (accessed October 2019), https://sicodis.dnp.gov.co/ReportesSGP/SGP_Historicos.aspx.

Local governments are not investing enough resources in education quality. The misalignment of pedagogical functions and budgetary allocations to schools from the national government would not be a major concern if local governments transferred some of their investment resources to schools or invested directly in curricular or pedagogical projects that met schools' needs. However, not all CTEs receive quality transfers, and the available data show that quality investments are not a priority for municipal governments.

Municipal governments use their total investment resources (quality transfers, local resources, general-purpose transfers, royalties, and cofinancing resources) mostly to finance the school food program and infrastructure maintenance rather than for pedagogical or quality investments. Municipal governments can choose to transfer part of their resources to schools in the form of a gratuity transfer, which is different from the gratuity transfers made by the national government to schools. However, this kind of investment is only fourth on the list of actual investments made by municipal governments, and quality improvement projects are only sixth. Teacher training and internet connectivity each represent only 1.25 percent of total investment spending (see table 7.6).

The performance-based formulas used to distribute quality and gratuity resources do not work as incentives for municipalities and principals because they fail to make resources conditional on behavior. There are three main reasons why the performance-based formulas already implemented to distribute quality and gratuity allocations do not create clear incentives for municipalities and school principals to maximize learning (World Bank 2021):

- *Formulas are highly complex and incorporate several targets, making it difficult for municipalities and school principals to understand which results they need to prioritize.* The formulas combine several variables related to increasing access and improving learning outcomes in ways that are difficult to understand (for example, they use deciles and quintiles for the performance of students on the national Saber tests and access variables only for upper secondary education). This complexity makes it very hard for a public servant or a school principal to understand exactly what to do to receive more resources in the future. In the absence of any guidance about how quality and gratuity transfers are distributed, municipalities and principals are unlikely to understand the improvements they need to make to receive more resources.
- *The ways in which exogenous variables like poverty and rurality are taken into account for the incentive might be confusing for local actors thus*

TABLE 7.6 **Municipal government uses of investment resources**

percent

	SOURCE OF FUNDS				
USE OF FUNDS	QUALITY TRANSFERS	LOCAL RESOURCES	GPS (UNCONDITIONAL)	ROYALTIES	COFINANCING
Food Program	3.59	18.18	40.01	12.68	70.18
Payroll-related expenditures	2.65	21.97	3.16	0.00	0.37
Infrastructure	17.62	9.51	20.73	62.18	20.06
Gratuity transfers to schools	38.38	0.59	0.15	0.00	0.00
Transportation	17.17	6.21	18.56	8.84	6.24
Quality improvement projects	5.86	12.61	5.76	2.74	1.19
Others	2.16	13.16	3.66	1.24	0.16
Utilities	9.07	5.23	2.64	0.15	0.00
Administrative expenses for the municipal education authority	0.12	6.15	1.95	7.47	1.03
Information systems	0.16	2.94	0.13	0.00	0.00
Teacher training	2.41	1.00	0.76	2.19	0.00
Connectivity	0.09	2.00	0.55	0.00	0.01
Consultancies and studies	0.65	0.38	1.44	2.41	0.75
Endowments	0.07	0.07	0.48	0.08	0.00

Source: Investment Expenditures Database, Unique Territorial Form (accessed October 2019), https://sisfut.dnp.gov.co/app/login.
Note: GPS = General Participation System.

confounding the incentive and making it difficult to push for better outcomes. Including exogenous variables like poverty or rurality directly in the formula might be puzzling for local actors because these are variables over which they have no control. The use of these variables is desirable because the same outcomes might be more difficult to achieve in lower capability areas, and that effort should be rewarded. It would be simpler, however, to have preestablished "mark-up" values for each municipality and to transfer the resources accordingly instead of including the exogenous variables in the formula.

- *There is no pedagogy on the availability, and therefore relative distribution, of quality and gratuity resources.* As shown in figure 7.12, the amount of resources available for quality and gratuity transfers is decreasing. The distributions to individual municipalities or schools might decrease even if they have improved their outcomes because the overall pot of resources is shrinking. Each municipality and school principal competes with others for these limited resources; their performance relative to others determines how much they will receive. With no advice from the national government, however, few local education staff or school principals understand the situation. Instead, they see that they receive lower amounts of resources even though they are performing better, which negates the monetary incentive.

The complexity of the distribution formulas for gratuity and quality, together with the fact that the overall pot for both is shrinking, has resulted in a situation in which there is no clear correlation between these per capita transfers and changes in the scores of municipalities on the SIEQ, as illustrated in figures 7.16 and 7.17. The figures show that only 39 percent and 32 percent of municipalities received quality and gratuity transfers, respectively, commensurate with the improvement in their performance. More worrisome is the fact

FIGURE 7.16

Quality transfers to municipalities compared to performance

a. Graphic

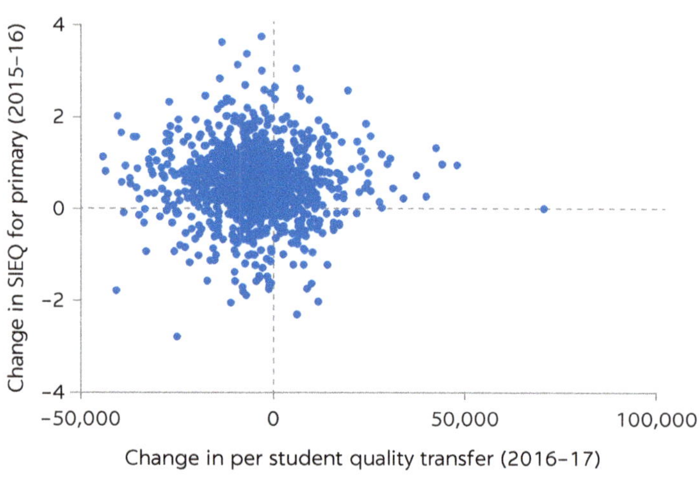

b. Numerical

Municipalities in sample 1,075		Change in SIEQ (2015–16)	
		Negative	Positive
Change in quality transfers (2016–17)	Negative	152 (14.1%)	574 (53.4%)
	Positive	80 (7.5%)	269 (25%)

Sources: SIEQ calculated by the Colombian Institute for Education Evaluation 2015–16; quality transfers data are from the Information and Consultation System for Distribution of Territorial Resources Database, National Planning Department, Bogotá (accessed October 2019), https://sicodis.dnp.gov.co/ReportesSGP/SGP_Historicos.aspx.
Note: SIEQ = Synthetic Index of Education Quality.

FIGURE 7.17

Gratuity transfers to municipalities compared to performance

a. Graphic

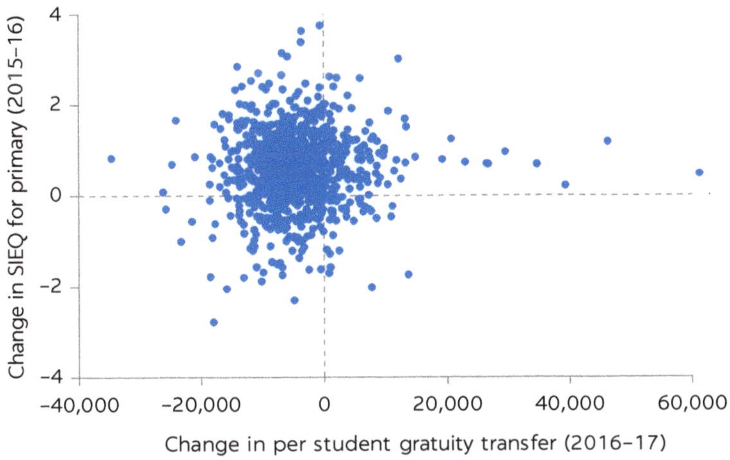

b. Numerical

Municipalities in sample 1,074		Change in SIEQ (2015–16)	
		Negative	Positive
Change in gratuity transfers (2016–17)	Negative	188 (17.5%)	685 (63.8%)
	Positive	43 (4%)	158 (14.7%)

Sources: SIEQ calculated by the Colombian Institute for Education Evaluation 2015–16; gratuity transfers data are from the Information and Consultation System for Distribution of Territorial Resources Database, National Planning Department, Bogotá (accessed October 2019), https://sicodis.dnp.gov.co/ReportesSGP/SGP_Historicos.aspx.
Note: SIEQ = Synthetic Index of Education Quality.

that 7.5 percent and 4 percent of municipalities received higher quality and gratuity transfers, respectively, even though their performance worsened. The use of performance-based incentives has some room for improvement.

EFFECTS OF DECENTRALIZED FINANCING SYSTEM ON SUBNATIONAL SPENDING AND EDUCATION OUTCOMES

Decreasing regional inequities in education funding and increasing access, efficiency, and learning are the main policy objectives of the transfer system. This section will analyze the extent to which these objectives have been met.

Decreasing regional inequities

Education expenditures per student vary widely among CTEs, as shown in figure 7.18. In this section we analyze the reasons behind this variation and its correlation with poverty.

We explore whether transfers decrease regional inequities in education funding by examining the distribution of provision of service, quality, and gratuity transfers compared to the poverty rate of the municipality. Next, we combine transfers with own-source resources from local governments to explore their impact on equity.

As shown in figure 7.19, in the absence of fiscal transfers, local government own-source resources spent on education are highly regressive: high poverty municipalities spend significantly less than rich municipalities on education from their own resources. Transfers compensate by providing more resources to

FIGURE 7.18
Per student public education expenditures, by CTE, 2017

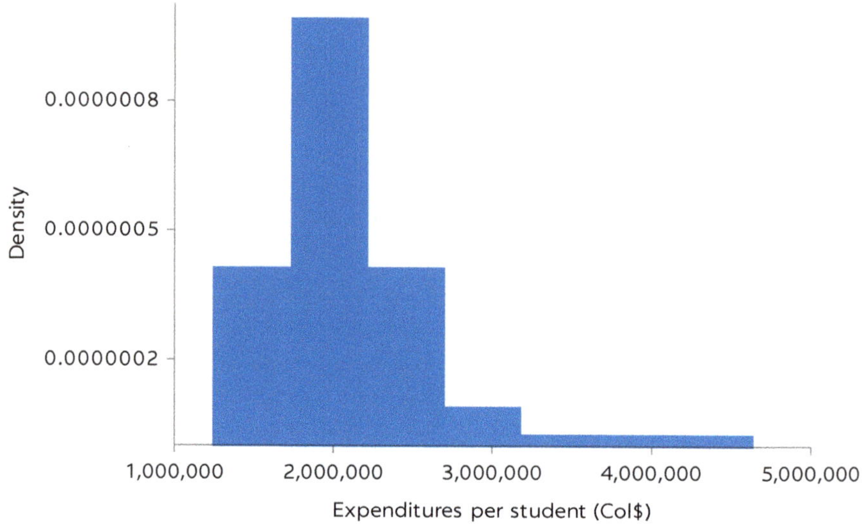

Source: Investment Expenditures Database, Unique Territorial Form (accessed October 2019), https://sisfut.dnp.gov.co/app/login.
Note: Col$ = Colombian peso; CTE = Certified Territorial Entity.

FIGURE 7.19
Interaction of education transfers with other regional income sources, 2017

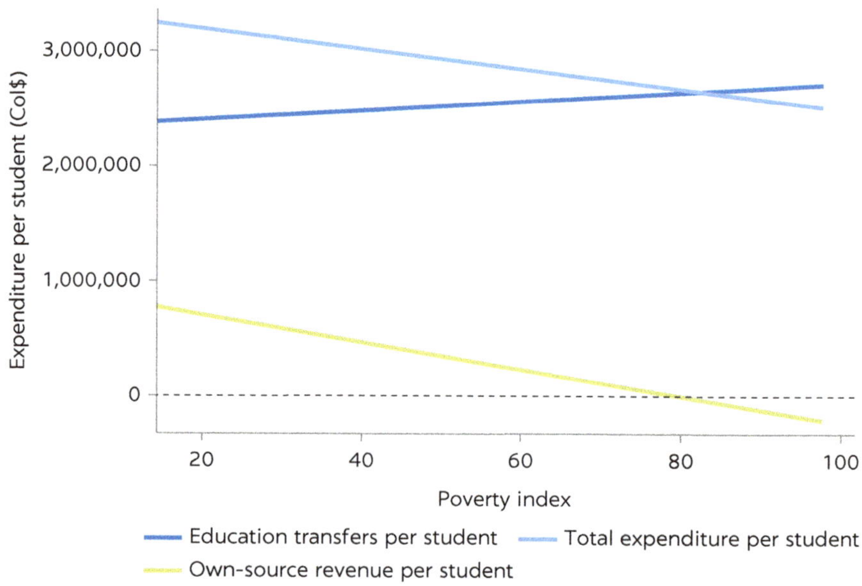

Sources: Expenditures and transfers data are from the Investment Expenditures Database, Unique Territorial Form (accessed October 2019), https://sisfut.dnp.gov.co/app/login; poverty index data are from Terridata (database), National Planning Department, Bogotá (accessed October 2019), https://terridata.dnp.gov.co/index-app.html#/descargas.

FIGURE 7.20
Students and teachers in the public sector, 2012–17

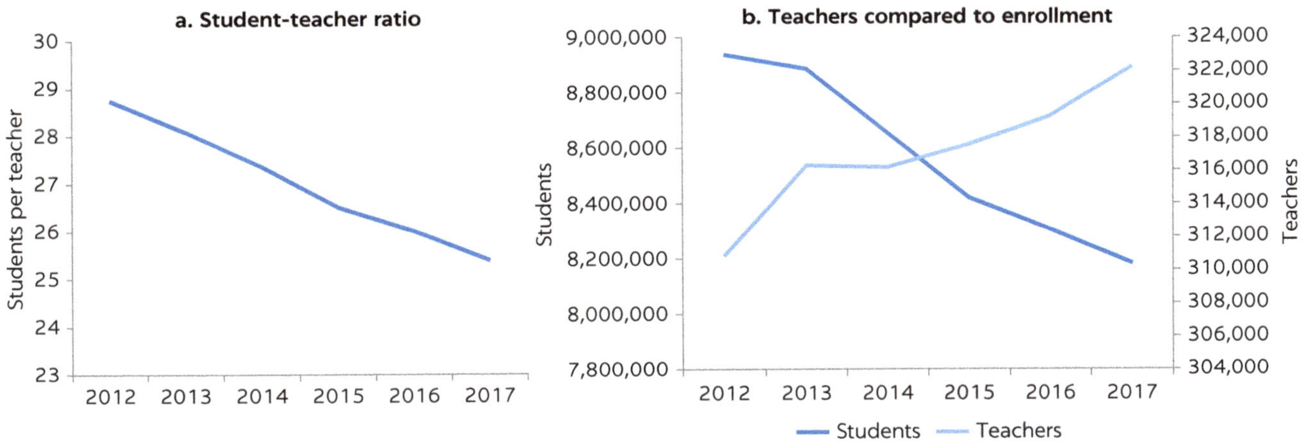

Sources: Public Teachers in Preschool, Basic, and Upper Higher Education Database, National Ministry of Education, Bogotá (accessed in October 2019), https://www.datos.gov.co/Educaci-n/MEN_DOCENTES-OFICIALES_EPBM/fjw5-pzau; enrollment data are from National Ministry of Education, Bogotá (accessed June 2020), https://www.mineducacion.gov.co/1759/w3-propertyname-3377.html?_noredirect=1.

high poverty municipalities. When the two are combined, overall education spending is still slightly regressive.

Increasing the efficiency of spending

One of the main objectives of using a funding formula instead of an input-based approach is to incentivize cost saving and increase the efficiency of education spending (Alonso and Sanchéz 2011). CTEs may be discouraged from engaging in cost-saving behavior, however, by inflexibility regarding teaching staff and by the resources transferred by the national government to cover additional costs through the complement. As a result, there is no reason to believe that there have been major efficiency improvements, especially because enrollment has been decreasing and the number of teachers has been increasing (see figure 7.20).

Even though we have no data for teacher attrition, the trends in figure 7.20 show that the system is facing dynamic inconsistency. Enrollment has been decreasing and is expected to keep decreasing because of the country's falling population. Although students are expected to remain in the system for 12 years, teachers on average stay in the system between 35 and 40 years. Eventually there will be a large teacher surplus that will need to be carefully managed to avoid extreme fiscal inefficiency.

Access and learning

We analyzed the impact of fiscal transfers on education outcomes in two specifications. In the first, we calculated the impact of fiscal transfers on total expenditures, and in the second, we calculated how total expenditure affects education outcomes—access and learning. For both specifications, we used three different models: (1) a pooled ordinary least squares (OLS) model; (2) a fixed-effects model; (3) and a dynamic panel data (DPD) model using a system generalized method of moments estimator (system GMM) in order to correct for the biases that may arise from the first two models.[19] Using the data available, we estimated the models from 2012 to 2017 for 1,101 municipalities using 2017 constant prices for all the monetary variables in the sample.[20]

Following the methodology found in Lewis (2017) and Lewis and Smoke (2017), we used total expenditures rather than education expenditures because spending on other sectors has positive externalities for the education sector and vice versa. Estimating the impact of fiscal transfers on total expenditures is necessary for analyzing whether fiscal transfers incentivize local governments to spend more or less and because transfers affect education outcomes only if they are spent.

Before analyzing the results from the econometric models, we looked at the correlations between transfers and total expenditures, own-source revenue, municipal value-added, poverty, mortality, and education outcomes. Figure 7.21 shows that consistent with our findings, poorer municipalities with lower taxing capabilities and higher mortality rates receive higher transfers, which are positively correlated with higher expenditure levels. For education transfers,

FIGURE 7.21

Correlation between fiscal transfers and key municipal variables, 2017

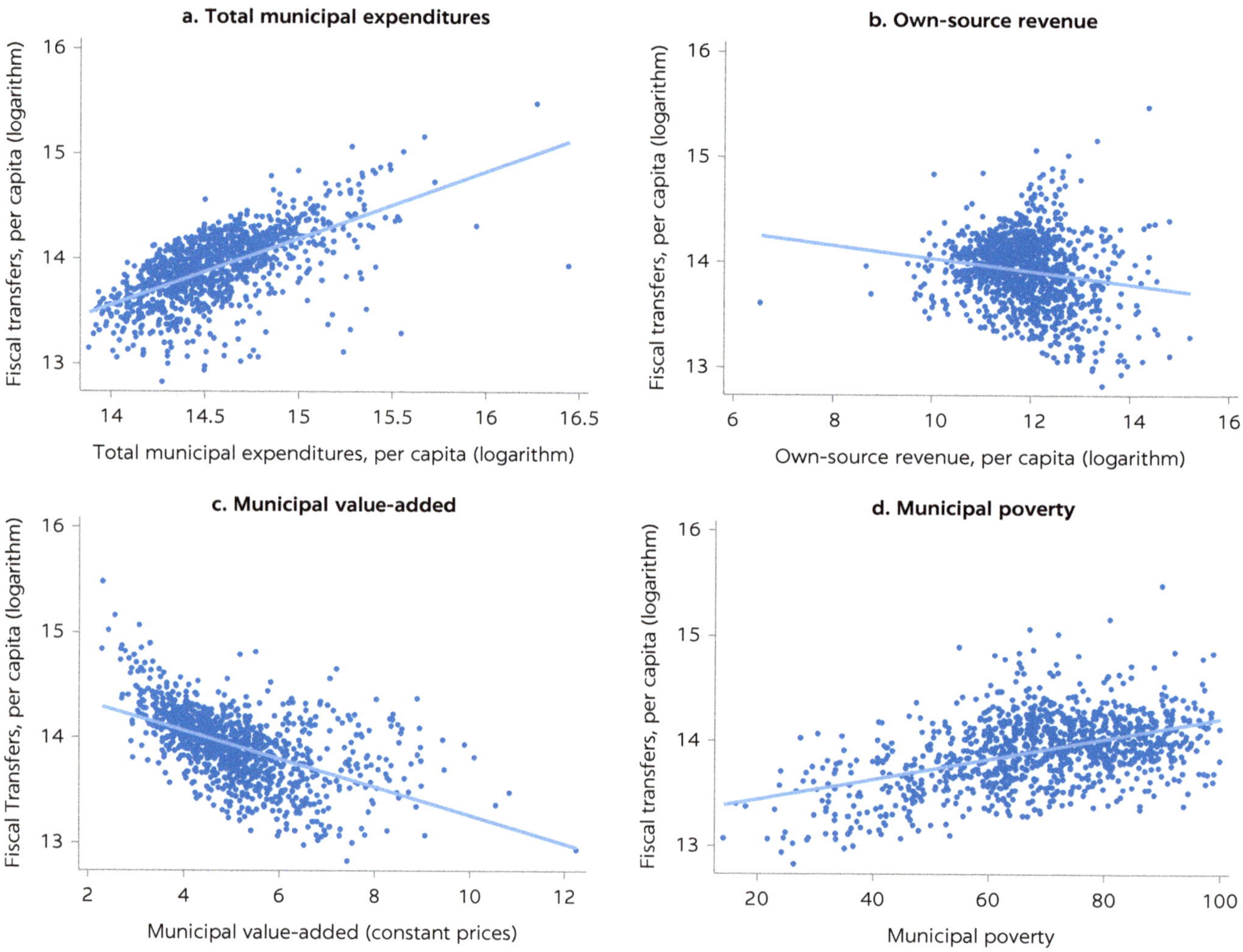

continued

FIGURE 7.21, *continued*

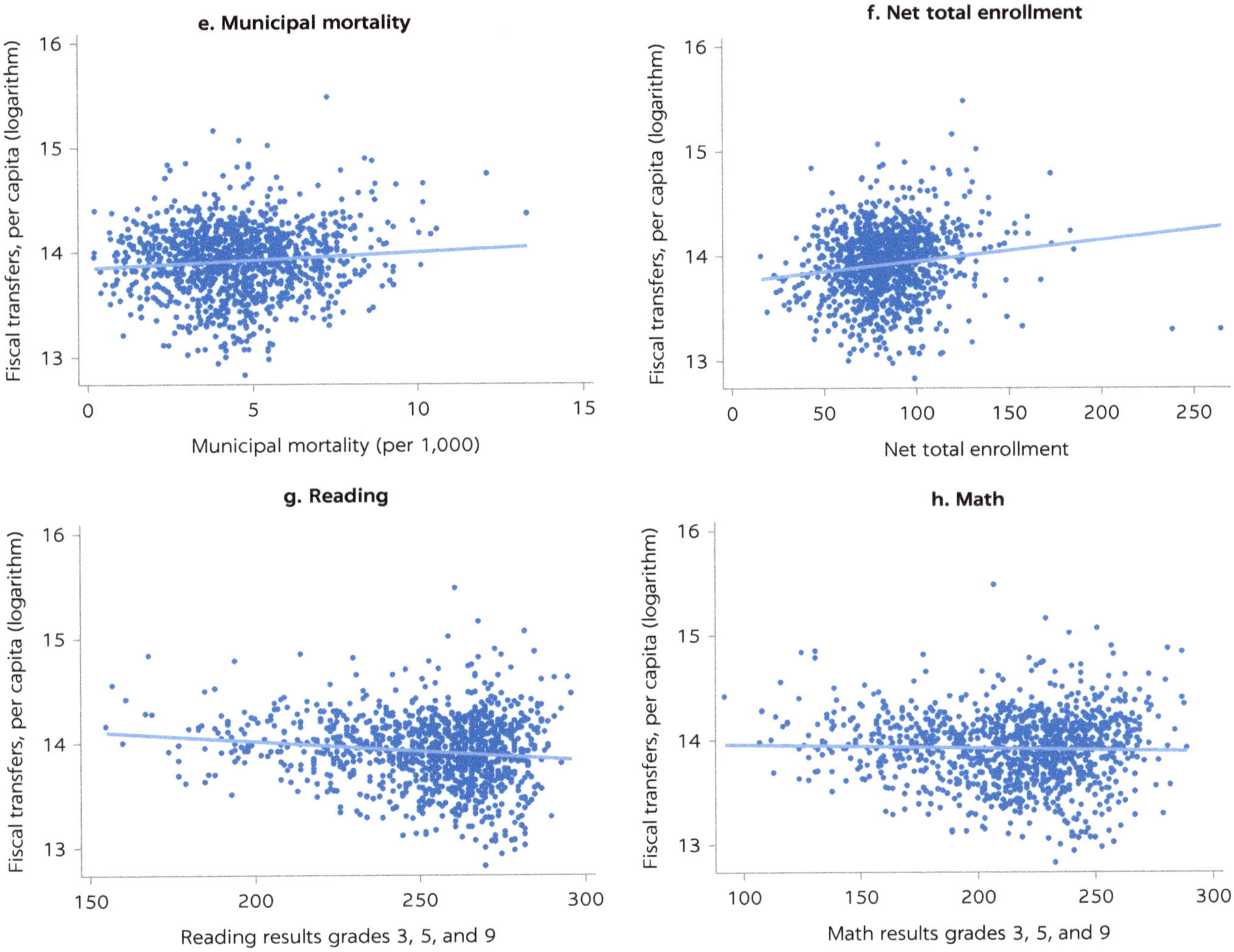

Sources: Expenditures, revenue, and transfers data from the Investment Expenditures Database, Unique Territorial Form (accessed October 2019), https://sisfut.dnp.gov.co/app/login; poverty index, mortality rate, and municipal value-added data are from the "Terridata" database from Terridata (database), National Planning Department, Bogotá (accessed October 2019), https://terridata.dnp.gov.co/index-app.html#/descargas; Municipal net enrollment rates are from the Municipal Statistics for Preschool, Basic, and Upper Higher Education Database, National Ministry of Education, Bogotá (accessed in October 2019), https://www.datos.gov.co/Educaci-n/MEN_ESTADISTICAS_EN_EDUCACION_EN_PREESCOLAR-B-SICA/nudc-7mev; reading and math results from the Saber 3, 5, and 9 standardized test are from the Colombian Institute for Education Evaluation.

the correlations show that higher transfers are positively correlated with net total enrollment rates, but negatively correlated with learning outcomes in reading and math for grades 3 to 9.

Impact of fiscal transfers on total expenditures

We used logarithms of per capita fiscal transfers and total expenditures to estimate the three models. The logarithms of total population and municipal value-added, as well as mortality per 100,000 habitants, water and internet coverage, rurality, and a poverty index, were used as controls (see table 7.7).

According to the OLS and DPD models, fiscal transfers have a significant positive impact on total expenditures, meaning that they incentivize CTEs to improve their fiscal performance. From the DPD model, it can be inferred that, on average, a 1 percent increase in total transfers from the national government increases local

TABLE 7.7 Impact of fiscal transfers on total local expenditures

	LN OF PER CAPITA TOTAL EXPENDITURE					
	OLS		FIXED EFFECTS		DPD	
	COEFFICIENT	*t*	COEFFICIENT	*t*	COEFFICIENT	*t*
Ln of per capita total expenditure (*t*−1)	0.6531668***	43.28	−0.0541123	−1.54	0.433954***	3.92
Ln of per capita national transfers	0.2556249***	17.19	0.2281262***	3.72	0.7998274***	3.57
Ln of population	−0.109068***	−13.79	−1.185435***	−4.74	−0.1184543***	−3.38
Ln of municipal value-added	0.0735142***	10.03	0.0558153***	2.87	0.1021636***	4.01
Mortality	−0.0098294***	−5.65	0.0000461	0.01	−0.0261444**	−2.67
Water coverage	−0.0000738	−0.85	−0.0001114	−0.80	0.0000476	0.41
Internet coverage	0.0067671***	7.21	0.0057751	0.97	0.0061338	1.44
Rurality	0.0085542**	2.54	n.a.	n.a.	−0.0086076	−0.56
Poverty index	−0.0009972***	−3.42	n.a.	n.a.	−0.0055301**	−2.63

Sources: Expenditure and transfer data are from the Investment Expenditures Database, Unique Territorial Form (accessed October 2019), https://sisfut.dnp.gov.co/app/login; poverty index, population, mortality rate, water coverage, internet coverage, rurality, and municipal value-added from Terridata (database), National Planning Department, Bogotá (accessed October 2019), https://terridata.dnp.gov.co/index-app.html#/descargas.
Note: DPD = dynamic panel data; n.a. = not applicable; OLS = ordinary least squares.
Significance level: * = 10 percent, ** = 5 percent, *** = 1 percent.

expenditure by 0.80 percent. Municipal value-added was found to have a positive significant effect on local expenditure, whereas poverty and mortality per 100,000 habitants were each found to have a significant negative impact.

Access

We measured the impact of total expenditures on access to education using net total enrollment. The logarithms of total population, municipal value-added, and rural public teachers as well as the mortality rates of children under age 1, water coverage, the size of the displaced population, a poverty index, a dummy for municipal certification, and rurality were used as controls (see table 7.8).

We found that total expenditure has a significant positive impact on total net enrollment in all models, which is not surprising because the transfer system is designed on a per student basis. According to the DPD model, on average, a 1 percent increase in per capita expenditure increases net enrollment by 5.88 percent. Furthermore, total population and the number of rural teachers were found to have a significant positive effect on enrollment. Finally, both municipal value-added and CTE status have a significant negative impact on enrollment, because in richer certified municipalities average enrollment is already so high that it is hard to increase it or keep it constant. For example, in 2017, average net enrollment in uncertified municipalities was 83 percent compared with 91 percent in certified municipalities.

Improving learning

To measure improvements in learning, we used the proportion of students in grades 3, 5, and 9 who scored above the passing rate on the Saber test in

TABLE 7.8 **Impact of total local expenditures on education access**

	NET TOTAL ENROLLMENT					
	OLS		FIXED EFFECTS		DPD	
	COEFFICIENT	*t*	COEFFICIENT	*t*	COEFFICIENT	*z*
Net total enrollment (*t*–1)	1.012863***	196.76	0.4390742***	9.43	1.011355***	43.73
Ln of per capita total expenditure	1.326306***	6.35	–0.1145145	–0.27	5.877762***	2.70
Ln of total population	0.4206454***	2.94	–8.517309**	–2.29	2.190015**	2.46
Ln of municipal value-added	–0.078969	–0.68	–0.6735837*	–1.90	–0.9523965*	–1.68
Rural teachers	0.2004358	–0.58	2.64671	1.56	1.014045*	1.67
Mortality under 1 year	0.0079038	1.05	0.0056203	0.62	–0.0172093	–1.02
Water coverage	0.0010673	–0.47	0.0017676	0.53	0.0019038	0.78
Displaced population	0.00000845	0.05	0.0002639**	2.08	–0.0000226	0.15
CTE	–0.6221256**	–2.32	n.a.	n.a.	–3.123263**	–2.19
Poverty index	–0.0074096	1.40	n.a.	n.a.	0.0066839	–0.50
Rurality	–0.099646	–1.07	n.a.	n.a.	–0.3478107	–1.40

Sources: Expenditures data are from the Investment Expenditures Database, Unique Territorial Form (accessed October 2019), https://sisfut.dnp.gov.co/app/login; poverty index, population, mortality rate under 1 year, municipal value-added, water coverage, displaced population, and rurality are from Terridata (database), National Planning Department, Bogotá (accessed October 2019), https://terridata.dnp.gov.co/index-app.html#/descargas; municipal net enrollment rates are from Municipal Statistics for Preschool, Basic, and Upper Higher Education Database, National Ministry of Education, Bogotá (accessed in October 2019), https://www.datos.gov.co/Educaci-n/MEN_ESTADISTICAS_EN_EDUCACION_EN_PREESCOLAR-B-SICA/nudc-7mev; rural teacher data are from the Public Teachers in Preschool, Basic, and Upper Higher Education Database, National Ministry of Education, Bogotá (accessed in October 2019), https://www.datos.gov.co/Educaci-n/MEN_DOCENTES-OFICIALES_EPBM/fjw5-pzau.
Note: CTE = Certified Territorial Entity; DPD = dynamic panel data; n.a. = not applicable; OLS = ordinary least squares.
Significance level: * = 10 percent, ** = 5 percent, *** = 1 percent.

reading and math (see tables 7.9 and 7.10).[21] As controls, we used the logarithms of total and public enrollment, logarithms of municipal value-added, logarithms of the number of public school teachers with a graduate degree, prenatal controls (number of times that pregnant women attend a medical consultation regarding their pregnancy), the proportion of minorities in total enrollment, the mortality rates of children under age 1, the size of the displaced population, a dummy for municipal certification, a poverty index, and municipal rurality.

In the case of both mathematics and reading, total expenditure does not seem to have a significant impact on learning outcomes. Prenatal controls and teachers with a graduate degree both have a significant positive impact, and the mortality of children under age 1 has a significant negative impact on both learning outcomes. Finally, the proportion of minorities enrolled in school has a negative impact only in the case of mathematics.

Although total expenditure is an important factor for promoting greater access, it does not improve learning outcomes, which are positively affected by variables related to health, early childhood care, and the proportion of teachers that hold a graduate degree. Total expenditure alone is not enough to achieve all the desired objectives; that fact needs to be taken into account in the design of education policies and reforms if Colombia is to improve its learning outcomes.

TABLE 7.9 **Impact of total local expenditure on reading**

	PERCENTAGE OF CHILDREN IN GRADES 3, 5, AND 9 SCORING ABOVE LOWEST ACHIEVEMENT LEVEL RATE IN READING					
	OLS		FIXED EFFECTS		DPD	
	COEFFICIENT	*t*	COEFFICIENT	*t*	COEFFICIENT	*t*
Percentage of children in grades 3, 5, and 9 scoring above lowest achievement level in reading (*t*−1)	0.7442651***	61.04	0.0504962**	2.21	0.7084338***	5.82
Ln of per capita total expenditure	0.1742293	0.22	−4.31737***	−2.60	5.682704	0.93
Ln of public enrollment	−1.608015***	−2.95	7.237776	1.61	−0.9597614	−0.52
Ln municipal value-added	0.6154466	1.47	2.32376	1.62	0.4038417	0.42
Prenatal controls	1.334119***	4.10	1.05966	1.46	2.37953**	2.37
Minority enrollment/total enrollment	−3.987472**	−2.38	26.95006*	1.89	−3.21142	−1.00
Mortality under 1 year	−0.1247323***	−3.50	−0.1441042***	−3.50	−0.1253349**	−2.56
Displaced population	−0.0004002*	−1.78	−0.0007656**	−2.39	−0.000538	−1.58
Ln teachers with graduate degree	0.8486343***	3.75	0.4867234	1.29	0.9629324*	1.81
CTE	2.708227***	3.28	n.a.	n.a.	1.201391	0.57
Poverty index	−0.1178591***	−5.47	n.a.	n.a.	−0.1394361	−1.00
Rurality	1.479624***	4.43	n.a.	n.a.	1.383466	1.45

Sources: Expenditure, revenue, and transfer data are from the Investment Expenditures Database, Unique Territorial Form (accessed October 2019), https://sisfut.dnp.gov.co/app/login; poverty index, mortality under 1 year, prenatal controls, municipal value-added, displaced population, and rurality data are from Terridata (database), National Planning Department, Bogotá (accessed October 2019), https://terridata.dnp.gov.co/index-app.html#/descargas; municipal public enrollment and minority enrollment rates are from the Municipal Statistics for Preschool, Basic, and Upper Higher Education Database, National Ministry of Education, Bogotá (accessed in October 2019), https://www.datos.gov.co/Educaci-n/MEN_ESTADISTICAS_EN_EDUCACION_EN_PREESCOLAR-B-SICA/nudc-7mev; teachers with graduate degrees data from the Public Teachers in Preschool, Basic, and Upper Higher Education Database, National Ministry of Education, Bogotá (accessed in October 2019), https://www.datos.gov.co/Educaci-n/MEN_DOCENTES-OFICIALES_EPBM/fjw5-pzau; reading results from the Saber 3, 5, and 9 standardized tests are from the Colombian Institute for Education Evaluation.
Note: CTE = Certified Territorial Entity; DPD = dynamic panel data; n.a. = not applicable; OLS = ordinary least squares.
Significance level: * = 10 percent, ** = 5 percent, *** = 1 percent.

Fiscal capacity and its correlation with learning outcomes

It is crucial to factor in the extent of local capacity when analyzing decentralization and its results. Local governments that have little or no capacity to implement public policies or effectively deliver social services will not improve their social outcomes regardless of the level of resources they receive and the number of functions allocated to them.

As the national government recognized in the National Development Plan 2018–22, local capacity in Colombia is a major concern for decentralization. The Plan identified inefficiency in public spending as one of the major causes of regional inequality, in addition to limitations in public management, limited capacity to identify local needs (leading to an inability to invest efficiently and improve results), and low levels of contract performance. The Plan also identified the lack of mechanisms to create and promote local capacity and attract quality human talent to the local public sector.

One way to analyze how capacity concerns explain education outcomes is through the relationship between the Municipal Fiscal Performance Index—an index that measures the capacity of municipalities to (1) spend resources; (2) have enough resources to finance their costs; (3) stay within the spending limits set by the national government; (4) raise sufficient own-source resources; (5) maintain high investment levels; (6) service their debt; and (7) produce savings—and the SIEQ (see figure 7.22).

TABLE 7.10 Impact of total expenditure on mathematics

	PERCENTAGE OF CHILDREN IN GRADES 3, 5, AND 9 SCORING ABOVE LOWEST ACHIEVEMENT LEVEL IN MATHEMATICS					
	OLS		FIXED EFFECTS		DPD	
	COEFFICIENT	*t*	COEFFICIENT	*t*	COEFFICIENT	*t*
Percentage of children in grades 3, 5, and 9 scoring above lowest achievement level in mathematics (*t*−1)	0.7678583***	69.09	0.0245192	0.99	0.6331355***	4.40
Ln of per capita total expenditure	1.814117*	1.95	−3.01828	−1.56	13.0501	1.02
Ln public enrollment	−2.20121***	−3.31	4.772328	0.91	−0.3434228	−0.10
Ln municipal value-added	0.4887888	0.99	1.510374	0.83	−1.013236	−0.51
Prenatal controls	1.419939***	3.63	1.201043	1.41	3.302537*	1.76
Minority enrollment/total enrollment	−7.154418***	−3.78	12.52049	0.86	−12.20824**	−2.11
Mortality under 1 year	−0.0890773**	−2.05	−0.0974657**	−1.99	−0.1560701*	−1.91
Displaced population	−0.0000701	−0.31	0.000000196	0.00	0.0001672	0.40
Ln teachers with graduate degree	1.015896***	3.83	0.4112422	0.96	1.505967*	1.84
CTE	3.036898***	3.12	n.a.	n.a.	0.610014	0.13
Poverty index	−0.1512268***	−5.61	n.a.	n.a.	−0.2767083*	−1.70
Rurality	1.57042***	3.84	n.a.	n.a.	2.02841	1.33

Source: Expenditure, revenue, and transfer data are from the Investment Expenditures Database, Unique Territorial Form (accessed October 2019), https://sisfut.dnp.gov.co/app/login;. poverty index, mortality under 1 year, prenatal controls, municipal value-added, displaced population, and rurality are from Terridata (database), National Planning Department, Bogotá (accessed October 2019), https://terridata.dnp.gov.co/index-app.html#/descargas; municipal public enrollment and minority enrollment rates are from the Municipal Statistics for Preschool, Basic, and Upper Higher Education Database, National Ministry of Education, Bogotá (accessed in October 2019), https://www.datos.gov.co/Educaci-n/MEN_ESTADISTICAS_EN_EDUCACION_EN_PREESCOLAR-B-SICA/nudc-7mev; teachers with graduate degrees data are from the Public Teachers in Preschool, Basic, and Upper Higher Education Database, National Ministry of Education, Bogotá (accessed in October 2019), https://www.datos.gov.co/Educaci-n/MEN_DOCENTES-OFICIALES_EPBM/fjw5-pzau; math results from the Saber 3, 5, and 9 standardized test are from the Colombian Institute for Education Evaluation.
Note: CTE = Certified Territorial Entity; DPD = dynamic panel data; n.a. = not applicable; OLS = ordinary least squares.
Significance level: * = 10 percent,** = 5 percent, *** = 1 percent.

FIGURE 7.22
Fiscal capacity and SIEQ results, 2015–16

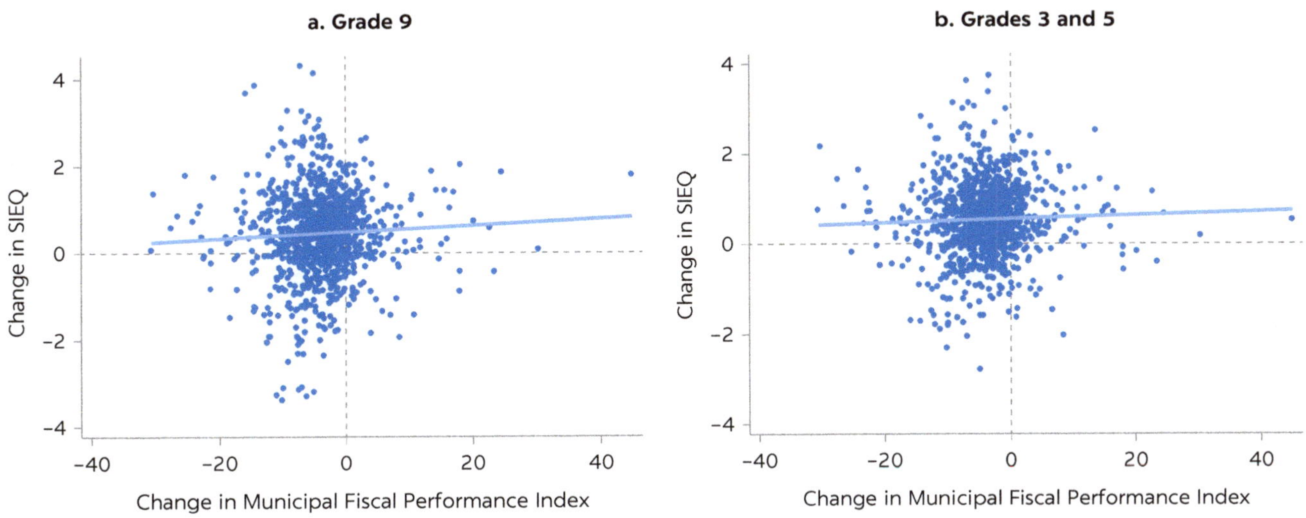

Sources: SIEQ calculated by the Colombian Institute for Education Evaluation 2015–16; Fiscal Performance Index from Terridata (database), National Planning Department, Bogotá (accessed October 2019), https://terridata.dnp.gov.co/index-app.html#/descargas.
Note: SIEQ = Synthetic Index of Education Quality.

The data show that there is a positive correlation between the capacity that municpalities have to use their resources and improved education outcomes. This relationship does not seem to be very strong, however, suggesting that not only spending, but the quality of spending, matters.

The National Development Plan 2018–22 establishes capacity building as one of its main pillars to improve the results of decentralization. The implementation of this pillar includes strategies aimed at achieving three main objectives: (1) fostering regional fiscal capacity to increase income; (2) promoting efficiency in local public spending; and (3) developing and implementing technical assistance to strengthen the capacity of human capital.[22]

CONCLUSION

There has been a growing debate about reforming the fiscal transfer system in Colombia. Many, including the teachers' union, argue in favor of a constitutional reform that would increase the total allocation from the national budget to fiscal transfers to improve social outcomes, particularly in health and education. Others argue in favor of a legal reform aimed at increasing the efficiency of the system to achieve better social outcomes without increasing the current amount

TABLE 7.11 **Lessons from the Colombia case study**

What worked?	Fiscal transfers have caused enrollment to increase, likely the result of a per student distribution formula that created a powerful incentive for CTEs to have more children in the public system
	Including socioeconomic variables such as poverty and rurality in the distribution formulas makes fiscal transfers progressive thus creating some level of horizontal equity
	Establishing a fiscal transfer that goes directly to schools provides a free education to vulnerable children around the country
	The fiscal reform undertaken in 2001 guaranteed a preestablished real annual real increase in transfers, giving the system more fiscal stability and a greater ability to plan and manage these resources
What can be improved?	Education transfers should not be distributed as a zero-sum game; forcing actors in the education sector to compete against each other for resources might affect the financing capability of key education functions
	When using a funding formula instead of an input-based approach for fiscal transfers to promote efficiency, avoid creating a complementary financing mechanism that might invalidate the efficiency incentive
	Teacher transfer mechanisms that allow human resource mobility across regions are necessary to promote efficiency
	Resources should be aligned with functions; in Colombia, quality transfers are received by uncertified municipalities that are responsible only for a few functions, whereas states receive no quality transfers despite having greater responsibilities
	Decentralization efforts require strong capacity-building programs to obtain their desired results
	New functions should not be assigned to actors without providing the resources to fund them, as was the case with the school feeding program and curricular autonomy in Colombia
	More important than how they are constructed, performance-based formulas should be predictable, transparent, aligned with objectives, and, especially, easy to understand for the entities whose actions are meant to be incentivized
	Performance-based formulas should be accompanied by communication or pedagogical campaigns that make it clear to local entities and actors that the resources they receive depend on measures of their performance
	Supporting systems and coordination in the form of data and management support are key; improving decision-making at the local government level requires the use of better data

Source: World Bank.
Note: CTE = Certified Territorial Entity.

TABLE 7.12 **Characteristics and shortcomings of types of transfers**

TYPE	PROVISION OF SERVICE SPECIFIC	QUALITY SPECIFIC	GRATUITY SPECIFIC
Objective 1	Equity	Performance	Performance
Objective 2	Efficiency	Equity	Equity
Determining the pool of funds	Endogenous	Discretionary; residual after distributing provision of service and gratuity resources	Discretionary; residual after distributing provision of service resources
Allocation of pool	Highly variable formula; no clarity about main components	Highly variable formula; no clarity about its main components	Highly variable formula; no clarity about main components
Incentive	Limited on equity and lack of incentives for efficiency	Unclear incentives for performance	Unclear incentives for performance
Who is incentivized?	CTEs	Municipalities	Schools
Impact	Equalizes per capita spending but no effect on efficiency	Some effects on equity but no apparent effect on learning	No effect on equity and no apparent effect on learning
Issues	Simplify formula, improve equity, and enforce efficiency	Strengthen incentives for performance and ensure clarity and consistency, especially for equality	Strengthen incentives for performance, improve equality, and ensure clarity

Source: World Bank.
Note: CTE = Certified Territorial Entity.

of transfers through constitutional reform. (The former government presented a proposal to increase efficiency without altering the overall amount for transfers. The bill was later withdrawn.)

This chapter illustrates that the pillars for a high-performing system exist, but it also makes a strong case for change. The system needs to provide more effective incentives and make complementary reforms to the management of the system, both of which will improve efficiency. The management of human resources is central to achieving these goals. Clarifying roles and responsibilities and aligning funding to those responsibilities is also key. Schools have a big mandate, including the design of their own curriculum, and they need more resources to do it effectively.

Table 7.11 details the lessons from the analysis of the Colombian fiscal transfer system that can be used by other countries that are considering decentralization reforms. Finally, table 7.12 presents a summary of the characteristics of the main earmarked education fiscal transfers in Colombia.

NOTES

1. We are especially thankful to Luis Piñeros for sharing his data and for numerous conversations about the decentralization in Colombia.
2. We use "municipalities" for *municipio* and "states" for *departamento*.
3. The proportion of total students enrolled in public schools was over 80 percent in those years.
4. National Quality of Life Survey 2018, NADS (National Administrative Department of Statistics), Bogotá, Colombia (accessed October 2019). https://www.dane.gov.co/index.php/estadisticas-por-tema/salud/calidad-de-vida-ecv/encuesta-nacional-de-calidad-de-vida-ecv-2018.
5. The SIEQ measures quality of education using levels of learning, changes in learning, dropout levels, and school environment. See Colombian Institute for Education Evaluation, https://www.icfes.gov.co/edicion-05-boletin-saber-en- breve, for the methodology.
6. Investment Expenditures Database, Unique Territorial Form (accessed October 2019), https://sisfut.dnp.gov.co/app/login.

7. Decree 2700 requires that municipalities seeking certification must have: (1) local development plans that conform to national education policies; (2) organized schools that provide primary through high school education; (3) a teaching payroll in line with national parameters; and (4) enough institutional capacity to administer the necessary organization processes and information systems in the education sector.
8. As of 2018, there were 96 CTEs. The municipality of Funza became certified in 2018. Because our data extends only until 2017, the rest of the analysis does not consider Funza to be a CTE.
9. Investment Expenditures Database, Unique Territorial Form (accessed October 2019), https://sisfut.dnp.gov.co/app/login.
10. Transfers made to the teachers' pension fund (FONPET) and expenditures from ministries other than the Ministry of Education are not included.
11. According to the Minister of Finance, this was the motivation behind Project No. 11 of 2006 to reform the National Constitution.
12. Investment Expenditures Database, Unique Territorial Form (accessed October 2019), https://sisfut.dnp.gov.co/app/login. The poorest municipalities can spend 42 percent of their general-purpose resources freely. The remaining resources must be spent according to the parameters established in the law as follows: 4 percent on sports and recreation, 3 percent on culture, and 10 percent on the pension fund (FONPET).
13. The SIEQ is constructed using four dimensions: (1) performance (the school's comparative performance on the Saber test); (2) progress (the school's results on the Saber test compared to the year before); (3) efficiency (the number of students who passed their level); and (4) the school environment.
14. A zero-sum game is a term commonly used in game theory to describe a situation in which two or more players engage in strategic interaction in which what one player wins the other loses.
15. The agreements signed between the main teacher's union and the government include: (1) a 12 percentage point real increase in the salary of all teachers, negotiated in 2015, to be applied incrementally from 2015 to 2019; (2) automatic promotions for teachers in grade 2 of the pay scale regulated under Decree 1278 of 2002 who complete graduate studies (with no evaluation required), negotiated between 2008 and 2014; (3) a new methodology to evaluate teachers for promotion, which increased the yearly percentage of teachers who were promoted from about 20 percent in 2015 to about 80 percent in 2016 (each promotion representing about a 28 percent increase in salary); (4) a yearly service bonus equivalent to 15 days of salary for all teaching staff, negotiated in 2013–14; (5) a "level 14" yearly bonus of 15 percent of salary for teachers in the last level of the pay scale regulated under Decree 2277 of 1979, negotiated in 2015; (6) a retirement bonus of one month's salary for retiring teachers in the last level of the pay scale regulated under Decree 2277 of 1979, negotiated in 2015; (7) a "remote area" monthly bonus of 15 percent of salary for teachers working in remote or difficult to access areas, negotiated in 2010.
16. Investment Expenditures Database, Unique Territorial Form (accessed October 2019), https://sisfut.dnp.gov.co/app/login.
17. The mandatory performance evaluation applies to teachers who are covered by Statute 1278, which was introduced in 2002. Teachers who joined the public system before 2002 are covered by Statute 2277, under which teachers are not evaluated.
18. A curricular mesh is a didactic complement to the learning standards for each grade and assignment. These tools were developed by the Ministry of Education to guide school principals and teachers in building curriculums aligned to the nonbinding national standards.
19. We avoided over instrumentation by using a reduced number of lags and collapsing them. All variables related to total expenditure were treated as endogenous, whereas all the other controls were treated as strictly exogenous.
20. The resources spent by states were incorporated into the model by dividing them among their municipalities according to the municipalities' population. A more detailed description of the data and methodology used as well as the results of the models can be found World Bank (2021).
21. The only data available combined results from students in both private and public schools.
22. Because the National Development Plan 2018–22 was adopted in 2019, no indicators are yet available to track progress toward achieving these objectives.

REFERENCES

Alonso, J.D., and A. Sanchéz. 2011. *Reforming Education Finance in Transition Countries: Six Case Studies in Per Capita Financing Systems*. Washington, DC: World Bank.

Cerdán-Infantes, P., and F. Zavala. 2017. *Reporte del Monitor Escolar*. Bogotá: World Bank.

Comptroller General of the Republic. 2017. *Redistributive Effect of the General Participation System: Results and Perspectives in Health and Education*. Bogotá: Comptroller General of the Republic.

Elacqua, G., H. Santos, I. Munevar, and F. Sanchéz. 2019. *The Impact of Decentralized Decision Making on Student Outcomes and Teacher Quality: Evidence from Colombia*. Washington, DC: Interamerican Development Bank.

Krugman, P.R., and M. Obstfeld. 2006. *Economía internacional: Teoría y Política*. Madrid: Pearson Educación.

Lewis, B.D. 2017. "Local Government Spending and Service Delivery in Indonesia: The Perverse Effects of Substantial Fiscal Resources." *Regional Studies* 51 (11): 1–13.

Lewis, B.D., and P. Smoke. 2017. "Intergovernmental Fiscal Transfers and Local Incentives and Responses: The Case of Indonesia." *Fiscal Studies* 38 (1): 111–39.

Mas-Collel, A., M.D. Whinston, and J.R. Green. 1995. *Microeconomic Theory*. New York: Oxford University Press.

Ministry of Finance and Public Credit. 2006. "*Exposición de motivos: Proyecto de Acto Legislativo No. 11*." Bogotá: Ministry of Finance and Public Credit.

——. 2018. "*Exposición de motivos: Proyecto de Ley para la reforma de la Ley 715 de 2001*." Bogotá: Ministry of Finance and Public Credit.

National Ministry of Education. 2016. *Guide No. 8*. Bogotá: National Ministry of Education.

National Planning Department. 2002. *Documento CONPES (Consejo Nacional de Política Económica y Social) 57*. Bogotá: National Planning Department.

——. 2013. *Documento CONPES (Consejo Nacional de Política Económica y Social) 159*. Bogotá: National Planning Department.

Olson, M. 1965. *The Logic of Collective Action*. Cambridge, MA: Harvard University Press.

World Bank. 2021. *The Role of Intergovernmental Fiscal Transfers in Improving Education Outcomes. Annex*. Washington, DC: World Bank.

8 Brazil Case Study

ANDRÉ LOUREIRO, LOUISEE CRUZ, AND URSULA MELLO

INTRODUCTION

This chapter describes Brazil's complex intergovernmental fiscal transfer system, which has improved regional and socioeconomic equity in education spending and outcomes and draws lessons that might be useful for other countries.[1] A key element of the Brazilian education financing framework is the Fund for the Development of Basic Education (FUNDEB), which has substantially reduced inequality in education spending across the country. The state of Ceará—a relatively poor state in Brazil—is a good example of how learning and other education outcomes can be substantially improved through increasing efficiency in education expenditures, that is, by increasing value for money. Using a panel data set at the municipal level, we find robust positive relationships between transfers and education spending and education outcomes in Brazil.

The Brazilian Constitution decentralizes preuniversity education provision to states and municipalities. The majority of Brazilian preuniversity students attend public schools. Out of the 48 million students in basic education (comprising the early childhood education (ECE), primary, and secondary levels), 16 million are enrolled in state schools and 24 million in municipal schools, representing 33 percent and 49 percent of total enrollment, respectively, according to the 2018 Brazilian Education Census. The Federal government has an oversight role of preuniversity education and concentrates its focus on tertiary education, with some exceptions.[2] Twenty-four percent of students in tertiary education are enrolled in public institutions.

Differences in the populations and economic size of municipalities and states result in substantial discrepancies between tax revenues and education investments, which means that transfers from the federal government are critical for promoting regional equity in spending per student. The level of income in Brazil can vary starkly across the regions and states, with the nine Northeastern states ranked lowest in per capita income. To alleviate regional imbalances in education spending FUNDEB pools municipal and state resources and redistributes the total based on student enrollment rates and education levels. An additional element of FUNDEB is the federal government's contribution of an amount that represents 10 percent of the sum of all subnational funds, which is redistributed according to the number of students enrolled in each school network, with the values varying by level of education.[3]

National financing instruments, particularly FUNDEB, have greatly helped to increase investment in education and reduce regional inequity in per student spending, but there is still room to increase equity and efficiency (Arvate, Mattos, and Rocha 2015; Cruz and Mereb 2018; Menezes-Filho 2007, 2012; World Bank 2017). Brazil allocates 16 percent of total public spending to education, which accounts for 6.2 percent of its gross domestic product (GDP). Over the last 15 years, education's share of GDP has increased by 2.3 percentage points, a 60 percent increase. FUNDEB is currently the largest source of funds for education and has helped to increase education investment, student enrollment, and teacher salaries, as well as reducing interregional spending inequality. Yet substantial equity gaps remain because, under FUNDEB's current distribution formula, richer municipalities in poor states receive more resources than poor municipalities in wealthy states.

The greatest challenge of education in Brazil is to increase the efficiency of education spending to achieve better learning outcomes. A constitutional rule mandates that the federal government allocates 18 percent of total tax revenues to education and that states and municipalities spend at least 25 percent of their revenues on the sector. These earmarks and the absence of any performance incentives in FUNDEB and other national financing mechanisms result in a highly inefficient use of resources. For any given level of spending, there is a wide variation in learning outcomes across the country. Educational achievement has increased at a much slower rate than spending, especially in secondary education. At the current rate, it will take Brazil 75 years to reach the average score in math for Organisation for Economic Co-operation and Development (OECD) countries and 263 years to reach the average score in reading (World Bank 2018).

The state of Ceará has implemented a results-based mechanism for intergovernmental transfers that is a role model for increasing efficiency in education spending. Ceará is a poor state with 9 million inhabitants in the northeast of Brazil that has implemented innovative education reforms since 2007. The state has devolved responsibility for all public primary and lower secondary schools to its municipalities and has established a framework of technical support and incentives to achieve learning goals. The state distributes shares of revenue from the Tax on the Circulation of Goods and Services (ICMS), the main source of revenue for Brazilian states, among municipalities based in part on their education performance. The share of the ICMS allocated to each municipality depends on the achievement of specified education, health, and environmental results, but there is no requirement that the municipalities use these transfers to improve education, health, or environmental outcomes. The ICMS transfers received by municipalities represent a substantial part of their total revenues, which gives them a substantial incentive to improve their education outcomes. As a result, the National Index of Education Quality (IDEB)[4] in Ceará has improved for both primary and lower secondary education (Lautharte, Oliveira, and Loureiro 2020). In 2017, 10 of the top 20 best-performing municipalities were in Ceará.[5]

THE BRAZILIAN EDUCATION SYSTEM

Responsibilities for service delivery

The Brazilian Constitution allocates responsibility for education to the federal, state, and municipal levels of government, which jointly provide public pretertiary education to 42 million students. Preuniversity education in Brazil consists of ECE for children from birth to age 5, primary and lower secondary education (grades 1 to 9) and upper secondary education (grades 10 to 12 on the general track or grades 10 to 13 for technical programs). The federal government is responsible for overall education planning and policy making, such as setting the minimum wage of teachers and the rules governing funding formulas. Municipalities are responsible for providing ECE and primary and lower secondary education, while states are responsible for providing lower and upper secondary education. Municipalities and states overlap in their responsibilities for lower secondary education because not all municipalities can afford to provide it.[6] Out of the 48 million students in preuniversity education, 16 million are enrolled in state school networks, 24 million in municipal school networks and 8 million are enrolled in private schools, which represent 33 percent, 50 percent and 17 percent of total national enrollment, respectively (see figure 8.1). The federal government manages a few mostly technical and military schools but focuses on providing tertiary education.[7]

Each level of government in Brazil is responsible for its students. The federal government sets the policy guidelines, monitors education quality, and provides financial assistance in specific areas. Nevertheless, most of the decisions regarding education delivery are taken at the state and municipal levels. At the policy level, they have autonomy to define the curriculum and teacher career and

FIGURE 8.1

Enrollment in public preuniversity education by level of government in Brazil, 2018

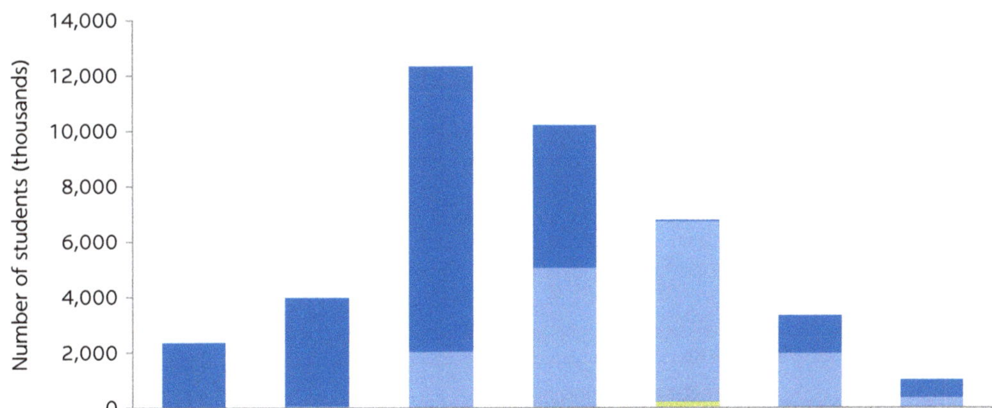

	Crèche (0–3 years)	Pre-school (4–5 years)	Primary (grades 1-5)	Lower secondary (grades 6-9)	Upper secondary (grades 10-13)	Young and adulthood education	Students with disabilities
Municipalities	2,346.9	3,915.9	10,284.0	5,143.2	41.5	1,354.7	631.3
State	3.9	52.4	2,030.9	5,031.4	6,527.1	1,956.6	355.8
Federal	1.2	1.6	7.3	15.1	209.4	13.0	5.0

■ Municipalities ■ State ■ Federal

Source: 2018 Education Census.

professional development as long as they are aligned with the national guidelines. At the implementation level, states and municipalities hire teachers, provide in-service training, and monitor their performance. They also maintain school infrastructure, manage the school calendar, and are responsible for providing meals, transportation, and uniforms to students. In monitoring the policy, the Ministry of Education (MEC) is responsible for conducting standardized student learning assessments, but many states have their own exams, and some states allow their municipalities to participate in the state exams. Municipal and state governments are responsible for expenditures, but the federal government plays a redistributive role by topping up resources for poorer states through FUNDEB and by providing education inputs through specific programs such as school meals, transportation, and textbooks, which are distributed according to student enrollment. The division of responsibility is shown in table 8.1.

TABLE 8.1 **Preuniversity education responsibilities of governments in Brazil**

FEDERAL GOVERNMENT	SUBNATIONAL GOVERNMENTS (STATE AND MUNICIPAL SCHOOL NETWORKS)
Policy formulation	
• National Education Plan with goals for pre university education • National Common Curricular Base (BNCC) • Teacher minimum wage • Funding formula rules • Terms and conditions for earmarked funding • Approval of national programs	• Curriculum • Teacher career and workload, including wages and incentives • Teacher training directives • School infrastructure directives
Policy implementation	
• Education delivery in a few federal schools only	• Teacher hiring and firing processes • Teacher training • Supervising and evaluating teachers • Selection and coordination of school leadership • Infrastructure and maintenance of schools • Textbook selection • Transportation for students • Student uniforms • School meals • School calendar • Budget management (including FUNDEB and own resources)
Monitoring	
• Assessment of learning outcomes through external evaluations of all students at the end of each education level (grades 3, 5, 9, and 12)	• Assessment of learning outcomes by some of the larger municipalities and most states in Brazil through their own standardized student evaluations; some states allow their municipal school networks to participate in the exams • School infrastructure • Teacher performance • Oversight of private schools (curriculum alignment, teachers' working conditions, and school infrastructure)

continued

TABLE 8.1, *continued*

FEDERAL GOVERNMENT	SUBNATIONAL GOVERNMENTS (STATE AND MUNICIPAL SCHOOL NETWORKS)
Financing	
• Tops up funding for poorer states through FUNDEB • Provides some school inputs, such as textbooks, school meals, and transportation through the National Fund for Education Development (FNDE), mostly based on student enrollment • Provides transfers directly to schools for small repairs or investments through the Money Direct to School Program (PDDE)	• Teacher salaries (partly covered by FUNDEB) • School utilities and maintenance (partly covered by FUNDEB) • School infrastructure • School meals, student transportation, and additional learning materials

Source: World Bank.
Note: FUNDEB = Fund for the Development of Basic Education.

Education spending and finance in Brazil

The Brazilian constitution establishes the decentralized provision and financing of preuniversity education and primary health care, with states and municipalities depending on a system of intergovernmental transfers to deliver these public services. The Constitution also mandated that subnational governments spend at least 25 percent of their revenues on education. The tax revenues of states and municipalities are not sufficient to cover the expenses of providing these services, especially at the municipal level (see figure 8.2), which is why a system of intergovernmental transfers was created.

Transfers from the federal government account for 63 percent and 22 percent of the current revenues of municipalities and states, respectively. States rely less on transfers than municipalities because they collect the ICMS, one of Brazil's two consumption taxes and the largest source of tax revenue in the country. The states that are most dependent on federal transfers are in the poorest regions of the country, the North and the Northeast, while almost all municipalities depend heavily on both federal and state transfers. About 88 percent of municipalities in Brazil have fewer than 50,000 inhabitants, and transfers account for 80 percent of their total revenue. The only exceptions are the most populous municipalities, which have a larger revenue base (see figures 8.2 and 8.3).

The smaller the subnational government, the greater the need for education transfers. Funding for education delivery at the state and municipal levels comes from both own-source revenues and intergovernmental transfers, with the relative shares greatly depending on the size and prosperity of the municipality or state. Larger and richer states and municipalities depend less on transfers, whereas they are vital for the smaller and poorer state and municipal governments. Poor and small municipalities also critically depend on state government transfers, regardless of the size of their state.

Municipalities carry most of the responsibility for education expenditure in Brazil. Almost 60 percent of preuniversity students are enrolled in municipal school networks, which also account for the highest share of education spending at 42 percent. Education represents 26 percent of the total spending of municipal governments, significantly higher than that for the states and the federal

FIGURE 8.2

Education and health spending compared with own revenues, by size of municipality, 2015

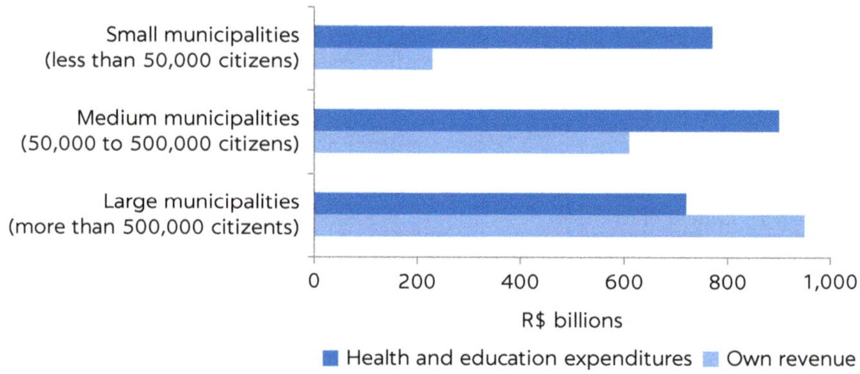

Source: 2015 National Public Sector Balance Sheet (BSPN), National Treasury of Brazil, Brasília.
Note: R$ = Brazilian real.

FIGURE 8.3

Current revenues, by government level, 2018

	Federal	State	Municipal
Taxes	507,174	505,170	146,092
Transfers	1,235	162,965	373,281
Others	1,027,254	100,474	62,306

■ Taxes ■ Transfers ■ Others

Source: 2018 National Public Sector Balance Sheet (BSPN), tables 9–10, National Treasury of Brazil, Brasília.
Note: Municipalities receive transfers from both federal and state governments. R$ = Brazilian real.

government with 13 percent and 3.6 percent, respectively (see figure 8.4). Breaking education spending down by government level, 90 percent of municipalities' and 61 percent of states' educational expenditures are allocated to the preuniversity levels (see figure 8.5).

Although spending per student in Brazil is relatively low in basic education, public expenditure on education has grown rapidly over the past decade, surpassing the OECD average in its share of GDP. In 2015, education represented approximately 6 percent of GDP (including higher education at 1.5 percent) and 16 percent of total expenditures by all levels of government (figure 8.6). Although total spending on education as a share of the budget is in line with Brazil's comparator countries, it is an outlier in terms of education spending as a share of GDP when compared to most of the other countries in Latin America or with

FIGURE 8.4

Education expenditures as a share of total expenditures, by government level, 2018

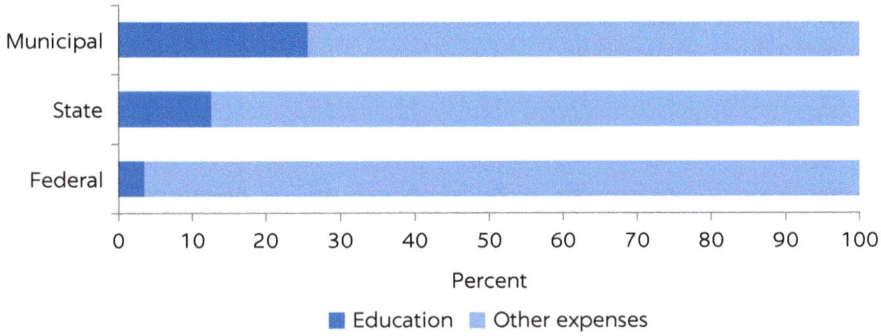

Source: World Bank calculations using 2018 National Public Sector Balance Sheet (BSPN), National Treasury of Brazil, Brasília.

FIGURE 8.5

Preuniversity expenditures compared to total education expenditure, by government level, 2018

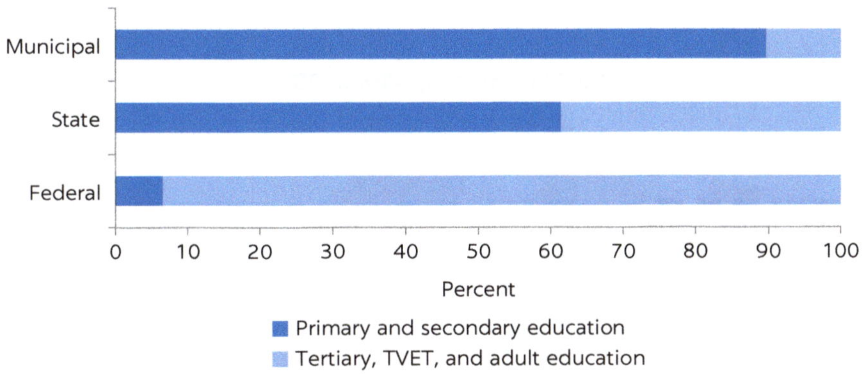

Source: World Bank calculations using 2018 National Public Sector Balance Sheet (BSPN), National Treasury of Brazil, Brasília.
Note: TVET = technical and vocational education and training.

FIGURE 8.6

Education expenditures as a share of GDP and of total government expenditures, 2002–18

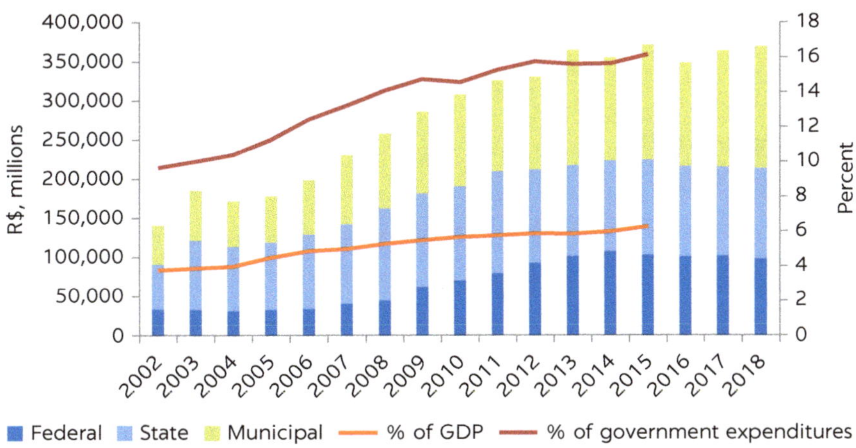

Source: World Bank calculations using data 2018 National Public Sector Balance Sheet (BSPN), National Treasury of Brazil, Brasília.
Note: GDP = gross domestic product; R$ = Brazilian real.

similar levels of income. In part, this is because the Brazilian public sector is larger than the government of many of its peers. In terms of trends, between 2002 and 2015, Brazil's education expenditure rose from 3.8 percent to 6.2 percent of GDP, the highest increase in public education spending among its comparator countries during that period.

Education outcomes and challenges

Despite a significant increase in education investments, Brazil faces a learning crisis and receives little value for its expenditures, which hinders labor productivity (World Bank 2017). Brazil has a high level of learning poverty, with 48 percent of 10-year-old Brazilian children unable to read or understand a simple text, and most of them live in the North and Northeast regions (see map 8.1). As measured by Brazilian students' results on the Programme for International Student Assessment (PISA), a worldwide standardized student assessment of the performance of 15-year-old students in mathematics, science, and reading, the quality of education improved between 2000 and 2018, but most of the improvement took place before 2009 (see figure 8.7).

MAP 8.1

Learning poverty in Brazilian municipalities, 2017

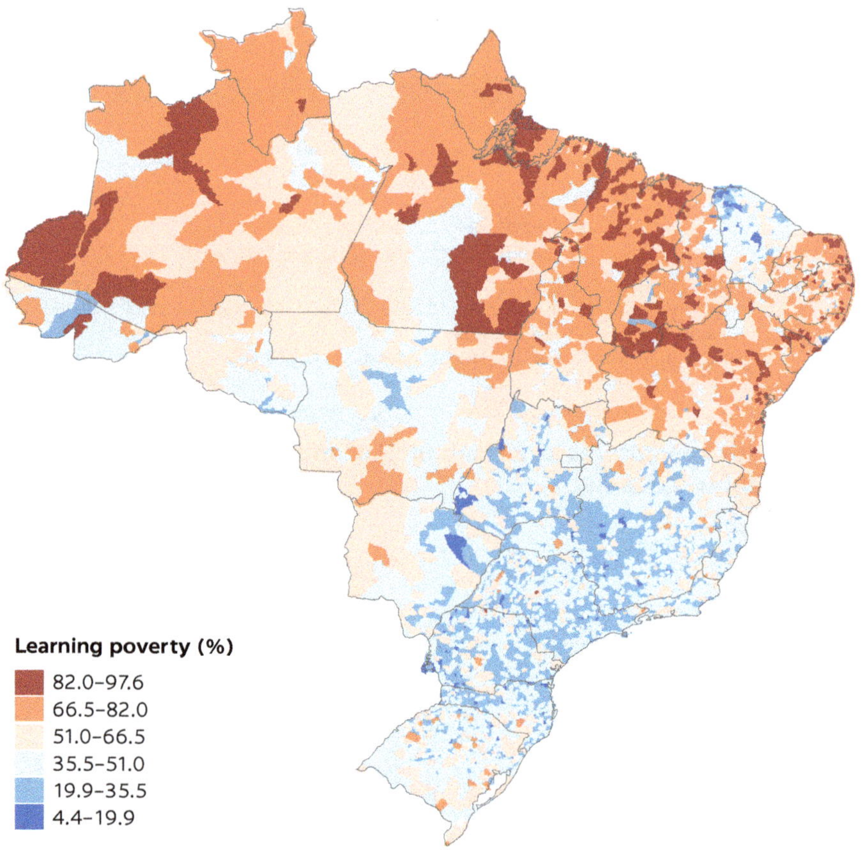

Source: World Bank calculations using data from the 2017 5th grade learning assessment for the Basic Education Evaluation System (SAEB) conducted by the National Institute of Educational Studies and Research (INEP).

Note: Legend indicates the percentage of learning poverty (share of students at age 10 that cannot read and understand a simple text).

FIGURE 8.7
Brazil's results on PISA, 2000–18

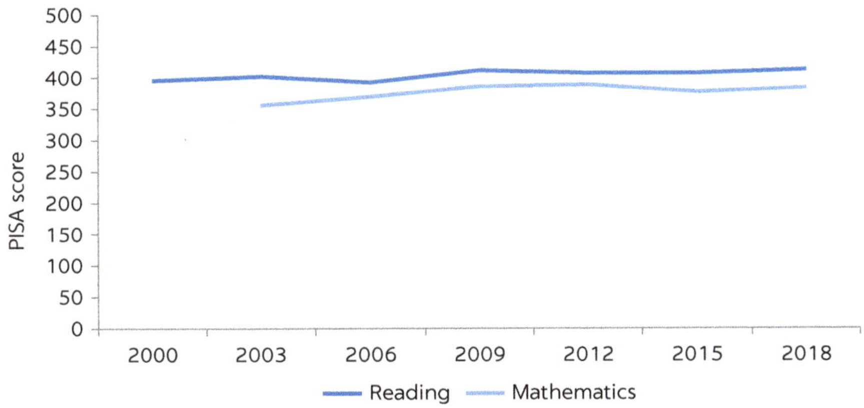

Source: World Bank calculations using data from the PISA Database, OECD, Paris, https://www.oecd.org/pisa/data/.
Note: OECD = Organisation for Economic Co-operation and Development; PISA = Programme for International Student Assessment.

The current intergovernmental transfer mechanism has reduced the equity gap in education financing, but there is still room for improvement. Brazil has high levels of inequality in education spending across states, and the richest states are the most inefficient. FUNDEB, the main education financing mechanism, has greatly increased education investment by redistributing funds for education within and across states, alleviating interregional inequality by providing poorer states with a federal top-up of resources. However, improvements are still needed. The earmarking in education spending ties education budgets to the ups and downs of the economic cycle, which obliges governments to increase their education spending in times of economic growth, mostly on personnel, making it difficult to retrench in harder economic times. Meanwhile, the federal top-up is allocated to poor states, which unfairly benefits rich municipalities in poor states and unfairly penalizes poor municipalities in rich states.

Part of the interstate inequality derives from a constitutional obligation to spend a fixed percentage of revenues on education, which contributes to inefficiency. A large proportion of subnational governments invest more than 25 percent of their total revenues on education, with some spending more than 35 percent (see figure 8.8). Wealthier municipalities and states spend considerably more per student than do poorer areas, and World Bank estimations indicate that up to 40 percent of education expenditure on primary and lower secondary education is inefficient, especially in rich areas in the South, Southeast, and Center-West regions (World Bank 2017).

The constitutional earmark is procyclical, which makes it hard for governments to adjust their education budgets. Because this earmark obliges governments to increase education spending in times of economic growth, generally with no planning or focus on results, the increased expenditure is often inefficient. This misallocation of resources is exacerbated by Brazil's rapid demographic transition to lower fertility rates, which raises public spending and increases its inefficiency.

FIGURE 8.8

Spending on education as a percentage of net revenue and spending per student, by municipal governments differentiated by region, 2019

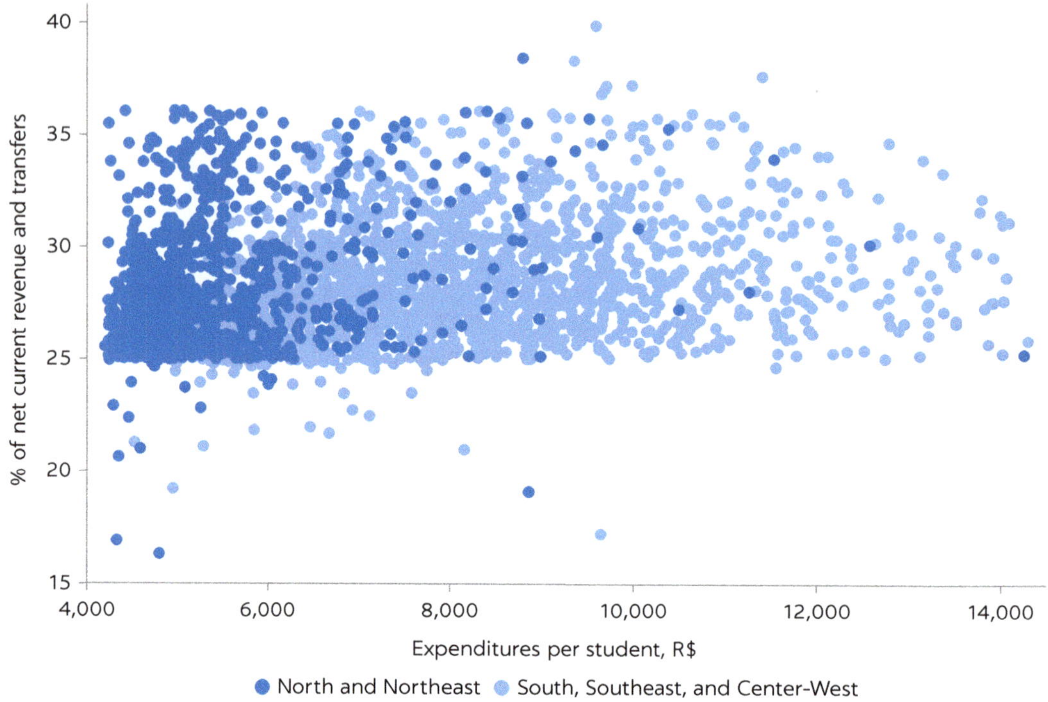

Source: World Bank calculations using 2019 National Public Sector Balance Sheet (BSPN), National Treasury of Brazil, Brasília.
Note: R$ = Brazilian real.

FISCAL TRANSFER MECHANISMS FOR EDUCATION

Main transfers in Brazil

The three largest intergovernmental transfers in Brazil are the ICMS, the Participatory Fund for Municipalities (the FPM), and the Participatory Fund for States (the FPE), in descending order of the size of their revenues. They have a few characteristics in common: all are mandatory transfers that share revenues among governmental entities with the purpose of improving equity. Additionally, they can be labeled as general transfers, meaning their resources can be spent on any governmental function. The ICMS is one of the two Brazilian value-added taxes. It is collected by the state governments, which share one-quarter of the revenues with their municipalities. The FPM and the FPE receive the revenues from two taxes collected by the federal government, the Income Tax (IR) and the value-added Industrialized Products Tax (IPI). The FPM receives 24.5 percent of those resources to allocate to municipalities, while the FPE receives 21 percent to distribute to the states. The FPM and FPE distribute these revenues in accordance with a rule designed to alleviate vertical and horizontal imbalances. For instance, the FPE allocates 85 percent of its resources to states in the North and Northeast regions because they have lower levels of socioeconomic development than the rest of the country. In 2018, the FPE and the FPM distributed approximately R$71 billion and R$83 billion, respectively.[8]

The largest intergovernmental transfer at the state level is the ICMS. Although the ICMS is collected at the state level, there is a constitutional obligation to transfer 25 percent of these resources to their municipalities (the ICMS quota). Seventy-five percent of the ICMS quota must be proportional to fiscal added value of each municipality, an indicator of their economic activity. The remaining 25 percent (the discretionary quota) can be redistributed according to states' own criteria, although most states use five or more criteria to apportion the discretionary quota, such as population size, environmental factors, and regional equity among others (Brandão 2014). Ceará decided to distribute these funds using a results-based mechanism that measures education, health, and environment outcomes in each municipality, with most weight given to education. This mechanism has fostered better education outcomes and more efficient spending in Ceará.

Nationwide transfers for education

Brazil has three earmarked transfers for financing public education at the subnational level: FUNDEB, the Salary Education Levy (Salário Educação), and transfers distributed by the National Fund for Education Development (FNDE). FUNDEB is the primary source of public education financing at the preuniversity level in Brazil, benefiting over 38 million students enrolled in schools managed by the state and municipal governments. Its legislation mandates that, in each state, 20 percent of the revenue collected by the main state and municipal taxes be set aside and the resources redistributed to state and municipal school networks based on student enrollment (for equalization within each state). For equalization between states, the federal government transfers additional resources to the states with the lowest levels of spending per student each year in an amount calculated as one-tenth of the total amount raised by the 27 state funds.[9] Another key source of funds for public education in Brazil is the Salary Education Levy, which collects a 2.5 percent payroll tax and was designed to provide support from private firms for preuniversity education. Forty percent of these revenues go to the federal government, while the remaining 60 percent is split among states and municipalities on the basis of their enrollment rates. The federal share is used to finance the FNDE, an autonomous entity linked to the Ministry of Education, which has a series of programs to provide textbooks, school meals, student transportation, and other material goods to states and municipalities. In most of the programs, the federal government transfers money to the subnational governments to implement the activities. Resources from FUNDEB and the Salary Education Levy are mandated and transferred automatically, but other transfers are discretionary and require subnational governments to subscribe to the respective programs. Figure 8.9 shows how these three transfers relate to the constitutional minimum spending requirements for each government level.

The main characteristics of the transfer mechanisms for education financing in Brazil are shown in table 8.2, including the results-based financing (RBF) model used in Ceará, which, although not specifically related to education financing, helped to improve education outcomes in the state.

FUNDEB was built upon a previous redistributive fund, the Fund for the Development of Primary and Lower Secondary Education (FUNDEF), which targeted primary and lower secondary education, and which substantially increased spending per student in the poorest areas. Before the creation of FUNDEF in 1996, differences in schooling coverage and tax revenues across jurisdictions created huge disparities in expenditure per student, even though

FIGURE 8.9

Preuniversity education financing in Brazil

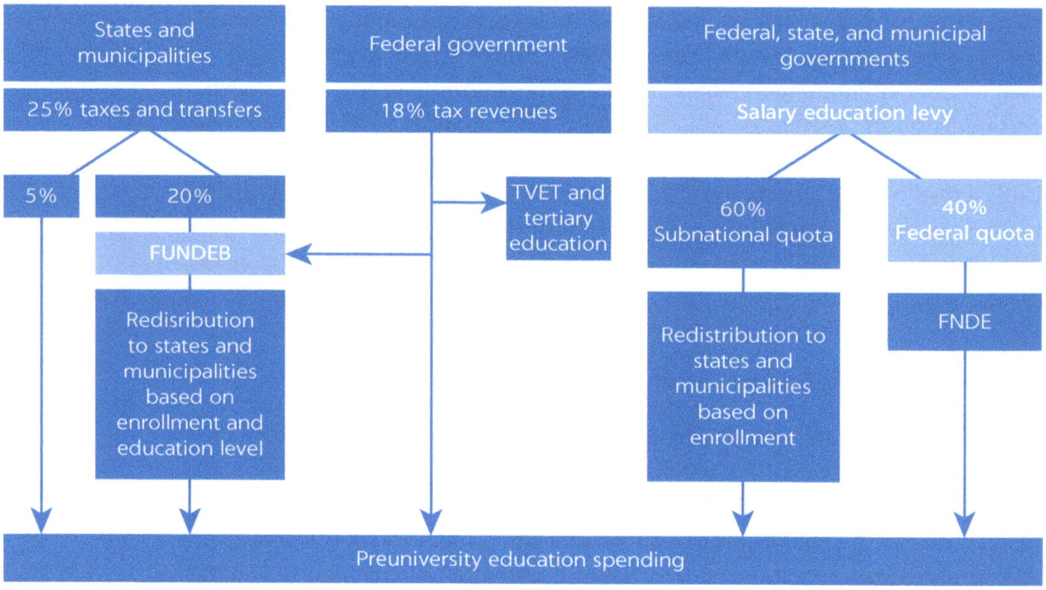

Source: World Bank based on Law 4440/1964; Law 76923/1975; Decree-Law 1422/1975; Brazilian Constitution of 1988, art. 212; Law 9766/1998; Law 10832/2003; Law 11494/2007.
Note: FNDE = National Fund for Education Development; FUNDEB = Fund for the Development of Basic Education; TVET = technical and vocational education and training.

TABLE 8.2 **Main transfer mechanisms in Brazil and the RBF model in Ceará**

TRANSFERS	FUNDEB	SALARY EDUCATION LEVY	FNDE TRANSFERS	CEARÁ RBF
Type	Specific to education	Specific to education	Specific to education	General
Objectives	To improve regional equity by increasing minimum spending per student in the municipal and state school networks of the poorest states (equity)	To provide resources for education (adequacy)	To provide financial support with technical assistance to subnational governments to incentivize certain policies (adequacy); aims for economies of scale in the acquisition of in-kind education inputs (efficiency)	To improve education, health, and environmental outcomes (performance)
Use of resources	60% to teachers' salaries; 40% to other expenses in preuniversity education	Any expenses in preuniversity education	Program-specific: school meals, transportation, textbooks, ECE facilities, school budgets	No restrictions
Determining the pool of funds	20% of a subset of government revenues at the state and municipal levels in each state plus a federal contribution of 10% of the sum of the 27 state funds	2.5% payroll tax	Availability of funds defined by the Ministry of Economy and the Ministry of Education	25% of ICMS quota that is distributed to municipalities (discretionary quota)

continued

TABLE 8.2, *continued*

TRANSFERS	FUNDEB	SALARY EDUCATION LEVY	FNDE TRANSFERS	CEARÁ RBF
Allocation of pool	Student enrollment, applying weights for each educational level	40% kept by federal government and 60% distributed to states and municipalities according to student enrollment rates	Varies with the program, but generally considers student enrollment rates, educational level, and demand and quality of application by subnational secretariat of education	72% of the discretionary quota distributed to education, 20% to health and 8% to environment outcomes; each category has an index and the amount transferred depends on improvements in indicators defined by index
Incentives	Increase enrollment	Increase enrollment	Increase and improve school inputs	Improve education outcomes
Who is incentivized?	All municipal and state governments that are responsible for primary and lower secondary education	Municipalities and states	Municipalities (mainly) and states	Mayors and other government officials within the municipal governments, because transfer spending is unconditional
Supporting systems	Education census data (student enrollment); FNDE for redistributing resources and monitoring system for allocation of resources; banking institutions to conduct direct transfers to states and municipalities	Brazilian Federal Revenue Office (tax collection and monitoring); FNDE; education census data (student enrollment); Banco do Brasil, which maintains accounts	Implementing agency; banking institutions; FNDE monitoring systems	Learning assessment; school census; banking institutions
Impact	Increase in education coverage to universal at ECE, primary and lower secondary levels; increase in per student investment in the poorest areas; reduction in interstate inequality in education spending; increased responsibility for provision to municipalities; improved learning outcomes and reduced learning poverty	Finances key preuniversity programs conducted by the FNDE	Increase availability of school inputs	Positive and significant impact on learning and other education outcomes
Issues and policy directions	Intrastate spending inequality remains; minimum spending level is endogenous and leads to unpredictability in funding levels	25% constitutional obligation drives inefficiency particularly in richer states and municipalities	Clear communication and support in the application processes are decisive for the effectiveness of the program, especially for small municipalities	Technical support strengthens the effectiveness of performance-based incentives; transparent criteria promote engagement and trust; freedom in the use of resources stimulates local politicians to prioritize policy fields included in the mechanism

Source: World Bank.
Note: ECE = early childhood education; FNDE = National Fund for Education Development; FUNDEB = Fund for the Development of Basic Education; ICMS = Tax on the Circulation of Goods and Services; RBF = results-based financing.

the constitution established a mandate to spend a minimum of 25 percent of revenues on education. Neighboring schools, one managed by the municipality and the other by the state, commonly had enormously different levels of resources and achievement. In its 10-year fixed term, FUNDEF increased the amount of education funds allocated to the poorest areas through a participatory fund in each state that was funded by a share of several state and municipal taxes and transfers. The federal government provided complementary funds for the states with the lowest spending per student. FUNDEF targeted primary and lower secondary education and distributed resources based on the previous year's student enrollment rates. Moreover, it stipulated that 60 percent of its resources be spent on teacher salaries.[10]

FUNDEB replaced FUNDEF in 2007 and extended its coverage to preprimary, upper secondary, and adult education. By the end of FUNDEF's term, it had increased student enrollment and equity of regional expenditure per child. This motivated the Congress to propose FUNDEB as a successor entity that would expand its coverage to include ECE, upper secondary, and adult education, thus increasing student coverage by 64 percent.[11] The government proposed to include more taxes in FUNDEB's basket[12] and to raise the share of both new and old taxes to be allocated to the fund from 15 to 20 percent, as well as increasing the federal budget's contribution. The federal top-up was gradually increased to 10 percent of total revenues collected by subnational governments as an equalization mechanism, a substantial increase from R$3.8 billion in 2007 to R$13.6 billion in 2018 (both measured in 2018 Brazilian *reals*).

The transfers are made to states and municipalities according to their student enrollment rates with no need for political bargaining. FUNDEB distributes the transfers automatically through periodic bank transfers to a specific account for each state and municipal government. The size of each allocation is calculated based on the enrollment rates recorded in the school census of the previous year conducted by the National Institute of Educational Studies and Research (INEP). The amount transferred to each school network varies annually depending on the level of revenue projected for the following year. In addition, two municipalities in a given state with identical numbers of students enrolled can get different amounts of transfers, because FUNDEB assigns a higher weight to students enrolled in schools where delivering education is more complex and therefore more costly. For example, students in ECE and upper secondary education have higher weights than those in lower secondary education, and students in rural and indigenous communities have higher weights, as do students with disabilities (see table 8.3). The weight for primary education in urban areas is equal to 1, while the other weights range from 0.8 to 1.3.

Each year *t*, the average value of FUNDEB transfer per student in state *i* is given by:

$$V_i^{FUNDEB} = \frac{F_i^{FUNDEB}}{\sum_v \sum_k \phi_{vk} N_{vk}^i} \tag{8.1}$$

where:

F_i^{FUNDEB} = Total funds available for FUNDEB in state i

ϕ_{vk} = weight for type of school k at school level V

N_{vk}^i = enrollment in school of type of school k at school level V in state i.

TABLE 8.3 Variables used to calculate the distribution of resources

FUNDEF	FUNDEB
• Available funds from tax revenues at state and federal level (federal revenues for the poorest states only) • Number of students enrolled in primary and lower secondary education • Weighting factors for enrollment: primary and lower secondary education in both rural and urban areas	• Available funds from tax revenues at state and federal level (federal revenues for the poorest states only) • Number of students enrolled in ECE, primary, and secondary education • Weighting factors for enrollment: 19 categories, according to education level, location, provision, and student's characteristics • Fund revenues estimated based on tax collection by states and municipalities • Clear rule for federal top-up • Guarantee of previous year's minimum federal top-up

Source: World Bank.
Note: ECE = early childhood education; FUNDEB = Fund for the Development of Basic Education; FUNDEF = Fund for the Development of Primary and Lower Secondary Education.

The federal government allocates 10 percent of the sum of the 27 state level funds in each year t to support the states with the lowest levels of V_i^{FUNDEB}:

$$FS_t = \frac{1}{10} \cdot \sum_{i=1}^{27} F_i^{FUNDEB} \tag{8.2}$$

The resources allocated by the federal government are distributed to the states with the following rules:

Step 1: Funds from FS_t are allocated to state i with the lowest V_i^{FUNDEB} until is equalized with the state with the second-lowest V_i^{FUNDEB};

Step 2: Funds from FS_t are allocated until to the two states with the lowest V_i^{FUNDEB} after receiving funds from FS_t in step 1 until it is equalized with the third-lowest value of V_i^{FUNDEB};

⋮

Step R: Funds from FS_t are allocated until to the R states with the lowest V_i^{FUNDEB} after receiving funds from FS_t in step R−1 until it is equalized with the (R+1)nd lowest (or next highest) value of V_i^{FUNDEB} and the sum of funds allocated in step R is equal to FS_t.

Generally, 9 or 10 out of 27 states received funds from FS_t.

By defining $V_i^{FUNDEB+FS}$ as the average value of FUNDEB transfer per student in state i after the federal support, the amount transferred in year t to school network s (state network + n^i municipal school networks) in state i is given by:

$$T_{s,i}^{FUNDEB} = \frac{\sum_v \sum_k \phi_{vk} N_{vk}^s}{\sum_{s=1}^{n^i+1} \sum_v \sum_k \phi_{vk} N_{vk}^s} \cdot F_i^{FUNDEB+FS} \tag{8.3}$$

Note that for states that do not receive federal support,

$$F_i^{FUNDEB+FS} = F_i^{FUNDEB}. \tag{8.4}$$

The steps for FUNDEF were similar to the ones explained above, but without considering ECE and upper secondary education and with different values for ϕ_{vk} and the percentage/amount of federal support.

Since FUNDEB's creation, its resources have constantly increased, which makes it a significant financing source for small municipalities and poor states. Between 2007 and 2017, the resources allocated to FUNDEB increased from approximately R$81 billion to more than R$132 billion. In the same period, the federal contribution increased from R$3.6 billion to approximately R$12.8 billion (see figure 8.10). These represent substantial increases for small municipalities and poor states. Currently one-third of the states, mostly those in the North and Northeast regions, receive the federal top-up. In municipalities with fewer than 50,000 inhabitants, FUNDEB's resources represent 89 percent of their education budgets. In contrast, in municipalities with more than 1 million citizens, FUNDEB accounts for 44 percent of their education budgets.

A recent amendment to the Brazilian constitution increases the federal contribution to FUNDEB, makes it more equitable, and mandates a results-based component for all Brazilian states. The amendment addresses equity more directly by allocating additional resources to municipal school networks with low spending and setting higher weights for enrollment of disadvantaged students, acknowledging that it is more costly to achieve high education outcomes in poor and marginalized contexts. The amendment (1) increases the federal top-up every year to 23 percent by 2026, starting with 12 percent in 2021; (2) improves the regional equity generated by the federal top-up by transferring 10.5 percentage points of the additional funds to the municipal school networks with the lowest spending per student, rather than assigning the 10 percent federal contribution to the states with the lowest spending per student, which gave rich municipalities in poor states additional federal support but left poor municipalities in rich states without additional funds; (3) allocates 2.5 percentage points out of the 13 percent additional federal top-up to transfers to school networks according to improvements in education results; (4) changes the constitutional article related to the ICMS transfers to municipalities, linking them to improvements in education results (as in Ceará's results-based model), and obligating all states to have at least 10 percent (and up to 35 percent) of the transfers linked to education outcomes; and (5) establishes an exogenous minimum spending level per student, to be defined by state law.[13]

FIGURE 8.10

Federal contributions to FUNDEB, 2007–17

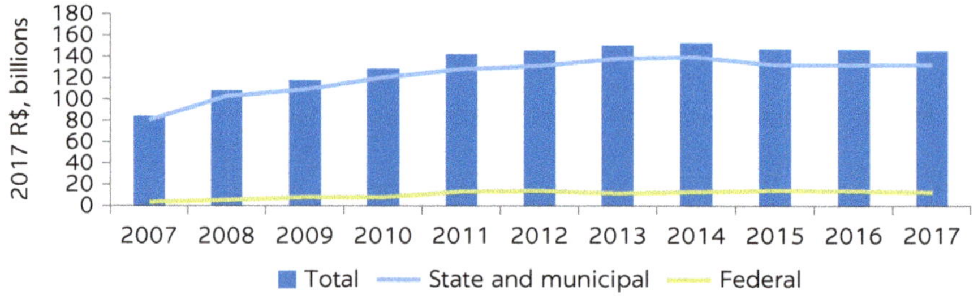

Source: FUNDEB Financial Statements 2007–17.
Note: FUNDEB = Fund for the Development of Basic Education; R$ = Brazilian real.

The results-based education financing framework in Ceará

The state of Ceará introduced an innovative method for splitting its ICMS revenue among its municipalities that makes the size of the transfers dependent on education outcomes. The ICMS is the largest source of revenue for state governments in Brazil; the national constitution mandates that states transfer 25 percent of these funds to their municipal governments (ICMS quota), which the municipal governments can use in any sector. The criteria of redistribution have one feature common to all states—75 percent of the ICMS quota distributed to municipalities must be proportional to their fiscal added value, an indicator of their economic activity. The remaining 25 percent (the discretionary quota) can be redistributed according to states' own criteria, such as population size and income level (see figure 8.11). Ceará was the first state in Brazil to use performance-based criteria for education, health, and environmental indicators to redistribute the discretionary quota.[14] Eighteen percent of the ICMS received by municipalities is linked to education outcomes, 5 percent to health outcomes, and 2 percent to environmental outcomes. Thus, when municipalities improve their education outcomes, they receive a higher share of ICMS revenue, and these resources can be allocated to any sector.

The development of results-based criteria for redistributing the ICMS quota was part of a wider education reform in Ceará that was aimed at increasing literacy rates. In 2007, the then-newly elected government of the state of Ceará set a clear goal for the state—to ensure that all students finish grade 2 with proper literacy skills. To achieve this goal, the state established three main policies that were aligned with global evidence on the effective use of RBF in education: (1) using RBF to provide municipalities with fiscal incentives to achieve established goals; (2) providing municipalities, especially those with limited technical capacity, with technical assistance, teacher training, and structured materials for improving the literacy process through the Literacy at the Right Age Program (PAIC)[15]; and (3) establishing a solid and reliable monitoring and evaluation system that continuously measures key education outcomes, including student learning. A key aspect of this strategy was the devolution of authority for managing primary and lower secondary schools to municipal governments with clear

FIGURE 8.11

Criteria for redistributing ICMS revenues among municipalities in Ceará

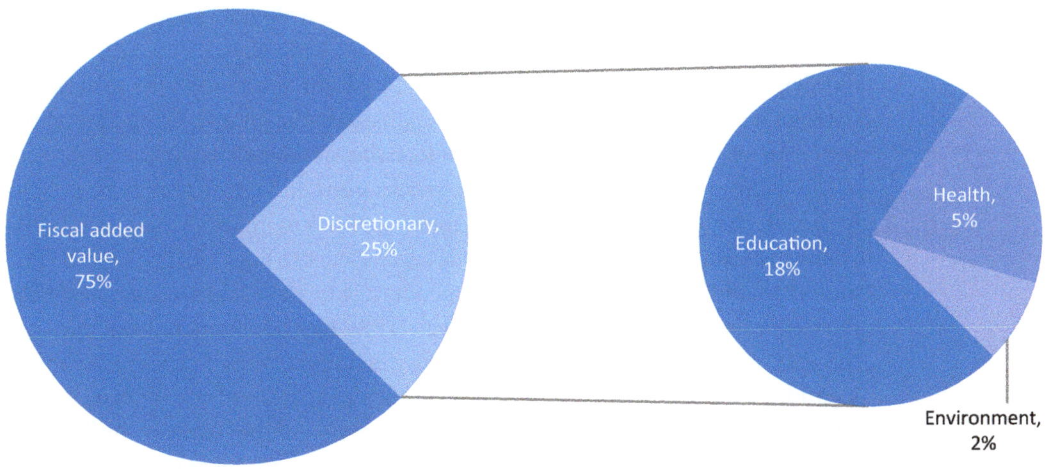

Source: World Bank based on information from the Ceará Institute of Economic Research (IPECE).
Note: ICMS = Tax on the Circulation of Goods and Services.

roles and responsibilities assigned to each government level and a strong collaborative strategy in which the state government supported municipal governments in providing primary and lower secondary education.[16] Last but not least, sustained political leadership and focus was a crucial element at the heart of this series of reforms.[17]

To operationalize the fiscal incentive mechanism, Ceará selected clear indicators and expanded the state's monitoring and evaluation systems. For each category of the ICMS quota redistribution, an index was created to define the rules and the amount received by each municipality. The health index took into account mostly improvements in the child mortality rate, while the environmental index focused on appropriate waste disposal. Education accounts for the largest amount of resources, and the Education Quality Index (IQE) takes into account literacy in grade 2, achievements in reading and mathematics in grade 5, and passing rates from grades 1 to 5. The focus was clear: municipal governments should improve literacy, reading, and mathematics among all students and not only a few, since high repetition rates or increasing inequality would penalize the performance results. To allow the calculation of the index, the state strengthened its monitoring and evaluation systems. In education, it expanded its Permanent Basic Education Assessment System (SPAECE), which previously assessed students in grades 5, 9, and 12, to include students in grade 2. SPAECE also assesses student achievement in Portuguese language and mathematics based on the state's curriculum. The state required the evaluation to take place every year and to evaluate all students in the relevant grades, including those in rural areas. To avoid municipal interference in the exam, the state covers all of the costs related to the evaluation and sends its own evaluators to schools. For the grade-to-grade progression rate indicator, less effort was needed because schools are already mandated to report progression rates annually to the Ministry of Education.

The design of the IQE was decisive in engaging municipalities because it provided evidence of which dimensions needed to be improved. IQE captures both the level of achievement (test scores and progression rates between grades) and improvement (changes in the test scores). It also gives different weights to each of the three indicators (literacy in grade 2, achievements in reading and mathematics in grade 5, and progression rates from grades 1 to 5) but prioritizes literacy. When the incentive mechanism was first created, the formula gave most weight to improvements in literacy to stimulate municipalities with poor education outcomes (see figure 8.12). As the quality of education improved in the state, the formula was redesigned to give more weight to increasing levels of literacy at grade 2 and achievement in grade 5 (see figure 8.13). To prevent municipalities from improving outcomes by sending only the best students to take the learning assessments, IQE also considers the share of students taking the exam and the standard deviation of learning outcomes in each school.

The RBF mechanism needed to be transparent and consistent to be seen as legitimate. To generate incentives for municipalities to improve their results, the system needed to be trustworthy. It was key in Ceará to have clear rules and clear indicators that were collected by independent external evaluators. Additionally, the Ceará Institute of Economic Research (IPECE), which created and operates the RBF mechanism, employs skilled professionals, which confers technical legitimacy and political independence on the calculation of the indexes. Lastly, IPECE makes all of the calculations available to the public. For each indicator, it publishes a list with the scores of each municipality and the amount of funds to be transferred.[18]

FIGURE 8.12

Components of the IQE for the results-based distribution of funds in Ceará, 2008–11

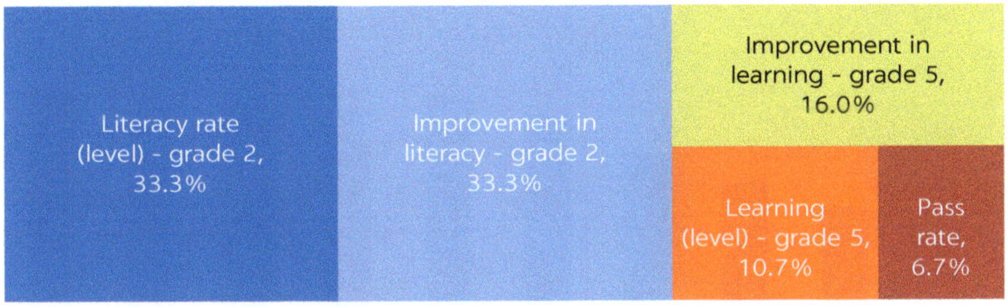

Source: World Bank based on State Law 14023/2007 and State Decree 29881/2009 on the RBF mechanism, 2008–11.
Note: IQE = Education Quality Index; RBF = results-based financing.

FIGURE 8.13

Components of the IQE for the results-based distribution of funds in Ceará, 2012–19

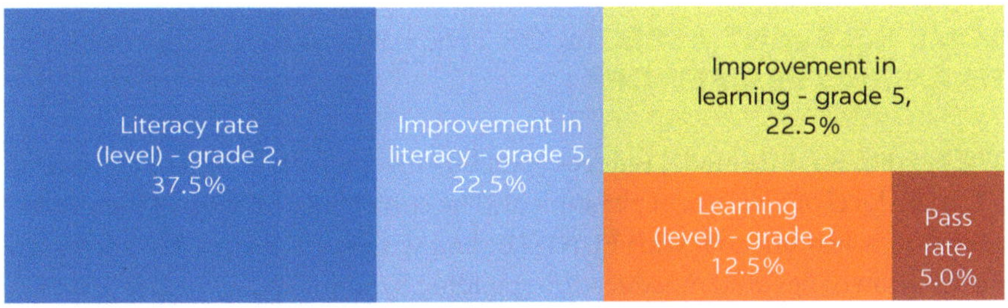

Source: World Bank based on State Decree 30796/2011 on the RBF mechanism, 2012–19.
Note: IQE = Education Quality Index; RBF = results-based financing.

The total sum of all transfers from the state government to the municipalities based on their education outcomes each year is usually higher than US$100 million, and for some municipalities, particularly the poorest, the transfer can be higher than one-third of their revenue from all sources. Every year the state government of Ceará transfers more than US$100 million to the municipal governments upon the achievement of specified outcomes (see figure 8.14). Depending on how well a municipality performed on the key indicators and on its income level, the transfer can amount to more than one-third of its total revenues.

The incentive mechanism puts a strong emphasis on increasing spending equity among municipalities and gives the municipal governments complete freedom in how to use the resources. The results-based framework rewards the efforts of municipal governments to reduce the level of learning outcomes that are below acceptable minimum levels, and it has a strong focus on improvements over time rather than on absolute levels of indicators. In addition, the state provides municipalities with technical assistance through PAIC to build the capacity of municipal secretariats of education. Municipalities also have complete freedom to choose how to use the additional resources. Overall, the mechanism creates incentives for municipalities to spend their resources to improve results in a positive competitive environment, in which all municipalities are encouraged to believe that they can do well.

FIGURE 8.14

Amounts transferred to municipalities in Ceará upon achievement of results, 2009–17

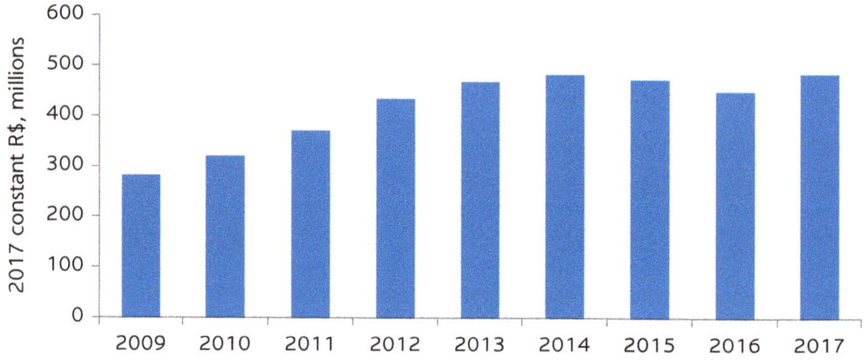

Source: World Bank based on Tax on the Circulation of Goods and Services (ICMS) quota reports, Ceará Institute of Economic Research (IPECE).
Note: R$1 = US$0.25, as of October 2019. R$ = Brazilian real; US$ = US dollar.

SOME RELEVANT ASPECTS OF THE BRAZILIAN EDUCATION FINANCING FRAMEWORK

The current funding model reduces spending inequality but does not ensure an adequate level of investment per student. The current distribution of per student spending is less unequal with FUNDEB than without it. Figure 8.15 shows the distribution of per student education spending by municipality before and after the FUNDEB redistribution and the improvement in equity and the increase in the lowest levels of spending. However, many municipalities have low per student investment even after the FUNDEB allocations. Because FUNDEB redistributes only 20 percent of a subset of revenues (which excludes key municipal taxes) and all subnational governments have to spend only 25 percent of their revenue on education, inequality is still substantial between school networks, and the lowest level of per student spending by municipalities is still below an adequate level. A quarter of all Brazilian students (about 10 million) benefit from less than R$4,300 per year. Also, because the amount allocated by FUNDEB each year depends on the available revenue, which, in turn, depends on economic cycles, the resulting minimum amount of spending per student varies considerably over time, causing significant instability in the poorest municipalities, as shown in figure 8.16.

The link between the current funding framework and revenues creates distortions and inefficiencies. The constitutional rule that requires states and municipalities to spend at least 25 percent of their revenues on education creates incentives for subnational governments to increase their spending when their revenues are unexpectedly higher without any planning or focus on results. The state and municipal courts prosecute any governor, mayor, or secretary of education who fails to comply with the 25 percent rule. This unplanned spending can be observed in a spike in the last two months of every calendar year, which coincides with the end of the fiscal year.

The exogenous increase in revenue results in high spending that is not related to results and is irreversible in the short term. If local governments are forced to increase their education spending in times of economic growth, especially on personnel, without linking them to results, it will be extremely difficult

FIGURE 8.15
Distribution of per student education spending, by municipalities with and without FUNDEB

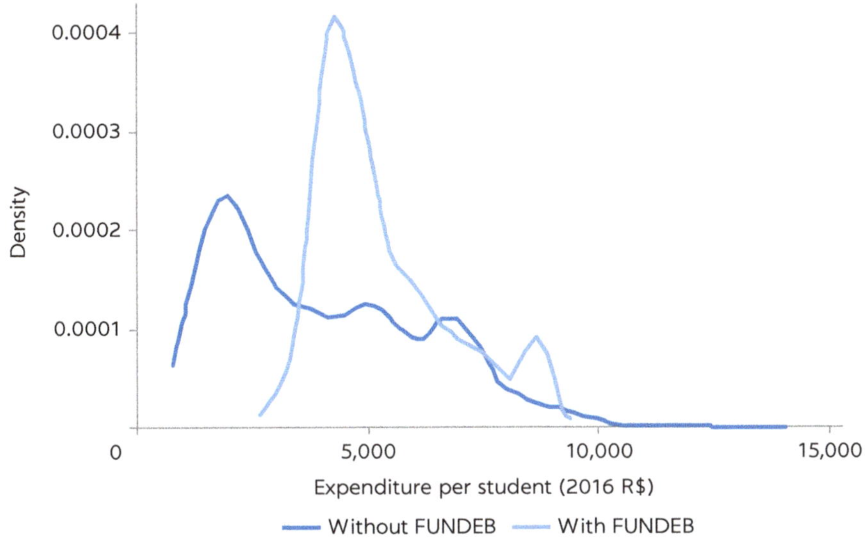

Source: World Bank using Summary Report on Budget Execution (RREO) from the Information System on Education Budgets (SIOPE).
Note: FUNDEB = Fund for the Development of Basic Education; R$ = Brazilian real.

FIGURE 8.16
Lowest spending per student in Brazilian municipalities after FUNDEB transfers, 2008–30

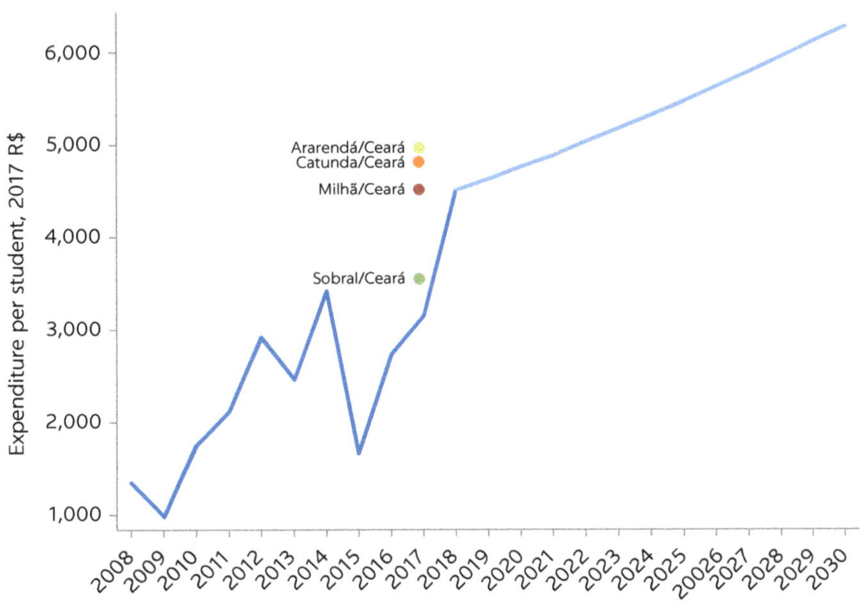

Source: World Bank using FNDE data.
Note: Data through 2017 are actual levels of expenditure per student in the municipalities with the lowest levels after receiving FUNDEB transfers. The data from 2018 on are projections for these values. The projections do not take into account COVID-19 shocks. FNDE = National Fund for Education Development; FUNDEB = Fund for the Development of Basic Education; R$ = Brazilian real.

for them to retrench when there is an economic crisis or a decrease in the number of students.

Most subnational governments allocate between 25 percent and 35 percent of their net revenues to education, with some exceeding 35 percent. Many of them spend more than 25 percent of their revenues because their spending is linked to the economic cycle. Many municipalities that spend almost R$10,000 or more per student are close to the 25 percent, suggesting that the rule is causing generally unplanned increases in salaries. At the same time, there are some municipalities that need to spend more than 35 percent of their net revenues to achieve a minimally adequate level of per student spending.

IMPACT OF BRAZIL'S DECENTRALIZED FINANCING SYSTEM ON SUBNATIONAL SPENDING AND EDUCATION OUTCOMES

Impact of FUNDEB and FUNDEF transfers on education spending

FUNDEB and its predecessor FUNDEF have made significant contributions to raising student enrollment and financing. Access, completion, and learning have increased substantially at all levels of preuniversity education, particularly in primary and lower secondary education. FUNDEB considerably reduced the gap in per student spending between rich and poor states and municipalities, but significant differences remain among municipalities. Average per student spending is relatively high, but many states and municipalities are spending well below the average; other municipalities have spending levels comparable to those of OECD countries but produce education results that are no better than Brazil's other school networks. This indicates there is substantial room for improving quality through increased efficiency.

FUNDEF created incentives for municipalities to increase student enrollment. By 2000, access to education for children aged between 7 and 14 years was universal. The North and Northeast regions experienced the steepest growth between 1997 and 2000, with 10 and 16 percentage point increases, respectively. Besides increasing overall enrollment, FUNDEF caused a shift of primary students from state-run schools to municipal schools, because it granted to municipal governments the financial means to afford education provision. Between 1997 and 2000, primary and lower secondary enrollment in municipal school networks increased by 4.3 million students. Although 2.1 million of the new students were new enrollees, the remaining 2.2 million students came from state school networks, for a 34.5 percent increase in municipal enrollments.

FUNDEF and FUNDEB have increased total expenditures on education, particularly in poorer regions, which have had a substantial increase in per student spending. Between 1996 and 2000, per student expenditure increased by approximately 40 percent. Figure 8.15 shows the distribution of per student spending in Brazilian municipalities both with and without FUNDEB and clearly shows how FUNDEB has helped to raise per student spending in the poorer municipalities, thus reducing regional spending inequity. Moreover, at the municipal level, overall net transfers are strongly and positively correlated with per student spending and mainly benefit smaller Brazilian school networks (see figure 8.17).

Empirical evidence suggests that educational transfers have a greater impact on education spending than general intergovernmental transfers. Table 8.4 presents our results from different statistical models in which the log of per

FIGURE 8.17

Per capita transfers, by per student spending and size of municipality, 2016

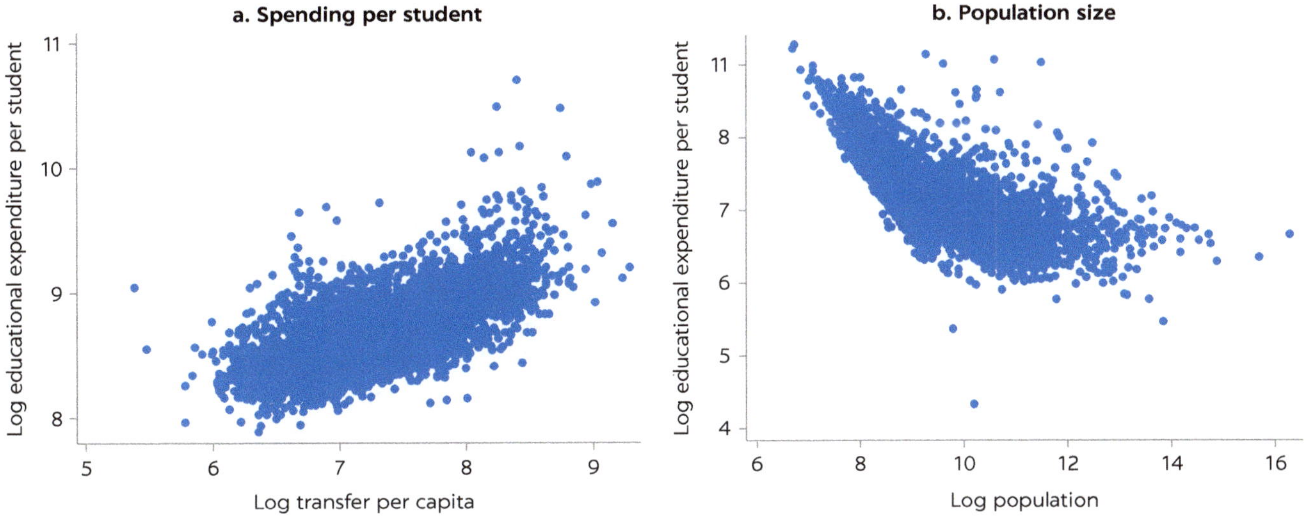

Sources: National Institute of Educational Studies and Research, Ministry of Education, and Brazilian Institute of Geography and Statistics.
Note: Per capita transfers include all net transfers to municipalities.

TABLE 8.4 **Explaining log municipal per capita education spending, 2012–17**

	OLS		FIXED EFFECTS		DYNAMIC PANEL	
	(1)	(2)	(3)	(4)	(5)	(6)
Log educational transfers per capita	0.636***	0.656***	0.302***	0.302***	0.642***	0.681***
	(0.00831)	(0.00876)	(0.0111)	(0.0111)	(0.0634)	(0.0717)
Log general transfers per capita	0.391***		0.209***		0.379***	
	(0.0113)		(0.0277)		(0.0127)	
Log general transfers from federal government per capita		0.215***		0.00899		0.185***
		(0.0184)		(0.00937)		(0.0216)
Log general transfers from state government per capita		0.119***		0.117***		0.125***
		(0.00639)		(0.0137)		(0.0116)
Exogenous controls	Yes	Yes	Yes	Yes	Yes	Yes
Time fixed effects	Yes	Yes	Yes	Yes	Yes	Yes
Municipality fixed effects	No	No	Yes	Yes	Yes	Yes
Number of observations	31,408	31,408	31,408	31,408	31,408	31,408
Number of cross-section units	5,552	5,552	5,552	5,552	5,552	5,552
Number of instruments	0	0	0	0	13	14

Source: World Bank.
Note: All fiscal and economic variables are measured in constant 2017 values. Standard errors are robust and clustered at the municipality level. Exogenous controls include log of population, log of GDP per capita, and percentage of value-added in the local economy that comes from agriculture and from industry. Ordinary least squares (OLS) and fixed-effects models assume all explanatory variables are exogenous. Dynamic panel assumes that educational transfers are endogenous. Second and third lagged values of endogenous variables (in differences and levels) serve as instruments for endogenous educational transfers. GDP = gross domestic product.
Significance level: *** = 1 percent.

capita municipal educational spending is regressed on the log of educational and general transfers. The estimates can be interpreted as elasticities. Our preferred estimates are from the dynamic panel in columns (5) and (6). Column (5) shows that an increase of 1 percent in educational transfers yields an increase of 0.64 percent in educational spending, while a 1 percent increase in general transfers is associated with an increase of 0.38 percent in educational spending. Column (6) presents results after disaggregating the general transfers into the federal and the state components. Although both are relevant for increasing educational spending, the elasticity of the federal transfers seems to be higher.

These findings are similar to the results of other recent studies. Using data from Brazilian municipalities between 2002 and 2008, Arvate, Mattos, and Rocha (2015) found that the impact on education spending of the unconditional Participatory Fund for Municipalities (FPM) and royalty transfers is smaller than the effect of education-specific transfers. Cruz and Mereb (2018) showed that a 1 percent increase in FUNDEB leads to a 0.678 percent rise in municipal education expenditure. Moreover, they showed that FUNDEB transfers are more relevant than FNDE transfers and the local revenues associated with the 25 percent minimum spending defined by the constitution.

FUNDEF and FUNDEB's requirements for states and municipalities to spend 60 percent of the transfers on teacher salaries increased wages and attracted better teachers. FUNDEF had the positive effect of raising the wages of teachers in public schools (Menezes-Filho 2007) and in the hiring of more qualified professionals (Gordon and Vegas 2005). In 2008, the federal government established a minimum wage for teachers with annual increases mandated by law. As a result, between 2009 and 2012, the minimum wage for teachers increased by 52 percent, whereas the inflation rate increased by only 17 percent (Menezes-Filho 2012).

Despite FUNDEB's significant contributions, there are still high levels of inequality between states in education spending, with the richest states being the most inefficient. The considerable heterogeneity occurs despite FUNDEB's equalizing goals; the level of per student spending stemming from the FUNDEB mandate is lower than what states actually spend by an amount ranging from 800 to almost 5,000 purchasing power parity (PPP) US dollars per year among public primary and lower secondary networks. In wealthier states and municipalities, per student expenditure is often high but not efficient, as shown in figure 8.18, with the light-blue bars indicating inefficient expenditure (World Bank 2017).

Impact of FUNDEB and FUNDEF transfers on education outcomes

Transfers are positively associated with higher spending in education, which, in turn, has a positive relationship with education outcomes. Table 8.5 shows the results of different statistical models that confirm the relationship between educational spending and outcomes. We prefer the specifications from the dynamic panel framework in columns (5) and (6). Column (5) shows that, conditional on total spending, a 1 percentage point increase in the education budget share leads to a 0.055 increase in the municipal school network's average score on the IDEB, which ranges from 0 to 10. Moreover, column (6) shows that a 1 percent increase in per capita education spending leads to an increase of 0.0011 in the average IDEB score. This positive relationship can also be observed in figure 8.19.

FIGURE 8.18

Per student education expenditure in public primary and lower secondary schools, by state, 2013

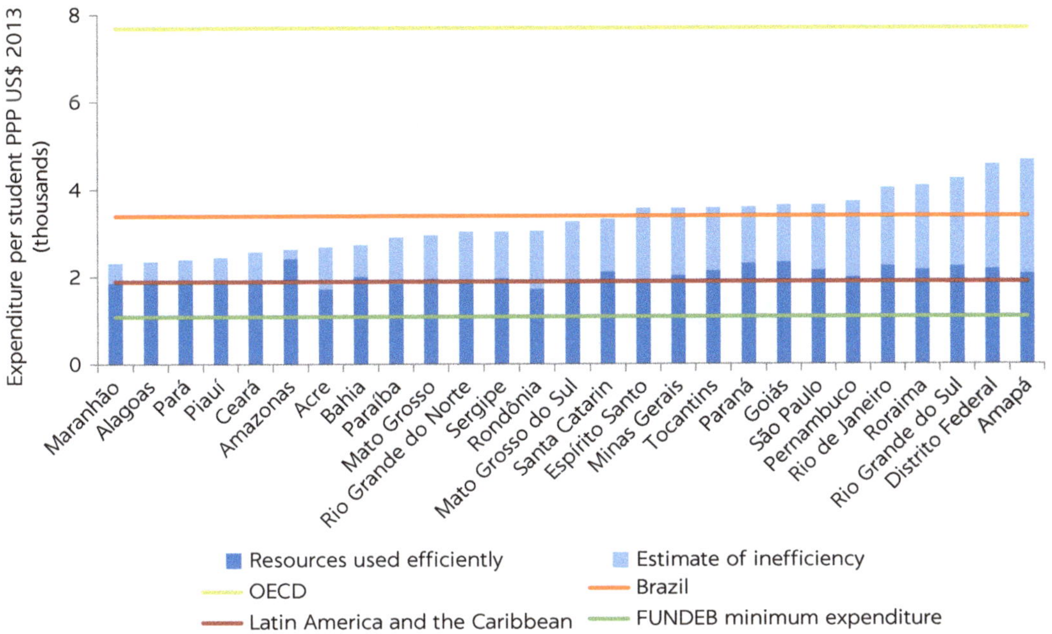

Source: World Bank 2017.
Note: FUNDEB = Fund for the Development of Basic Education; OECD = Organisation for Economic Co-operation and Development; PPP = purchasing power parity; US$ = US dollar.

TABLE 8.5 **Municipalities' IDEB outcomes**

	OLS		FIXED EFFECTS		DYNAMIC PANEL	
	(1)	(2)	(3)	(4)	(5)	(6)
Lag of log total spending per capita	−0.0504***		0.0873***		0.421***	
	(0.0131)		(0.0302)		(0.131)	
Lag of educational share	−0.0175		0.0138***		0.0554***	
	(0.0113)		(0.00522)		(0.0212)	
Lag of log educational spending per capita		−0.0628***		0.0609***		0.112**
		(0.0108)		(0.0232)		(0.0447)
Exogenous controls	Yes	Yes	Yes	Yes	Yes	Yes
Time fixed effects	Yes	Yes	Yes	Yes	Yes	Yes
Municipality fixed effects	No	No	Yes	Yes	Yes	Yes
Lagged educational outcome	Yes	Yes	Yes	Yes	Yes	Yes
Number of observations	18,383	18,336	18,383	18,336	18,383	18,336
Number of cross-section units	5,152	5,152	5,152	5,152	5,152	5,152
Number of instruments	0	0	0	0	15	12

Source: World Bank.
Note: All fiscal and economic variables are measured in constant 2017 values. Standard errors are robust and clustered at the municipality level. Exogenous controls include log of population, log of GDP per capita, and percentage of value added in the local economy that comes from agriculture and from industry. Ordinary least squares (OLS) and fixed-effects models assume all explanatory variables are exogenous. Dynamic panel assumes that spending variables are endogenous. Second and third lagged values of endogenous variables (in differences and levels) serve as instruments. GDP = gross domestic product; IDEB = National Index of Education Quality.
Significance level: ** = 5 percent, *** = 1 percent.

FIGURE 8.19

IDEB scores and per student education expenditure in municipal primary schools, Ceará municipalities highlighted, 2013–17 total

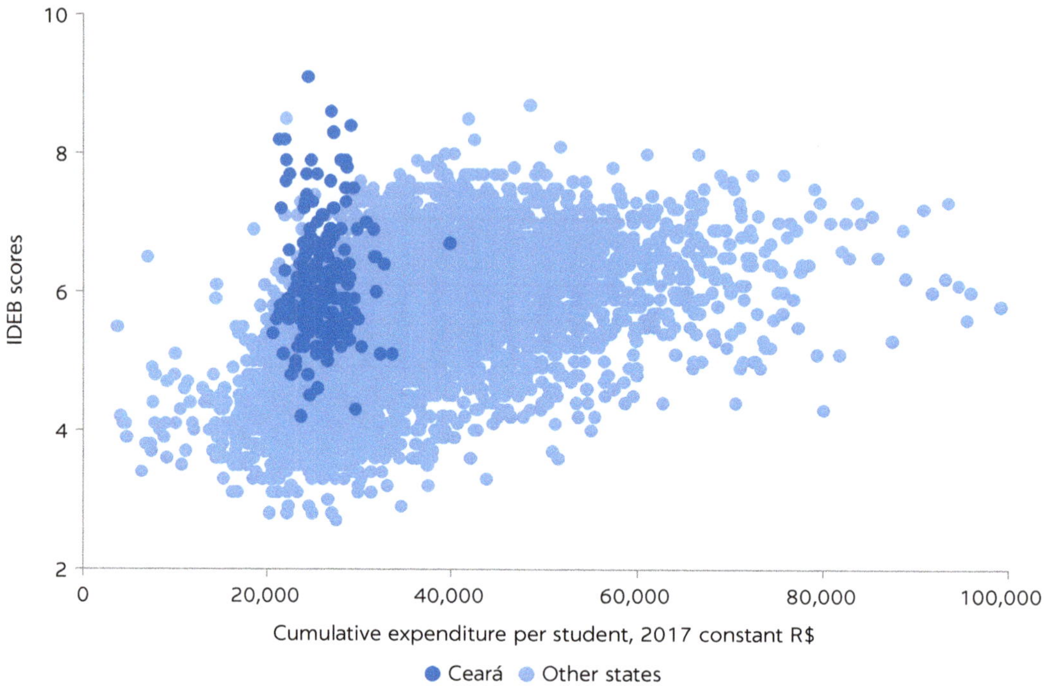

Source: World Bank using Summary Report on Budget Execution (RREO) from the Information System on Education Budgets (SIOPE).
Note: IDEB = National Index of Education Quality; R$ = Brazilian real.

FUNDEB and FUNDEF are strongly associated with increases in completion rates and other positive education outcomes. In an impact evaluation of FUNDEB's effect on upper secondary students between 2005 and 2011, Silveira et al. (2017) showed that FUNDEB raised students' test scores on the nationwide standardized test, Basic Education Evaluation System (SAEB), in Portuguese and mathematics by 12 and 18 points, respectively.

Despite substantial improvements, Brazil is performing below the outcomes that could reasonably be expected given the current levels of per student spending. Brazilian public primary and lower secondary students should be achieving IDEB scores that are approximately 40 percent higher than current levels.[19] If all municipalities used their resources as well as the most efficient municipalities, then primary and secondary education could be significantly improved without any additional spending. Inefficient municipalities and states should emulate the best management and resource allocation practices, particularly those used in the state of Ceará.

Impact of RBF on education spending in Ceará

The incentives for mayors to improve education outcomes in their municipalities led to increases in education spending. The state of Ceará's results-based framework created incentives to improve education outcomes, leading to an increase in overall education spending on primary and lower secondary education in all of the state's municipalities even though they were free to use the additional resources on other budget items (Lautharte, Oliveira, and Loureiro 2020). The reform also benefitted small municipalities with good education outcomes, which had previously received lower transfers based on their small populations and low levels of economic activity (Albuquerque 2009; Sales 2011). Research also indicates that the policy promoted a more egalitarian share of resources (Franca 2014; Nogueira 2012), and the revenues received as a result of the RBF mechanism are higher than the investment that municipalities need to improve health and education indicators (Garcia, Simonassi, and Costa 2015).

Impact of RBF on education outcomes in Ceará

Ceará's municipalities had the greatest improvement in the quality of primary and lower secondary education since 2005 and, collectively, have the best education quality index in the country when socioeconomic conditions are taken into consideration. Ceará's municipalities had the largest increase in IDEB scores between 2005 and 2017 among all 5,570 Brazilian municipalities, with one of its municipalities, Sobral, reaching first place in 2017, the latest IDEB ranking, and with 10 of its municipalities among the top 20. Map 8.2 shows the change in the IDEB scores of Brazilian municipalities between 2005 and 2017 and demonstrates that Ceará, in the Northeast region, had the largest improvement. When socioeconomic conditions are taken into account, as measured by the Human Development Index, Ceará had the best municipal primary and lower education

MAP 8.2

Change in IDEB scores, 2005–17

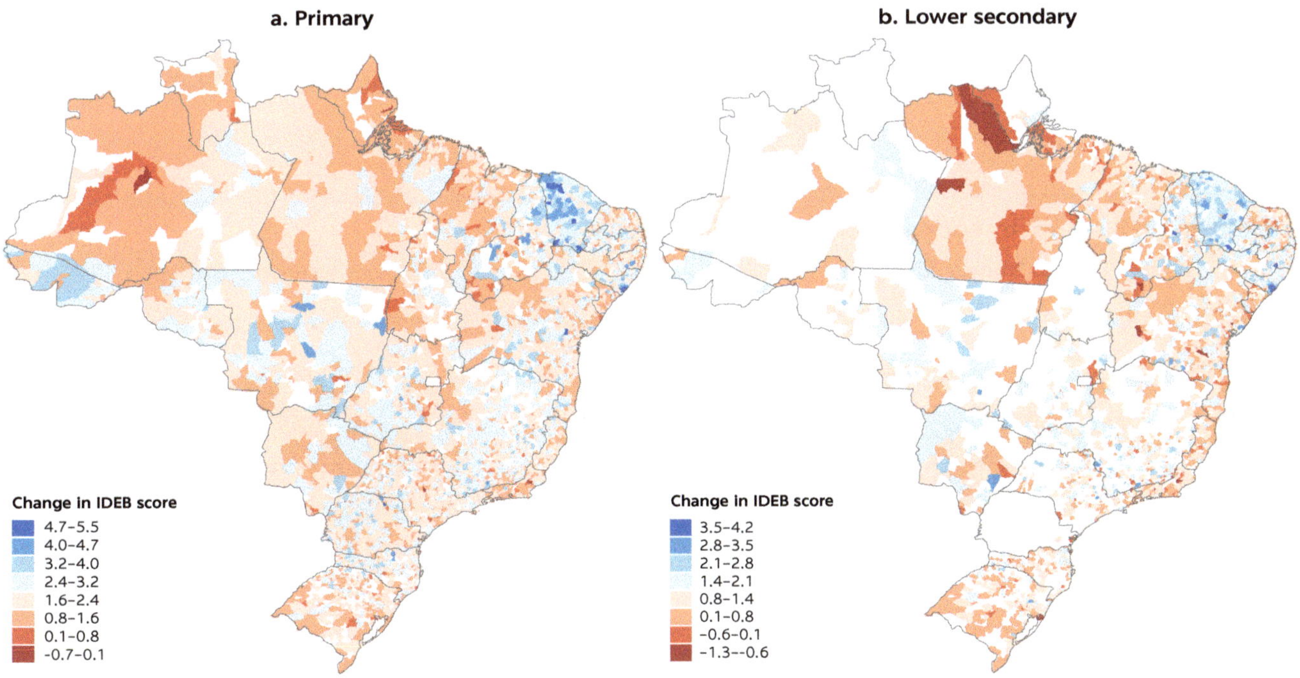

Sources: World Bank with data from 2005 and 2017 IDEB and INEP in primary and lower secondary education.

Note: Legends indicate the change in IDEB scores. IDEB = National Index of Education Quality; INEP = National Institute of Educational Studies and Research system among all Brazilian states in the latest round of IDEB. The top performing municipalities in Ceará are also those that showed the greatest improvement between 2005 and 2017 in the learning component of the IDEB, and many of these municipalities were poor (see figure 8.20).

The results-based transfer mechanism in Ceará had a positive and significant impact on education outcomes, even in municipalities that are poor or have lost resources. There is compelling evidence that the new ICMS rule in Ceará had a significant impact on student learning measured by SAEB (Lautharte, Oliveira, and Loureiro 2020; Petterini and Irffi 2013; Shirasu, Irffi, and Petterini 2013). By adopting different control groups and expanding the range of the analysis to 1995 to 2009, Carneiro and Irffi (2017) also reveal a positive impact.[20] Quasi-experimental evaluations show that the ICMS mandate contributed to increasing literacy rates as well as improving scores in Portuguese and mathematics (Brandão 2014; Petterini and Irffi 2013; Carneiro and Irffi 2017). Even municipalities that lost resources after the introduction of the new ICMS rule improved their education performance. The rule also helped to reduce the achievement gap between poor and rich municipalities (Brandão 2014). A quasi-experimental study analyzed students' learning scores from 2007 to 2011 and found that the PAIC had a positive impact on student achievement in Portuguese and mathematics (Costa and Carnoy 2015).

The ICMS policy was also successful for poor municipalities and those that initially lost resources. In her impact evaluation, Brandão (2014) disaggregated her analysis between winner and loser and richer and poorer municipalities. Winner municipalities were those that received a higher share of ICMS resources after the rule change, whereas losers were those that lost resources. The evaluation found that the policy was successful in improving education outcomes for both groups of municipalities when compared to neighboring municipalities in other states. The study found that the policy had a positive impact on both rich and poor municipalities, but the results for rich municipalities were statistically significant from 2009 on, whereas they did not become statistically significant for poor municipalities until 2011.[21]

FIGURE 8.20

Change in IDEB scores, by socioeconomic conditions, 2005–17

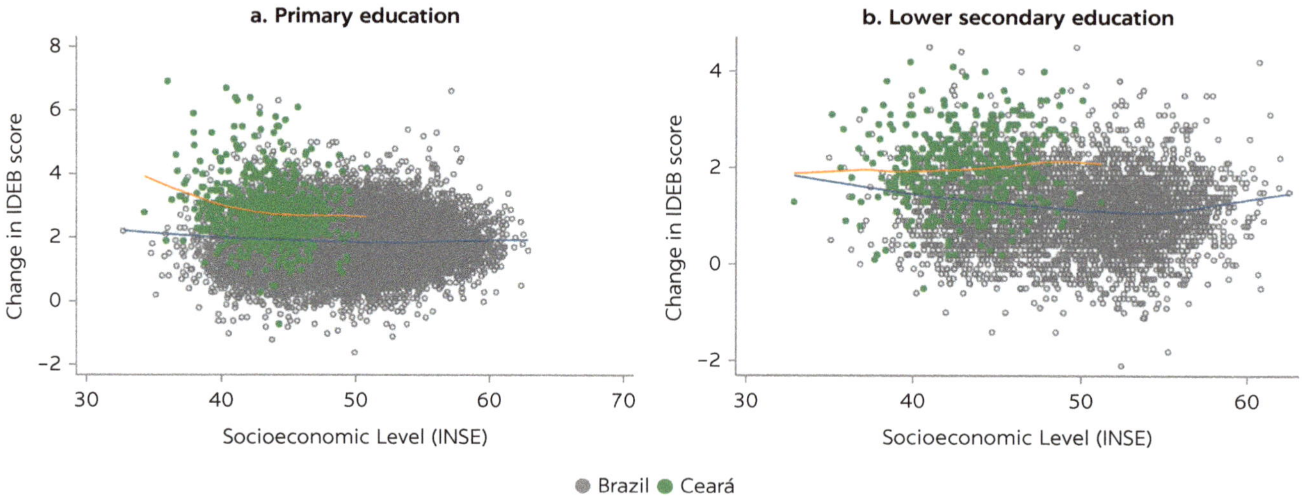

Source: World Bank using data from National Institute of Educational Studies and Research and the Ministry of Education.
Note: IDEB = National Index of Education Quality; INSE = indicator of level of socioeconomic status of schools.

The existing evidence indicates that the incentive mechanism and the provision of technical assistance, implemented simultaneously, have had a greater impact on learning than they would have had if adopted separately. An important aspect of Ceará's education model is the complementary impact of its various policy pillars (incentives, technical assistance, learning monitoring, the decentralization of education provision, and strong political leadership) on learning. World Bank research strongly suggests that implementing the full package has a greater impact on learning than implementing one pillar alone (Lautharte, Oliveira, and Loureiro, 2020). Comparing schools at the border between Ceará and neighboring states, Lautharte, Oliveira, and Loureiro (2020) have shown that when the incentive model with technical assistance was introduced in schools in Ceará, it produced an impact two to three times greater than that when the same schools had only RBF in place. These results hold for the performance of primary and lower secondary students on both the Portuguese and mathematics SAEB tests.

CONCLUSION

The experience of the Brazilian education finance framework shows that it is possible to substantially improve the regional equity of education spending. The main lessons from the Brazilian education finance system include:

- Pooling resources from distinct governmental levels to redistribute them according to a per capita rule with a minimum level of spending per student is an effective and transparent way of reducing inequalities in education spending, especially in systems with high regional inequality at the baseline.
- Applying higher weights for disadvantaged students when redistributing funds can foster a more equitable expansion of education provision and enrollment.
- Strengthening information systems, increasing transparency, and allowing direct bank transfers are key to eliminating political bargaining over intergovernmental transfers in education.
- Replacing the earmarking of revenues for education expenditures with an exogenous minimum level of education spending per student that is compatible with the amount of total resources allocated to the education sector can effectively increase efficiency and equity.

The RBF mechanism implemented in the state of Ceará can teach us important lessons on how to substantially improve learning and other education outcomes by using resources rationally, especially in a context of fiscal constraint. The main lessons from the Ceará case are:

- There is a high level of complementarity between financial incentives and technical assistance. Creating well-designed incentives aimed at improving education outcomes in the absence of technical support can still improve average education outcomes, but some municipalities can become discouraged and lag behind, thus undermining the overall benefits of the policy. Conversely, providing high-quality technical support without strong and attractive incentives for improvement can yield some gains, particularly in municipalities with limited capacity and poor education outcomes. However, municipalities that are doing slightly better in education outcomes may be less likely to engage in the technical assistance program.

- A crucial element of Ceará's RBF mechanism is the use of general transfers as an incentive to improve education. Ceará's incentive mechanism links general transfers to education results, allowing mayors to use the transfers in any sector, even one not directly related to education. Such freedom provides incentives for all of municipal government, including the mayors and secretaries of finance.
- Two necessary preconditions for establishing a results-based mechanism in education are a decentralized school system and a robust monitoring and evaluation system. A system of incentives requires that subnational governments have autonomy over how to manage their schools. The Ceará case shows that a highly decentralized system with well-designed incentives and support to the municipalities can be very successful in improving student learning. In addition, the state government of Ceará has a monitoring and evaluation system, which is critical for establishing incentives based on education results and identifying municipalities that need more support.

NOTES

1. This chapter benefited from comments and suggestions from Samer Al-Samarrai, Blane Lewis, Lars Sondergaard, Halsey Rogers, Pedro Cerdán-Infantes, Emanuela di Gropello, Pablo Acosta, Kjetil Hansen, and Fabiano Colbano.
2. The exceptions include federal schools that provide primary and upper secondary education. Many states and a few municipal governments also have their own universities and vocational training institutes.
3. The Brazilian National Congress has recently approved a reform of FUNDEB under which the federal contribution will gradually increase to 23 percent by 2026, starting with 12 percent in 2021.
4. The IDEB is calculated at the school, municipal, state, and national levels and is based on two components: student performance on the nationwide Basic Education Evaluation System (SAEB) and student passing rates ($IDEB = N \cdot P$, where N = normalized student performance at the end of each school cycle, $0 \leq N \leq 10$ and P = harmonic mean of student progression of all grades in each school cycle, $0 \leq P \leq 1$). The index is calculated every two years and is coupled with targets that make it possible to assess whether schools, municipalities, states, and the country are making progress toward improving education quality.
5. For more details on the Ceará education model, see Loureiro et al. (2020).
6. The establishment of the Fund for the Development of Primary and Lower Secondary Education (FUNDEF) and, later, FUNDEB has minimized this issue. Since the establishment of these funds, there has been an ongoing process of devolving lower secondary education to municipalities. However, there is wide variation among states. According to the 2018 Education Census, the share of municipal enrollment compared to total public enrollment in lower secondary education ranges from as low as 2 percent in Paraná to 28.5 percent in São Paulo, 44 percent in Mato Grosso do Sul, and 49 percent in Amazonas, and as high as 74 percent in Rio de Janeiro and 94 percent in Ceará.
7. Public universities have enrolled 24.3 percent of the country's 8 million tertiary students. The federal government is the main public provider of higher education, accounting for 62 percent of the enrollment in public institutions, followed by the states with 32 percent, and the municipalities with 6 percent.
8. For a broader discussion of the general transfers in Brazil, see World Bank (2020).
9. The amount transferred by federal government to the states is defined each year using the following algorithm: (1) the states are ranked by value per student (amount of FUNDEB resources in the state divided by total enrollment) considering both the state network and the municipalities in each state; (2) the federal government calculates the amount of resources that would need to be transferred to the state with the lowest value per student to reach the amount per student in the state with the second-lowest value per student;

(3) the equalization process is repeated comparing the value per student in each state with the value per student in the next-highest state; (4) the process stops when the top-up funds allocated by the federal government would exceed the total allocated amount for the federal contribution to FUNDEB.

10. Because FUNDEB is procyclical, that is, the total amount of funds available each year is a fraction of government revenues, the minimum spending per student is defined endogenously by a top-down approach, rather than by a bottom-up approach, under which the amount to be allocated for education is defined on the basis of an "ideal cost." This choice is made relevant by Brazil's strong fiscal constraints. See World Bank (2020).
11. According to education census data, there were 46.6 million students enrolled in public basic education in 2007 under FUNDEB, while 28.4 million were in primary and lower secondary education under FUNDEF. Therefore, FUNDEB covered 64 percent more students than those covered by FUNDEF.
12. Added were the Causa Mortis and Donations Tax (ITCMD), the Motor Vehicles Property Tax (IPVA) and a 50 percent quota of the Rural Lands Tax (IITR).
13. The amendment also increased the minimum percentage of spending on teacher salaries with FUNDEB funds from 60 percent to 70 percent.
14. As of 2019, states such as Pernambuco, Alagoas, Espírito Santo, and Amapá had changed their ICMS redistribution criteria, following Ceará's experience.
15. TPAIC was organized under three main components: literacy support, pedagogical use of student assessment, and strengthened governance. Literacy support comprises a series of activities, such as designing and delivering textbooks, strengthening teacher training with a focus on classroom practice, fostering the reading culture, and supporting the expansion of ECE. The pedagogical use of student assessment involved financial and technical support for the implementation of local learning assessments and training municipal and school professionals to make a systematic use of assessment results. Strengthened governance included a cascade model to support and train municipal teams and incentives for exchanging best practices among schools. See Loureiro et al. (2020).
16. The devolution of primary and lower secondary education to municipalities is one of the main results of FUNDEB policy, but this process evolved differently in different Brazilian states. Ceará was one of the few states that already had high levels of decentralization in 2007. Since then, other states have devolved the responsibility for managing primary and lower secondary education to municipal governments, but none of them has established a framework of collaboration between the state and municipal governments with concrete technical support as Ceará did. Having seen Ceará's outstanding education results, some other states have recently started to design similar frameworks.
17. For more details on the education reforms in Ceará, see Loureiro et al. (2020).
18. For a discussion of how information systems and accountability can reduce political bargaining, see Toral (2019).
19. Data envelopment analysis showed that if all municipal and state networks used best practices in resource allocation and management, the average IDEB score of primary and lower secondary students in Brazil would rise from 4.5 to 6.4. When disaggregating the results for lower (1st to 5th) and upper grades (6th to 9th), there is evidence that IDEB scores could increase from 5 to 7 and from 4 to 6, respectively. For details, see World Bank (2017).
20. Carneiro and Irffi (2017) use four different control groups and apply a difference-in-differences approach. The first control consisted of municipal schools from all Brazilian states with an ICMS rule different from Ceará's. The second was restricted to states in the Northeast, which have regional similarities. The third removed from the previous groups states that had external learning evaluations on the assumption that this policy might have affected the schools' scores. The fourth compared Ceará's municipal schools with schools run by the state. In the first and the second control groups, the authors considered two scenarios, one with and another without propensity score matching.
21. Brandão (2014) used a difference-in-differences model and two control groups picked from Ceará's neighboring states: Piaui, Pernambuco, Paraiba, and Rio Grande do Norte. The first control consisted of municipalities right at the border that belong to the same microregion, according to the Brazilian Institute of Geography and Statistics (IBGE) classification. The second was formed through propensity score matching. As the latter was more balanced with treated municipalities, the author considered the control group formed through propensity score matching to conduct the winner-loser and richer-poorer subgroup analysis. The education variable consisted of SAEB scores in Portuguese and math.

REFERENCES

Albuquerque, M.T.P.R. 2009. *Uma análise da cota-parte do ICMS dos municípios Cearenses.* Fortaleza, Brazil: Universidade Federal do Ceará.

Arvate, P.R., E. Mattos, and F. Rocha. 2015. "Intergovernmental Transfers and Public Spending in Brazilian Municipalities." Working Paper No. 377, Fundação Getúlio Vargas, São Paulo, Brazil.

Brandão, J.B. 2014. *O rateio de ICMS por desempenho de municípios no Ceará e seu impacto em indicadores do sistema de avaliação da educação.* Rio de Janeiro, Brazil: Fundação Getúlio Vargas.

Bruns, B., and J. Luque. 2014. *Great Teachers: How to Raise Student Learning in Latin America and the Caribbean.* Washington, DC: World Bank. https://openknowledge.worldbank.org/handle/10986/20488.

Carneiro, D., and G. Irffi. 2017. *Avaliação comparativa das leis de incentivo à educação no Ceará.* Fortaleza, Brazil: Universidade Federal do Ceará.

Costa, L.O., and M. Carnoy. 2015. "The Effectiveness of an Early-Grade Literacy Intervention on the Cognitive Achievement of Brazilian Students." *Educational Evaluation and Policy Analysis* 37 (4): 567–590. https://doi.org/10.3102/0162373715571437.

Cruz, T., and T. Mereb. 2020. "Minimum Spending in Education and the Flypaper Effect." *Economics of Education Review* 77 (August): 102012.

Franca, E.M. 2014. *Repasse da cota-parte do ICMS aos municípios Cearenses: Avaliação das mudanças ocorridas no período de 2009 a 2011.* Fortaleza, Brazil: Universidade Federal do Ceará. http://www.repositorio.ufc.br/handle/riufc/15161.

Garcia, F.G., A.G. Simonassi, and R.F.R. da Costa. 2015. "A lei 14.023/07 e os investimentos em educação fundamental e saúde nos municípios Cearenses: Uma análise no período 2006–2010." *Revista Economia e Desenvolvimento* 14 (1). https://periodicos.ufpb.br/ojs2/index.php/economia/article/view/27510.

Gordon, N., and E. Vegas. 2005. "Education Finance Equalization, Spending, Teacher Quality, and Student Outcomes: The Case of Brazil's FUNDEF." In *Incentives to Improve Teaching: Lessons from Latin America*, edited by Emiliana Vegas, 151–86. Washington, DC: World Bank.

Lautharte, I., V.H. de Oliveira, A. Loureiro. 2021. "Incentives for Mayors to Improve Learning: Evidence from State Reforms in Ceará, Brazil." Policy Research Working Paper 9509, World Bank, Washington, DC. https://openknowledge.worldbank.org/handle/10986/35024.

Loureiro, A., L. Cruz, I. Lautharte, and D.K. Evans. 2020. "The State of Ceara in Brazil is a Role Model for Reducing Learning Poverty." World Bank, Washington, DC. https://openknowledge.worldbank.org/handle/10986/34156.

Menezes-Filho, N.A. 2007. "Os determinantes do desempenho escolar do Brasil." Instituto Futuro Brasil, Ibmec-SP e FEA-USP. http://www.cepe.ecn.br/seminarioiv/download/menezes_filho.pdf.

——. 2012. "O piso salarial dos professores." Instituto de Ensino e Pesquisa, Insper., São Paulo, Brazil.

Menezes-Filho, N., and E. Pazello. 2007. "Do Teachers' Wages Matter for Proficiency? Evidence from a Funding Reform in Brazil." *Economics of Education Review* 26 (6): 660–72. https://doi.org/10.1016/j.econedurev.2007.08.003.

Nogueira, C.A.G. 2012. "Efeitos distributivos das políticas públicas: O caso da nova metodologia de cálculo da cota parte do ICMS do Ceará." *Revista FSA* (Centro Universitário Santo Agostinho) 9 (1): 55–69.

Petterini, F.C., and G.D. Irffi. 2013. "Evaluating the Impact of a Change in the ICMS Tax Law in the State of Ceará in Municipal Education and Health Indicators." *EconomiA* 14 (3): 171–84. https://doi.org/10.1016/j.econ.2013.10.003.

Sales, P.S.T. 2011. *Avaliação da distribuição das cotas-parte do ICMS devidas aos municípios cearenses: Cenários alternativos.* Fortaleza, Brazil: Universidade Federal do Ceará. http://www.repositorio.ufc.br/handle/riufc/5768.

Shirasu, M., G.D. Irffi, and F.C. Petterini. 2013. *Melhorando a qualidade da educação por meio do incentivo orçamentário aos prefeitos: O caso da Lei do ICMS no Ceará*. Fortaleza, Brazil: Universidade Federal do Ceará.

Silveira, I.M. da, J.E. de Lima, E.C. Teixeira, and R.G. da Silva. 2017. "Avaliação do efeito do FUNDEB sobre o desempenho dos alunos do ensino médio no Brasil." Institute of Applied Economic Research. http://repositorio.ipea.gov.br/handle/11058/8009.

Toral, G. 2019. "Information, Oversight, and Compliance: A Field Experiment on Horizontal Accountability in Brazil." https://ssrn.com/abstract=3462008.

World Bank. 2017. "A Fair Adjustment: Efficiency and Equity of Public Spending in Brazil: Volume 1—Overview." Working Paper 121480, World Bank, Washington, DC. http://documents.worldbank.org/curated/en/643471520429223428/Volume-1-Overview.

——. 2018. *World Development Report 2018: Learning to Realize Education's Promise*. Washington, DC: World Bank. http://www.worldbank.org/en/publication/wdr2018.

——. 2020. *Diagnostic and Reform Options for the System of Intergovernmental Fiscal Transfers to Brazilian States*. Internal report. Brasília, Brazil: World Bank.

9 Bulgaria Case Study

ASSENKA HRISTOVA AND LARS SONDERGAARD

INTRODUCTION

Municipalities in Bulgaria are highly dependent on the transfers they receive from the central government to fund the education provided in comprehensive schools. These transfers are specifically earmarked for comprehensive schooling and, together with European Union (EU) grants, cover 98 percent of municipalities' spending on comprehensive education. Although municipalities are free to top up the resources they receive from the central government, 30 percent of municipalities do not, and those that do contribute very little (on average only 15 leva per student or 2 percent of their total spending).[1] Because municipalities rely heavily on transfers from the central government, the central government is in a position to vary its funding formula to ensure that its transfers are equitably distributed—both for ensuring that similar students are supported with the same amount of funding (horizontal equity) but also for ensuring that students with greater needs are supported with more resources (vertical equity).

This chapter sheds light on the mechanisms by which these vital intergovernmental transfers affect local spending on education in Bulgaria. In doing so, the chapter seeks to identify the strengths and weaknesses of the current system and proposes ways to improve it.

The chapter is organized as follows. First, we describe the decentralized system in Bulgaria, highlighting the roles and responsibilities of central and local actors. Next we describe the fiscal transfer system. The next section presents evidence on the extent to which the transfer system influences education outcomes, and the last section presents proposals to improve the system.

DECENTRALIZATION IN THE EDUCATION SECTOR

In Bulgaria, the government guarantees free access to education. Education is compulsory for children between the ages of 5 and 16 and consists of two years of preschool education, seven years of basic education, and three to five years of upper secondary education (see figure 9.1). For "comprehensive education," the focus of this chapter, the public sector (either through the central government or the municipalities) honors that guarantee by financing a large number of public schools. In addition to providing funding for the delivery of public education, the government subsidizes the provision of free textbooks to students in grades 1 to 7 and free breakfasts to students in grades 1 to 4. Local authorities can also choose to provide free transportation to students travelling to schools in another settlement. Private schools are also entitled to public funding at their request on the condition that they provide free education to 20 percent of the students whom they enroll.

The responsibility for delivering public education is shared between the central government and the 265 municipalities, with some parts of the education system more decentralized than others. The municipalities are responsible for the delivery of early childhood education and primary, lower, and upper secondary general education. The delivery of vocational education is a shared responsibility between the state and municipalities. A number of specialized schools and schools of national and regional significance are funded by the state through the Ministry of Education and Science (MoES), the Ministry of Culture (MoC), and the Ministry of Youth and Sports (MoYS). According to MoES data for the 2018–19 school year, 88 percent of the 2,281 public schools are funded by municipalities, with the remaining (mainly vocational schools) funded by the three ministries (see table 9.1).

On paper, there is a clear and logical division of roles and responsibilities between the different entities in the system (see table 9.2). At the top, the Council of Ministers is responsible for setting policy and priorities and of

FIGURE 9.1
Organization of Bulgaria's school system

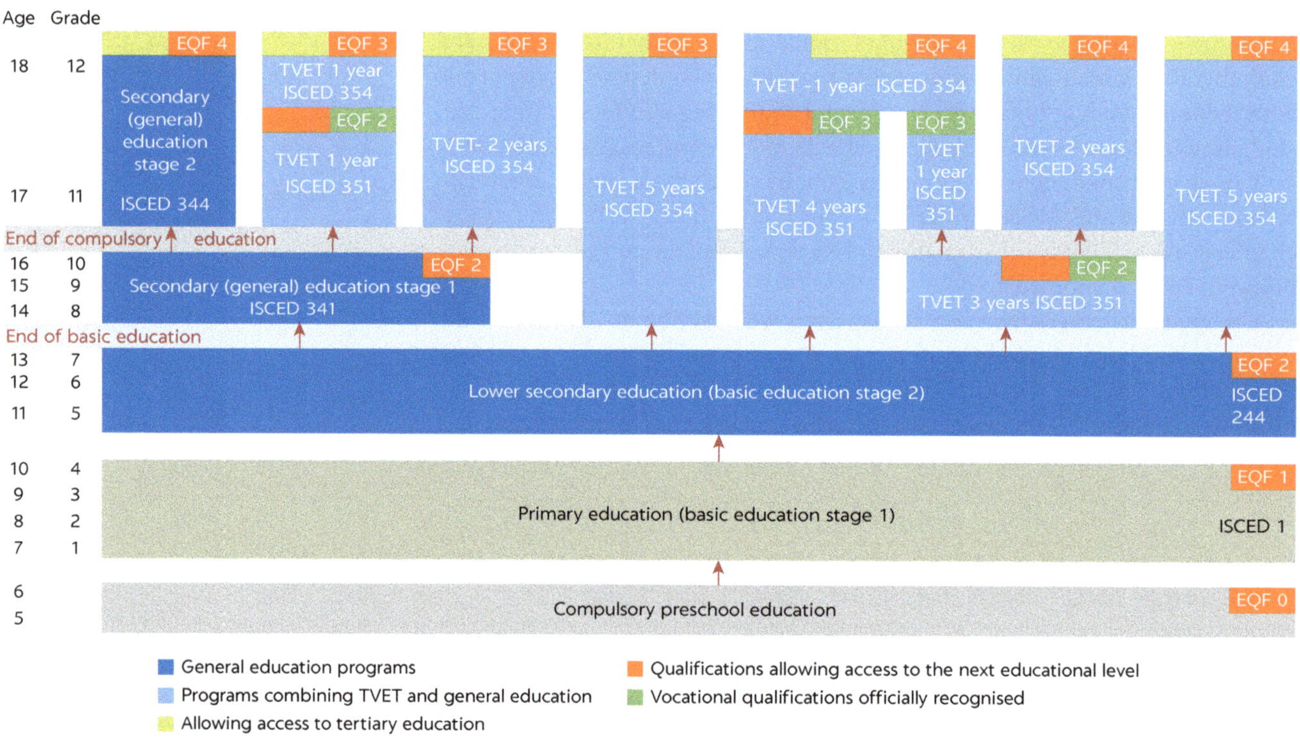

Source: Adapted from CEDEFOP 2019.
Note: EQF = European Qualifications Framework; ISCED = International Standard Classification of Education; TVET = technical and vocational education and training.

TABLE 9.1 **Structure of Bulgaria's public school network, by level of government, 2018–19**

TYPE OF SCHOOL	FUNDING BODY (FLSU)	NUMBER OF SCHOOLS
Municipal schools	***Local governments***	***2005***
Primary schools (grades 1–4)	Municipalities	127
Basic schools (grades 1–7)	Municipalities	1,132
Integrated schools (grades 1–10)	Municipalities	68
Special profile gymnasiums (grades 8–12)	Municipalities	92
Secondary general schools (grades 1–12)	Municipalities	443
Secondary vocational schools (grades 8–12)	Municipalities	124
Sports schools	Municipalities	19
State-owned schools	***Central government***	***276***
Basic schools (grades 1–7)	MoES	1
Special profile gymnasiums (grades 8–12)	MoES	3
Secondary general schools (grades 1–12)	MoES	5
Secondary vocational schools (grades 8–12)	MoES	220
Art and culture schools	MoC	23
Sports schools	MoYS	6
Spiritual schools	MoES	2
Prison schools	MoES	7
Special schools	MoES	9

Source: Based on data from MoES.
Note: FLSU = First-level spending unit; MoC = Ministry of Culture; MoES = Ministry of Education and Science; MoYS = Ministry of Youth and Sports.

mobilizing and distributing resources based on financing standards that they define. Next, the Minister of Education and Science is responsible for implementing the policy set by the Council of Ministers. The minister plays a leading role in developing the state educational standards (SES) and in ensuring that educational institutions function in compliance with the legislation. To carry out that role, MoES has 28 deconcentrated branches to support its work, as well as 9 specialized agencies.[2] Third, the 265 municipalities have authority over the allocation of spending for the delivery of education and are responsible for incorporating local needs and local policy considerations in their spending decisions. Finally, since 2007–08, when the school-based management (SBM) model was introduced, schools have had a relatively high level of autonomy. School principals are responsible for hiring and firing teachers and of determining teacher salaries (within a salary range set by the Collective Labour Contract). Schools are also responsible for organizing and putting aside resources to fund teacher in-service development and training. Schools have the power to determine their profiles and occupations and to choose their syllabuses. Schools and their teachers can decide which textbooks to use. Although a substantial amount of responsibility has been shifted to schools, their authority over resource allocation is constrained by predefined limitations within the country's educational standards and rules as determined by the central government. Most of those requirements and limitations affect the distribution of school spending, such as the proportion of the school budget that can be spent on personnel.

TABLE 9.2 **Education roles and responsibilities of national and subnational governments**

FUNCTION	CENTRAL GOVERNMENT	SUBNATIONAL GOVERNMENTS
Policy	Sets national education policy and the Minister of Education determines most SES	Can establish local policy priorities within the centrally defined education policy and SES
Financing	Determines state educational standard for financing; defines UCSs and additional financing standards and rates; defines allocation rules; transfers earmarked funding from the central budget; approves national programs for the development of education	Develops local allocation formulas for distribution of earmarked transfers, allocates earmarked funding for schools, can provide additional funding to schools from own revenues, and controls spending
Curriculum	MoES defines framework curricula by classes, stages, and levels of education; curricula for compulsory and specialized subjects and modules in general education and for compulsory TVET training modules	Responsible for resourcing implementation of the curriculum through delegation of funding for state-mandated activities and distribution of other funds to schools
Facilities and Infrastructure	Provision of funding for improvement of facilities and infrastructure	Responsible for maintenance of facilities and infrastructure
Teachers and education staff	MoES and its deconcentrated structures are responsible for defining priority areas for teachers' professional development and provision of teacher training; not responsible for teaching workforce management	Responsible for provision of teacher training, but not for teaching workforce management
Quality assurance	Provided through school inspections	n.a.

Source: Preschool and School Education Act and state educational standards.
Note: MoES = Ministry of Education and Science; n.a. = not applicable; SES = state educational standards; TVET = technical and vocational education and training; UCS = unified cost standard.

Municipalities' role in addressing rising inequality and poor learning outcomes

Municipalities are responsible for ensuring access to and participation in education, the implementation of delegated financing and the distribution of other budget funds, and the provision of equipment, security, medical services, food, sport, and transportation. However, they play only a limited or no role in managing and controlling schools; selecting staff or appointing principals; overseeing the quality of the education provided in municipal schools; or intervening with targeted policy measures to address problems such as struggling students, the poor quality of teaching, or poor performing schools. Municipalities also play a limited role in strengthening teachers' continuing professional development.

Of particular concern is the fact that Bulgaria still lacks a clear and coherent approach to quality assurance in education that would: integrate all school-level and system-level quality goals and standards; equip all entities (the central government, municipalities, and schools) with effective tools and indicators to provide comparable evidence to ensure the quality, equity, and efficiency of educational programs and processes; and make it possible to make informed decisions about allocating funding and improving teaching and learning. The current system emphasizes "control and compliance" rather than "diagnosing and supporting." The underlying presumption is that control of resources (inputs) and processes (activities) by the central government and the municipalities will result in the required outcomes for equity and quality.

No common goals are being set between the central government and the municipalities for student assessment results or other measures of achievement. The Council of Ministers has established the National Inspectorate of Education

(NIE) to conduct independent assessments of the quality of education at the kindergartens and schools and, importantly, to develop guidelines for improvement. The school inspections are expected to yield essential data to inform results-based resource allocation. However, the first round of inspections started only recently, and it will be at least five years after the 2019–20 school year before they cover all kindergartens and schools. Under the 2016 Preschool and School Education Act (PSEA), the MoES is required to introduce a mechanism for ensuring the openness, transparency, and annual analysis of the results of the national external assessments for quality monitoring and improvement. However, there are currently no publicly available comprehensive analyses of these results to inform policy and funding decisions at the national and subnational levels.

Moreover, "accountability" still focuses largely on fiduciary or fiscal accountability rather than on accountability for results. Municipalities are expected to exercise control over the spending of resources allocated to both public schools and private schools receiving public funding. Although they are responsible for the expenditure of state grants earmarked for education, they play no role in evaluating and monitoring the quality of education and school leadership or in developing guidelines for school improvements to increase efficiency. The responsibility for monitoring and analyzing student achievement results at the municipal level is held by the regional units of the MoES. The municipalities have limited capacity to reward a school's good performance or to hold a principal accountable for a school's dismal educational outcomes.

The narrow understanding of "responsible for delivering education services"

In Bulgaria, as in other countries in the region, municipalities are considered to be responsible for ensuring compliance with norms and standards, including school buildings operating at the right hours and for the full school year, complying with sanitary, hygiene, and safety standards, and having the correct number of students in accordance with classroom norms. However, they are not considered to be responsible for ensuring that quality learning is taking place. This definition of what it means to deliver education services is not unique to Bulgaria. In Lithuania, for example, a similar division exists, with the Ministry of Education responsible for the costs associated with the "education process" and the municipalities in charge of the "education environment."

Alignment of funding with delivery of education services

Comprehensive education is funded almost exclusively by special-purpose transfers from the central government to municipalities (see figure 9.2). The amount transferred to each municipality is estimated by the central government based on unified cost standards (UCSs), per student rates, and other predefined criteria. The transfers are intended to fund activities rather than to reward results and are not conditional on school-level performance indicators. The UCS represents the per student cost to municipalities of maintaining their schools, including staff costs, as estimated by the central government. The municipalities are each supposed to adopt and apply their own formula for distributing the earmarked transfers among their schools. However, they have only limited discretion to make education policy using this formula.

This funding framework is well-aligned with the management functions of local authorities that were laid out explicitly in the PSEA. These functions include "providing for" and "controlling" (1) the conditions and organization of educational activities; (2) outreach to children of compulsory school age; (3) the physical environment needed for the functioning of schools; (4) the conditions needed for the full-day organization of studies; (5) the security of students; (6) health services in schools; (7) catering, recreation, and sports in schools; and (8) free transportation for students.

The funding model is based on separating different levels of financial allocation and management; attributing specific governance competencies to different levels of education administration; and sharing tasks among the different levels.

Within Bulgaria's Consolidated Fiscal Program, education is financed at two levels. At the first level, the central government allocates specific earmarked transfers to municipalities to fund state- mandated educational activities. The amount of these transfers is based on the centrally defined UCSs per student, per class, and per institution and on the number of students, number of classes, and number of institutions in the given municipality. The unified standards are the backbone of the funding relationship between the central government and the municipalities in which funding is provided to municipalities to cover the costs of maintaining their schools, including staff costs.

At the second level, municipalities (and, in the case of some funds, the sectoral ministries) allocate these earmarked transfers as lump sum amounts to local schools based on allocation formulas devised by each municipality. These specific-purpose transfers from the central government make up 92 percent of what is spent on comprehensive schools. Funds from the EU make up another 6 percent, leaving only 2 percent of spending financed from municipalities' own sources.[3]

Just as the scope of the education governance responsibilities of municipalities is narrow, their authority over the management of the transfers received from the central government is also limited. Every municipality is required to distribute 100 percent of the transfer designated for comprehensive schools to their local comprehensive schools. Municipalities may not transfer funds received for one education activity or function to another (for example, from comprehensive schools to kindergartens). A centrally defined rule stipulates that municipalities delegate at least 85 percent of earmarked education funding on a per student, per class, and per institution basis, but they are free to allocate the remaining 15 percent among schools according to local policy considerations.

Level of education spending

On average, EU members spent 4.7 percent of their gross domestic product (GDP) and 10.2 percent of their government budgets on education in 2018.[4] Bulgaria's allocation to education of only 3.5 percent of GDP (and about 9.7 percent of the government budget) makes it one of the lowest spenders in Europe (see figure 9.3). Most of the resources spent on education in Bulgaria come from public resources. The government provides funding for about 77 percent of total spending on all levels of education and 90 percent of spending on preschool and all levels of education combined.[5] Private sources account for only 20.5 percent of overall educational spending, with the largest portion (73.2 percent) allocated to tertiary education. External funding (mainly from the EU) accounts for the remaining funding for education.

FIGURE 9.2
Public funding flows for school education in Bulgaria, as of 2020

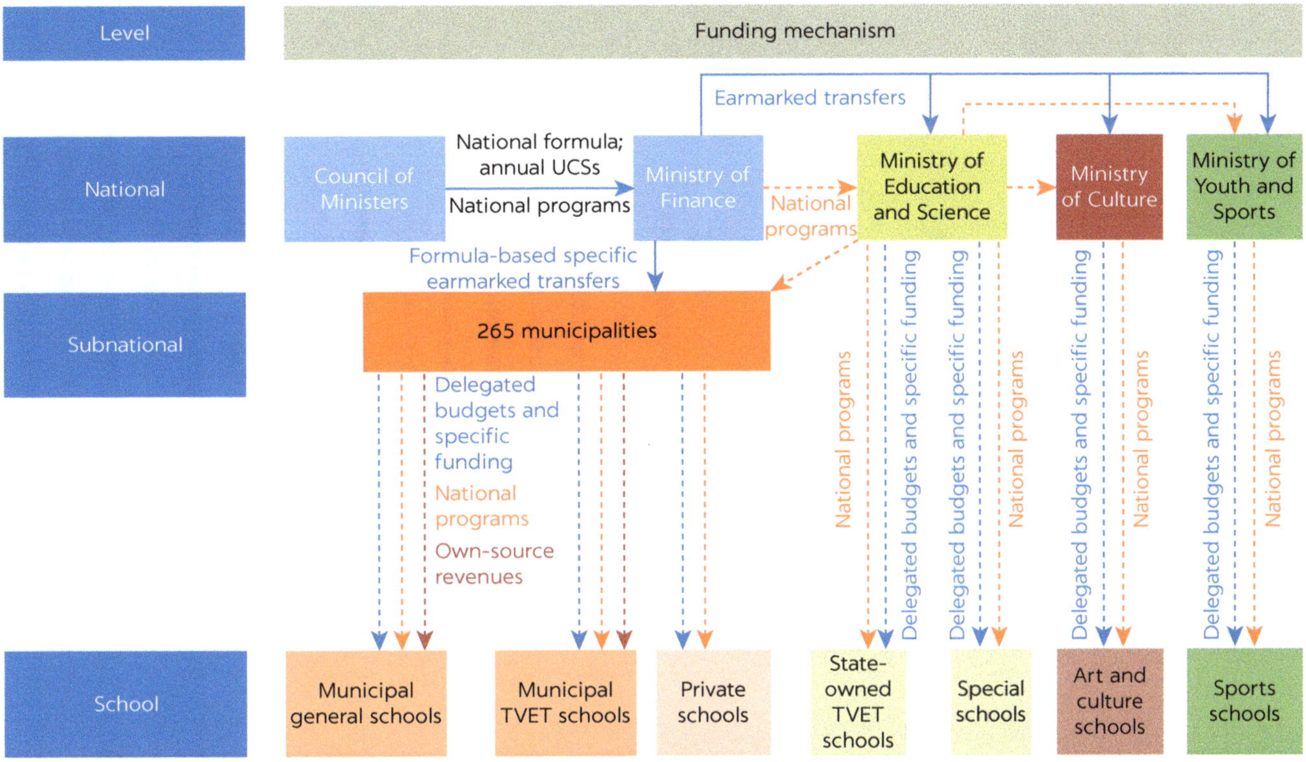

Source: World Bank.
Note: TVET = technical and vocational education and training; UCS = unified cost standard.

Bulgaria joined the EU in 2007, and until 2015, it spent approximately Lev 1.2 billion (€613.5 million) in EU grants on education. EU funding has become an even more important source of funds for education since the beginning of the new EU funds program period in 2014. Until 2018, an additional Lev 1.16 billion (€593 million) of EU funds were invested in Bulgarian education. In 2018 alone, approximately 9 percent of total public spending on education was financed by EU funds (see figure 9.4).

Education sector challenges

Learning outcomes have not improved for more than a decade, and educational inequities remain high. Bulgaria's scores on the Programme for International Student Assessment (PISA), which measures the learning achievement of 15-year-olds, have remained flat since 2006, with the share of poor performers hovering above 40 percent of the student population in reading, math, and sciences (see figure 9.5).[6] The country's Progress in International Reading Literacy Study (PIRLS) scores (which measure the learning outcomes of 4th graders) show that 5 percent of 4th graders have not yet learned to read, a percentage that has remained unchanged since 2001.[7] Similarly, the share of early school leavers (young people aged between 18 and 24 with at most a lower secondary education who are not involved in further education or training) has been hovering at about 12 percent since 2010 (see figure 9.6). The high number of children who have never enrolled in school also remains a serious source of concern (Hristova et al. 2019). Sixty-seven percent of Roma students (European

FIGURE 9.3

Education spending as percentage of GDP, Bulgaria and EU countries

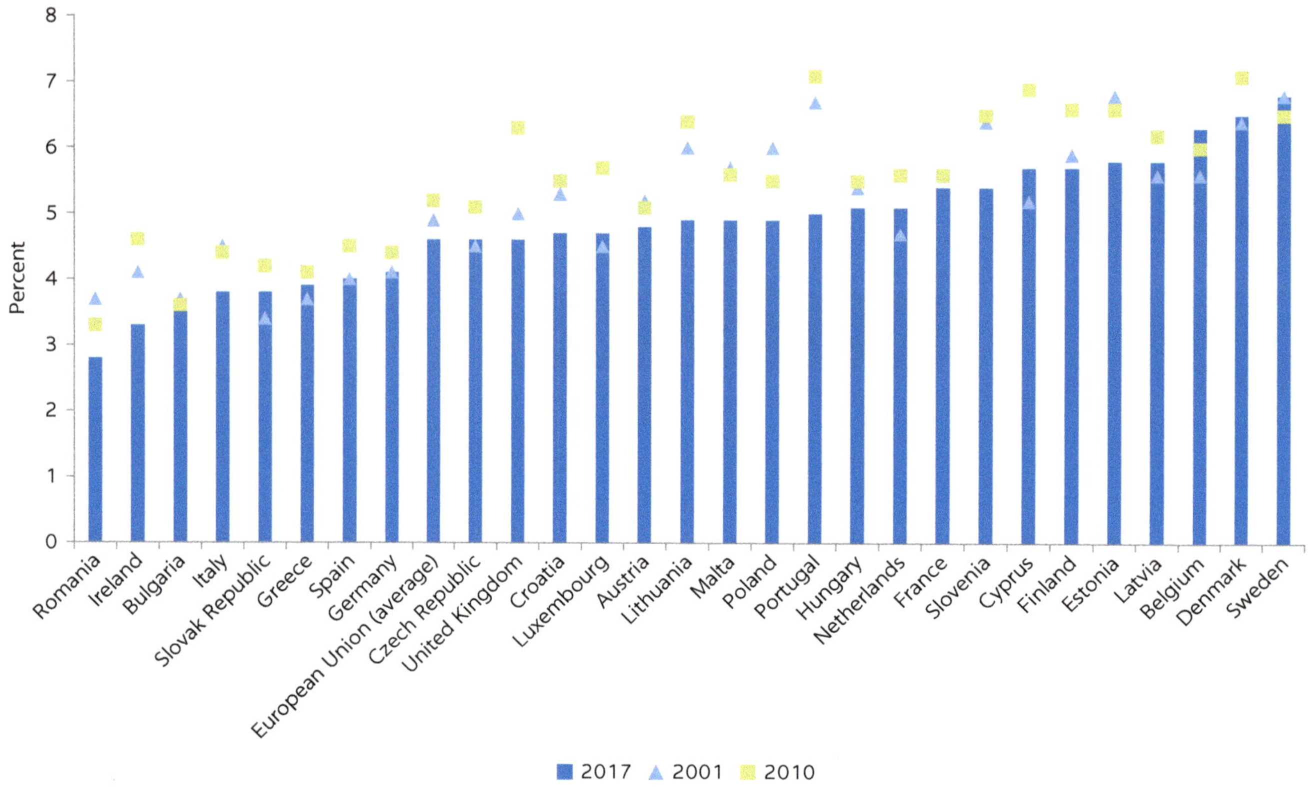

Source: COFOG, Eurostat Database, European Commission, Brussels, https://ec.europa.eu/eurostat/data/database.
Note: COFOG = Classification of the Functions of Government; GDP = gross domestic product.

FIGURE 9.4

EU funding for education, 2008–18

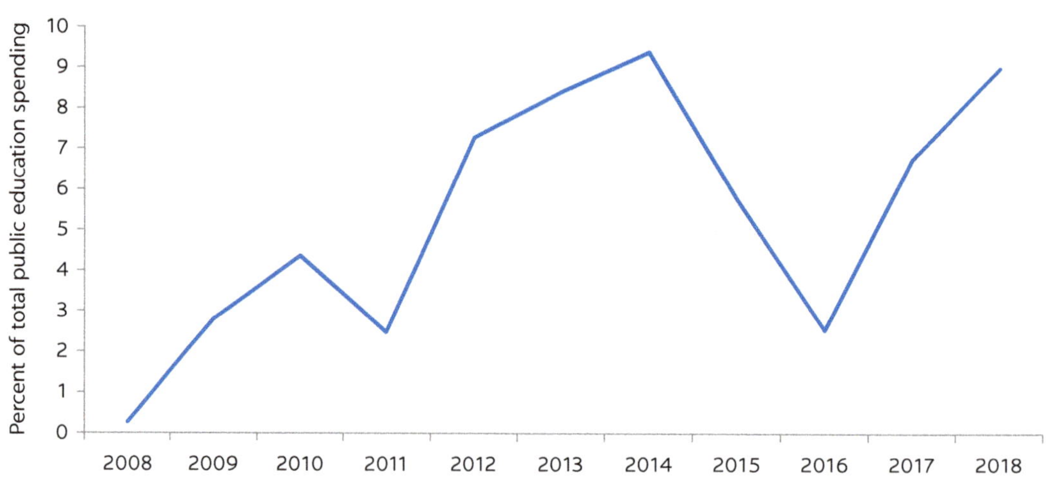

Source: Based on data from the Ministry of Finance.
Note: EU = European Union.

FIGURE 9.5
PISA test scores, 2006–18

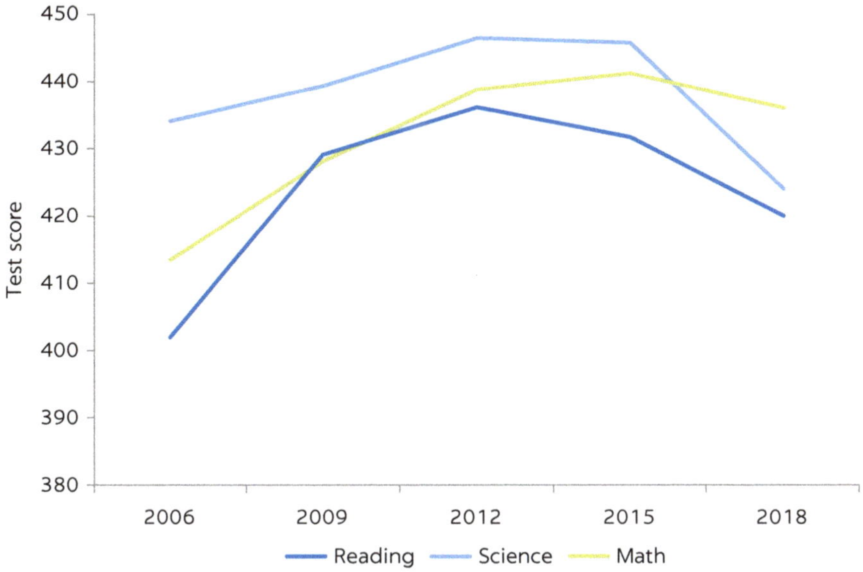

Source: PISA Database, OECD, Paris, https://www.oecd.org/pisa/data/.
Note: OECD = Organisation for Economic Co-operation and Development; PISA = Programme for International Student Assessment.

FIGURE 9.6
Early leavers from education and training, ages 18 to 24, Bulgaria and EU countries, 2002–18

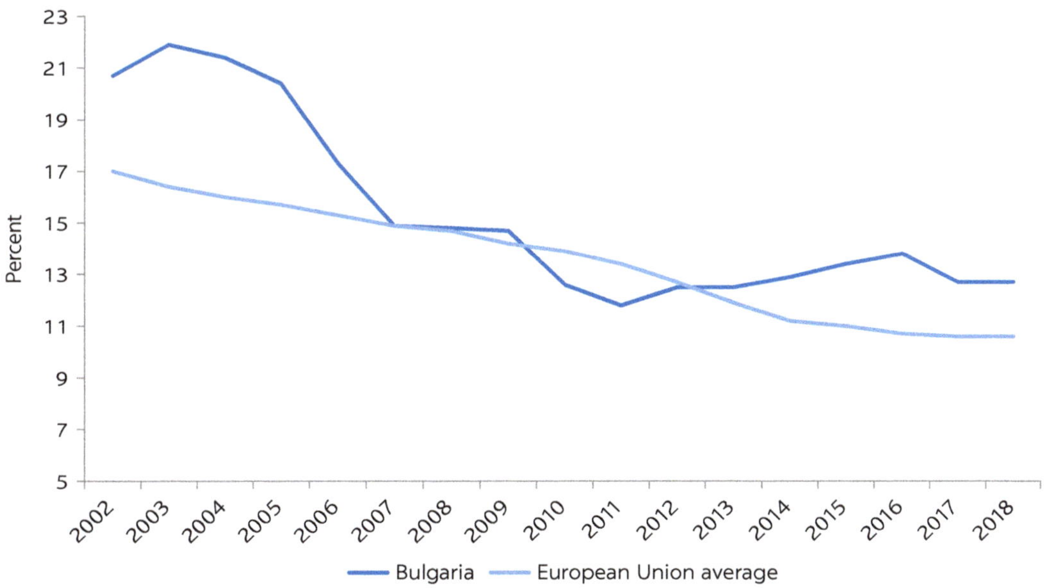

Source: Eurostat Database, European Commission, Brussels, https://ec.europa.eu/eurostat/web/products-datasets/-/edat_lfse_30.

Union Agency for Fundamental Rights 2016) and about half of all children with disabilities (European Commission 2019) drop out of education early, a sign of specific educational vulnerabilities that need to be tackled.

By several measures, the school system delivers some of the most inequitable outcomes in Europe. Students from socioeconomically weak backgrounds in Bulgaria are the most likely in Europe to study with other disadvantaged students and, not surprisingly, are the least likely to succeed academically. Also, worryingly, even though resources are equitably distributed, these socioeconomic gaps remain large. First, the relationship between performance and socioeconomic background is strong. Bulgaria has the largest share in Europe of underachievers in reading concentrated in the bottom socioeconomic quarter, with the gap between the share of underachievers in the bottom and top socioeconomic quarters being the highest among all EU countries. Second, the share of academically resilient students, defined as disadvantaged students who scored in the top quarter of performance in reading among students in their own country in PISA 2018, is the lowest in Europe. Third, academic segregation in Bulgarian schools is among the highest in Europe, with between-school differences accounting for 54.7 percent of the total variation in student performance. Fourth, the difference between the mean reading score of students attending schools in urban areas and those attending schools in rural areas is equivalent to more than three years of schooling. And fifth, Bulgaria has one of the largest indexes of school social segregation in the EU, with low-achieving students from disadvantaged backgrounds often concentrated in schools different from those attended by high-achieving students from better-off households.

The lack of improvement in key sector outcome indicators for more than a decade and the clear signs of inequities in the system suggest the need to rethink the country's fiscal transfer mechanisms.

Beyond the education sector, Bulgaria faces two large, demographic structural challenges that complicate the delivery of quality education. First is a considerable shrinkage in the school-age population, which is diminishing demand for educational services and putting significant pressure on the financial sustainability of schools in some municipalities. Changing demographics combined with increased out-migration has resulted in a decline of 33 percent in the total number of students over the last two decades (see figure 9.7). The rural population fell 16.5 percent from 2007 to 2017, considerably more than the urban population, which fell 4.1 percent in the same decade. These trends have had serious implications for enrollment, especially in rural areas. Between 2010 and 2018, the total number of students enrolled in rural schools declined by 19 percent, compared with an average decline of 6 percent countrywide. Many schools in rural areas and small towns are also enrolling increasing numbers of students from the Roma and Turkish ethnic minority groups, which will require more investments aimed at making learning more inclusive.

The second challenge also relates to demographics. Although Bulgaria's population has declined by 14 percent since 2000, the number of municipalities has increased. As a result, Bulgaria has an increasing number of very small, financially weak (and even unviable) municipalities. A growing number of these municipalities manage very few schools. In the 2000–01 school year, the median municipality had seven comprehensive schools under its jurisdiction, while 28 municipalities had two or fewer. In 2018–19, the number of schools in the median municipality decreased to four schools, with 71 municipalities having only two or fewer schools. The number of students enrolled in the median municipality's schools shrank by 44.4 percent, and the student-teacher ratio decreased from 13.7:1 to 9.9:1 between 2000 and 2018 (see table 9.3). The number of "protected" schools (small schools that receive additional funding to keep them open to guarantee access to education) increased from 90 schools in 2010 to 161 in 2019–20.

FIGURE 9.7

Decline in population ages 5 to 19 in Europe

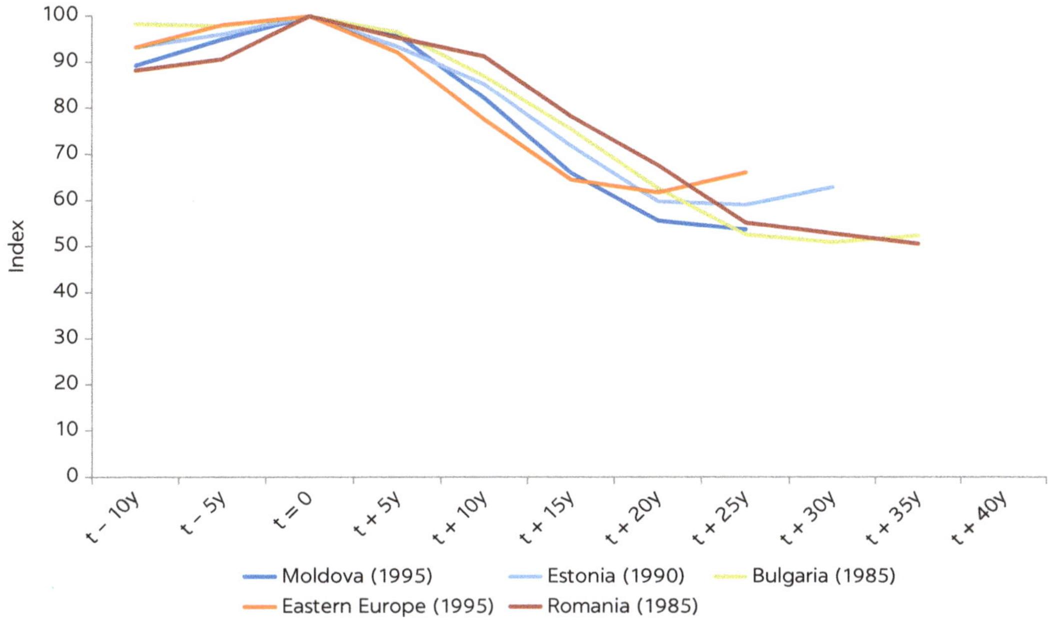

Source: United Nations 2018.
Note: Index = 100 in the peak population year corresponding to the dates in legend.

TABLE 9.3 **Selected demographic indicators for Bulgaria, 2000–19**

	2000–01	2010–11	2018–19
General demographics			
Number of municipalities	262	264	265
Total population	8,149,468	7,504,868	7,000,039
Population of median municipality	14,225	12,103	10,095
School demographics per median municipality			
Comprehensive schools	7	5	4
Classes	69	44	41
Teachers	105	73	80
Students	1,429	916	795
Students per teacher	13.7	12.5	9.9
Students per class	20.7	20.8	19.4

Source: World Bank based on data from National Statistical Institute, Sofia, https://www.nsi.bg.

FLOW OF FISCAL EDUCATION TRANSFERS

Evolution of Bulgaria's decentralized system for financing of education

Bulgaria has been implementing formula-based funding in education for almost 25 years. The general system of intergovernmental fiscal transfers in the country was set up in the early 1990s with the process of territorial restructuring and the adoption of the legal framework providing for local self-governance. The first steps toward introducing a system of delegated budgets in schools were taken in

1995 in a pilot initiative involving 20 municipalities, in which municipal schools were granted the authority to manage their property and financial resources and to raise additional revenues (Danchev and Ivanov 2009). Over the next decade, only a limited number of municipalities adopted discretionary formula-based funding of schools. Most of these formulas were per student–based, but some municipalities factored in the educational level of the school, the school size, the type and profile of the class, and the remoteness of the school, among others. Those early efforts were limited in breadth and depth, and the MoES retained the management of all teacher deployment and financing.

In 2002, a comprehensive fiscal decentralization reform package and action plan was launched. The reforms (1) improved the assignment of intergovernmental roles and responsibilities; (2) created incentives for municipalities to increase local revenues; (3) distinguished between state-delegated and locally financed public services; (4) strengthened the financial capacity of local authorities; and (5) enhanced the transparency of the flow of funds. Before 2002, municipal schools were funded exclusively from the country's general budget revenue. Moreover, the intergovernmental fiscal transfer mechanism lacked clear rules for allocating shared taxes and general subsidies among the municipalities (Danchev and Ivanov 2009). The 2002 fiscal decentralization process introduced fundamentally new principles for devolving service provision and funding responsibilities to municipalities, new rules for assigning expenditures and revenues across different levels of government, and mechanisms for allocating fiscal transfers from the central government budget to municipal budgets.

In 2007, a mechanism was adopted for delegating decision-making power from the central government to the local authorities that distinguished between local tasks and mandated activities. Local tasks were noncompulsory and would be funded entirely by municipalities' own revenues. Mandated activities were compulsory (such as the provision of education) or of national importance (such as the provision of healthcare and social assistance) and were to be funded by the central government through earmarked fiscal transfers or from the municipalities own revenues, or both. Under the 2007 mechanism, intergovernmental transfers for mandated activities are allocated based on UCSs, and local authorities have very little discretion over how those resources are spent. Education transfers must be spent on schools, but municipalities have a limited amount of discretion over how to distribute the funds among schools. The central government also provides municipalities with a general, formula-based equalization subsidy, the main purpose of which is to reduce inequalities in per capita local revenues between municipalities and thus to keep horizontal fiscal balance. As with own-source revenues, municipalities are free to decide how to spend this subsidy.

In line with the general decentralization reform, the Bulgarian government implemented a sweeping reform of education finance in 2007–08. A vital aspect of the reform was a new way of funding the system, which had the explicit aim of providing stronger incentives for both schools and municipalities to respond appropriately to the declines in student numbers in classes and schools, which had been plummeting for decades as a result of falling birth rates. The reform shifted away from funding municipalities on the basis of the size of their teaching and nonteaching staff and toward a quasi-voucher system based on the number of students in each municipality. This gave municipalities an immediate incentive to cut overspending and reduce fixed costs by closing schools and merging classes (Levačić 2008).

Distribution of central government funds to local authorities

All intergovernmental fiscal transfers for education in Bulgaria are specific-purpose grants. The PSEA established a "conceptual" funding framework based on four pillars defined according to the purpose of funding: (1) carrying out activities aimed at the education and upbringing of children and pupils; (2) ensuring equal access to schooling and supporting the development of the child's personality; (3) developing kindergartens, schools, and personality development support centers; and (4) implementing national programs for education development (see table 9.4). Within each pillar, there are different funding streams aimed at providing the resources needed to achieve the defined purpose.

The first pillar constitutes the main funding streams for school education. Most of these funds are allocated to the municipalities based on UCSs for each type of educational institution. Each municipality receives its own allocation based on a per student UCS disaggregated by different types of education institutions.[8] Once the municipality receives the funds, it transfers them to schools based on its own formula. As well as the stream of funds for the provision of basic education, this pillar also covers additional streams of funds for students from vulnerable groups, for the maintenance of protected schools, and for the maintenance of technical and vocational education and training (TVET) classes that provide training in protected professions and in professions that are expected to be short of workers in the labor market.

Within the second pillar, various specific-purpose grants are transferred to municipalities to ensure equal access to education and foster personality development. These grants cover scholarships, transportation for students, the provision of free textbooks and educational materials, the full-day organization of education and meals, recreation, and sports, personal development support, and support for talented students.

The funding streams within the third pillar are intended to support the development of educational institutions. This includes funding for improving school facilities, purchasing or funding capital repairs of fixed tangible assets, resourcing libraries and information services, funding teacher in-service training and development, providing teachers with support for transportation and rent, and meeting other costs aimed at improving the physical environment and the quality of the educational process. Some elements of result-based funding have been legally introduced, but because there is no quality assessment mechanism, they are still not being enforced.

Under the fourth pillar, funding is provided for the implementation of centrally defined national programs for the development of education by providing grants to schools or resourcing centrally implemented programs. This is a flexible mechanism for resourcing interventions and school activities that cannot be financed by the institutional funding provided under the first three pillars. National programs could also provide resources to municipal education development programs when the measures and activities of the national program could be implemented more efficiently at the municipal level. The terms and conditions for the allocation of funds are set out in each national program. Funds are transfers from the state budget to the MoES budget and from the MoES to a municipality for approved school projects. Municipalities then transfer the funds from the MoES budget to schools but have only a limited say in how the funds are allocated.

TABLE 9.4 **Pillars for central government education transfers to municipalities**

PILLAR 1	PILLAR 2	PILLAR 3	PILLAR 4
Objectives			
Maintenance of activities for education and upbringing of children and students	Support for equal access to education and personal development	Development of kindergartens, schools, and personal development support centers	Implementation of national programs for the development of education
Purpose of grant			
Basic education services Students from vulnerable groups Maintenance of protected schools Maintenance of TVET classes providing training in protected professions and professions that are expected to be short of workers in the labor market	Transportation for students Scholarships Free textbooks and educational materials Full-day organization of educational process and provision of meals Personal development support Recreation and sports Programs to prevent early dropout Support for students with outstanding talent	Improvement of school facilities Improvement of quality of education and educational outcomes Teacher in-service training, development, and support Libraries and information services Other costs of improving the physical environment and the educational process	Specific-purpose grants
Determination of pool			
UCSs per student, per class, and per institution; additional standards and rates per student	Additional standards and rates per student and rates per institution	Additional standards or rates per student; performance-based funding (not enforced); capital subsidy	Scope and amount of funding for each national program determined and adopted by the Council of Ministers
Allocation of funds			
Allocation rule (2007–17) transfer to municipalities: UCS per student X number of students Allocation rule (since 2018) for transfers to municipalities: (UCS per student X number of students) + (UCS per class X number of classes) + (UCS per institution X number of institutions) For work with students from vulnerable groups, allocation based on the concentration of parents with low educational attainment Funding for the maintenance of protected schools according to rules adopted by the Council of Ministers For the maintenance of TVET classes providing training in protected professions and professions that are expected to be short of workers in the labor market according to a list of professions, approved annually by the Council of Ministers	Terms and conditions for the allocation of resources, including the additional spending standards or rates per student, as set out by the Council of Ministers	Allocation of funds for: teacher development as a percentage of personnel costs; performance-based funding based on results of school inspections (not enforced); per student rate for infrastructure and facilities or according to municipal investment program	Terms and conditions as set out in the respective national program; school projects are approved by the MoES; municipal governments are involved in transfer of funds from the MoES budget to school budgets but play no decision-making role in the allocation of funds

continued

TABLE 9.4, *continued*

PILLAR 1	PILLAR 2	PILLAR 3	PILLAR 4
Use of funds			
Personnel costs, maintenance costs, fixed costs, additional remuneration for work with students from vulnerable groups, and expenses for external services	Transportation costs and maintenance of buses, scholarships, expenditures for textbooks and educational materials, personnel costs, maintenance costs, costs of meals, spending on external services, and costs of materials and subscriptions	Expenditures for the acquisition of fixed tangible assets, the capital repair of fixed tangible assets, the construction of infrastructure, costs of external services, costs of in-service teacher training, transportation, and rent	Expenditures for the implementation of school- based interventions and activities that could not be implemented within the institutional funding

Source: PSEA and state educational standards for financing institutions.
Note: MoES = Ministry of Education and Science; PSEA = Preschool and School Education Act; TVET = technical and vocational education and training; UCS = unified cost standard.

The four pillars are categories used in the legal framework to provide a "conceptual model" for the system of school finance. However, budgets are not formally presented according to the pillars, and spending is not tracked by these pillars in the treasury system. Therefore, it was not possible for us to directly quantify the magnitude of funding in each pillar over time or to analyze spending by pillar in our analysis of spending versus outcomes. Different education-related transfers are embedded within the budget classification's general categories of transfers. The supplementary subsidy for state-mandated activities integrates the funds earmarked to cover the expenses involved in maintaining schools but also contains funding for other mandated tasks. This is the most important transfer, which accounted for 75 percent of transfers across all sectors in 2018. The bulk of education-related funds under this transfer would come under pillar 1.

Targeted transfers for capital expenditures provide schools with funding for capital spending, among all other capital expenditures at the municipal level. Funding under national programs for the development of education is allocated with other targeted transfers from the central budget, including miscellaneous transfers. As a rough estimate, we believe that pillar 3, which focuses on capital spending, makes up about 5 percent of total transfers, with the remaining two pillars accounting for the remaining approximately 20 percent.

How is the system designed to achieve equity?

The model for the public financing of comprehensive school education in Bulgaria is designed to compensate for various naturally occurring inequalities in educational opportunities. It involves different mechanisms for allocating extra resources to municipalities and schools with less fiscal capacity or higher expenditure needs, or both, so that their ability to provide basic education service is increased and equalized.

The specific-purpose grants from the central government to municipalities are intended to cover all the costs of running comprehensive schools, with no expectation that municipalities will top up the resources. Thus, by providing grants that are intended to fully fund the cost of providing comprehensive education, the central government is reducing the risk that poor municipalities will spend less than rich municipalities.

The funding mechanism uses different groupings of municipalities and a weighting system to reflect inequality in access to education arising from their specific characteristics. Initially, the system of UCSs, introduced in 2007, divided all the municipalities into four categories according to their size, population density, peripheral location, and mountainous terrain. Three of the UCSs—two for types of kindergartens and one for comprehensive schools—were differentiated for all four categories of municipalities, with smaller municipalities receiving more money per student to compensate for the higher costs associated with small schools and partially filled classes. This grouping has evolved to allow for greater differentiation of municipal needs, which has also added complexity. In 2013, the initial four categories of municipalities were expanded to seven (see table 9.5), depending on the number of settlements and the number of population.

In 2018, MoES and the Ministry of Finance (MoF) made some additional changes to the formula, with the end result that local authorities face weaker incentives to downsize classes and schools. First, the number of categories of municipalities was expanded to eight, because some municipalities needed more resources than others to finance their schools. Second, the formula abandoned the simplicity that had been a hallmark of the 2007 reforms. Instead of relying solely on the number of students enrolled, it introduced a more complex formula involving both the number of students but also "norms" for average "acceptable" class sizes.

Additional funds are now granted to schools with over 20 percent of students from vulnerable groups, with the amount of funding depending on the exact percentage. Vulnerability is assessed using proxies such as the low educational status of parents. Schools may use these additional resources to fund extra remuneration for teachers, to pay mediators or social workers, to participate in

TABLE 9.5 Number of municipalities and allocation to students by category, 2007 and 2013

GROUP	PER STUDENT AMOUNT		NUMBER OF MUNICIPALITIES
	BULGARIAN LEV	US$	
2007			
Group 1 (large urban areas)	796	531	15
Group 2	849	566	40
Group 3	894	596	139
Group 4 (small mountainous areas)	958	639	70
2013			
Group 1	1,274	867	6
Group 2	1,298	883	6
Group 3	1,335	908	6
Group 4	1,365	929	28
Group 5	1,442	981	60
Group 6	1,465	997	43
Group 7	1,570	1,068	115

Source: Council of Ministers' regulations and Bulgarian National Bank.

outreach to identify and include vulnerable children and students in education, or to provide them with additional training in the Bulgarian language.

A special group of "protected" schools is given additional funding beyond the UCS transfers to keep them open and functioning. A school is eligible for protected status if its closure would risk restricting access to education. The list of protected schools is adopted annually by the Council of Ministers.

In addition to the specific-purpose grants that are meant to fully cover the cost of providing comprehensive education, poorer municipalities also have access to a general equalization subsidy. This subsidy is designed to equalize their revenue and spending capacity to guarantee a minimum "portfolio" of public services. It consists of two components: (1) the equalization of revenue potential, which is allocated to those municipalities that have per capita tax revenue below a predefined national per capita tax revenue threshold[9]; and (2) the equalization of service provision potential. The latter component is calculated in accordance with the municipality's spending needs, which are estimated using such indicators as the number of children under 5 years of age, the number of children between 6 and 14 years of age, the number of adults age 65 and older, area of the municipality, the length of municipal roads, and the municipality's population. In practice, the general equalization subsidy is the only intergovernmental transfer over which the local governments have full spending discretion. Until 2019, all municipalities had access to general equalization funds. A new eligibility rule has been introduced, however, that grants the subsidy only to those municipalities whose permanent tax revenues per capita are less than 120 percent of the national per capita tax revenues.

Municipal discretion to complement or reallocate central government transfers

Municipalities have full discretion to complement the specific-purpose transfers they receive from the central government with their own resources, but they have no discretion to reallocate the specific-purpose grants themselves (see box 9.1). In other words, municipalities cannot use the funds they have received for comprehensive education to fund, for example, social protection, because those funds have to be used for their comprehensive schools. However, even though municipalities may top up the earmarked funds they receive for comprehensive education with other revenue, they do not seem to be doing so. This suggests that municipalities are using their own-source revenue and the equalization grant to fund other mandated expenditures for which they either receive no specific-purpose grants or do not receive enough to cover their costs.

Information and support mechanisms for the funding system

Information and support mechanisms enable the planning and allocation of intergovernmental fiscal transfers in Bulgaria. The National Electronic Information System for Pre-School and School Education (maintained by the MoES) contains information on the number of institutions, classes, and students for each type of cost standard applied. To determine the need for targeted support to vulnerable students, the MoES collects voluntary data about the educational attainment of parents. Municipalities are supported by the Municipal Finance Directorate in the Ministry of Finance, which collects and maintains information on municipal budgets and municipal capital expenditures as well as

BOX 9.1

Evolution of the allocation mechanism in school finance

When the delegated budget system was first introduced, the specific-purpose grants from central budgets to municipal budgets for the provision of basic education services were calculated by multiplying the UCS per student by the number of students. Municipalities were obliged to distribute 100 percent of the UCS-based transfers they received among their schools using their own local formula, but they were required to allocate a minimum of 80 percent of the funds according to the UCS per student and number of students, and had discretion over only 20 percent to be distributed according to local preferences and differences between schools (such as the type of heating system, the school location, the area, or the numbers of students from vulnerable backgrounds).

Over the next decade, various modifications and adjustments were made to the funding mechanism, but no significant change was made to the per student principle. The allocation mechanism was gradually becoming more complex, with the addition of more UCSs (increasing from 36 in 2010 to 49 in 2017) and the introduction of various supplementary components.

In 2018, a significant change in the funding formula design was introduced, adding per class and per institution UCSs to the per student standard that had been in use since 2007. The mandatory distribution of 100 percent of the funds remained unchanged. The scope of municipalities' discretion to reallocate funds has been slightly restricted, however, with the new distribution rule requiring at least 85 percent of the funding to be allocated on a per student, per class, and per institution basis and up to 15 percent of the funding to be allocated according to local needs and circumstances.

preparing monthly and quarterly reports on the implementation of municipal budgets. The Directorate also (1) coordinates all activities related to the preparation and implementation of municipal budgets; (2) develops the mechanisms for allocating subsidies; (3) negotiates with the National Association of Municipalities in the Republic of Bulgaria (NAMRB) on the allocation of subsidies; and (4) provides methodological support to the municipalities. NAMRB offers a wide range of information, methodological, and consultancy support to municipal governments, including training. It also maintains an online information system that contains data on municipal finances.

Researchers interested in quantifying the intergovernmental funding flows in education face two main problems. First, the four funding pillars are not coded in Bulgaria's budget classification system, which makes it difficult to quantify or track the amounts of funding provided under each pillar. Second, the main intergovernmental transfer covers municipalities' expenditures on "state-mandated activities." Although the transfer is functionally earmarked, the code for tracking the transfer is not.

Patterns and trends in the flow of funds through the transfer system

Municipalities in Bulgaria have very limited fiscal autonomy. Their own-source revenue is tiny (except for a few municipalities that include resorts or strong economic centers), and most of the transfers they receive from the central government are for a specific purpose. The own-source revenues from the local tax base of the median Bulgarian municipality in 2018 accounted for only

24.2 percent of the local budget, with the remaining 75.8 percent coming from various transfers from the central budget (see table 9.6). The transfer entitled "total supplementary subsidy for state-mandated activities" is the most important, accounting for 75 percent of intergovernmental transfers in 2018 and for 50.5 percent of the revenues of the median municipality. By comparison, the general equalization subsidy—over which municipalities have full discretion—accounted for only 8.5 percent of the total revenues of the median municipality as of 2018.

The most significant state-mandated activity is education, which is evident when municipal spending is broken down by funding source (that is, whether the funds to finance the spending were from own sources, transfers, or EU funds). The breakdown shows that, in 2018, spending on education—financed by the earmarked transfers—amounted to 69 percent of total spending (see table 9.7).

TABLE 9.6 **Revenue structure of Bulgaria's municipalities, 2018**

	ALL MUNICIPALITIES (AGGREGATED) (%)	MEDIAN MUNICIPALITY (%)	RESTRICTIONS ON USE
Own-source revenues (local base)	38	24	No
Central government transfers	62	76	For most transfers
Total supplementary subsidy for state-mandated activities	47	51	Yes, mandated activity only
General equalization subsidy	5	9	No
Targeted transfers for capital expenditure	3	4	Yes, capital expenditures
Other targeted transfers from central budget (including transfer for national programs for the development of education)	6	7	Yes, specified spending[a]
Other targeted subsidies (including transfers for free transport of students)	2	1	Yes, transport-related activities[b]

Source: World Bank, based on data from the Ministry of Finance.
Note: Subnational transfers do not add up to central government transfers because of rounding.
a. Includes targeted transfers to cover: (1) differences in housing prices; (2) costs associated with disaster prevention and management; (3) spending on cultural activities; (4) funding for infrastructure projects; (5) funding from national programs for the development of education; and (6) other specified spending.
b. Includes subsidies for urban, suburban, or intercity public passenger transport, compensation for the free transportation of students up to 16 years of age, and compensation for free or reduced-price passenger transport.

TABLE 9.7 **Local spending on state-mandated activities financed by earmarked transfers**

PURPOSE OF SPENDING	2018 (LEV)	SHARE OF TOTAL (%)
General public services	270,525,911	9
Defense and security	57,358,660	2
Education	2,176,576,697	69
Healthcare	135,946,800	4
Social protection	376,780,700	12
Housing, public works, utilities, and environmental protection	269,791	0
Recreation, resorts, culture, and religious activities	116,502,940	4
Economic activities and services	28,715,623	1
Expenditures not classified elsewhere	121,579	0
Total	3,162,798,701	100

Source: World Bank, based on data from the Ministry of Finance.
Note: Percentage total does not add to 100 because of rounding.

TABLE 9.8 **Local spending on comprehensive education by source**

	2018 (LEV)	SHARE OF TOTAL (%)
Special-purpose grants from the central government	1,406,130,381	92
Own-source revenue	29,651,289	2
EU structural funds and other international organizations	96,411,984	6
Total	1,532,193,654	100

Source: World Bank, based on data from the Ministry of Finance.
Note: EU = European Union.

For comprehensive education, municipalities rely almost exclusively on funding from either the central government or from EU structural funds (see table 9.8). In 2018, 92 percent of municipal spending on comprehensive schools was financed from special-purpose grants, another 6 percent from EU structural funds, and only 2 percent from own-source funds (or the equalization fund). In 2018, 78 municipalities (30 percent) contributed no additional funds, and the remaining municipalities contributed an average of only 15 leva per student (covering 2 percent of all costs).

EFFECTS OF THE DECENTRALIZED FINANCING SYSTEM

Effects of transfers on subnational spending

Because the specific-purpose grants finance 92 percent of what municipalities spend on comprehensive schools, their significance is clear—they pay teachers' salaries and keep the lights on in schools. Without transfers, spending per student would likely favor financially better-off municipalities.

To further underscore the importance of these fiscal transfers, we used a regression model to estimate the impact of total transfer revenues per capita on total local spending per capita and education spending per student in Bulgaria (see World Bank 2021). We found that, after controlling for municipality-specific characteristics, a 1 percent increase in total transfer revenues per capita results in a 0.45 percent increase in total local spending per capita and a 0.15 percent increase in total education spending per student.

Effects of transfers on education outcomes

Despite transfers' strong impact on increasing subnational education spending, their effects on outcomes are mixed.

On the positive side, transfers take into account local characteristics that either result in higher costs (such as low population density) or a more challenging education environment (such as having more disadvantaged students). This strong feature of the Bulgarian system ensures that spending is pro-poor because poorer municipalities have the highest per student spending.

Also on the positive side, the transfers have reduced inefficiencies in the system as measured by low average class sizes. Bulgaria has done uniquely well in reducing the number of classes, teachers, and schools in response to the significant decline in its school-age population. The introduction of the "money follows the student" principle in education finance triggered a process of optimization in the school network and a related decline in the number of classes and teaching staff. As transfers became tied to numbers of students rather than schools, classes, or teachers, municipal officials were forced to identify those schools that could be merged or closed. Indeed, Bulgaria's downsizing is especially impressive when compared to other EU member states that have also experienced large declines in their student populations. For example, figure 9.8 shows the changes in Croatia in comparison with those in Bulgaria in figure 9.9. Croatia's decline in student numbers was not as drastic as that in Bulgaria, but, unlike Bulgaria, Croatia has not reduced the number of its schools, teachers, and classes in response to the decline in its student numbers.

The funding system has not, however, helped municipalities address the challenges outlined in the section titled *Education Sector Challenges*. The education system remains highly segregated, there are many failing schools, and learning outcomes are not improving. These problems are not entirely caused by weaknesses in the funding system but, tellingly, the size of the transfers given to municipalities does not appear to have any relationship to the education outcomes that municipalities achieve. Using a range of different statistical methods, we found no evidence that increased spending leads to improved learning outcomes at the subnational level. At first sight, it even appears that providing more resources may be counterproductive. Our simple bivariate correlations indicate that those municipalities that spend more on a per student basis

FIGURE 9.8

Change in education metrics, Croatia, 2000/01–2017/18

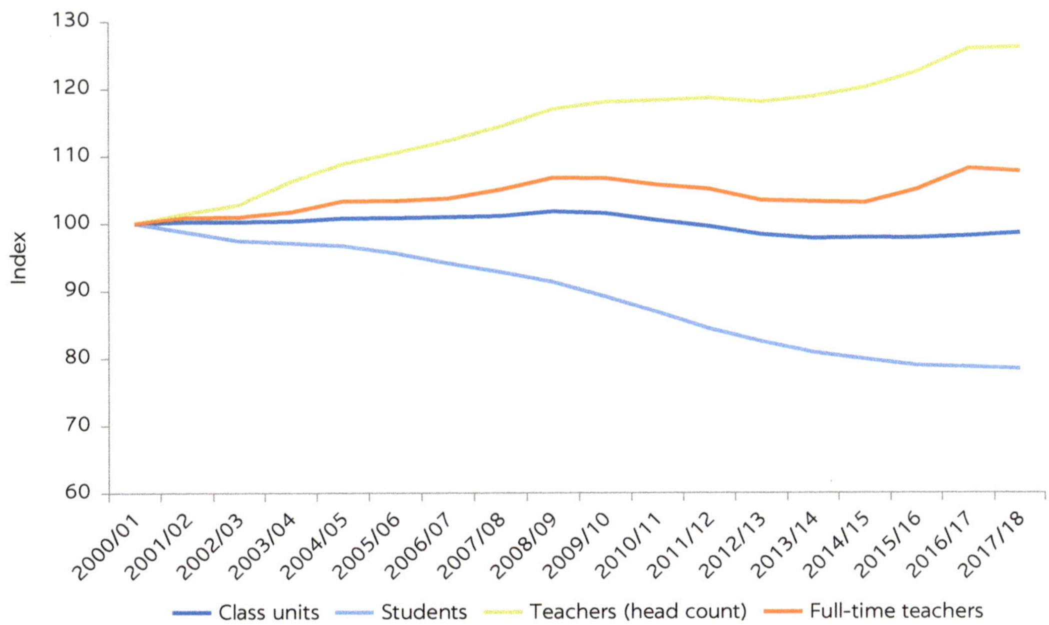

Source: Statistical Yearbook of the Republic of Croatia, Croatian Bureau of Statistics, https://www.dzs.hr/Eng/Publication/stat_year.htm.
Note: Index = 100 for 2000–01.

FIGURE 9.9
Change in education metrics, Bulgaria, 2000/01–2008/19

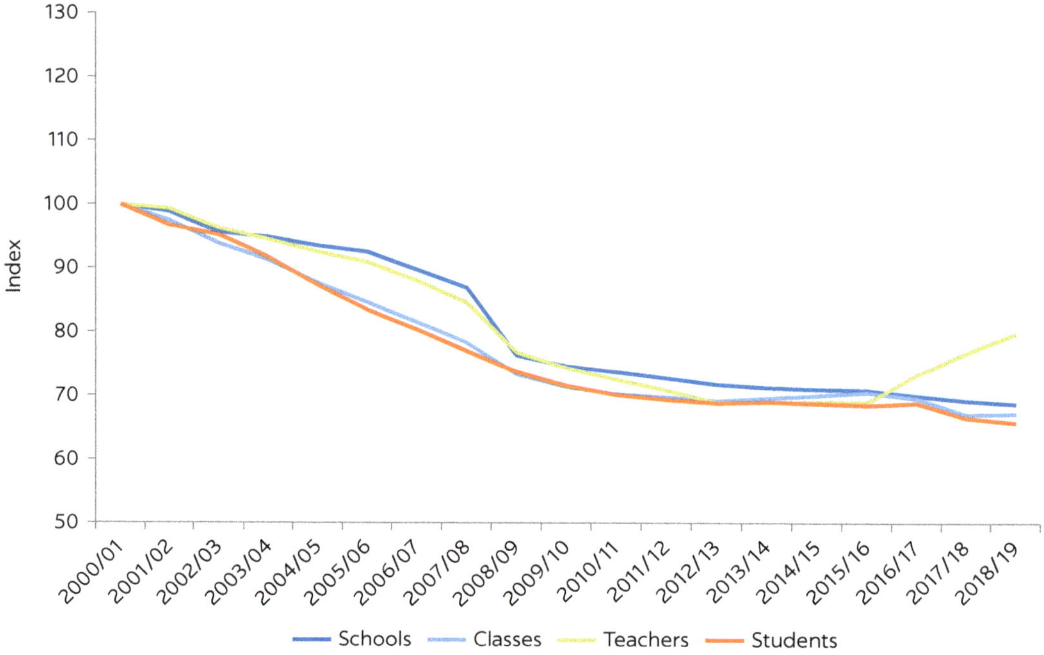

Source: World Bank based on data from National Statistical Institute, Sofia, www.nsi.bg.
Note: Index = 100 for 2000/01.

produce the lowest scores on grade 7 assessments in math and the Bulgarian language (see figure 9.10).

However, the bivariate relationship depicted in figure 9.10 is potentially misleading because it does not take into account other potential factors that could drive test score results. Therefore, we used a multivariate regression approach to explore the statistical relationship between municipalities' level of spending from the transfers they receive from the central government and the results they achieve after controlling for other factors that are likely to influence students' test scores. We found no evidence of a positive impact of spending on test scores. In fact, in several of the specifications used, we were unable to reject the conclusion that there is a negative relationship. Specifically, we designed several regression models to evaluate the impact of intergovernmental transfers on education outcomes. The results of all of them suggested that these transfers had no impact on the average scores on the Bulgarian language exam in the 2018–19 school year. One of the models is presented in more detail in World Bank (2021). After controlling for factor variables such as student-teacher ratio and average class size as well as contextual factors (such as the type of municipality, its population, the poverty rate among those between birth and age 17, and the share of students with parents with low educational attainment), the coefficients of the share of education spending in the municipal budget and total spending per capita were both insignificant. Put more bluntly, spending does not seem to play any role in driving educational performance as measured by test scores.

FIGURE 9.10
Local spending from transfers and educational outcomes, 2018/19

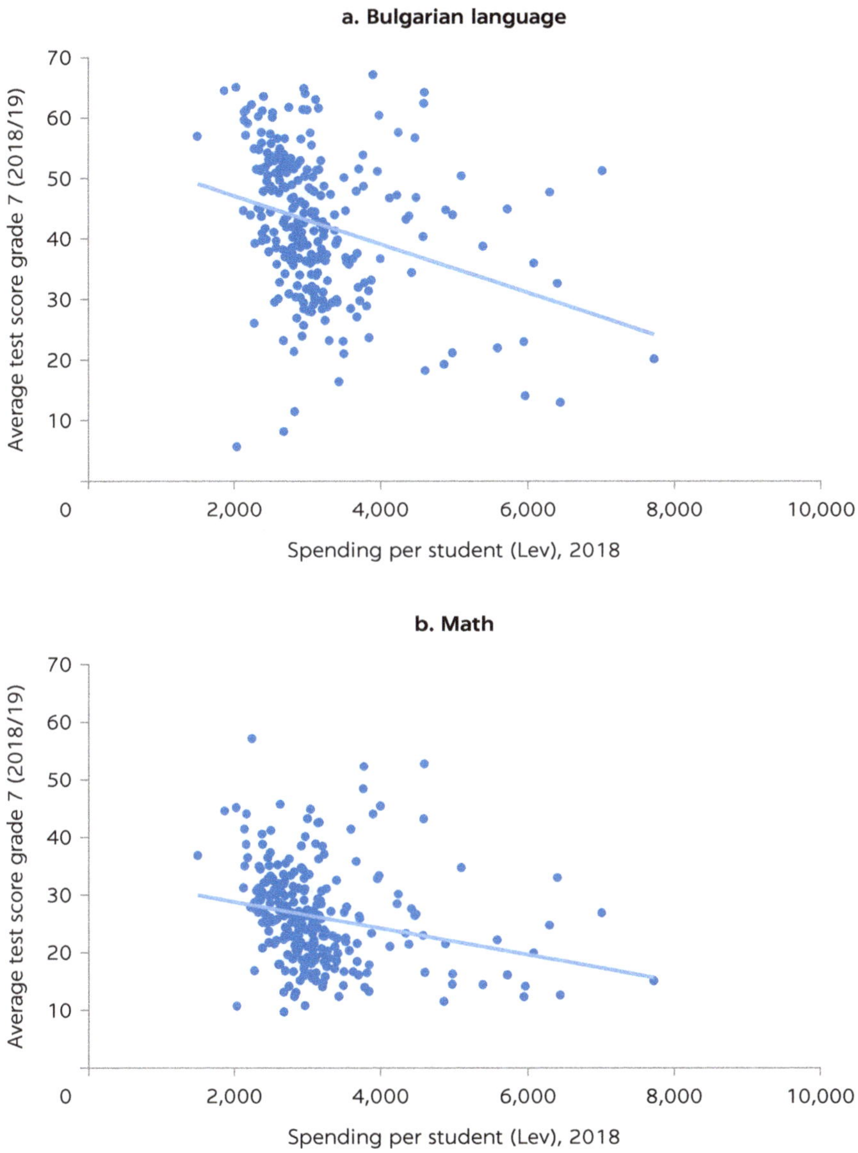

Source: Expenditures are based on data received from the Ministry of Finance; data on the number of students and average test scores were provided by the Ministry of Education and Science.

Why has the funding system not had a bigger impact on education outcomes?

There are several reasons why the education funding system has not improved the performance of Bulgaria's students. First, the funding system provides no incentives to any of the key actors in the system to improve outcomes, including ministers, state inspectors, mayors, municipal education teams, principals, and teachers. For the main flows in the system, the bulk of financing is allocated entirely according to inputs (the number of enrolled students, the number of classes, and school characteristics), with no adjustments made on the basis of what is or is not achieved. Although the foundations have been formally established for the implementation of a results-based approach to education finance, they are unclear in scope and are still not being enforced.[10] For example, the government has introduced a remuneration mechanism that enables school principals to reward good teaching. However, the financial incentives provided to teachers are not aligned with any credible measure of student performance.

Second, the system lacks an integrated and coherent evaluation and assessment framework to enable the credible verification and monitoring of what students are (or are not) learning. The current external evaluation results (available annually for students in grades 4, 7, 10 and 12) are not used to inform or evaluate education finance policies at either the national or subnational level. Moreover, given the dismal outcomes produced by Bulgarian students in the PISA language and mathematics tests, the system could benefit from testing reading and numeracy skills in grades 1 and 2 to identify and rectify any weaknesses earlier in the education cycle. Third, despite the key role that municipalities play in providing education in Bulgaria, the system gives them hardly any role in addressing the big challenges related to poor learning and inequities. This is a missed opportunity to tap into their creativity and local knowledge. Currently, municipalities play a limited role in the management of their schools. They have no power to evaluate the performance of schools or school leadership and, hence, have no way to drive schools to improve. The benefit of decentralization lies in the assumption that local governments are best placed to identify local strengths and needs, but Bulgaria seems to have missed the opportunity to empower municipalities to do more than distribute predefined funding in education. Municipalities have been given no incentive to take on a bigger role, and in any case, they lack the capacity to reward schools for good education outcomes[11] or to hold principals accountable for dismal educational outcomes.[12]

Currently, municipalities' responsibilities are largely fiduciary and administrative, and they are not focused on improving learning performance in their schools. Moreover, the central government makes no effort to nudge municipalities to improve the learning performance of their students. For example, the central government does not prepare and publish comparisons of student performance on tests by municipality. Also, there is no warning system to identify municipalities that are underperforming in student achievement and to put those municipalities under further scrutiny and offer more support. The scope of local education policy making and service provision is mostly micromanaged by the central government and predefined by input-based financial instruments over which local governments have limited discretion or authority (NALAS 2018).

KEY POLICY DIRECTIONS TO STRENGTHEN DECENTRALIZED EDUCATION FINANCING

Simply tweaking the intergovernmental transfer system will not address the multiple underlying causes of Bulgaria's poor educational performance. However, rethinking how funds are allocated and distributed could trigger exactly the types of broader reforms Bulgaria needs. The following questions are important: What role could municipalities play beyond the narrow administrative roles they currently have? What information is needed to shift their focus to learning outcomes? How can all actors in the system be incentivized to focus on narrowing inequities in the system and on increasing what students know and can do at the end of each grade? Four proposals for how the system could be improved follow.

Introduce a results-based approach to the funding mechanism with features that incentivize the poorest performing schools and municipalities to improve their performance

The 2007 decentralization reforms jolted municipalities into taking aggressive action to make their spending more efficient. The central government changed to a per student funding formula and deliberately set the per student amount so low that several municipalities were unable to maintain their large number of schools. Municipalities were prompted to take decisive action, and a record number of schools were merged or closed in 2008 and 2009. Bulgaria has done exceptionally well relative to other EU member states in downsizing its school network to match the declining student population.

Bulgaria's education system needs a new jolt to give municipalities an incentive to desegregate their schools (so that disadvantaged students and high-achieving students are not concentrated in separate schools), reduce dropouts, and improve learning outcomes. The central government must take bold action through its intergovernmental fiscal transfer system to galvanize municipalities into action.

The experience of Ceará—a relatively poor state in Brazil with 9 million inhabitants and 184 municipalities—provides some lessons for how the Bulgarian government could reform its intergovernmental fiscal transfer system in a way that incentivizes municipalities and schools to achieve better results. In 2007, Ceará began linking part of its fiscal transfers to municipalities to their education performance. Since then, the state has had some of the country's biggest improvements in the quality of education, with 9 of its municipalities having ranked among Brazil's top 20 in 2017. The Ministry of Education uses a simple funding formula that takes into account both improvements in test scores and reductions in dropout rates to incentivize municipalities to make progress on both fronts. Municipalities cannot "game the system" by trying to improve their test score results by letting its weakest students drop out. This ensures that every municipality—not only the top performers—has an incentive to improve. Moreover, it ensures that municipalities need to make improvements every year to maintain the previous year's funding level.

It is important to recognize that Ceará did not achieve its impressive results simply by changing its funding system. Not only did it use the funding system to incentivize mayors and municipal councils to focus on improving learning outcomes and reducing dropout rates, but it also provided municipal education teams with technical assistance on *how* to make progress (see box 9.2).

In 2017, closer to Bulgaria, Denmark launched a Program for Lifting the Academically Weakest Students, combining technical assistance to schools with a pay-for-performance program. Under this program, a school can receive a prize of between €175,000 and €200,000 (depending on the size of the school). To get the prize, a school must reduce the proportion of students who perform poorly on Denmark's standardized examination.

BOX 9.2

Improving education outcomes in Ceará, Brazil

Each year, the state of Ceará in Brazil distributes a fixed sum of money to its municipalities, placing the municipalities in competition with one another for those resources. To receive more resources, municipalities need not have the highest test scores or the lowest dropout rates; they merely need to show improvement. Those that show improvement each year receive more funds, and those that rest on their laurels will likely lose funding.

The distribution of funds is based on a formula that includes two results indicators—test scores and dropout rates. The formula takes into account both the levels of the indicators (a municipality with high test scores and low dropout rates will receive more funding) and the changes in the indicators (a municipality that improves test scores and lowers dropout rates will receive more funding).

Importantly, the state does not rely solely on the results-based mechanism but also provides technical assistance to municipalities, particularly under its Program to Achieving Literacy at the Right Age. The program provides schools with learning materials that define a clear timetable for classes and prioritizes basic skills, especially literacy in the early grades. Teachers undergo regular training on how to use these materials, including classroom observation with feedback. Municipalities with low-performing schools get additional support, while those with high-performing schools must ensure that these schools assist their low-performing counterparts to qualify for additional rewards from the state.

The state also works with municipalities to improve the management of their education systems. It provides training and materials to municipal education secretariats, with the goal of increasing classroom teaching time, reducing the number of multigrade classes, adopting meritocratic selection criteria for school principals, and offering financial and nonfinancial incentives to teachers whose students meet literacy targets.

Source: Loureiro, Cruz, and Lautharte 2020.

Develop reliable quality indicators and measurement instruments and set clear targets

To increase the system's focus on learning outcomes, better data will be needed to quantify and track learning. Without better data, problems will continue to go unnoticed and unaddressed. As of 2018–19 school year, for example, national assessments were carried out in grades 4, 7, and 12. (The external assessment for students in grade 10 was pending.) The 2018 grade 7 assessment results for Bulgarian language showed that there are a large number of failing schools. The scores of these schools were so low that it is hard to determine whether *any* learning took place during those seven years.

Introducing early grade reading and numeracy assessments and setting clear and easy to understand targets for what all 2nd graders should be able to do would be an important step. Such early grade assessments were critically important in motivating mayors and communities to take action in Ceará, but they are also used by countries that are among the top education performers (such as Singapore) to identify and quantify challenges and take rapid action. These assessments help to quantify problem areas, allowing teachers and teacher training to identify topics or students that need more focus.

More broadly, Bulgaria needs a credible and trusted assessment system and to use the data generated from that system to inform decision-making. Assessments should place more emphasize on students' mastery of desired skills and less emphasis on students' ability to memorize and reproduce facts. Assessments should also be designed so that results can be compared across time. And actors need to use the data that have been generated to improve outcomes, such as by informing changes to curriculum and teaching practices. The government has taken the first steps to develop such a system, but these efforts need to be accelerated if actors in the system are to be rewarded in accordance with their achievements.

Empower municipalities to play a bigger role in reducing inequality and improving students' results

For results-based financing to work, municipalities need to play a bigger role. Specifically, if they are to be incentivized to narrow the learning gaps between rich and poor students and improve the overall quality of education, they will need to participate in three areas in which they are not currently involved: (1) overseeing the quality of education provided by the schools under their jurisdiction; (2) holding school principals accountable for low achievement in their schools; and (3) intervening with targeted policy measures to address problem areas. Municipalities will need to build increased capacity to match their strengthened management and decision-making authority. The government may also consider implementing a warning system that would identify underperforming municipalities on an ongoing basis and trigger the provision of additional targeted support.

Consolidate municipalities into larger entities that are more financially and administratively viable

A growing number of very small, financially unviable municipalities in Bulgaria manage only one school. Alarmingly, many of these municipalities spend more on administrative costs than on their school. The future looks even more challenging because Bulgaria is expected to experience one of the largest population declines in the world. In 2050, its population is expected to be 23 percent smaller than in 2019 (United Nations 2019).

The preconditions necessary for incentives to work are that municipalities be financially viable and have a certain necessary level of administrative capacity. Although these goals are beyond the purview of the education sector, it is closely related to its future development. A "whole of government" approach will be needed (1) to create a national dialogue about the need for fewer municipalities; (2) to create incentives for municipalities to merge; and (3) to establish a timetable for the voluntary amalgamation of municipalities or for the government to step in and force mergers.

Administrative-territorial reform is not on the current policy agenda; an intermediate step might be to foster partnerships between local governments to share services (including education), coordinate the management of educational infrastructure, and implement joint projects (such as those related to infrastructure). Combining the capacity and resources of different municipalities could increase the efficiency of delivered services. Some of these efforts might lead municipalities to create the preconditions for further consolidation.

NOTES

1. Based on data obtained from the Ministry of Finance. The data on student enrollment in comprehensive schools come from National Statistical Institute, Sofia, www.nsi.bg.
2. These nine agencies are: (1) the National Inspectorate for Education (NIE); (2) the National Agency for Vocational Education and Training (NAVET); (3) the Center for Assessment of Preschool and School Education (CAPSE); (4) the Center for Educational Information; (5) the National Center for Information and Documentation (NACID); (6) the National Center for Teacher Qualification; (7) the Center for the Educational Integration of Children and Pupils from Ethnic Minorities; (8) the Human Resource Development Center, and (9) the Implementation Agency for the Operational Program titled Science and Education for Smart Growth.
3. BOOST Public Expenditure Database, World Bank, Washington, DC, https://datacatalog.worldbank.org/group/boost-public-expenditure-database.
4. Based on data from General Government of Finance and Statistics according to the Classification of the Functions of Government (COFOG), Eurostat Database, European Commission, Brussels, https://ec.europa.eu/eurostat/data/database.
5. Based on statistics from UNESCO-OECD, Eurostat Database, European Commission, Brussels, https://ec.europa.eu/eurostat/data/database.
6. The shares of Bulgarian students performing below the critical proficiency level 2 in PISA 2018 were 47.1 percent in reading, 44.4 percent in mathematics, and 46.6 percent in science, while only 2 percent in reading and sciences and 4 percent in mathematics were high achievers.
7. Learning Poverty: Historical Data and Subcomponents (database), World Bank, Washington, DC, https://datacatalog.worldbank.org/dataset/learning-poverty.
8. According to the Bulgarian budget classification, the functional subdivisions of the education sector consist of: (1) full-day kindergartens and combined children's establishments; (2) special kindergartens; (3) half-day kindergartens; (4) seasonal kindergartens; (5) preschool half-day training for 6-year-old children; (6) special schools; (7) comprehensive schools; (8) art and culture schools; (9) sports schools; (10) schools abroad; (11) vocational schools and professional courses in secondary comprehensive education schools; (12) schools in prisons; (13) hostels; (14) canteens; (15) extracurricular activities; (16) resource assistance; and (17) other educational activities.
9. As of 2019, the amount of revenue potential equalization is calculated using the following formula: (120 percent × national per capita tax revenues – municipal tax revenues per capita) × number of the municipal population.
10. Enforcement is on hold until 2025 when the first round of large-scale school inspections will be completed.
11. The salaries of the principals of municipal schools are set by the MoES, but the performance-based component is decided by the head of the relevant Regional Division of Education.
12. The labor contracts of principals of municipal schools are signed and can be terminated by the head of the relevant Regional Division of Education.

REFERENCES

CEDEFOP (European Centre for the Development of Vocational Training). 2019. *Spotlight on VET—2018 Compilation: Vocational Education and Training Systems in Europe*. Luxembourg: CEDEFOP.

Danchev, P., and S. Ivanov. 2009. "Financing Public Education in Bulgaria." In *Public Money for Public Schools*, edited by Casandra Bischoff. Budapest: Central European University Press.

European Commission. 2019. *Compulsory Education in Europe, 2019/20*. Luxembourg: European Union.

European Union Agency for Fundamental Rights. 2016. *Second European Union Minorities and Discrimination Survey*. Vienna: European Union Agency for Fundamental Rights.

Hristova, A., S. Baev, S. Petrova, and E. Tosheva. 2019. *Challenges for Bulgaria's Preschool and School Education and Possible Solutions*. Sofia: Institute for Research in Education.

Levačić, R. 2008. *Assessing Progress in Implementing Financing and Governance Reforms in Bulgaria's Education Sector*. Washington, DC: World Bank.

Loureiro, A., L. Cruz, and I. Lautharte. 2020. *The State of Ceará in Brazil is a Role Model for Reducing Learning Poverty*. Washington, DC: World Bank.

NALAS (Network of Associations of Local Authorities of South-East Europe). 2018. *Fiscal Decentralization Indicators for South-East Europe, 2006–2017, 7th ed.* North Macedonia: NALAS. http://www.nalas.eu/Publications/Books/FDReport_18.

United Nations. 2018. *World Urbanization Prospects: The 2018 Revision*. New York: United Nations.

——. 2019. *World Population Prospects 2019: Highlights*. New York: United Nations. https://population.un.org/wpp/Publications/Files/WPP2019_Highlights.pdf.

World Bank. 2021. *The Role of Intergovernmental Fiscal Transfers in Improving Education Outcomes. Annex*. Washington, DC: World Bank.

10 China Case Study

XIAOXIA WANG AND BINZHEN WU

INTRODUCTION

China has the largest education system in the world, with 270 million students and 16 million teachers working in 514,000 educational institutions as of 2018. It achieved universal coverage of nine-year compulsory education in 2011, a remarkable increase over the gross enrollment rate of only 66 percent in junior high schools in 1978. In the 40 years from 1978 to 2018, the gross enrollment rate for senior high schools more than doubled (from 34 percent to 88 percent), the rate for higher education increased 17 times (from 2.7 percent to 46 percent), and the rate for kindergartens increased sevenfold (from 11 percent to 80 percent). The number of undergraduates in regular higher education institutions was 9 million in 2019, more than 20 times the number in 1978. China now sends more students abroad than any other country.[1]

Government funds are the main revenue source for schools, accounting for more than 70 percent of total education expenditure since 2008. Education in China is managed mostly by the state-run public education system, although the number of nonpublic schools has increased steadily in recent years. In 2017, about 95 percent of primary schools were public schools. The proportion of public schools declines with the level of education, dropping to about 70 percent for higher education. Financing such a large public education system has been a challenge for the Chinese government, and it became even more difficult after China exempted students from tuition fees for compulsory education and abolished rural agricultural taxes and fees in the 2000s.

Nevertheless, there has been a tremendous increase in government expenditure on education in China, and the educational system has become increasingly reliant on the government. Figure 10.1 shows that government expenditure per student for all education levels (kindergarten to university) increased by almost 15 times in nominal terms from ¥ 826 in 1998 to ¥ 13,091 in 2018. Government educational expenditure as a share of total educational expenditure increased from 69 percent in 1998 to 80 percent in 2018. Government educational expenditure as a share of gross domestic product (GDP) increased from 2.4 percent in 1998 to 4 percent in 2018. In addition, the government spent a larger share of its budget on education after 2000, increasing from 13.8 percent in 2000 to a peak of 16.3 percent in 2011 before dropping to 14.5 percent in 2018. These figures

FIGURE 10.1

Per student and government education expenditure, 1998–2018

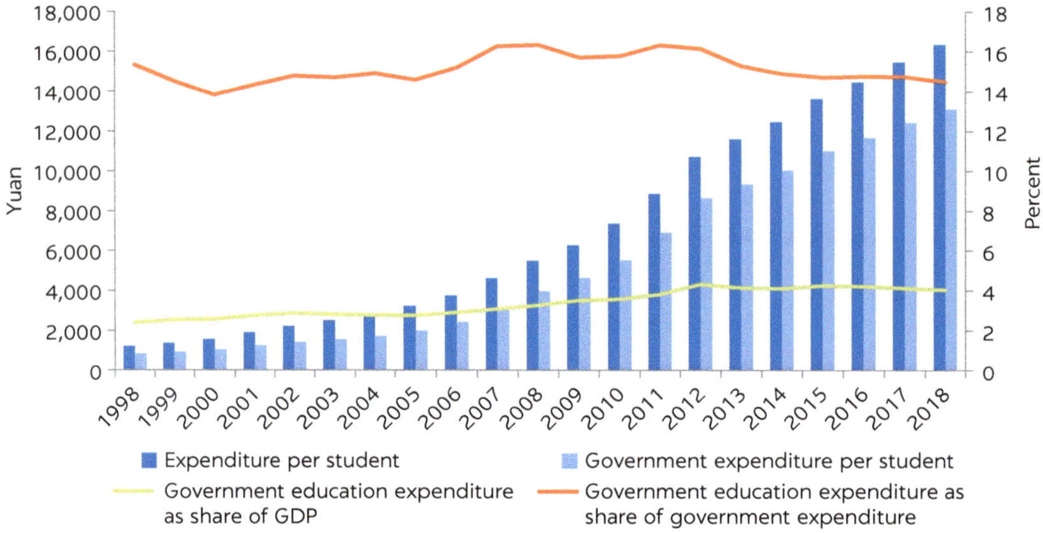

Source: National Bureau of Statistics.
Note: Per student expenditure includes students from kindergarten to university. GDP = gross domestic product.

indicate that the Chinese government is playing a more active and supportive role in education than before.

Challenges remain, however, concerning the adequacy and equity of educational expenditure. Government educational spending as a share of GDP still lags behind the world average of 4.5 percent in 2017.[2] In addition, disparities still prevail in education spending and access to high quality education. Moreover, China needs to improve its management system to systemically monitor student outcomes and use the information for school accountability and management purposes.

This chapter shows how China improved the adequacy and equity of government educational expenditure and how the changes improved education outcomes. We first describe the education finance system and how it has changed over time. We focus on pretertiary education and on the decentralization of education funding and provision. Subnational governments, particularly counties, are primarily responsible for the financing and administration of pretertiary education. However, there is a large and growing cascading system of financial transfers from the central government to local governments that aims to help equalize educational financing across regions. Next, we discuss how the education finance system and its evolution has affected the adequacy and equity of education spending and development. Finally, we discuss the challenges to the current system, particularly with regard to equity, and propose some potential policy solutions.

Our figures and tables at the national level are based on various years of the Educational Statistics Yearbook of China, the China Educational Finance Statistical Yearbook, and the webpages of the National Bureau of Statistics, the Ministry of Education, and the Ministry of Finance. The education finance information at the county level comes mainly from the dataset of the Fiscal Statistics for Prefectures, Municipalities, and Counties of China (FSPMC) 1993–2007. Unfortunately, no reliable county-level information is available after 2007. As a compromise, we used a case study of a prefecture in Shandong province to illustrate the current situation.

CHARACTERISTICS OF THE EDUCATION DECENTRALIZATION SYSTEM

In China, the administrative structure of subnational and local governments consists of four levels: (1) the provincial level (including provinces, autonomous regions, and municipalities); (2) the prefectural level; (3) the county level (including county-level cities and districts in a prefecture-level city); and (4) the township level (including districts in county-level cities and subdistricts in prefecture-level cities). At the end of 2019, there were 31 provincial administrations, 333 prefectures, 2,851 counties, and 39,945 townships.[3] There have been changes in the vertical administrative hierarchies, but counties have remained China's most stable administrative unit (Li, Lu, and Wang 2016; Lin, Liu, and Tao 2013; Xu 2011;). Villages are not statutory levels of government, but they played an important role in the provision of primary education before 2001.

Fiscal arrangements generally follow the hierarchical administration system (see figure 10.2), except that some counties are financially supervised directly by provinces rather than prefectures, and most townships are financially managed by counties (Liu and Alm 2015).[4] The tax-sharing reform in 1994 clearly divided revenue assignments and expenditure responsibilities between the central and provincial governments. Provincial governments are granted the authority to set up fiscal relationships within their borders. As a result, the degree of within-province decentralization varies between provinces (Martinez-Vazquez, Qiao, and Zhang 2008; Liu, Martinez-Vazquez, and Qiao 2014).

Subnational governments are responsible for providing public goods such as education, health care, pensions, and infrastructure within their jurisdictions. They also have the authority to formulate and enforce public policies in accordance with the principles and guidelines specified by the State Council. However,

FIGURE 10.2
Administrative structure of Chinese government for education

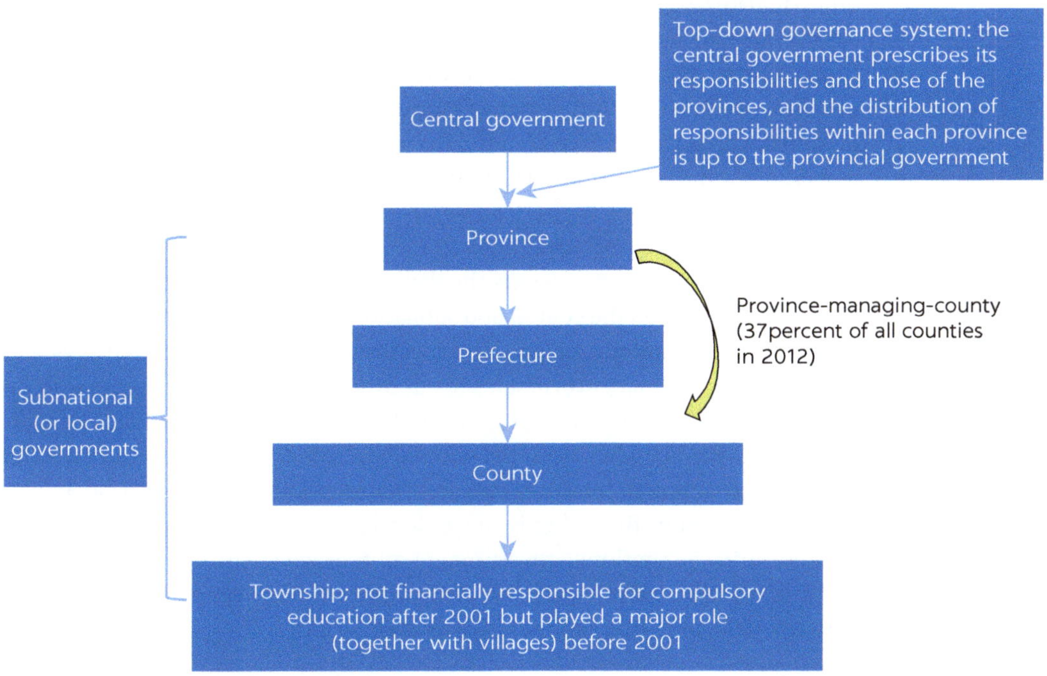

Source: Original illustration for this publication.

because the promotion of local government officials depends crucially on how they are evaluated by their superior government, they have a strong incentive to follow the policies specified by those governments.

Current decentralized education system

In the education sector, the extent of decentralization varies by education level. As stipulated in the Compulsory Education Law enacted in 1986 and the Education Law enacted in 1995, counties have the primary responsibility for the provision, financing, and administration of pretertiary public education in their jurisdictions.[5] (Townships currently do not bear any financial responsibility for compulsory education, although they played a major role before 2001.) Nearly all counties set up their own senior high schools and bear the corresponding responsibility, but there are also a few senior high schools affiliated with higher-level governments. Preschools are administered mostly by townships. Central or provincial governments are responsible for financing higher education institutions in accordance with university affiliation, although provincial governments often help to finance the state-affiliated colleges located in their provinces, and the central government helps to support some non-state-affiliated colleges through transfers. In addition, the central and provincial governments distribute substantial amounts of fiscal transfers to counties to expand their fiscal capacity and help them finance compulsory education.

Although the management of pretertiary schools is highly decentralized and localized, the upper-level governments, particularly the central and provincial governments, are responsible for setting the standards and developing the guidelines that subordinate governments must follow, as well as for enforcing regulations and for providing the financing necessary to guarantee the provision of education, especially compulsory education. For example, the central authorities formulate the nationwide standard for (1) the amount of administrative expenditure per student (consisting mainly of schools' operating costs); (2) quality standards for running schools, construction, and teacher qualifications; (3) the guidelines for the curriculum, textbooks, and examinations; and (4) plans for educational reform and development. Considerable autonomy is given to the provincial governments to develop province-wide education policies, guidelines, and standards. For example, provinces can set a standard for administrative expenditure per student as long as it is no lower than the national standard. They also allocate financing responsibilities and determine the transfer system within their borders. These arrangements are described in table 10.1.

Panel a of figure 10.3 presents the distribution of government educational expenditure between the central and subnational governments since 1999. Total government educational expenditure increased by 21 times between 1999 and 2018. The subnational governments spent over 90 percent of the total, and the ratio increased from about 92 percent in 1999 to 95 percent after 2012. In addition, this share is higher than the subnational governments' share of overall expenditure, although the latter also grew substantially over this period, implying that education financing is more decentralized than other government expenditures. Subnational governments on average spent 16 percent of their budgets on education, while the central government spent only 4 percent between 1999 and 2018, and these shares were stable.

TABLE 10.1 **Government responsibility for pretertiary education**

FUNCTION	CENTRAL	SUBNATIONAL (PROVINCIAL)	SUBPROVINCIAL (MAINLY COUNTY)
Policies including principles, guidelines, and standards	Nationwide policies	Province-wide polices, in accordance with policies set by the central government	Local policies, in accordance with policies set by upper-level governments
Financing	Mainly provide financial support through transfers	Mainly provide financial support through transfers	Assume the primary responsibility for financing schools in the jurisdiction
Administration[a]			
Curriculum	Stipulate nationwide subjects	Stipulate provincially arranged subjects (not common)	Stipulate locally arranged subjects (not common)
Admissions	No	No for most provinces	Yes
Exams	No, except for the national college entrance exam	College entrance exam[b]	Organize and manage exams
Facilities and infrastructure	No	No	Yes
Teachers and education staff	No	No	Yes
Quality assurance	No	No	Yes

Sources: Compulsory Education Law of 1986, Education Law of 1995, and websites of education departments at various levels of government.

a. Although the central and provincial governments are not involved in the administration of curriculum, admissions, exams, facilities, teachers, and quality assurance, they formulate principles, guidelines, and standards and enforce regulations.

b. College entrance exams are organized by provinces but highly regulated by the central government, which sets the exam dates, chooses exam subjects, and even suggests exam questions that provinces can choose to follow. Most provinces do not conduct province-wide entrance exams for pretertiary education.

Data are available only from 1999 to 2007 for the distribution of government expenditure on education within provinces. Panel b of figure 10.3 shows that counties were always the main contributors and that the distribution was quite stable. Counties spent between 64 and 67 percent of total government expenditure on education in this period. The prefectural, provincial, and central governments spent between 11 and 13 percent, 15 and 16 percent, and 6 and 8 percent, respectively. However, the stable expenditure shares did not reflect any changes in revenue source. In fact, an increasing amount of counties' expenditure was financed by upper-level governments through transfers. Within provinces, educational expenditure is more decentralized than other kinds of expenditure. Counties' share of total government expenditure grew in this period, from 33 percent to 42 percent, but was still much lower than their approximately 66 percent share of educational expenditure. On average, 22 percent of counties' expenditure was spent on education, while the share was only 9 percent for prefectural governments, 10 percent for provincial governments, and 3 percent for the central government during this period. These shares were stable.

FIGURE 10.3

Fiscal decentralization for education in China

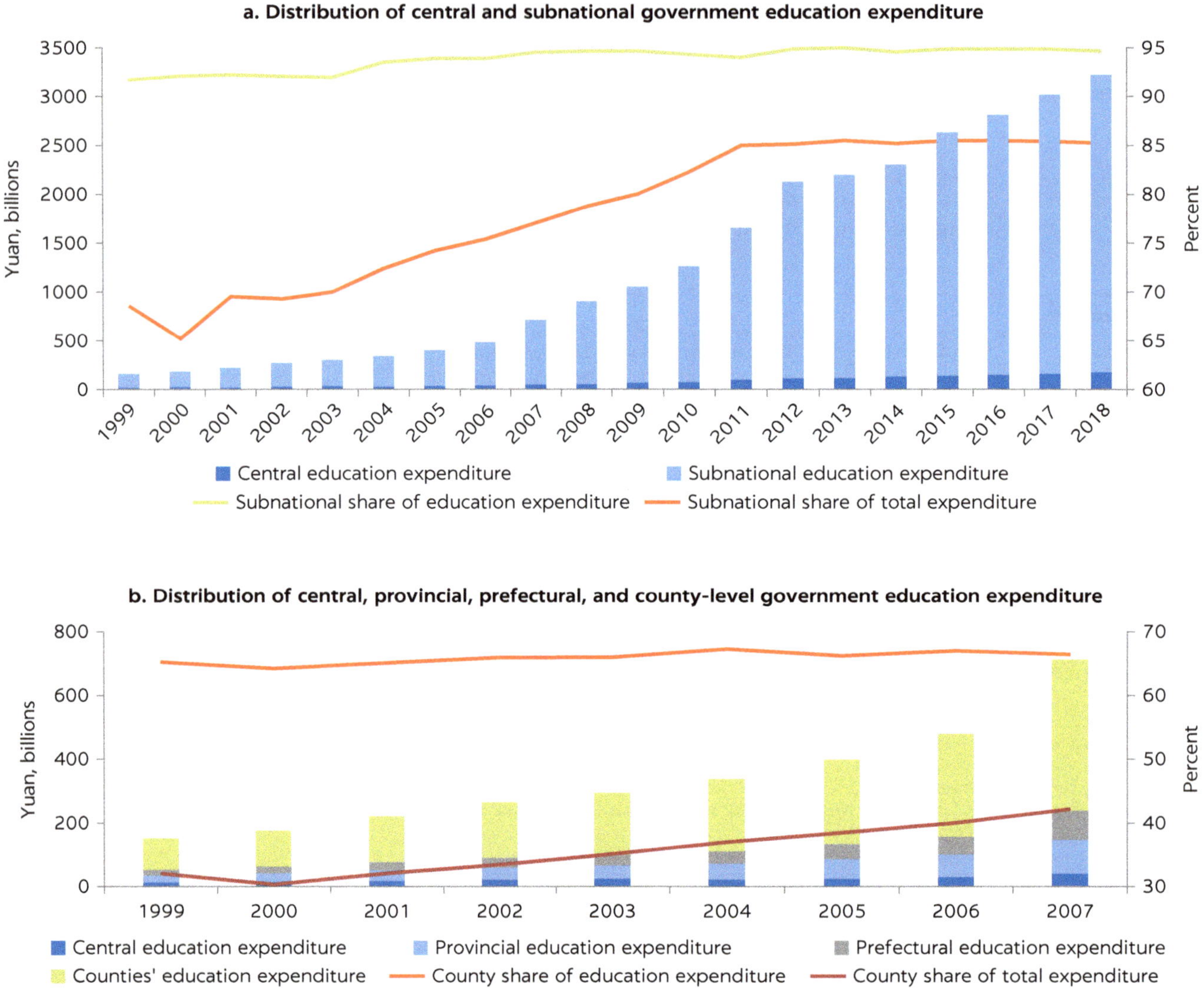

Source: Ministry of Finance and Fiscal Statistics for Prefectures, Municipalities, and Counties, 1993–2007.

Note: Education expenditure includes all education levels, including tertiary education. Only government expenditure is shown in the figure.

Because no data are available on current financing responsibilities within provinces, we use Shandong province in the east of China and the prefecture of Rizhao in Shandong to illustrate the current organization of decentralization as of 2018. As shown in table 10.2, 88 percent of government educational expenditure in Shandong was attributable to subprovincial governments in 2018. Counties spent 84 percent of government educational expenditure in Rizhao. Assuming that Rizhao is representative of Shandong, we can assume that counties spent 74 percent (88 percent of 84 percent) of government education expenditure in the province, similar to the national average in 2007. In Rizhao in 2018, counties' share of educational expenditure was lower than their share of total expenditure. Similarly, subprovincial governments' share of educational expenditure was lower than their share of total expenditure in Shandong.

TABLE 10.2 **Education expenditure in Shandong, 2018**

SHANDONG PROVINCE			PREFECTURE OF RIZHAO		
	LEVEL (¥, BILLION)	SHARE (%)		LEVEL (¥, BILLION)	SHARE (%)
Total government expenditure	1,010.1		Total government expenditure	25.96	
Provincial	90.9	9.0	Prefectural	1.12	4.3
Subprovincial	919.2	91.0	County level	24.83	95.7
Government educational expenditure	200.7		Government educational expenditure	5.39	
Provincial	23.1	11.5	Prefectural	0.86	15.9
Subprovincial	177.5	88.5	County level	4.53	84.1

Source: Shandong Provincial Department of Finance and Rizhao Municipal Bureau of Finance.
Note: Some columns do not total because of rounding. ¥ = Chinese yuan.

Other government expenditure may have become more decentralized than educational expenditure, which would be a reversal of the overall national situation in 2007. We cannot be sure whether this is true elsewhere, but it is consistent with the central government's attempt to reduce the degree of decentralization in the education sector after 2005.

Changes over time

China's education finance system has always aimed to promote adequacy and equity of education finance and provision. Adequacy is defined as the expenditure of sufficient funds to attain the desired level of educational development in a given region or nationally. Equity is defined as achieving a more even distribution of educational resources and outcomes among regions and schools. Resource constraints often force governments to choose between equity and adequacy and to focus on only one objective at a time, shifting the focus when the balance changes significantly.

In the wake of the economic reform that started in 1978, education policy makers prioritized adequacy, which was consistent with the emphasis of efficiency or economic growth for other major policy reforms. The decentralization of education finance and the diversification of financing sources (or marketization) were two defining features of the reforms (Tsang 1996; Ngok 2007). The reforms were very effective in mobilizing various resources to develop education, but decentralization was blamed for the glaring surge in educational inequity in the 1990s, which resulted from substantial regional disparities in economic development (Mok 2001; Hanson 2000). The central government switched its focus to combating inequality in the 2000s and, in the process, reversed the trend of decentralization in education financing.

The change in the decentralization structure was marked by the turning points in the mid-1980s and the early 2000s, both of which had a remarkable impact on compulsory education. Before the mid-1980s, China had a highly centralized fiscal system with a narrow revenue base, consistent with a planned economy. In the mid-1980s, the structure of education finance was rapidly decentralized, and the revenue base was diversified and marketized. This restructuring, prescribed in the Compulsory Education Law of 1986, was driven by a scarcity of resources for educational investment and a rising demand for education (Ngok 2007). The change gave local governments the authority to administer local schools and shifted financing responsibility downward, with each level of government trying to devolve the financing responsibility to its subordinate governments. The usual structure was that primary schools were mainly financed by villages, junior high schools by townships, senior high schools by counties, and higher education by provinces (Ngok 2007; Tsang 1996). According to a survey carried out by the State Council in 1998, 78 percent of compulsory education costs were paid by townships and villages, 9 percent by counties, and 11 percent by the provinces, with only 2 percent borne by the central government.

The financial burden on the grassroots governments incentivized them to mobilize all kinds of resources to finance education, including encouraging the development of nonpublic education (Hu 2012). Nevertheless, many townships and villages failed to collect adequate revenue for education, which was the main reason for the glaring disparities in education development across regions in 1990s (Mok 2001; Hanson 2000). Many students in poor rural areas suffered as a result of the inferior education and dropped out of school (Ngok 2007). In 1995, expenditure per student in the highest-spending province was 8.6 times of that in the lowest-spending province for primary education (¥ 1,248 versus ¥ 145), and 5.0 times of that for junior high education (¥ 1,595 versus ¥ 322 yuan). The gross enrollment rate in junior high school was only 78 percent in 1995. These statistics propelled China to launch the massive Compulsory Education Project for Poor Regions in 1995. This program provided conditional transfers to 865 "national impoverished counties," with the major focus to improve school facilities. However, it did not change the financing structure of the decentralization system, nor did it relieve the financial burden on rural areas other than the national impoverished counties. The regional disparity in government education expenditure continued to grow between 1995 and 2000. The ratio of government expenditure per student between the highest and the lowest spending province rose to 10.7 and 6.7 for primary and junior high education, respectively, in 2000.

Another trigger for the reform of the decentralized financing system was rural tax reform, which began in 2000, and the introduction of exemptions from tuition fees for compulsory education, both of which made it much harder for grassroots governments to finance education from their own resources. The first stage of rural tax reform abolished the major revenue resources—educational surcharges and fundraising for education—that had enabled townships and villages to finance education. As a result, the responsibility for financing rural compulsory education was shifted from townships and villages to counties. This may help reduce within-county disparities in educational development, particularly the rural-urban gap, because the entire county now shared resources. The second stage of rural tax reform in 2003 abolished agricultural taxes and related fees, which eroded a substantial share of counties' revenue. The exemptions from tuition fees for compulsory education was initially provided for students from poor rural areas in 2005 and was extended to all rural students in 2007 and to urban students in 2008. This further reduced the financial resources available to fund education, adding urgency to reform the decentralized system.

The New Mechanism to Guarantee Rural Compulsory Education Financing (the New Mechanism), a major reform in compulsory education financing, was announced at the end of 2005 and implemented in 2006. The reform was launched in the less-developed western provinces in 2006 and expanded to the entire country in 2007. In the New Mechanism, the central government clearly expressed its responsibility to finance compulsory education through the compulsory education transfer. Provincial governments were also required to take more responsibility to increase the equity of educational financing within each province by giving more transfers to poor regions. The policies have centered around the goal of "no children left behind," that is, no children dropping out of school because of poverty.

Panel a of table 10.3 illustrates the financing responsibilities of the central government. To reach a guaranteed level of administrative expenditure per student and to compensate for revenues lost through the tuition fee exemption, the central government committed to pay 80 percent of the guaranteed level of administrative expenditure of the western provinces (the least developed areas), 60 percent of the guaranteed level of the central provinces, and none of the costs of most of the eastern provinces (although this was increased to 50 percent for 2016). The central government also helped to finance free textbooks and school infrastructure. However, the reform did not modify the central government's lack of responsibility for financing personnel costs, which constitute over 60 percent of total compulsory education costs, mainly consisting of teachers' salaries. Therefore, teachers' salaries continued to be a heavy burden for local governments.

The details of the system have changed over time. For example, the standards for administrative expenditure per rural student have increased over time (see table 10.3, panel b). The amounts were set in each province by the provincial governments between 2006 and 2008. After 2009, the central government announced uniform standards, by region and by urban or rural school. In 2016, the central government unified the urban and rural standards and started to contribute 50 percent of the standard to the eastern provinces. The standard was unified nationwide in 2020. Depending on the area, the central government contributed 50 percent or 100 percent of the subsistence allowance for poor students after 2016. In 2019, China grouped provinces into five tiers rather than the traditional western, central, and eastern tiers, with the level of the central government's financing responsibility differing among the tiers.

The national standard for administrative expenditure is a minimum requirement. Each level of government is free to set its own standard as long as it is no lower than the level set by upper-level governments. Upper-level governments usually do not help finance anything at a level higher than their own standards. In practice, local standards vary substantially. For example, in 2016, the highest levels were in Shanghai (at ¥ 1,600 for primary education and ¥ 1,800 for junior high education), which were much higher than the national levels (at ¥ 650 for primary and ¥ 850 for junior high). A higher local standard means that the local government must bear a larger share of administrative expenditure, which may leave less money available for other educational expenses, such as personnel costs. Therefore, it is likely that the New Mechanism increased the share of administrative expenditure in total government education expenditure.

The aim of the transfer system was to help poor regions, and the role of the central government in financing education in rich regions did not change much. In general, the New Mechanism increased the financing responsibility of local

TABLE 10.3 **Education financing responsibilities under the New Mechanism**

a. Central government's share of expenditure by functions

EXPENDITURE BY FUNCTION	SUBCATEGORY	CENTRAL GOVERNMENT SHARE (%)
Administrative expenditure	Administrative expenditure subsidy per student; revenue loss from tuition fee exemptions	Western provinces: 80 Central provinces: 60 Most eastern provinces: 0
Personnel expenditure	Free textbooks	Central and western provinces: 100 Eastern provinces: 0
	Teachers' salaries	0
Infrastructure	Major maintenance and renovation costs	Central and western provinces: 50 Eastern provinces: 0

b. National standards for administrative expenditure per student for compulsory education

EDUCATION LEVEL	REGION	RURAL (YUAN) 2009	2010	2011	2013	2014	URBAN AND RURAL (YUAN) 2016	2020
Primary	Central and western provinces	300	400	500	560	600	600	650 (whole country)
	Eastern provinces	350	450	550	610	650	650	
Junior high	Central and western provinces	550	600	700	760	800	800	850 (whole country)
	Eastern provinces	500	650	750	810	850	850	

Source: Ministry of Education of China, Ministry of Finance of China and compilations based on published government documents.
Note: Administrative expenditure consists mainly of schools' operating costs.

governments above the level of counties. Nevertheless, it barely changed the degree of decentralization as measured by the distribution of educational expenditure because help from the upper-level governments came in the form of transfers, which were reflected only in the revenue and not in the expenditure of subnational governments.

The trend of bringing the central government and the provinces back into educational provision affected not only financing, but also the power to make policy decisions. Before the 2000s, although the devolution of decision-making power was much slower than the devolution of financial responsibility, the increased financial autonomy of local governments over education inevitably eroded the power and influence of upper-level governments over local education policies (Tsang 1996). After 2005, the policy-making power tilted back to higher-level governments. The central and provincial governments intervened more frequently and thoroughly. These changes were illustrated by the way China achieved its goal of raising government spending on education to over 4 percent of GDP (see box 10.1). In addition, Zhang and Feng (2018) show that, from 1985 to 2018, the central government issued 562 policy statements regarding the financial equity and adequacy of pretertiary education, and the number of statements rose significantly after 2001. The statements focused on teacher incentives and quality, student funding, funding guarantees, funding growth,

BOX 10.1

How did China achieve the goal of spending 4 percent of GDP on education?

In 1993, the central government set a target of raising government expenditure on education from 2.4 percent to 4 percent of gross domestic product (GDP)—the world average at that time—by 2000. However, by 2000, government educational expenditure was only 2.6 percent of GDP. In 2001, the central government recommitted to reaching the target by 2005 but failed again, reaching only 2.8 percent by 2005. The failure was related to the highly decentralized nature of the education system; grassroots governments did not have much room in their budgets for more educational investment; the central government's emphasis on increasing educational investment was hindered by its failure to provide financial support to local governments.

In 2006, the central government proposed the 4 percent target again and reemphasized the requirement of three increases in local government education budgets: appropriations for education should increase at a faster rate than revenues; average expenditure per student should increase steadily; and teacher salaries and the average administrative expenditure per student should both increase steadily. The central government also emphasized the need for increases in two ratios: government educational expenditure as a share of GDP; and government educational expenditure as a share of total government expenditure. Government educational expenditure as a share of GDP increased steadily to 3.5 percent in 2009.

In 2010, the central government set a deadline of two years to meet the 4 percent target and exploited several new instruments. First, the central government encouraged local governments to expand their revenue for education by expanding the tax base for the educational surcharge; collecting a local educational surcharge; and using 10 percent of local net revenue from land sales. Second, the central government gave local governments an incentive to hit the target: basing the evaluation of local government performance and promotion of local government officials on a weighted average of four indexes: (1) the growth in government educational expenditure (30 percent); (2) the increase in government educational expenditure as a share of total government expenditure (50 percent); (3) the educational surcharge rate (10 percent); and (4) the completion rate of extracting 10 percent of revenue from land sales (10 percent). Third, the central government established an administration office focusing on achieving the 4 percent goal, which coordinated different departments and supervised and monitored local governments to reach the 4 percent target. These instruments were very effective, and China finally achieved the goal in 2012, when government expenditure on education reached 4.3 percent of GDP.

At the end of 2013, the central government decided to remove pegged links between public expenditure on education and fiscal revenue or GDP. Nevertheless, government educational expenditure as a share of GDP has remained over 4 percent since 2012.

sources of funding, and institutions. The statements also made stipulations regarding the use of funds, school building, and management.

The shift away from the decentralization of compulsory education was followed by a considerable increase in government education spending and noticeable improvements in education outcomes in poor regions. The ratio of government expenditure per student between the highest and the lowest provinces dropped from a peak of 10.6 in 2005 to 5.3 in 2016 in primary education and from 9.6 in 2005 to 5.7 in 2015 in junior high education. Meanwhile, the gross enrollment rate rose from 95 percent in 2005 to 104 percent in 2016 for junior high schools and from 53 percent in 2005 to 88 percent in 2016 for senior high schools.

Great efforts have been made through the education finance and administration systems both to improve equity and to increase adequacy. The system had focused on decentralizing to increase adequacy for more than 20 years since the beginning of economic reform, but in the 2000s, it shifted its focus to improving equity without significantly reducing adequacy. This was not an easy task. The incentives for local governments, especially counties, to pursue both adequacy and efficiency were retained—they remained primarily responsible for local education development and continued to be vested with decentralized administration authority. In addressing equity, China has adopted a fiscal transfer system under which the central government shares education costs with local governments and balances financial resources between regions to ensure a minimum basic level of education for all students.

FISCAL TRANSFER MECHANISMS

Although government expenditure is highly decentralized in the Chinese fiscal system, government revenue is far less so, and this contrast has increased over time. As shown in panel a of figure 10.4, subnational governments were responsible for 85 percent of total government expenditure in 2018, while their revenue share was only 58 percent.[6] The expenditure-revenue gap was equivalent to 44 percent of subnational governments' expenditure. In 2000, subnational governments were responsible for 55 percent of total government expenditure and received 67 percent of total government revenue, and the expenditure-revenue gap was only 15 percent of subnational expenditure.

Local governments rely heavily on transfers from higher-level governments to fill the expenditure-revenue gap. In the Chinese cascading fiscal transferring system, each upper-level government disburses substantial transfers to its subordinate governments. The central and provincial governments are the major sources of such transfers. Nevertheless, information on the transfers within provinces is not publicly available, so we focus on the transfers from the central government to all subnational governments. The ratio of the central government's transfers to subnational governments' expenditure was 22 percent in 2000, rose to a peak of 39 percent in 2009, and then declined slowly to 33 percent in 2018 (figure 10.4, panel a). However, there was still a substantial unfilled gap after 2015, which reached nearly 11 percent of subnational expenditure in 2018, posing a risk of rising subnational government debt. The unfilled gap was quite small before 2015, and negative before 2010.

Panel b of figure 10.4 shows the situation of counties for which information was available between 1999 and 2007. Counties were responsible for 42 percent of total government expenditure in 2007 and received 23 percent of total government revenue. The expenditure-revenue gap was about 45 percent of counties' expenditure in 2007, increasing from 34 percent in 2000. Transfers were important in filling some of the gap, but they were not sufficient before 2005. As a result, counties ran deficits or resorted to raising extra-budgetary funds to make ends meet. After 2005, with governments above counties taking more responsibility for education financing, the situation for counties improved. Transfers started to exceed the gap and reached 49 percent of counties' expenditure in 2007.

FIGURE 10.4
Subnational and county government expenditure and revenue

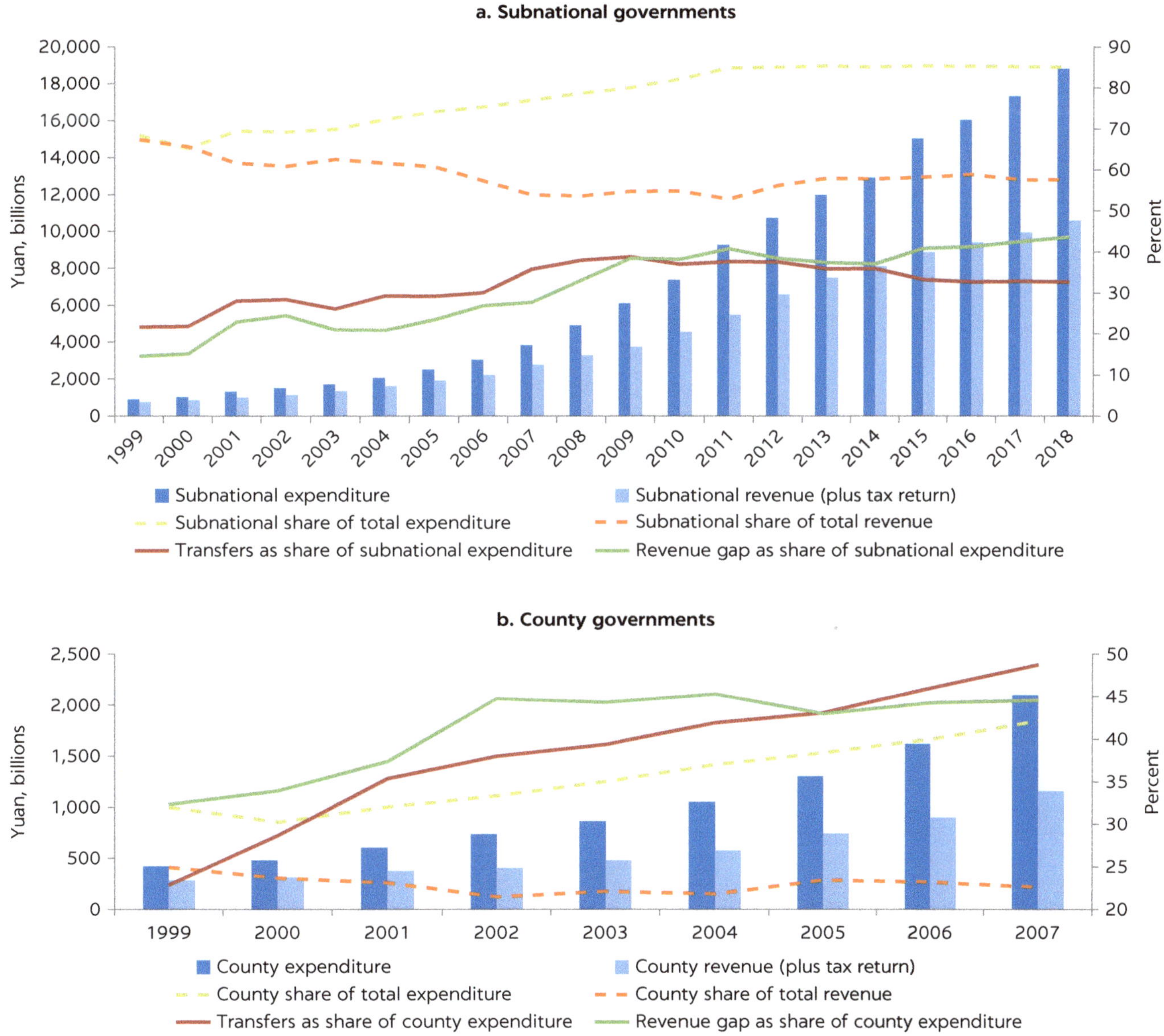

Source: Ministry of Finance and Fiscal Statistics for Prefectures, Municipalities, and Counties 1993–2007.

Structure

Transfers in China are either general transfers or conditional, or specific, transfers. General transfers aim mainly to equalize fiscal capacity between governments by allocating more resources to those with larger fiscal expenditure-revenue gaps. The allocation usually follows a predetermined formula, with regional characteristics as the main determinants. In principle, higher-level governments give full discretion to subordinate governments to decide how to spend the transfers, implying that general transfers may not differ much from regular fiscal revenues for the receiving governments. In contrast, conditional transfers come with clear spending restrictions intended to ensure adequate spending on designated projects, such as ensuring the provision of compulsory education for rural areas.

They are motivated by the concern that some local governments, especially those in the less developed regions, may not invest enough on the targeted projects. The allocation rules of conditional transfers were usually less transparent than those of general transfers. Less transparency often led to more manipulation and distortions. In addition, conditional transfers often required local governments to match spending, which could increase local fiscal pressure. China has been revising the transfer system in the last two decades, to reduce conditional transfers and expand general transfers.[7] Transfers in education have followed the same trend.

Panel a of figure 10.5 shows the structure of central to provincial transfers. General transfers have continually grown, while conditional transfers increased before 2012 but have been stable since. As a result, the share of general transfers out of total transfers has increased substantially from 37 percent in 2000 to 63 percent in 2018. The share has generally been over 50 percent since 2005. Panel b shows the structure of transfers to counties before 2007. General transfers accounted for 54 percent of total transfers to counties in 2000, and the proportion rose to 63 percent in 2007.

Table 10.4 shows a further breakdown of the general and conditional transfers from the central government to the provinces. The largest component of general transfers is the equalizing transfer. The allocation of the equalizing transfer follows a formula, which can be very complicated, that depends on a province's fiscal gap, economic development, altitude, and population, among

FIGURE 10.5
Structure of transfers

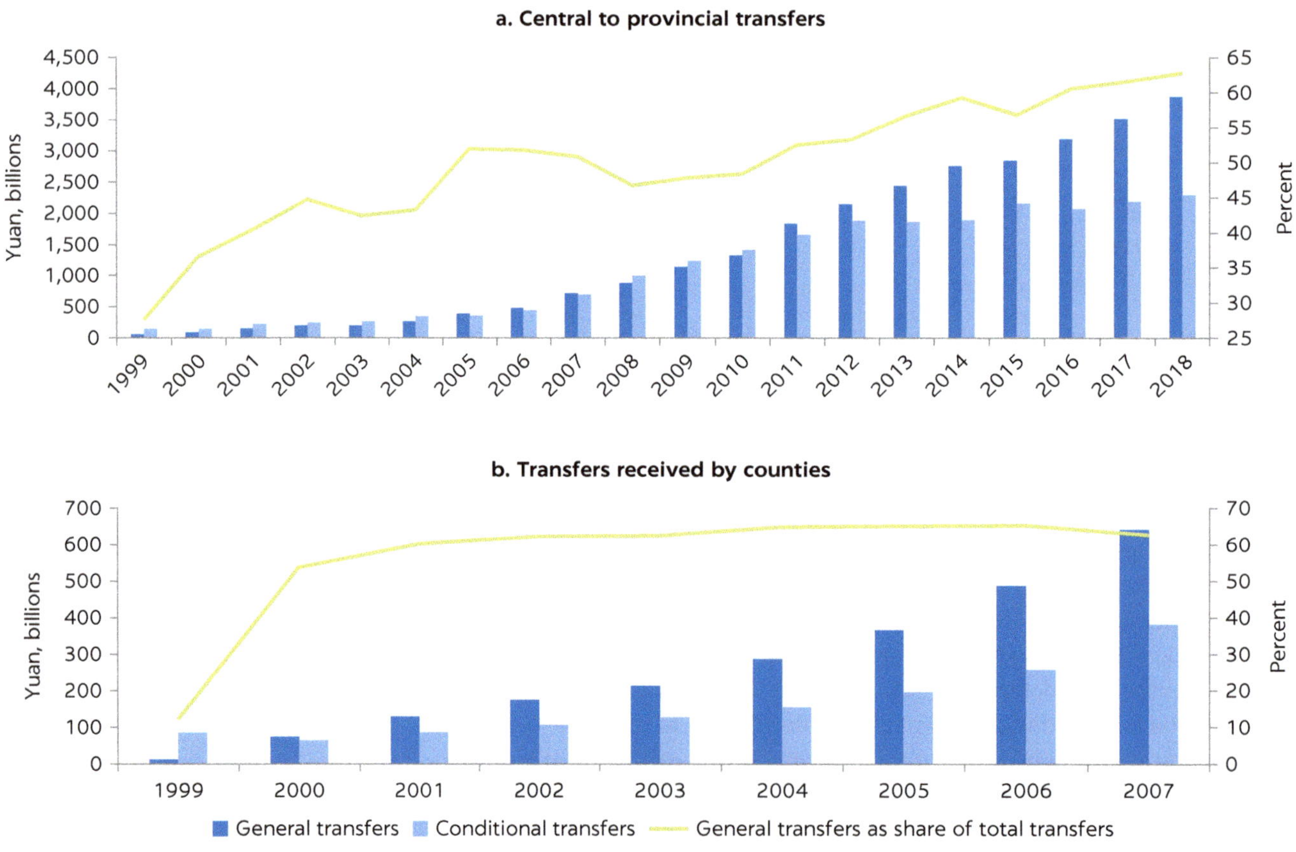

Source: Ministry of Finance and Fiscal Statistics for Prefectures, Municipalities, and Counties 1993–2007.

TABLE 10.4 **Structure of central to provincial transfers**

TYPE	COMPONENTS	ALLOCATION FORMULA?	2008 AMOUNT (¥, BILLIONS)	2008 PROPORTION (%)	2018 AMOUNT (¥, BILLIONS)	2018 PROPORTION (%)
General transfers			874.6	100	3,872.2	100
	Compulsory education transfers (mislabeled conditional transfers)	Yes	41.9	4.8	146.3	3.8
	Transfers for other noneducational purposes (mislabeled conditional transfers)	Yes	285.5	32.6	1,223.7	31.6
	Other (general, redistributive)	Yes, for the majority	547.2	62.6	2,502.2	64.6
Conditional transfers		n.a.	996.2	100	2,292.7	100
Conditional education transfers for education		n.a.	69.3	7.0	156.0	6.8
	Fund for supporting preschool education	Yes	n.a.	n.a.	14.9	0.6
	Subsidy for weak rural compulsory school renovation	Yes	n.a.	n.a.	36.1	1.6
	Fund for improving the conditions for academic senior high schools	Yes	n.a.	n.a.	5.0	0.2
	Funds for national training plan of teachers in kindergarten, primary, and secondary schools	Yes	n.a.	n.a.	1.99	0.1
	Fund for quality improvement plan of vocational education	Yes	n.a.	n.a.	18.7	0.8
	Subsidy for special education	Yes	n.a.	n.a.	0.4	0.0
	Subsidy for student aid	Yes	n.a.	n.a.	42.3	1.8
	Fund to support local college development	Yes	n.a.	n.a.	36.7	1.6
Conditional transfers for noneducational purposes		n.a.	n.a.	n.a.	2,136.7	93.2
	Conditional transfers for infrastructure	No	n.a.	n.a.	410.9	17.9

Sources: Data for 2018 are from Tax Rebates and Transfer Payments in General Public Budget from Central Government to Local Governments in 2018, Ministry of Finance, Beijing, http://yss.mof.gov.cn/2018czjs/201907/t20190718_3303311.htm; data for 2008 are from 2008 National Financial Revenue Final Accounts, Ministry of Finance, Beijing, http://yss.mof.gov.cn/caizhengshuju/200907/t20090707_176723.htm.
Note: Some columns do not total because of rounding; n.a. = not applicable; ¥ = Chinese yuan.

other characteristics. In practice, some conditional transfers are mislabeled as general transfers. The largest of the mislabeled general transfers for education is the compulsory education transfer, which dates to 2006, when China rolled out the New Mechanism. This compulsory education transfer amounted to 3.8 percent of total general transfers in 2018, down from 4.8 percent in 2008. The decline reflects a feature of transfer restructuring reform—expanding general transfers relative to conditional transfers. The compulsory education transfer constituted 4.8 percent of total education expenditure in 2018, similar to its 4.9 percent share in 2008. Other conditional transfers mislabeled as general transfers accounted for 31.6 percent of total general transfers in 2018, similar to the share of 32.6 percent in 2008. The true general transfers constituted the remaining 64.6 percent of total general transfers in 2018, while the share was 62.6 percent in 2008.

The conditional transfers from the central government to provinces target different education stages (see table 10.4). In 2018, conditional education transfers amounted to ¥ 156 billion, 6.8 percent of all conditional transfers from the central government to the provinces, similar to the 7 percent share in 2008. Transfers for student aid constituted the largest conditional educational transfers, accounting for 1.8 percent of all conditional transfers in 2018. Conditional educational transfers are usually established to achieve a goal such as promoting compulsory education in poor rural areas. According to the World Bank (2002), the transfers in the Compulsory Education Project for Poor Regions were among the largest of conditional transfers in the mid-1990s. In 2010, China launched the National Teacher Training Plan to improve the quality of teachers in rural primary and junior high schools and, later, in rural preschools. Also in 2010, China initiated the Renovation Project for Weak Rural Compulsory Schools, with a transfer accounting for 1.6 percent of all government conditional transfers to provinces in 2018.

No information exists on what portion of the general transfers is spent on education. However, we could roughly estimate the magnitude based on some assumptions. First, we deduct the mislabeled compulsory education transfer from the general transfers and add them to the conditional transfers to get adjusted general and conditional transfers. Then, we deduct the adjusted conditional educational transfers from local government education expenditure to get the education expenditure financed by local fiscal revenue and adjusted general transfers. Finally, by assuming that the proportion of adjusted general transfers allocated to education is the same as that of local fiscal revenue, we derive how much adjusted general transfer was allocated to education.

By our calculations, in 2018, 12.4 percent (¥ 302 billion) of the adjusted conditional transfers were used for educational purposes, while 19.1 percent (¥ 2,742 billion) of the sum of adjusted general transfers (¥ 3,726 billion) plus local fiscal revenue (¥ 10,593 billion) were allocated to education. As shown in panel a of figure 10.6, the contribution of conditional transfers to subnational education expenditure has been declining since 2010, mainly because of the drop in the contribution of compulsory education transfers,[8] while the contribution of general transfers has been climbing since 2007.

From 2007 to 2018, the share of all transfers in subnational government education expenditure increased moderately from 28.3 percent to 33.4 percent (falling from 11.6 percent to 9.9 percent for conditional transfers and increasing from 16.7 percent to 23.4 percent for general transfers), slightly reducing the financial burden on subnational governments for education. The educational expenditure share of total subnational government expenditure has remained stable at about 16 percent. No information was available on conditional transfers for education at the county level, but we infer that general transfers contributed 25 to 35 percent of county-level education expenditure from 2001 to 2007 (see panel b of figure 10.6). The educational expenditure share of total county government expenditure remained stable at about 22 percent.

Provincial governments are required by the central government to state the rules by which they deliver transfers to subordinate governments. However, neither the specific rules nor any data are available to present a full view of the within-province structure of transfers after 2007. Therefore, we again use the prefecture of Rizhao in Shandong province, as shown in table 10.5. In 2018, received transfers constituted 32 percent of total expenditure by the counties, 37 percent by the prefecture, and 23 percent by the province. Note that the

FIGURE 10.6

General and conditional transfers spent on education

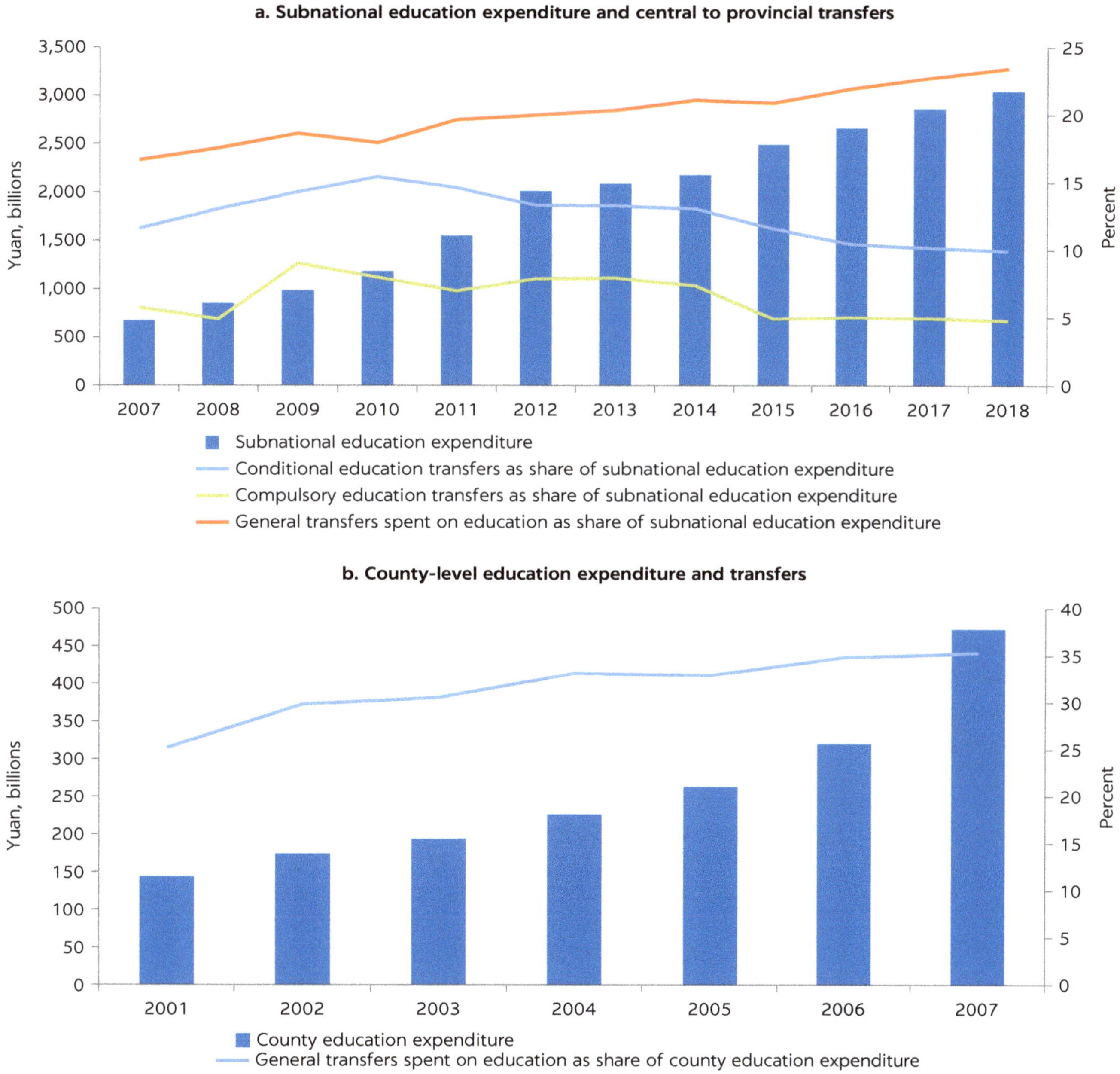

Source: Ministry of Finance and Fiscal Statistics for Prefectures, Municipalities, and Counties 1993–2007.
Note: Information about central to provincial educational conditional transfers before 2008 is not available. Full information on educational conditional transfers to county-level governments is also not available.

counties' reliance on transfers in Rizhao was much lower than the national average of counties in 2007 (49 percent as shown in panel b of figure 10.4). Similarly, the reliance of Shandong province on transfers was much lower than the national average of provinces in 2018 (at 33 percent as shown in panel a of figure 10.4). These numbers are not surprising; the literature indicates that western provinces depend much more on transfers than eastern provinces such as Shandong. In education, adjusted conditional transfers and adjusted general transfers contributed 6.5 percent and 13.3 percent, respectively, to the province's education expenditure. Conditional transfers and general transfers contributed 9.6 percent

TABLE 10.5 **Transfer structure in Shandong and Rizhao, 2018**

ITEM	CALCULATIONS OF TRANSFERS	SHANDONG PROVINCE (¥, BILLIONS)	PREFECTURE OF RIZHAO (¥, BILLIONS)	COUNTIES IN RIZHAO (¥, BILLIONS)
Fiscal expenditure	(1)	1,010.1	26.0	19.4
Education expenditure	(2)	200.7	5.4	4.5
Fiscal revenue without tax return	(4)	648.5	16.0	14.9
Tax return	(5)	57.7	1.0	0.4
Fiscal revenue (including tax return)	(6) = (4)+(5)	706.3	16.9	15.2
Transfer from upper-level government (excluding tax return)	(7) = (8)+(10)	229.2	9.7	6.3
General transfer (original)	(8)	123.9	5.1	2.9
Compulsory education transfer	(9)	6.6	0.4	0.4
Conditional transfer (original)	(10)	105.3	4.6	3.4
Conditional transfer for education (original)	(11)	6.5	0.1	0.05
Conditional transfer for education (adjusted)	(12) = (9)+(11)	13.0	0.5	0.5
General transfer (adjusted)	(13) = (8)–(9)	117.3	4.7	2.5
General transfer assumed to be spent on education	(14) = (13)*[((2)–(12))/((6)+(13))]	26.7	1.1	0.6
Fiscal gap/expenditure (%)	(15) = [(1)–(6)]/(1)	30.1	34.7	21.5
Transfer from upper-level government/expenditure (%)	(16) = (7)/(1)	22.7	37.4	32.2
Transfer from upper-level government/revenue (%)	(17) = (7)/(6)	32.5	57.3	41.1
Conditional transfer for education/education expenditure (%)	(18) = (12)/(2)	6.5	9.6	10.0
General transfer on education/education expenditure (%)	(14)/(2)	13.3	19.7	12.6
Education expenditure as share of total (%)	(3) = (2)/(1)	19.9	20.8	23.3

Source: Shandong Provincial Department of Finance, Rizhao Municipal Bureau of Finance.
Note: ¥ = Chinese yuan.

and 19.7 percent, respectively, to the prefecture's education expenditure and 10 percent and 12.6 percent, respectively, to the education expenditure of the counties in Rizhao. Therefore, a total of 22.6 percent of the counties' educational expenditure was covered by transfers, much lower than the national average of 35 percent in 2007 (see panel b of figure 10.4).

Adequacy and equity in the allocation of transfers

Transfers are generally intended to relieve the financial burden on local governments by increasing the adequacy of their budgets. This was a major objective of the New Mechanism. After the New Mechanism, however, although financial transfers for education from the central and provincial governments increased, the financial burden on local governments may not have declined substantially in poor regions and has definitely increased in rich regions. Before the reform, the administrative expenditure of local governments were largely covered by tuition fees, but the reform exempted most students from these fees, and central government transfers compensated for at most 80 percent of the revenue loss. More importantly, the New Mechanism did not require governments above the county level to share the cost of teachers' salaries, which constituted over 60 percent of the total cost of education provision. In 2009, China implemented a performance-based pay system for compulsory education teachers and required that their salaries be at least equal to those of civil servants. This resulted in a sharp increase in teacher salaries in pretertiary education (see figure 10.7), which has probably outweighed the effects of rising transfers. This may be why the subnational expenditure–revenue gap in panel a of figure 10.4 increased faster than transfers after 2007 and why the transfers were unable to fill the gap after 2010.

Different transfers have different objectives, with general transfers designed to increase equity and conditional transfers designed to increase adequacy. In China, however, conditional transfers tend to be delivered to poor counties for targeted projects. As a result, for both general transfers and conditional transfers, rich regions receive transfers that are much lower than their contributions to the tax revenue of their superior governments, whereas poor regions receive transfers of a higher value than their tax revenue contributions. The change in the structure of the transfers indicates that the central government has put more emphasis on equity over time.

China's transfers on average play a redistributive role to promote equity as shown in both the data and the literature (Mao, Wang, and Bai 2011; Su and Xie 2015). Figure 10.8 illustrates the evolution of this redistributive role by relating transfers per capita received by provinces to GDP per capita in 2005 (panel a) and 2017 (panel b).[9] The relationship was negative in both years, though more strongly so in 2017. Figure 10.8 also examines the relationship between transfers and the fiscal gap (measured by the difference between expenditure and revenue) on a per capita basis by province in panels c and d. The relationship was positive in both years, meaning that transfers tended to fill the subnational fiscal gap. For transfers to counties, information was available only before 2007, but a significant redistributive role is also seen in these results (World Bank 2021).

The compulsory education transfer, which is the largest single educational transfer, aims to guarantee the provision of the basic level of compulsory education. Therefore, its objective combines adequacy and equity. Similar to the equalizing transfer, the compulsory education transfer is also allocated based on a formula that incorporates regional factors. Figure 10.9 shows that the compulsory education transfers to provinces (panel a) and counties (panel b) declined as their economic development increased, thus confirming the redistributive feature of the transfer.

FIGURE 10.7

Teachers' salaries as a share of civil servants' salaries, 1995–2017

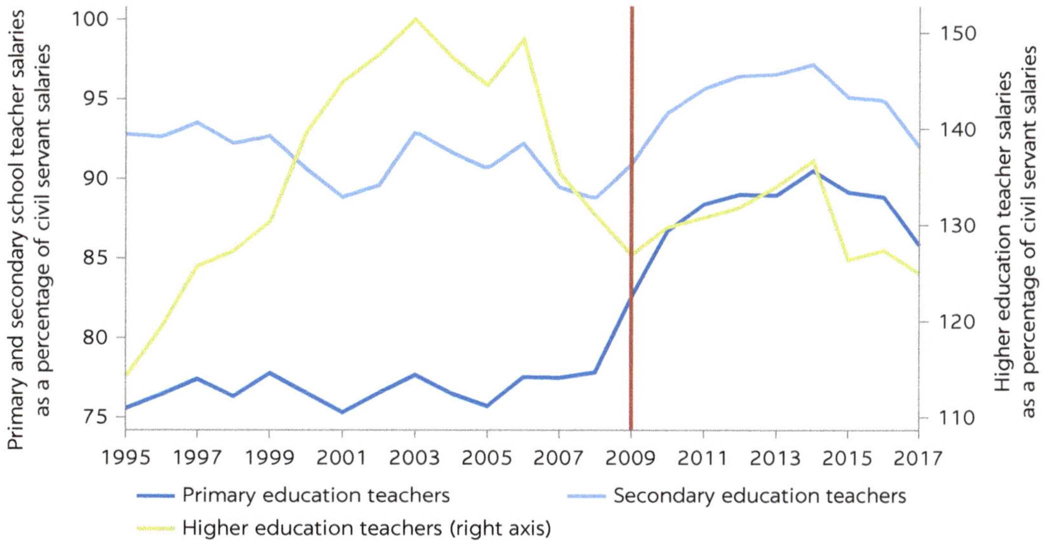

Source: China Labor Statistics Yearbook.

FIGURE 10.8

Redistributive features of transfers across provinces, 2005 and 2017

yuan

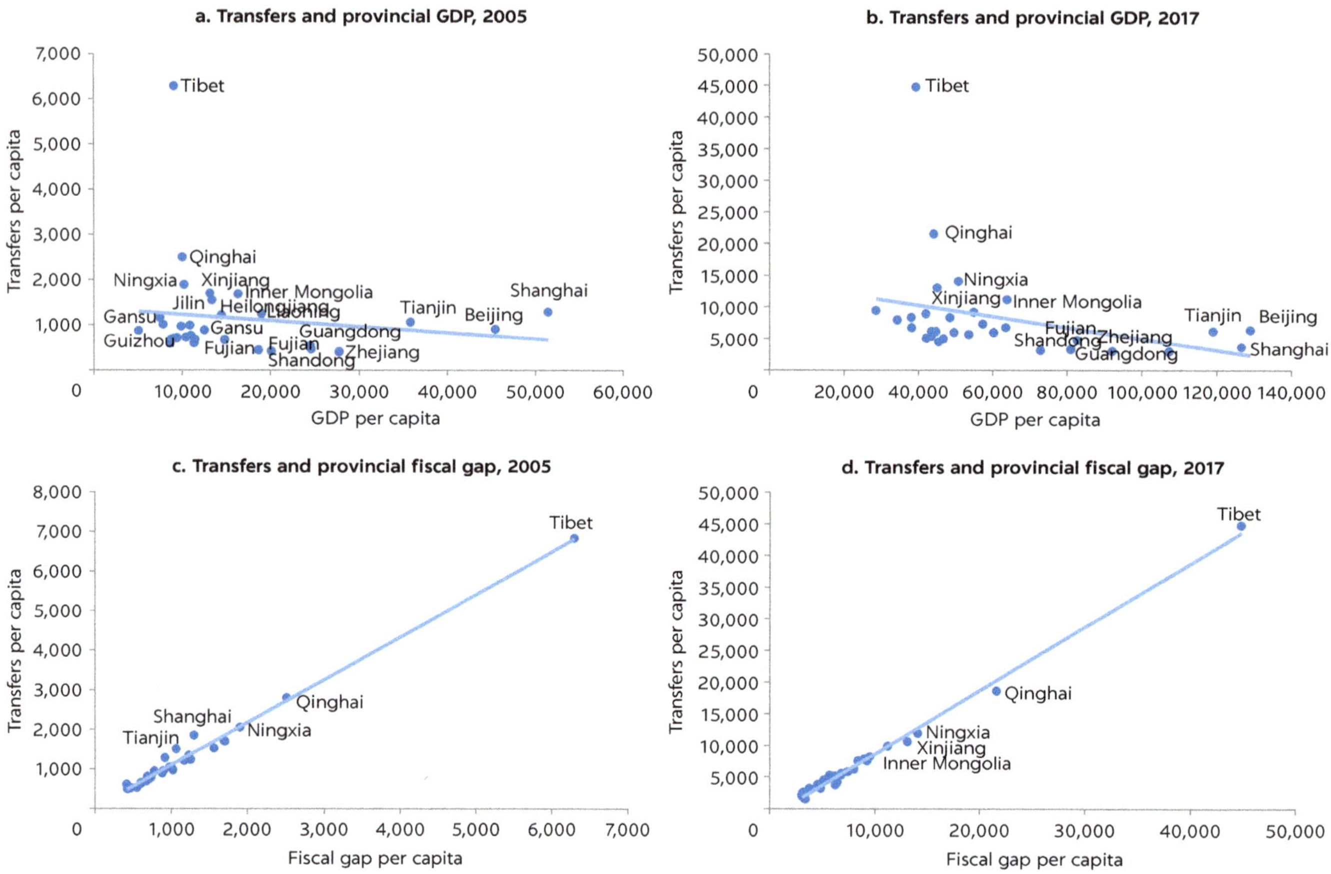

Source: Fiscal Yearbook of China.
Note: GDP = gross domestic product.

The New Mechanism of 2005 required governments higher than counties to allocate the compulsory education transfer within their borders. There are two types of allocation rules: those that help the poor and those that reward the outstanding. Under the former rule, more transfers are allocated to counties with worse economic or educational development, while under the latter rule, more transfers are allocated to counties that have demonstrated considerable educational improvement or have implemented a key policy effectively. Shaanxi province, in western China, allocates transfers based on counties' compliance with the province's rules for using the compulsory education transfer. Hunan province, in central China, disburses transfers to rich counties that successfully implement tuition exemptions. Zhao (2017) illustrates that Zhejiang province, in eastern China and one of China's richest, allocates the compulsory education transfer to promote equality by giving much higher transfers to poor counties than to rich counties. To prevent transfers from crowding out local governments' own revenue, receiving counties are required to provide matching funds in proportion to the transfers they receive. The transfers have an amplifying effect on total education spending, but this matching system can increase the financial pressure on poor counties. Yin and Tang (2016) find that "rewarding the outstanding" system dominated in 423 counties in central China in 2007.

FIGURE 10.9

Redistributive features of the compulsory education transfer

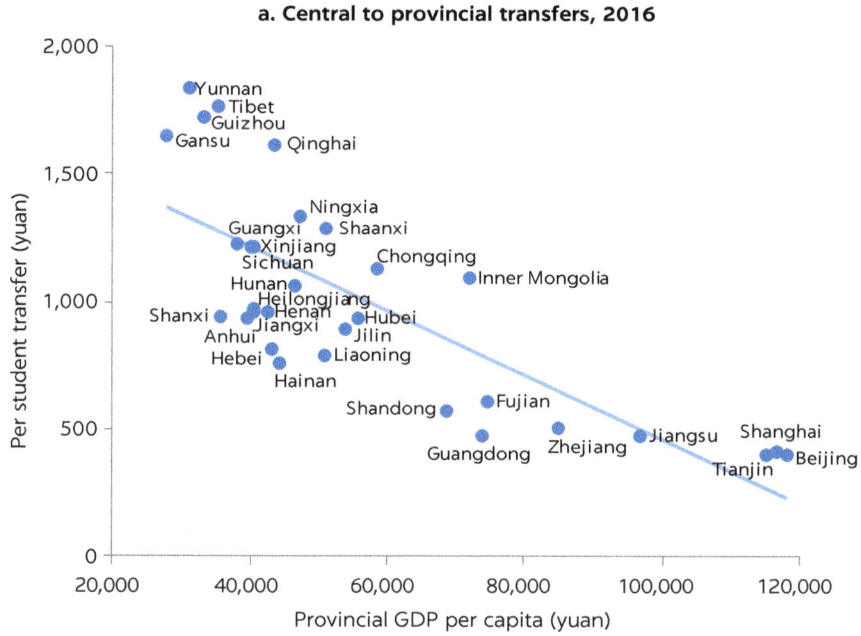

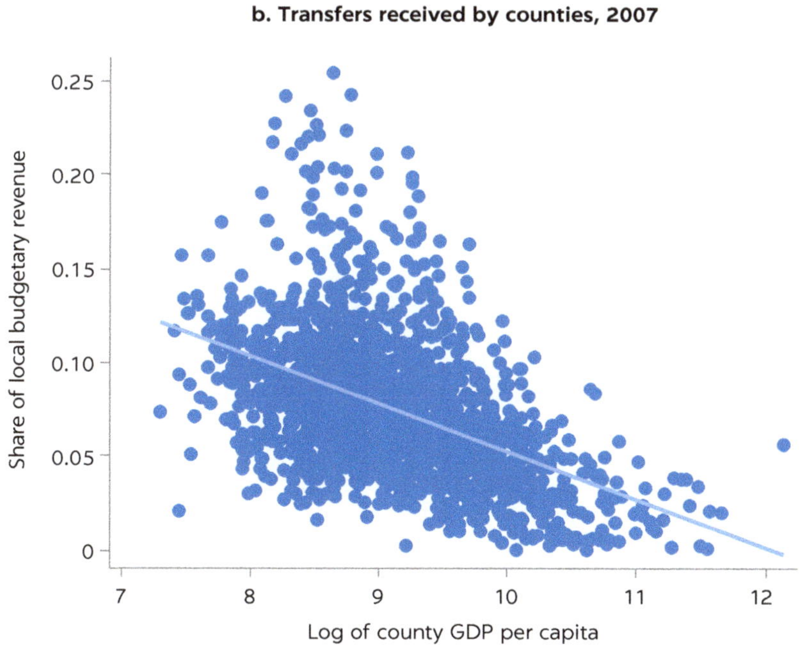

Source: Ministry of Finance and Fiscal Statistics for Prefectures, Municipalities, and Counties 1993–2007.
Note: GDP = gross domestic product.

EFFECTS OF THE DECENTRALIZED FINANCING SYSTEM

Equity and adequacy are the two most important objectives for the Chinese education system. In this section, we first discuss how the decentralization of the system and subsequent reforms have affected the adequacy, equity, and structure of education spending. Then we investigate how they have affected the adequacy and equity of education outcomes.

Effects on education spending

Adequacy

When China started to decentralize the education system in the mid-1980s, policy makers gave priority to increasing adequacy. The decentralization reform led to the mobilization of various resources and resulted in a remarkable growth in education expenditure. The average nominal annual growth rate of government educational expenditure per student was 15.7 percent in the 1980s and 13.8 percent in the 1990s (see figure 10.10). When nongovernment expenditure is included, the average annual growth rate in the 1990s was 16.9 percent.

The highly decentralized system was reversed to an extent in the early 2000s and overhauled after the implementation of the New Mechanism in 2005. These reforms were intended to help poor regions, particularly in rural areas, to invest more in education, while keeping the decentralization structure in place for richer regions. As intended, adequacy was further increased after these reforms. The government education expenditure as a share of GDP achieved the 4 percent goal for the first time in 2012. Between 2000 and 2012, government expenditure per student grew by 18.7 percent annually in nominal terms (see figure 10.10), while expenditure financed by nonpublic resources fell slightly, and total expenditure per student grew by 17.2 percent per year. Both government expenditure per student and total expenditure per student grew at a faster pace than GDP in most years of this period.

The key element of the New Mechanism was the introduction of the compulsory education transfer scheme. A major concern was that conditional transfers might crowd out local governments' own spending with the same objectives and in net lead to a smaller than intended increase in spending on the targeted objective.

FIGURE 10.10

Growth of education expenditure in China, 1978–2017

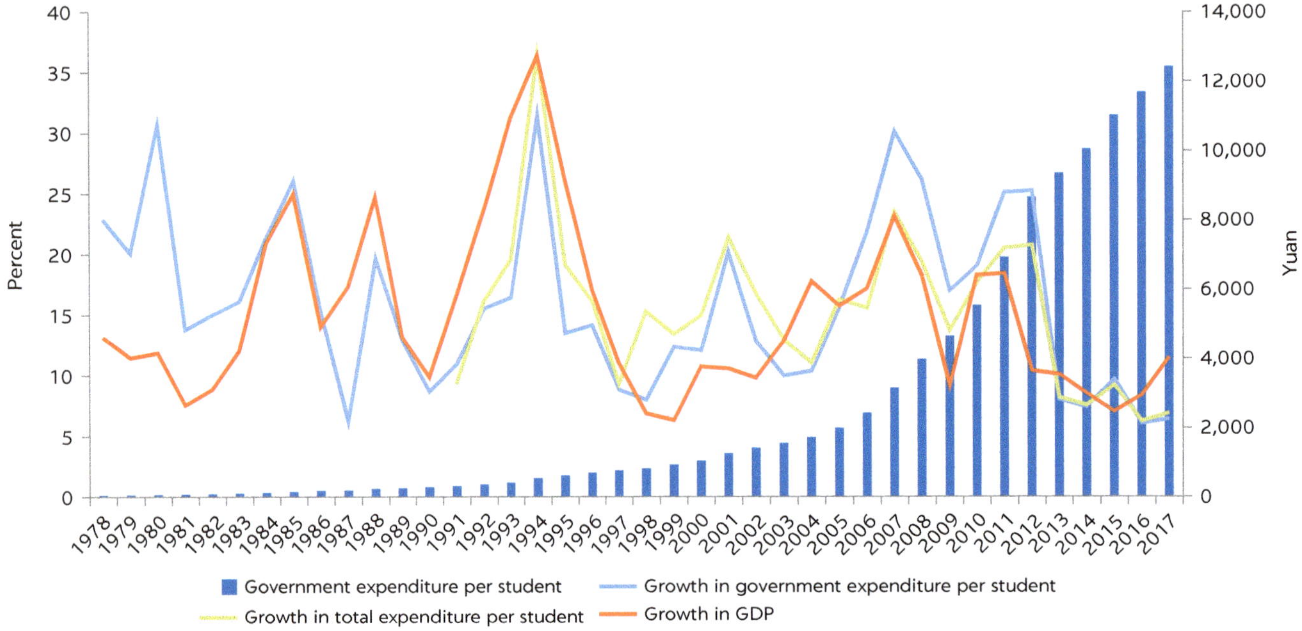

Source: Ministry of Finance, National Bureau of Statistics, and China Educational Finance Statistical Yearbook.
Note: GDP = gross domestic product.

Table 10.6 shows the regression of government education expenditure on the compulsory education transfer using county-level data. It indicates that, instead of a crowding-out effect, the compulsory education transfer in China had the "flypaper" effect of attracting more funds. For each additional unit of compulsory education transfer, local government education expenditure increased by ¥1.16. Yang, Ha, and Wu (2017) conduct a similar analysis based on a county-level sample in western China and find a larger effect.

To examine the causal effect of the New Mechanism on education expenditure, most previous studies exploit the phase-in stage of the reform and use the difference-in-differences strategy. Regions receiving central transfers were the treated group, and those that did not were the control group. However, the data sources, observation periods, and identification details vary between studies, which may have led to inconsistencies in their findings. For example, the New Mechanism was not a randomized experiment. Some studies address the selection bias problem by using propensity score matching but others do not. The reform may also have changed the migrating behavior of families with school-age children, which would have affected education expenditure per student. However, this problem has rarely been considered in the existing studies.

Some studies in the literature find that the New Mechanism increased total educational spending or administrative expenditure (Huang, Miao, and Jin 2017; Lu 2014). Others, however, have different findings. For example, Yang and Ha (2017) and Ha and Liu (2018a) find that the New Mechanism did not change educational spending for junior high education or primary education in the short run. Ding, Lu, and Ye (2020) conclude that the reform did not even

TABLE 10.6 Relationship between county education expenditure and transfers

	DEPENDENT VARIABLE: COUNTY EDUCATION EXPENDITURE	
	1997–2005	2006–07
Compulsory education transfer	0.510***	1.157***
	(0.068)	(0.144)
General transfer	0.121***	0.095***
	(0.002)	(0.007)
Local fiscal revenue	0.080***	0.056***
	(0.001)	(0.003)
GDP	0.003***	0.004***
	(0.000)	(0.000)
ln(population)	1,734.707***	4,556.714***
	(22.981)	(185.809)
Constant	3,658.941***	10,840.960***
	(194.019)	(1,131.132)
Number of observations	20,994	3,162
R-squared	0.907	0.914

Source: Fiscal Statistics for Prefectures, Municipalities, and Counties 1993–2007.
Note: Standard errors in parentheses. GDP = gross domestic product.
*** $p < 0.01$.

increase administrative expenditure in rural primary schools. These studies indicate that the transfers increased government administrative expenditure but may crowd out education expenditure funded by other sources or nonadministrative expenditure.

General transfers may also affect education spending despite not targeting at education specifically. If poor local governments spend a larger proportion of fiscal revenue on education than rich governments, equalizing general transfers can increase the average share of educational spending. General transfers may give local governments a disincentive to collect own-source revenue, which means that local expenditure does not increase as much as the transfers. However, most studies, including those using either provincial data or county-level data, find that general transfers had a flypaper effect or no significant crowding-out of local government spending (Wu, Liu, and Fan 2019; Fu and Shen 2012; Liu and Ma 2015; Mao, Lv, and Ma 2015).

The use of general transfers for local government education expenditure may also be affected by productive expenditure bias (Yin and Zhu 2012; Fu and Shen 2012). Local governments often give priority to economic growth, which is the most important element in performance evaluations for promotion of local officials (Li and Zhou 2005; Zhou 2007). Therefore, local governments may prefer to spend general transfers on productive local projects such as building infrastructure or subsidizing firms rather than on education. Some studies, such as Guo and Jia (2008), find that general transfers suffer from productive expenditure bias. Nevertheless, other studies find that, compared with local fiscal revenue or conditional transfers, general transfers are more likely to be spent for residents' well-being, such as on health care and education (Ma, Guo, and Liu 2016; Zhang and Wu 2019).

Equity

The effect of a highly decentralized financing system is double-edged. Without transfers from upper-level governments, the country's huge disparities in economic development, such as the rural-urban gap, inevitably led to substantial inequality in education financing, as was the case before the mid-2000s. Panel a of figure 10.11 shows that the expenditure of rural compulsory schools lagged significantly behind those of urban schools in 2000. Expenditure per student in rural primary schools was only 64 percent of that in urban primary schools, and the ratio was even lower for junior high schools at 58 percent. Disparities in education expenditure also existed among provinces in the early 2000s, as can be seen in the Gini coefficient in panel b of figure 10.11. For all education levels, the disparity among provinces in per student education expenditure reached its peak in about 2004.

After the introduction of the New Mechanism in the mid-2000s, equity increased significantly. In 2016, as shown in panel a of figure 10.11, the rural-urban ratio of expenditure per student was 88 percent for primary education and 86 percent for junior high schools, an increase of 24 and 28 percentage points, respectively, compared to the ratios in 2000. Panel b of figure 10.11 shows a substantial decline in inequality across provinces. The Gini coefficient declined from 0.24 in 2003 to 0.17 in 2017 for primary education, from 0.25 in 2004 to 0.17 in 2017 for junior high education, from 0.24 in 2004 to 0.18 in 2017 for senior high education, and from 0.2 in 2005 to 0.16 in 2017 for tertiary education. We also calculate the Gini coefficients of prefecture-level education expenditure per student and again find a similar steady decline in inequality after 2005.

Panel c of figure 10.11 shows the ratio of counties' education expenditure relative to their own fiscal revenue (including tax returns) in 2000 and 2007. The ratio was higher for poor counties on average. The difference was more pronounced in 2007. The higher ratio in poor counties was partially attributed to the larger educational transfers provided to poor counties after the introduction of the New Mechanism. This proportionately higher education expenditure helped poor counties catch up with the expenditure of their rich counterparts, which echoes the increased equity between rural and urban areas in education expenditure.

Only a few studies have rigorously investigated the effect of the New Mechanism on the equity of education expenditure. These studies find evidence that overall equity increased after the reform but that disparities may

FIGURE 10.11

Distribution of education expenditure in China

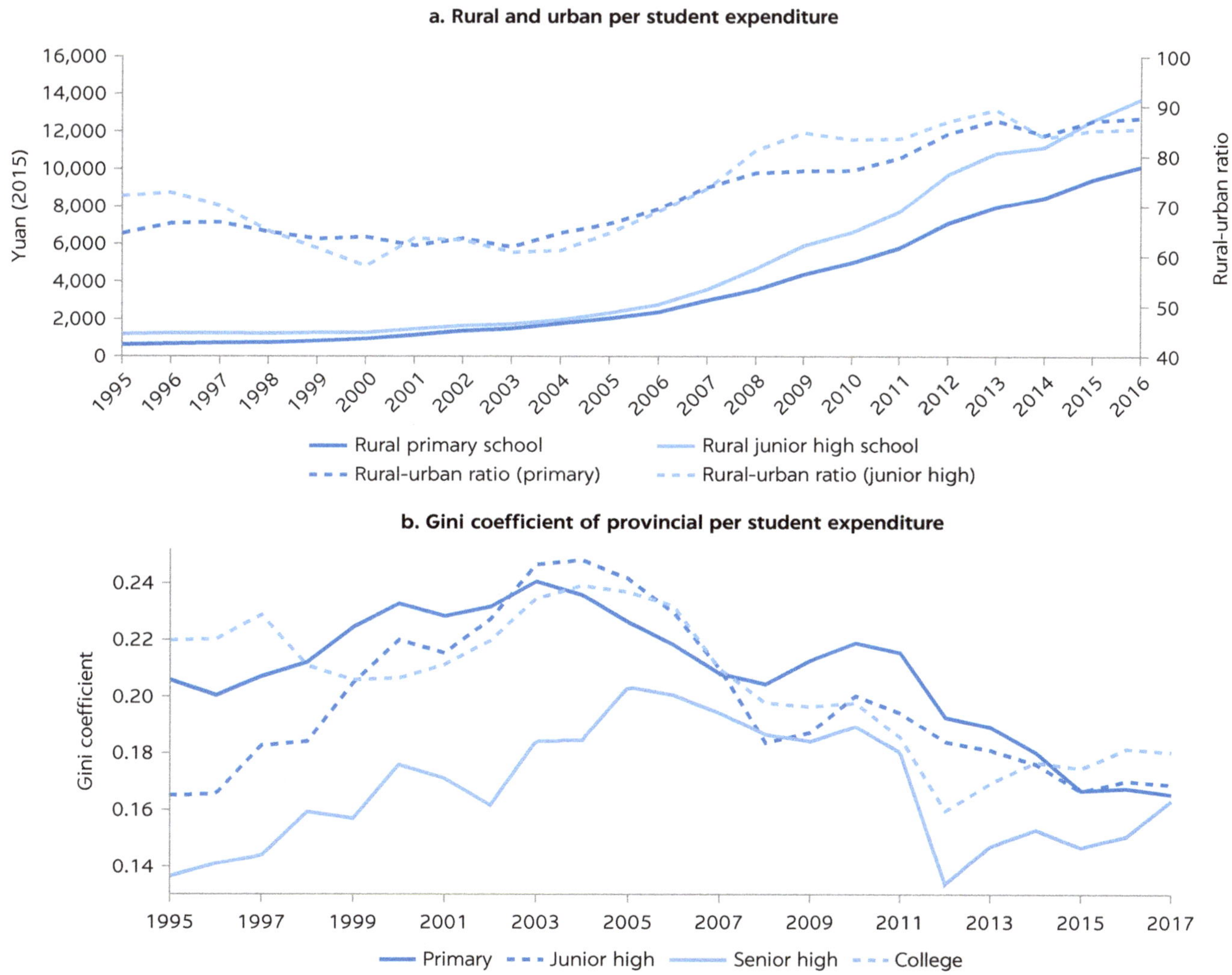

Note: The Gini coefficient is calculated using the number of students in each province as a weight.

continued

FIGURE 10.11, *continued*

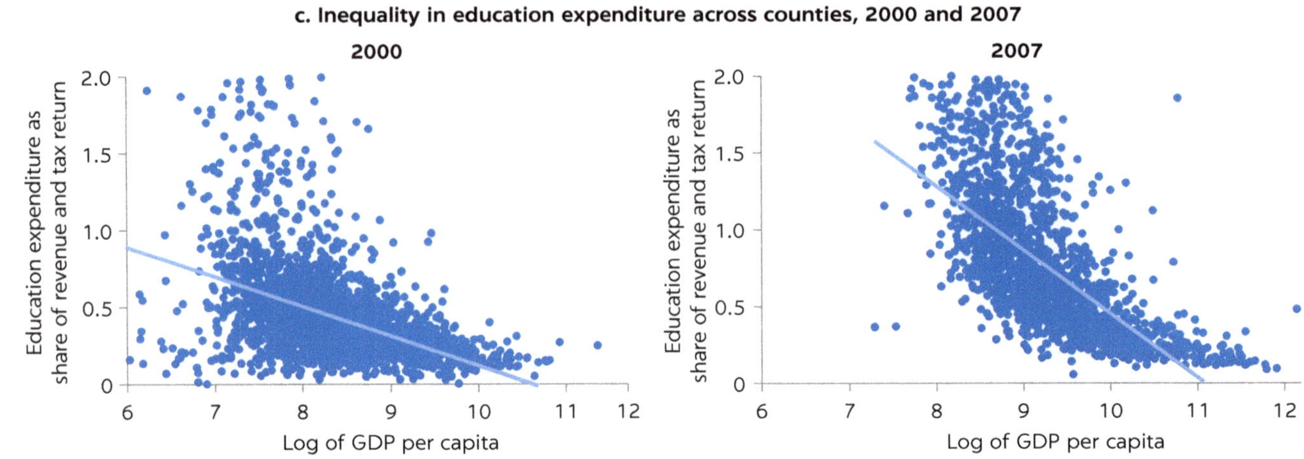

Sources: China Educational Finance Statistical Yearbook, Educational Statistics Yearbook of China, and Fiscal Statistics for Prefectures, Municipalities, and Counties 1993–2007.
Note: GDP = gross domestic product.

have remained or even widened from other perspectives. For example, Lu (2014) examines primary schools in the provinces of Zhejiang, Hubei, and Guangxi and finds that the New Mechanism reduced inequality across the provinces but had an insignificant effect on the within-county inequality of education spending. Based on nationwide county-level data in 2005 and 2006, Huang, Miao, and Jin (2017) find that the reform reduced the eastern-western disparity in primary education but had no effect on the disparity in junior high education. The urban-rural differences in administrative expenditure also did not shrink.

To examine the evolution of inequality in education expenditure under the New Mechanism, Zhao et al. (2015) investigate a western province from 2008 to 2013. They find wide differences in education spending per student within the province that were mainly driven by rising cross-county differences in administrative expenditure. However, the study finds that the least developed counties had gradually caught up with medium-developed counties in education expenditure. The authors also find increasing disparities in per student expenditure among schools, which raises concerns about unequal within-county resource allocation. Moreover, the disparity in facilities between schools was larger than the disparity in education expenditure, which raises the question of the magnitude of the effect of compulsory education transfers on improving educational outcomes.

Expenditure structure

In addition to adequacy and equity, the decentralization reforms have also affected the structure of education spending. We find that, under the New Mechanism, more education funds came from the government, and more education resources were spent on administrative expenditure and on providing compulsory education.

Panel a of figure 10.12 shows that, after 2005, government education expenditure as a share of total education expenditure increased significantly for primary education, which is not surprising because the reform exempted students from tuition fees and shifted the tuition burden from students to governments. The share for junior high education is similar. Panel b of figure 10.12 shows that, under the New Mechanism, for government education expenditure, the share of administrative expenditure increased from 12 percent in 2005 to 27 percent in 2015, while the share of personnel expenditure decreased from 85 percent in 2005 to 72 percent in 2015. There was a much smaller structural change in total education expenditure, which implies that funding from other sources may have compensated for the change in government expenditure. These structural changes have been confirmed in some rigorous studies. Based on county-level data in central and western China in 2005 and 2006, Yang and Ha (2017) find that the New Mechanism raised government administrative expenditure per student, but administrative expenditure from other funding sources dropped and teachers' salaries were negatively affected. Ding, Lu, and Ye (2020) use county-level data over a longer time span and find similar structural changes.

FIGURE 10.12

Structure of primary education expenditure, 1995–2017

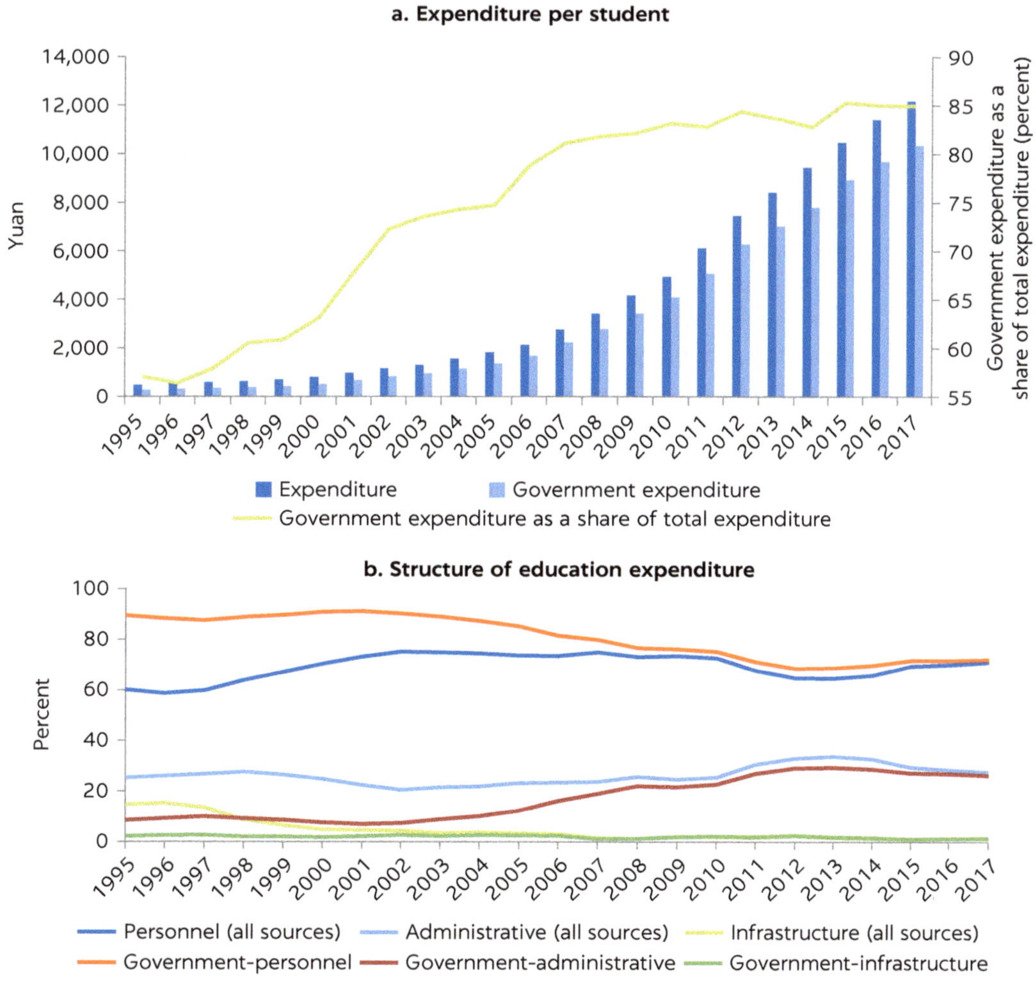

Source: China Educational Finance Statistical Yearbook.

Effects on education outcomes

The decentralization process since the mid-1980s has been accompanied by a remarkable improvement in education outcomes. The net enrollment rate of school-age children in primary school, for example, increased from 94 percent in 1980 to 99 percent in 2000. Figure 10.13 shows that the graduation rate to junior high school increased from 76 percent in 1980 to nearly 100 percent after 2006. The graduation rate to senior high school grew from 46 percent in 1980 to 51 percent in 2000 and to 95 percent in 2018. The graduation rate from senior high school to college increased from 27 percent in 1990 to 73 percent in 2000 and to 94.5 percent in 2016.[10] In 2011, China achieved universal compulsory education. The gross enrollment rate reached 89 percent for senior high school and 48 percent for higher education in 2018.

Figure 10.14 compares the graduation rate to senior high school with expenditure per junior high student in each province in 2005, 2010, and 2015. There is a clear positive correlation between the two variables, although the correlation weakened slightly in later years. The pattern is similar if we switch the horizontal axis to report three-year lagged per student expenditure to account for the time taken to complete junior high school.

Several studies provide evidence that the series of education financing reforms increased education attainment (the number of years spent in school). For the Compulsory Education Project for Poor Regions that focused on improving school facilities from 1995 to 2005, Wang, Zou, and Mao (2019) find that the project had a significant long-term positive effect in increasing the schooling years of the cohort in question by 0.7 years. Chyi and Zhou (2014) find that the tuition exemption policy increased school enrollment among rural children, with a stronger effect for girls. Shi (2016) finds that tuition exemption had a significant positive impact on the school enrollment of students between ages 13 and 16 but no such impact on children between ages 9 and 12.

Under the New Mechanism, Xiao, Li, and Zhao (2017) find that exposure to one additional semester increased the probability of a student graduating from high school by 7.9 percentage points, increased the number of school years attained by 0.56 years, and increased math test scores by 0.12 standard deviations. The schooling effect was stronger for children with less educated

FIGURE 10.13

Graduation and gross enrollment rates in China, 1978–2018

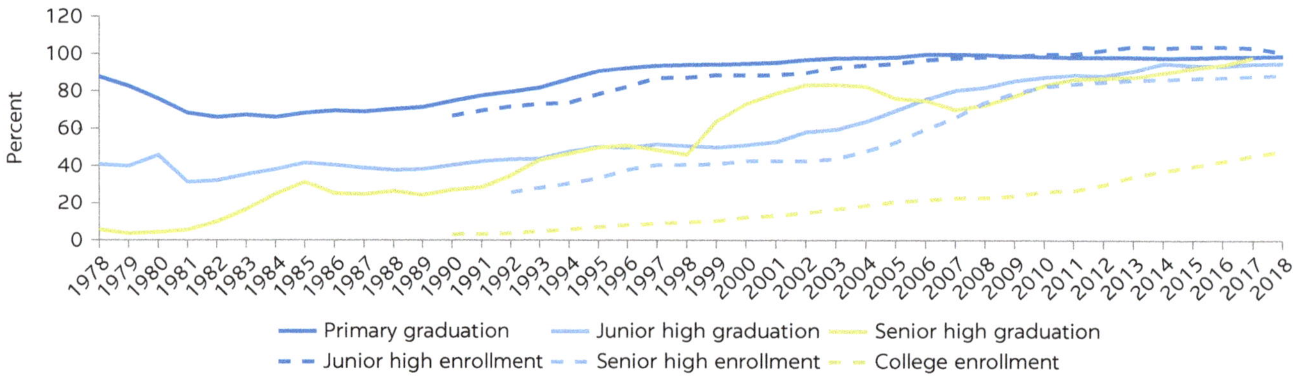

Source: Educational Statistics Yearbooks of China.

FIGURE 10.14

Junior high school education expenditure and graduation rates, by province

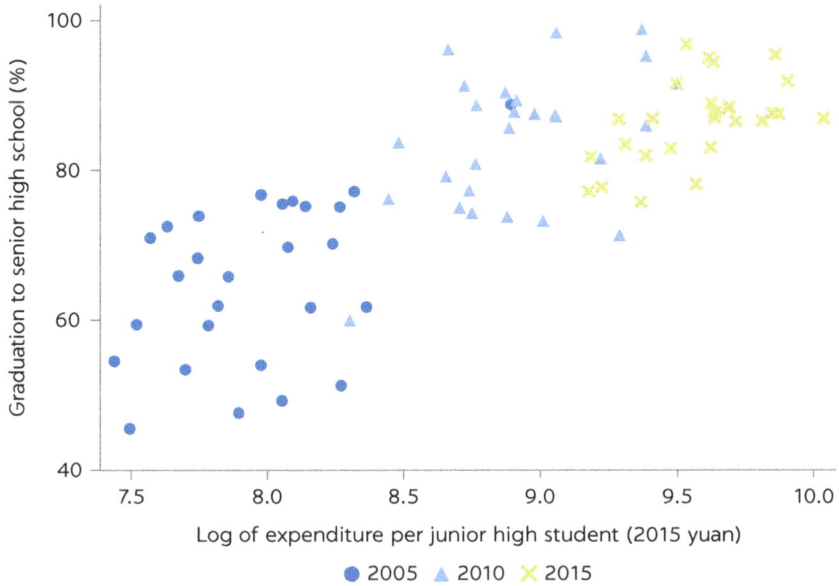

Source: Educational Statistics Yearbook of China and China Educational Finance Statistical Yearbook.

fathers, implying that the reform might have promoted intergenerational mobility. Ha and Yan (2018) find that for every 20-percentage point increase in the financing share of administrative expenditure by governments above counties, students' number of schooling years increased by 0.11 years, and the probability of completing compulsory education increased by 2.2 percentage points. Similarly, Ha and Liu (2018b) find that for each ¥ 100 increase in the transfer received by prefecture governments, the probability of students completing compulsory education rose by 0.8 percentage points.

The decentralized financing system has affected education outcomes in two ways. First, the system has increased the adequacy of school spending and thus improved school conditions. Wang and Wu (2020) find that, for a 1 percent increase in junior high expenditure per student, the graduation rate to senior high school increased by 0.17 to 0.2 percentage points. Among all expenditure items, increase in personnel expenditure was most effective. The increasing expenditure has resulted in substantial improvements in school facilities, reductions in the student-teacher ratio, and continuous growth in per student school building area, fixed assets, and volume of library books after 2003 (see panel a of figure 10.15). The cross-province disparity in teacher quality narrowed as well, as shown by a declining standard deviation in the provincial share of junior high school teachers with appropriate qualifications in panel b of figure 10.15.

Second, the decentralization reforms may have affected education outcomes by altering the behavior of students and households. The reforms not only reduced the burden of education spending on households but also improved households' opinions about school quality. In a field investigation in western China after the tuition exemption and the New Mechanism reform Sun (2008) finds that 89.3 percent of the 3,293 parents interviewed became more willing to send their children to school. Shi (2012) finds an

FIGURE 10.15

Changes in junior high school outcomes

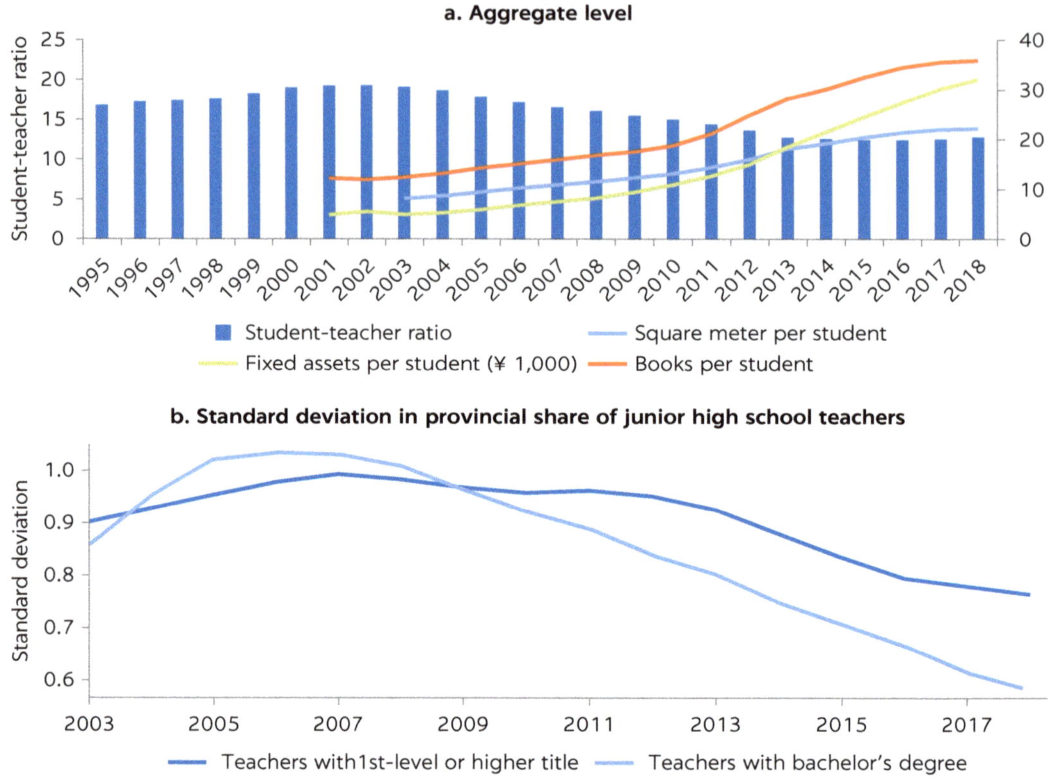

Source: Educational Statistics Yearbook of China.

intrahousehold flypaper effect of the tuition exemption policy. When tuition expenditure was reduced by ¥ 1, families would increase their other educational expenditure by ¥ 0.65.

In contrast with the improving education outcomes since the 1980s, the trend in inequality in education outcomes is not monotonic. Figure 10.16 shows the Gini coefficient based on the graduation rate to senior high school in each province. The Gini coefficient increased until 2001 and declined thereafter. Under the New Mechanism, it continued to decline from 0.09 in 2005 to less than 0.04 in 2015. For the graduation rate to college, the peak of provincial disparities was earlier, in 1997, possibly related to the massive college expansion at that time. Because the New Mechanism allocated more central and provincial resources to poorer regions, education outcomes there were more likely to improve. As a result, the provincial variations in education outcomes narrowed.

Although the provincial disparities in education attainment have been declining considerably since the 2000s, substantial disparities remain both across and within provinces. According to unified tests conducted by the nationally representative China Family Panel Studies in 2014, there were sizable disparities in education performance between the different regions of China, between urban and rural areas, and between urban and migrant students (see figure 10.17).

FIGURE 10.16
Gini coefficient of provincial graduation rates in China, 1995–2017

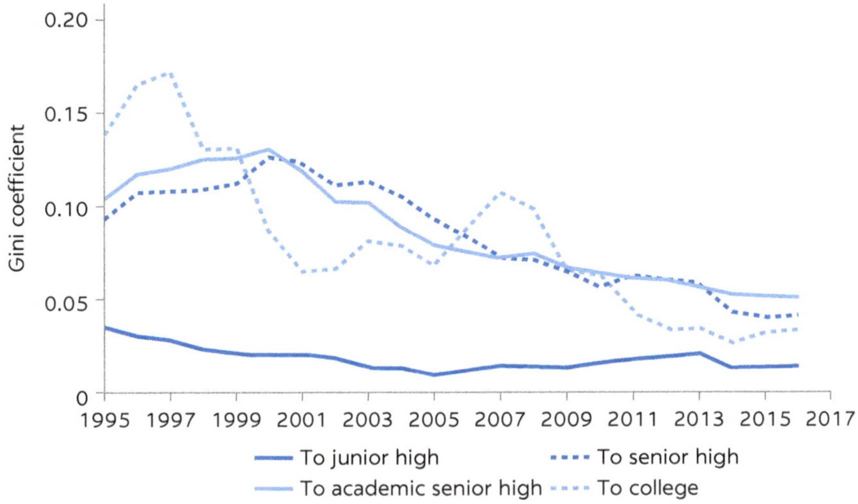

Source: Educational Statistics Yearbook of China.

FIGURE 10.17
Education performance in China, 2014

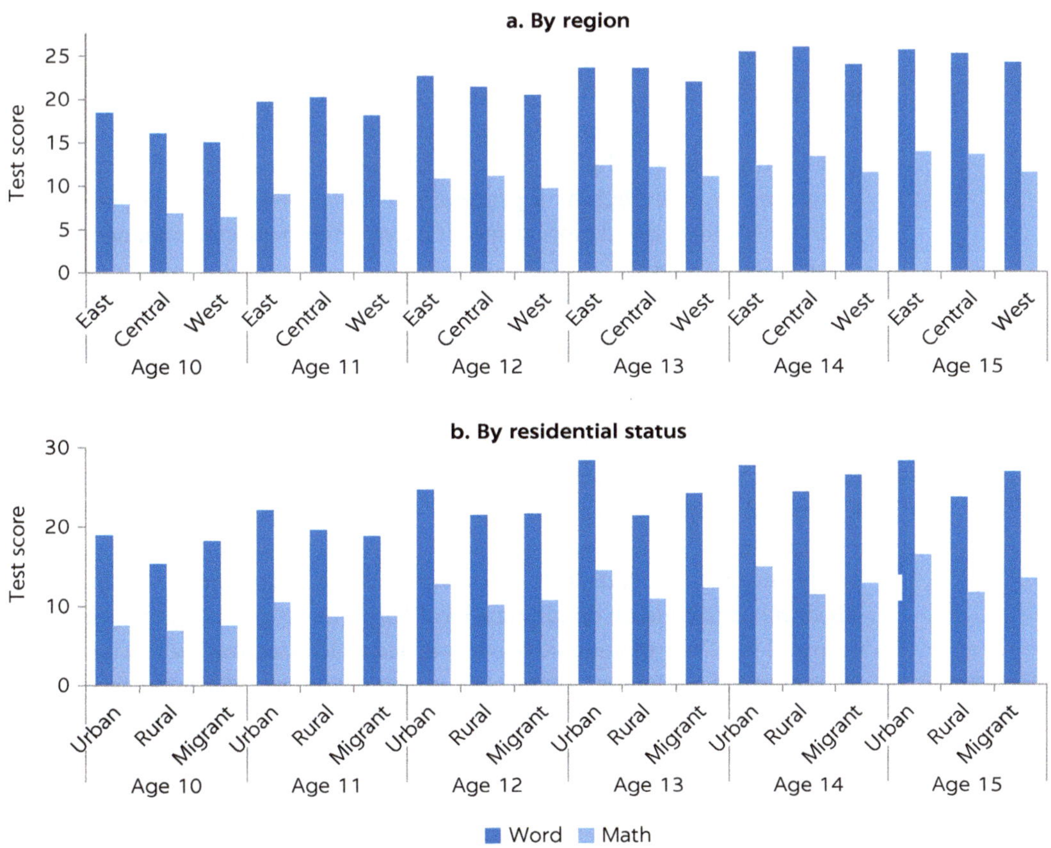

Source: China Family Panel Studies.
Note: "Migrant students" are those whose parents have migrated from rural areas to urban areas. They live and study in the urban area but do not hold an officially issued residential certificate in the residing place.

KEY POLICY DIRECTIONS

Chinese education financing reforms have aimed to increase adequacy and equity. Before the early 2000s, the policy focus was on increasing adequacy, and inequity grew. Since the early 2000s, increasing equity has been the focus, although the adequacy goal was not neglected. The timely adjustment to the policy orientation of educational finance system contributed to the improvement in both adequacy and equity.

Nevertheless, inequality is still one of China's biggest challenges. The inequality challenges have three elements. First, substantial disparities remain in total education expenditure and education outcomes across regions. Second, migrant children are falling behind. Third, within-county inequality is substantial and seems to be rising. In urban areas, school sorting is common, and differences in school quality lead to disparities in housing prices. This so-called "capitalization of education" leads to worries about residential segregation and education inequality (Ha, Wu, and Yu 2015; Ha and Yu 2017; Hu, Zheng, and Wang 2014; Zhang, Chen, and Shi 2016). In rural areas, there is a growing outflow of high-quality teachers and students, which is increasing the rural-urban gap in school performance.

The first two issues will require the central and provincial governments to make important decisions involving redistribution across regions. More equalizing transfers might be a possible solution. The equalizing transfers would need to focus on personnel expenditure, which are the largest component of education expenditure. Additional equalizing transfers would help poor rural counties attract and retain good teachers. Improving incentives could also be helpful, such as giving teachers who choose to work in poor areas extra credits in their promotion assessments or making the experience of serving in poor regions a prerequisite for promotion. Schools in poor regions should be given more discretion over their personnel management to attract good teachers.

The inability of migrant children to access local schools has been a social issue for a long time. There were more than 240 million migrant workers in China in 2018.[11] Under the residential certificate system (*hukou* in Chinese), the children of migrant parents often have no equal access to local public education in the areas where the migrant parent lives. This is the most important reason that a large number of rural children do not migrate with their parents and are left behind in their hometowns. The number of children left behind was nearly 7 million in 2018. This situation has not improved significantly despite various policy endeavors. In late 2019, cities with populations of under 3 million abolished the restriction on obtaining a local *hukou* for migrants, but migrant children still face insurmountable barriers to access local education in larger cities. The central government has created a national student identity system to track students and facilitate the portability of the standard level of administrative expenses. Ideally, the system works like a large-scale school voucher program. However, given the substantial differences between the standard level and local governments' actual amount of administrative costs, and the fact that administrative expenses constitute no more than 40 percent of the total cost, local governments in high-cost regions have little incentive to accept migrant children with a portable low-value voucher. Upper-level governments could compensate local governments for the cost of providing education to migrant children. They could also establish a coordination mechanism between local governments.

The solution demands collaboration among the Ministry of Education, the Ministry of Finance, and the bureau in charge of *hukou* system, because it needs not only an equity-oriented education administration system, but also an education finance system that provides equal resources.

The central or upper-level governments may not know the best solution for within-county inequality because they lack local information. Local governments should be given incentives to achieve a good balance between equity and adequacy. One potential solution is to preserve the Tiebout mechanism (Tiebout 1956) or "voting by feet": mobility restrictions should be removed to allow people to live where they prefer. In addition, upper-level governments could encourage policies that promote within-county equality, such as school-based affirmative action (such as the Texas Ten Percent plan in the United States[12]) and policies that rotate teachers to different schools within the same county. Moreover, it is beneficial and necessary to monitor student outcomes and use the information continuously and systemically for school accountability and management purposes.

Within-county inequality is closely related to the issue of how to regulate private schools and public schools to increase the supply, or adequacy, of high-quality education. The desire to promote equity has restricted the development of private schools. High-end private schools attract the best teachers and the best or richest students, while low-end private schools provide a substandard education. Private schools are at a disadvantage compared to public schools because they receive much lower government subsidies and face restrictions on their development. Private schools have the advantage, however, of much more discretion in how to manage their affairs and incentivize the teachers. It might be difficult to fully level the playing field and to find the best balance of provision between public and private schools because of the multiple social responsibilities of public schools. However, it is clear that the provision of high-quality education in either sector falls well short of demand. The shortage has been increasing as more families are willing to pay higher prices for better education. The education finance system, together with the administration system, surely has an important role to play here, but the best solution is still being hotly debated.

The last challenge, though not least, is the declining economic growth rate in China. The significant increases in education expenditure since 2006 have been possible because of an economic growth rate of over 10 percent in the 2000s. However, economic growth has slowed since 2012, making it difficult to sustain the high growth in education spending. The current education finance system must change accordingly. On the one hand, it is time to reconsider the balance between "helping the poor" and "rewarding the outstanding" in the transfer system. On the other hand, it is also essential that the Ministry of Education create a unified and standardized system for evaluating education performance and then ensure that the results guide decisions about the allocation of education transfers. This calls for the joint efforts of the Ministry of Finance and the Ministry of Education.

NOTES

1. Number and Rates of International Mobile Students (Inbound and Outbound), UNESCO Institute for Statistics Database, UNESCO, Paris, data.uis.unesco.org.

2. Government Expenditure on Education as a Percentage of GDP, UNESCO Institute for Statistics Database, UNESCO, Paris, data.uis.unesco.org.
3. The divisions of provinces and prefectures are usually stable, while counties and townships can merge or divide. At the end of 2000 (as compared to 1990), there were 31 (30) provinces, 333 (336) prefectures, 2,861 (2,833) counties, and 49,668 (65,188) townships in mainland China.
4. In 2003, China started a pilot reform that shifted the management and supervision of township finance upward to counties, although the township was still regarded as an independent accounting entity. In the same year, the government resumed a pilot reform aimed at "flattening the governance hierarchies," which required designated provinces to directly supervise some counties as well as their direct subordinate prefectures. By 2012, about 72 percent of townships were financially managed by counties, and about 37 percent of counties were directly supervised by provincial governments.
5. There are a small number of centrally affiliated pretertiary schools. The expenditure on these schools was less than 0.5 percent of the total expenditure on pretertiary schools in 2016.
6. As compensation for the reduction in local tax revenues under tax reform, a special form of transfer, known as tax return, is allocated to subnational governments based on a predetermined formula. We treated tax return the same way as other government revenues and did not consider it transfer. The scale of tax return has been declining substantially. In 2018, it amounted to only about 11.5 percent of total transfers and 7.6 percent of the subnational revenue, including tax return.
7. Opinions of the State Council on Reforming and Improving the Central-to-Local Transfer Payment System, Guofa [2014] No. 71, http://www.gov.cn/zhengce/content/2015-02/02/content_9445.htm.
8. In 2009, there was a sizable increase in the compulsory education transfer, which might be related to the three-year Safe School Building Project. It declined gradually thereafter.
9. Data limitations prevented us from distinguishing between general and conditional transfers at the provincial level.
10. China launched the massive college expansion in 1999–2005. The promotion rate for senior high school students increased from 46 percent in 1998 to 79 percent in 2001.
11. Report on China's Migrant Population Development 2018, National Health Commission of China, http://www.nhc.gov.cn/wjw/xwdt/201812/a32a43b225a740c4bff8f2168b0e9688.shtml.
12. Under the Texas Ten Percent Plan, students in the top 10 percent of their high school class are guaranteed admission to any public university in the state.

REFERENCES

Chyi, Hau, and Bo Zhou. 2014. "The Effects of Tuition Reforms on School Enrollment in Rural China." *Economics of Education Review* 38 (February): 104–23.

Ding, Yanqing, Fengming Lu, and Xiaoyang Ye. 2020. "Intergovernmental Transfer under Heterogeneous Accountabilities: The Effects of the 2006 Chinese Education Finance Reform." *Economics of Education Review* 77 (August): 101985.

Fu, Wenlin, and Kunrong Shen. 2012. "Equalizing Transfer Payment and the Structure of Local Government's Expenditure." *Economic Research Journal* (5): 45–57.

Guo, Qingwang, and Ruixue Jia. 2008. "Central Government's Fiscal Transfers and the Provision of Local Public Services." *Journal of World Economy* (9): 74–84.

Ha, Wei, Hongbin Wu, and RenZhe Yu. 2015. "A New Research on the Capitalization of School Quality in Housing Prices: An Empirical Study Based on Repeated Cross-Sectional Data in Beijing." *Education and Economy* (5): 3–10.

Ha, Wei, and Ye Liu. 2018a. "Impact Evaluation of Rural Education Finance Guarantee Scheme on Compulsory Education Expenditure in Rural China: Evidence from Provincial Panel Data." *China Economics of Education Review* (4): 46–63.

——. 2018b. "Does the "New Mechanism" Facilitate the Completion of Compulsory Education? An Investigation based on the Prefectural Data in Central and Western China." *Journal of the Chinese Society of Education* (11): 62–69.

Ha, Wei, and Fang Yan. 2018. "Does Money Matter? The Effects of Block Grants on Education Attainment in Rural China: Evidence from Intercensal Population Survey 2015." *International Journal of Educational Development* 62 (September): 174–83.

Ha, Wei, and Renzhe Yu. 2017. "How Much Is an Improved School Worth? Evidence from the Comprehensive Reform in Compulsory Education in Beijing." *Peking University Education Review* 15 (3): 137–53.

Hanson, E. Mark. 2000. *Educational Decentralization around the Pacific Rim*. Washington, DC: World Bank.

Hu, Wanyang, Siqi Zheng, and Rui Wang. 2014. "The Capitalization of School Quality in Home Value: A Matching Regression Approach with Housing Price-Rent Comparison." *China Economic Quarterly* 13 (3): 1195–1214.

Hu, Yifan. 2012. "The Difficult Knot of Rural Compulsory Education." *Caijing Magazine,* June 12. http://finance.sina.com.cn/g/20020612/219860.html.

Huang, Bin, Jingjing Miao, and Jun Jin. 2017. "A Causal Effect Analysis of the "New Mechanism" Reform on Rural Primary and Secondary Education Expenditure: Based on Quasi-Experimental Research Design." *Journal of the Chinese Society of Education* (11): 38–46.

Li, Hongbin, and Li-An Zhou. 2005. "Political Turnover and Economic Performance: The Incentive Role of Personnel Control in China." *Journal of Public Economics* 89 (9–10): 1743–62.

Li, Pei, Yi Lu, and Jin Wang. 2016. "Does Flattening Government Improve Economic Performance? Evidence from China." *Journal of Development Economics* 123 (November): 18–37.

Lin, Justin, Mingxing Liu, and Ran Tao. 2013. "Deregulation, Decentralization, and China's Growth in Transition." In *Law and Economics with Chinese Characteristics: Institutions for Promoting Development in the Twenty-First Century,* edited by D. Kennedy and J.E. Stiglitz, 466–90. Oxford: Oxford University Press.

Liu, Chang, and Guangrong Ma. 2015. "Does Intergovernmental Transfer in China Have Flypaper Effect? Quasi-Experimental Evidence from China's Designation of National Poor Counties." *China Journal of Economics* (1): 25–46.

Liu, Yongzheng, and James Alm. 2015. "Fiscal Reform, Land Expansion, and Urban Growth in China." Working Paper, Renmin University, Beijing, China.

Liu, Yongzheng, Jorge Martinez-Vazquez, and Baoyun Qiao. 2014. "Falling Short: Intergovernmental Transfers in China." *Public Finance and Management* 14 (4): 374–98.

Lu, Ke. 2014. "Evaluation of the Impact of the 'New Mechanism' on the Balanced Allocation of Educational Financial Resources: An Estimation based on a Matching Model." *Peking University Education Review* (1): 156–66.

Ma, Guangrong, Qingwang Guo, and Chang Liu. 2016. "The Structure of Fiscal Payments and Regional Economic Growth." *Social Sciences in China* (9): 105–25.

Mao, Jie, Bingyang Lv, and Guangrong Ma. 2015. "Transfer and Government Expansion: An Investigation based on the 'Price Effect.'" *Management World* (7): 29–41.

Mao, Jie, Dehua Wang, and Chong-En Bai. 2011. "Intergovernmental Transfers for Ethnic Regions, Public Spending Difference and Economic Development Gap." *Economic Research Journal* (S2): 75–87.

Martinez-Vazquez, J., B. Qiao, and L. Zhang. 2008. "The Role of Provincial Policies in Fiscal Equalization Outcomes in China." *China Review* 8 (2): 135–67.

Mok, Ka-Ho. 2001. "Education Policy Reform." In *The Market in Chinese Social Policy,* edited by L. Wong and N. Flynn, 88–111. Houndmills: Palgrave.

Ngok, Kinglun. 2007. "Chinese Education Policy in the Context of Decentralization and Marketization: Evolution and Implications." *Asia Pacific Education Review*, 8 (1): 142–57.

Shi, Xinzheng. 2012. "Does an Intra-Household Flypaper Effect Exist? Evidence from the Educational Fee Reduction Reform in Rural China." *Journal of Development Economics* 99 (2): 459–73. http://dx.doi.org/10.1016/j.jdeveco.2012.05.006.

———. 2016. "The Impact of Educational Fee Reduction Reform on School Enrolment in Rural China." *Journal of Development Studies* 52 (12): 1791–1809. http://dx.doi.org/10.1080/00220388.2016.1156094.

Su, Chunhong, and E Xie. 2015. "Fiscal Mobility, Public Transfers, and Their Efficiency in Alleviating Poverty: Analysis Based on Micro-data of Rural China." *Journal of Financial Research* (4): 34–49.

Sun, Baicai. 2008. "The Effect of the New Mechanism on Enrollment in Rural Western China." *The World of Survey and Research* (12): 9–10.

Tiebout, Charles M. 1956. "A Pure Theory of Local Expenditures." *Journal of Political Economy* 64 (5): 416–24.

Tsang, Mun. 1996. "Financial Reform of Basic Education in China." *Economics of Education Review* 15 (4): 423–44.

Wang, Dehua, Jie Zou, and Zhonggen Mao. 2019. "Schooling and Income Effect of Education Development in China: Evidence from the National Compulsory Education Project in China's Poor Areas." *Economic Research Journal* (9): 155–70.

Wang, Xiaoxia, and Binzhen Wu. 2020. "The Effect of Various Education Expenditures on Education Outcomes." Working Paper, Tsinghua University, Beijing.

World Bank. 2002. *China: National Development and Sub-National Finance: A Review of Provincial Expenditures.* Washington, DC: World Bank. https://openknowledge.worldbank.org/bitstream/handle/10986/15423/multi0page.pdf?sequence= 1.

———. 2021. *The Role of Intergovernmental Fiscal Transfers in Improving Education Outcomes. Annex.* Washington, DC: World Bank.

Wu, Min, Chang Liu, and Ziying Fan. 2019. "Intergovernmental Transfers and the Expansion of Subnational Government Expenditure: An Empirical Explanation based on China's Budgetary System." *Journal of Financial Research* 465 (3): 74–91.

Xiao, Yun, Li Li, and Liqiu Zhao. 2017. "Education on the Cheap: The Long-Run Effects of a Free Compulsory Education Reform in Rural China." *Journal of Comparative Economics* 45 (3): 544–62.

Xu, Chenggang. 2011. "The Fundamental Institutions of China's Reforms and Development." *Journal of Economic Literature* 49 (4): 1076–1151.

Yang, Jin, and Wei Ha. 2017. "Impact Evaluation of Intergovernmental Grants on Compulsory Education Expenditure in Rural China: Evidence from County-Level Panel Data." *Research in Educational Development* (8): 46–55.

Yang, Jin, Wei Ha, and Yinhuo Wu. 2017. "The Effect of Financial Transfer Payments on Compulsory Education Expenditure at County Level: An Analysis Based on County-Level Data in Western China." *Education Research Monthly* (7): 13–22.

Yin, Heng, and Hong Zhu. 2012. "A Study of Productive Expenditure Bias in County-Level Finance in China." *Social Sciences in China* 33 (1): 127–47.

Yin, Zhendong, and Yugang Tang. 2016. "Earmarked Grants and Local Government Spending Behavior: Evidence from China's Rural Compulsory Education Aid Program." *Economic Research Journal* (4): 47–59.

Zhang, Muyang, Jie Chen, and Wei Shi. 2016. "The Values of Good School from the Perspective of Rent Yields Discounts: Empirical Evidence from the Second-Hand Housing Market in Shanghai." Journal of Financial Research 432 (6): 97–111.

Zhang, Rongxin, and Xiao Feng. 2018. "Equity and Adequacy of K12 Education Finance in China: Central Government's Policy and Impact." Working Paper. https://aefpweb.org/sites/default/files/webform/Equity%20and%20Adequacy%20of%20K12%20Education%20Finance%20in%20China--Central%20Government's%20Policy%20and%20Impact.pdf.

Zhang, Yuan, and Binzhen Wu. 2019. 'How Do Different Types of Fiscal Transfers Affect the Structure of Local Government's Revenue and Expenditure?" Working Paper, Tsinghua University, Beijing.

Zhao, Haili. 2017. "Transfer Payments of Compulsory Education and Input Equilibrium: Based on the Data of Zhejiang Province." *Educational Research* (9): 46–54.

Zhao, Litao, Ling Li, Chen Huang, Naiqing Song, and Yiran Zhao. 2015. "The Distributive Effect of the Overall Planning Reform of Provincial-Level Educational Funding." *Social Sciences in China* 239 (11): 111–27.

Zhou, Li'An. 2007. "Governing China's Local Officials: An Analysis of the Promotion Tournament Model." *Economic Research Journal* (7): 36–49.

www.ingramcontent.com/pod-product-compliance
Ingram Content Group UK Ltd.
Pitfield, Milton Keynes, MK11 3LW, UK
UKHW050037060726
472907UK00008B/300

9 781464 8169